11/27/70 J5

DATE DUE

BIRD APR 29 '88

DUMBARTON OAKS STUDIES

ᦞ XII ᦞ

COINAGE AND MONEY
IN THE
BYZANTINE EMPIRE
1081–1261

COINAGE AND MONEY
IN THE
BYZANTINE EMPIRE
1081-1261

BY

MICHAEL F. HENDY

Dumbarton Oaks
Center for Byzantine Studies
Trustees for Harvard University
Washington, District of Columbia
1969

Distributed by
J. J. Augustin, Publisher
Locust Valley, New York

Library of Congress Catalogue Card Number 62-17509
Printed in Germany *at* J. J. Augustin, Glückstadt

Acknowledgements

Since the informal groundwork for this volume was already under way while I was still an undergraduate at Oxford, a considerable element of thanks must go to my former tutor, John Prestwich of The Queen's College, for aiding and abetting my interest in the Byzantine state and its coinage—even to the detriment of the fundamentals of historical research which he was endeavoring to inculcate.

My chief debt of gratitude is due to Philip Grierson, Reader in Mediaeval Numismatics at Cambridge University. That formal work was begun is almost entirely due to his encouragement, and that it was completed owes much to his friendly support over the past three years.

Alfred R. Bellinger, Professor at Yale University and Visiting Scholar at Dumbarton Oaks, not only performed the unenviable task of reading through the work while it was still in manuscript, but also showed himself willing to lend a sympathetic ear to extravagant ideas and to ensure their discarding with humor and kindliness.

Michael Metcalf, Assistant Keeper of Coins in the Ashmolean Museum, Oxford, was the first to draw my attention to the possibility of using the numismatic material in Bulgarian museums and has been most generous in providing me with information regarding the coins in the Ashmolean Museum itself, including those from the Goodacre Collection now on loan from Mrs. N. J. Goodacre.

That this volume contains as much new hoard material as it does is the result of an extremely pleasant stay of seven months in the People's Republic of Bulgaria under the terms of a graduate exchange scholarship. That once there I was actually able to fulfil the possibilities offered by the immense amount of material available both at Sofia and in the provincial museums is largely because of the guidance and efforts of Dr. Todor Gerassimov, Head of the Coin Cabinet at the Archaeological Museum of the Academy of Sciences. Warm thanks for cooperation, and in many cases for personal hospitality, are also due to the staff of the Archaeological Museums at Plovdiv, Pazardzhik, Stara Zagora, Kazanluk, Turnovo, Assenovgrad, Nova Zagora, Sliven, and Blagoevgrad. Particular thanks must go to Messrs. Dzhambov and Kolev of Plovdiv, Nikolov of Stara Zagora, and Getov of Kazanluk, and to Mme Gizdova of Pazardzhik.

The possibility of turning this into a book is very largely due to the generosity of Dumbarton Oaks in electing me to a Junior Fellowship and in prolonging it over two years. For most Byzantine scholars such a stay means the provision of admirable working conditions and the use of a splendid library; for a numismatist it means, in addition, the privilege of access to one of the great coin collections of the world. I am also profoundly grateful to the Publications Committee for accepting the volume for publication in their series of Studies.

Special mention must be made of the indefatigable efforts of Mrs. Margaret Ševčenko who not only typed my manuscript but also attempted at that late stage to correct the major blemishes of language that had hitherto escaped.

Photographs of coins in the Münzkabinett, Berlin, were obtained through the kind offices of Dr. Peter Berghaus of Münster.

I owe Plates 48–50 to the generosity of Paul A. Underwood, Professor at Dumbarton Oaks.*

Messrs. Wallace Lane and Richard Amt, the Dumbarton Oaks photographers, have exercised their skill (and patience) in providing the photographic plates for the volume mainly by direct photography rather than by the more usual process utilizing plaster casts. The casting of over four hundred scyphate coins, many in lamentable style and regrettable state of preservation, would have been a gigantic task.

Messrs. John Wilson and Robert Halpin of Dumbarton Oaks have used their admirable talents in drawing the maps at the end of the volume.

Finally, my thanks must be extended to the authorities of the various museums and institutions that have allowed me to illustrate material from their coin cabinets: the British Museum, the Ashmolean Museum, the Bibliothèque Nationale, the American Numismatic Society, and the Johns Hopkins University Museum. Mr. Philip Whitting also kindly gave me the freedom of his considerable collection. To Mme Cécile Morrisson of the Bibliothèque Nationale the author owes a particular debt of gratitude for friendly hospitality and cooperation.

24 May 1967
M. F. Hendy
Dumbarton Oaks

* Since the above was written, we regret to announce the death of Professor Underwood in September 1968.   *Ed.*

Table of Contents

Acknowledgements v

List of Plates xi

Selected Numismatic Bibliography xiii

List of Abbreviations xvii

List of Ligatured Letters Used in Inscriptions xviii

Section I: PRELIMINARIES

CHAPTER 1   The Eleventh Century: Monetary Crisis . . .   3

CHAPTER 2   Specific Gravity Determinations: Gold and Electrum
Nomismata *ca.* 1081–1203   10

CHAPTER 3   The Twelfth Century: Monetary Recovery. . .   14

CHAPTER 4   The Monetary Terminology of the Twelfth Century.   26

CHAPTER 5   The Date of the Alexian Monetary Reform . .   39

CHAPTER 6   The *Palaia kai Nea Logarike*   50

CHAPTER 7   Imperial Ceremonial Costume   65

Section II: THE COINS 1081–1204

CHAPTER 8   The Comneni   71

    (i)   Alexius I, Pre-reform, 1081–1092. . . .   71

    (ii)   Alexius I, Post-reform, 1092–1118   81

    (iii)   John II (1118–1143)   102

    (iv)   Manuel I (1143–1180)   111

    (v)   Alexius II (1180–1184)   131

    (vi)   Andronicus I (1183–1185)   132

    (vii)   Isaac, Usurper in Cyprus (1184–1191). . . .   136

CHAPTER 9   The Angeli and Ducae   143

    (i)   Isaac II (1185–1195)   143

    (ii)   Uncertain Attribution: Isaac Comnenus or Isaac
Angelus   147

(iii) Theodore Mangaphas, Usurper in Philadelphia (1189–
1190)   149
(iv) Alexius III (1195–1203)   150
(v) Isaac II, Alexius IV (1203–1204)   156
(vi) Alexius V (1204)   156

CHAPTER 10   The Internal Organization of the Metropolitan Mint   157

SECTION III: THE COINS 1204–1261

CHAPTER 11 (i)   The Imitative Coinage of the Period of the Latin
Emperors (1204–1261) and Kings of Thessalonica
(1204–1224)   191
(ii)   The Imitative Coinage of the Period of the Asenid
Tsars of Bulgaria (ca. 1195–?)   218
(iii) Summary   223

CHAPTER 12   The Empires of Nicaea and Thessalonica   .   .   .   224
(i)   The Empire of Nicaea   227
Theodore I (1208–1222)   227
John III (1222–1254)   237
Theodore II (1254–1258)   256
John IV (1258/59)   261
Michael VIII (1258/59–1261).   261
Uncertain Nicaean Attribution   264
The Family Names of the Emperors of Nicaea .   .   266
(ii)   The Empire of Thessalonica   267
Theodore Ducas (1224–1230).   268
Manuel Ducas (1230–1237)   274
John Ducas (1237–1244)   279
Demetrius Ducas (1244–1246)   288
Uncertain Thessalonican Attribution   289
(iii) Thessalonica under the Emperors of Nicaea   .   .   290
John III (1246–1254)   290
Theodore II (1254–1258)   295
Michael VIII (1258/59–1261).   295
(iv) Other Rulers   296
The "Despots" of Epirus   296
Leo and John Gavalas, Rulers of Rhodes (ca. 1204–
ca. 1250)   296
Ivan II Asen, Tsar of Bulgaria (1218–1241)   .   .   296
"Stefan Ducas Rex"   297

SECTION IV: GENERAL CONSIDERATIONS

CHAPTER 13   *Apodesmoi* and *Apokombia*   301

CHAPTER 14   The Coinage and the Economy   315

SECTION V: MATERIALS

CHAPTER 15   List of Hoards   325
SUPPLEMENTARY NOTE   405
Key to Plates   411
Indexes   431
    I.   Rulers, Mints, and Denominations
    II. Hoards
    III. Imperial Ceremonial Costume
    IV. Religious Figures
    V.   General
Plates
Maps
    The Lands of the Byzantine Empire 1081–1261
    Hoard Locations

List of Plates

1–3.   Alexius I (Pre-reform)

3–8.   Alexius I (Post-reform)

9–11. John II

12–18. Manuel I

18–19. Andronicus I; Isaac Comnenus of Cyprus

20–21. Isaac II; Uncertain—Isaac II, Isaac Comnenus

22–23. Alexius III

24–25. "Bulgarian" Imitative

25–28. Latin Imitative (Larger Module)

29.   Latin Imitative (Smaller Module)

30–31. Theodore I (of Nicaea)

31–34. John III

34–35. Theodore II

36.   Michael VIII; Uncertain Nicaean Attribution

37–38. Theodore Comnenus-Ducas (of Thessalonica)

39.   Manuel Comnenus-Ducas

40–41. John Comnenus-Ducas; Demetrius Comnenus-Ducas; Uncertain Thessalonican Attribution

42–43. John III; Theodore II

44–45. Clipped Coins; Roger II of Sicily (Ducat)

45–46. Debased Hyperpyra, Thirteenth-fourteenth Century; Overstrikes; Ivan II, Asen

47.   Stefan "Rex"; Miscellaneous Eleventh Century; Hugh I of Cyprus (Besant)

48.   Hagia Sophia. "Constantine IX" and Zoë

49.   Hagia Sophia. "Constantine IX" and Zoë, detail of *Apokombion*

50.   Hagia Sophia. John II and Irene

51.   Supplementary Material

Selected Numismatic Bibliography

PRIMARY SOURCES

(Greek)

Acta et Diplomata Graeca Medii Aevi, eds. F. Miklosich, and G. Müller, 3 (Vienna, 1865), 4 (1871), 5 (1887), 6 (1890)

Actes de Lavra, eds. G. Rouillard, and P. Collomp, 1 (Paris, 1937)

CHONIATES, NICETAS. *Corpus Scriptorum Historiae Byzantinae* (Bonn, 1835)

Ius Graeco-Romanum, ed. C. E. Zachariä von Lingenthal, 3 (Leipzig, 1857)

Opisanie liturgicheskikh rukopisei khranyashchikhsya v bibliotekakh pravoslavnogo Vostoka, ed. A. Dimitrievskii, 1: Τυπικά (Kiev, 1895)

PACHYMERES, GEORGE. *Corpus Scriptorum Historiae Byzantinae* (Bonn, 1835)

"Typikon de Grégoire Pacourianos pour le monastère de Pétritzos (Bačkovo) en Bulgarie," ed. L. Petit, *Vizantiiskii Vremennik*, 11 (1904), Supplement 1

ZONARAS, JOHN. *Corpus Scriptorum Historiae Byzantinae* (Bonn, 1841)

(Western)

Acta Imperii Inedita, ed. E. Winkelmann, 1 (Innsbruck, 1880)

De Profectione Ludovici VII in Orientem, ed. V. G. Berry, Records of Civilization, Sources and Studies, no. 42 (New York, 1948)

Documenti sulle relazione della città toscane coll'Oriente Cristiano e coi Turchi, ed. G. Müller (Florence, 1879)

Gesta Francorum et aliorum Hierosolimitanorum, ed. R. Hill (London, 1962)

Historia de Expeditione Friderici Imperatoris, ed. A. Chroust, MGH, *Scriptores Rerum Germanicarum*, New Series, 5 (Berlin, 1928)

Historia Hierosolymitana, Fulcher of Chartres, ed. H. Hagenmeyer (Heidelberg, 1913)

La pratica della mercatura, Francesco Balducci Pegolotti, ed. A. Evans, Mediaeval Academy of America, publ. no. 24 (Cambridge, Mass., 1936)

Urkunden zur älteren Handels- und Staatsgeschichte der Republik Venedig mit besonderer Beziehung auf Byzanz und die Levante, eds. G. Tafel and G. Thomas, Fontes Rerum Austriacarum (Vienna, 1856), vols. 1, 2

SECONDARY MATERIAL

AHRWEILER-GLYKATZI, H. "Nouvelle hypothèse sur le tétartèron d'or et la politique monétaire de Nicéphore Phocas," *Recueil des travaux de l'Institut d'Etudes Byzantines*, 8 (= Mélanges G. Ostrogorsky, 1) (Belgrade, 1963), pp. 1–9

BALLING, J. "A Byzantine Double Hoard from Lindos," *Nordisk Numismatisk Årsskrift* (1963), pp. 13–41

BELL, H. W. *Sardis*, vol. 11, pt. 1, *Coins* (Leiden, 1916)

BELLINGER, A. R. *Catalogue of the Coins Found at Corinth, 1925* (New Haven, Conn., 1930)

―――― "A Hoard of Silver Coins of the Empire of Nicaea," *Centennial Publication of the American Numismatic Society*, ed. H. Ingholt (New York, 1958), pp. 73–81

BELLINGER, A. R. "Three Hoards of Byzantine Bronze Coins," *Greek and Byzantine Studies*, 1 (1958), pp. 163–71
———— "Three More Hoards of Byzantine Copper Coins," ANS, *Museum Notes*, 11 (1964), pp. 207–26
———— and METCALF, D. M. "A Hoard of Byzantine Scyphate Bronze Coins from Arcadia," *NC*[6], 19 (1959), pp. 155–64
BERTELÈ, T. "Costantino il Grande e S. Elena su alcune monete bizantine," *Numismatica*, 14 (1948), pp. 91–106
———— "*L'imperatore alato nella numismatica bizantina* (Rome, 1951)
———— "L'imperatore con una palma su una bulla e monete bizantine del sec. XIII," *Polychronion: Festschrift Franz Dölger zum 75. Geburtstag*, ed. P. Wirth (Heidelberg, 1966), pp. 82–89
———— "Lineamenti principali della numismatica bizantina," *RIN*, 66 (1964), pp. 33–118
———— "Una moneta dei despoti di Epiro," *Numismatica*, 17–18 (1951–52), pp. 17–18
———— "Monete bizantine inedite o rare," *Zeitschrift für Numismatik*, 36 (1926), pp. 1–36
———— "Monete di Giovanni Comneno Duca imperatore di Salonicco (1237–1244)," *Numismatica*, 16 (1950), pp. 61–79
———— "Il titolo degli iperperi della zecca di Nicea," *Thirteenth International Congress of Byzantine Studies* (Oxford, 1966), *Supplementary Papers, Summaries*, pp. 95–97
———— "La Vergine Aghiosoritissa nella numismatica bizantina," *Revue des études byzantines*, 16 (1958) (= Mélanges S. Salaville), pp. 233–34
———— and GOODACRE, H. "Monete degli imperatori di Nicea," *Numismatica*, 2 (1936), pp. 91–94
———— *see also*, LATHOUD, D.
BORRELL, H. P. "Unedited Coins of the Lower Empire," *NC*, 4 (1841), pp. 15–22
BLAKE, R. P. "Some Byzantine Accounting Practices Illustrated from Georgian Sources," *Harvard Studies in Classical Philology*, 51 (1940), pp. 11–33
BRUNETTI, L. "Nuovi orientamenti statistici nella monetazione antica," *RIN*, 52–53 (1950–51), pp. 3–74
COX, D. H. *Coins from the Excavations at Curium, 1932–1953*, ANS, *Numismatic Notes and Monographs*, no. 145 (New York, 1959)
DE GUADAN, M. "Nomisma d'argento di Isacco II Angelo, e le coniazione di Teodoro Ducas Mankaphas," *Italia numismatica*, 9 (1960), pp. 117–20
———— "Una nueva moneda de cobre de Miguel VIII Paléologo, acuñada en Nicea," *Numisma*, yr. 3, no. 8 (1953), pp. 19–25
DÖLGER, F. "Finanzgeschichtliches aus der byzantinischen Kaiserkanzlei des 11. Jahrhunderts," in his *Paraspora* (Ettal, 1961), pp. 326–49. First published as no. 1 of the *Bayerische Akademie d. Wissenschaften: Philos.-Hist. Klasse, Sitzungsberichte, Jahrgang 1956*
DONALD, P. J. *See* WHITTING, P. D.
DU CANGE, C. *De Imperatorum Constantinopolitanorum Numismatibus Dissertatio* (Rome, 1755)
EHRENKREUTZ, A. S. "Byzantine *Tetartera* and Islamic *Dīnārs*," *Journal of the Economic and Social History of the Orient*, 7 (1964), pp. 183–90
EDWARDS, K. M. "A Remarkable Coin of Manuel I Comnenus," *Classical Studies in Honor of E. Capps* (Princeton, 1936), pp. 103–105
———— *Corinth*, 6, *Coins* (Cambridge, Mass., 1933)

FRŒHNER, W. *Monnaies byzantines de la collection Photiadès Pacha.* Sale Catalogue
  (Paris, 23–24 May 1890)
FROLOW, A. "Les noms de monnaies dans le typicon du Pantocrator," *Byzantinoslavica,*
  10 (1949), pp. 241–53
GERASSIMOV, T. D. "Contribution à l'étude de la numismatique de l'Empire byzantin de
  Salonique," *Studia in honorem M. S. Drinov* (Sofia, 1960), pp. 381–98
———— "Un problème de numismatique byzantine," XIIᵉ *Congrès International des Études
  Byzantines (Ochride, 1961): Résumés des communications* (Belgrade-Ochrid, 1961),
  pp. 35–36
GOITEIN, S. D. "Bankers' Accounts from the Eleventh Century A.D.," *Journal of the
  Economic and Social History of the Orient,* 9 (1966), pp. 28–66
———— *A Mediterranean Society,* 1, *Economic Foundations* (Berkeley, 1967)
GOODACRE, H. "The Flat Bronze Coinage of Nicaea," *NC⁵,* 18 (1938), pp. 159–64
———— *A Handbook of the Coinage of the Byzantine Empire,* 2nd. ed. (London, 1957)
———— "Irene Dukaina, Wife of the Emperor Alexius I," *NC⁵,* 19 (1939), pp. 105–11
———— "Notes on some Byzantine Coins," *NC⁶,* 5 (1945), pp. 34–40
———— *see also,* BERTELÈ, T.
GRIERSON, P. "Byzantine Coinage as Source Material," *Thirteenth International Congress
  of Byzantine Studies* (Oxford, 1966), *Main Papers,* 10, pp. 1–17
———— "The Debasement of the Bezant in the Eleventh Century," *BZ,* 47 (1954), pp.
  379–94
———— "A Follis of Nicephorus Bryennius (?)," *NC⁶,* 10 (1950), pp. 305–11
———— "Nomisma, tetartèron et dinar: un plaidoyer pour Nicéphore Phocas," *RBN,*
  100 (1954), pp. 75–84
———— "Notes on the Fineness of the Byzantine Solidus," *BZ,* 54 (1961), pp. 91–97
HARRIS, J. "A Gold Hoard from Corinth," *American Journal of Archaeology,* 43 (1939),
  pp. 268–77
ILIESCU, O. "Le dernier hyperpère de l'Empire byzantin de Nicée," *Byzantinoslavica,*
  26 (1965), pp. 94–99
LAMBROS, S. P. Ἀνέκδοτα νομίσματα τοῦ μεσαιωνικοῦ βασιλείου τῆς Κύπρου, in K. Sathas,
  Mesaionike Bibliotheke, 2 (Venice, 1873), pp. 547–96
———— "Monnaies et bulles inédites de Neopatras et de Carytaena," *RN²,* 14 (1869) pp.
  184–193
LATHOUD, D. and BERTELÈ, T. "Les clefs de Saint Pierre sur une monnaie de Jean III
  Doucas Vatatzès, empereur de Nicée (1222–1254)," *Unitas,* 1 (1948), pp. 189–96
LAURENT, V. "Bulle et monnaies inédites de Jean Ducas Comnène empereur de Thessaloni-
  que (1240–1244)," *Cronica Numismatică și Arheologică,* 125/126 (1943), pp. 3–14
———— "Bulletin de numismatique byzantine (1940–1949)," *Revue des études byzantines,*
  9 (1951), pp. 192–251
———— "L'Emblème du lis dans la numismatique byzantine: son origine," *Centennial
  Publication of the American Numismatic Society,* ed. H. Ingholt (New York, 1958),
  pp. 417–27
———— "Le 'Juste poids' de l'hyperpyron trachy," *Congrès international de numismatique,
  1953, Actes,* 2 (Paris, 1957), pp. 299–307
———— "Les monnaies tricéphales de Jean II Comnène," *RN⁵,* 13 (1951), pp. 97–108
LONGUET, H. "Deux monnaies de Manuel l'Ange Comnène Ducas, empereur de Thes-
  salonique (1230–1262 [*sic*])," *RN⁵,* 7 (1943), pp. 137–44
———— "Notes de numismatique byzantine," *RN⁵,* 2 (1938), pp. 1–22

LONGUET, H. "Die unedierten byzantinischen Münzen des Wiener Kabinettes," *NZ*, 77
        (1957), pp. 28–57
LOPEZ, R. S. "La crise du besant au Xe siècle et la date du Livre du Préfet," *Annuaire de
        l'Institut de Philologie et d'Histoire Orientales et Slaves*, 10 (1950) (= Mélanges
        Henri Grégoire, 2), pp. 403–18
———— "The Dollar of the Middle Ages," *Journal of Economic History*, 11 (1951), pp. 209–34
———— "Harmenopoulos and the Downfall of the Bezant," Τόμος Κωνσταντίνου Ἁρμε-
        νοπούλου (Thessaloniki, 1952), pp. 111–125
MARIĆ, R. "Novci Solunskog Tsara Teodora Angela," *Starinar*, N.S., 5–6 (1954–55), pp.
        351–52
MATTINGLY, H. "The Lazania Hoard of Byzantine Coins," *Report of the Dept. of Antiquities,
        Cyprus, 1937–39* (Nicosia, 1951), pp. 22–23
———— "A Find of Thirteenth-century Coins at Arta in Epirus," *NC⁵*, 3 (1923), pp. 31–46
METCALF, D. M. "The Brauron Hoard and the Petty Currency of Central Greece,
        1143–1204," *NC⁷*, 4 (1964), pp. 251–59
———— "Byzantine Scyphate Bronze Coinage in Greece," *Annual of the British School of
        Archaeology at Athens*, 56 (1961), pp. 42–63
———— *Classification of Byzantine Stamena in the Light of a Hoard Found in Southern
        Serbia* (= Situla [Dissertationes Musei Nationalis Labacensis] 9), Ljubljana, 1967
———— *Coinage in the Balkans, 820–1355* (Thessaloniki, 1965)
———— "John Vatatzes and John Comnenus: Questions of Style and Detail in Byzantine
        Numismatics," *Greek, Roman and Byzantine Studies*, 3 (1960), pp. 203–14
———— "The Reformed Gold Coinage of Alexius I Comnenus," *HBN*, 16 (1962), pp. 271–84
———— *see also*, BELLINGER, A. R.
MOSSER, S. McA. *A Bibliography of Byzantine Coin Hoards*, ANS, *Numismatic Notes and
        Monographs*, No. 67 (New York, 1935)
RATTO, R. *Monnaies byzantines et d'autres pays contemporaines à l'époque byzantine*. Sale
        Catalogue (Lugano, 9 December 30. Reprinted Amsterdam, 1959)
ROLLIN, G. "Monnoies d'or des empereurs de Nicée pendant l'occupation de Constanti-
        nople par les princes croisés," *RN* (1841), pp. 171–76
SABATIER, J. "Alexis Ier Comnène, Irène et Jean," *Annuaire de la Société Française de
        Numismatique et d'Archéologie*, 3 (1868), pp. 291–92
———— *Description générale des monnaies byzantines*, 2 vols. (Paris, 1862)
SCHINDLER, L. "Ein byzantinischer Münzfund," *Mitteilungen der Numismatischen Gesell-
        schaft in Wien*, 15 (1923), pp. 229, 232
———— "Die Stamma, eine byzantinische schüsselförmige Weisskupfermünze," *NZ*, 73
        (1949), pp. 107–10
SHERBORN, C. DAVIES. "New Byzantine Bronze of Isaac II," *Numismatic Circular*, 40
        (1932), p. 341
SVORONOS, J. N. Βυζαντιακὰ νομισματικὰ ζητήματα, *Journal international d'archéologie
        numismatique*, 2 (1899), pp. 341–401
SVORONOS, N. G. "Recherches sur le cadastre byzantin et la fiscalité aux XIe et XIIe
        siècles: le cadastre de Thèbes," *BCH*, 83 (1959), pp. 1–145, etc.
THOMPSON, M. *The Athenian Agora, 2, Coins from the Roman through the Venetian Period*
        (Princeton, 1954)
TIVCHEV, P. and TSANKOVA-PETKOVA, G. "Au sujet des relations féodales dans les
        territoires bulgares sous la domination byzantine à la fin du XIe et pendant la
        première moitié du XIIe siècle," *Byzantinobulgarica*, 2 (1966), pp. 107–25

WAAGE, D. B. *Antioch-on-the-Orontes*, 4, pt. 2, *Greek, Roman, Byzantine and Crusaders' Coins* (Princeton, 1952)

WARREN, F. "Notes on Some Mediaeval Coins of Cyprus," *NC³*, 12 (1892), pp. 209–19

WHITTING, P. D. "A Bronze of Isaac II," *Numismatic Circular*, 60 (1952), p. 512

——— and DONALD, P. J. "Two Coins of John IV of Nicaea," *Numismatic Circular*, 75 (1967), p. 32

WROTH, W. *Catalogue of the Coins of the Vandals, Ostrogoths and Lombards and of the Empires of Thessalonica, Nicaea and Trebizond in the British Museum* (London, 1911)

——— *Catalogue of the Imperial Byzantine Coins in the British Museum*, 2 vols. (London, 1908)

WULFING, J. M. "A Hoard of Eighty Byzantine Gold Coins," *The Numismatist*, 39 (1926), pp. 49–54

ZAKYTHINOS, D. A. *Crise monétaire et crise économique à Byzance du XIIIᵉ au XVᵉ siècle* (Athens, 1948)

List of Abbreviations

ANS	— American Numismatic Society
BCH	— *Bulletin de correspondance hellénique*
BMCV	— *Catalogue of the Coins of the Vandals, Ostrogoths, and Lombards and of the Empires of Thessalonica, Nicaea and Trebizond in the British Museum*
BZ	— *Byzantinische Zeitschrift*
HBN	— *Hamburger Beiträge zur Numismatik*
IBAD	— *Izvestiya na Bulgarskoto Arkheologichesko Druzhestvo* (1910–20). vols. 1–7; continued as
IBAI	— *Izvestiya na Bulgarskiya Arkheologicheski Institut* (1921–50), vols, 1–16; continued as
IAI	— *Izvestiya na Arkheologicheskiya Institut* (1950), vol. 17
MGH, SS	— Monumenta Germaniae Historica, *Scriptores*
NC	— *Numismatic Chronicle*
NZ	— *Numismatische Zeitschrift*
RBN	— *Revue belge de numismatique*
RIN	— *Rivista italiana di numismatica*
RN	— *Revue numismatique*

List of Ligatured Letters used in Inscriptions

Since this publication does not contain a detailed catalogue, and a "typical" inscription only is given for each type of coin, the list makes no claim to be exhaustive. It does, however, include most of the commoner combinations.

Ѧ	— ΑΛ		ΜΡ	— MP
Ᵽ, �ₚ	— AP		NH	— NH
Ⅎ	— ΓШP		Ø, Ꝋ	— OA
∆ᚺ	— ΔH		ꙮ	— OV
ᚺⅯ	— HM		Ϙ	— CT
ⅯH, ᚺᚺ	— MH		Ħ	— TH
ⅯP, ᚺP	— MHP		Ᵽ	— TP
ⅯN	— MN		Ʇ, Ꞁ	— TШ
ⅯNH	— MNH		⚓	— ΦШ
ⅯNᚺN	— MNHN		ℬ	— ШP

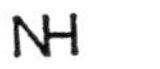

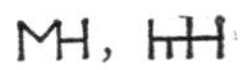

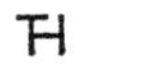

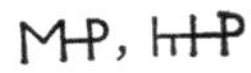

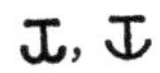

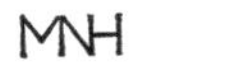

xviii

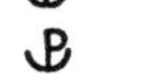

COINAGE AND MONEY
IN THE
BYZANTINE EMPIRE
1081–1261

SECTION I

PRELIMINARIES

CHAPTER ONE

THE ELEVENTH CENTURY: MONETARY CRISIS

On Easter Sunday, 4 April 1081, after a period of looting and riot, Alexius Comnenus was crowned Emperor of the Romans by the Patriarch Cosmas in the Great Church at Constantinople.

It was not an enviable heritage into which he entered: externally, the Empire was threatened from several sides simultaneously; from the west by the Normans, from the north by the Patzinaks, and from the east by the Seljuk Turks. Internally, the situation was little better: an empty treasury and a wildly debased coinage; an army reduced by the conscious efforts of his predecessors, and by the losses and confusion of the disastrous defeat of Manzikert and its aftermath; considerable disaffection among the powerful landed nobility, to many of whom he must himself have appeared something of an upstart and hardly a permanent figure. It is, in itself, a measure of his achievement that, on his death in 1118, he was able to hand on the Empire to his son John II (1118–43) with at least no threat to the dynastic succession as such. The fact that the position of the Empire then bore no resemblance to that of the chaotic and dangerous years of the eighth and ninth decades of the eleventh century, renders the extent of his success comparable to those of Heraclius and Leo III.

Yet the period of a little over a century during which the Comneni and Angeli ruled the Eastern Empire is customarily regarded very much as a time of temporary respite—an age of superficial brilliance, all but hiding an essential and ever-increasing decadence, culminating naturally in the sack of Constantinople by the armies of the Fourth Crusade. It was in spite of this decadence (so runs the argument) that the dynasty was for long able to play a leading part in the politics of the Mediterranean, to maintain a sumptuous court which dazzled east and west alike, and to act as a generous and energetic patron of art. Stripped of its outward glamor, however, the period was marked by an unhealthy increase in the power of the military nobility at the expense of the central government; the decline of the war fleet and mercantile marine in the face of neglect and of the privileged competition of the Italian trading republics; the loss of revenue as a result of the widespread granting of tax immunities, both to those same republics and to the lay and ecclesiastical nobility, and of the shifting of trade routes to areas outside the control of the Empire. The precarious financial position of the Comneni was marked by the large-scale debasement of the coinage, which, if they did not originate,

1*   3

they certainly encouraged and increased. Such a conception of twelfth-century Byzantium is perhaps best illustrated by Runciman's well known phrase that "Under the capable rule of Alexius's son, John II, the decadence barely showed."[1]

The supposed debasement of the coinage under these two dynasties is a widely accepted assumption, and generally held as one of the most obvious illustrations of the Empire's economic debility—and although it is true that views dissenting from the traditional have been, and are, expressed, no exhaustive examination of the coinage and monetary system of the late eleventh and the twelfth century has yet been undertaken. It was still possible in 1951 for R. S. Lopez, one of the leading authorities on the economics of the period, to state: "We have specimens of seven different types of the nomisma struck by Alexius I, and of thirteen struck by Manuel. Presumably all of them were intended to pass as good bezants, but most of them were of bronze, billon, silver, or pale gold."[2] Commendably, with a little more reserve, N. G. Svoronos wrote, in 1959, in an article on the cadastral registers of Thebes:

> Certains renseignements autorisent néamoins à penser que la monnaie d'or d'Alexis devait être de toute façon inférieure en titre à celle d'avant la dévaluation de Monomaque et peut-être même à celle de Michel VII Ducas, puisque Bohémond exige le versement annuel stipulé au traité de paix de 1108 en pièces d'or à l'effigie de cet empereur ou bien de Michel IV. D'autre part, étant donné les nombreux types de nomismata de bas aloi émis par Alexis Ier, on peut se demander si les monnaies à base d'or et de bon poids n'avaient pas dans l'Empire un cours limité, étant réservées aux payements extérieurs, et si le numéraire en nomismata vraiment en circulation ne consistait pas justement dans ces monnaies de bas aloi, dont la valeur intrinsèque ne pouvait pas atteindre un niveau élevé....[3]

As long ago as 1951 L. Schindler suggested that the coinage of the period might fit into a fractional system, and even drew up a table of denominational values and relationships,[4] recently modified by T. Bertelè.[5] Unfortunately, however, neither Schindler's nor Bertelè's studies have been in any way exhaustive, and their hypothetical systems do not appear to have been accepted with any great enthusiasm by other numismatists and economic historians. At the moment, the question apparently rests.

---

[1] S. Runciman, *Byzantine Civilization* (London, 1933), p. 53.

[2] R. S. Lopez, "Harmenopoulos and the Downfall of the Bezant," Τόμος Κωνσταντίνου Ἁρμενοπούλου (Thessaloniki, 1952), p. 123.

[3] N. G. Svoronos, "Recherches sur le cadastre byzantin et la fiscalité aux XIe et XIIe siècles: le cadastre de Thèbes," *BCH*, 83 (1959), p. 104.

[4] L. Schindler, "Die Stamma, eine byzantinische schüsselförmige Weisskupfermünze," *NZ*, 73 (1949), pp. 107–10.

[5] T. Bertelè, in "Lineamenti principali della numismatica bizantina," *RIN*, 66 (1964), pp. 33–118.

The coinage and monetary system of the period ought not to be considered in isolation, but rather against the background of that of the preceding century, during which time the first signs of strain occur in the traditional monetary pattern, and at the end of which it lay in chaos. In addition, a comparison should be made between the pattern of coinage of the period *c.* 1034–1081, and that of Alexius and his successors up to 1204, for even with a cursory examination several important differences meet the eye.

The coinage of the Byzantine Empire during the eleventh century until the reign of Michael IV (1034–41) very largely conformed to a pattern set in the preceding centuries. The standard gold nomisma of 24 "keratia" weight and 24 carats fine, called in documentary sources the "(hi)stamenon nomisma" (τὸ νόμισμα [ἱ]στάμενον), was evidently still struck at the Constantinian rate of 72 to the pound—although it may well be that the Byzantine pound had become somewhat lighter than the Roman by this time, since the average weight of the stamenon (*c.* 4.40 gm.) gives a pound of 316.80 gm. as opposed to 327.45 gm. From the reign of Nicephorus II, Phocas (963–69), there had been issued parallel to the stamenon a light weight gold coin known from the sources as the "tetarteron nomisma" (τὸ νόμισμα τεταρτηρόν)—light by $^1/_{12}$, or 2 keratia, and, according to recent research, probably the result of an attempt by Nicephorus to bring the weight of the nomisma into line with that of the Fatimid dinar.[6] Since the later part of the joint reign of Basil II and Constantine VIII (976–1025), the two denominations had been clearly distinguishable, the stamenon taking a thin, spread fabric, the tetarteron a thicker and smaller one.

The silver "miliaresion," a coin of thin, flat fabric, continued to be accounted at the rate of 12 to the stamenon; the copper "follis" (of large, flat fabric), at the rate of 288 to the same, which is also 24 to the miliaresion. Both silver and copper coinages were of a token nature, their nominal value being considerably in excess of their intrinsic worth.

There is every reason to believe that at this time (1034), the coinage was functioning normally, and that the government was having no difficulty in maintaining the weight and purity of its precious-metal denominations. The Emperor Basil II, at his death in 1025, left what was considered the enormous sum of 200,000 lbs. of gold in the treasury—possibly several years' revenue.[7]

[6] P. Grierson, "Nomisma, tetartèron et dinar: un plaidoyer pour Nicéphore Phocas," *RBN*, 100 (1954), pp. 75–84. Later modified by H. Ahrweiler-Glykatzi, "Nouvelle hypothèse sur le tétartèron d'or et la politique monétaire de Nicéphore Phocas," *Recueil des travaux de l'Institut d'Études Byzantines*, 8 (= *Mélanges G. Ostrogorsky*, 1) (Belgrade, 1963), pp. 1–9. Even more recently, however, A. S. Ehrenkreutz has cast doubts on the connection between the tetarteron and dinar: "Byzantine *Tetartera* and Islamic *Dīnārs*," *Journal of the Economic and Social History of the Orient*, 7 (1964), pp. 183–90.

[7] The bulk of the figures for the debasement of the eleventh century is taken from two articles by P. Grierson in the *Byzantinische Zeitschrift*: "The Debasement of the Bezant in the Eleventh Century," *BZ*, 47 (1954), pp. 379–94; later modified by "Notes on the Fineness of the Byzantine Solidus," *BZ*, 54 (1961), pp. 91–97.

Despite the depredations of Constantine VIII during his short sole reign (1025–28), there seems no doubt that the bulk of this treasure remained to Michael IV on his accession; indeed, the chronicler Psellus repeatedly affirms that most of it remained at the beginning of the reign of Constantine IX, Monomachus (1042–55). Nevertheless, the reign of Michael IV marks the beginnings of the debasement of the gold coinage, which seems to have hovered somewhere between the theoretical 24 carats fine and an actual 19½ at this time. The debasement was extended by Constantine IX, at the end of whose reign the purity of the gold coinage remained at approximately 18 carats. This situation lasted until late in the reign of Romanus IV, Diogenes (1067–71), when a new slide began, which, with increasing rapidity, was extended by his two successors Michael VII, Ducas (1071–78) and Nicephorus III, Botaneiates (1078–81). At the commencement of the reign of Alexius, the fineness of the gold coinage had been reduced to about 8 carats, although the full weight of 24 keratia (4.40 gm.) had been retained. The tetarteron nomisma fell in much the same way as the stamenon.

Under Michael IV, the stamenon had assumed a new fabric and had become very spread, and also slightly scyphate (cup-shaped). It seems probable that the new shape was adopted when it became necessary for the treasury to distinguish between the old, and hence pure stamena, and the new, debased ones. The emperor who systematized the debasement (Constantine IX) definitively adopted the new fabric and even accentuated it—possibly to stop the fraudulent battering of the scyphate into a flat piece of supposedly pure content. There can be no doubt that these gold scyphates are to be identified with the "nomisma trachy" (τὸ νόμισμα τραχύ) of documentary sources, and it would appear reasonable to assume that the description "uneven" (τραχύ) referred to the scyphate fabric of these issues.[8] The debased tetarteron continued to be struck in the old fabric, the problem of distinction not arising.

There is, unfortunately, no contemporary evidence bearing directly upon the effect that the debasement of the gold coinage had upon either the system of account, or upon the system of silver and copper denominations hitherto dependent upon the stamenon nomisma. Given the circumstances, however, it is not too difficult to ascertain the course that events must have taken.

Throughout the period c. 1034–81, the government would have paid its debts in the debased coinage of the day. Although a given number of currently issued nomismata, during the reign of Romanus III, Argyrus (1028–34), would still have held the same value as under his predecessors, the same number of currently issued pieces under Theodora or Isaac I, Comnenus (i.e., 1055–59), would have held only ⅚ of its former worth, and under Nicephorus III it would have represented barely one half. Although the government might eventually

[8] Chap. 4, pp. 29–31.

have been compelled to increase the number of nomismata in its payments in order to offset the decline in their actual, as opposed to theoretical, value, it would have been impossible to ensure that it did so at a rate sufficient to keep pace with the decline. On the other hand, the government at no period appears to have demonetized and called in the intrinsically more valuable issues of its predecessors. Consequently, despite the gradual operation of Gresham's law tending toward the withdrawal of the least debased issues from circulation, the circulating medium, during the reign of Nicephorus III, for example, would have contained issues ranging in fineness from the full 24 carats down to 8 carats. The Byzantine theory of coinage had for so long been based on the notion that the value of a gold coin was equivalent to the amount of metal that it contained as bullion, that it is difficult to believe that the authorities could have enforced the circulation of debased pieces at the same rate as those of pure gold. Instead, a hierarchical principle would eventually have been evolved, with the standard based on the value of the old pure gold stamenon nomisma as a unit of account, the value of each new issue, once in circulation, being estimated according to its intrinsic worth. It would have been on this basis that the government would have demanded payments made to it. Thus a trachy of Nicephorus III, at a fineness of 8 carats, although paid out as a nomisma of full value, would have been counted, once in circulation, as worth its 8 keratia weight of pure gold—possibly plus the value of the silver which went to make up the rest of the alloy. Sixteen keratia of silver being approximately equivalent in value to $1\frac{1}{2}$ gold keration, the total value of the trachy would have been $9\frac{1}{2}$ (i.e., $8+1\frac{1}{2}$) keratia—or 114 folleis.

The fact that the government must have operated some such system seems to be indicated by the general custom of accompanying a further debasement by a change in the type of the gold coin. Had the authorities counted pure and debased coins indifferently as worth a full standard nomisma during the collection of taxes, for instance, this would have been superfluous.

The miliaresion and follis being, in any case, denominations of a token nature, they would have tended to remain stable, pegged to the traditional standard, acting as units in which the value of the debased trachea were estimated.

The debasement of the nomisma between c. 1034 and 1081 involved a fall from a theoretical 24 carats to an actual 8. The pattern for the Comneni and Angeli is noticeably different: there exist nomismata of gold, electrum, and low grade alloys of varying proportions of silver and copper (billon), for each reign over a period exceeding a hundred years. Clearly a complete debasement from gold to billon over the whole period is out of the question: equally, a complete debasement within each reign, no matter how long or short it might be, would be logically absurd, implying as it does either foreknowledge of the length of the reign, or the existence of a quite incredible series of coincidences.

On the other hand, the assumption that coins of what is apparently good gold, of electrum, and of billon, could circulate together—all being invested with the same theoretical value of a nomisma of pure gold[9]—is completely unrealistic, and it is to be wondered how such a conception could possibly last as long as it has. In this kind of situation the tendency is for the less debased pieces to disappear from circulation in favor of the more debased (Gresham's law). To ensure otherwise would necessitate an omnipotent and omnipresent government and a population of superhuman honesty. Furthermore, the possibilities of illegal profit would have been obvious, enormous, and accessible to all with sufficient capital to buy a quantity of base metal and the ability to manufacture a presentable pair of dies.

It must also be pointed out that if the Byzantine government were fortunate enough to be able to enforce the circulation of billon coins at the same rate of exchange as those of gold and electrum, it is difficult to imagine any convincing reasons for it continuing to strike pieces of high intrinsic value at all.

Nor is the suggestion that coins of gold were for external use and those of base metals for internal circulation[10] any more convincing. Although gold was occasionally exported, even officially, it is hard to conceive of the imperial government with its long tradition of forbidding, or at least discouraging, the export of that precious metal, actually aiding such a movement by the production of special coins—even if it were in the greatest difficulties. To accept this theory is also to ignore the large amounts of gold found on imperial territory. A system by which gold was formally reserved for the use of the higher ranks of society, particularly the official, while those of lower status were obliged to make do with a currency of base metal, is similarly, on examination, improbable, if not quite impossible. Restrictions of this type would scarcely have been feasible: the whole point of coinage is that (at least theoretically) it can circulate in a society.

Alternatively, it might be supposed that, once put into circulation by a fraudulent government at a grossly enhanced rate, each coin found its own level of value, dependent on its intrinsic worth. This, of course, would have meant that each piece in a transaction would have had to have been tested as to its actual value. At any given moment, therefore, there would have existed almost as many levels of value as there were coins in circulation. In these circumstances, it would be surprising not to find the fabric of the Empire shattered and commerce at a standstill within a decade, let alone a century.

[9] See note 2.
[10] See note 3.

On dealing with any large series of these coins, or better, with a series of hoards, it soon becomes evident that although the Comneni and Angeli undoubtedly struck coins of the same size, weight, and fabric, in several metals or alloys, issues of a particular combination of obverse and reverse types are, with only rare exceptions, struck in one metal or alloy only. Small, carefully selected collections naturally tend to obscure this, for "odd" coins are naturally preferred. Given the above, there would seem to be an unanswerable case for treating the series as fractional in type: that is, that there should exist a regular rate of exchange from the point of view of both issue and circulation, between coins of the same size, weight, and fabric, but distinguished by the particular combination of their obverse and reverse designs and by a fixed metal content. The crucial point is, obviously, to establish whether issues of each metal or alloy were struck according to a regular standard, and whether that standard bears any fairly simple fractional relationship, as far as intrinsic worth is concerned, to issues of other metals.

CHAPTER TWO

SPECIFIC GRAVITY DETERMINATIONS: GOLD AND ELECTRUM NOMISMATA
c. 1081–1203

The table below involves over seventy gold and electrum coins of the late eleventh and twelfth centuries the specific gravities of which were determined by the author and by Mrs. E. West Fitz Hugh of the Freer Gallery of Art. Also included are the figures for several coins already published by Brunetti.[1] The theory of the process used is well known: determination of the specific gravity of an alloy of two known metals enables the relative proportions of the metals in the alloy to be calculated. The practical aspects and the limitations of the process are perhaps less familiar, and for this reason a short report has been appended.

No.	Coll.	Ruler and Denomination	Wt. in Air	Wt. in CCl_4	Sp. gr.	% $A\!\!\!/$	Fineness Carats
1	D.O.	Alexius I, Comnenus	4.400	3.990	17.1	85	20.5
2	D.O.	(1081–1118)	4.425	4.004	16.8	82	19.5
3	D.O.		4.226	3.824	16.8	82	19.5
4	D.O.		4.451	4.044	17.5	88	21.0
5	A.M.		4.312	3.908	17.0	84	20.0
6	A.M.		4.386	3.974	17.0	84	20.0
7	G.C.	$A\!\!\!/$ (Pl. 3.4–Pl. 5.14)	4.283	3.875	16.7	81	19.5
8	G.C.		4.350	3.982	18.9	97	23.5
9	G.C.		4.236	3.833	16.8	82	20.0
10	M.H.		4.335	3.911	16.3	78	19.0
11	L.B.		4.493	4.226	16.8	82	20.0
12	L.B.		4.286	4.029	16.7	81	19.5
13	L.B.		4.192	3.947	17.1	85	20.5
14	D.O.		4.504	3.912	12.1	29	7.0
15	A.M.	(Pl. 6.2–5)	4.410	3.820	11.9	26	6.5
16	G.C.	El.	4.240	3.567	10.0	—	—
17	D.O.	(Pl. 6.6–9)	4.344	3.763	11.9	26	6.5

[1] L. Brunetti, "Nuovi orientamenti statistici nella monetazione antica," *RIN*, 52–53 (1950–51), p. 9: the figures are based on the use of distilled water rather than CCl_4.

No.	Coll.	Ruler and Denomination	Wt. in Air	Wt. in CCl$_4$	Sp. gr.	% A͵	Fineness Carats
18	D.O.	John II, Comnenus	4.406	3.995	17.1	85	20.5
19	D.O.	(1118–1143)	4.315	3.910	17.0	84	20.0
20	D.O.		4.334	3.930	17.1	85	20.5
21	D.O.	(Pl. 9.*1–3*)	4.157	3.769	17.1	85	20.5
22	G.C.		4.332	3.919	16.7	81	19.5
23	L.B.		4.356	4.101	17.1	85	20.5
24	L.B.		4.382	4.119	16.7	81	19.5
25	D.O.	A͵	4.223	3.836	17.4	87	21.0
26	D.O.		4.432	4.012	16.8	82	20.0
27	D.O.	(Pl. 9.*4–9*)	4.336	3.935	17.3	86	20.5
28	D.O.		4.365	3.954	16.9	83	20.0
29	A.M.		4.114	3.723	16.8	82	20.0
30	G.C.		4.045	3.662	16.8	82	20.0
31	D.O.	(Pl. 9.*10*)	4.324	3.916	16.9	83	20.0
32	D.O.		4.248	3.841	16.6	80	19.5
33	G.C.	El. (Pl. 10.*1–6*)	4.267	3.688	11.7	23	5.5
34	G.C.		2.842	2.458	11.8	24	6.0
35	D.O.	Manuel I, Comnenus	3.486	3.160	17.1	85	20.5
36	D.O.	(1143–1180)	4.108	3.721	16.9	83	20.0
37	D.O.		4.307	3.903	17.0	84	20.0
38	D.O.	A͵ (Pl. 12.*1–12*)	4.340	3.933	17.0	84	20.0
39	A.M.		4.225	3.824	16.8	82	20.0
40	G.C.		3.116	2.813	16.4	78	19.0
41	M.H.		4.389	3.970	16.7	81	19.5
42	L.B.		4.232	3.980	16.8	82	20.0
43	D.O.		4.375	3.781	11.8	24	6.0
44	G.C.	(Pl. 13.*1*, *2*)	4.095	3.534	11.6	21	5.0
45	G.C.		4.327	3.733	11.6	21	5.0
46	G.C.	(Pl. 13.*3*, *4*)	4.489	3.864	11.5	19	5.0
47	A.M.		4.038	3.485	11.6	21	5.0
48	G.C.	(Pl. 13.*5–9*)	4.163	3.585	11.5	19	5.0
49	M.H.	El.	4.614	3.982	11.6	21	5.0
50	D.O.		4.578	3.954	11.7	23	5.5
51	A.M.	(Pl. 13.*10–12*)	4.236	3.645	11.4	18	4.5
52	G.C.		4.226	3.644	11.6	21	5.0
53	D.O.	(Pl. 14.*1–4*)	4.419	3.821	11.8	24	6.0
54	G.C.	(Pl. 14.*7–9*)	4.365	3.761	11.6	21	5.0

No.	Coll.	Ruler and Denomination	Wt. in Air	Wt. in CCl₄	Sp. gr.	% Aʹ	Fineness Carats
55	D.O.	Andronicus I,	4.387	3.965	16.9	83	20.0
56	D.O.	Comnenus	4.393	3.981	17.0	84	20.0
57	D.O.	(1183–1185)	4.158	3.762	16.8	82	20.0
58	D.O.	Aʹ (Pl. 18.9, 10)	4.326	3.918	16.9	83	20.0
59	G.C.		4.315	3.900	16.6	80	19.5
60	G.C.	El. (Pl. 18.11, 12)	3.957	3.417	11.7	23	5.5
61	D.O.	Isaac II, Angelus	3.808	3.444	16.7	81	19.5
62	D.O.	(1185–1195)	4.148	3.759	17.0	84	20.0
63	D.O.	Aʹ (Pl. 20.1–4)	4.538	4.109	16.9	83	20.0
64	D.O.		4.358	3.946	16.9	83	20.0
65	G.C.		4.393	3.971	16.6	80	19.5
66	A.M.		4.450	3.839	11.6	21	5.0
67	G.C.	El. (Pl. 20.5–8)	3.840	3.281	11.0	9	2.5
68	G.C.		3.783	3.256	11.4	18	4.5
69	D.O.	Alexius III, Angelus	4.298	3.894	17.0	84	20.0
70	D.O.	(1195–1203)	4.280	3.877	16.9	83	20.0
71	D.O.		4.427	4.005	16.7	81	19.5
72	D.O.	Aʹ (Pl. 22.1–3)	4.344	3.930	16.7	81	19.5
73	G.C.		4.191	3.791	16.7	81	19.5
74	L.B.		4.274	4.016	16.5	79	19.0
75	D.O.		4.188	3.585	11.1	12	3.0
76	D.O.	El. (Pl. 22.4–7)	4.533	3.808	10.0	—	—
77	M.H.		4.158	3.542	11.0	9	2.5
78	D.O.	John III, Ducas-Vatatzes Emperor of Nicaea	4.261	3.829	15.7	73	17.5
79	D.O.	(1222–1254)	4.401	3.951	15.6	72	17.5
80	D.O.	Aʹ (Pl. 31.13–15:	4.343	3.892	15.4	70	17.0
81	D.O.	Pl. 32.1–5)	4.346	3.896	15.4	70	17.0

Key:

D.O. — Dumbarton Oaks Collection
A.M. — Ashmolean Museum Collection
G.C. — Goodacre Collection
M.H. — Author's Collection
L.B. — L. Brunetti (*art. cit.*)

Method: The weight of the coin in air is obtained by the usual method. To obtain the weight in carbon tetrachloride, the coin is suspended in the liquid by means of a length of fine copper wire. The weight of the wire alone in carbon tetrachloride is also determined and subtracted, to give the weight of the coin alone. The formula used for calculation of the specific gravity of the coin is: $\dfrac{\text{wt. in air}}{\text{wt. in air} - \text{wt. in CCl}_4} \times 1.595$.

The factor 1.595 is the density of the carbon tetrachloride, which is denser than water, and used for the following reasons: it has less surface tension, and there is, therefore, less likelihood of an accumulation of air bubbles around the wire, or on the surface of the coin—which would cause low weights; it evaporates more quickly than water, and so time need not be wasted in drying the coin after weighing; because it is denser than water, the results tend to be more accurate.

There are, however, still several sources of error possible in the specific gravity method; the presence of impurities in the metal, or the existence of hidden cavities may affect the weight of a coin. Careful inspection of the pieces to be used showed slight superficial incrustation in some cases, but never in amounts large enough to influence the result. The most obvious source of error is uncertainty as to the composition of the alloy. Silver alone may be used, or copper alone, or a mixture of the two in unknown proportions. If the alloy has a high gold content, then the error is not serious, but it becomes increasingly so as gold content decreases.[2] The one case of detailed chemical analysis of the gold denomination (a piece of Alexius I, from the Gornoslav hoard),[3] betrays the existence of only minute quantities of metals other than gold and silver, and to judge from the appearance of the coins themselves, this is the case throughout the twelfth century. At the point in the thirteenth century when there is documentary evidence for the commencement of an admixture of copper, it becomes immediately apparent both visually, and in the specific gravity determinations themselves. The case of the electrum is less certain, but documentary sources seem to suggest that only with the reign of Isaac II, Angelus (1185–95) was there any attempt to add copper to the gold/silver alloy. Again, this is evident in the table of results.

Specific gravity measurements have less value in determining the silver content of alloys of silver and base metals;[4] the small difference between the specific gravities of silver and copper considerably affecting the reliability of the results.

Specific gravities: Gold – 19.3, Silver – 10.5, Copper – 8.9.

M. F. Hendy

E. West FitzHugh (Assistant in Technical Research, Freer Gallery of Art, Smithsonian Institution, Washington D. C.)

[2] E. R. Caley, "Validity of the Specific Gravity Method for the Determination of the Fineness of Gold Objects," *Ohio Journal of Science*, 49, 2 (March 1949), pp. 73–82.

[3] Ch. Dzhambov, reporting the discovery of the Gornoslav (Bulgaria) hoard in *Arkheologiya*, yr. III, bk. 4 (1961), pp. 1–5, mentions the chemical analysis of a gold scyphate from the hoard. The composition was as follows: gold, 75.2%; silver, 23.1%; copper, 1.2%. The balance was presumably taken up by trace metals, etc. It is also worth noting at this point that, of a hoard of thirty gold scyphates of Manuel I found at Corinth in 1938, all apparently gave an approximate density of 17—that is, 20 carats fine. See: J. Harris, "A Gold Hoard from Corinth," *AJA*, 43, 2 (April-June 1939), p. 271.

[4] Caley, "Estimation of Composition of Ancient Metal Objects: Utility of Specific Gravity Measurements," *Analytical Chemistry*, 24 (April 1952), pp. 676–81.

CHAPTER THREE

THE TWELFTH CENTURY: MONETARY RECOVERY

The figures in the table of fineness produce incontestable evidence that the gold nomisma was struck according to a regular standard of somewhere between 19 and 21 carats throughout the late eleventh and the twelfth century. This is much the same as the standard of the nomisma during the fourth decade of the eleventh century, before the period of greatest debasement, and therefore represents a considerable improvement.

In point of fact, this should not be unsuspected, for western documents of the period continually give a standing of between *c.* 38 and *c.* 60 grams of silver to a Byzantine coin termed "perperum," "purpuratus," or "yperperum."[1] This can only be the issue referred to in the Byzantine sources themselves as τὸ νόμισμα ὑπέρπυρον (hyperpyron nomisma). It is impossible to draw any detailed conclusions regarding the hyperpyron from these exchange rates alone, but it is clear that they involve a coin of relatively high gold content, and not, for instance, the electrum issue discussed below: for this reason, the identification of the gold coin in the table of fineness as the hyperpyron nomisma of the sources must be regarded as conclusive.

It is equally evident that, at least from the reign of Alexius I to that of Isaac II, Angelus (1185–95), the electrum nomisma was also struck on a consistent standard. The readings in the table are a little less regular than those for the gold, but this may well be accounted for by the difficulty of ensuring a uniform mixture of the gold and silver during the preparation of the alloy.

---

[1] The exchange values of the hyperpyron were:

1097: fifteen solidi of deniers (Tournois?), *c.* 60 gm. Æ; *Gesta Francorum et aliorum Hierosolimitanorum,* ed. R. Hill (London, 1962), p. 33.

1155: eighteen solidi of deniers (Veronese), *c.* 28 gm. Æ; R. M. della Rocca, A. Lombardo, *Documenti del commercio veneziano nei secoli XI–XIII,* 1 (Turin, 1940), p. 119.

1156: ten solidi of deniers (Genoese), *c.* 40 gm. Æ; *Historiae Patriae Monumenta,* Chartarum, II, no. 316, col. 332.

1157: 9½ solidi of deniers (Gen.), *c.* 38 gm. Æ; *ibid.,* no. 440, col. 402.

1190: 2/11 mark (Cologne) of Æ, *c.* 42 gm.; *infra,* p. 21, note 20.

1196: forty solidi of deniers (Venetian), *c.* 43 gm. Æ; G. Tafel and G. Thomas, *Urkunden zur älteren Handels- und Staatsgeschichte der Republik Venedig mit besonderer Beziehung auf Byzanz und die Levante,* 1, Fontes Rerum Austriacarum (Vienna, 1856), no. 78, p. 218.

1204: ¼ mark (Col.) of Æ, *c.* 57 gm.; Günther of Pairis, *De Expugnatione Urbis Constantinopolitanae,* ed. Riant (Geneva, 1877), p. 78.

1204: three solidi of deniers (English), *c.* 50 gm. Æ; Ralph of Coggeshall, *Chronicon Anglicanum,* Rerum Britannicarum Medii Aevi Scriptores (London, 1875), p. 150.

As long as the correct proportions were used for each melting, however, this would be of little moment, for the standard would average out. A level of somewhere between 4¹/₂ and 7 carats seems to be suggested. The varied color of these issues—from silver to gold—is therefore probably to be explained by the degree of preferential surface corrosion of the silver of the alloy, and not by large variations in the quality of the alloy itself, as hitherto supposed.

It is impossible to gain more precise figures for the theoretical standard of the gold hyperpyron from contemporary Greek sources: there does exist, however, a probable western connection of considerable interest, from a slightly later period.

During the years 1231–32, Frederick II of Hohenstaufen, the German Emperor, ordered that a gold coin known as the "augustalis" should be struck and put into circulation in the kingdom of Sicily. Both events are recorded by Richard of San Germano:[2]

> (1231): *Mense Decembris...nummi aurei, qui augustales vocantur, de mandato imperatoris in utraque sycla, Brundusii et Messane, cuduntur.*

> (1232): *Mense Iunii quidam Thomas de Pando civis Scalensis novam monetam auri que augustalis dicitur ad Sanctum Germanum detulit distribuendam per totam abbatiam et per Sanctum Germanum, ut ipsa moneta utantur homines in emptionibus et venditionibus suis. . . .*

Pegolotti, in the *Pratica della mercatura*, quotes the augustalis as being of 20¹/₂ carats fine[3] ("Agostantini [for Agostari] d'oro a carati 20 e ¹/₂"). The *Statuta Officiorum*, a document dated to Frederick's own reign, is even more specific:[4]

> *Augustales auri, qui laborantur in predictis siclis, fiunt de caratis viginti et medio, ita quod quelibet libra auri in pondere tenet de puro et fino auro uncias x. tarenos vii ¹/₂; reliqua vero uncia una et tareni viginti duo et medius sunt in quarta parte de ere et in tribus partibus de argento fino sicut in tarenis.*

The exact proportions of the metals forming the alloy of the augustalis are, according to the above, 20¹/₂ carats gold, 2⁵/₈ carats silver and ⁷/₈ carat copper.

The assumption of this curious standard has never been satisfactorily explained, the traditional fineness of the Sicilian tari being 16²/₃ carats. Lopez has connected it with a treaty signed in 1231 between Frederick and the Hafsid state of Tunis (possibly a renewal of a previous agreement of 1221), by which the Emperor was assured a regular tribute of gold.[5] It is not known

[2] Richard of San Germano, *Annales*, MGH, *SS*, 19, pp. 365, 368.
[3] Francesco Balducci Pegolotti, *La pratica della mercatura*, ed. A. Evans, Mediaeval Academy of America, publ. no. 24 (Cambridge, Mass., 1936), p. 288.
[4] *Acta Imperii Inedita*, ed. E. Winkelmann, I (Innsbruck, 1880; photographic reprint Aalen, 1964), no. 1004, p. 766.
[5] R. S. Lopez, "Back to Gold 1252," *Ec.Hist.Rev.²*, IX, 2 (Dec. 1956), p. 227.

in what form the gold was to be paid, but conceivably a part at least might have been in gold dust from the Senegalese river gravels—the famous *aurum de Paleola* of the medieval period—which was apparently obtained as a natural alloy of between 20 and 21 carats gold, with the rest mainly silver, but small amounts of copper being present. The implication that the standard of the augustalis was based upon that of the Senegalese gold dust is attractive, certainly, but hardly convincing. It is unlikely in the extreme that the mint authorities would have trusted the natural standard of the *aurum de Paleola* to the extent that they would use the gold dust for the manufacture of augustales without first refining and then re-alloying—a process which would have destroyed any convenience that such a standard might have had, for an augustalis of proven, manufactured alloy would have always been worth more than an equivalent weight of *aurum de Paleola* of identical, but natural, alloy. Neither of the contemporary North African states, Hafsid or Muwahid, struck coins of 20½ carats fine,[6] despite the fact that they were the main recipients of the Senegalese dust. Both appear to have issued coins of a 24 carat standard, in which the tribute may have been paid in any case.

On the other hand, when it is realized that in the third decade of the thirteenth century the only gold coin of international repute struck by a Christian power was the Byzantine hyperpyron; that it had been struck on what was evidently the same standard as that utilized for the augustalis for over a century at the time of the Fourth Crusade, and had possibly been continued by the emperors of Nicaea;[7] that Frederick had notoriously ambitious designs on the Latin Levant, and had been there as recently as 1228–29 on a crusade, a connection between the two denominations, the hyperpyron and the augustalis, becomes much more probable than that proposed between the augustalis and the *aurum de Paleola*.

Such a proposition does not necessarily destroy the importance of the treaty of 1231: it may well be that it was this assurance of a regular supply of gold that gave or confirmed in Frederick the intention to issue a gold coinage, and it is quite possible that the weight of gold in an augustalis (approximately 4.5 gm.) was meant to equal that of the Hafsid double dinar (4.5–4.75 gm.). A Byzantine standard of fineness and a Muslim standard of bullion value wonld have given the augustalis the best of both worlds.

The hyperpyron of the Comneni and Angeli was, then, probably struck at a theoretical standard of 20½ carats fineness. In addition, the remaining carats of silver (approx. 2½), would possibly have been taken into account with

[6] H. W. Hazard, *The Numismatic History of Late Mediaeval North Africa*, ANS, Numismatic Studies, no. 8 (New York, 1952), p. 48.

[7] Chap. 12, pp. 248–49.

regard to the total value of the denomination. It is difficult to estimate the contemporary ratio between the value of gold and silver, but in Italy at this time it apparently hovered between 11 and 10:1. Calculations based on this rate will not be too far wrong. The silver of the alloy would therefore have been approximately equivalent in value to $\frac{1}{4}$ keration weight of gold, the total value of the coin therefore being approximately equivalent to $20\frac{3}{4}$ keratia weight of gold—or very nearly $\frac{7}{8}$ that of the stamenon nomisma of the pre-debasement period.[8]

This still leaves unknown the reasons behind the original assumption of the curious standard of $20\frac{1}{2}$ carats. It is clear, however, that it was not a matter of Alexius being incapable of restoring the full 24 carat standard, for, as will be seen below, the reform involved an improvement from appreciably less than 8 carats. The improvement being so large, it is certain that, had he so wished, Alexius could have restored the full fineness without much more difficulty. It may tentatively be suggested that Alexius was returning to the standard of fineness as introduced by Michael IV, under whom the fineness of the gold was reduced in the first place—but even this connection, if accepted, still brings a solution to the original problem no nearer.

A further point of crucial importance for the correct understanding of the monetary system used by Alexius I and his successors is the question of the rôle of their hyperpyron. Had it replaced the old Constantinian stamenon as the lynch-pin of the system, or did it itself fit into the traditional framework? In the first case, the subordinate denominations would have been fractions of the hyperpyron itself; in the second case, fractions of the Constantinian coin, by now merely a coin of account, the hyperpyron being reckoned as worth so many miliaresia and/or folleis of the traditional value. Two considerations swing the decision decisively in favor of the first possibility.

In 1136, a coin termed "the currently most valued gold nomisma" was, according to an imperial document, worth 48 "aspra trachea."[9] The care taken over the description of the two denominations, and the particular phrasing used, indicates that the gold nomisma in question was definitely a current coin, and not a coin of account. As such, it can only have been the hyperpyron. If the hyperpyron was so integrated into the duodecimal pattern as to be worth forty-eight of any denomination, in view of its rather awkward intrinsic value, it follows that it must have stood at the head of the monetary system, and that it had become the standard coin.

---

[8] It should be understood that the keration was basically neither a coin nor a fixed value, but a weight ($\frac{1}{24}$ stamenon nomisma). Consequently, a keration based on the hyperpyron nomisma weighed the same as that based on the old stamenon, but was in fact equivalent in value to only approximately $\frac{7}{8}$ of the latter. Similarly, the twenty-four keratia of gold alloy contained in a hyperpyron were equivalent in value to only $20\frac{3}{4}$ of the twenty-four contained in the old stamenon.

[9] The typicon of the Pantocrator Monastery; see note 17.

2

This is undoubtedly confirmed by a group of western documents dated to the last decade of the twelfth century: two Pisan, the other Venetian.[10] They are all accounts, rendered in "yperpera" and "karates"—the latter without exception in whole units. In several cases, sums of 20 keratia are mentioned which would have been given as "yperperum 1" if the hyperpyron were reckoned as worth no more than 20 keratia. In addition, however, sums of so many yperpera *et quartum, et tertium, et medium*, occur (see also pp. 35, 36 for the Pantocrator typicon). Only if the yperperum were accounted as being of 24 keratia would the accounts be consistent, for the whole number of keratia greater than twenty simply divisible by four, three, and two is of course twenty-four.

The question of the electrum nomisma remains to be discussed in detail. If, as now appears likely, the Comnenian system of scyphates was fractional in type, and the basis of that system was the hyperpyron, then it might reasonably be expected that the electrum coin should bear some comparatively simple fractional relationship to the hyperpyron.

Probably during, or shortly after, the year 1182/83, a still extant treatise was drawn up concerning a radical overhaul of the system of minor taxes (dependent for their reckoning upon the amount charged for the main land-tax) which had been undertaken between indictions XIV and II (September 1105– September 1109) of the Emperor Alexius I. The author was apparently a civil servant with access to the imperial archives, for besides providing a kind of commentary consisting of practical examples of the reckoning of taxes under both the old and the new systems, and information on the monetary system, he quotes several of the imperial lyseis which effected the changes involved. The document is unquestionably of fundamental importance, and as such will be examined later: one point is, however, immediately relevant; a nomisma termed "trachy aspron" is clearly identified as being worth 4 miliaresia or 96 folleis—that is, $^1/_3$ part of the standard nomisma.[11]

There is good reason to believe that "trachy aspron"—white scyphate— occasionally involves scyphate billon coins—which were of relatively low value.[12] In this case, however, the combination of description and value ensures that the white scyphate mentioned must be identified with the electrum nomisma. Although at first sight it might appear unlikely, both electrum and billon denominations do have a white appearance in common, for the billon pieces regularly appear to have been silvered or blanched.

---

[10] For the Pisan, see: G. Müller, *Documenti sulle relazioni delle città toscane coll'Oriente cristiano e coi Turchi* (Florence, 1879), nos. 46, 47. For the Venetian, see: Tafel and Thomas, *Urkunden,* I, no. 78, pp. 218–24.

[11] Chap. 6, p. 57.

[12] *Infra,* pp. 20, 21.

It is relatively simple to calculate the alloy necessary for a denomination worth $1/3$ of a hyperpyron—assuming that the latter coin was already the standard. As seen above, the hyperpyron was equivalent in value approximately to $20^3/_4$ keratia weight of gold: $1/3$ part would obviously be equivalent to approximately 7. The gold content of such a coin should therefore be, on the average, somewhere between 5 and 6 carats fine, if the remaining carats of silver provided the balance. The specific gravity determinations in the table are, for the period Alexius I–Isaac II, perfectly consistent with the standard suggested and, on this occasion, the identification of the aspron trachy nomisma with the electrum issues of the late eleventh and the twelfth centuries need consequently not be doubted.

Judging from the specific gravity determinations, the electrum nomisma continued to be struck at the same standard until the reign of Isaac II, under whom the readings suddenly become erratic, remaining so under Alexius III, Angelus-Comnenus (1195–1203), his successor. The chronicler Nicetas Choniates reports that Isaac, by adulteration of the silver coin, struck an illegal nomisma: Ἀλλὰ καὶ τὸ ἀργύριον κιβδηλεύσας ἀδόκιμον τὸ νόμισμα κέκοφε,[13] which would seem to be a clear reference to the process reflected in the table. Precisely how the debasement was accomplished is uncertain: on the basis of the very low readings for the majority of the coins struck between 1185–1203, it appears that copper must have been introduced into the alloy. If the "bisanti d'oro copoluti di Cipri a carati 4" of Pegolotti's coin list,[14] which were struck by the Lusignan kings of Cyprus until early in the reign of Henry II (1285–1324), were the successors of the electrum nomisma as struck under the Angeli, then a reduction in gold content is also implied. Equally unclear is whether the government attempted to maintain the now artificial rate of 1:3 for the hyperpyron and electrum nomisma, or whether debasement was followed by eventual official readjustment—which would probably only be following what had happened on the free market. Choniates' statement is, in fact, frequently used without adequate analysis to illustrate the hopeless debasement and confusion of the contemporary coinage: there is, however, no evidence to suggest that the hyperpyron—the basis of the monetary system—was affected in any way.

A Pisan document of 1199 provides sufficient information for it to be accepted as fairly certain that a coin known as the "manuellatus" was circulating at the rate of 8 keratia (of gold of hyperpyron standard).[15] Once

[13] Nicetas Choniates, Bonn ed., p. 584.

[14] Pegolotti, *Pratica*, p. 288.

[15] *Infra*, pp. 22 (note 23), 23. Rhabdas, in a mathematical treatise dated 1304, remarks that the sum of $5^7/_{13}$ keratia is approximately equal to $2/_3$ trachy — which results in a trachy of approximately $8^4/_{13}$ keratia (presumably for 8 keratia). Doubtless he refers to a monetary situation already long past. See: P. Tannery, *Mémoires scientifiques*, 4 (Paris, 1920), *Sciences exactes chez les Byzantins*, pp. 148–49.

2*

again, it is a question of the electrum denomination, with the same value as before, but precisely what the term implies is not quite clear. The manuellatus could be an electrum coin of Manuel; an electrum coin of any emperor prior to Isaac II, and so called because Manuel was the last emperor to have struck electrum coins of the old quality in any number, or, quite simply an electrum coin of any quality or emperor, but so termed because those of Manuel I were still the most common in circulation, since he reigned so long and struck so many types in electrum. The evidence is conflicting, and quite possibly the term had no precise connotations: during the early thirteenth century it might also have been applied to the hyperpyron.

The series of scyphates struck in billon and/or copper has already been identified by Schindler[16] with the "staminum" of Latin documentary sources. The term's obvious derivation is from (ἱ)στάμενον formerly denoting the standard gold nomisma of the eleventh century—and presumably used to describe these billon coins because they were theoretically of the same weight as the original, although of different metal. There are few definite instances of the term being used of these coins in contemporary Byzantine sources, although it would seem that the Latins can only have been following current Byzantine usage. Rather, in official documents at least, they are referred to as "trachea." In order to avoid confusion, they will be referred to in the text as "billon trachea," or "billon nomismata." In point of fact, until some time in the reign of Manuel, coins of this denomination of regular imperial mintage seem to have been mainly of billon in which the silver was easily visible: after this period they were of copper, or billon in which the silver was of such minute proportions that it was invisible. Many of the latter period seem to have been put through a process of silvering—either by dipping or by blanching. Throughout the life of the denomination, however, it was nominally of billon, and will be referred to as such in the text.

The typicon of the Pantocrator Monastery in Constantinople, founded in 1136 by the Emperor John II and his wife Irene, contains numerous and detailed references to the salaries of the officials and inmates of the institution, and to sums of money to be set aside, or spent, for certain specific purposes. For the candles and incense to be used at the thrice-yearly commemoration of the dead, it is ordered that the Monastery spend:... νομίσματα τραχέα ἄσπρα δύο, ἢ τοῦ κατὰ τὴν ἡμέραν προτιμωμένου χρυσοῦ νομίσματος μέρος εἰκοστὸν τέταρτον, —"two aspra trachea nomismata being the twenty-fourth part of the most valued gold nomisma of the day."[17] As already pointed out, the gold nomisma in question can only be the hyperpyron: equally the aspron trachy can, on

---

[16] Schindler, "Die Stamma." See chap. 1, p. 4 (note 4).

[17] A. Dimitrievskii, *Opisanie liturgicheskikh rukopisei khranyashchikhsya v bibliotekakh pravoslavnogo Vostoka*, I: Τυπικά (Kiev, 1895), p. 689.

this occasion, only be the billon nomisma, since the electrum aspron trachy is worth $1/_3$ of the hyperpyron, not $1/_{48}$. H. Mattingly, in a report on the Lazania (Cyprus) hoard of billon coins of this denomination, published figures for the chemical analysis of six pieces:[18] two each of two types of John II, and two of an early type of Manuel I. All except one piece (of John) show a remarkably consistent silver content, which, excluding the abnormal coin, averages at 6.3%. Despite the hazardous nature of any calculations attempting to arrive at the intrinsic value of these coins, it does appear that the silver content is not of the order that might be expected if their intrinsic value closely approached their theoretical and official value—as in the cases of the hyperpyron and the electrum nomisma. The denomination is therefore to be recognized as in part, at least, a token one.

The partly token nature of the billon trachy may to some extent explain the complaints of the western chronicler Odo of Deuil,[19] a participant in the Second Crusade (1147). He states that the westerners almost invariably lost on the exchange rate between the denier and the staminum. The crusaders would naturally have expected a rate based on the intrinsic value of each of the denominations: the Byzantines, on the other hand, a rate giving the billon trachy its official value of $1/_{48}$ part of the hyperpyron. It was only at Constantinople, where some special arrangement might have been made, that a relatively satisfactory rate of exchange was encountered. Here, they gave less than two deniers for a billon trachy instead of the five that they had given while making their way down through the Balkan peninsula, and the five or six which they were to give once well into Asia Minor.

The *Historia de Expeditione Friderici Imperatoris* mentions that Frederick Barbarossa the German emperor, while travelling through the Balkans in 1190 on his way to the Levant, came to an agreement with the Emperor Isaac II. Among the conditions was the following, relating to coinage:[20] *Et quod argenti marca emetur pro yperperis quinque et dimidio, et quod mutabitur yperperum pro staminibus centum et viginti, nulla differentia existente inter nova et vetera stamina.* The staminum is unequivocally quoted here as being worth $1/_{120}$ hyperpyron.

[18] H. Mattingly, "The Lazania Hoard of Byzantine Coins," *Report of the Dept. of Antiquities, Cyprus, 1937–39* (Nicosia, 1951), pp. 22–23. The analyses were as follows:
John II: First coinage, Æ: 88.2% Æ: 10.8%
                : 93.9%   : 5.8%
John II: Second coinage, : 93.0%   : 6.3%
                : 93.1%   : 6.4%
Manuel I: First coinage, : 92.1%   : 6.8%
                : 92.9%   : 6.2%
[19] Odo of Deuil, *De Profectione Ludovici VII in Orientem*, ed. V. G. Berry, Records of Civilization, Sources and Studies, no. 42 (New York, 1948), pp. 40 and 66.
[20] *Historia de Expeditione Friderici Imperatoris*, ed. A. Chroust, MGH, *SS* (N.S.), 5, p. 66.

Since both rates of exchange—that of 1136 and that of 1190—are apparently official ones, it would not be possible to argue with any probability that the one represents an official rate, the other a commercial. The denial that there should be any difference between old and new stamina furnishes the solution, implying as it does, that some difference could be thought to exist. Clearly, a revaluation of the billon trachy vis-à-vis the hyperpyron had taken place: possibly for some legitimate monetary reason, possibly as the result of a debasement of the denomination which had caused the difference between its intrinsic and theoretical values to become too wide and which the government had eventually been compelled to admit by a readjustment of the rate of exchange. The question must be reserved for discussion later, but briefly, it does appear from hoard evidence, and from a consideration of the coins themselves, that it is a matter of a revaluation legitimately carried out.[21] It may well have been this action which prompted Nicetas Choniates to charge Manuel with having put debased silver into the coinage: ἀργύριον ἀδόκιμον εἰς νόμισμα κέκοφε.[22] In fact, however, the revaluation cannot have taken place as early as Choniates places it, for he states that Manuel attempted to defraud the crusaders (of 1147) with these coins: numismatic evidence, on the other hand, indicates that the change in value of the billon trachy occurred a good deal later than 1147. There is during this reign no sign of any debasement of the gold or electrum coin—on a permanent basis at least—and Choniates' accusation must either be regarded as completely baseless, or a mistaken appreciation of the revaluation of the billon nomisma.

One of the Pisan documents of account mentioned above, and dated to 1199, bears the following entry: *Item, Guido dedit Alberto sol[idos] LXXI staminorum, que sunt yperpera IIII et kar[ates] XV.*[23]

$$
\begin{aligned}
\text{Now, 4 hyperpyra 15 keratia} &= \text{71 solidi of stamina} \\
4\ ^{15}/_{24}\ \text{hyperpyra} &= 71 \times 12\ \text{stamina} \\
4^{5}/_{8}\ \text{hyperpyra} &= 852\ \text{stamina} \\
\therefore\ 1\ \text{hyperpyron} &= \tfrac{852}{4^{5}/_{8}}\ \text{stamina} \\
&= 184^{8}/_{37}\ \text{stamina or 184 stamina to the} \\
&\qquad\text{nearest whole number.}
\end{aligned}
$$

Thus, by 1199 the value of the billon trachy had again fallen—this time to $1/_{184}$ hyperpyron. In contrast to the two previously mentioned rates of 1136 and 1190, this document being definitely non-imperial, it is arguable that the value given may have been the commercial rate of the trachy. However, in default of further evidence, the equivalence should be accepted as official, and

[21] Chap. 10, pp. 170–71.
[22] Nicetas Choniates, Bonn ed., p. 89.
[23] Müller, *op. cit.*, p. 77.

indeed numismatic evidence—presented below—suggests that a debasement had taken place over a period of time.[24]

The same document contains a useful check on the validity of the case for a fractional system under the Comneni and Angeli in the form of a series of entries which remain unmutilated in the text and relatively uncomplicated in form:

Item, ego Gerardus feci debitum, cum veniebam cum Clanni et Torscello Pisis Constantinupolim, yperpera XXV, que reddidi domino Romano.

Item, dedi Octoviano et Alberto pro expensis, quando exierunt Constantinupoli causa revertendi Pisas, yperpera XX et stam[ina] CII.

Item, dedi cursori quem misimus ad Scium pro navi imperiali, yperpera XX et quartum.

Item, dedi scribis curie manuellatos VI.

Item, dedi pro preparare navem Grandeorgolii, communi consilio bonorum omnium Pisanorum concivium et imperiali precepto, yperpera XXXIIII.

Item, dedi domino Iacobi interpreti, consilio multorum bonorum Pisanorum, yperpera XX, cum filiam suam coniugavit.

Item, in duobus sendatis pro vexillo imperialis navis yperpera V.

Summa bizan. CXXVI et kar. XX.

Although the final total is indeed 126 bizanti (hyperpyra), 20 karates, a less compressed form would be $124^1/_4$ hyperpyra, 6 manuellati, 102 stamina. Now $^1/_4$ hyperpyron = 6 keratia, and, according to the rate of exchange between the hyperpyron and the stamenon contained in this same document, 102 stamina = approximately $13^1/_3$ keratia ($\frac{102 \times 24}{184}$ ker.). Therefore:

$$
\begin{array}{rl}
6 \text{ manuellati} = & 126 \text{ hyp. } 20 \text{ ker.} \\
- & 124 \text{ hyp. } 19^1/_3 \text{ ker. (i.e., } 6+13^1/_3 \text{ ker.)} \\
\hline
= & 2 \text{ hyp. } ^2/_3 \text{ ker.}
\end{array}
$$

Two hyperpyra contain 48 keratia; therefore 1 manuellatus equals approximately 8 keratia, which is the value given to the electrum trachy by the treatise on taxation mentioned above.

The case for the existence of at least three denominations in the scyphate series therefore appears conclusive.

Throughout the period there were also issued small, thick, flat copper coins. The Pantocrator typicon mentions that charity distributed at the gates of the monastery on feast days should be in the form of tetartera noummia: (διὰ) νουμμίων ἢ τεταρτηρῶν.[25] Similarly, at the feasts of the Presentation and the Transfiguration the personnel of the monastery hospital were to receive sums

[24] Chap. 10, p. 180.
[25] Dimitrievskii, *op. cit.*, pp. 661–62.

of 309 and 920 tetartera nomismata respectively.[26] It is quite clear that during the eleventh century, the tetarteron nomisma was the light weight coin of gold: the scale of the payments made in the typicon at this point, however, indicates that the term by 1136 involved a coin of very small value, and there is little doubt that the small copper coins described above were the tetartera of the Comneni and Angeli. The gold tetarteron not having been struck since the early years of the reign of Alexius I, the term had been appropriated to describe the copper pieces resembling the gold coins in fabric.

Confirmation again comes from western sources: Fulcher of Chartres, one of the chroniclers of the First Crusade, describes how in 1097, *Iussit imperator de auro suo et argento atque palliis proceribus nostris dari; peditibus quoque distribui fecit de nummis suis aeneis, quos vocant tartarones.*[27] Precisely what their value was in relation to the hyperpyron is impossible to ascertain. Certainly they were worth less than the traditional follis, which, like the gold tetarteron and the silver miliaresion, had no place in the reformed coinage of Alexius—as an actual coin. It is noticeable that the treatise on taxation mentioned above employs the term follis for the formal estimates, but actual payments are demanded: διὰ νουμίων χαλκῶν—a much vaguer term.[28] In addition, fractions of the follis are an appreciable factor of the taxation reforms of the Emperor—which they had not been previously—an evident indication that denominations of a smaller value were by then in existence. Since the same taxation treatise still quotes the standard nomisma and the miliaresion in terms of the noummion (6,000 to the nomisma),[29] it seems reasonable to assume that the tetarteron was a multiple of this traditional monetary division—which itself had long since ceased to be represented by an actual coin. The follis must therefore be regarded as a unit of account, for there exist no coins struck by the Comneni and Angeli bearing any resemblance to its former weight, and it seems unlikely that at the time of the reform of the rest of the coinage, it should sink to the insignificant standard represented by the copper tetarteron. Precisely the same is to be observed of the miliaresion of the new monetary system.

There is reason to believe that there existed fractions of the copper tetarteron as part of the new system—the half being quite recognizable.[30]

The coinage system as established by the reforms of Alexius I would thus seem to have been as follows:

[26] *Ibid.*, p. 692.

[27] Fulcher of Chartres, *Historia Hierosolymitana*, ed. H. Hagenmeyer (Heidelberg, 1913), lib. I, cap. x, pp. 188–89.

[28] Chap. 6, p. 57.

[29] *Ibid.*, p. 61, table 1.

[30] Chap. 8, pp. 109–10.

N Hyper-pyron	El. Aspron Trachy	(Miliare-sion)	(Kera-tion)	Bill. Aspron Trachy	(Follis)	Æ Tetarteron Noummion	Æ Half-tetarteron	(Noummion)
I	3	12	24	48	288			6,000
	I	4	8	16	96			2,000
		I	2	4	24			500
			I	2	12			250
				I	6			125
					I			
						I	2	
							I	
								I

El. Aspron trachy: 1185/95, debased.

Bill. Aspron trachy: 1190, $\frac{1}{120}$ hyperpyron; 1199, $\frac{1}{184}$ hyperpyron.

CHAPTER FOUR

The Monetary Terminology of the Twelfth Century

'Η φόλλις: the follis

$\frac{1}{288}$ standard nomisma. A unit of account, not represented by a coin after the establishment of the new monetary system based on the hyperpyron nomisma.

Τὸ κεράτιον
Karatus etc.} : the keration (carat)

Primarily a weight ($\frac{1}{24}$ standard nomisma), but used as a unit of value dependent upon the worth of a keration weight of a given metal or alloy. Thus the hyperpyron-keration was worth approximately $\frac{7}{8}$ of a keration of pure gold. Likewise, a hyperpyron of 24 keratia weight was worth approximately $20\frac{3}{4}$ keratia weight of pure gold. Not represented by a coin.

Τὸ μιλλιαρήσιον: the miliaresion

One-twelfth standard nomisma. A unit of account, not represented by a coin after the establishment of the new monetary system based on the hyperpyron nomisma. By the second half of the twelfth century, it had largely given way to the keration: surviving accounts—both Byzantine and Latin—are, by then, kept in nomismata (hyperpyra) and keratia.[1]

Dimitraton: the nomisma of St. Demetrius type

A term found in Georgian documents of account, but presumably having its origin in current Byzantine terminology.[2] To be identified with the Thessalonican electrum issue of Manuel I portraying, as the reverse type, the Emperor and St. Demetrius (Pl. 14.7–9).

Τὸ νόμισμα (κομνηνᾶτον) θεοτόκιον: the (Comnenian) theotokion nomisma

A grant of twenty-four Komnenata theotokia nomismata is mentioned in a chrysobull of John II in favor of the Monastery of Patmos (July 1119?).[3]

---

[1] For the Byzantine, see: F. Miklosich and G. Müller, *Acta et Diplomata Graeca Medii Aevi*, 5 (Vienna, 1887), pp. 389–91. For the Latin, see Müller, *Documenti*, pp. 74–78; Tafel and Thomas, *Urkunden*, 1, pp. 218–24.

[2] R. P. Blake, "Some Byzantine Accounting Practices Illustrated from Georgian Sources," *Harvard Studies in Classical Philology*, 51 (1940), p. 30.

[3] Miklosich and Müller, *Acta et Diplomata*, 6 (Vienna, 1890), p. 100. See also, *ibid.*, p. 98.

Chrysobulls of the succeeding emperors award similar grants of "most esteemed" trikephala (1157); "recent" trikephala—which are also "the most
valued of the day" (1161); and again, "recent" trikephala (1197).[4] The sums
in the chrysobulls of 1157 and 1161 can only involve the electrum nomisma—
since the contemporary hyperpyron portrayed two heads or figures, rather
than three: it therefore seems reasonable to assume that the chrysobull of
1119? should involve the same denomination; in which case the issue in question is probably the Constantinopolitan issue of Alexius I—depicting the
Theotokos as the obverse type (Pl. 6.2–5).

The theotokia nomismata mentioned in the typicon of the Pantocrator
Monastery (1136),[5] possibly involve hyperpyra of John II, the reverses of
which depict the Emperor and the Theotokos (Pl. 9. 1–14).

Τὸ νόμισμα (ὑπέρπυρον) μανοηλᾶτον ⎫
Manuellatus, manolatus, manlat ⎬ : the (hyperpyron) nomisma of Manuel

The term is rare in Byzantine sources, but is certainly used by the poet
Theodore Prodromus.[6] When "manuellatus" is used in Latin sources, it is
possibly applicable to either the electrum nomisma or the hyperpyron: in
1199 certainly to the former, in 1219 possibly to the latter.[7] It probably means
little more than "of the weight and purity employed during the reign of
Emperor Manuel," and need not necessarily refer to an actual coin of that
Emperor. The origin of the term lay not in the fact that Manuel struck coins of
abnormal standard, but that his long reign saw the production of a proportionally large amount of coin, particularly of the electrum denomination,
therefore making up a large part of the circulating medium for several decades,
even after his death.

The stauro-manuellatus, mentioned in a Venetian document of 1157, is almost
certainly to be identified with the second electrum coinage of Manuel, on the
reverse of which the Emperor and Virgin hold between them a large patriarchal
cross (Pl. 13. 3,4). An alternative identification is type C (Pl. 13. 5–9).

Stafratus: the nomisma of cross type
A term found in a Venetian document of 1143, but presumably having its
origin in current Byzantine terminology. The issue in question can only be the
metropolitan electrum (hagiogeorgaton) type of John II—on the reverse of
which the Emperor and St. George hold a large patriarchal cross (Pl. 10. 1–4).

For the stauro-manuellatus, see *supra*.

[4] *Infra*, pp. 33, 34.
[5] Dimitrievskii, *op. cit.*, p. 687.
[6] Eds. D. C. Hesseling and H. Pernot, *Poèmes prodromiques en grec vulgaire* (Amsterdam, 1910), no. IV, p. 74.
[7] Chap. 12, pp. 225–26. See also Chap. 5, p. 49 (note 30).

Τὸ νόμισμα (ἱ)στάμενον ⎫
Staminum, etc.   ⎬ : the stamenon nomisma

The nomisma of standard ([ἱ]στάμενον = fixed or standard) weight. The term seems to have appeared during the first quarter of the eleventh century and to have been used to denote the nomisma of full weight, as opposed to the light weight tetarteron. When the standard coin assumed a scyphate fabric the term "stamenon" apparently gave place to "trachy." "Stamenon" did continue to be used, however, for as late as 1083, Gregory Pacourianus mentions the "scyphate of standard weight" (τὸ ἱστάμενον τραχύ), when describing the rule under which the Monastery of Petritzos (Bachkovo), which he was founding, was to be run.[8] Georgian documents of the late eleventh and early twelfth centuries from the Iviron Monastery of Mt. Athos describe gold issues that are clearly scyphate as "stamenoni," e.g., "stamenoni ek'ust'avi" and "alek'sati."[9] As in the case of the tetarteron, the term soon began to be applied to another denomination, the billon scyphate first struck by Alexius I, which was of the same weight and fabric as the original trachy. Presumably it became redundant as far as the gold coinage was concerned when the term "hyperpyron" came into vogue. This change had certainly taken place by 1147—when Odo of Deuil, the historian of the Second Crusade, described the "staminas" as "cuprea moneta."[10] The name is quite commonly used in western commercial documents of the twelfth century, but seems little used by the Byzantines themselves, who generally refer to τὸ νόμισμα τραχύ.[11] The reference in a Pisan document of 1162 to "dimidium staminum"[12] should not be taken as proving the existence of such a denomination as a coin: the sum was probably paid in tetartera.

Τὸ νόμισμα τεταρτηρόν ⎫
Tartaron, tetartaron   ⎬ : the tetarteron nomisma (or νουμμίον/noummion)

Originally a gold coin, lighter than the stamenon nomisma by $1/_{12}$, it was first struck by Nicephorus II, and continued until early in the reign of Alexius I. At some point after this, the name was appropriated to describe a copper coin of similar small, thick fabric, first struck by Alexius as an element of his reformed coinage. This change had taken place by 1097, when the tetarteron in its new form was mentioned by Fulcher of Chartres, a western chronicler of the First Crusade, under the transliteration "tartaron."[13] During the late eleventh and the twelfth centuries it was worth a fraction of the follis.

---

[8] L. Petit, "Typikon de Grégoire Pacourianos pour le monastère de Pétritzos (Bačkovo) en Bulgarie," *Vizantiiskii Vremennik*, 11 (1904), p. 26.

[9] Blake, "Accounting Practices," pp. 27, 29.

[10] Chap. 3, p. 21.

[11] *Infra*, pp. 30, 31.

[12] Müller, *Documenti*, p. 10.

[13] Chap. 3, p. 24.

In the normal course of affairs sums equivalent to a coin of higher value were, naturally, paid out in copper tetartera. Thus the typicon of the Pantocrator Monastery records the payment of gold nomismata (hyperpyra) in this way: ... καὶ νουμίων ἢ τεταρτηρῶν χρυσοῦ νομίσματος ἑνός ....[14] The typicon of the Monastery of Our Lady of the Altars of Elijah (Anatolia, 1160) mentions: τεταρτηρὰ τρικέφαλα,[15] which under the circumstances can only be trikephala of, or in, tetartera. For the gold tetarteron had not been struck for nearly eighty years, and it is difficult to imagine any qualification of type being made concerning a copper tetarteron worth at most $1/2$ follis. In addition, it must be pointed out that no copper tetarteron type of Manuel depicts three figures or heads.

The copper coin weight (3.90 gm.) published by Schlumberger[16] and bearing the inscription: + ΠΑΛΑΙΟΝ ΟΛΟΤΡΑΧΟΝ ΕΛΑΦΡΟΝ, "the old, unmutilated, light weight coin," should probably be dated to the first quarter of the twelfth century. The description can refer to the gold tetarteron only at a time when it was no longer issued, but still in circulation: hence παλαιόν. The weight is perfectly satisfactory.

Τὸ (νόμισμα) τραχύ: the trachy (scyphate) nomisma

The scyphate fabric first occurs regularly under Michael IV and, until the reign of Alexius I, is almost entirely confined to the debased gold nomisma of standard weight. With the reform no less than three scyphate denominations appear: the gold; the electrum third, and the billon forty-eighth.

In 1065, by a chrysobull of the Emperor Constantine X, the monks of the Iviron Monastery of Mt. Athos were granted the right of paying an annual sum of sixty nomismata: .... τὰ μὲν τριάκοντ(α) ἱστάμενα τὰ δὲ ἕτερα τριάκοντα τεταρτ(η)ρ(ά)[17]. Half, then, was to be paid in histamena, half in tetartera.

In 1077, Michael Attaleiates ruled, in the Diataxis of the monastery which he was founding at Rodosto, that the stipends of the clergy were to be paid: τὰ μὲν ἡμίση τραχέα τὰ δὲ ἡμίση τέταρτα,[18] or half in trachea, half in tetartera.

In 1083, Gregory Pacourianus mentions in the typicon of the monastery that he was founding at Petritzos (Bachkovo), that, on his appointment as Duke of Theodosiopolis, he confided the management of his effects and treasure to his brother. The money consisted of: παλαιὸν λογάριον ῥωμανᾶτον, τραχὺ μονομαχᾶτον, δουκᾶτόν τε καὶ σκηπτρᾶτον, πρὸς δὲ καὶ μιχαηλᾶτον[19]—"old money of

---

[14] Dimitrievskii, op. cit., p. 661.

[15] Ibid., pp. 767, 769.

[16] G. Schlumberger, Mélanges d'archéologie byzantine, I (Paris, 1895), pp. 31–32.

[17] F. Dölger, Finanzgeschichtliches aus der byzantinischen Kaiserkanzlei des 11. Jahrhunderts, Sitzungsberichte der Bayerischen Akademie der Wissenschaften (Phil.-Hist. Klasse), I (Munich, 1956), p. 6.

[18] K. Sathas, Mesaionike Bibliotheke, I (Venice, 1872), p. 35.

[19] Petit, "Typikon de Grégoire Pacourianos," p. 13.

Romanus [III]; the trachy of [Constantine IX], Monomachus; of [Constantine X], Ducas; the 'sceptre' trachy, and that of Michael [VII, Ducas]." The stipends of the monks were to be paid in the ἱστάμενον τραχύ.[20]

A coin weight published by Laurent bears the legend: ΔΙΚΑΙΟC CΤΑΘΜΟC ΤΥ ΤΡΑΧΕΟC ΥΠΕΡΠΥΡΟΥ—"the just weight of the trachy hyperpyron."

A lysis of Alexius I, dated to 1108/09, reckons the τραχὺ ἄσπρον νόμισμα as worth ⅓ standard nomisma.

The typicon of the Pantocrator Monastery (1136) reckons a further aspron trachy nomisma as worth ¹⁄₄₈ standard nomisma.

The last three denominations have already been identified as the gold, electrum, and billon scyphates, respectively, of the reformed coinage.[21] On the basis of the reference of 1065, which distinguishes between the stamenon and the tetarteron, it might be supposed that the similarly phrased reference of 1077, distinguishing the trachy and the tetarteron, should be comparable in some degree. The typicon of Pacourianus acts in direct confirmation of this supposition, for it is clear, on the basis of the references found there, that the trachy is also a coin of standard weight (stamenon): in effect, therefore, the distinction made in 1077 was the same as that made in 1065. Now the only coins of standard weight attributable to Constantine IX, Constantine X, and Michael VII are, in fact, the scyphate, debased gold pieces of those Emperors. In other words, there are six occasions, from both the pre-reform and post-reform periods, where the trachy can be identified with some degree of certainty. When it is considered that all these trachea possess two major characteristics in common: that they are of standard weight and also scyphate, the implication of the description "trachy" (= "rough" or "uneven") becomes immediately clear; it means, quite simply, "scyphate," in opposition to the smooth, flat fabric of the tetarteron. The elaborate theories constructed in order to provide the trachy with an identity are, therefore, quite unnecessary.

Although, theoretically, the term "trachy" could have been applied to all three scyphate denominations of the Comnenian reformed coinage, in practice it seems to have been rarely used of the gold or the electrum, but frequently of the billon. The typicon of the Monastery of the Virgin Full of Grace (founded in Constantinople during the reign of Alexius I by his wife Irene) mentions the sum of: ... νομίσματα τραχέα εἴκοσι τέσσαρα καὶ ... νόμισμα ἓν ὑπέρπυρον,[22] clearly using the term to denote a denomination which is quite separate from the hyperpyron, and which, in the context, can only be the billon. The scale on which payments of trachea—only once qualified by "aspron"—occur in the typicon of the Pantocrator, renders it almost certain that, once again, it

[20] *Supra*, p. 28, note 8.
[21] Chap. 3, pp. 14, 18, 20–21.
[22] Miklosich and Müller, *op. cit.*, 5, p. 372.

is the billon which is implied. The typicon of the Cosmosotira Monastery, founded in Thrace by the Sebastocrator Isaac, in 1152/53, also mentions payments in trachea.[23]

Τὸ νόμισμα τραχὺ ἄσπρον⎫
Albus   ⎬ : the white, scyphate nomisma

The earliest occurrence of the term is apparently to be found in a chryso-bull of Alexius I in favor of the Athonite monastery of the Lavra, dated to July, 1104 (... ἄ[σπρ]α ... τραχέα νομίσματ[α]).[24] This seems to involve the electrum nomisma. Two further instances, of 1108/09 and 1136, mention the aspron trachy as worth $\frac{1}{3}$ and $\frac{1}{48}$ (hyperpyron) nomisma, respectively. In fact, two denominations are obviously involved, the electrum and the billon, both of which were white and scyphate.[25] The sense of the passage in which the term is used must, therefore, obviously determine the interpretation placed on it.

Τὸ νόμισμα τρικέφαλον⎫
Trimenus   ⎬ : the trikephalon nomisma

A term concerning which there has already been a certain amount of discussion. The traditional interpretation is that the expression describes any coin on which there appeared three heads or figures, the "Nummus trino capite insignitus" of Du Cange.[26] Frolow, in his article on the monetary terms used in the Pantocrator typicon, put forward the theory that the term was derived from τρεῖς + κεφαλαί, equivalent to the Latin tremissis, the third of the unit.[27] Laurent, however, in what was apparently the last word on the subject, wrote in 1951 that he admitted with "légère hésitation" the interpretation based on iconography.[28] Clearly, with the identification of the electrum denomination as the third part of the standard nomisma, some further examination of the question is necessary.

John II, in a chrysobull confirming that of his father of March 1093, in favor of the Monastery of St. John on Patmos, continued an annual grant of twenty-four κομνηνάτα θεοτοκία—to be paid by the duke of Crete from the revenues of the island. In this instance, the expression "Comnenian theotokion" can have applied only to the electrum issue of his father depicting

[23] L. Petit, "Typikon du monastère de la Kosmosotira près d'Aenos (1152)," *Izvestiya russkago arkheologicheskago instituta v Konstantinopole*, 13 (1908), pp. 24 and 54.
[24] G. Rouillard and P. Collomp, *Actes de Lavra*, 1 (Paris, 1937), p. 143.
[25] Chap. 3, pp. 18, 20–21.
[26] C. Du Cange, *Glossarium ad Scriptores Mediae et Infimae Graecitatis*, 2 (Lyons, 1688; reprint, Bratislava, 1891), col. 1605.
[27] A. Frolow, "Les noms de monnaies dans le typicon du Pantocrator," *Byzantinoslavica*, 10, 2 (1949), p. 247.
[28] V. Laurent, "Bulletin de numismatique byzantine (1940–1949)," *Revue des études byzantines*, 9 (1951), p. 205.

as its obverse type the Theotokos seated upon a throne (Pl. 6.*2–5*).[29] In September 1157, however, Theoctistus, the abbot of Patmos, again mentioned the annual grant made by Alexius and John, but describes the sum as twenty-four νομίσματα τρικέφαλα προτιμηταῖα[30]—"the most esteemed trikephala nomismata," which would seem to indicate that, on this occasion at least, the term "trikephalon" implied an electrum issue.

John II mentions in the Pantocrator typicon that fifty hyperpyra are to be set aside to pay for the ceremonies involving the procession of the icon of the Virgin Hodegetria to the tombs of the founders and of their son Alexius. After sums of six, twenty-four, and two hyperpyra are set aside for specific purposes, it is ruled that the remaining eighteen are to be changed into hagiogeorgata nomismata (ὑπαλλαττέσθωσαν εἰς ἁγιογεωργάτα νομίσματα),[31] and used for the purchase (presumably) of icons and/or banners. It necessarily follows that the hagiogeorgaton was of lower value than the hyperpyron, since the latter could hardly be changed into pieces of higher value.

In March of the same year, it is recorded that a manuscript changed hands for the sum of eight νομίσματ(α) τρικέφα(λα) τῆς προτιμομέ(νης) χαραγ(ῆς) τοῦ κρατ(αιοῦ) ἡμῶν βα(σι)λ(έως) ἤτοι ἁγιογεωργάτ(α),[32]—"trikephala nomismata of the most valued coining of our mighty Emperor, and of hagiogeorgaton type."

The hagiogeorgaton of the last two documents can only be that issue of John II depicting on the reverse the Emperor and St. George holding between them a cross, or labarum (Pl. 10.*1–6*). There is no doubt that the issue is in general an electrum one: a few gold, and even copper specimens have been recorded, but several at least of these are, in fact, gilded. No gold or copper examples have ever been found in hoards—which present a far more reliable picture of the circulating medium than the trays of a collection: were they eventually to be found, they would have to be counted as hyperpyra and billon trachea respectively, not as examples of imperial fraud. The reference from the typicon indicates the lesser value of the hagiogeorgaton vis-à-vis the hyperpyron: since there were only two denominations of precious metal, it is certain that the book changed hands for $2\frac{2}{3}$ hyperpyra and that the imperial instructions meant in effect that the eighteen hyperpyra in question were to be changed into fifty-four hagiogeorgata. The crucial point, however, is that the issue was also a trikephalon.

The typicon of the Monastery of St. Mamas in Constantinople (1158/59) records that each monk should receive annually for clothing the sum of: νομίσματα ὑπέρπυρα δύο and: τρικέφαλα παλαιὰ δύο in two instalments of one

[29] *Supra*, pp. 26, 27.

[30] Miklosich and Müller, *op. cit.*, 6, p. 107.

[31] Dimitrievskii, *op. cit.*, p. 682.

[32] V. Laurent, "Les monnaies tricéphales de Jean II Comnène," *RN*[5], 13 (1951), p. 98.

hyperpyron and one trikephalon. If the monastery were to become more prosperous, however, then each was to receive the annual sum of τρία ὑπέρπυρα.[33] It follows that the trikephalon was worth less than ½ hyperpyron and, therefore, must once more be identified with the electrum denomination.

In May, 1161, Manuel I confirmed by chrysobull the grants made to the Monastery of Patmos by his father and grandfather, apparently increasing the sum of money to two pounds of the currently most valued trikephala nomismata (νομίσματα τρικέφαλα τὰ κατὰ τὴν ἡμέραν προτιμώμενα λίτραι δύο). In the same document a few lines later, the sum is referred to as being: ... δύο τρικεφάλων καινουργίων λιτρῶν,—"new trikephala."[34] Now, in 1161 "new" trikephala could only be electrum pieces, since the hyperpyron of Manuel depicted only two figures: that of Christ Emmanuel on the obverse and of the Emperor on the reverse.

Yet, a crucial reference in a document of the Monastery of St. Paul, near Miletus, renders it certain that the trikephalon cannot be directly equated with the electrum denomination, the third, and that the iconographical interpretation must prevail. The Emperor Isaac Angelus (1185–95), confirming the monastery in possession of some property, mentions the sum of thirty-six ὑπέρπυρα τρικέφαλα.[35] Isaac's gold hyperpyra do, indeed, depict three figures or "heads"—the Virgin on the obverse, the Emperor and St. Michael on the reverse. Clearly, therefore, the term could describe the gold as well as the electrum denomination.

Perhaps even more important than the identification of the trikephalon is the fact that the qualifying descriptions applied to it are the same as those for the hyperpyron,[36] even when the denomination referred to is undoubtedly the electrum:

1136 (Cypriot MS) νομίσματ(α) τρικέφα(λα) τῆς προτιμομέ(νης) χαραγ(ῆς)

1157 (Abb. Theoctistus) τρικέφαλα προτιμηταῖα

1158/59 (St. Mamas typicon) τρικέφαλα παλαιά

1161 (Manuel: chrysobull) νομίσματα τρικέφαλα τὰ κατὰ τὴν ἡμέραν προτιμώμενα—
... τρικεφάλων καινουργίων ...

Other documents where the identification of the denomination is uncertain:

1160 (Our Lady of Pity typicon)[37] νομίσματα τρικέφαλα τὰ κατὰ τὴν ἡμέραν προτιμώμενα

---

[33] S. Eustratiades, "Τυπικὸν τῆς ἐν Κωνσταντινουπόλει Μονῆς τοῦ Ἁγίου Μεγαλομάρτυρος Μάμαντος," *Hellenika*, I, 2 (1928), p. 283.

[34] Miklosich and Müller, *op. cit.*, 6, p. 118.

[35] *Ibid.*, 4 (Vienna, 1871), p. 320.

[36] *Infra*, pp. 35, 36.

[37] L. Petit, "Le monastère de Notre Dame de Pitié," *Izvestiya russkago arkheologicheskago instituta v Konstantinopole*, 6, 1 (1900), p. 31.

1193 (Private document of sale)[38] παλαιὰ τρικέφαλα νομίσματα

1197 (Written order of the *Megas Logariastes*)[39] τρικέφαλοι καινούργιαι (λίτραι)

It should be noted that the last two quotations are from a period when the debasement of the electrum coinage may have complicated the issue: a factor which does not apply to the others.

The equivalent Latin term seems to have been "trimenus," which, combined with "perperus" in Venetian documents of 1121 and 1136, must refer to the various gold issues of John II (Pl. 9. *1–14*).

Τὸ νόμισμα (τρικέφαλον) ἁγιογεωργάτον : the (trikephalon) nomisma of St. George type

An electrum scyphate issue depicting the Emperor John II and St. George as the reverse type (Pl. 10.*1–6*).

Τὸ νόμισμα (τραχὺ) ὑπέρπυρον
Purpuratus, perperum, yperperum } : the (scyphate) nomisma of refined gold

The standard scyphate nomisma of $20^{1}/_{2}$ carats fine, was introduced by Alexius I, probably during the course of the year 1092.[40] The first use of the term occurs in the will of St. Christodoulos of Patmos, datable to March 1093: (...νομίσματα τεσσαράκοντα δύο ὑπέρ[πυρα]).[41] Byzantine authors with any pretension to style tend to avoid the term, however, possibly considering it "common." Even the imperial chancery was to some extent affected by this prejudice, and it is consequently not until well into the twelfth century that the name occurs at all frequently. Western sources exhibit less fastidiousness, and from 1097 onward the various transliterations of the word are comparatively common in chronicles and commercial documents. Byzantine documents dated to 1017, 1018/19, and 1081, from the Athonite monastery of the Lavra, apparently containing the term are, as their editors point out, later copies and must therefore be regarded as containing intrusive terminology. There is no reason to believe that the introduction of the term antedated the reign of Alexius in general, and the issue of the reformed gold in particular.

The derivation of the term as suggested by Du Cange—that ὑπέρ + πῦρ : ("above + fire") represents the refined gold or "aurum coctum" of late Roman and mediaeval sources[42]—is perfectly satisfactory. The theory advanced by A. Frolow giving it a western derivation (perperum=something deformed: the scyphate as seen by Western eyes),[43] is entertaining in its ingenuity but has

---

[38] Miklosich and Müller, *op. cit.*, 6, p. 125.

[39] *Ibid.*, p. 140.

[40] Chap. 5, p. 46.

[41] Miklosich and Müller, *op. cit.*, 6, p. 82.

[42] C. Du Cange, *De Imperatorum Constantinopolitanorum Numismatibus Dissertatio* (Rome, 1755), p. 123: Codex Theodosianus, 12, 7 (1).

[43] Frolow, "Les noms de monnaies," pp. 245–46.

nothing else to recommend it. Apart from the fact that there already existed a perfectly good phrase in the West to describe this fabric ("nummus" or "aureus scyphatus"), it must be pointed out that the earliest Western sources generally use the variant "purpuratus," "perperum" tending to be a later form. The implication of high gold content given by the term assures its identification as the reformed gold issue of the Comneni, for it could hardly be applied to any other denomination, the nomisma of the preceding forty years always having been less pure than 20 ½ carats, and often lamentably so: likewise it could not apply to the electrum denomination of the reformed coinage.

The adjective τραχύ occurs only once in relation to the hyperpyron—on a bronze coin-weight bearing the inscription: (ὁ) δίκαιος σταθμὸς τοῦ τραχέως ὑπερπύρου ("the just weight of the scyphate hyperpyron"). On the basis of its rather light weight (3.83 gm.), Laurent has postulated the existence of a gold denomination outside the normal stamenon/tetarteron pattern, in order to provide the trachy hyperpyron with an identity:[44] fortunately, with the identification of the term τραχύ as meaning "scyphate," this necessity is removed. It can only be assumed that the light weight of the piece in question results from corrosion and/or wear, to which processes copper is particularly prone. The weight cannot antedate the reign of Alexius according to the present state of knowledge, and is quite at home in a twelfth- to fourteenth-century context.

The Pantocrator typicon provides several more references to the hyperpyron: at first sight they are in fact so varied and numerous that they have been cited as an illustration of the confusion of the Byzantine coinage under the Comneni. Frolow, attempting to produce some kind of order, wrote: "Rien ne pourrait mieux illustrer, peut-être, le désarroi des finances byzantines à la veille de la quatrième Croisade que cette diversité d'unités en cours."[45] Such an attempt was probably bound to fail without at least some concept of the Comnenian monetary system—which Frolow conspicuously lacked. With the identification of the main denominations, the disorder can be seen as only apparent. The following references clearly describe the gold hyperpyron:

... νομίσματα χρυσᾶ, τὰ κατὰ τὴν ἡμέραν προτιμώμενα πάντων, ἑπτὰ ἥμισυ
"seven and a half gold nomismata, currently the most valued of all"

Dimitrievskii, *Opisanie*, p. 689.

... νομίσματος ὁμοίου τὸ ἥμισυ
"half a nomisma of similar type"   *Ibid.*, p. 689.

... νομίσματος ὁμοίου τέταρτον
"a quarter of a nomisma of similar type"   *Ibid.*, p. 690.

---

[44] V. Laurent, "Le 'Juste poids' de l'hyperpyron trachy," *Congrès International de Numismatique, 1953, Actes*, 2 (Paris, 1957), pp. 299–307.
[45] Frolow, "Les noms de monnaies," p. 242.

3*

... νομίσματα ὅμοια τρία ἥμισυ τρίτον
"three and a sixth nomismata of similar type"   *Ibid.*, p. 690.
... τὸ κατὰ τὴν ἡμέραν προτιμώμενον χρυσοῦν νόμισμα
"the currently most valued gold nomisma"   *Ibid.*, p. 686.
... νομίσματα ὑπέρπυρα
"hyperpyra nomismata"   *Ibid.*, p. 694.
... νομίσματος ὑπερπύρου τὸ ἥμισυ
"half a hyperpyron nomisma"   *Ibid.*, p. 689.
... νομίσματα καινούργια, τὰ κατὰ τὴν ἡμέραν προτιμώμενα δύο ἥμισυ
"two and a half new nomismata, currently the most valued"   *Ibid.*, p. 690.
... νομίσματα ὅμοια τρία τρίτον
"three and a third nomismata of similar type"   *Ibid.*, p. 690.
... νομίσματα ὅμοια δύο ἥμισυ
"two and a half nomismata of similar type"   *Ibid.*, p. 690.
... νομίσματα ὑπέρπυρα καινούργια δύο τρίτον
"two and a third new hyperpyra nomismata"   *Ibid.*, p. 691.
... νόμισμα ὑπέρπυρον καινούργιον ἓν πρὸς τὸ ἥμισυ
"one and a half new hyperpyron nomisma"   *Ibid.*, p. 692.
... νομίσματα ὑπέρπυρα καινούργια ὅμοια τρία τρίτον
"three and a third new hyperpyra nomismata of similar type"   *Ibid.*, p. 692.
... νομίσματα ὑπέρπυρα παλαιά
"old hyperpyra nomismata"   *Ibid.*, p. 690.

Such an abundant selection of quotations has been included only to demonstrate, from similarity in phrasing, that despite several variations, all references do in fact refer to the hyperpyron, and to confirm Western documents in regarding the hyperpyron as the standard coin upon which fractional sums are based.

The hyperpyron pound (of seventy-two pieces) is also mentioned in the typicon (... λίτρας ὑπερπύρους δύο).[46]

Latin commercial documents exhibit their own customary qualifying descriptions of the perperum or yperperum. The usual Venetian phrase seems to have been *perperi auri boni veteres pesantes* ("hyperpyra of good gold, weighing as of old" [i.e., of customary weight]). A small group of documents do in fact read *perperi auri boni novi pesantes*, which does not imply the existence of a new standard of weight, since they are chronologically sandwiched between examples of the more usual phrase. This group is in fact by the hand of one person—Gyslando Carnello—and reflects the personal formula used by him. The translation should probably read "hyperpyra of good gold, weighing as new," implying freshly minted pieces, presumably therefore of customary

---

[46] Dimitrievskii, *op. cit.*, p. 688.

weight. The two formulae in effect mean the same. The Pisan notaries, on the other hand, seemed to have preferred *yperpera auri bene ponderata ad rectas pensas de Constantinopoli* ("hyperpera of gold, correctly weighed, according to the established standards of Constantinople")[47] or some similar phrase.

These qualifications were purely customary, ensuring that the coins changing hands were genuine and of full weight.

Τὸ νόμισμα $\begin{Bmatrix} \text{ὑπέρπυρον} \\ \text{τρικέφαλον} \end{Bmatrix}$ προτιμώμενον; προτιμηταῖον; παλαιόν; καινούργιον

Throughout the twelfth century, the gold hyperpyron, and the trikephalon even where demonstrably of electrum, are both frequently qualified by the descriptions: "currently the most valued (of all)," "the most esteemed," "old," "new," etc.[48] In the majority of cases —all those connected with the hyperpyron and most of those connected with the trikephalon—these qualifications cannot have been the expressions of a preference for issues of pure or debased title, as has generally been assumed.

It is perhaps significant that, whereas the term (τὸ νόμισμα) καινούργιον is occasionally qualified by some such description as τὸ κατὰ τὴν ἡμέραν προτι-μώμενον, or, as in the case of a chrysobull of Manuel I for the Monastery of Patmos, the one is used apparently interchangeably with the other, the adjective παλαιόν remains without further qualification.[49] There does, therefore, seem to be some consistent distinction between new issues—which are also currently the most valued—and old issues. The implication would seem to be that a distinction long forbidden was being applied: the custom that coins of the reigning emperor, or of recent mintage—generally not widely circulated and therefore without wear—should pass at a slight premium over older coins— generally the more widely circulated and worn.

The most explicit condemnation of the custom mentioned above is found in Novel 14 (i) of Valentinian III, dated to 445:

> *De pretio solidi et nequis solidum integrum recuset.*
>
> *Impp. Theod(osius) et Valent(inianus) Aa. ad populum Romanum. Frequens ad nos, Quirites, temerarii ausus querela pervenit, ut in parentum nostrorum contumeliam insigniti solidi eorum nominibus ab omni emptore recusentur: quod diu impunitum esse non patimur. Hoc ergo edicto agnoscat universitas capitale manere supplicium, si quisquam vel domini patris mei*

---

[47] For the Venetian, see: Tafel and Thomas, *Urkunden*, I, nos. LII, LIII, LIV, LXIX, LXXVII; A. Lombardo and R. M. della Rocca, *Nuovi documenti del commercio Veneto dei sec. XI–XIII* (Venice, 1953), nos. 5, 7, 10, 15, 21, 24, 40. Gyslando Carnello accounts for nos. LII, LIII, LIV, 10. For the Pisan, see: Müller, *Documenti*, nos. 14, 38, 42.

[48] For the hyperpyron, see *supra*, pp. 35, 36; for the trikephalon, see *supra*, pp. 33, 34.

[49] *Ibid*, pp. 33, 34, 36.

Theodosii vel sacrarum necessitudinum nostrarum vel superiorum principum solidum aureum integri ponderis refutandum esse crediderit vel pretio minori taxaverit . . .

The *Codex Justinianus* (11, x [i]) mentions an earlier enactment of Valentinian I to the same effect, and as late as the ninth century Leo VI (886–912) found it necessary to issue the same prohibition (Novel 52)—if the above interpretation of the descriptive phrases found in twelfth-century sources is correct, with so little success that, by the latter period, the custom had become officially condoned and even recognized.

This distinction between new or fresh coins and old or worn ones is very probably to be connected with the circulation of sealed purses of coin, which would have contained pieces of choice quality, as opposed to that of loose coin, which would have been in a far more variable state of preservation. Such, at least, appears to be the implication of the eleventh edict of Justinian—to be discussed *infra*, chap. 13, pp. 304–05.

Τὸ χρυσοῦν νόμισμα τραχὺ χιάτον: the gold scyphate nomisma "with a X"

This occurs on two occasions, in documents dated March 1093, and March 1094.[50] Although early, their dates put them quite definitely into the post-reform period, and the description "gold" alone probably justifies the identification of these pieces with the hyperpyron. Mme Morrisson, in an as yet unpublished paper, given to the Byzantine Congress at Oxford in 1966, has also suggested, however, that the description "with a X" refers to the letter in the abbreviation ĪC/XC, found on the obverse of the hyperpyron of Alexius, his electrum having instead M͞P/Θ͞V, and therefore that the term is, in fact, a description of the still recently issued hyperpyron.

Τὸ νόμισμα χάραγμα: the coined nomisma

The marked or engraved nomisma, hence an actual coined piece as opposed to a unit of account. Used particularly of the hyperpyron and the electrum denomination, e.g., of the latter: . . . τὸ μὲν χάραγμα νόμισμα διὰ τραχέων ἄσπρων νομισμάτων ἀπαιτεῖσθαι.[51]

Τὸ νόμισμα χρυσοῦν: the gold nomisma.
The hyperpyron.[52]

[50] Miklosich and Müller, *op. cit.*, 6, pp. 82, 92.
[51] Chap. 6, p. 57.
[52] Dimitrievskii, *op. cit.*, p. 686.

CHAPTER FIVE

THE DATE OF THE ALEXIAN MONETARY REFORM

The primary division in the coinage of Alexius I is between issues of traditional type, and those representing innovation. The first group—by far the smaller—consists of debased trachea (Pl. *1.1–12*); debased tetartera (Pl. 2. *1–12*); flat silver miliaresia (Pl. *2.14–17*); coins of base silver, slightly scyphate, continuing a tradition commenced by Constantine IX (Pl. *2.13*); and the large, flat, copper folleis, of both the named and the anonymous series (Pls. *2.18–22*, 3. *1–3*). The second group has already been described in dealing with the new monetary system, and in brief is marked by the appearance of the gold hyperpyron, the electrum and billon fractional scyphates, and the copper tetarteron. The only issue to some extent common to both groups is the electrum trachy, but, whereas under Nicephorus III and Alexius I prior to his reform, it was a coin of debased character, subsequent to the reform its legal value was more or less identical with that of the bullion contained in it; $1/3$ part of the hyperpyron nomisma.

Several general points emerge. Since it is the group of denominations representing innovation that is continued by the successors of Alexius I, it would seem reasonable to assume that, in general, it is the later. The relatively small number of pieces of traditional type remaining suggests, prima facie, that the reform began at a relatively early stage in the reign. Finally, the fundamental change in the monetary pattern brought about by the introduction of fractional scyphates was, nevertheless, basically the result of the application of an extremely simple concept, and there is, therefore, no general reason why the introduction of the new system should not have been complete within a relatively short period of time, rather than the piecemeal product of an extended period. This is particularly true of the fractional pieces, which could hardly have been introduced before the hyperpyron upon which they were dependent.

The question of the date of the monetary reform of Alexius has apparently not previously been discussed in detail. Metcalf, in a short study of the gold coinage, suggested that it was introduced in *c.* 1097 as a result of the territorial gains for the Empire brought about by the First Crusade.[1] In a further publication, he suggested that the issue of "bronze," fractional scyphates ante-

---

[1] D. M. Metcalf, "The Reformed Gold Coinage of Alexius I Comnenus," *HBN*, 16 (1962), pp. 271–84.

dated this by some appreciable time.[2] The latter, at least, is unlikely on the grounds put forward in the paragraph preceding this.

The resolution of the problem is unfortunately hampered by the universal practice among Byzantine authors of dealing only with such subjects as were considered "acceptable"—which economic and monetary affairs were not— and of making use of elliptical or consciously archaic terms when forced to deal with subjects which both they and their readers would have considered disagreeably "common." Very little evidence is therefore to be gained from contemporary authors, and scarcely more from other documentary sources.

The first occurrence of the purpuratus in Latin documents is in 1097:[3] the ὑπέρπυρον appears for the first time in original Byzantine documentary sources in March, 1093.[4]

The electrum τραχὺ ἄσπρον first occurs specifically in July, 1104,[5] although its existence may be inferred as early as March, 1093.[6]

The copper tartaron had succeeded the follis by 1097.[7]

Fortunately, the coins themselves provide a good deal more information than these somewhat meagre indications.

There exists a rare issue of scyphates—evidently commemorative—in electrum and billon depicting, as the obverse type, the young Emperor John II crowned by Christ and, as the reverse, the Emperor Alexius I and his wife Irene Ducaina (Pl. 6.*1, 10, 11*). A specimen of the electrum issue was described by Sabatier in 1868 and is now in the possession of the Bibliothèque Nationale.[8] A further example of the general type was published by Goodacre in 1939 and was described as being of gold. Unfortunately, the piece in the Goodacre Collection—now on loan to the Ashmolean Museum—proves, on examination, to be a gilded specimen of the billon issue, which is relatively common.[9] If hyperpyra of the type were struck, therefore, they remain to come to light. In fact, the lack of the hyperpyron is of no great importance since the existence of the electrum third and the billon forty-eighth indicates that the unit upon which they were fractionally dependent must already have been in circulation. The only convincing date for the issue of this commemorative type is September 1092, when Alexius crowned his young son John (b. 1087) as emperor, in

---

[2] *Idem, Coinage in the Balkans, 820–1355* (Thessaloniki, 1965), p. 92.

[3] Chap. 3, p. 14 (note 1).

[4] Chap. 4, p. 34.

[5] *Ibid.*, p. 31.

[6] *Ibid.*, p. 26, 31.

[7] Chap. 3, p. 24.

[8] J. Sabatier, in *Annuaire de la société française de numismatique* (1868), p. 292. An approximate specific gravity determination of the piece in question results in a reading of 8 carats fine, which, in view of the appalling debasement of the pre-reform trachea of Alexius, necessitates its acceptance as a part of the reformed series.

[9] H. Goodacre, "Irene Dukaina, Wife of the Emperor Alexius I," *NC*[5], 19 (1939), p. 110.

defiance of the rights of his ward and colleague Constantine Ducas, the son of Michael VII;[10] the new monetary system was therefore in existence at that date.

The identification of the pre-reform trachea of Alexius here becomes a matter of some importance. The Sofia hoard of 1897 contained 205 stamena and stamena trachea of the Emperors Romanus III, Constantine IX, Constantine X, Eudocia and her sons, Romanus IV, Nicephorus III, and Alexius I, together with one reformed hyperpyron of the last-named Emperor.[11] The heavily alloyed trachea of Alexius were of two types only, the one depicting the Emperor holding a jewelled stellate scepter (Pl. 1.*1–4*), the other of similar type but differing in the form of scepter (Pl. 1.*5–8*). Since the bulk of the hoard was composed of the debased stamena trachea of preceding emperors and there was only one piece (the hyperpyron) which was recognizably of the reformed coinage, it seems reasonable to assume that these two heavily alloyed types constitute the pre-reform issues. The first type is in general an electrum issue, but of variable gold content, one analyzed piece containing a mere 3 carats of gold, another being apparently of a gold (?), silver, and copper alloy.[12] The second type is seemingly only of a silver/copper alloy, although one specimen of the eight present at Dumbarton Oaks may contain some gold. This latter type, at least, has no place within the reformed coinage. The evidence suggests, therefore, that Alexius, while at first attempting to continue the standard of the electrum trachea of Nicephorus III, was forced to debase even further—at the same time, as was now customary, changing the design of the coin.

Further confirmation exists.

The *British Museum Catalogue* attributes to Alexius III, Angelus-Comnenus, an apparently unique miliaresion of traditional, flat fabric, together with two varieties of scyphate in debased metal.[13] All three depict St. Demetrius in military dress, handing a labarum, a patriarchal cross, or a cross, to an Alexius Comnenus: iconographically and stylistically, the coins are closely related (Pls. 1.*9–12*, 2.*17*).

The attribution will, however, not stand up to examination. The last miliaresia of flat fabric (other than the type under discussion) are to be dated to the early years of Alexius I, belonging as they do to a group of coins marked by traditional characteristics of fabric, weight, and type. Thus, when Alexius III obtained the throne in 1195, the denomination had not been struck for approximately a century. The scyphates which are so closely related to it are similarly

[10] F. Chalandon, *Essai sur le règne d'Alexis Ier Comnène* (Paris, 1900), pp. 121–22, 137–39.
[11] Chap. 15, p. 383.
[12] Both in the collection at Dumbarton Oaks.
[13] W. Wroth, *Catalogue of the Imperial Byzantine Coins in the British Museum* (London, 1908), vol. 2, pl. LXXIII. *4–6, 13*.

alien to the issues of Alexius III, whose trachea, whether of gold, electrum, or billon, all depict the Emperor with St. Constantine.[14] While the issues of Alexius III are of a relatively large, spread fabric, these "St. Demetrius" scyphates are smaller and thicker.

Whatever judgment is finally passed on the competence of the Angeli—and that on Isaac II may prove more favorable than the one now favored—it would appear unlikely that an emperor of the somewhat dubious caliber of Alexius III should exert himself to the extent of reviving two denominations which were quite out of place in a system of coinage which had, by then, been in operation for a full century. Clearly, a reattribution to Alexius I should be considered.

The scyphates in question have one major characteristic of detail—in addition to several smaller points of detail and style—which ally them to a small but distinct series already attributed to Alexius I. The imperial name is to be found on the obverse side—which is contrary to normal practice. The other issues of the group are in billon (Pl. 7.8, 9), in electrum (Pl. 6.6–9), and even in gold (Pl. 5.5). The last is certainly the most significant, since these specimens form part of a series of hyperpyra sharing a general chronological development of legend with coins of obvious metropolitan manufacture, but which themselves, in points of detail and style, demonstrate an independence explicable only on the assumption that they were issued by a separate mint.[15] It would therefore appear reasonable to expect that all the issues in the group should emanate from the same source, and, moreover, belong to the same period: the reign of Alexius I.

Incidental proof of the correctness of the reattribution of the "St. Demetrius" scyphates to Alexius I, rather than to Alexius II or III, is to be found among the coins of the Norman kingdom of Sicily.

The silver alloy scyphate ducat (ducalis) of Roger II (1130–54) is as follows:

Obv. +IC·XC·RG· / IN·ÆTRN (*Iesus Christus regnat / in aeternum*). Bust of Christ, bearded and nimbate, wearing tunic and colobion; holds Gospels in left hand.

Rev. R·DVX·Ҏ / R·R·SLS (*Rogerius dux Apuliae / Rogerius rex Siciliae*). $\begin{smallmatrix} AN \\ R \\ X \end{smallmatrix}$ (*Anno regni X*) in field.
    Full-length figure of king Roger on right and of duke Roger of Apulia (his son), holding between them patriarchal cross on long shaft and three steps. King Roger wears stemma, divitision, and jewelled loros of simplified type (details blundered); holds globus cruciger in left hand. Duke Roger wears short military tunic and breastplate; holds sword in right hand. The king is represented frontally, the duke laterally (Pl. 45.*11*).

[14] Pls. 22.*1–12*, 23.*1–7*.
[15] Chap. 8, pp. 90–95.

The whole coin—fabric, type, and style—is of Byzantine origin, and there is little doubt that the original is to be found in the "St. Demetrius" scyphate issues under discussion. The only conceivable alternative original is the hagio-georgaton type of John II (Pl. 10.*1–4*), but comparison shows obvious and decisive differences between the hagiogeorgaton and the ducat. On the other hand, the differences between the "St. Demetrius" issues and the ducat are minimal: the necessary alteration of the inscriptions; the globus cruciger held by King Roger—a simple addition; the cross on three steps rather than two; Duke Roger holding the sword in his right hand rather than his left.

The ducat was first struck in the tenth year of the reign of Roger II (*anno regni X*), that is, in 1140. There is, therefore, no possibility of the "St. Demet-rius" issue belonging to any other emperor than Alexius I, Comnenus, the original being of necessity earlier than the copy.

Now the two varieties of scyphate depicting St. Demetrius possess a develop-ment of metal content parallel to the debased products of the metropolitan mint. That variety in which the Saint hands a labarum to Alexius, although generally of a silver/copper alloy, definitely includes electrum specimens, for the one coin in the collection at Dumbarton Oaks is of that metal. The other (a good deal more common) in which St. Demetrius hands a patriarchal cross to the Emperor is, in all known cases, however, of the silver/copper alloy. The further stage in the debasement of the trachy is, therefore, apparently illus-trated within both the metropolitan and the provincial mint.

The presence of St. Demetrius on both the traditional miliaresion and the scyphates is of crucial importance in dealing with this group. The earliest representation of the Saint, on coins other than these, occurs on the copper half-tetartera of John II (Pl. 11. *15–17*); his first appearance on coins of precious metal dates from the reign of John's successor Manuel I, when he is found on the electrum coinage (Pl. 14.7–*9*).

An ideal solution to the problem of the identification of this mint, between the two termini of 1081 and 1092, in harmony with both the historical and numismatic factors, at once emerges. When Alexius came to the throne in April 1081, he inherited—besides the less imminent if no less real dangers—the threat of an almost immediate invasion of Epirus by the Normans of southern Italy. This invasion, although decently furnished with an excuse from Byzan-tine domestic politics, was in fact a war of conquest.

Robert Guiscard, at the head of a considerable army, laid siege to Dyrrh-achium in June 1081,[16] after seizing Avlona and the island of Corfu. Alexius, according to Anna Comnena, left Constantinople for Thessalonica in August.[17] After a short stay in the latter city he proceeded to the scene of the campaign,

[16] Anna Comnena, IV, 1; Bonn ed., 1, pp. 187–88.
[17] *Ibid.*, IV, 4; Bonn ed., 1, p. 198.

almost immediately meeting with a severe defeat under the walls of Dyrrh-achium (October).[18] He returned to Thessalonica to reorganize his army. At this point Anna enters into a rather lengthy and embarrassed account of events in Constantinople which, to put it briefly, seem to have occurred as follows:[19] Alexius needed money more than ever, but there was none to be had from the imperial treasury, thoroughly depleted by Nicephorus III. He therefore requested his brother, the Sebastocrator Isaac, and his mother, the regent Anna Dalassena, whom he had left in Constantinople, to procure as much as possible by whatever means lay at hand. The regents managed to gather a little from their own possessions and from those of their supporters and duly sent what there was to the mint. The total was, however, quite insufficient for the pressing needs of the moment. Recourse was therefore had to that canon which permitted the confiscation of church property for the redemption of prisoners of war from the enemy. An unknown amount was obtained on the basis of the sale of "surplus" church vessels. The Emperor shortly after returned to the capital. Robert, in turn, was forced to return to Italy to deal with disturbances within his possessions, and the threatened invasion of Henry IV of Germany; both initiated at the request and encouragement of Alexius.

By May 1082,[20] Alexius had again left Constantinople, for Ioannina, but once more met with defeat and returned to the capital to organize further resistance. It was apparently at this point (August 1082) that, depressed by his setbacks, he issued a chrysobull forbidding future alienation of ecclesiastical property.[21]

Profiting by the defeats suffered by the Emperor, Bohemund, in charge of the Norman army in the absence of his father, after strengthening his position by the acquisition of various towns in Thessaly, laid siege to Larissa. The siege, according to Anna, began in April 1083 (the festival of St. George the Martyr)[22] and continued for six months, at the end of which it was raised by Alexius (presumably in September 1083). After this, his first appreciable military success, the Emperor returned to Thessalonica and from there attempted to tamper with the loyalty of Bohemund's lieutenants—with some considerable effect, for Castoria was restored to the Empire by Bohemund's own men. This was apparently the last military event of the year, since Alexius was back in the capital by the beginning of December.[23]

---

[18] *Ibid.*, IV, 6; Bonn ed., 1, p. 208.

[19] *Ibid.*, V, 1–2; Bonn ed., 1, pp. 225–31.

[20] *Ibid.*, V, 4; Bonn ed., 1, p. 237.

[21] C. E. Zachariä von Lingenthal, *Ius Graeco-Romanum*, 3 (Leipzig, 1857), pp. 355–58. For the chronology, see: V. Grumel, "L'affaire de Léon de Chalcédoine," *Études byzantines*, 2 (1944), pp. 126–33.

[22] Anna Comnena, V, 5; Bonn ed., 1, p. 244.

[23] *Ibid.*, VI, 8; Bonn ed., 1, p. 295.

Bohemund returned to Italy on receipt of the news of Castoria, but was back in Epirus with his father in 1084. In 1085, however, with little achieved, Robert died,[24] and the territory occupied by the Normans was recovered without too much difficulty.

Alexius himself, therefore, was in Thessalonica at least three times, twice in 1081 and once in 1083: in addition, it is clear that the second city of the Empire was the main base of munitions and supplies for the Norman war. Both the existence of a separate mint (for at least some of the period 1081–92) and the iconographical characteristics of some of its products are entirely explicable if it is assumed that that mint was situated at Thessalonica.

It should be observed at this point that not only is the appearance of St. Demetrius on the coinage unprecedented at this time, but the design itself, on all three issues, is somewhat unusual. The normal aspect of both saint and emperor in the numismatic iconography of the successors of Alexius (when the presence of saints becomes more common) is purely frontal—even if something is held between them. This holds good throughout the eleventh and twelfth centuries.[25] The aspect of the saint on coins of this group is somewhat different: he is represented laterally. The implication is plain: St. Demetrius, the patron saint of the city of Thessalonica, in full military dress, sword in hand, is actually handing the labarum or cross to Alexius. The Norman war was bitter, the outcome crucial, with the Empire fighting for its very existence. Under the circumstances nothing would be more natural than this iconographical scene.

As to the reasons for the Normans copying these rather rare issues, it should be remembered that for the best part of the period of the first Norman war they would have been the current trachea nomismata in the area of conflict, and that the invaders would, therefore, have come across them comparatively frequently.

The following sequence of events would thus seem to be indicated: at some time shortly after the commencement of the Norman campaign—probably during either the first or second visit of the Emperor (August–September 1081 and October 1081–early 1082)—a precious-metal mint was brought into operation at Thessalonica. This was in time to produce a short issue of trachea depicting the military St. Demetrius handing a labarum to the Emperor, which paralleled the first metropolitan coinage of Alexius, who was attempting to equal the standard of gold content used by Nicephorus III. The further debasement then occurred at both Constantinople and Thessalonica, accom-

---

[24] Chalandon, *op. cit.*, p. 93.

[25] Cf. John II with St. George (Pl. 10.*1–6* [electrum]); Manuel I with St. Theodore (Pl. 13.*5–9* [electrum]), with St. Demetrius (Pl. 14.*7–9* [electrum]); Isaac Comnenus of Cyprus with St. George (Pl. 19.*6, 7* [billon]); Isaac II with St. Michael (Pl. 20.*1–8* [gold and electrum]); Alexius III with St. Constantine (Pl. 22.*1–12*, etc. [gold, electrum, and billon]).

panied by the customary changes in design. The debasement itself possibly occurred during the winter 1081/82, when, following the defeat of Dyrrhachium the Emperor, according to Anna, was particularly short of money. The second type at Thessalonica—depicting St. Demetrius handing a patriarchal cross to the Emperor—would therefore probably have been struck at least until 1084/85, when the Norman war came to an end, and the corresponding metropolitan issue right up until the date of the coinage reform.

Although this analysis renders certain the attribution of particular types of trachea to the pre-reform period of the reign, and gives some indication, at least, of the length of the first two coinages, the actual date of the reform still remains uncertain, but, on the evidence above, should lie at some point between 1084/85 and 1092.

It is, however, difficult to detect any point during that period at which Alexius might have had the resources and the opportunity to put the reform into effect. No sooner was the Norman war finished than the Empire was involved with a long struggle against the Patzinaks. Several campaigns have been distinguished.[26] That of 1085/86 involved incursions into the Thracian plain aided by discontented Paulician elements and resulted in the defeat and death of the Grand Domestic of the West, Gregory Pacourianus: the general, Taticius, who was sent to recover the situation, found it necessary to pay the troops a year's wages in order to persuade them to fight. 1087 saw further attacks by the Patzinaks and the dispossessed king of Hungary, Saloman, reaching right down the Thracian plain, almost to the coast: although this alliance was dispersed, the Emperor's defeat in northern Bulgaria, at Silistria, followed shortly, after which he was forced to ransom such captured troops as had been left alive by the nomads. A short peace in 1089 was followed by a reopening of the war: in 1090 the area of the campaign was the region around Adrianople; conflict was only brought to an end in April 1091 by the decisive victory at Levunium, where the Patzinaks were virtually exterminated with the aid of the Cumans. The years 1090/91 had also seen an attempt by the Seljuk Emir of Smyrna, Tzachas, to blockade the capital by means of the considerable fleet which he had had constructed.

It is, therefore, hardly conceivable that Alexius would have been able to institute the new coinage between 1084/85 and 1091. The only acceptable solution is therefore to consider the commemorative issue of September 1092— used probably for imperial largess distributed in the coronation celebrations— as inaugurating the new system, and to suppose that this small issue of electrum and billon trachea (and hyperpyra, assuming that they were struck), was then followed by the regular series which formed the pattern for the coinage of the next century and a half.

[26] Chalandon, *op. cit.*, pp. 95–136. The chronology 1085–91 remains controversial.

There are, finally, several contemporary sources which are widely accepted as referring to the debased state of the coinage under Alexius—even at a relatively late date in the reign, when, according to the arguments employed above, the reformed coinage should have been in circulation. In fact none are decisively against either the reform or the relatively early date postulated for it.

In anticipation of the campaign against Robert Guiscard, Anna Comnena mentions that Alexius, soon after his accession, sent to Henry IV of Germany 144,000 nomismata to encourage the latter to open a diversionary campaign in southern Italy. This sum was paid διά τε εἰργασμένου ἀργυρίου καὶ Ῥωμανάτου παλαιᾶς ποιότητος—"in worked silver and Romanata of old quality."[27] That there could exist an old quality suggests that there existed a new and necessarily lower one. This interpretation may be correct, but it should be observed that the date of the occasion (before August 1081) is prior to that suggested for the monetary reform, and is therefore irrelevant to any discussion concerning its existence. The coins in question were probably stamena nomismata of the Emperor Romanus III, the last ruler to have struck pieces of 24 carats fine.

It is also pointed out that, subsequent to the second Norman war, by the provisions of the treaty signed at Deavolis in September 1108, Alexius promised to pay Bohemund the annual sum: ἀπὸ τῶν βασιλικῶν θησαυρῶν τάλαντα διακόσια τοῦ προβεβασιλευκότος κυρίου Μιχαὴλ ποιότητά τε καὶ χαραγὴν ἀποφέροντα —"two hundred talents [of nomismata] of the former Emperor, the lord Michael, of his quality and bearing his stamp, from the imperial treasury."[28] According to Zakythinos and Svoronos, for instance, this indicates the debasement of the coinage being issued currently, to which Bohemund preferred the older, purer coins. It is generally forgotten that Bohemund was hardly in a position to demand any such distinction—he had just suffered a humiliating defeat—and the payment was an obvious gilding to the remaining clauses of the treaty, which were heavily weighted in favor of the Empire. It is, of course, not certain which Emperor Michael was referred to, but possibly it was Michael IV —whose gold coins fluctuated between a theoretical 24 carats fine and an actual 19½—rather than Michael VII, whose coinage is of a mere 13 or 14 carats.

It would be as well to exercise care when approaching terminology such as the above two examples and others quoted elsewhere in this publication: it is true that Anna might actually be referring to particular coins of these emperors —but equally well she could be describing their particular metallic quality. Other cases might be cited: for instance, it is evident that John II could not have expected certain expenses of the Pantocrator Monastery to have always been paid in his hagiogeorgata, and that the grant that Alexius I made to the Monastery of Patmos could not have been forever paid in Komnenata theo-

[27] Anna Comnena, III, 10; Bonn ed., 1, p. 175.
[28] Ibid., XIII, 12; Bonn ed., 2, p. 243.

tokia; it is probable that the term "manuellatus," as used by the Latin sources, referred to coins other than those actually struck by that Emperor. Apparently, then, the reference was indeed to the particular standard of metal content as much as to the actual issue. It may well be, therefore, in consideration of the reluctance of the Byzantines to employ the vulgar term hyperpyron, that Anna was employing a circumlocution, since the hyperpyron was of much the same purity as the coinage of Michael IV. Possibly, she was merely repeating a euphemism already employed in the copy of the treaty to which she obviously had access.

The chronicler Zonaras states that Alexius, upon finding the coinage debased by his predecessors, struck a nomisma of copper, which he used in imperial expenses, while demanding taxes sometimes in good gold, sometimes in half gold, even in copper.[29] Unfortunately, the stage of the reign at which this is supposed to have occurred is not mentioned. It is possible that Zonaras was referring to the further debasement which took place in the coinage of Constantinople and Thessalonica during the winter 1081/82. This certainly implied the removal of most of the gold formerly used for the monetary alloy, and the substitution of an appreciable amount of copper. The imperial government would quite possibly have demanded payment of taxes in coins of better standard—those of the predecessors of Alexius.

The further information, that Alexius used metal gained from the melting down of public monuments and "obols" (folleis?) for the manufacture of nomismata, is in this case perfectly plausible: certainly at this stage the government must have been quite desperate to lay hands on any metal within its reach.

Alternatively, and more probably, however, it may be supposed that Zonaras is giving an erroneous interpretation of the reformed coinage itself. Distinction is made between nomismata of good gold, of half gold, and of copper. This is, of course, precisely the pattern taken by the reformed currency. According to this alternative interpretation, the nomisma of good gold would have been the hyperpyron, that of half-gold a loose description of the electrum, that of copper a similar one of the billon. The land tax was paid in electrum and billon. It may even be that the passage gives some clue as to the methods by which the new coinage was put into circulation: quite simply, imperial expenses were paid in varying proportions of the three denominations. As long as this was done according to official exchange rates based on the bullion value of the

---

[29] Zonaras, XVIII, 22; Bonn ed., 3, p. 738: οὗτος ὁ βασιλεὺς καὶ τὸ νόμισμα κεκιβδηλευμένον παρὰ τῶν πρὸ αὐτοῦ εὑρηκὼς χάλκεον ἔθετο, ᾧ εἰς τὰ τῆς βασιλείας ἐκέχρητο ἀναλώματα, τοὺς δέ γε φόρους διὰ χρυσίνων δοκίμων εἰσέπραττε, πῇ δέ γε καὶ δι' ἑτέρων, χρυσίνων μὲν κἀκείνων, ἀλλ' ἡμιχρύσων, ἔστι δ' οὗ καὶ διὰ τῶν χαλκέων ἐδασμοφόρει. ὅθεν χαλκοῦ δεόμενος πλείονος τοὺς ὀβολοὺς εἰς νόμισμα μετετύπωσε καί τινα τῶν δημοσίων ἔργων, τῶν χαλκουργημάτων φημί, κατασπάσας εἰς στατῆρας συνέκοψε καὶ νέας δεκάτας ἐκαίνισεν.

pieces involved, there would have been no fraud—although the conservative minded might well have objected to the practice.[30] The observation concerning the melting down of "obols"—frequently a euphemism for folleis—for manufacture into nomismata would in this case probably be a blundered reference to the abolition of the follis in favor of the billon trachy and the copper tetarteron.

The new taxes which the same passage mentions Alexius as establishing may well be a reference to the provisions of the *Nea Logarike*, which remain to be discussed in the next chapter.

Whatever the correct interpretation, it can no longer be doubted that at some comparatively early stage of the reign, Alexius was able to institute a reform of the coinage according to an unprecedented pattern, one which provided the basis of its ultimate period of splendor.

---

[30] What is apparently a gloss on the astrological writer Astrampsychus and which is quoted by Du Cange, terms the electrum (aspron trikephalon) denomination "wasteful" or "destructive" — καὶ περὶ ἀπωλείας πραγμάτων δηλονότι ἄσπρων ἢ τρικεφάλων καὶ τῶν ὁμοίων. See: Du Cange, *Glossarium ...Graecitatis*, 2, col. 1605.

The western writer Arnold of Lübeck also describes the electrum (manlat) in a disparaging and not entirely accurate fashion: *Est autem manlat de viliori nummismate, qui nec totus sit aureus, nec totus cupreus, sed quasi de confusa et vili constat materia*: In *Chronica Slavorum*, IV, 12; ed. Pertz, MGH, *SS*, 21, p. 174.

Monetary alloys of this kind, however honest in origin, tended to be unpopular on principle since they lent themselves so easily to subsequent manipulations that were extremely difficult to detect. On this subject see, for instance, Nicholas Oresme, *De Moneta*, caps. 3, 13; ed. C. Johnson (London, 1956), pp. 7–8, 20–22.

CHAPTER SIX

THE *PALAIA KAI NEA LOGARIKE*

Taking into account the date of the monetary reform of Alexius I, the pattern which it took, and the changes inevitably resulting in the circulating medium, it should now be possible to undertake an examination of the treatise known as the Παλαιὰ καὶ Νέα Λογαρική,[1] avoiding the excesses of hypothetical complication which have so far marked the question.

The treatise is a practical excursus into the estimation of certain kinds of tax liability and the reforms carried through by Alexius in that field. According to N. Svoronos, it must be dated to a period subsequent to 1182/83, which is the last year mentioned in a treatise on lunar cycles accompanying it and in the same hand.[2] It was certainly written after the death of Alexius, for he is referred to as: ὁ ἀοίδιμος βασιλεύς—the regular term for deceased emperors.[3] A reference occurs to indictions XII and XIII,[4] which, in the circumstances, probably applies to the years 1118/19 and 1119/20; that is, during the early part of the reign of John II.

There has been a certain amount of disagreement as to the particular indictional cycles referred to in the lyseis contained in the treatise. Von Lingenthal preferred those two commencing in September 1077 and ending September 1107; Dölger those commencing in September 1092 and ending September 1122.[5] There is, in fact, no question but that Dölger is correct, as correlation of the weekdays, months, and years mentioned clearly demonstrates. This is of some importance, for it requires that the treatise should be interpreted within the context of the reformed coinage, and not according to the coinage of the period of debasement (1081–92), as hitherto assumed.

The first part, entitled: Ἀρχὴ σὺν θεῷ τῆς παλαιᾶς λογαρικῆς τοῦ αὐγούστου καίσαρος,—"The commencement, with God's help, of the old [method of] reckoning of Augustus Caesar"—opens with a table showing the relation of the standard gold nomisma to its subdivisions (Table 1, p. 59).[6] That the traditional

---

[1] Published and tabulated by von Lingenthal: *Ius Graeco-Romanum*, 3, pp. 385–400.

[2] Svoronos, "Recherches," p. 79.

[3] Von Lingenthal, *op. cit.*, p. 393.

[4] *Ibid.*, p. 400.

[5] F. Dölger, *Regesten der Kaiserurkunden des oströmischen Reiches*, 2 (Munich-Berlin, 1925), nos. 1230, 1234, 1245, 1246, 1247.

[6] Von Lingenthal, *op. cit.*, p. 386. The equivalents in noummia—not published by von Lingenthal—are given by Svoronos ("Recherches," p. 79).

relationships: 1 nomisma=12 miliaresia=288 folleis should remain in force, in theory at least, so far into the reign of Alexius need occasion no surprise: indeed, the system outlasted the Comneni and Angeli (although its dating back to the reign of Augustus is, of course, incorrect). The fractional system based formerly upon a nomisma of 24 keratia weight of pure gold had merely been transferred to a coin of 24 keratia weight of gold of the standard of the hyperpyron. The fact that the hyperpyron itself is not mentioned casts no reflection on the fact of its existence, and results merely from there being no need to use any other term for it than χάραγμα νόμισμα—worth the traditional number of miliaresia and folleis.

The treatise then proceeds to deal with the actual estimation of tax liability. The taxes concerned are those termed παρακολουθήματα, directly dependent on the sum levied for the basic land-tax (δημόσιος κανών, δημόσιον). The first mentioned is the δικέρατον, levied, as might be expected, at the rate of 2 keratia per nomisma of the basic tax; that is, $1/_{12}$. Amounts involving fractions of the follis were raised to the next whole number, a practice presumably dating from a time when there existed no coin of smaller value (Table 2, p. 59).[7]

The second subsidiary tax, the ἑξάφολλον (instituted by Leo III), was collected only when the basic tax rose above the sum of $2/_3$ nomisma, and, as its name indicates, was levied at a rate of six folleis per nomisma of the basic tax. Unlike the *dikeraton*, the *hexafollon* recognized no fractions of the nomisma, fractions lower than one-half being ignored, those between the half and the unit being counted as the unit itself. The table, therefore, commencing at a basic tax of $2/_3$ nomisma, charges six folleis, until a sum of $1^1/_2$ nomisma is reached, where the charge increases to twelve folleis.

The issue is somewhat complicated by the institutions known as χάραγμα and στροφή or ἀντιστροφή. It was evidently the practice for the tax collector to demand the next whole number of coined nomismata when the total tax amounted to a sum of nomismata and upwards of two-thirds: hence *charagma*. The difference was returned in small change: hence *strophe*, etc. Thus, for a total tax (basic + *dikeraton* + *hexafollon*) of $1^2/_3$ nomisma, two whole nomismata would have been demanded, and $1/_3$ nomisma returned in change. The preference of the imperial government for payment of taxes in gold is a noticeable phenomenon from late Roman times onward (Table 3, pp. 60–61).[8]

A further table illustrates the estimation of the amount charged for the *dikeraton* and *hexafollon* on sums between two and 10,000 whole nomismata of basic tax. The calculations are relatively simple: no fractions of the nomisma being involved as far as the basic tax is concerned, the more complicated as-

[7] *Ibid.*, p. 386.
[8] *Ibid.*, pp. 387–88.

4*

pects of *dikeraton, hexafollon, charagma,* and *strophe* do not occur. Only a representative number of instances are therefore given here (Table 4, p. 61).[9]

The remaining two subsidiary taxes, the συνήθεια and the ἐλατικόν, differ in one important respect from the *dikeraton* and *hexafollon*: originally to the profit of the tax collector and his agents, they had later been annexed to the profit of the government. The distinction still appeared subsequently, however, in that they do not seem to have been taken into account in the estimation of the *charagma,* and were apparently always paid in small change.

Unlike the other two subsidiary taxes, the *synetheia* and *elatikon* did not go beyond certain fixed ceilings; nine nomismata in the case of the former, one nomisma in that of the latter. From one to five nomismata of the basic land-tax, the *synetheia* was levied at a rate of one miliaresion per nomisma, and from then on at a flat rate, as seen in the table. The *elatikon* was levied at a flat rate of twelve folleis between one and five nomismata of the basic tax, and from then as in the table (Table 5, p. 61).[10]

The final table of the *Palaia Logarike* provides instances of the assessment of all the subsidiary taxes together (Table 6, p. 62).[11]

As regards the payment of taxes under the system of the *Palaia Logarike,* three distinct phases should be considered. The first, prior to the debasement of the coinage under Constantine IX, presents no problems: payment would have been made in stamena nomismata of 24 keratia weight, and 24 carats fine, and in current miliaresia and folleis. The second, stretching from some point in the reign of Constantine IX—when the debasement became systematic—until 1092, when Alexius I carried out his monetary reform, is considerably more involved. The situation revealed at the commencement of the process resulting eventually in the establishment of the *Nea Logarike,* tends to confirm the suggestion made above,[12] that the trachea of various degrees of debasement were generally treated as worth their bullion value only, as far as normal circulation and the collection of taxes were concerned, and not as worth the purely theoretical value given them on their issue. The dichotomy between the theoretical and actual value of the precious metal coinage would not have been such a great cause of difficulty as might at first be supposed—at least as far as the system of reckoning was concerned. Once a given issue of trachy had received, in the course of circulation, a value in miliaresia or folleis (based on the old stamenon nomisma) which commanded general acceptance, it would have been quite possible to make up the sum demanded, for instance, by the tax collector. The only aspect which would

---

[9] *Ibid.,* pp. 389–91.
[10] *Ibid.,* p. 391.
[11] *Ibid.,* p. 392.
[12] Chap. I, p. 7.

have caused obvious difficulty would have been the payment of the *charagma*; the problems involved in the exact making up, in debased trachea, of any given sum of charagmata nomismata would have been formidable.

The third period, that subsequent to the monetary reform of Alexius but prior to the establishment of the *Nea Logarike*, should have been relatively simple, with the hyperpyron as the standard charagma nomisma. That a resumption of the old system did not, in practice, occur was not, as has generally been assumed, the result of a debased and chaotic coinage, but rather of the lack of any standard rate for the levy of the land-tax and its subsidiaries. This situation had certainly been brought about by the debasement of the preceding period, but had been perpetuated, despite the reform of the coinage, by the prevailing social trends current in the Empire. The final establishment of the *Nea Logarike* marked the resumption of control by the imperial government over those elements which had escaped it in the chaotic political and economic conditions of the last decades of the eleventh century.

The second part of the treatise, entitled: Καὶ ἀρχὴ τῆς νέας τῆς νῦν ἀπαιτουμένης διὰ προστάξεως τοῦ ἀοιδίμου βασιλέως κυροῦ ἀλεξίου τοῦ κομνηνοῦ —"And the beginning of the new and present system of collection through the command of the famed Emperor, the lord Alexius Comnenus,"[13]—consists of a series of reports (ὑπομνηστικά) made by the treasury officials, and imperial rulings in the form of λύσεις.

The first report, made by John Tzirithon and dated March of indiction II (i.e., March 1109),[14] describes the fiscal situation in the *dioikeseis* of Thrace and Macedonia prior to the establishment of the *Nea Logarike*, and also the first measures taken in the formation of the latter. The position preceding these measures seems to have been as follows. The taxes were being collected according to customary methods. Demetrius Camaterus had obtained the farm of taxes for the indiction XIII (1104/05), having promised to double the amount formerly collected, but, having failed in his engagement, he had had his palace near to the hippodrome confiscated. The collection for indiction XIV (1105/06) had been confided to the *proedros* Nicephorus Artavasdus, who, having accomplished his task, reapplied for indiction XV (1106/07). Artavasdus had himself relied on the system inherited from his predecessors, according to a report that he made. Consequently his agents had collected in certain fiscal units (χωρία), instead of one miliaresion, one nomisma;[15] in others, instead of two miliaresia, one trachy nomisma; in others, instead of three miliaresia, one

---

[13] Von Lingenthal, *op. cit.*, p. 393.

[14] *Ibid.*, pp. 393–96.

[15] *Ibid.*, p. 393: ... ἔν τισι μὲν τῶν χωρίων ἀντὶ μιλλιαρησίου ἑνὸς νόμισμα ἕν, ἐν ἑτέροις δὲ χωρίοις ἀντὶ μιλλιαρησίων β′ τραχὺ νόμισμα ἕν, ἐν ἄλλοις ἀντὶ μιλλιαρησίων γ′ νόμισμα α′, καὶ ἐν ἑτέροις ἀντὶ μιλλιαρησίων δ′ νόμισμα ἕν, πάντα δὲ τὰ πρόσωπα καὶ τὰ μοναστήρια καί τινα τῶν χωρίων ἀντὶ μιλλιαρησίων ιβ′ τραχὺ νόμισμα ἕν.

nomisma; and in yet others, instead of four miliaresia, one nomisma. In the case of "personages" (πρόσωπα), monasteries, and certain other units, however, one trachy nomisma had been collected instead of twelve miliaresia. Artavasdus had therefore asked for instructions as to the collection for indiction XV.

Since the list of miliaresia charged by the collectors is arranged in a regularly ascending order, it is clear that the νόμισμα and the τραχὺ νόμισμα of the report are one and the same denomination. It is also clear from the development of the text that this nomisma is to be identified with the νόμισμα τραχὺ ἄσπρον of the lysis quoted a little further on in the same report, which is expressly stated to be worth four milaresia or ninety-six folleis; that is, the third part of the standard nomisma—which can only be the hyperpyron. The sense of the passage is therefore that variously for every one, two, three, or four miliaresia of their tax liability, the majority of fiscal units were paying one aspron trachy nomisma worth four miliaresia: that is, they were paying the normal rate (one aspron trachy for four miliaresia); one and one-third times the normal (one aspron trachy instead of three miliaresia); twice the normal (one aspron trachy instead of two miliaresia); even four times the normal (one aspron trachy instead of one miliaresion). The *prosopa* and monasteries, on the other hand, forming independent fiscal units, were being assessed at—or paying, which is not the same—a mere third of the normal rate, or one aspron trachy instead of twelve miliaresia. It is fortunately relatively easy to reconstruct the stages by which this situation had come about.

As the actual value of the trachy declined increasingly throughout the period *c.* 1042–1092, so the collection of taxes would have been progressively more affected. The general tendency, as explained above, would have been for the collector to reckon the money paid in to him at its bullion value, which, although causing considerable hardship to the taxpayer, who saw his income steadily declining in purchasing power in any case, would have left both the state revenue and the theoretical monetary system relatively unchanged. Had this been the only characteristic of the period, both the *Palaia Logarike* and the rate of taxation might have remained intact. It appears, however, that the *prosopa* and monasteries were in a position to complicate matters. Both benefited from the weakness of the central government and this became more and more apparent as the second half of the century proceeded. The situation revealed in Thrace and Macedonia, in the *hypomnestikon* of John Tzirithon, prior to the establishment of the *Nea Logarike*, is entirely explicable if it is assumed that these classes were sufficiently powerful to be able to enforce the collection of their taxes according to the theoretical, as opposed to the actual, value of current money; in other words, if for a tax liability of one hundred standard nomismata, they paid one hundred trachea of Constantine X (actually worth about nine miliaresia each) during his reign; one hundred trachea of Michael VII (worth seven to eight miliaresia each) during his; and during the reign of Nicephorus III, one hundred current trachea (worth barely five miliaresia each), and so on. In these circumstances, since the farmer of taxes was engaged to procure a fixed amount of money (doubtless reckoned according to its bullion value) from his province, his only recourse would have been to increase the rate of taxation in those fiscal units which could be coerced: no doubt charging the highest rate that each could be forced to pay—a variable level, as seen in the report submitted by Artavasdus.

The position would not have eased even when the reformed coinage came into general use: the *prosopa* having increased their power and influence over the last decades, it would have been impossible to coerce them into paying a full standard hyperpyron for the nomisma or twelve miliaresia of tax, when, during the reign of Nicephorus III and prior to the coinage reform of Alexius, they had been paying a debased trachy worth five miliaresia or less. Doubtless, they paid that coin in the new system which most resembled the debased trachy in value—the aspron trachy worth four miliaresia. The unfortunate remainder would therefore of necessity have continued to pay the high rates given in the report. The tax collector and even the government probably preferred payment of aspra trachea rather than hyperpyra, since they stood to gain a greater proportion of bullion vis-à-vis the total amount collected, owing to the fact that the level at which the taxpayer was forced to pay a piece of precious metal had now sunk from eight miliaresia (the old rate of the *charagma*) to four miliaresia at the highest. In addition, payment at the rate of one hyperpyron instead of one miliaresion—a rate twelve times the normal—would have been beyond the bounds of possibility, as pointed out by Svoronos.

What one is in the presence of during indiction XIV and the preceding period, is therefore basically not monetary confusion, but wildly differing rates of taxation.[16]

Faced with Artavasdus' report, there were three main courses open to the Emperor: to permit the continuation of the situation as described; to re-establish a uniform rate based on the *Palaia Logarike* with the hyperpyron as the charagma nomisma (which might well have diminished the total collected, since, by now, the high rates paid by the majority probably more than balanced the amount lost to the *prosopa*); or to establish some uniform rate which was nevertheless higher than that prevailing before the debasement. It was, in fact, the last which he took.

The lysis to the effect, presumably issued late in indiction XIV or early in indiction XV—if it was meant to be in time to regulate the collection of taxes

[16] A fact of which Chalandon, in dealing with the treatise, could not be aware, without some knowledge of the monetary reforms undertaken by Alexius. Hence the evident confusion of his account. Svoronos was under the same disadvantage.

for the latter indiction—is unfortunately only reported at second hand by Tzirithon, but appears to have been phrased as follows: where previously one silver coin or miliaresion had been taken, there was now to be collected—from all *choria* and *prosopa*—one nomisma, with its *dikeratohexafollon, synetheia,* and *elatikon*. The nomisma in question was the τραχὺ παλαιόν.[17]

The sense is by no means clear, but nevertheless what seems to have been meant was that where there had previously been taken one miliaresion for the basic tax, there was now to be collected one trachy palaion. The trachy palaion can, once more, only have been the electrum coin worth the third part of the hyperpyron—perhaps "old" in relation to the "new" reformed hyperpyron. The term *palaion* is obviously used generically on this occasion, and cannot therefore refer to the condition of individual pieces. The rate of taxation had, in effect, been quadrupled and all were now paying at a rate comparable to the highest paid by the *choria* prior to the issue of the lysis.

However, the lysis was evidently insufficiently clear, for another was soon issued. The relevant parts are quoted in full by Tzirithon. Before continuing, it is necessary to mention that this second lysis definitely marked the end of the *charagma* in its old form. The term in future refers to those sums of the basic tax involving whole nomismata. Those involving fractions were termed λεπτὰ ψηφία. The *lepta psephia* were always accounted separately, even when, in total, they amounted to more than a nomisma.

The second lysis[18] ordered that the *lepta psephia* of the basic tax were to be collected in copper coins (διὰ χαλκῶν νουμίων), the *charagma* in nomismata (διὰ νομισμάτων). The *lepta psephia* (expressed in the accounts as fractions of the nomisma) were to be reckoned at a rate of four miliaresia to the nomisma; that is, on the basis of the same nomisma—the electrum — as the *charagma,* although they were always paid in copper. This lysis was to apply to *prosopa* and *choria* without distinction.

Even this second lysis was insufficient. Apparently some agents understood or pretended to understand the Emperor to mean that the *lepta psephia* were only to be reckoned at the rate of four miliaresia to the nomisma when their sum amounted to a whole number of nomismata, but that otherwise, fractions were to be reckoned at the old rate—half a nomisma equalling six miliaresia, a third equalling four miliaresia, and so on. By this method more was paid for the fraction than the whole. Others (correctly) understood the Emperor to mean that whatever the total of the *lepta psephia,* it was to be treated as four

[17] Von Lingenthal, *op. cit.,* p. 394: ... ἀπὸ πάντων τῶν τε χωριτῶν καὶ τῶν προσώπων ἀντὶ ἀργυροῦ ἑνὸς ἤτοι μιλλιαρησίου ἑνὸς νόμισμα ἓν εἰσπράττεσθαι διά τε τοῦ δικερατοεξαφόλλου, συνηθείας τε καὶ ἐλατικοῦ· ἐπὶ δὲ τῇ ἀπαιτήσει τῶν νομισμάτων τὸ τραχὺ παλαιὸν ἓν ἀπαιτεῖσθαι νόμισμα μετὰ τῶν παρακολουθημάτων αὐτοῦ.

[18] *Ibid.:* ... διὰ χαλκῶν νουμίων ἀπαιτεῖσθαι τὰ λεπτὰ ψηφία τῶν τελουμένων δημοσίων, καὶ πάλιν οὕτως ἰδοὺ διορίζεται ἀπαιτεῖσθαι· τὸ μὲν χάραγμα διὰ νομισμάτων, τὰ δὲ λεπτὰ ψηφία ὡς εἴρηται διὰ νουμίων· πλὴν ἐπὶ τῶν δ′ μιλλιαρησίων τῷ νομίσματι.

miliaresia to the nomisma—half a nomisma equalling two miliaresia, a quarter, one miliaresion, and so on. Since the Emperor was absent from the city (involved in the preparations for the second Norman war), the question was incapable of solution, and the taxes for indictions XV and I (1106–08), were calculated according to the rate most advantageous to the state.

It was only in February of indiction II (1108/09) that the Emperor was able to formulate a reply, which marked the establishment, in its main principles, of the *Nea Logarike*. The translation is as follows:[19]

Rescript

The former rescript of my majesty is clearly complete and unambiguous, for my majesty decreed this: that on the one hand the coined (*charagma*) nomisma is to be collected in aspra trachea nomismata, and on the other hand fractional sums (*lepta psephia*) in copper coins, and that the [copper] coins are to be reckoned at four miliaresia to the nomisma; that one who owes $\frac{1}{2}$ nomisma gives two miliaresia of copper coins; that for $\frac{1}{3}$ is paid one miliaresion, eight folleis; for $\frac{1}{4}$, one miliaresion; for $\frac{1}{6}$, sixteen folleis; for $\frac{1}{8}$, twelve folleis; for $\frac{1}{12}$, eight folleis; for $\frac{1}{24}$, four folleis; for $\frac{1}{48}$, two folleis . . . .

The meaning is indeed unambiguous: the *charagma* was to be collected in electrum trachea, the *lepta psephia* in copper coins, at the rate of four miliaresia to the nomisma, whatever their total. The *lepta psephia* were therefore to be reckoned at the same rate as the *charagma*—but collected in a different form.

Little remained toward the establishment of the *Nea Logarike* in its final form. A second *hypomnestikon* was drawn up by George Spanopoulus, *Logothetes tou genikou*, in August of indiction II, concerning payment of the *dikeratohexafollon, synetheia* and *elatikon*.[20] In brief, it appears that certain taxpayers who delivered their taxes directly to the central authorities in the city, had objected to paying the *dikeratohexafollon* at the old rate of thirty folleis (twenty-four and six respectively) to the nomisma, as had apparently continued to be the case, despite the impression given by the first lysis, that the *parakolouthemata* were to be paid at a rate appropriate to the (aspron trachy) nomisma which now, otherwise, formed the basis of reckoning. They demanded that since the nomisma on which the tax was now based was the electrum coin worth one-third of the standard, they should pay ten folleis per nomisma; one-

[19] *Ibid.*, p. 395: Ἡ προγεγονυῖα λύσις τῆς βασιλείας μου σαφής ἐστι πάντη καὶ ἀναμφίβολος. τοῦτο γὰρ προσέταξεν ἡ βασιλεία μου, τὸ μὲν χάραγμα νόμισμα διὰ τραχέων ἄσπρων νομισμάτων ἀπαιτεῖσθαι, τὰ δὲ λεπτὰ ψηφία διὰ νουμίων χαλκῶν· καταλογίζεσθαι δὲ τὰ νουμία ἐπὶ τῶν δ' μιλλιαρησίων τῷ νομίσματι, ὥστε τὸν χρεωστοῦντα ἥμισυ νομίσματος διδόναι μιλλιαρήσια β' νουμίων χαλκῶν, καὶ ὑπὲρ τοῦ τριμοίρου τελεῖσθαι μιλλιαρήσιον α' φόλλεις η', ὑπὲρ τοῦ τετάρτου μιλλιαρήσιον α', ὑπὲρ τοῦ ἕκτου φόλλεις ις', ὑπὲρ τοῦ ὀγδόου φόλλεις ιβ', ὑπὲρ τοῦ δωδεκάτου φόλλεις η', ὑπὲρ τοῦ κδ'' φόλλεις δ', ὑπὲρ τοῦ μη'' φόλλεις β'.

[20] *Ibid.*, pp. 396–98.

third of the former rate. A similar complaint was made concerning the *synetheia* and *elatikon*. By a further lysis (June, ind. II), the Emperor compromised in fixing the rate for the *dikeratohexafollon* at fifteen folleis per nomisma, in place of the former thirty folleis, and, for the *synetheia* and *elatikon*, eighteen folleis per nomisma in place of the thirty-six previously paid. *Dikeratohexafollon*, *synetheia* and *elatikon* were to be collected in noummia, whatever their total.

With this ultimate lysis, the *Nea Logarike* took its final form. The new system was marked by a higher rate than its predecessor; by the simplification of its calculations (as shown *infra*.); and by its application to all fiscal units not already covered by imperial decree granting a favorable rate of taxation—for, in default of positive evidence to the contrary, there is no reason to suspect that the injunction enforcing the new measures upon all *prosopa* and *choria* was not applied to all those who had been illegally evading their liabilities. It took the place of a system the theory of which had become divorced from practice.

The principal features of the new system as demonstrated in the final table are that the *parakolouthemata* are, in effect, all combined in a charge of thirty-three folleis $(15+18)$ per nomisma, their former idiosyncracies being ignored. The term *charagma* refers only to the whole nomismata of the basic tax, the *lepta psephia* always being reckoned in folleis, whatever their final total. The nomisma on which all parts of the table are based is the electrum aspron trachy, of four miliaresia or ninety-six folleis (Table 7, p. 63).[21]

The first of the examples for the calculation of *parakolouthemata* under the *Nea Logarike* concerns a hypothetical monastery.[22]

Basic tax on various properties	$= 1 + \frac{1}{2} + \frac{1}{3} + \frac{1}{12}$ nom.
	$2 + \frac{1}{2} + \frac{1}{4}$ nom.
	$4 + \frac{1}{2} + \frac{1}{4} + \frac{1}{24}$ nom.
	$\frac{1}{3} + \frac{1}{8}$ nom.
Charagma	$= 7$ nomismata trachea $(1 + 2 + 4$ nom.$)$
Parakolouthemata on 7 coined trachea at 33 folleis per nomisma	$= 231$ folleis
Lepta psephia in miliaresia	$= 11\frac{2}{3}$ miliaresia $= 280$ folleis
Parakolouthemata on $11\frac{2}{3}$ mil. (280 folleis or $2 + \frac{1}{2} + \frac{1}{3} + \frac{1}{12}$ nom.)	$= 96\frac{1}{4}$ folleis
Total (*charagma* + *lepta psephia* + *parakolouthemata*)	$= 7$ trachea, $607\frac{1}{4}$ folleis
At 1 trachy for 16 folleis, $607\frac{1}{4}$ folleis	$= 38$ trachea (to next whole number)
Total	$= 45$ whole trachea $(7 + 38)$.

(The text is continued after the tables, on page 64.)

[21] *Ibid.*, p. 399.
[22] *Ibid.*, p. 400, for both examples.

Figures in parentheses and addition signs in the following tables are insertions by the author.

TABLE 1

Nomisma	(Total)	Miliaresia	Folleis	Noummia
$1/48$		—	6	
$1/24$		—	12	
$1/24+1/48$	$(1/16)$	—	18	
$1/8$		—	36	
$1/8+1/48$	$(7/48)$	—	42	
$1/12$		1	—	500
$1/6$		2	—	1000
$1/4$		3	—	1500
$1/3$		4	—	2000
$1/3+1/12$	$(5/12)$	5	—	2500
$1/2$		6	—	3000
$1/2+1/12$	$(7/12)$	7	—	3500
$1/2+1/6$	$(2/3)$	8	—	4000
$1/2+1/4$	$(3/4)$	9	—	4500
$1/2+1/3$	$(5/6)$	10	—	5000
$1/2+1/3+1/12$	$(11/12)$	11	—	5500
$1/2+1/3+1/6$	(unit)	12	—	6000

= 1 coined nomisma (χάραγμα νόμισμα)

TABLE 2

Nomisma (Basic Land-tax)	( )	Dikeraton in Folleis	Total Nomisma	( )	Folleis	=	Miliaresia	Folleis
A $1/48$	$(1/48)$	1 (r. $1/2$)	—		7	=	—	—
$1/24$	$(2/48)$	1	—		13	=	—	—
$1/24+1/48$	$(3/48)$	2 (r. $1\,1/2$)	—		20	=	—	—
$1/12$	$(4/48)$	2	—		26	=	1	2
$1/12+1/48$	$(5/48)$	3 (r. $2\,1/2$)	—		33	=	1	9
$1/8$	$(6/48)$	3	—		39	=	1	15
$1/8+1/48$	$(7/48)$	4 (r. $3\,1/2$)	—		46	=	1	22
$1/6$	$(8/48)$	4	—		52	=	2	4
B $1/4$	$(12/48)$	6	$1/4+1/48$	$(13/48)$	—	=	3	6
C $1/3$	$(16/48)$	8	$1/3+1/48$	$(17/48)$	2	=	4	8
$1/3+1/12$	$(20/48)$	10	$1/3+1/12+1/48$	$(21/48)$	4	=	5	10
$1/2$	$(24/48)$	12	$1/2+1/24$	$(26/48)$	—	=	6	12
$1/2+1/48$	$(25/48)$	13 (r. $12\,1/2$)	$1/2+1/24+1/48$	$(27/48)$	1	=	6	19
$1/2+1/24$	$(26/48)$	13	$1/2+1/12$	$(28/48)$	1	=	7	1
$1/2+1/24+1/48$	$(27/48)$	14 (r. $13\,1/2$)	$1/2+1/12+1/48$	$(29/48)$	2	=	7	8
$1/2+1/12$	$(28/48)$	14	$1/2+1/8$	$(30/48)$	2	=	7	14
$1/2+1/8$	$(30/48)$	15	$1/2+1/6$	$(32/48)$	3	=	8	3
$1/2+1/8+1/48$	$(31/48)$	16 (r. $15\,1/2$)	$1/2+1/6+1/48$	$(33/48)$	4	=	8	10

A Since $1/48$ nomisma = 6 folleis, the *dikeraton* tax amounts to $1/12$ of 6 folleis, or theoretically $1/2$ follis: because the tax recognizes no fractions of the follis, however, the next whole number is collected (i.e., 1 follis).

B From this point on, the total tax is calculated in fractions of the nomisma, to the smallest available fraction (i.e., $1/48$ nomisma = 6 folleis).

C Where the total does not fall exactly into forty-eighths, the extra is given in folleis.

TABLE 3

	1. Nomisma (Basic Land-tax)	1. ( )	2. Dikeration Nomisma	2. ( )	2. Folleis	3. Hexafolion Folleis	3. Hexafolion Nomisma	4. Total (Basic+Dikeration+Hexafolion) Nomisma	4. ( )	4. Folleis	5. Miliaresia	5. Folleis	6. Charagma Nomisma	7. Change (Strophe) Nomisma	7. ( )	7. Folleis
A	$1/2+1/6$ $(2/3)$	$(32/48)$	—	—	16	6	—	$1/2+1/6+1/24+1/48$	$(35/48)$	4	8	22	1	$1/4$	$(12/48)$	2
	$1/2+1/6+1/48$	$(33/48)$	—	—	17 (v. 16½)	6	—	$1/2+1/4$	$(36/48)$	5	9	5	1	$1/6+1/24+1/48$	$(11/48)$	1
	$1/2+1/6+1/24$	$(34/48)$	—	—	17	6	—	$1/2+1/4+1/48$	$(37/48)$	5	9	11	1	$1/6+1/24$	$(10/48)$	1
	$1/2+1/6+1/24+1/48$	$(35/48)$	—	—	18 (v. 17½)	6	—	$1/2+1/4+1/24+1/48$	$(39/48)$	—	9	18	1	$1/6+1/48$	$(9/48)$	—
	$1/2+1/4$	$(36/48)$	—	—	18	6	—	$1/2+1/3$	$(40/48)$	1	10	—	1	$1/6$	$(8/48)$	—
	$1/2+1/4+1/48$	$(37/48)$	—	—	19 (v. 18½)	6	—	$1/2+1/3+1/48$	$(41/48)$	1	10	7	1	$1/8$	$(6/48)$	5
	$1/2+1/4+1/24$	$(38/48)$	—	—	19	6	—	$1/2+1/3+1/24$	$(42/48)$	2	10	13	1	$1/12+1/48$	$(5/48)$	5
	$1/2+1/4+1/24+1/48$	$(39/48)$	—	—	20 (v. 19½)	6	—	$1/2+1/3+1/24+1/48$	$(43/48)$	2	10	20	1	$1/12$	$(4/48)$	4
	$1/2+1/3$	$(40/48)$	—	—	20	6	—	$1/2+1/3+1/12$	$(44/48)$	3	11	2	1	$1/24+1/48$	$(3/48)$	4
	$1/2+1/3+1/48$	$(41/48)$	—	—	21 (v. 20½)	6	—	$1/2+1/3+1/12+1/48$	$(45/48)$	3	11	9	1	$1/24$	$(2/48)$	3
	$1/2+1/3+1/24$	$(42/48)$	—	—	21	6	—	$1/2+1/3+1/8$	$(46/48)$	4	11	15	1	—	—	9
	$1/2+1/3+1/24+1/48$	$(43/48)$	—	—	22 (v. 21½)	6	—	$1/2+1/3+1/8+1/48$	$(47/48)$	4	—	22	—	—	—	2
B	$1/2+1/3+1/12$	$(44/48)$	—	—	22	6	—	1	—	17	—	—	—	—	—	—
	$1/2+1/3+1/8$	$(46/48)$	—	—	23	6	—	1	—	—	—	—	—	—	—	—
	$1/2+1/3+1/8+1/48$	$(47/48)$	—	—	24 (v. 23½)	6	—	$1+1/12$	$(1\ 4/48)$	2	—	—	—	—	—	—
C	1	(1)	$1/12$	$(4/48)$	2	6	$1/48$	$1+1/12+1/48$	$(1\ 5/48)$	4	—	—	—	—	—	—
D	$1+1/12$	$(1\ 4/48)$	$1/12$	$(4/48)$	4	—	$1/48$	$1+1/6+1/48$	$(1\ 9/48)$	—	—	—	—	—	—	—
	$1+1/6$	$(1\ 8/48)$	$1/12$	$(4/48)$	—	—	$1/48$	$1+1/4+1/48$	$(1\ 13/48)$	2	—	—	—	—	—	—
	$1+1/4$	$(1\ 12/48)$	$1/12+1/48$	$(5/48)$	2	—	$1/48$	$1+1/3+1/24$	$(1\ 18/48)$	4	—	—	—	—	—	—
E	$1+1/3+1/12$	$(1\ 16/48)$	$1/12+1/48$	$(5/48)$	4	—	$1/48$	$1+1/3+1/8$	$(1\ 22/48)$	1	—	—	2	$1/3$	$(16/48)$	5
	$1+1/3+1/8$	$(1\ 20/48)$	$1/12+1/48$	$(5/48)$	1 (v. ½)	—	$1/48$	$1+1/2+1/24$	$(1\ 26/48)$	1	—	—	2	$1/4+1/24$	$(14/48)$	5
	$1+1/2$	$(1\ 24/48)$	$1/8$	$(6/48)$	1	—	$1/24$	$1+1/2+1/6$	$(1\ 32/48)$	2	—	—	2	$1/4+1/48$	$(13/48)$	4
	$1+1/2+1/48$	$(1\ 25/48)$	$1/8$	$(6/48)$	2 (v. 1½)	—	$1/24$	$1+1/2+1/6+1/48$	$(1\ 33/48)$	2	—	—	2	$1/4$	$(12/48)$	4
	$1+1/2+1/24$	$(1\ 26/48)$	$1/8$	$(6/48)$	2	—	$1/24$	$1+1/2+1/6+1/24$	$(1\ 34/48)$	3	—	—	2	$1/6+1/24+1/48$	$(11/48)$	3
	$1+1/2+1/24+1/48$	$(1\ 27/48)$	$1/8$	$(6/48)$	3	—	$1/24$	$1+1/2+1/6+1/24+1/48$	$(1\ 35/48)$	4	—	—	2	$1/6+1/48$	$(9/48)$	2
	$1+1/2+1/12$	$(1\ 28/48)$	$1/8$	$(6/48)$	4 (v. 3½)	—	$1/24$	$1+1/2+1/4$	$(1\ 36/48)$	4	—	—	2	$1/6$	$(8/48)$	2
	$1+1/2+1/8$	$(1\ 30/48)$	$1/8$	$(6/48)$	4	—	$1/24$	$1+1/2+1/4+1/24$	$(1\ 38/48)$	—	—	—	2	$1/8+1/48$	$(7/48)$	—
	$1+1/2+1/8+1/48$	$(1\ 31/48)$	$1/8+1/48$	$(7/48)$	—	—	$1/24$	$1+1/2+1/4+1/24+1/48$	$(1\ 39/48)$	8	—	—	—	$1/24+1/48$	$(3/48)$	—
	$1+1/2+1/6$	$(1\ 32/48)$	$1/8+1/48$	$(7/48)$	2	—	$1/24$	$1+1/2+1/3$	$(1\ 40/48)$	4	—	—	—	—	—	—
	$1+1/2+1/4$	$(1\ 36/48)$	$1/8+1/48$	$(7/48)$	4	—	$1/24$	$1+1/2+1/3+1/12+1/48$	$(1\ 45/48)$	—	—	—	—	—	—	—
	$1+1/2+1/3$	$(1\ 40/48)$	—	—	2	—	$1/24$	2	(2)	8	—	—	—	—	—	—
	$1+1/2+1/3+1/12$	$(1\ 44/48)$	—	—	4	—	$1/24$	$2+1/12+1/48$	$(2\ 5/48)$	4	—	—	—	—	—	—

Explanatory Note to Table 3

A *Column 1* gives the basic land-tax in fractions of a nomisma, the totals of the fractions in parentheses ($^{32}/_{48}$ nom. = 192 folleis).

  Column 2 is the *dikeraton* tax on the basic land-tax, the numbers in parentheses being, as in the previous table, the theoretical halves which are, in practice, raised to the next highest unit: $^{1}/_{12}$ of 192 folleis = 16 folleis.

  Column 3 is the *hexafollon* tax on the basic land-tax: 6 folleis until that tax equals $1\frac{1}{2}$ nomismata.

  Column 4 gives the sum of these as $^{1}/_{2}+^{1}/_{6}+^{1}/_{24}+^{1}/_{48}$ nom. (= $^{35}/_{48}$ nom. = 210 folleis). There are four extra folleis.

  Column 5 gives this sum in miliaresia and folleis.

  Column 6. The practice of *charagma* occurs as explained above: in this case, the taxpayer gives the treasury 1 nomisma.

  Column 7. The treasury then refunds the difference to the taxpayer *strophe*: $^{1}/_{4}$ nom. and 2 folleis.

B (*Columns 5-7*). Since the total tax has now reached the sum of 1 nomisma (actually 1 nom., 4 folleis), the *charagma* is no longer collected, and the taxpayer is not therefore entitled to a refund.

C The *hexafollon* for C and D is calculated both in folleis and in fractions of the nomisma; otherwise, the calculation from here on is in fractions of the nomisma alone.

D See C.

E The *charagma* again comes into operation, the total tax having reached $1\frac{2}{3}$ nom. The taxpayer is again entitled to a refund (*strophe*) of the excess, which he has paid in the form of 2 nomismata (see *Columns 6, 7*).

TABLE 4

Nomismata (Basic Tax)	Dikeraton	Hexafollon	Total
2	$^{1}/_{6}$	$^{1}/_{24}$	$2+^{1}/_{6}+^{1}/_{24}$
10	$^{1}/_{2}+^{1}/_{3}$	$^{1}/_{6}+^{1}/_{24}$	$11+^{1}/_{24}$
50	$4+^{1}/_{6}$	$1+^{1}/_{24}$	$55+^{1}/_{6}+^{1}/_{24}$
100	$8+^{1}/_{3}$	$2+^{1}/_{12}$	$110+^{1}/_{3}+^{1}/_{12}$
500	$41+^{1}/_{2}+^{1}/_{6}$	$10+^{1}/_{3}+^{1}/_{12}$	$552+^{1}/_{12}$
1,000	$83+^{1}/_{3}$	$20+^{1}/_{2}+^{1}/_{3}$	$1,104+^{1}/_{6}$
5,000	$416+^{1}/_{2}+^{1}/_{6}$	$104+^{1}/_{6}$	$5,520+^{1}/_{2}+^{1}/_{3}$
10,000	$833+^{1}/_{3}$	$208+^{1}/_{3}$	$11,041+^{1}/_{2}+^{1}/_{6}$

TABLE 5

Nomismata (Basic Tax)	Synetheia	Elatikon	
1	$^{1}/_{12}$ (1 miliaresion)	$^{1}/_{24}$ (12 folleis)	
2	$^{1}/_{6}$	$^{1}/_{24}$	
3	$^{1}/_{4}$	$^{1}/_{24}$	
4	$^{1}/_{3}$	$^{1}/_{24}$	
5	$^{1}/_{3}+^{1}/_{12}$	$^{1}/_{24}$	
6	1	$^{1}/_{2}$	the same until nomismata 10
$10+^{1}/_{2}$	2	1	the same until nomismata 30
$30+^{1}/_{2}$	3	1	the same until nomismata 100
$100+^{1}/_{2}$	6	1	the same until nomismata 200
$200+^{1}/_{2}$	9	1	fixed sum.

TABLE 6

Nomis- mata (Basic Tax)	Dikeraton	Hexafollon	Syne- theia	Ela- tikon	Total	( )
1	$1/12$	$1/48$	$1/12$	$1/24$	$1+1/6+1/24+1/48$	$(1^{11}/48)$
2	$1/6$	$1/24$	$1/6$	$1/24$	$2+1/3+1/12$	$(2^{20}/48)$
3	$1/4$	$1/24+1/48$	$1/4$	$1/24$	$3+1/2+1/12+1/48$	$(3^{29}/48)$
4	$1/3$	$1/12$	$1/3$	$1/24$	$4+1/2+1/4+1/24$	$(4^{38}/48)$
5	$1/3+1/12$	$1/12+1/48$	$1/3+1/12$	$1/24$	$5+1/2+1/3+1/8+1/48$	$(5^{47}/48)$
6	$1/2$	$1/8$	1	$1/2$	$8+1/8$	$(8^{6}/48)$
7	$1/2+1/12$	$1/8+1/48$	1	$1/2$	$9+1/6+1/24+1/48$	$(9^{11}/48)$
8	$1/2+1/6$	$1/6$	1	$1/2$	$10+1/3$	$(10^{16}/48)$
9	$1/2+1/4$	$1/6+1/48$	1	$1/2$	$11+1/3+1/12+1/48$	$(11^{21}/48)$
10	$1/2+1/3$	$1/6+1/24$	1	$1/2$	$12+1/2+1/24$	$(12^{26}/48)$
$10+1/2$	$1/2+1/3+1/24$	$1/6+1/24+1/48$	2	1	$14+1/2+1/12+1/48$	$(14^{29}/48)$
15	$1+1/4$	$1/4+1/24+1/48$	2	1	$19+1/2+1/24+1/48$	$(19^{27}/48)$
20	$1+1/2+1/6$	$1/3+1/12$	2	1	$25+1/12$	$(25^{4}/48)$
25	$2+1/12$	$1/2+1/48$	2	1	$30+1/2+1/12+1/48$	$(30^{29}/48)$
30	$2+1/2$	$1/2+1/8$	2	1	$36+1/8$	$(36^{6}/48)$
$30+1/2$	$2+1/2+1/24$	$1/2+1/8+1/48$	3	1	$37+1/2+1/6+1/48$	$(37^{33}/48)$
35	$2+1/2+1/3+1/12$	$1/2+1/6+1/24+1/48$	3	1	$42+1/2+1/8+1/48$	$(42^{31}/48)$
40	$3+1/3$	$1/2+1/3$	3	1	$48+1/6$	$(48^{8}/48)$
45	$3+1/2+1/4$	$1/2+1/3+1/12+1/48$	3	1	$53+1/2+1/6+1/48$	$(53^{33}/48)$
50	$4+1/6$	$1+1/24$	3	1	$59+1/6+1/24$	$(59^{10}/48)$
55	$4+1/2+1/12$	$1+1/8+1/48$	3	1	$64+1/2+1/6+1/24+1/48$	$(64^{35}/48)$
60	5	$1+1/4$	3	1	$70+1/4$	$(70^{12}/48)$
65	$5+1/3+1/12$	$1+1/3+1/48$	3	1	$75+1/2+1/4+1/48$	$(75^{37}/48)$
70	$5+1/2+1/3$	$1+1/3+1/8$	3	1	$81+1/4+1/24$	$(81^{14}/48)$
75	$6+1/4$	$1+1/2+1/24+1/48$	3	1	$86+1/2+1/4+1/24+1/48$	$(86^{39}/48)$
80	$6+1/2+1/6$	$1+1/2+1/6$	3	1	$92+1/3$	$(92^{16}/48)$
85	$7+1/12$	$1+1/2+1/4+1/48$	3	1	$97+1/2+1/3+1/48$	$(97^{41}/48)$
90	$7+1/3$	$1+1/2+1/3+1/24$	3	1	$103+1/3+1/24$	$(103^{18}/48)$
95	$7+1/2+1/3+1/12$	$1+1/2+1/3+1/8+1/48$	3	1	$108+1/2+1/3+1/24+1/48$	$(108^{43}/48)$
100	$8+1/3$	$2+1/12$	3	1	$114+1/3+1/12$	$(114^{20}/48)$
$100+1/2$	$8+1/3+1/24$	$2+1/12+1/48$	6	1	$117+1/2+1/3+1/8+1/48$	$(117^{47}/48)$

TABLE 7

Nomisma (Basic Tax)	( )	Charagma Nom. Trachy	Miliaresia	Folleis	= Nom.	= Foll.	Parakolouthemata in Folleis	Charagma Nom.	Total Folleis	( )
$1/48$	$(1/48)$	—	—	2	—	—	$1/2+1/6+1/48$	—	$2+1/2+1/6+1/48$	$(2^{33}/48)$
$1/24$	$(2/48)$	—	—	4	—	—	$1+1/4+1/8$	—	$5+1/4+1/8 \ (=1/3+1/24)$	$(5^{18}/48)$
$1/24+1/48$	$(3/48)$	—	—	6	—	—	$2+1/16$	—	$8+1/16$	$(8^3/48)$
$1/12$	$(4/48)$	—	—	8	—	—	$2+1/2+1/4$	—	$10+1/2+1/4$	$(10^{36}/48)$
$1/12+1/48$	$(5/48)$	—	—	10	—	—	$3+1/3+1/12+1/48$	—	$13+1/3+1/12+1/48$	$(13^{21}/48)$
$1/8$	$(6/48)$	—	—	12	—	—	$4+1/8$	—	$16+1/8$	$(16^6/48)$
$1/8+1/48$	$(7/48)$	—	—	14	—	—	$4+1/2+1/4+1/24+1/48$	—	$18+1/2+1/4+1/24+1/48$	$(18^{39}/48)$
$1/6$	$(8/48)$	—	—	16	—	—	$5+1/2$	—	$21+1/2$	$(21^{24}/48)$
$1/4$	$(12/48)$	—	1	—	—	24	$8+1/4$	—	$32+1/4$	$(32^{12}/48)$
$1/3$	$(16/48)$	—	1	8	—	32	11	—	43	(43)
$1/3+1/12$	$(20/48)$	—	1	16	—	40	$13+1/2+1/4$	—	$53+1/2+1/4$	$(53^{36}/48)$
$1/3+1/8$	$(22/48)$	—	1	20	—	44	$15+1/8$	—	$59+1/8$	$(59^6/48)$
$1/3+1/8+1/48$	$(23/48)$	—	1	22	—	46	$15+1/2+1/4+1/24+1/48$	—	$61+1/2+1/4+1/24+1/48$	$(61^{39}/48)$
$1/2$	$(24/48)$	—	2	—	—	48	$16+1/2$	—	$64+1/2$	$(64^{24}/48)$
$1/2+1/48$	$(25/48)$	—	2	2	—	50	$17+1/6+1/48$	—	$67+1/6+1/48$	$(67^9/48)$
$1/2+1/24$	$(26/48)$	—	2	4	—	52	$17+1/2+1/4+1/8$	—	$69+1/2+1/4+1/8$	$(69^{42}/48)$
$1/2+1/24+1/48$	$(27/48)$	—	2	6	—	54	$18+1/2+1/24+1/48$	—	$72+1/2+1/24+1/48$	$(72^{27}/48)$
$1/2+1/12$	$(28/48)$	—	2	8	—	56	$19+1/4$	—	$75+1/4$	$(75^{12}/48)$
$1/2+1/12+1/48$	$(29/48)$	—	2	10	—	58	$19+1/2+1/3+1/12+1/48$	—	$77+1/2+1/3+1/12+1/48$	$(77^{45}/48)$
$1/2+1/8$	$(30/48)$	—	2	12	—	60	$20+1/2+1/8$	—	$80+1/2+1/8$	$(80^{30}/48)$
$1/2+1/8+1/48$	$(31/48)$	—	2	14	—	62	$21+1/4+1/24+1/48$	—	$83+1/4+1/24+1/48$	$(83^{15}/48)$
$1/2+1/6$	$(32/48)$	—	2	16	—	64	22	—	86	(86)
$1/2+1/4$	$(36/48)$	—	3	—	—	72	$24+1/2+1/4$	—	$96+1/2+1/4$	$(96^{36}/48)$
$1/2+1/3$	$(40/48)$	—	3	8	—	80	$27+1/2$	—	$107+1/2$	$(107^{24}/48)$
$1/2+1/3+1/12$	$(44/48)$	—	3	16	—	88	$30+1/4$	—	$118+1/4$	$(118^{12}/48)$
$1/2+1/3+1/12+1/48$	$(45/48)$	—	3	18	—	90	$30+1/2+1/3+1/12+1/48$	—	$120+1/2+1/3+1/12+1/48$	$(120^{45}/48)$
$1/2+1/3+1/8$	$(46/48)$	—	3	20	—	92	$31+1/2+1/8$	—	$123+1/2+1/8$	$(123^{30}/48)$
$1/2+1/3+1/8+1/48$	$(47/48)$	—	3	22	—	94	$32+1/4+1/24+1/48$	—	$126+1/4+1/24+1/48$	$(126^{15}/48)$
1	(1)	1	—	—	—	—	33	1	33	(33)
$1+1/12$	$(1^4/48)$	1	—	8	—	—	$35+1/2+1/4$	1	$43+1/2+1/4$	$(43^{36}/48)$
$1+1/6$	$(1^8/48)$	1	—	16	—	—	$38+1/2$	1	$54+1/2$	$(54^{24}/48)$
$1+1/4$	$(1^{12}/48)$	1	1	—	—	—	$41+1/4$	1	$65+1/4$	$(65^{12}/48)$
$1+1/3$	$(1^{16}/48)$	1	1	8	1	32	44	1	76	(76)
$1+1/3+1/12$	$(1^{20}/48)$	1	1	16	1	40	$46+1/2+1/4$	1	$86+1/2+1/4$	$(86^{36}/48)$
$1+1/3+1/8$	$(1^{22}/48)$	1	1	20	1	44	$48+1/8$	1	$92+1/8$	$(92^6/48)$
$1+1/3+1/8+1/48$	$(1^{23}/48)$	1	1	22	1	46	$48+1/2+1/4+1/24+1/48$	1	$94+1/2+1/4+1/24+1/48$	$(94^{39}/48)$
$1+1/2$	$(1^{24}/48)$	1	2	—	—	—	$49+1/2$	1	$97+1/2$	$(97^{24}/48)$
$1+1/2+1/12$	$(1^{28}/48)$	1	2	8	—	—	$52+1/4$	1	$108+1/4$	$(108^{12}/48)$
$1+1/2+1/6$	$(1^{32}/48)$	1	2	16	—	—	55	1	119	(119)
$1+1/2+1/4$	$(1^{36}/48)$	1	3	—	—	—	$57+1/2+1/4$	1	$129+1/2+1/4$	$(129^{36}/48)$
$1+1/2+1/3$	$(1^{40}/48)$	1	3	8	—	—	$60+1/2$	1	$140+1/2$	$(140^{24}/48)$
$1+1/2+1/3+1/12$	$(1^{44}/48)$	1	3	16	—	—	$63+1/4$	1	$151+1/4$	$(151^{12}/48)$
$1+1/2+1/3+1/8$	$(1^{46}/48)$	1	3	20	—	—	$64+1/2+1/8$	1	$156+1/2+1/8$	$(156^{30}/48)$
$1+1/2+1/3+1/8+1/48$	$(1^{47}/48)$	1	3	22	—	—	$65+1/4+1/24+1/48$	1	$159+1/4+1/24+1/48$	$(159^{15}/48)$
2	(2)	2	—	—	—	—	66	2	66	(66)
$2+1/2$	$(2^{24}/48)$	2	2	—	—	—	$82+1/2$	2	$130+1/2$	$(130^{24}/48)$
$2+1/2+1/4$	$(2^{36}/48)$	2	3	—	—	—	$90+1/2+1/4$	2	$162+1/2+1/4$	$(162^{36}/48)$
3	(3)	3	—	—	—	—	99	3	99	(99)

A distinctly odd feature of the table above is the occurrence of fractions of the follis which will cancel no further than the denominator 16. It is uncertain whether even the coin of smallest value—the copper half-tetarteron—was of such a minute value, and it might therefore be assumed that payment was made according to the next half-tetarteron, tetarteron, or follis.

The trachy which was collected for every sixteen folleis of the *lepta psephia* + *parakolouthemata* can hardly have been the aspron trachy nomisma of the *charagma*—a tax of thirty-eight on a mere seven is outside the order of the possible. It seems certain that it is to be identified with the billon trachy, although why it is given the enhanced value of sixteen folleis, instead of the normal six, is uncertain. Possibly it was in the form of a tax concession (συμπάθεια or κλάσμα), or an encouragement to pay in billon trachea rather than copper tetartera noummia. The same observation is valid for the second example, where the trachy is given the value of twelve folleis.

The second example concerns a liability for the basic tax of one nomisma *charagma*, nine miliaresia *lepta psephia*.

For indictions XII and XIII (that is, including one year's arrears):

Charagma	= 2 nom. or 2 (aspra) trachea
Lepta psephia	= 18 miliaresia
Parakolouthemata on two coined trachea	= 66 folleis
18 miliaresia (4 + ½ nom.)	= 432 folleis
Parakolouthemata on 432 folleis	= 148 ½ folleis
Total *parakolouthemata* + *lepta psephia*	= 646 ½ folleis
At 1 trachy for 12 folleis, 646 ½ folleis	= 54 trachea (to next whole number)
Total	= 56 whole trachea (2 + 54).

CHAPTER SEVEN

IMPERIAL CEREMONIAL COSTUME

Documentary sources for the study of imperial ceremonial costume are few in number: those of sufficient length and detail to be more than merely incidental are only two—the tenth-century *De Caerimoniis* of Constantine VII, and the fourteenth-century *De Officiis*, long attributed to George Codinus. Comparison of the two demonstrates only too clearly that, although the form of dress might remain relatively constant, nomenclature was considerably less standardized. It is consequently often difficult, sometimes impossible, to be sure of the fourteenth-century equivalent of any given piece of tenth-century costume: the complete twelfth-century usage is unknown. The *De Caerimoniis* —the more detailed and intelligible of the two sources— does allow of some degree of certainty in the identification of nomenclature with actual dress and, for this reason, the terminology of the tenth century will be used in describing the coin types of the Comneni and Angeli. Anomalies—in the light of future research—will no doubt appear, but the convenience of using a term involving a single word rather than a lengthy paraphrase must outweigh this consideration.

The three main outer garments seem to have been the chlamys, the loros, and the sagion.

The chlamys (χλαμύς), as may be readily understood from the *De Caerimoniis*, was the most frequently used of all the imperial ceremonial costumes:[1] it was, in addition, the chlamys together with the stemma (q.v.) which were the chief symbols of the coronation. Although still in the sixth and seventh centuries a cloak of full dimensions, by the tenth and eleventh it had gone through a process of stylization and appears merely as a narrow, triangular, ankle-length stretch of cloth, caught at the wearer's right shoulder by a fibula (φίβλα). The borders are generally represented as being heavily jewelled or embroidered. An excellent example of the stylized garment is to be seen worn by Nicephorus III in the Coislin MS 79 (fols. 1, 2). The square inset on the border hanging from the right shoulder of the wearer was termed "tablion" (ταβλίον) and was of a color different from the rest of the garment, the combination being determined by the rank of the wearer: the imperial chlamys seems generally to have been purple with a gold tablion. The fourteenth-century equivalent of the chlamys was apparently the mandyas (μανδύας).

[1] Particularly, *De Caerimoniis*, I, 37; Bonn ed., pp. 187–91.

The loros (λῶρος) likewise presents little difficulty in identification, being a heavily embroidered and jewelled strip of cloth several yards in length, wound round the body and allowed to drape to the ankles in front. Apparently of far more limited use than the chlamys, the loros was, according to the *De Caerimoniis*, regularly used only on Easter Sunday. The same section[2] mentions that the loros, in its shape, represented the Burial of Christ (i.e., the winding-sheet), and in the richness of its embroidery and jewellery, the Resurrection: an alternative explanation—that the loros was derived from the old Roman consular dress—is also advanced, and this is confirmed by a glance at the latter, as seen in the fifth- and sixth-century consular diptychs. The narrow strip of cloth, the *trabea*, proceeds from ankle height in front, to the wearer's right shoulder, over, down, and under the same arm, diagonally across the front of the body to the left shoulder, over and diagonally across the back, round and across the waist, draping finally across the left arm. Precisely the same is to be seen in the coronation panel of Constantine VII himself, in the Hermitage, and worn by Nicephorus III in the Coislin MS 79 (fol. 1ᵛ). The *trabea*/loros seems to have been of purple or of gold, but was always heavily embroidered or jewelled, or both. As in the case of the chlamys, the use of the loros was not confined to the emperor.

There remains unexplained the apparent co-existence of two kinds of loros over a period of three hundred years. The traditional form has been described above: the newer is also the simpler, and is perhaps best seen in the Romanus II and Eudocia ivory in the Cabinet des Médailles, but is also worn by Constantine IX and John II in their respective mosaic panels in Hagia Sophia (Pls. 48, 50). This new pattern first appears on the coinage of Basil I (867–86) and only completely replaces the other in the thirteenth century. Belyaev suggested that the adoption of the simpler form was the result of the loros becoming so heavy with gold and gems that it became inconvenient to wind it round the body.[3] This does not explain the apparent survival of the older form, which appears simultaneously with the other even in the same medium. It must be admitted, however, that, this oddity apart, there is no evidence to suggest that the two are in fact different costumes.

The suggestion put forward by Ebersolt—that the kite-shaped piece of cloth seen on the dress of the empress when wearing the loros should be identified with the θωράκιον of Constantine VII—is, as de Jerphanion has shown, without foundation:[4] it is quite apparent that it is, in fact, the train of the loros, which, instead of draping across the waist and over the left arm as in the case of the emperor, is pulled round and caught at the waist by a fibula.

---

[2] *De Caerimoniis*, II, 40; Bonn ed., pp. 637–39.

[3] D. F. Belyaev, *Byzantina*, 2 (St. Petersburg, 1893), p. 213.

[4] G. de Jerphanion, "Le 'Thorakion,'" *Mélanges Ch. Diehl*, 2 (Paris, 1930), p. 79.

At the beginning of the twelfth century the loros tends to lose its panelled pattern, the jewellery, however, remains.

The sagion (σαγίον) is again easily identifiable, the derivation of the term obviously being from the Latin *sagum*, or cloak, generally of the short military type. According to Constantine VII, the borders could contrast with the purple color of the rest of the garment by being embroidered in gold (χρυσο-περικλείστον). An unmistakable example of this kind of sagion is to be seen on the twelfth-century Angheran roundel.

There were evidently two forms of tunic in imperial use, the divitision (διβητήσιον) and the scaramangion (σκαραμάγγιον). According to Constantine VII, the divitision of white or purple was generally worn under the chlamys and was apparently an ankle-length tunic. The fourteenth-century equivalent was the saccos (σάκκος).

The question of the scaramangion has already been examined in considerable detail by Kondakov,[5] who identified its origins in the "kaftan" of the steppes, a long over-tunic, generally richly colored and decorated, belted, full-sleeved, and slashed at the front or sides to permit horse riding. It seems to have been used by the Byzantine emperors, often under the sagion, when making their short ceremonial processions to the various parts of the city by horse or by ship: for example to the Great Church, the Church of the Holy Apostles, the Golden Gate or Blachernae, etc. As far as imperial portraits are concerned, little distinction seems to have been made between the divitision and the scaramangion, but the *De Caerimoniis* does give the impression that the scaramangion tended to be more varied in color than the divitision: it could evidently be of gold, purple, red, or white, and also gold embroidered. In addition, the stemma could be worn with it alone, which was apparently not the case with the divitision. An unmistakable example of the scaramangion is to be seen worn by Nicephorus III in the Coislin MS 79 (fol. 2ᵛ). The four-teenth-century equivalent seems to have been the scaranicon (σκαράνικον).

The anexikakia (ἀνεξικακία), as described in the *De Caerimoniis* and the *De Officiis*,[6] was a small roll of parchment, wrapped in cloth and filled with dust: a symbol of mortality. It was clearly a development of the rather similar piece of consular regalia, the *mappa*.

The stemma (στέμμα), or crown, existed in several colors and was presumably therefore of the type known as "camelaucion," having a cloth covering to the area within the circlet. An extremely interesting description of the crown occurs in Anna Comnena, the translation being as follows:

---

[5] N. P. Kondakov, "Les costumes orientaux à la cour byzantine," *Byzantion*, I (1924), p. 19. The fact that scaramangion and stemma are worn together in the *De Caerimoniis* precludes it from being an item of headwear. Cf. J. Verpeaux, *Traité des offices* (Paris, 1966), p. 145, note 2.

[6] *De Caerimoniis*, II, 40; Bonn ed., p. 638: *De Officiis*, 6; Bonn ed., p. 51.

Further he [Alexius] ordered that on the public festivals both the Sebastocrator and the Caesar should wear crowns which were, however, very inferior in grandeur to the diadem he wore himself. The imperial diadem, or tiara, was like a semi-spherical close-fitting cap, and profusely adorned with pearls and jewels, some inserted and some pendent; on either side at the temples two lappets [ὁρμαθοί] of pearls and jewels hung down on the cheeks. This diadem is the essentially distinctive feature of the Imperial dress. But the coronets of the Sebastocrators and Caesars are but sparingly decorated with pearls and jewels, and have no globe.[7]

The stemma, as represented on the coins, always has pendilia (πρεπενδούλια),[8] although the globe and the cross surmounting it on the top center of the cap are sometimes present, sometimes absent. The crown worn by the empress differs slightly in that it is surmounted by triangular ornaments.

Examination of the mosaic panels portraying Constantine IX and John II betrays the existence of yet another article of dress in the collar-piece, which is rather similar to the ancient Egyptian pectoral. Such a collar-piece is frequently used with the loros of simplified type, but, even if worn with the traditional pattern of loros, would not be visible owing to the shape of the latter. On the coinage, the collar-piece apparently occurs not only with the simplified loros, but also with the chlamys. Comparison between the two main sub-varieties of the hyperpyron of Alexius I (Pls. 3.4–4.2) demonstrates, however, that on these occasions the "collar-piece" is, in fact, merely the jewelled border of the chlamys which is pulled across the neck to be fastened by the fibula at the emperor's right shoulder.

An altogether different set of imperial dress was required for military purposes, and although this can hardly be described as purely ceremonial, since it appears on the coins, some attempt must be made to describe it here.

The best illustration is to be found in the *Menologium* of Basil II in the Biblioteca Marciana at Venice. The Emperor appears dressed in the stemma, a short military tunic, and mail breastplate, with a short cloak—probably the sagion—fastened by a fibula at the center of the chest. On the coins the sagion generally appears to be fastened at the shoulder. The Emperor's feet are shod with the scarlet buskins or campagia (καμπάγια)[9] which the coin portraits are rarely sufficiently detailed to record. He also wears breeches—the old Roman *bracae*.

[7] Anna Comnena, III, 4; Bonn ed., pp. 147–48. The translation from: E. A. S. Dawes, *The Alexiad of the Princess Anna Comnena* (London, 1928), p. 78.

[8] *De Caerimoniis*, I, 41; Bonn ed., p. 209. (In this instance, at least, referring to the crown of the empress.)

[9] *Ibid.*, I, 92; Bonn ed., p. 423. II, 40; p. 639.

Section II
THE COINS 1081–1204

CHAPTER EIGHT

THE COMNENI

(i)

THE PRE-REFORM COINAGE OF ALEXIUS I, COMNENUS
1081–1092

EL. or Æ DEBASED TRACHY

MINT OF CONSTANTINOPLE

First coinage (1081–?)

Obv. ĪC XC in field.

Christ, bearded and nimbate, wearing tunic and colobion, seated upon throne with back; holds Gospels in left hand.

Rev. +ΛΛΕΞΙѠΔΕC ΠΟΤ,ΤѠΚΜ – or var.

Bust of emperor wearing stemma, divitision, and chlamys; holds in right hand scepter, the head of which is composed of a series of globules forming a star, and in left, globus cruciger.

Pl. 1.*1–4*,
Pl. 51.*3*

Second coinage (?–1092)

Obv. ĪC XC in field.

Bust of Christ, bearded and nimbate, wearing tunic and colobion; holds Gospels in left hand.

Rev. +ΛΛΕΞΙѠΔΕC ΠΟΤ,ΤѠΚΜ – or var.

Bust of emperor wearing stemma, divitision, and chlamys; holds in right hand scepter, the head of which is composed of a leaved cross, and in left, globus cruciger.

Pl. 1.*5–8*

MINT OF THESSALONICA

First coinage (1081/82–?)

Obv. ∴KERO ΛΛΕΞΙѠ – or var. ĪC XC in field.

Bust of Christ, bearded and nimbate, wearing tunic and colobion; holds Gospels in left hand.

Rev. MI
$$\begin{array}{cc} \cdot & \Delta \\ \Delta & \in C \\ MI & \Pi \\ TI & T \\ I & H \end{array}$$ – or var.

Full-length figure of emperor facing, on right, and of Saint Demetrius, beardless and nimbate, turned to right and handing to emperor labarum on long shaft standing on globule. Emperor wears stemma, divitision, collar-piece and jewelled loros of simplified type; saint wears short military tunic, breastplate and sagion; holds sword in left hand.

Pl. 1.*9*

Second coinage (?–1092)

Obv.

As first coinage.

Rev.

As first coinage, but St. Demetrius hands to emperor patriarchal cross on long shaft standing on globule and two steps.

Pl. 1.*10–12*

EL. or Æ DEBASED TETARTERON

MINT OF CONSTANTINOPLE

First coinage (1081–?)

Obv. ĪC X̄C in field.

Bust of Christ, bearded and nimbate, wearing tunic and colobion; holds Gospels in left hand.

Rev. +ΛΛЄΞΙѠΔЄC ΠΟΤΤѠΚΟΜ – or var.

Bust of emperor wearing stemma, divitision, and chlamys; holds in right hand scepter cruciger, and in left, globus cruciger.

Pl. 2.*1,2*

Second coinage (?–1092)

Obv. +ЄΜΜΛ ΝΟΥΗΛ – or var. ĪC X̄C in field.

Full-length figure of Christ, bearded and nimbate, wearing tunic and colobion, standing on dais; holds Gospels in left hand.

Rev. +ΛΛЄΞΙѠΔЄC ΠΟΤΤѠΚΟΜΝΗ+ – or var.

Full-length figure of emperor wearing stemma, divitision, collar-piece, and jewelled loros of simplified type; holds in right hand scepter cruciger, and in left, globus cruciger.

Pl. 2.*3–5*

MINT OF THESSALONICA

First coinage (1081/82–?)

Obv. M̄P̄ Θ̄V̄ in field.

Bust of Virgin nimbate, orans, wearing tunic and maphorion; beardless, nimbate head of Christ on breast.

Rev. +ΛΛΕΞΙШΔ ΠΟΤΤШΚ – or var.

Bust of emperor wearing stemma, divitision, and chlamys; holds in right hand jewelled scepter, and in left, globus cruciger.

Pl. *2.6–9*

Second coinage (?–1092)

Obv. ĪC X̄C in field.

Christ, bearded and nimbate, wearing tunic and colobion, seated upon throne without back; holds Gospels in left hand.

Rev. +ΛΛΕΞ ΔΕCΠΟΤΤΟΚ – or var. ✳ ✳ in field.

Bust of emperor wearing stemma, divitision, collar-piece, and jewelled loros of simplified type; holds in right hand labarum-headed scepter, and in left, anexikakia.

Pl. *2.10–12*

Æ ALLOY LIGHT WEIGHT SCYPHATE
(presumably bearing some relation to the miliaresion)

MINT OF CONSTANTINOPLE

Obv. +ΘΚΕΡΟΗΘΕΙ ΤШCШΔΟVΛШ – or var. M̄P̄ Θ̄V̄ in field.

Full-length figure of Virgin, nimbate, orans, wearing tunic and maphorion.

Rev. +ΛΛΕΞΙШΔΕC ΠΟΤΤШΚΟΜΝ – or var.

Full-length figure of emperor wearing stemma, short military tunic, breastplate, and sagion; holds in right hand cross on long shaft, and in left, sheathed sword, point resting on ground.

Pl. *2.13*

Æ ALLOY MILIARESION or FRACTION

MINT OF CONSTANTINOPLE

Type A

Obv. M̄ Θ̄ in field.

Bust of Virgin nimbate, orans, wearing tunic and maphorion; beardless, nimbate head of Christ on breast.

Rev. +O̅K̅E̅
ROHΘEI
ΛΛEΞIШ
ΔECΠOT
TШKOM
NHN(Ш)

Pl. *2.14*

Type B

Obv. +ΘKE ROHΘ – or var. M̅P̅ Θ̅V̅ in field.

Three-quarter-length figure of Virgin nimbate, orans, wearing tunic and maphorion; beardless, nimbate head of Christ on breast.

Rev. — + —
ΛΛEΞI
ШΔECΠO
THTШKO
MNHNШ
— · —

Pl. *2.15,16*

MINT OF THESSALONICA

Obv. IMHΔϽOITΛO ΛΛEΞIШΔECΠ

Half-length figure of emperor facing on right, and of Saint Demetrius, beardless and nimbate, turned to right and handing to emperor cross on long shaft. Emperor wears stemma, divitision, collar-piece, and jewelled loros of simplified type: saint wears uncertain dress, probably tunic, breastplate, and sagion.

Rev. +X̅E̅
ROHΘEI
ΛΛEΞIШ
ΔECΠOTH
TШKOMN̅H̅
NШ

Pl. *2.17*

Æ FOLLIS

MINT OF CONSTANTINOPLE

First coinage (1081–?)

Obv. I̅C̅ X̅C̅ in field.

Bust of Christ, bearded, with cross behind head, wearing tunic and colobion; Ͻ C in field of cross.

Rev.

Cross over crescent, surrounded by globules.

Pl. *2.18, 19*

Second coinage
  Obv. ĪC X̄C in field.
    Bust of Christ, bearded and nimbate, wearing tunic and colobion; holds Gospels in left hand; all within border of large globules.
  Rev. M̄P ⊕V̄ in field.
    Three-quarter-length figure of Virgin nimbate, orans, wearing tunic and maphorion; all within border of large globules.

Pl. *2.20, 21*

Third coinage (?–1092)
  Obv. ĪC X̄C in field.
    Bust of Christ, bearded and nimbate, wearing tunic and colobion.
  Rev. IC
      NI KΛ
         XC
    Cross pattée.

Pl. *2.22*

MINT OF THESSALONICA

Type A
  Obv. M̄P ⊕V̄ in field.
    Bust of Virgin nimbate, wearing tunic and maphorion; holds beardless, nimbate head of Christ on breast.
  Rev. +ΛΛЄ⊐I ΔЄCΠOTTⱲK – or var.
    Full-length figure of emperor wearing stemma, divitision, collar-piece, and jewelled loros of simplified type; holds in right hand labarum on long shaft, and in left, globus cruciger.

Pl. *3.1*

Type B
  Obv. C Φ

       Ⱳ Δ
    Jewelled cross on steps, all within border of large globules.
  Rev. +Λ
    Bust of emperor wearing stemma, divitision, and jewelled loros of traditional type; holds in right hand scepter cruciger, and in left, globus cruciger. All within border of large globules.

Pl. *3.2*

EASTERN MINT? / THESSALONICA?

Obv.   I̅C̅   X̅C̅
         N̅I̅   K̅Λ̅
    Cross on steps.
Rev.   +
         C̅E̅P̅C̅V̅N̅
         E̅P̅Γ̅E̅I̅B̅Λ̅
         C̅I̅Λ̅E̅I̅Λ̅Λ̅
           E̅Ξ̅I̅U̅

Pl. 3.3

THE PRE-REFORM COINAGE OF ALEXIUS I: COMMENTARY

EL. DEBASED TRACHY

The first and second coinages of the mints of both Constantinople and Thessalonica have already been identified on the bases of such little hoard evidence as is available and of metal content.[1]

An entry for a further (anomalous) type, represented by an apparently unique coin in the Münzkabinett at Berlin which has come to light since this book went to press, will be found on page 405, in the Supplementary Note.

EL. DEBASED TETARTERON

There are four types of debased tetarteron for the pre-reform period. The first is presumably that with a bust of Christ on the obverse, and on the reverse, a bust of the Emperor in chlamys holding a scepter and globus cruciger (Pl. 2.*1*, *2*). This type has been identified in electrum; although most specimens appear to have had quantities of copper added to the alloy, as well as silver.

Three types remain. In consideration of the fact that there are four types of debased trachy, which break down into two each for the mints of the capital and of Thessalonica, there is an obvious case for inquiring whether such a breakdown might not be possible also for the four tetarteron types.

For a definite indication as to the correct origin of these pieces, an examination of the copper tetartera of the post-reform period is required. Metropolitan types A, B, and C all have, as the reverse type, a bust of the Emperor holding a scepter (Pls. 7.*10*, *11*; 8.*1–4*). On all these issues the position of the right arm is characteristic—held away from the body so that the elbow juts out at an angle. Precisely this posture is adopted on two types of debased tetartera (Pl. 2.*1–5*), and it would therefore appear reasonable to assign these, at least, to the mint of the capital. On the first and third coinages of the Thessalonican reformed tetartera the position of the right arm is totally different. On the

[1] Chap. 5, pp. 41–45.

first coinage (Pl. 8.*7*, *8*), the arm is held across the body, the scepter resting in the crook of the arm—a rather more natural posture than that evinced in the products of the metropolitan mint. In addition, some pains have been taken to render the individual fingers and thumb of the hand holding the scepter. The third coinage of reformed copper tetartera (Pl. 8.*10*, *11*) utilizes yet another method of representing the position of the arm: it is doubled and held close to the body. Exactly these two positions are paralleled in the two remaining issues of debased tetartera in question (Pl. 2.*6–12*). It would therefore seem certain that the mint of Thessalonica followed that of the metropolis as regards the number of types of both precious metal denominations.

As to the order of the two issues of debased Thessalonican tetartera, the eight specimens of Plate 2.*6–9* present in the collection at Dumbarton Oaks are of slightly but definitely better alloy than the five of Plate 2.*10–12*. The order is presumably therefore in descending quality of alloy—as in the case of both trachea and tetartera of the metropolitan mint and the St. Demetrius trachea of the Thessalonican.

It should be pointed out that while occasional examples of the debased tetartera of the pre-reform period are of such poor alloy that they appear to be entirely of copper, and similarly, a few pieces of the reformed copper series appear to contain small amounts of silver, the general distinction between the two series remains valid.

Æ ALLOY LIGHT WEIGHT SCYPHATE

There is nothing that can be said about this denomination except that it is presumably of metropolitan origin.

Æ ALLOY MILIARESION or FRACTION

There is no certain order for the two metropolitan issues: type A, which resembles an issue of Nicephorus III, may be the earlier.[2] The type having the figures of Alexius and St. Demetrius as the obverse design is attributed to the mint of Thessalonica on grounds stated in Chapter Five (pp. 41–45).

Æ FOLLIS

The follis in its late eleventh-century form was still largely based on the pattern introduced by John I (969–76), who, as is confirmed by documentary sources, commenced the series known as the "anonymous bronze." This group of coins, as might be expected from the name which it has acquired, consists of issues on which the name of the imperial issuer does not appear, and the normal imperial portrait is replaced by a religious motif of some kind. How-

[2] J. Sabatier, *Description générale des monnaies byzantines*, 2 (Paris, 1862), p. 181, no. 8 (pl. LI, 17).

ever, with the reign of Constantine X (1059–67), the series of named coins—with imperial portraits or monograms—recommences, and to all appearances, continues simultaneously with the anonymous pieces. The imperial monogram occurs together with the cross on coins of Romanus IV (Pl. 47.2), of Nicephorus III (Pl. 47.3), and of Alexius I himself (Pl. 3.2). Now, as will be argued below, there are convincing reasons for the suspicion that a mint other than the capital was producing a large proportion of the copper tetarteron coinage of the post-reform period of Alexius I; the evidence points to Thessalonica as being in the main responsible. It will also be pointed out that all those issues marked by the cross or an imperial monogram, or both, occur in the group attributable to Thessalonica.[3] There is therefore an excellent case for assuming that the pre-reform folleis with the same characteristics were the product of the same mint. It so happens that the case can be tested—for which a return must be made to the years immediately preceeding the elevation of Alexius Comnenus in 1081.

During the closing months of his reign the Emperor Michael VII sent out from the capital a general named Nicephorus Basilacius to effect the capture of the Duke of Dyrrhachium, Nicephorus Bryennius, whose loyalty the Emperor had good reason to suspect.[4] On receipt of this news Bryennius, with the intent evidently of rallying his supporters, set out for his estates in Thrace. The affair resolved itself into a race between the two Nicephori for the city of Thessalonica. Basilacius was the winner and, although defeated outside the city by the forces of Bryennius, managed to hold the walls. The resulting stalemate was ended when Bryennius (who had everything to lose by delay) came to some form of unspecified agreement with Basilacius and left for Thrace, being proclaimed emperor at Trajanopolis and soon gaining admittance to his native Adrianople. An attack was subsequently made on the capital.

However, despite his swift movements, Bryennius lost out to a third Nicephorus—whose surname was Botaneiates—the former governor of the Anatolic theme, who gained admission to the capital in early 1078 and was duly crowned emperor. This still left Bryennius in opposition, for he refused the offer of the title of Caesar made by the successful Botaneiates. The young Alexius Comnenus was then sent out against the fractious Bryennius and soon succeeded in defeating and capturing him near Selymbria. Immediately afterward he was ordered—rather than return to the capital—to proceed against Basilacius who had evidently remained in Thessalonica, had since been reinforced by the remnants of the army of Bryennius, and had proclaimed himself emperor. Basilacius was once more defeated outside the walls of

[3] *Infra*, p. 100.
[4] The sequence of events is related by Nicephorus Bryennius (the Younger) III, 8 – IV, 28; Bonn ed., pp. 109–156: and by Anna Comnena, I, 4–9; Bonn ed., 1, pp. 23–48.

Thessalonica and again retired inside the city. The citizens were, however, evidently tiring of what threatened to become a routine, for they soon opened the gates to Comnenus, and, after attempting to hold out in the citadel, Basilacius was captured and removed, along with his hoard of coin.

It is difficult to ascertain precisely how long the rebellions of Bryennius and Basilacius lasted, but probably somewhere in the region of six months. For an appreciable time, therefore, the city of Thessalonica—which very probably possessed a mint—was in the hands of a Nicephorus whose loyalty to the reigning emperor was at first unalloyed, then compromised, and finally definitely withdrawn: on the basis of these facts it is logical to inquire whether, for the ultimate stage at least, there might not be a coinage to accompany his pretensions. Such an issue of copper folleis does in fact exist.

Obv. IC XC in field.

Bust of Christ, bearded and nimbate, wearing tunic and colobion; right hand raised in benediction, holds scroll in left.

Rev. C B

N B

Jewelled patriarchal cross, radiate, on base and step.

Pl. 47.4

This type has already been published by Grierson, who, on the assumption that it must belong to either Nicephorus Botaneiates or Nicephorus Bryennius, finally assigned it to the latter.[5] He was certainly correct in ruling out another usurper, Nicephorus Melissenus (1080/81), as a possible candidate, since the few provenances are exclusively European, and Melissenus, although certainly issuing coinage, was confined to the Asian provinces. Apparently, however, Grierson completely mislaid Nicephorus Basilacius.

The crux is that it would seem certain that Thessalonica was issuing copper coinage subsequent to the monetary reforms of Alexius I in 1092, and highly probable that the pre-reform folleis of Alexius and his predecessors which are of the same characteristic designs, were also products of this mint. Thessalonica was in the hands of a usurper during the last months of the reign of Michael VII and the first of Nicephorus III. There is a small issue of coins of characteristic Thessalonican design which is admirably suited for an attribution to a short reign. The attribution to Nicephorus Bryennius—who was never in control of the city—should therefore be revoked in favor of Nicephorus Basilacius, who was.

With the above observations in mind, the six types of follis attributed to Alexius fall into two general groups. The type having a cross and monogram as its obverse design (Pl. 3.2) should be assigned to the mint of Thessalonica—

[5] Ph. Grierson, "A Follis of Nicephorus Bryennius(?)" *NC*⁶, 10 (1950), pp. 305–11.

particularly since the same motif was reused for the third coinage of the group of reformed tetartera identified as emanating from this mint. Clearly related to this is the follis having a full-length figure of Alexius as its reverse type (Pl. 3.1); both designs are surrounded by a characteristic border of large globules. The attribution of a third type (Pl. 3.3) is more problematic. Despite the fact that the design is of the kind which has been identified as largely Thessalonican, provenances are commonly eastern. True, two specimens came from the Athenian Agora excavations,[6] but one was among the few late finds from Antioch,[7] and at least one author has commented on their turning up in the bazaars of Beirut. In addition, a specimen published by Sabatier has an Arabic countermark,[8] as does a further example in the Dumbarton Oaks Collection. The suggestion made by Wroth that the type was struck at Antioch at the time of the First Crusade is only in part likely. Why these crusaders should strike coins in the name of the reigning Byzantine emperor has never been adequately explained—the tradition that they did dies hard. Besides, it must be pointed out that the follis as a current imperial denomination had certainly ceased to be struck by 1097, probably by 1092. However, Antioch had been, between the accession of Alexius in 1081 and its fall to the Seljuks in 1084/85, an almost independent and isolated fragment of the Empire under the Armenian, Philaretus. The type in question could therefore have been struck there, but a Thessalonican origin should not be ruled out, particularly since the reverse inscription would be entirely apposite in the context of the Norman war and the "St. Demetrius" coinage.

Three types of anonymous bronze remain (Pl. 2.18–22). In consideration of the fact that they continue the tradition established by John I and issued in unbroken series by his successors, they should in all probability be assigned to the mint of the capital. The order of striking is agreed upon by Bellinger, Thompson, and Whitting.[9]

[6] M. Thompson, *The Athenian Agora*, 2, *Coins* (Princeton, 1954), p. 74.

[7] D. B. Waage, *Antioch-on-the-Orontes*, 4, pt. 2 (Princeton, 1952), p. 168.

[8] Sabatier, *Description générale*, 2, p. 191, no. 21 (pl. LI, 19).

[9] There are three widely recognized works dealing with the anonymous bronze: A. R. Bellinger, *The Anonymous Byzantine Bronze Coinage*, A.N.S. Numismatic Notes and Monographs, No. 35 (New York, 1928); M. Thompson, *op. cit.*, pp. 109–115; P. D. Whitting, "The Anonymous Byzantine Bronze," *NC*[6], 15 (1955), pp. 89–99. The types in question form Thompson's classes J, K, and L.

THE POST-REFORM COINAGE OF ALEXIUS I

1092–1118

N HYPERPYRON

MINT OF CONSTANTINOPLE

First Coinage (1092/93)
  Obv.
      As *first coinage of electrum and billon trachea.*
  Rev.

Second coinage (1092/93–1118)
  Obv. +KЄRO HΘЄI. I͞C X͞C in upper field.
      Christ, bearded and nimbate, wearing tunic and colobion, seated on throne
      without back; right hand raised in benediction, holds Gospels in left.
  Rev. ΛΛЄΞIШ ΔЄCΠOTH TШ KOMNHNШ in two columnar groups.
      Full-length figure of emperor wearing stemma, divitision, and chlamys;
      holds in right hand labarum-headed scepter, and in left, globus cruciger.
      Manus Dei in upper right field.

Characteristics normally peculiar to the metropolitan mint for this issue
are: the form of the left- and right-hand columnar inscriptions

Λ   TШ;
ΛЄ KO'
ΞIШ M-H
ΔЄC NШ
ΠO
TH

the dots on the scepter shaft and below the tablion; the chlamys bordered
on two sides as it drapes from the emperor's right elbow. The chlamys-border
forming the collar is always decorated with three jewels; the pendilia are
normally of the form: .⌡.⌡., although defective varieties such as: .⌡ ⌡. do, very
rarely, occur.

  Var. I (A)
      The border of the chlamys leading to the right shoulder interrupts that

      forming the collar (⌐), and the tablion tends to a spread form (◫).

  Var. I (B)
      The border of the chlamys leading to the right shoulder is interrupted

      by that forming the collar (⌐), and the tablion tends to a narrower

      form (◫).

Both I (A) and I (B) are marked by a diagonal fold on the chlamys as it drapes from the emperor's left arm, and both undergo a development in the ending of the left-hand columnar inscription which is apparently, in general, chronological. The first stage of the development (i) ends: T; the second (ii) ends: T,; the third (iii): TH. Simultaneously the jewelling of the right-hand chlamys-border—at first of small jewels—becomes more and more exaggerated in size.

I (A) (i)	Pl. 3.*4*	I (B) (i)	Pl. 3.*9*
I (A) (ii)	Pl. 3.*5*	I (B) (ii)	Pl. 3.*10*
I (A) (iii)	Pl. 3.*6–8*	I (B) (iii)	Pl. 4.*1, 2*

Var. II

As above, but marked by the ultimate degree of exaggerated jewelling; the disappearance of the diagonal fold on the chlamys, and the columnar inscription always ending (iii). Collar as I (A). (The second and smaller of the two dots beneath the tablion, as seen occasionally in this variety, is probably only a "centralizing dot" and of no significance except to the die-cutter.)

Pl. 4.*3–5*

MINT OF THESSALONICA (1092/93–1118)

Types as second metropolitan coinage. Characteristics normally peculiar to the issues of this mint are: the form of the left- and right-hand columnar inscriptions Λ　　T , including the frequent use of the ligature MN in place

ΛЄ　Ш
ΞΙ　KO
Ш　MN
ΔЄC　N
ΠO　Ш
TH

of MH; the chlamys bordered on only one side as it drapes from the emperor's right elbow; the lack of dots on the labarum shaft and below the tablion. The cross on the globus is often much larger, or the stem of the cross much longer, than is usual in the case of the metropolitan issues (†).

Var. I

The earliest specimens of this variety are recognizably smaller and thicker than the later ones and the metropolitan pieces. The chlamys lacks the diagonal fold as it drapes from the emperor's left arm; the collar usually has five jewels (but four or six are known). Two specimens from the Gornoslav hoard betray a subsequently erased attempt to decorate the edges of the chlamys on two sides, as in the metropolitan issues (Pl. 4.9). Inscription ends: (i) or (ii).

Pl. 4.*6–10*

Var. II

As above, but diagonal fold on chlamys. Inscription ends: (i) or (ii).

Pl. 5.*1, 2* (*rev.* only)

Var. III

As above, but four jewels on collar. Inscription ends: (i) or (ii).

Var. IV

(*A*) As above, but three jewels on collar. Inscription ends: (i), (ii), or
(iii)—T_H; right-hand columnar inscr. reads: T‿ω or T‿ω.
KO   KO
M‿H   M‿H
N   N
‿ω

Pl. 5.*3, 4* (*revs.* only)

(*B*) As above, but obv. inscr. reads +KЄROHΘ ΛΛЄΞIω.
Rev. inscr. ends: (i), (ii), or (iii). One specimen from the Gornoslav
hoard had a dot on the labarum staff and below the tablion, as in the
metropolitan issues (Pl. 5.*6* [*rev.* only]).

Pl. 5.*5* (*obv.* only), *6* (*rev.* only)

Var. V

As metropolitan var. I (A), medium jewelling, *rev.* inscr. ends (iii),
pendilia ⌡⌡ .

Pl. 5.*7, 8* (*rev.* only)

Var. VI

As metropolitan var. II, but jewelling less exaggerated, and large cross
on globus.

Pl. 5.*9, 10*

MINT OF PHILIPPOPOLIS?

Types as second metropolitan coinage.

Var. I

Characterized by four jewels in collar; proportionally large head **and**
labarum; squat but large cross surmounting globus. The left-hand
columnar inscription is of the form normally used by the Thessalonican
mint in its earlier stages, and ends as (i) or (ii); the right-hand is, for
the gold, however, largely peculiar to this mint: T‿ω or T‿ω. Pendilia
often ⌡⌡ .   KO   KO
M   M‿N
N   N

Pl. 5.*11, 12* (*revs.* only)

6*

Var. II

A "caricature" of the normal imperial figure: gigantic head and squat body. The form of the labarum allies it to the above var. Known from only one specimen, in the Gornoslav hoard, which had a collar of three jewels and inscr.:

$$\begin{matrix} \Lambda & & \\ \Lambda \epsilon & \mathsf{T}\omega\dot{} \\ \overline{\underline{}}\mathsf{I} & \mathsf{KO} \\ \omega & \mathsf{M}\mathsf{N}\mathsf{H} \\ \Delta\epsilon\mathsf{C} & \mathsf{N} \\ \Pi\mathsf{O} & \omega \\ \mathsf{T} & \end{matrix}$$

Pl. 5.*13* (*rev.* only)

UNKNOWN MINT

Characterized by squat style, but much less grotesque than the previous. Known only from two specimens, in the Gornoslav hoard, which were, however, from different dies. Left-hand columnar inscription of metropolitan form, and ends (i) or (ii). Right-hand:

$$\begin{matrix} \mathsf{T}\dot{} \\ \omega \\ \mathsf{KO} \\ \mathsf{M}\mathsf{N} \\ \mathsf{N} \end{matrix}$$

Pl. 5.*14* (*rev.* only)

EL. ASPRON TRACHY

MINT OF CONSTANTINOPLE

First coinage (1092/93)

Obv. IѠΔЄϹΠT +ΚЄΡΟΗΘЄΙ. ĪĊ X̄Ċ in upper center field.

Full-length figure of John II beardless, standing on dais, on left, crowned by Christ, bearded and nimbate. Emperor wears stemma, divitision, collar-piece, and jewelled loros of simplified type; holds in right hand labarum-headed scepter, and in left, globus cruciger. Christ wears tunic and colobion; holds Gospels in left hand.

Rev. +ΛΛЄΞΙѠΔЄ ЄΙΡΗΝΙΛVΓΛ

Full-length figures of Alexius I, on left, and of Irene, holding between them patriarchal cross on long shaft. Both wear stemma, divitision, collar-piece, and jewelled loros as above. Emperor holds anexikakia in right hand.

Pl. 6.*1*

Second coinage (1092/93–1118)

Obv. M̄P̄ Θ̄V̄ in field.

Virgin nimbate, wearing tunic and maphorion, seated upon throne without back; holds beardless, nimbate head of Christ on breast.

Rev. Λ   – or var.
ΛЄ   ΤШ
ͼΙШ   ΚΟ
ΔЄⅭ   ΜͶ
ΠΟ   Ν
Τ

Full-length figure of emperor wearing stemma, scaramangion or divition, and sagion; holds in right hand jewelled scepter, and in left, globus cruciger.

Pl. 6.*2–5*

MINT OF THESSALONICA

Obv. +ΚЄΡΟ ΛΛЄͼΙШ. Īͼ X̄Ͼ in upper field.
Christ, bearded and nimbate, wearing tunic and colobion, seated on throne with back; holds Gospels in left hand.

Rev. +ΔЄⅭΠΟΤΗ ΤШΚΟΜͶΗ – or var. ΜΘ or Μ in upper center field.
Full-length figure of emperor on left, crowned by Virgin nimbate. Emperor wears stemma, divitision, collar-piece, and jewelled loros of simplified type; Virgin wears tunic and maphorion. Only five specimens apparently known: the piece in the British Museum has a large star in the upper center field of the reverse—between the emperor and the Virgin.

Pl. 6.*6–9*,
Pl. 51.*4*

BILL. ASPRON TRACHY

MINT OF CONSTANTINOPLE

First coinage (1092/93)

Obv. ΙШΔЄⅭΠΤ +ΚЄΡΟΗΘЄΙ – or var. Īͼ X̄Ͼ in upper center field.
Full-length figure of John II beardless, standing on dais, on left, crowned by Christ, bearded and nimbate. Emperor wears stemma, divitision, collar-piece, and jewelled loros of simplified type; holds in right hand labarum-headed scepter, and in left, globus cruciger. Christ wears tunic and colobion; holds Gospels in left hand.

Rev. +ΛΛЄͼΙШΔЄ ЄΙΡΗΝΙΛVΓU – or var.
Full-length figures of Alexius I, on left, and of Irene, holding between them patriarchal cross on long shaft. Both wear stemma, divitision, collar-piece, and jewelled loros as above. Emperor holds anexikakia in right hand.

Pl. 6.*10, 11*

Second coinage

   Obv. I̅C̅ X̅C̅ in upper field.

      Christ, bearded and nimbate, wearing tunic and colobion, seated on throne with back; holds Gospels in left hand.

   Rev. — or var.

      Full-length figure of emperor wearing stemma, scaramangion or divitision, and sagion; holds in right hand jewelled scepter on long shaft; left hand apparently rests on hip.

Pl. 7.1

Third coinage

   Obv. I̅C̅ X̅C̅ in upper field.

      Christ, bearded and nimbate, wearing tunic and colobion, seated on throne with back; holds Gospels in left hand.

   Rev. +ΛΛЄ⊐IѠ ΔЄСΠТ or +ΛΛЄ ΔЄС – or var.

      Bust of emperor wearing stemma, divitision, and chlamys; holds in right hand scepter cruciger, and in left, globus cruciger.

Pl. 7.2–4

Fourth coinage

   Obv. +КЄRО НΘЄI. I̅C̅ X̅C̅ in field.

      Bust of Christ, bearded and nimbate, wearing tunic and colobion; holds Gospels in left hand.

   Rev. +ΛΛЄ ΔЄС – or var.

      Bust of emperor wearing stemma, divitision, collar-piece, and panelled loros of simplified type; holds in right hand labarum-headed scepter, and in left, globus cruciger.

Pl. 7.5, 6

MINT OF THESSALONICA

   Obv. I̅C̅ X̅C̅ in field.

      Full-length figure of Christ, bearded and nimbate, wearing tunic and colobion (holds Gospels in left hand?).

   Rev. ? ѠI⊐ƎΛΛ+

      Full-length figure of emperor on right, and of Virgin nimbate, holding between them labarum on long shaft. Emperor wears stemma, divitision, collar-piece, and jewelled loros of simplified type; Virgin wears tunic and maphorion.

Pl. 7.7

MINT OF PHILIPPOPOLIS?

Obv. +KЄRO ΛΛЄⳆIⱲ. Ī͞C X͞C in field.

Christ, bearded and nimbate, wearing tunic and colobion, seated on throne without back; holds Gospels in left hand.

Rev. Δ TⱲ   – or var.
ЄC KO
ΠO MN
TH N

Full-length figure of emperor wearing stemma, divitision, collar-piece, and panelled loros of simplified type; holds in right hand, scepter with large labarum as head—in which generally a cross; in left hand, globus cruciger.

Pl. *7.8, 9*

Æ TETARTERON

MINT OF CONSTANTINOPLE

Type A

Obv. Ī͞C X͞C in field.

Bust of Christ, bearded and nimbate, wearing tunic and colobion; holds Gospels in left hand.

Rev. +ΛΛЄ ΔЄC – or var.

Bust of emperor wearing stemma, divitision, collar-piece, and panelled loros of simplified type; holds in right hand labarum-headed scepter, and in left, globus cruciger.

Pl. *7.10, 11*

Type B

Obv. Ī͞C X͞C in field.

Bust of Christ, bearded, with cross behind head, wearing tunic and colobion; holds Gospels in left hand. Ɔ C in field of cross.

Rev. +ΛΛЄⳆIⱲ ΔЄC – or var.

Bust of emperor wearing stemma, divitision, collar-piece, and jewelled loros of simplified type; holds in right hand jewelled scepter, and in left, globus cruciger.

Pl. *8.1, 2*

Type C

Obv. Ī͞C X͞C in field.

Christ, bearded and nimbate, wearing tunic and colobion, seated on throne without back; holds Gospels in left hand.

Rev. +ΛΛΕΞΙШ ΔΕC – or var.

Bust of emperor wearing stemma, divitision, and chlamys; holds in right hand scepter cruciger, and in left, globus cruciger.

Pl. 8.*3, 4*

Type D

Obv. ĪC X̄C in field.

Christ, bearded and nimbate, wearing tunic and colobion, seated on throne without back; right hand raised in benediction, holds Gospels in left.

Rev. +ΛΛΕΞΙШ ΔΕCΠΟΤΤШΚ – or var.

Full-length figure of emperor wearing stemma, divitision, jewelled loros of simplified type, and sagion; holds in right hand labarum on long shaft, and in left, globus cruciger.

Pl. 8.*5, 6*

MINT OF THESSALONICA

First coinage

Obv. ĪC X̄C in field.

Bust of Christ, bearded and nimbate, wearing tunic and colobion; holds Gospels in left hand.

Rev. +ΛΛΕΞ – or var.

Bust of emperor wearing stemma, divitision, and chlamys; holds in right hand scepter cruciger, and in left, globus cruciger.

Pl. 8.*7, 8*

Second coinage

Obv. M̄P̄ Θ̄V̄ in field.

Bust of Virgin nimbate, orans, wearing tunic and maphorion.

Rev. +Λ ΔΕC – or var.

Bust of emperor wearing stemma, divitision, and chlamys; holds in right hand labarum on long shaft, and in left, globus cruciger.

Pl. 8.*9*

Third coinage

Obv.   C   Φ   – or var.

　　　　Ⲙ Δ

Jewelled cross on steps.

Rev. +TШKO MNH – or var.

Bust of emperor wearing stemma, divitision, and jewelled loros of traditional type; holds in right hand scepter cruciger, and in left, globus cruciger.

Pl. 8.*10–12*

Type D

Obv.   Λ   Δ   – or var.

        Κ   Φ

Patriarchal cross on steps.

Rev. +ΛΛЄ ⊐Ι – or var.

Bust of emperor wearing stemma, divitision, and jewelled loros of traditional type; holds in right hand jewelled scepter, and in left, globus cruciger.

Pl. 8.*13–15*

Type E

Obv. ĪC X̄C in field.

Full-length figure of Christ, bearded and nimbate, wearing tunic and colobion; holds Gospels in left hand.

Rev. +ΛΛЄ ⊐ΙШΔЄC – or var.

Full-length figure of emperor wearing stemma, divitision, collar-piece, and jewelled loros of simplified type; holds in right hand labarum on long shaft, and in left, globus cruciger.

Pl. 8.*16*

Æ HALF-TETARTERON

MINT OF THESSALONICA

Obv. M̄P ΘV̄ in field.

Bust of Virgin nimbate, wearing tunic and maphorion.

Rev.   ΛΛЄ

Bust of emperor wearing stemma, divitision, and chlamys; holds in right hand labarum on long shaft, and in left, globus cruciger.

Pl. 8.*17*

THE POST-REFORM COINAGE OF ALEXIUS I: COMMENTARY

N̄ HYPERPYRON

Despite the fact that no examples of the hyperpyron with the commemorative types of 1092/93 have as yet come to light, the existence of specimens of both the electrum and the billon denominations renders it probable that the gold was, in fact, struck.

The main hyperpyron type of Alexius I having been struck over a period in excess of twenty years, a considerable degree of chronological development is apparent, as might be expected. Two chronological features are of particular importance: the ending of the left-hand columnar inscription and the relative size of the jewelling on the chlamys-border as it drapes from the Emperor's left arm.

Examination of the metropolitan second coinage vars. I (A) and I (B) clearly establishes the development of the ending of the left-hand columnar inscription through the stages (i)–(iii) as being approximately parallel to the increasing exaggeration of the jewelling. The Gornoslav hoard of 1961[1] contained forty-seven specimens of I (A) and forty-eight of I (B), from a total of 239 hyperpyra of Alexius I. A division made in both groups, according to the size of the jewelling, renders it apparent that the specimens in which the jewelling is composed of comparatively small globules contain all three inscriptional endings, while those in which the jewelling is of medium or large size globules contain only ending (iii). The small amount of additional hoard evidence available tends to support this evidence. There are only two hoards of any size whose composition would seem to indicate deposition during the early years of the monetary reform: that from Sofia of 1897,[2] and that from Khissar of 1922.[3] The Sofia hoard contained a total of 206 stamena of Romanus III, debased stamena trachea of Constantine IX, Constantine X, Eudocia with her sons, Romanus IV, Nicephorus III, and Alexius I (both metropolitan debased coinages), but included a single hyperpyron of var. I (B) with the inscriptional ending (iii), but without exaggerated jewelling. The part of the Khissar hoard that was recovered consisted of a single debased stamenon trachy of Michael VII, fifty-eight of Nicephorus III and a single specimen of Alexius I: also present were five hyperpyra of Alexius I, the only specimen of which a full description is extant being a specimen of var. I (A), with the inscriptional ending (ii).

The existence of this chronological development is further supported by analysis of the earlier group (vars. I–IV) attributed to Thessalonica. In general, the earliest varieties of this group are those that differ most from the Constantinopolitan. The first specimens of var. I are of smaller, thicker fabric (c. 26–28 mm.) than the later issues (c. 30–32 mm.), and than all those of the metropolitan mint; the chlamys, as it drapes from the left arm, lacks the diagonal fold which, in the case of the metropolitan issues, is a clear inheritance from the debased trachea of Nicephorus III (Pl. 47.5); the chlamys is bordered on only one side on the left, as opposed to two sides in the Constantinopolitan pieces; the collar has the greatest number of jewels (four to six); the right-hand columnar inscription begins $_{\omega}^{\mathrm{T}}$. Var. II—a small one, but nevertheless certainly consisting of more than one reverse die—varies from its predecessor only in its larger fabric (permanent from now on), and the addition of the diagonal fold to

[1] Chap. 15, pp. 343–44.
[2] Ibid., p. 383.
[3] Ibid., p. 354.

the chlamys. Var. III consistently has a smaller number of collar jewels (four). Var. IV has the same number of collar jewels as the metropolitan coins (three), and also acquires the metropolitan form of the beginning of the right-hand columnar inscription (TꞶ as opposed to $\underset{\omega}{\mathsf{T}}$). The ligature ꟽH also becomes more common on the later varieties, ꟽN having been a characteristic of the earlier Thessalonican issues.

In addition to these substantive varieties, small, unrepeated borrowings from the Constantinopolitan techniques appear: var. I includes specimens showing a subsequently erased attempt to decorate the chlamys on two borders on the left side, and one specimen of var. IV (B) actually includes the dots on the labarum-shaft and below the tablion which are, at this stage of the issue, otherwise confined to the metropolitan series.

Analysis of the Thessalonican coins of the Gornoslav hoard with regard to the varieties of inscriptional endings provides the following facts: of twenty-one specimens of var. I, eighteen end (i) and three end (ii). Of the nine specimens of the next variety represented in reasonable numbers, var. III, one ends (i) and eight end (ii). Of six specimens of var. IV (A), one ends (i), and five end (iii). Var. IV (B)—of which four specimens were present—remains unrepresentative, since a single reverse die accounted for three specimens reading (i).

Despite the regrettably small numbers involved, it does, therefore, appear that the development T, T₁, TH, or T_H presents a roughly chronological sequence.

Metcalf attributes vars. I (A) and I (B) to separate mints—Constantinople and Nicaea respectively.[4] The differences between I (A) and I (B) have already been enumerated: whether these are sufficient to support the existence of a further provincial mint is most doubtful. Certainly the provisional attribution to Nicaea is untenable simply because at the time of the commencement of the reformed coinage (1092) Nicaea was in the hands of the Seljuks, and remained so until 1097, along with all but a very small portion of the Empire's former Asiatic holdings. Both varieties are of the same fabric; on both, the left side of the chlamys is decorated on two borders; both have the diagonal fold to the right, the same number of jewels for the collar, the metropolitan form of inscription, the dots on the labarum shaft and below the tablion. The similarities are far more striking than the differences, and another explanation than that of separate mints is called for.

The proportional output of the two main provincial mints as present in the Gornoslav hoard presents a consistent picture: Thessalonica var. I, twenty-one specimens, var. III, nine; var. IV, ten; var. V, six. Philippopolis (?) var. I, nine (six ending [i], three ending [ii]); var. II, one. The impression given is of a concentration at the commencement of the reform, followed by a decline

---

4 Metcalf, "Alexius I," p. 276.

in output that eventually saw the survival of Thessalonica only. This is precisely the kind of pattern that might be expected from a general recoinage for which temporary mints were set up to effect a swift and efficient reform.

The pattern for the metropolitan mint—as represented by var. I(A)—is somewhat different. The figures are as follows: inscriptional ending (i), nine; (ii), five; (iii), thirty-three. The pattern for I (B) is rather similar: inscriptional ending (i), fifteen; (ii), nine; (iii), twenty-four. With this similarity in mind, and in view of the close resemblance between I (A) and I (B), it would seem almost certain that both are the product of the same mint (Constantinople), but each the issue of a separate administrative division (officina).

The identification of I (B)—rather than I (A)—as the product of a temporary officina is made for two main reasons: the fact that in the succeeding variety (II) only the collar type (A) is represented, and also on consideration of the increasing exaggeration of the jewelling of the chlamys border. If the Gornoslav specimens of I (A) and I (B) are arranged according to the degree of exaggeration of jewelling, a valuable point emerges: whereas the chronological development of the inscriptional ending is amply confirmed, the proportions are entirely different: I (A) small jewelling, sixteen; medium jewelling, three; large jewelling, twenty-eight; I (B) small jewelling, thirty-four; medium jewelling, thirteen; large jewelling, one. This pattern is confirmed by two more bodies of evidence: the catalogue of examples used by Metcalf in his examination of the hyperpyra of Alexius I, and the Dumbarton Oaks Collection. In both, whereas specimens of I (A) distinguishable by their large jewelling are comparatively numerous, the similar group in I (B) is almost non-existent. It would seem, therefore, that the officina producing var. I (B) systematically lagged behind that producing I (A) in the exaggeration of the jewelling. The secondary nature of officina I (B) is, then, apparent: it was officina I (A) that set the pace in the exaggeration of jewelling; it was the distinctive feature (the collar) of the same officina that survived into the following variety. Officina I (B) was created to aid in the reform of the gold coinage, and with that accomplished, it was dismantled.

Metcalf has also suggested that the issue here described as var. II of the second metropolitan coinage should be considered the product of a mint other than the capital, on the grounds that the decoration of the divitision in certain specimens of var. II is more pronounced than that on the late specimens of var. I (A). This mint is provisionally attributed to Greece, at either Thebes or Corinth.[5] The unlikely nature of such an attribution becomes apparent when the output of this mint is assessed in relation to the others. As Metcalf himself observes, and the Gornoslav hoard confirms, var. II is a very common variety, and therefore, in all probability, originally issued in large numbers.

[5] *Ibid.*, p. 278.

One is therefore presented with the problem of a provincial mint set up at a comparatively late stage of the reformed coinage (the issues of which were marked by the latest inscriptional variety, [iii], and the ultimate stage in the exaggeration of the jewelling) which nevertheless managed to produce almost as large a volume of coinage as Constantinople itself, and which exceeded that of other provincial mints by far. This is in the highest degree unlikely from what is known of the position of Greece in the economy of the twelfth-century Empire—true, it contained the prosperous trading centers of Thebes and Corinth (one of which possibly did possess a mint for copper), but even they could not have borne comparison with either Thessalonica or Constantinople. What seems far more likely is that the introduction of var. II at the capital was immediately subsequent to the dismantling of the officina which had been producing coins of var. I (B)—or its coalition with that producing var. I (A). It is noticeable that the commencement of var. II saw the disappearance of the diagonal chlamys fold: clearly what had happened was that the exaggeration of the jewelling had reduced the horizontal space available for the fold, which now became difficult to fit in. Var. II was, therefore, not the issue of a separate mint but the result of the introduction of another pattern for the combined die-cutters of the formerly separate officinae.

Metcalf's attribution to Trebizond[6] of the distinctive group here attributed to Thessalonica is equally unlikely, although it must be admitted that it was made before adequate reports of the contents of the Gornoslav hoard were available. The occurrence of such a large proportion (forty-seven specimens) of this rather scarce group in that hoard at once throws suspicion on the attribution. Coins of this group have also been found in the Corinth excavations.[7] The only evidence for their presence in Asia Minor is the finding of four specimens, together with a hyperpyron of John II, at Gurdzhaani in Georgia.[8] The date of the Thessalonican coins in question should be soon after 1092; the date of their deposition subsequent to 1118. They had adequate time to make the journey. It should, in addition, be pointed out that during the reign of Alexius I, at least, Trebizond was a city of uncertain loyalty. Twice during the reign it was the scene of contemplated or actual rebellion; on the first occasion by Theodore and Gregory Gavras (1091–93?)—Anna Comnena mentions expressly that the elder Gavras was sent to Trebizond to get him out of the way[9]—and, on the second occasion, by Gregory Taronites (indictions XII–XIV [1103–06]).[10] It is, therefore, hardly likely that the bullion

[6] *Ibid.*, p. 276.

[7] K. M. Edwards, *Corinth, 6, Coins* (Cambridge, Mass., 1933), p. 141, no. 116.

[8] T. Ya. Abramishchvili, "Nakhodka Vizantiiskikh zolot'ikh monet v Gurdzhaani," *Viz. Vrem.*, 13 (1958), pp. 282–85.

[9] Anna Comnena, VIII, 9; Bonn ed., 1, pp. 417–22.

[10] *Ibid.*, XII, 7; Bonn ed., 2, pp. 161–64. Almost certainly identical with the Gregory above.

necessary for the maintenance of a precious-metal mint would be entrusted to a city of this caliber, the hinterland of which was so limited as to be capable of being supplied from the capital without difficulty.

The general attribution of the above group to a provincial mint is made on the grounds of the great differences in fabric, arrangement of inscription, and details of design between the known issues of the metropolitan mint and the numerous varieties of this series. The number of varieties of which it is comprised, together with the relatively high proportion of die-links found in this series, is perhaps the strongest argument in favor of a provincial attribution, for the metropolitan series shows both a good deal less variation, and is the product of a larger number of dies. The attribution to Thessalonica in particular is based on the fact that, given the commencement of the reformed coinage in 1092, the mint concerned can only have been in the European territories of the Empire. The only city justifiably capable of putting out a small but fairly continuous series of hyperpyra would have been Thessalonica, the second city of the Empire. In addition, var. IV (B) has the imperial name on the obverse, which, if not entirely confined to the mint identified as Thessalonica, nevertheless connects the variety with the St. Demetrius debased trachea of the immediately preceding period. There are also stylistic connections between the two, as may be seen by comparing the debased trachea (Pl. 1.*9–12*) with the earlier reformed hyperpyra of the series (Pl. 4.*6–10*).

The attribution of vars. V and VI to Thessalonica, which has been made above, is certainly more problematical. On the assumption, however, that the commencement of the reformed gold coinage saw the reopening or expansion of a precious-metal mint in the city—represented by vars. I–IV—and that there was certainly some European mint other than the capital—probably Thessalonica—active during the reign of John II, there would seem to exist a chronological hiatus of some size between var. IV of Alexius I and the first coinage of John II. None of the coins of vars. I–IV exhibit any signs of the exaggerated jewelling so characteristic of the later products of the metropolitan mint—despite the fact that the constant tendency of the Thessalonican mint is to emulate the characteristics of those of the capital. Only var. IV has the final form of the left hand inscriptional ending (iii). It would seem to be a reasonable assumption that the inscriptional development apparent at Thessalonica did not occur at too great a distance in time from that at Constantinople: indeed, it may well be that the provincial development was the result of the directions of the central authorities, and therefore more or less contemporary with that of the metropolitan mint.

In the Gornoslav hoard there were six specimens of that stage of the issue represented by the medium jewelling of the chlamys border and the inscription ending (iii), but which showed two unusual features. The first was in the form of the pendilia, the normal metropolitan variety being ⋅ḷ⋅ḷ⋅, although ⋅ḷ ḷ⋅ occasionally occurs. This group, however, all possessed the unusual form ḷ ḷ (Pl. 5.*8* [*rev.* only]). A further example came from the Suedinenie hoard of 1955,[11] and there is yet another in the collection at Dumbarton Oaks (Pl. 5.7). The second was in the unusually long stem to the cross surmounting the globus which is found in this group. This latter is a noticeable feature of many specimens of Thessalonican vars. I–IV, and it would therefore seem probable that these coins (var. V) represent a further stage in the trend of Thessalonican issues toward complete identity with the products of the metropolitan mint. The ultimate stage is therefore probably seen in var. VI which in all points of detail is the same as the metropolitan second coinage var. II—but which still has the characteristic long stem to the cross (Pl. 5.*9, 10*). It is this stage that is continued in the reign of John II. It might be added, at this point, that the only other regular examples of the ḷ ḷ pendilia form occur in a series of copper trachea which, there is strong reason to believe, emanates from the mint of Thessalonica during the early thirteenth century.

The existence of a temporary mint at Philippopolis (Plovdiv) seems indicated by the following considerations: the specimens assigned to this mint are distinctive in style and inscriptional form from metropolitan issues—and yet do not fit well into the Thessalonican series; they are related to an extremely rare issue of billon trachea; both hyperpyra (Pl. 5.*11–13*) and billon trachea (Pl. 7.*8, 9*) seem to be connected by provenance with the Thracian plain in general, and with Philippopolis in particular.

As observed above, the nine specimens of var. I present in the Gornoslav hoard seem to indicate a date of production very early in the reformed coinage—six having the inscriptional development (i), and three having (ii). This is the stage already represented by Thessalonican var. I. The early inscriptional forms, however, clash with elements that are, at the Thessalonican mint, distinctly later: the larger fabric; the four jewels of the collar; the diagonal chlamys fold; the form of the right-hand inscription reading TШ. On the other hand, there are features characteristic of this group alone: the proportionally large head and labarum; the squat but large cross surmounting the globus; the arrangement of the right-hand inscription TШ or TШ. Precisely

$$\begin{matrix} \text{TШ} & & \text{TШ} \\ \text{KO} & & \text{KO} \\ \text{M} & & \text{MN} \\ \text{N} & & \text{N} \end{matrix}$$

these features are shared by the billon trachea. Only one specimen of the hyperpyron was previously known;[12] yet there were ten present in the hoard from Gornoslav, which is less than twenty-five miles distant from

---

[11] Chap. 15, pp. 386–87.

[12] Metcalf, "Alexius I," no. 62, p. 283 (pl. 11): from the British Museum Collection.

Plovdiv. The billon trachy was formerly known from perhaps half a dozen specimens: in 1955 a hoard of twenty-one pieces in uniformly fresh condition was found on Bounardzhik hill, actually within the limits of mediaeval Philippopolis.[13] The attribution of a temporary mint to the Thracian plain is entirely compatible with what is known of the contemporary monetary and economic situation: Thessalonica was, as far as the supply of coinage was concerned, administratively tied to Greece, and the setting up of a temporary mint at Philippopolis to effect the recoinage in the Thracian plain would, therefore, have been a matter of extreme convenience.

The identity of the temporary mint here labelled "unknown" (Pl. 5.*14*) cannot even be guessed at, the present state of knowledge of its products being based upon only two specimens from the Gornoslav hoard which were, however, from different dies. It was apparently of the early, temporary, provincial class.

EL. ASPRON TRACHY

There are extant three types of the electrum trachy which are attributable to Alexius I. The first and second require little comment, and are here attributed to the metropolitan mint: the columnar inscription of the second is of a form only slightly modified from that used for the hyperpyron.

The third (Pls. 6.*6–9*, 51.*4*), of great rarity, is also of considerably more interest. The most noticeable feature is the obverse inscription which contains the imperial name—normally the mark of mints other than the metropolitan, and in particular of Thessalonica or Philippopolis. The style is rather poor, the figures being ill-proportioned and sketchily executed. The great difference between the five known specimens is the presence of an enormous star in the upper center field of the reverse of the British Museum specimen (Pl. 6.*9*). Stellate decorations are in general rather uncommon in the Byzantine numismatic iconography of the period, and confined to the debased tetartera of Alexius (Pl. 2.*10–12*); the electrum trachea of Manuel I (Pl. 13.*6–9*); the billon trachea of the same Emperor (Pl. 16.*10–13*), and those of Isaac II (Pl. 21.*1–4*, 7). In the majority of cases these stellate ornaments are balanced by being in pairs; are comparatively unobtrusive; and are consistently present within the type. The star of the specimen in question is anything but unobtrusive for it is placed in a most inconvenient position between the Emperor and the Virgin who is attempting to crown him—it seems to be almost an afterthought, despite its rather elaborate form. Moreover, it occurs on only one die out of five. An unprovable but attractive hypothesis springs to mind.

---

[13] Chap. 15, p. 379. The type was apparently first published by H. Longuet ("Notes de numismatique byzantine," *RN*[5], 2 [1938], p. 10, nos. 12, 13).

The period of the reign concerned is that covering the preparations made by Alexius for opposing the invasion of Epirus by the Normans under Bohemund during the years 1107/08 (the second Norman war). In preparation for the landing, Alexius left Constantinople for Thessalonica in September of indiction XIV (1105),[14] remaining at the latter city or on the Dalmatian frontiers for a year and two months. Thessalonica was, as in the first Norman war, the main base of supply and munition. Soon after his arrival at Thessalonica, according to Anna Comnena, a large comet—the largest ever seen— appeared in the heavens, and remained there as a bright and conspicuous object for forty days. The considerable speculation as to its meaning was eventually resolved in favor of the Empire. It has already been noted that the die-cutters of the Thessalonican mint were under considerably less restraint than their colleagues of the capital. It is, therefore, quite possible that the star of the specimen in question represents the comet—which would date the particular die to some point within the years 1105–08.

Bill. Aspron Trachy

There are altogether six types attributable to Alexius I—four almost certainly metropolitan, one probably Thessalonican, the other probably a product of a temporary mint at Philippopolis.

The first metropolitan coinage is presumably the commemorative issue of 1092/93 (Pl. 6.*10, 11*). Thus, the second is probably that with the full-length figure of the Emperor and the double columnar inscription (Pl. *7.1*): in this case the reformed coinage would have commenced its first regular types in all metals with a complete set of conspicuous designs, and with the new, full, columnar inscriptions. As in the case of the electrum trachy, the inscriptional arrangement is a modified form of that used on the metropolitan hyperpyra. Of the remaining two metropolitan coinages, it would appear that the one having as its reverse type a bust of the Emperor wearing a chlamys (Pl. *7.2–4*) should be considered the third coinage, since the obverse type of Christ enthroned is identical in detail and similar in style to that used for the second coinage. In addition, it frequently has the fuller form of imperial inscription (+ΛΛΕΞΙѠ ΔΕϹΠΤ) as well as the simpler form (+ΛΛΕ ΔΕϹ). Specimens of that issue having as the reverse type a bust of the Emperor wearing a panelled loros (Pl. *7.5, 6*) have the simpler inscription and are of slightly cruder style. It should, therefore, probably be considered the fourth and last coinage.

[14] The episode is treated in Anna Comnena, XII, 3, 4; Bonn ed., 2, pp. 140–49. It is noticeable that the Empress Irene is reported as leaving the capital: διὰ χρυσοῦ καὶ ἄλλης ποιότητος .... χάραγμα (p. 145)—with coined money of gold and other quality. This seems a probable reference to the fractional scyphates, although it, and a further incident referred to in XIV, 2, could still quite well have involved debased pieces of the pre-reform period that had remained in circulation.

The type attributed to Thessalonica (Pl. *7.7*) has a retrograde inscription—uncommon on the scyphates of the eleventh and twelfth centuries—and is probably to be linked with the "St. Demetrius" miliaresion of the pre-reform coinage, which has the same feature (Pl. *2.17*). It is also related to this miliaresion, and to the debased trachea depicting St. Demetrius, in a further characteristic aspect: all four types have the Saint or the Virgin on the left side of the reverse—as opposed to the more usual right. The only exception to this feature within the Thessalonican group of issues is the electrum trachy of the reformed coinage: in this case the Virgin stands on the right.

The type attributed to Philippopolis (Pl. *7.8, 9*) has already been discussed when dealing with the hyperpyron to which it is obviously related—it would not be surprising, in a mint of temporary nature and evidently small output, if the dies of both denominations were the product of a single die-cutter. Certainly, the characteristic style, which seems to be common to all known specimens of this group, tends to support this hypothesis.

Æ TETARTERON

There are a large number of types of copper tetarteron which are assigned to Alexius I. On examination of a series of these coins, a clear division into two general groups becomes apparent. The first consists of coins of four types, all of relatively small, thick, boldly clipped fabric, and of neat style. The second is composed of broader, thinner, and frequently less elegant pieces, and covers the remaining types. This division continues into the reign of John II, to a lesser extent into that of Manuel I, and can occasionally be glimpsed on series of even later date.

The major source of information concerning the distribution of copper tetartera comes from the excavations at Athens and Corinth—enormous quantities of this denomination having been recovered from both sites. When the numbers of the two groups of tetartera found during these excavations are put into tabular form, the differences in fabric and style are confirmed and augmented to an astonishing extent by evidence of distribution.[15]

Quite clearly, those types distinguished by their small, thick fabric and neat style do not occur in significant proportions at either Athens or Corinth. On the other hand, those marked by their broader, thinner fabric frequently occur in appreciable numbers, sometimes in enormous proportions. There is, therefore, an excellent case for considering these two groups the products of separate mints.

The fact that the group of copper tetartera of the post-reform period marked by its small, thick fabric does not appear on Greek sites renders it very

---

[15] The evidence presented opposite in tabular form is based on that given by Thompson (*The Athenian Agora*, pp. 74, 75) and by Edwards (*Corinth*, pp. 141–46).

		Athens (to 1949)	Corinth (to 1929)
Alexius I			
Small, thick fabric; elegant style.	Type A	12	8
	Type B	0	1
	Type C	1	0
	Type D	1	0
Broad, spread fabric; less elegant style.	First coinage	180	85
	Second coinage	96	61
	Third coinage	602	372
	Type D	7	2
	Type E	34	6
John II			
Small, thick fabric.	Type A	2	0
	Type B	0	2
Broad, spread fabric.		114	83
Manuel I			
	First coinage	17	12
	Type B	0	0
	Type C	4	6
	Type D	8	17
	Obv.: Monogram	1699	493
	Obv.: St. George	1387	494
	Obv.: Christ, bust	307	137
	Obv.: Cross-on-steps	161	66

probable that this is the group which should be considered the product of the mint of the capital. It is, in fact, precisely this group which continues the fabric of the old, debased tetartera of the metropolitan mint, and it would seem clear that the administrative division that had previously produced tetartera of precious metal was now assigned the task of producing the new copper coins of the Comnenian monetary system.

The obvious corollary is to attribute the second group to Thessalonica. However, examination of the coinages of Alexius and Manuel reveals the existence of a further group—distinguishable by its roughly clipped fabric, crude and blundered style and its light weight—within the wider context of that larger group of issues regularly appearing in large numbers at Athens and Corinth, and in Greek hoards in general. The heavier coins, of better style, are no doubt Thessalonican; the lighter coins, of crude style, and very probably including a high proportion of half-tetartera, would appear to emanate from a central Greek mint of uncertain identity—but probably Athens, Corinth, or Thebes—the practice of which was to follow the combination of obverse and reverse types in current use at Thessalonica. The Thessalonican coins appear regularly in larger numbers than the Constantinopolitan in Greece, but are themselves heavily outnumbered by the issues of the Greek mint.

Unfortunately, however, the division between the products of the mint of Thessalonica and those of the mint situated probably in central Greece is not as consistent during this reign as it later becomes: the situation undoubtedly needs the kind of clarification that will come only from the detailed analysis of a very large body of material evidence. It has therefore been thought more consistent with the present state of knowledge to group the whole series of non-metropolitan tetartera—together with the half-tetartera of the same types—under the mint of Thessalonica. A preliminary analysis follows:

MINT OF THESSALONICA

First coinage *Second coinage*	Apparently entirely of the heavier, better style series and therefore probably all to be attributed to Thessalonica.
Third coinage *Type D* *Type E*	Includes both the heavier, better style series, and the lighter, cruder style, clipped series. The essential differences between the two are to be seen in comparing Pl. 8.*7–11* with Pl. 8.*12*, *15*. Some, if not all, of the lighter coins are almost certainly half-tetartera.

The existence of the type listed by Sabatier as no. 3 of Alexius III[16] (which together with his no. 4 [type D] is in fact clearly to be attributed to Alexius I) must be regarded as dubious until an undoubted specimen should come to light. There are no specimens of this type present in the standard catalogues, nor are there any in the collection at Dumbarton Oaks: none turned up in the excavations at Athens, and only a single specimen is reported from Corinth. In view of the appalling condition of most excavation coins and the similarity of no. 3 to type D—with which it might, therefore, easily have been confused—it would seem best to reserve the position, rather than to confirm what may possibly be a "mythical" type.

Finally, several iconographical characteristics confirm the existence of the two major groups of issues—the Constantinopolitan and the Thessalonican/ Greek. Firstly, it should be noted that the latter group accounts for all those tetartera and half-tetartera distinguished by the type of a cross, or a monogram, or both (i.e., Alexius I, third tetarteron coinage, and type D; Manuel I, tetarteron type B and half-tetarteron type A). Obviously, both were motifs

16 Sabatier, *Description générale*, 2, p. 230 (pl. LVIII, 10).

favored by this mint. Secondly, that the traditional form of loros appears in two types from a total of five for this group under Alexius I (again third tetarteron coinage and type D). The metropolitan mint, however, is consistent in its use of the simplified loros (types A, B, and D). Thirdly, that, while the beardless bust type occurs on the first coinages of Manuel I in the electrum and billon trachy coinages, it occurs twice on the tetarteron and half-tetarteron series—once on a type of that group distinguished by its small, thick fabric (rare in Greece) and once on a type of the spread, thin group (common in Greece). It is evident, therefore, that they form the first coinages of two separate series of issues.

Little is known concerning the chronology of the various types of the metropolitan mint. Type D, with a standing imperial figure and fuller form of inscription on the reverse, possibly represents the first coinage—in which case type A, with short inscription, might be the last. The evidence for the Thessalonican/Greek series is more substantial: on the basis of overstrikes occurring among the pieces found in the excavation of the Athenian agora, the sequence for the first three coinages seems securely established.[17]

The exact nature of the abbreviated invocations found on the obverses of the Thessalonican types has been studied by Zacos and Veglery.[18]

Æ HALF-TETARTERON

The attribution of this issue—distinct from the unit by its obverse and reverse types—to Thessalonica, is based on the consideration that this is the pattern which later becomes customary at that mint, extending even into the thirteenth century. The weight of the two specimens in the collection at Dumbarton Oaks (1.6 and 2.2 gm.) places them quite firmly in the half-tetarteron series. Both apparently read: ΛΛЄ, and the rather long, bearded face is much more typical of Alexius than of John, who is generally given a rounder face, and who provides the only alternative attribution.

---

[17] Thompson, *op. cit.*, p. 115.

[18] G. Zacos and A. Veglery, "C for Σ on Coins of the Eleventh Century," *Numismatic Circular*, 68 (1960), pp. 154–57.

THE COINAGE OF JOHN II, COMNENUS

1118–1143

A̸ HYPERPYRON

MINT OF CONSTANTINOPLE

First coinage

Obv. I̅C̅ X̅C̅ in upper field.

Christ, bearded and nimbate, wearing tunic and colobion, seated upon throne without back; right hand raised in benediction, holds Gospels in left.

Rev. +IѠΔЄCΠOTH – or var. Θ̅V̅ M̅P̅ in right field.

Half-length figure of emperor on left, and of Virgin nimbate, holding between them patriarchal cross on long shaft. Emperor wears stemma, divitision, collar-piece and panelled loros of simplified type; holds anexikakia in right hand. Virgin wears tunic and maphorion. *Manus Dei* in upper left field; dot on lower portion of shaft of cross, in most, if not all cases.

Pl. 9.*1–3*

Second coinage

Obv. I̅C̅ X̅C̅ in upper field.

Christ, bearded and nimbate, wearing tunic and colobion, seated upon throne without back; right hand raised in benediction, holds Gospels in left.

Rev.
I̅Ѱ̅	ФV
ΔЄC	PO
ΠOT	ГЄ
TѠ	NH
Π	T

– or var. M̅ Θ̅ in upper center field.

Full-length figure of emperor on left, crowned by Virgin nimbate. Emperor wears stemma, divitision, collar-piece, and panelled loros of simplified type; holds in right hand labarum on long shaft, and in left, anexikakia. Virgin wears tunic and maphorion.

Pl. 9.*4, 5*

Third coinage

Obv. +KЄPO HΘЄI. I̅C̅ X̅C̅ in upper field.

Christ, bearded and nimbate, wearing tunic and colobion, seated upon throne with back; holds Gospels in left hand.

Rev.
$$\overline{\text{IW}}$$
ΔEC
ΠO
TH
– or var.

Full-length figure of emperor on left, crowned by Virgin nimbate. Emperor wears stemma, divitision, collar-piece, and panelled loros of simplified type; holds in right hand globus cruciger. Virgin wears tunic and maphorion. This coinage differs from the two preceding in being of two main varieties:

Var. A

Collar-piece has four jewels ⌣, and globus cruciger either ∴ or ∴ Normally ΘV MP in field.

Pl. 9.*6, 7*

Var. B

Collar-piece has five jewels ⌣, but globus cruciger apparently always ∴ Normally VΘ ϘM or MP in field.

Pl. 9.*8, 9*

MINT OF THESSALONICA

First coinage

As metropolitan first coinage, but of smaller, thicker fabric: shaft of cross generally lacks dot.

Pl. 9.*10*

Second coinage

As metropolitan second coinage, but of smaller, thicker fabric.

Pl. 9.*11*

Transitional coinage (second/third)

As metropolitan second coinage, but of smaller, thicker fabric; emperor holds globus cruciger in left hand, only the left-hand columnar inscription is present. ΘV MP etc. in field.

Pl. 9.*12*

Third coinage

As metropolitan third coinage, but of smaller, thicker fabric.

Pl. 9.*13, 14*

EL. ASPRON TRACHY

MINT OF CONSTANTINOPLE

Obv. I̅C̅ X̅C̅ in field.

Christ, bearded and nimbate, wearing tunic and colobion, seated upon throne without back; right hand raised in benediction, holds Gospels in left.

Rev.
$$\begin{matrix} \overline{IW} & \odot & \odot \\ \Delta\in C & \Im\daleth & \Gamma\in \\ \Pi O & \Phi W & W P \\ TH & \Pi & \Gamma\Pi \end{matrix} \quad \text{or} \quad \text{– or var.}$$

Two main varieties; both having two sub-varieties, (*A*) lacking the dot below the tablion of the chlamys, which (*B*) always possesses:

Var. I

Rev.

Full-length figure of emperor on left, and of Saint George, beardless and nimbate, holding between them patriarchal cross on long shaft at the base of which a small globe. Emperor wears stemma, divitision, and chlamys; saint wears short military tunic, breastplate, and sagion, holds sword in left hand.

I (A) Pl. 10.*1*;
I (B) Pl. 10.*2*

Var. II

Rev.

As above, but emperor and saint hold between them patriarchal cross on long shaft, at the base of which three steps.

II (A) Pl. 10.*3*;
II (B) Pl. 10.*4*

MINT OF THESSALONICA

Rev.

As above, but emperor and saint hold between them labarum on long shaft, at the base of which a small globe.

Pl. 10.*5, 6*

BILL. ASPRON TRACHY

MINT OF CONSTANTINOPLE

First coinage

Obv. M̅P̅ Θ̅V̅ in field.

Virgin nimbate, wearing tunic and maphorion, seated upon throne without back; holds beardless, nimbate head of Christ on breast.

Rev.
```
ΙѠ   ΦV
ΔЄC  PO
ΠO   ГЄ   – or var.
TH   NH
TѠ   T
Π
```

Full-length figure of emperor wearing stemma, short military tunic, and sagion; holds in right hand labarum on long shaft, and in left, globus cruciger.

Pl. 10.7, *8*

Second coinage

Obv. ĪC X̄C in field.

Bust of Christ, bearded and nimbate, wearing tunic and colobion; holds Gospels in left hand.

Rev. +ΙѠΔЄCΠOTT ΠΦVPOГNT – or var.

Bust of emperor wearing stemma, divitision, collar-piece, and panelled loros of simplified type; holds in right hand scepter cruciger, and in left, globus cruciger.

Two varieties:

Var. A

Rev.

Scepter cruciger has plain shaft, collar-piece normally has six jewels 𐍈.

Var. B

Rev.

Scepter has transverse stroke on shaft, collar-piece normally has five jewels 𐍈.

Var. A Pl. 10.*9, 10*;
Var. B Pl. 10.*11*,
Pl. 11.*1, 2*

MINT OF THESSALONICA

Obv. M̄P ѲV in field.

Virgin nimbate, wearing tunic and maphorion, seated upon throne without back; holds beardless, nimbate head of Christ on breast.

Rev.
```
ΙѠ   ΦV
ΔЄC  PO
ΠOT  ГЄ   – or var.
TѠ   NH
ΠOP  T
```

Full-length figure of emperor wearing stemma, divitision, and jewelled loros of traditional type; holds in right hand labarum-headed scepter, and in left, anexikakia.

Pl. 11.*3, 4*

Æ Tetarteron

Type A

Obv. I̅C̅ X̅C̅ in field.

Full-length figure of Christ, standing on dais, bearded and nimbate, wearing tunic and colobion; holds Gospels in left hand.

Rev. +IѠΔЄCΠΟΤ ΤѠΠΟΡΦVΡΟΓΝΤ – or var.

Full-length figure of emperor wearing stemma, divitision, collar-piece, and jewelled loros of simplified type; holds in right hand scepter cruciger, and in left, globus cruciger.

Pl. 11.*5–7*

Type B

Obv. M̅P̅ Θ̅V̅ in field.

Bust of Virgin nimbate, orans, wearing tunic and maphorion.

Rev.
I̅Ѡ̅ ΦV
ΔЄC PO
ΠΟΤ ΓЄ – or var.
ΤѠ ΝΗ
ΠΟΡ Τ

Full-length figure of emperor wearing stemma, divitision, and chlamys; holds in right hand jewelled scepter, and in left, globus cruciger.

Pl. 11.*8–10*

Obv. I̅C̅ X̅C̅ in field.

Bust of Christ, bearded and nimbate, wearing tunic and colobion; holds Gospels in left hand.

Rev. +IѠΔЄC ΠΟΤ – or var.

Bust of emperor wearing stemma, divitision, and chlamys; holds in right hand jewelled scepter on long shaft, and in left, globus cruciger.

Pl. 11.*11, 12*

Æ Half-tetarteron

Type A

Obv. I̅C̅ X̅C̅ in field.

Full-length figure of Christ, standing on dais, bearded and nimbate, wearing tunic and colobion; holds Gospels in left hand.

Rev. +IШΔЄC ΠOTH – or var.

> Bust of emperor wearing stemma, divitision, and chlamys; holds in right hand labarum-headed scepter, and in left, globus cruciger.

Pl. 11.13, 14

Type B

Obv.
ΔΙ ΡΙ
ΜΙ Ο
О Т
∫
– or var.

> Bust of Saint Demetrius, beardless and nimbate, wearing tunic, breast-plate, and sagion; holds in right hand sword, and in left, shield.

Rev. +IШ ΔЄC – or var.

> Bust of emperor wearing stemma, divitision, collar-piece, and panelled loros of simplified type; holds in right hand labarum-headed scepter, and in left, globus cruciger.

Pl. 11.15–17

THE COINAGE OF JOHN II: COMMENTARY

Ν HYPERPYRON

The three main coinages of hyperpyra issued by John II present remarkably few problems. The first and the last coinages are distinguishable, and the chronological sequence is therefore secure. The last coinage is undoubtedly that issued from two administrative divisions (officinae) of the mint—an arrangement seen previously in var. I of the main metropolitan coinage of Alexius I, but which was also followed by John's successor, Manuel I. The first coinage is presumably that portraying the half-length figures of the Emperor and the Virgin (Pl. 9.*1–3*), for the form of throne on the obverse continues that seen on the hyperpyra of Alexius I (i.e., with two horizontal bars). In all cases, the arrangement of the reverse inscription is as strictly controlled as it had been during the later years of Alexius and variations are small and rare.

There is a small group of specimens of all three coinages distinguished by their relatively small, thick fabric (*c.* 28 mm. as opposed to *c.* 30–33 mm.).[1] Four examples of the first coinage and three examples of the third were present in the Gornoslav hoard. A specimen of the small, thick variety of the first coinage also occurred in the Lakité hoard.[2] On the basis of these two provenances for the series, an attribution to the mint of Thessalonica is indicated—since, as already shown, it had already been in operation during the reign of Alexius.

---

[1] Pl. 9.*10–14*.
[2] Chap. 15, pp. 359–60.

Within this group, the products of at least two pairs of dies form a type showing features that are transitional between those of the normal second and third coinages (Pl. 9.*12*). The throne on the obverse belongs to the second coinage, as does the labarum on long shaft on the reverse. On the other hand, the globus cruciger and the single column of inscription on the reverse clearly belong to the third coinage. In the case of the piece illustrated there has been a schematic attempt made, by the addition of a back, to convert the form of the throne from that on the second coinage to that on the third.

These Thessalonican coins are also connected with an anomalous issue of the hyperpyron type of Manuel (Pl. 12.*12*), by the occurrence of an exaggerated "radiate" cross in the nimbus of Christ, on the obverse. Presumably, therefore, all are products of the same mint.

El. Aspron Trachy

The electrum coinage divides into three main varieties. On the evidence of a coin from re-cut dies in the Nicosia (I) hoard of the early nineteen-twenties,[3] it would appear that the variety in which the Emperor and Saint hold between them a patriarchal cross on steps is later than that on which they hold a patriarchal cross on globe. Both are apparently the product of two officinae.

The variety in which the Emperor and Saint hold a labarum on globe seems to betray Thessalonican connections in the rather characteristic elongated, raised form of the labarum-head (cf. Pls. 1.*9*; 4.*6–10*; 5.*1–6*; 10.5, 6). The Nicosia hoard contained seventy-eight specimens of both metropolitan varieties, but none of that attributed to Thessalonica: a preliminary source of support for the attribution itself.

Bill. Aspron Trachy

There are three types of billon scyphate. The later of the two metropolitan coinages is presumably that capable of division into two varieties according to the officina distinction.

The remaining metropolitan issue is too scarce for the observation of possible officina distinctions—but it may at least be said that none are obvious, and that the following type therefore probably represents the first occasion on which two officinae were active for this denomination.

The type which has been attributed to Thessalonica definitely seems to be a separate issue, on the basis of hoard evidence. Two large hoards from Cyprus totally lack specimens while containing large numbers of both metropolitan types. The Lazania hoard of the late thirties[4] contained a total of no less

---

[3] Chap. 15, pp. 371–372. Information from Mr. P. D. Whitting.
[4] *Ibid.*, p. 360.

than 403 specimens of the first metropolitan coinage, and 229 of the second. A parcel of coins in the hands of P. D. Whitting,[5] which is one of several similar reliably reported as having come from a large hoard found in Nicosia within the last decade, contains thirteen specimens of the first metropolitan coinage and 169 of the second.

It is also noticeable that the Emperor wears a loros of traditional type on the issue in question. This is distinctly unusual at such a late date, but can be paralleled on both the pre-reform folleis and the post-reform tetartera of Alexius I which have been attributed to the mint of Thessalonica (Pls. *3.2*; *8.10–15*). Perhaps more important, it also re-occurs on the coinage of the thirteenth-century emperors of Thessalonica (Pls. *37.1, 2*; *39.10, 11*; *42.1–4*). The attribution therefore seems well authenticated.

Æ Tetarteron

There is no doubt that the differences noticed between the groups assigned to Constantinople and Thessalonica under Alexius I continue to operate during the reign of John II. The twenty-seven specimens of metropolitan type A and the nine specimens of type B present in the collection at Dumbarton Oaks are of the characteristic small, thick fabric, while the nine specimens of the type attributed to Thessalonica display the larger, thinner fabric (although the style is by now distinctly neater): the metropolitan types do not occur in appreciable numbers at either Athens or Corinth, while the Thessalonican type occurs in comparatively large numbers at both.[6] There is no evidence bearing on the relative chronological order of types A and B.

Æ Half-tetarteron

The reign of John II is crucial for the case for the existence of the half-tetarteron denomination. There are two issues to be taken into consideration: in both cases the reverse type is of a bust of the Emperor holding a labarum-headed scepter and globus cruciger (Pl. *11.13–17*). Examination of a series of the coins shows that the flans of these two types are appreciably smaller than either the Thessalonican or the Constantinopolitan series of tetartera. The reduced flan is not balanced by any increase in thickness, and the average weight is definitely below that of the normal tetarteron. The figures are as follows:

(Tetarteron)

Metropolitan type A (27 specimens) average weight = 3.8 gm.
B (9 specimens) average weight = 3.7 gm.
Thessalonican type (9 specimens) average weight = 3.6 gm.

[5] *Ibid.*, p. 372.
[6] *Supra*, p. 99.

(Half-tetarteron)

Type A (14 specimens)	average weight = 1.9 gm.
Type B (13 specimens)	average weight = 1.9 gm.

Despite the rather small number of specimens involved, the evidence would seem sufficient to indicate that the two issues in question were struck at a standard of weight appreciably lower than that of the normal tetarteron types, and although the average for the lower standard is slightly over half that of the higher, there need be little doubt that they do in fact represent the half denomination.

The obverse and reverse types do not in themselves provide any decisive indications for an attribution to either Constantinople or Thessalonica. On type A, the obverse type of the standing figure of Christ is similar to that on the metropolitan tetarteron type A, but the imperial bust on the reverse is closely similar to that seen on the Thessalonican type. The bust of St. Demetrius on the obverse of the half-tetarteron type B would obviously be an attractive reason for a Thessalonican attribution, but cannot be considered decisive without supplementary evidence. Indeed to counter this, it might be pointed out that on this type the posture of the Emperor's arm as he holds the scepter is that which had been largely characteristic of the metropolitan mint during the previous reign.

The numbers of coins of these rather scarce types occurring at Athens and Corinth do, however, favor a Thessalonican origin: eleven specimens of type A, and ten of type B were recovered from the excavations at Athens,[7] while eleven specimens of type A and three of type B were found at Corinth.[8] Although these proportions do not approach those of the Thessalonican tetartera recovered from these sites, they are nevertheless appreciably in excess of those for the coins of the Constantinopolitan series.

Two further considerations swing the decision in favor of Thessalonica: that the evidence for the striking of half-tetartera prior to 1204 is confined to the Thessalonican/Greek group of coins, and that there are definite indications that the Thessalonican emperor, Theodore Comnenus-Ducas (1224–30) produced coins of the general tetarteron fabric on two distinctive standards of weight which can only be the unit and the half.[9]

[7] Thompson, *The Athenian Agora*, p. 74.
[8] Edwards, *Corinth*, p. 144.
[9] Chap. 12, p. 274.

THE COINAGE OF MANUEL I, COMNENUS

1143–1180

A̸ HYPERPYRON

MINT OF CONSTANTINOPLE

Obv. +KЄRO HΘЄI. ĪC XC in field.

Bust of Christ, beardless and nimbate, wearing tunic and colobion; holds scroll in left hand. Pattern in nimbus-cross normally ∴ but occasionally a single dot as in contemporary electrum (see p. 183).

Rev. MΛNᴙHΛ ΔЄCΠOTH TШ ΠOPΦVPOΓЄNNHTШ – in two columnar groups. Full-length figure of emperor, bearded, wearing stemma, divitision, and chlamys; holds in right hand labarum-headed scepter, and in left, globus surmounted by patriarchal cross. *Manus Dei* in upper right field.

Five main varieties:

Var. I

The portion of the chlamys-border forming the collar has six jewels ⌣. The right-hand columnar inscription normally commences TШ although $\overset{T}{Ш}$ is known.

Pl. 12.1–4

Var. II

The collar has five jewels; general inscription as above, but the right-hand column frequently begins with the ligature Ⴀ or Ⴀ.

Pl. 12.5, 6

Var. III

The collar has four jewels; the right-hand column normally begins with the ligature.

Two main sub-varieties, (*A*) lacking the dot on the divitision, below the point of the chlamys, which (*B*) always possesses.

III (A) Pl. 12.7;
III (B) Pl. 12.8

Var. IV

The collar has three jewels; inscription as above.

Pl. 12.9

Var. V

The collar has 8–12 jewels; inscription as above. The fabric is generally slightly thicker and smaller than the preceding, the style distinguished by its neat and jewel-like quality.

Pl. 12.*10, 11*

MINT OF THESSALONICA

Obv.

As above.

Rev.

As above, but globus surmounted by single-barred cross.

Pl. 12.*12*

EL. ASPRON TRACHY

MINT OF CONSTANTINOPLE

First coinage

Obv. $\begin{matrix} \overline{IC} & \overline{XC} \\ O & N\forall \\ \in M & H\Lambda \\ M\Lambda \end{matrix}$ – or var., in field.

Bust of Christ Emmanuel, beardless and nimbate, wearing tunic and colobion; holds scroll in left hand.

Rev. MΛNΫHΛ ΔЄCΠOTH – or var. $\overline{MP}$ $\overline{\Theta V}$ in upper center field.

Full-length figure of emperor, beardless, on left, crowned by Virgin. Emperor wears stemma, divitision, collar-piece, and jewelled loros of simplified type; holds in right hand labarum-headed scepter, and in left, anexikakia. Virgin wears tunic and maphorion.

Two main varieties:

Var. A
   Rev.
      Scepter shaft lacks dot.

Pl. 13.*1*

Var. B
   Rev.
      Scepter shaft has dot.

Pl. 13.*2*

Second coinage

Obv. $\overline{IC}$ $\overline{XC}$ in field.

Christ, bearded and nimbate, wearing tunic and colobion, seated upon throne without back; right hand raised in benediction, holds Gospels in left.

Rev. MΛNЧHΛ ΔЄCΠOTH – or var. M̄ ⊖V̄ in upper field.

Full-length figure of emperor, bearded, on left, and of Virgin nimbate, holding between them patriarchal cross on long shaft at the base of which a small globe. Emperor wears stemma, divitision, collar-piece, and jewelled loros of simplified type; holds anexikakia in right hand. Virgin wears tunic and maphorion.

Two main varieties:

> *Var. A*
> > *Rev.*
> > > Collar-piece has four jewels ⬭.

Pl. 13.3

> *Var. B*
> > *Rev.*
> > > Collar-piece has five jewels.

Pl. 13.4

Type C (Third coinage?)

Obv. ĪC̄ X̄C̄ in field.

Full-length figure of Christ, standing on dais, bearded and nimbate, wearing tunic and colobion; holds Gospels in left hand. ✳ ✳ in field.

Rev. MΛNЧHΛ   O ⊖Є O Δ Ш P O ∫   – or var.

Full-length figure of emperor, bearded, on left, and of St. Theodore, bearded and nimbate, holding between them patriarchal cross on long shaft at base of which a large globe. Emperor wears stemma, divitision, collar-piece, and jewelled loros of simplified type; holds sheathed sword in right hand. Saint wears short military tunic and breastplate; holds sheathed sword in left hand.

Three main varieties:

> *Var. A*
> > *Rev.*
> > > No dot on shaft of patriarchal cross. Includes sub-variety lacking asterisks on obverse.

Pl. 13.5, 6

8

Var. B
   Rev.
      One dot on shaft of patriarchal cross.

Pl. 13.7, *8*

Var. C
   Rev.
      Two dots on shaft of patriarchal cross.

Pl. 13.9

Type D (Fourth coinage?)

Obv. Ī͞C X͞C / O NȢ / ЄM HΛ / MΛ – or var., in field.

Bust of Christ Emmanuel, beardless and nimbate, wearing tunic and colobion; holds scroll in left hand.

Rev. MΛNȢHΛ ΔЄCΠOTHC O ΠOPΦVPOΓЄNNHTOC – in two columnar groups.

Full-length figure of emperor, bearded, wearing stemma, scaramangion or divitision, and sagion; holds in right hand labarum-headed scepter, and in left, anexikakia. *Manus Dei* in upper right field.

Three main varieties:

Var. A
   Rev.
      One dot on shaft of scepter near head.

Pl. 13.*10*

Var. B
   Rev.
      Two dots on shaft of scepter near head.

Pl. 13.*11*

Var. C
   Rev.
      Three dots on shaft of scepter near head.

Pl. 13.*12*

Type E (Fifth coinage?)

Obv. Ī͞C X͞C in upper field.

Christ, bearded and nimbate, wearing tunic and colobion, seated upon throne with back; holds Gospels in left hand.

Rev. MΛΝѴΗΛ ΔЄСΠΟΤ – or var. M̅P̅ Θ̅V̅ in upper field.

Full-length figure of emperor, bearded, on left, crowned by Virgin nimbate. Emperor wears stemma, divitision, and chlamys; holds in right hand labarum on long shaft, and in left, globus cruciger. Virgin wears tunic and maphorion.

Three main varieties:

   Var. A
      Rev.
         The portion of the chlamys-border forming the collar has three jewels ⬚—often square. Includes sub-variety in which the labarum shaft has dot.

                                          Pl. 14.*1, 2*

   Var. B
      Rev.
         Collar ⬚.

                                          Pl. 14.*3*

   Var. C
      Rev.
         Collar ⬚.

                                          Pl. 14.*4*

MINT OF THESSALONICA

Electrum products of this mint are characterized by an extremely thin, deep, scyphate fabric, and by the frequent use of small obverse dies.

First coinage
      As first metropolitan coinage, but of characteristic fabric.

                                          Pl. 14.*5*

Second coinage
      As second metropolitan coinage but of characteristic fabric.

                                          Pl. 14.*6*

Type C (Third coinage?)
      Obv. M̅P̅ Θ̅V̅ in field.
         Virgin nimbate, wearing tunic and maphorion, seated upon throne without back; holds beardless, nimbate head of Christ on breast.

8*

Rev. MΛNЧHΛΔЄCΠOTH  – or var.

Full-length figure of emperor bearded, on left, and of St. Demetrius, beardless and nimbate, holding between them labarum on long shaft. Emperor wears stemma, divitision, and chlamys; holds anexikakia in right hand. Saint wears short military tunic and breastplate.

Pl. 14.7–9

BILL. ASPRON TRACHY

MINT OF CONSTANTINOPLE

First coinage

Obv. I̅C̅ X̅C̅ in field.

Bust of Christ, beardless and nimbate, wearing tunic and colobion; holds scroll in left hand.

Rev. MΛNЧHΛ ΔЄCΠ – or var.

Bust of emperor, beardless, wearing stemma, divitision, and chlamys; holds in right hand labarum-headed scepter, and in left, globus cruciger. Two main varieties:

Var. A

Rev.

Labarum shaft has no dots; portion of chlamys-border forming collar normally has three jewels ⌒ .

Pl. 14.*10, 11*

Var. B

Rev.

Labarum shaft has two dots—one near head of labarum, the other between the hand and shoulder; collar normally has four jewels.

Pl. 14.*12, 13*

Second coinage

Obv. I̅C̅ X̅C̅ in upper field.

Christ, bearded and nimbate, wearing tunic and colobion, seated upon throne with back; holds Gospels in left hand.

Rev. MΛNЧHΛ ΔЄCΠOTH – or var.

Full-length figure of emperor, bearded, wearing stemma, divitision, collar-piece, jewelled loros of simplified type, and sagion; holds in right hand scepter cruciger, and in left, globus cruciger.

Two main varieties:

> *Var. A*
> > *Rev.*
> > > Collar piece has four jewels ⌣; globus cruciger of ✚ or ✚ form.
> > > > Pl. 15.*1, 2*

> *Var. B*
> > *Rev.*
> > > Collar-piece has five jewels; globus cruciger of ✚ form.
> > > > Pl. 15.*3, 4*

Third coinage (first phase)

Obv. M͞P Θ͞V in upper field.

Virgin nimbate, wearing tunic and maphorion, seated upon throne without back; holds beardless, nimbate head of Christ on breast.

Rev. MΛNЧHΛ ΔЄCΠOTHC – or var.

Full-length figure of emperor, bearded, wearing stemma, divitision, and chlamys; holds in right hand labarum on long shaft, and in left, globus surmounted by patriarchal cross.

Three main varieties:

> *Var. A*
> > *Rev.*
> > > Labarum shaft lacks dots.
> > > > Pl. 15.5, *6*

> *Var. B*
> > *Rev.*
> > > Labarum shaft has one dot.
> > > > Pl. 15.7–*9*

> *Var. C*
> > *Rev.*
> > > Labarum shaft has two dots (occasionally, as in the piece illustrated, waisted ⦙).
> > > > Pl. 15.*10*

Third coinage (second phase)
  Rev.
    Emperor holds globus surmounted by single-barred cross in left hand. Four main varieties:

  Var. A
    Rev.
      Labarum shaft lacks dots.

  Var. B
    Rev.
      Labarum shaft has one dot.

Pl. 15.*11*

  Var. C
    Rev.
      Labarum shaft has two dots.

Pl. 15.*12*

  Var. D
    Rev.
      Labarum shaft has three dots.

Pl. 15.*13*

Fourth coinage
  Obv. ĪC XC in field.
    Christ, bearded and nimbate, wearing tunic and colobion, seated upon throne without back; holds Gospels in left hand.
  Rev. MΛNЧHΛ ΔЄCΠOT – or var. M̅P̅ Θ̅V̅ in upper right field.
    Full-length figure of emperor, bearded, on left, crowned by Virgin nimbate. Emperor wears stemma, divitision, collar-piece, and jewelled loros of simplified type; holds in right hand labarum-headed scepter, and in left, globus cruciger. Virgin wears tunic and maphorion. Four main varieties:

  Var. A
    Rev.
      Three jewels on emperor's loros between waist and collar-piece; loros-waist ⊠ or ⊡.

Pl. 16.*1–6*

  Var. B
    Rev.
      One jewel on emperor's loros between waist and collar-piece; loros-waist ⊡ or ⊠.

Pl. 16.*7–9*

Var. C
> *Obv.*
>> Asterisk above throne on left, or right, or both.
>
> *Rev.*
>> One jewel on emperor's loros between waist and collar-piece; loros-waist ⊡.

Pl. 16.10–13

Var. D
> *Rev.*
>> Jewel-within-circle on collar-piece; on loros between waist and collar-piece; on both collar-piece and loros; on loros-waist. One jewel on emperor's loros between waist and collar-piece; loros-waist ▣ or ⊡.

Pl. 16.14, 15;
Pl. 17.1–4

Æ Tetarteron

MINT OF CONSTANTINOPLE

First coinage
> *Obv.* I̅C̅ X̅C̅ in field.
>> Bust of Christ, beardless and nimbate, wearing tunic and colobion; holds scroll in left hand.
>
> *Rev.* MΛNЧHΛ ΔECΠ – or var.
>> Bust of emperor, beardless, wearing stemma, divitision, collar-piece, and panelled loros of simplified type; holds in right hand labarum on long shaft, and in left, globus cruciger.

Pl. 17.5, 6

Type B
> *Obv.* M̅P̅ Θ̅V̅ in field.
>> Full-length figure of Virgin nimbate, orans, wearing tunic and maphorion, turned to right. *Manus Dei* in upper right field.
>
> *Rev.* MΛNЧHΛ ΔECΠOTHC – or var.
>> Full-length figure of emperor, bearded, wearing stemma, divitision, collar-piece, jewelled loros of simplified type and sagion; holds in right hand scepter cruciger, and in left, anexikakia.

Pl. 17.7, 8

Type C

Obv. ĪC XC in field.

    Full-length figure of Christ, standing on dais, bearded and nimbate, wearing tunic and colobion; holds Gospels in left hand.

Rev. MΛNЧHΛ ΔЄCΠOTH – or var.

    Full-length figure of emperor, bearded, wearing stemma, divitision, collar-piece, and jewelled loros of simplified type; holds in right hand labarum on long shaft, on which X, and in left, globus cruciger.

Pl. 17.9, 10

Type D

Obv. M̄P Θ̄V in field.

    Bust of Virgin nimbate, orans, wearing tunic and maphorion.

Rev. MΛNЧHΛ ΔЄC – or var.

    Bust of emperor, bearded, wearing stemma, divitision, and chlamys; holds in right hand labarum-headed scepter, and in left, globus cruciger, or, more rarely, globus surmounted by patriarchal cross.

Pl. 17.11, 12

MINT OF THESSALONICA

Type A (Heavy standard)

Obv. Γ O Є / Γ Ψ I O / ∫ – or var.

    Bust of St. George, beardless and nimbate, wearing tunic, breastplate, and sagion; holds in right hand spear, and in left, shield.

Rev. MΛNЧHΛ ΔЄCΠOT – or var.

    Bust of emperor, bearded, wearing stemma, divitision, collar-piece, and jewelled loros of simplified type; holds in right hand labarum-headed scepter, and in left, globus cruciger.

Pl. 17.13, 14

Type B (Heavy standard)

Obv. ĪC XC in field.

    Cross, radiate, on three steps.

Rev. MΛNЧHΛ ΔЄCΠOTH – or var.

    Half-length figure of emperor, bearded, wearing stemma, divitision, collar-piece, and jewelled loros of simplified type; holds in right hand labarum on long shaft, and in left, globus cruciger.

Pl. 17.15, 16

Æ Half-tetarteron

MINT OF THESSALONICA

Type A (Heavy standard)

Obv. Ⰰ – small, neat letters. M[ΛNЧH]Λ Δ[ECΠOTHC] Π[OPΦVPOΓEN-
NHTOC O] K[OMNHNOC]

Rev.
    Bust of emperor, beardless, wearing stemma, divitision, collar-piece (most frequently decorated with five jewels ⏝), and panelled loros of simplified type; holds in right hand labarum on long shaft, and in left, globus cruciger.

                               Pl. 17.*17, 18*

Type B (Heavy standard)
Obv. ĪC X̄C in field.
    Bust of Christ, beardless and nimbate, wearing tunic and colobion; holds scroll in left hand.
Rev. MΛNЧHΛ ΔECΠOTH – or var.
    Full-length figure of emperor, bearded, wearing uncertain dress (stemma, short military tunic, breastplate, and sagion?); holds in right hand scepter cruciger, and in left, globus cruciger.

                               Pl. 17.*19, 20*

UNCERTAIN GREEK MINT

Type A (Light standard; as Thessalonican half-tetarteron type A)

Obv. Ⰰ – large, often ill-formed letters.

Rev.
    Bust of emperor, beardless, wearing stemma, divitision, collar-piece (most frequently decorated with six jewels ⏝), and panelled loros of simplified type; holds in right hand labarum on long shaft, and in left, globus cruciger.

                                 Pl. 18.*1, 2*

Type B (Light standard; as Thessalonican tetarteron type A)

Obv. ΓΕΟ ΓΙΟϚ – or var.

    Bust of St. George, beardless and nimbate, wearing tunic, breastplate, and sagion; holds in right hand spear, and in left, shield.

Rev. MANЫHΛ ΔЄCΠOT – or var.

Bust of emperor, bearded, wearing stemma, divitision, collar-piece and jewelled loros of simplified type; holds in right hand labarum-headed scepter, and in left, globus cruciger.

Pl. 18.*3, 4*

Type C (Light standard; as Thessalonican half-tetarteron type B)

Obv. ĪĊ X̄Ċ in field.

Bust of Christ, beardless and nimbate, wearing tunic and colobion; holds scroll in left hand.

Rev. MANЫHΛ ΔЄCΠOTH – or var.

Full-length figure of emperor, bearded, wearing uncertain dress (stemma, short military tunic, breastplate, and sagion?); holds in right hand scepter cruciger, and in left, globus cruciger.

Pl. 18.*5, 6*

Type D (Light standard; as Thessalonican tetarteron type B)

Obv. ĪĊ X̄Ċ in field.

Cross, radiate, on three steps.

Rev. MANЫHΛ ΔЄCΠOTH – or var.

Half-length figure of emperor, bearded, wearing stemma, divitision, collar-piece, and jewelled loros of simplified type; holds in right hand labarum on long shaft, and in left, globus cruciger.

Pl. 18.*7, 8*

THE COINAGE OF MANUEL I: COMMENTARY

AV HYPERPYRON

Information on the hyperpyron of Manuel I is mainly derived from two hoards: that from Gornoslav which contained 264 pieces, and that from Corinth of 1938,[1] which amounted to thirty. As might be expected, in the light of the issues of the long reign of Alexius I, a considerable chronological development is evident. The most general indication of the sequence of issues is based on the fact that the last metropolitan coinage of hyperpyra of John II is of large fabric (30–33 mm.), only slightly scyphate, and characterized by a style which might be termed "spread," while the hyperpyra of Andronicus I are uniformly of slightly smaller fabric (few specimens exceed 30 mm.), deeper, and of a neat, confined, bejewelled style. It might well be expected there-

[1] Chap. 15, p. 335.

fore that the earlier coins of Manuel I should betray the characteristics of the coinage of John, while the later ones should anticipate, to some extent at least, the peculiarities of the coinage of Andronicus.

Examination of the specimens in the Gornoslav hoard revealed a division into five varieties—apparently in chronological succession—according to the number of jewels on the border of the chlamys forming the collar. Of the Gornoslav hoard, sixty-two specimens were of var. I (six jewels), eighty of var. II (five jewels), eighteen of var. III (four jewels), sixty-five of var. IV (three jewels), and thirty-five of var. V (eight to twelve jewels). Although the proportions occurring in the Corinth hoard were different (var. I, two specimens; var. II, nine; var. III, one; var. IV, three; var. V, fifteen), the same general divisions occurred. Vars. I and II are of a fabric and style indistinguishable from the last coinage of John II, while var. V is of a distinctly smaller, deeper fabric, and of a neat, jewelled style: that is, bearing an obvious relationship to the hyperpyra of Andronicus I.

The two specimens of var. I in the Corinth hoard and the six in the collection at Dumbarton Oaks all have the right-hand columnar inscription commencing ⲦⲰ. Of the seven specimens of var. II in the Corinth hoard which were from different dies, and the six at Dumbarton Oaks, six similarly read ⲦⲰ in the right-hand column, but in seven cases the ligature ⳁ or ⳁ has replaced the separate letters which had been characteristic of the reformed coinages of Alexius I and John II as well as of var. I of Manuel. Common to all the specimens of vars. I and II from Gornoslav, Corinth, and Dumbarton Oaks are the small devices •, ▪, ✗, ❟, ∫, ∫ on the chlamys immediately below the tablion—presumably some form of officina distinction.

Logically the next variety should be that in which the collar is decorated with four jewels. Possibly a less numerous coinage than the rest, only eighteen specimens occurred in the Gornoslav hoard. Such evidence as it has been possible to gather regarding the inscriptional varieties suggests that the ligature ⳁ or ⳁ becomes dominant during the course of this coinage.

Var. IV has three jewels to the collar, and in general continues the trends in the inscription evident in the previous coinage, ⳁ or ⳁ predominating.

Var. V is undoubtedly the latest issue, and, as mentioned above, is related to the coinage of Andronicus I, by fabric and style. The number of jewels in the collar having diminished from six to three over four varieties, the only possibility remaining to the authorities of the mint in order to retain the distinction between them would have been to increase the number to a total above that used in the first (var. I, six jewels)—a collar of two jewels would have been unprecedented! With the advent of var. V whatever remains of the originally strict control over the arrangement of the inscription finally breaks down. While the use of the ligature ⳁ or ⳁ is almost uniform, the fifteen specimens in the Corinth hoard and the ten at Dumbarton Oaks provide eleven examples of the form of the left-hand inscription commencing $\frac{MΛ}{NႱ}$, six of $\frac{MΛ}{NOV}$, six of $\frac{MΛ}{NႱHΛ}$, and two of $\frac{MΛ}{NႱH}$. Although the traditional pendilia form **.!.!.** apparently dominates vars. I and II, by the stage of the issue represented by var. V several new forms have appeared. Metcalf suggests a provincial mint as the possible source of var. V, but this is unlikely if only in view of the large numbers occurring in both the Gornoslav and Corinth hoards. Thessalonica, the only provincial gold mint operating to any extent continuously during the preceding reigns, is conspicuous by the small volume of its products; besides, the issue fits perfectly well into the metropolitan series.

There were two specimens present in the Gornoslav hoard, on which the globus held by the Emperor on the reverse was surmounted by a single-barred cross, rather than a patriarchal cross: these are far more likely than var. V to have been the products of Thessalonica. The attribution to a mint other than that of the capital is assured by the fact that coins of this group stand outside the chronological developments seen in the products of that mint. The specimen illustrated (Pl. 12.*12*), for instance, has a collar of six jewels (the earliest variety at the capital)—but is of smaller module than normal for the variety. The ligature ⵊ on the reverse is also normally a later feature. Finally, the curious exaggeratedly "radiate" effect of the cross in the nimbus of Christ links this variety with the provincial series of hyperpyra of John II (Pl. 9.*10, 14*). Coins of this variety were probably the last hyperpyra struck outside the capital, for there are no further series assignable to provincial mints.

El. Aspron Trachy

Two hoards provide the major portion of the available information on the electrum coinages of Manuel: the first, the Lindos (Rhodes) hoard of 1902;[2] the second, the Nicosia (I) hoard of the early nineteen-twenties.

There is no doubt concerning the identification of the first coinage: the young Emperor is represented as beardless. The second coinage, moreover, is, owing to the similarity of its reverse type in detail, style, and fabric to that of the first coinage, equally certainly attributed. The electrum trachea of John II were the products of two officinae, and it would appear reasonable to assume that this number was involved in the production of at least the first coinages of the succeeding Emperor. Analysis confirms that both of the issues mentioned above were indeed the products of two officinae, and, moreover, that the remainder of the metropolitan issues were the product of three officinae. The last coinage, the fifth, should therefore be that in which the three officinae appear to operate at a roughly equal rate (type E). The third coinage

---

[2] Chap. 15, p. 361.

is, in this case, presumably that in which the products of the third officina appear only rarely (type C)—either because it had only commenced to operate toward the end of that coinage, or because its organization at this stage was not as settled and efficient as that of the remainder, which had been in operation for many years without interruption. The other issue (type D) should logically form the fourth coinage.

The only type failing to reflect the characteristics of the metropolitan mint is that on which the standing figures of the Emperor and St. Demetrius appear (Pl. 14.7–9). In a rather similar fashion to metropolitan type D, a number of dots occur beneath the head of the labarum held between the Emperor and Saint, but the twenty specimens in the Nicosia hoard, together with the seven in the collection at Dumbarton Oaks, fail to reveal whether they conform to any systematic pattern. Examination of the pieces in question reveals that the type, however, has a distinct fabric—no larger in diameter than normal, but very deeply scyphate in form, and therefore considerably thinner. The inscription is frequently extremely small and neat. These characteristics also appear in a small group of coins the types of which are the same as those of the first and second metropolitan coinages (Pl. 14.5, 6).

A document of the Georgian monastery of Iviron on Mt. Athos mentions a coin called the "dimitraton" no less than four times in a list of gifts made to the monastery:

(3) 2 mules worth 180 dimitrati
(59) 200 drakhani (nomismata) dimitrati
(75) 200 drakhani dimitrati
(136) 300 drakhani dimitrati

According to Blake, the author of the article on Byzantine accounting practices as illustrated by this document, the four entries are all "late" and probably Comnenian.[3] The term must refer to an issue on which St. Demetrius was present, and, moreover, an issue of high value, for, *pace* Blake, all the other entries of the document refer to coins of that description. The only issue fulfilling these qualifications is, in fact, the electrum trachy mentioned above. Certain base silver, billon, or copper scyphates of the empire of Thessalonica might conceivably have been candidates for identification were it not for the consideration of value. This very consideration is itself, however, confirmed by another entry. No. (144), which is datable to *c.* 1170, mentions an ass's colt bought for fifteen perperay (hyperpyra).[4] Entry (3), however, refers to two mules worth 180 dimitrati. Assuming the identity of the dimitraton and the electrum trachy in question, the price of a mule works

[3] Blake, "Accounting Practices," p. 30.
[4] *Ibid.*, p. 24.

out at thirty hyperpyra $(90 \div 3)^5$—which, in view of the generally recognized superiority of the mule over the ass, might well represent a reasonable price.

It is particularly interesting that the dimitraton should appear on four occasions in the accounts of an Athonite monastery—supplying the only extant references to the issue. Entry no. (3) is crucial—"two mules worth 180 dimitrati". It is theoretically possible that, on the three other occasions of the term's use, coins of this particular issue sent from different parts of the Empire were involved. On this occasion, however, the Athonite accountant clearly uses the term as a familiar way of reckoning value: these coins were therefore a recognizable element of the circulating medium with which he dealt. The Athonite peninsula is, of course, only about sixty miles distant from the city of Thessalonica, and, in view of the fact that the only other appearances of St. Demetrius on the Comnenian coinage occur on issues that can reasonably be connected with the city (Pl. 1.*9–12*; Pl. 11.*15–17*), a similar provisional attribution is here clearly indicated. This would include the varieties of the first and second electrum coinages distinguishable by their deeply scyphate, thin fabric.

The dimitraton was in all probability struck as a local counterpart to the metropolitan issue depicting the Emperor and St. Theodore: this provincial attribution has the fortunate result in balancing the five metropolitan varieties of the hyperpyron with five coinages of electrum trachea.

The widespread employment of the Christ Emmanuel type—whether labelled or not—on the coinage of this Emperor, and more particularly on his earlier coinage, is almost certainly a play on the words MANҰHΛ / ЄMMANҰHΛ; especially appropriate in view of his youth at the time of his accession.

Bill. Aspron Trachy

Manuel's series of billon trachea opens with the beardless bust type, which, in a similar fashion to the second coinage of John II, was the product of two officinae. The second coinage was also the product of two officinae, but the third and fourth involve the introduction of two more. The first phase of the third coinage was the product of three officinae, the second phase the product of four. The fourth coinage was throughout the product of four officinae.

Æ Tetarteron and Half-tetarteron

The first metropolitan coinage of tetartera portrays the young, beardless, imperial bust, but the sequence following this remains uncertain. The weight

---

[5] Utilizing the rate 1:3 which has been established between the hyperpyron and the electrum trachy. The absolute level of these two prices remains curiously high however.

standard is possibly slightly lower than for the coinage of John II, but not remarkably so:

First coinage, 14 specimens, average weight = 3.7 gm.
Type B   34 specimens, average weight = 3.4 gm.
Type C   11 specimens, average weight = 3.4 gm.
Type D   19 specimens, average weight = 3.4 gm.

As Metcalf has noticed, however, that group which is comprised of types which appear in the excavations at Athens and Corinth, and in Greek hoards generally, is a good deal more complicated, each type dividing approximately into a heavy and a light variety.[6] Moreover, the large, heavy coins of each type, although forming an appreciable element of Greek excavation and hoard finds, are heavily outnumbered by their light counterparts: this is well illustrated by the composition of the Brauron hoard of 1956, the Kalentzi hoard of 1927, and the Kastri hoard of 1952.[7]

The average weights for both heavy and light varieties of each type are as follows:[8]

I   (*Obv.*: monogram) heavy variety, average weight of
                                16 specimens = 2.7 gm.
I (a) (*Obv.*: monogram) light variety, average weight of
                                27 specimens = 1.8 gm.
II   (*Obv.*: Saint George) heavy variety, average weight of
                                23 specimens = 4.5 gm.
II (a) (*Obv.*: Saint George) light variety, average weight of
                                5 specimens = 1.9 gm.
III   (*Obv.*: Christ, bust) heavy variety, average weight of
                                4 specimens = 2.9 gm.
III (a) (*Obv.*: Christ, bust) light variety, average weight of
                                19 specimens = 1.9 gm.
IV   (*Obv.*: cross-on-steps) heavy variety, average weight of
                                24 specimens = 4.0 gm.
IV (a) (*Obv.*: cross-on-steps) light variety, average weight of
                                6 specimens = 1.9 gm.

The most easily distinguished varieties are the large, heavy St. George and cross-on-steps issues of fine style (II and IV). The heavy varieties of the monogram and Christ, bust types (I and III) are of equally fine style, but

[6] Metcalf, *Coinage in the Balkans*, p. 108.
[7] Chap. 15, pp. 330–31, 350, 352.
[8] I includes four specimens published by D. M. Metcalf in "The Brauron Hoard and the Petty Currency of Central Greece, 1143–1204," *NC*[7], 4 (1964), p. 253, note 2. III includes a specimen in the British Museum (*BMC*, 2, p. 578, no. 64).

despite the smaller numbers upon which their average weights are based, it is certain that whatever their theoretical weight, it was considerably less than the two types (II and IV) which they most resemble.

In order to establish the denominational identity of the four heavy varieties, it is necessary to consider the Thessalonican coinage of Manuel's predecessor, John II. That series—all of good style—included a tetarteron type, and two further types, distinct from each other and from the tetarteron, which, on the basis of their small flans and light weight, have been identified as half-tetartera.

Precisely this relationship is evident between the four heavy varieties in question: the St. George and cross-on-steps types are undoubtedly tetartera, the former type closely related by style and detail to the Thessalonican half-tetarteron of John II having a bust of St. Demetrius as its obverse type. Quite simply what has happened is that the standard of weight has been increased, putting the new, heavy tetarteron types in a favorable position as regards both their predecessors at Thessalonica, and their contemporaries at Constantinople, which show no signs of increased weight. The heavy, monogram and Christ bust types (av. wts. 2.7 gm. and 2.9 gm. respectively) are therefore clearly Thessalonican half-tetartera of a weight approximately proportional to their units.

The question of the attribution of the four light weight varieties (I a, II a, III a, and IV a) at once arises. The solution is obvious: they outnumber their heavier counterparts in most Greek hoards, and evidently in the Athens and Corinth excavations. The only reasonable explanation is that they are the products of a separate mint, as Metcalf has suggested. Their style is generally decidedly cruder than the heavy Thessalonican series; they are often of clipped fabric; they apparently maintain the weight standard of the old half-tetarteron of John II (c. 1.9 gm.). On the basis of overstrikes—mainly of this series—found during the excavations at Athens and Corinth, the order of issue would seem to be: *obv.* monogram; *obv.* St. George; *obv.* Christ, bust; *obv.* cross-on-steps.[9] The Greek mint was presumably merely copying the types of the current Thessalonican issue—whether tetarteron or half-tetarteron; this in turn seems to imply that the Thessalonican tetarteron and half-tetarteron types were not issued contemporaneously but successively. There is certainly nothing impossible in this.

There are no parallels to the Greek light series of half-tetartera for the reign of John II, but there is a striking resemblance in the coinage of Alexius I.[10] The first two coinages of Thessalonican copper tetartera are of uniformly

---

[9] Thompson, *The Athenian Agora*, p. 116. The position of the monogram type as the first issue is confirmed by its portraying the Emperor as beardless.

[10] *Supra*, pp. 99–100.

large, rounded fabric, and respectable, if not brilliant, style. The third coinage (*obv.*: jewelled cross) is of extremely varied style and fabric however; the minority compare quite favorably with the preceeding coinages, but the majority are of much cruder style, badly clipped fabric, and light in weight. The type having as its obverse a patriarchal cross suffers similarly.

The obvious explanation is that the third coinage saw the opening of the Greek mint—at either Athens, Corinth or Thebes—which began to strike its characteristically poor and light products. It is this coinage that comes to light in such large numbers in the excavation of both cities.

It is noticeable that the coinage of John II exists only in the Thessalonican style and fabric, and the implications of this are apparent in the Athens and Corinth excavation figures:[11] despite his twenty-three-year-reign the number of his coins from both sites is disproportionately small. Clearly the reign of John saw the closing down of the Greek mint, and only such Thessalonican tetartera and half-tetartera as reached central Greece by normal circulation are represented at these two cities (as in the case of the Corinth hoard of February 1937).[12] The explanation that the comparative rarity of coins of John from these excavations was the result of the peaceful nature of the reign is unsatisfactory: the Norman sack of Corinth in 1147 (only three years after John's death) took place at a time when his coinage should still have been the dominant element of the circulating medium at both Athens and Corinth, had the Greek mint been open during his reign. It was not, and the fact is reflected in the excavation figures.

The consequence presumably was that, by the commencement of the reign of Manuel, the Greek cities faced a serious shortage of small change, the last substantive supplies being datable to the reign of Alexius I. The enormous quantities of the first two coinages of Manuel showing the characteristics of the Greek mint found on Greek sites attests both the shortage and its alleviation by the reopening of that mint.

Metcalf, in publishing the Brauron hoard of 1956 (consisting mainly of half-tetartera of the monogram type of Manuel I), suggests Thessalonica as the source of the lightest and crudest varieties of half-tetartera.[13] It may be regarded as certain that Thessalonica was a Comnenian mint and very probable that there existed at least one other at Thebes, Athens, or Corinth—that much is common ground. However, Thessalonica cannot be regarded as the origin of these half-tetartera (not, as Metcalf assumes, "folles" of a light standard of weight). Throughout the late eleventh and the twelfth century, one mint besides that of the metropolis was producing a continuous series of copper

[11] Table, p. 99.
[12] Chap. 15, pp. 334–35.
[13] Metcalf, "The Brauron Hoard," p. 258.

tetartera of comparatively good style and weight, together with an occasional issue of half-tetartera distinguishable from the unit by type. Apart from the fact that one of these half-tetarteron types portrays St. Demetrius, the first coins of this series (the first and third coinages of Alexius I here attributed to Thessalonica) bear a strong resemblance, in certain points, to two types of debased tetartera for which there are plausible reasons in favor of an attribution to that city. It is this series which is continuous—that attributed to the Greek mint (or mints) does not appear during the reign of John II, and it again disappears during that of Isaac II. It would seem far more likely that it is the continuous series of good style that should be assigned to the second city of the Empire, which was quite capable of producing competent dies for its gold and electrum issues and therefore presumably for its copper.

ALEXIUS II, COMNENUS

1180–1184

Coins of this Emperor are unknown, and probably none were struck. It is possible that the last issues of his father continued in production into his reign. Those tetarteron types provisionally attributed to Alexius II by D. M. Metcalf (*Coinage in the Balkans*, pp. 88 and 118), should be retained in their more usual attributions. The types involved are, therefore, here assigned to Alexius I (Thessalonican types D and E), which in fact fit perfectly well into this series; and to Alexius III (the general Thessalonican tetarteron and half-tetarteron type), which in its chronological development conforms exactly to that noted for the other denominations of this Emperor.

THE COINAGE OF ANDRONICUS I, COMNENUS

1183–1185

A/ HYPERPYRON

MINT OF CONSTANTINOPLE

Obv. M͞P Θ͞V in upper field.

Virgin nimbate, wearing tunic and maphorion, seated upon throne with back; holds beardless, nimbate head of Christ on breast.

Rev. ΛΝΔΡΟΝΙΚΟC ΔЄCΠΟΤΗC – or var. Ι͞C Χ͞C in upper right field.

Full-length figure of emperor on left, crowned by Christ, bearded and nimbate. Emperor wears stemma, divitision, collar-piece, panelled loros of simplified type, and sagion; holds in right hand labarum-headed scepter, and in left, globus cruciger. Christ, wearing tunic and colobion, holds Gospels in left hand.

Pl. 18.*9, 10*

EL. ASPRON TRACHY

MINT OF CONSTANTINOPLE

Obv. +ΘΚЄRΟ ΗΘЄΙ. M͞P Θ͞V in upper field.

Full-length figure of Virgin nimbate and orans, wearing tunic and maphorion, standing on dais; beardless, nimbate head of Christ on breast.

Rev. ΛΝΔΡΟΝΙΚШ ΔЄCΠΟΤΗ – or var. Ι͞C Χ͞C in upper right field.

Full-length figure of emperor on left, crowned by Christ, bearded and nimbate. Emperor wears stemma, divitision, and chlamys; holds in right hand labarum on long shaft, and in left, anexikakia. Christ, wearing tunic and colobion, holds Gospels in left hand.

Two main varieties:

Var. A
Rev.
Labarum shaft lacks dot.

Pl. 18.*11*

Var. B
Rev.
Labarum shaft has dot.

Pl. 18.*12*

BILL. ASPRON TRACHY

MINT OF CONSTANTINOPLE

Obv. M̅P̅ Θ̅V̅ in field.

Full-length figure of Virgin nimbate, wearing tunic and maphorion, standing on dais; holds beardless, nimbate head of Christ on breast.

Rev. ΛΝΔΡΟΝΙΚΟC ΔЄCΠΟΤΗC – or var. I̅C̅ X̅C̅ in upper right field.

Full-length figure of emperor on left, crowned by Christ, bearded and nimbate. Emperor wears stemma, divitision, collar-piece, and jewelled loros of simplified type; holds in right hand labarum-headed scepter, and in left, globus cruciger. Christ, wearing tunic and colobion, holds Gospels in left hand.

Two main varieties:

Var. A
Rev.
Two jewels on loros between waist and collar-piece.

Pl. 18.*13, 14*

Var. B
Rev.
Three jewels on loros between waist and collar-piece.

Pl. 18.*15, 16*

Æ TETARTERON

MINT OF CONSTANTINOPLE

Obv. M̅P̅ Θ̅V̅ in field.

Full-length figure of Virgin nimbate, wearing tunic and maphorion, standing on dais; holds beardless, nimbate head of Christ on breast.

Rev. ΛΝΔΡΟΝΙΚΟC ΔЄCΠΟΤΗC⎱ – or var. I̅C̅ X̅C̅ in upper right field.
ΛΝΔΡΟ ΝΙΚΟC ⎰

Full-length figure of emperor on left, crowned by Christ, bearded and nimbate. Emperor wears stemma, divitision, and chlamys; holds in right hand labarum on long shaft, and in left, anexikakia. Christ, wearing tunic and colobion, holds Gospels in left hand.

Pl. 19.*1*

MINT OF THESSALONICA

Type A
Obv. M̅P̅ Θ̅V̅ in field.

Bust of Virgin nimbate, orans, wearing tunic and maphorion; beardless, nimbate head of Christ on breast.

Rev. ΛΝΔΡΟ ΝΙΚΟС – or var.

Bust of emperor wearing stemma, scaramangion or divitision, and sagion; holds in right hand labarum-headed scepter, and in left, globus cruciger.

Pl. 19.*2*

Type B

Obv.
```
      O
    ΛΓΙ  ꟼ
  O     Γ    – or var.
   ſ Γ  ſ
     Є
```

Bust of Saint George, beardless and nimbate, wearing tunic, breast-plate, and sagion; holds in right hand spear, and in left, shield.

Rev. ΛΝΔΡΟΝΙΚΟС (ΔЄСΠΟΤΗС ?) – or var.

Full-length figure of emperor wearing stemma, divitision, collar-piece, and jewelled loros of simplified type; holds in right hand labarum on long shaft, and in left, globus surmounted by patriarchal cross. *Manus Dei* in upper right field.

Pl. 19.*3*

Æ HALF-TETARTERON

UNCERTAIN GREEK MINT

Obv. M̅P̅ Θ̅V̅ in field.

Bust of Virgin nimbate, orans, wearing tunic and maphorion; beardless, nimbate head of Christ on breast.

Rev. ΛΝΔ – or var.

Bust of emperor wearing stemma, scaramangion or divitision, and sagion; holds in right hand labarum-headed scepter, and in left, globus cruciger.

(As Thessalonican tetarteron type A.)

Pl. 19.*4*

THE COINAGE OF ANDRONICUS I: COMMENTARY

N̸ HYPERPYRON

The number of specimens available for study is, in the case of both gold and electrum, lamentably small: there is, to all intents and purposes, no hoard evidence whatsoever.

It is, however, quite clear that the reign of Andronicus saw a reorganization of the administrative system behind the production of the metropolitan coinage, the effect on the officinae being particularly noticeable.[1]

---

[1] Chap. 10, pp. 172–73, etc.

The iconography of all the metropolitan denominations of this Emperor forms a compact theme: the Virgin as the obverse type, the Emperor crowned by Christ as the reverse. The distinction between denominations is maintained by the varying posture of the Virgin, and the different combinations of imperial dress.

As is well known, the beard worn by Andronicus was long and forked—a fact alluded to by the chronicler Choniates[2] and verified by its constant appearance on his coins. Andronicus is the only emperor to be portrayed with a beard of this type during the twelfth century, although the style was in vogue during the thirteenth.

Æ TETARTERON

The metropolitan tetarteron fits into the iconographical theme evident in the other products of this mint, while the Thessalonican series does not. The difference is confirmed by distribution, as seen in the results of the Athens and Corinth[3] excavations:

	Athens	Corinth
Metropolitan type	o	o
Thessalonican type A	74	19 (16+3)
Thessalonican type B	2	o

The exact proportions of Thessalonican tetartera and Greek half-tetartera of identical types represented in these figures is uncertain. Type B is attributed to Thessalonica because of the similarity of its obverse type to that of Manuel's type A from that mint, and despite the small numbers found at Athens, and the complete absence of the type from Corinth.

It should be noted that, if correctly read, the occurrence of a specimen of type B overstruck on type A, from among the Athens material, should give the order of issue.[4]

Æ HALF-TETARTERON

The Greek mint of uncertain identity continues to follow the obverse and reverse types of the current Thessalonican issue.

[2] Nicetas Choniates; Bonn ed., pp. 450–51. Choniates also notes (p. 453) that when the mob broke into the palace at the time of the downfall of Andronicus they found, among other valuables, twelve kentenaria of gold coins, thirty kentenaria of silver coins and two hundred kentenaria of copper coins. It seems very probable that this represents a description of the three scyphate denominations in gold, electrum, and billon.

[3] Thompson, *The Athenian Agora*, p. 75; Edwards, *Corinth*, p. 146.

[4] Thompson, *op. cit.*, p. 117.

THE COINAGE OF ISAAC COMNENUS, USURPER IN CYPRUS
1184–1191

EL. ASPRON TRACHY

MAIN MINT (Nicosia?)

Obv. M̅P̅ Θ̅V̅ in field.

Virgin nimbate, wearing tunic and maphorion, seated upon throne without back; holds beardless, nimbate head of Christ on breast.

Rev. CΛ ΛKI OC | I | ЄC Δ Π — or var.

Full-length figure of emperor wearing stemma, divitision, and chlamys; holds in right hand scepter cruciger, and in left, anexikakia.

Pl. 19.5

BILL. ASPRON TRACHY

MAIN MINT (Nicosia?)

Type A

Obv. M̅P̅ Θ̅V̅ in field.

Virgin nimbate, wearing tunic and maphorion, seated upon throne without back; holds beardless, nimbate head of Christ on breast.

Rev. ICΛΛKIOC ΟΓЄШΡΓΙΟC — or var.

Full-length figure of emperor on left, and of St. George, beardless and nimbate, holding between them patriarchal cross on long shaft at the base of which a small globe. Emperor wears stemma, divitision, and chlamys; holds anexikakia in right hand. Saint wears short military tunic and breastplate; holds sword in left hand.

Pl. 19.6, 7

Type B

Obv. ΙC ΟЄ MM Λ | X̅C̅ N४ HΛ — or var.

Beardless, nimbate bust of Christ Emmanuel, wearing tunic and colobion; holds scroll in left hand.

Rev.
```
      I    Δ
     CΛ   Є
     ΛΚΙ  C     – or var.
     OC   ΠΟ
          TH
          C
```

Full-length figure of emperor wearing stemma, scaramangion or divitision, and sagion; holds in right hand scepter cruciger, and in left, anexikakia. *Manus Dei* in upper right field.

Pl. 19.*8–10*

SECONDARY MINT

Obv. M̅P̅ Θ̅V̅ in field.

Full-length figure of Virgin nimbate, orans, wearing tunic and maphorion.

Rev.
```
      I    ΔЄC
     CΛ   ΠΟ
     ΛΚΙ  TH     – or var.
     OC   C
```

Full-length figure of emperor wearing stemma, divitision, and chlamys, standing on dais; holds in right hand cross on long shaft, and in left, globus cruciger. *Manus Dei* in upper right field.

Pl. 19.*11*

Æ TETARTERON

MAIN MINT (Nicosia?)

Type A

Obv. M̅P̅ Θ̅V̅ in field.

Bust of Virgin nimbate, orans, wearing tunic and maphorion.

Rev. ICΛΛΚΙΟC ΔЄC – or var.

Bust of emperor wearing stemma, divitision, and chlamys; holds in right hand scepter cruciger, and in left, globus cruciger.

Pl. 19.*12*

Type B

Obv.
```
     I̅C̅  X̅C̅
      +   +      in field.
```

Bust of Christ, bearded and nimbate, wearing tunic and colobion; right hand raised in benediction, holds Gospels in left.

Rev. ICΛΛΚΙΟC ΔЄC – or var.

Bust of emperor wearing stemma, scaramangion or divitision, and sagion; holds in right hand scepter cruciger, and in left(?).

Pl. 19.*13, 14*

SECONDARY MINT

Obv. M̄P̄ ΘV̄ in field.

Full-length figure of Virgin nimbate, orans, wearing tunic and maphorion, turned to right. *Manus Dei* in upper right field.

Rev.
I   ΔЄC
CΛ   ΠO
ΛKI TH
OC   C

Full-length figure of emperor wearing stemma, divitision, and chlamys, standing on dais; holds in right hand cross on long shaft, and in left, globus cruciger. *Manus Dei* in upper right field.

Pl. 19.*15*

THE COINAGE OF ISAAC COMNENUS: COMMENTARY

Isaac Comnenus was a grandson of the Sebastocrator Isaac, third son of the Emperor John II. At the accession of Andronicus I he was in the hands of the Templars, having been sold to them by the Armenians, by whom he had been captured in Cilicia. Ransomed by Andronicus, he was sent back to Cilicia with sufficient money to raise a small force in Isauria. Instead of using the money in the service of the Empire, Isaac crossed over to Cyprus (1184) and presented to the authorities there forged letters of appointment as governor. Once accepted in this position he proclaimed himself emperor and held the island until 1191 when he was deposed by Richard I of England during the course of the Third Crusade.[1]

Despite the sack of the island by Renauld of Chatillon/Antioch in 1155/56, there is considerable evidence that Cyprus remained wealthy—no doubt largely owing to its strategic position on the main trade routes from the Latin principalities in Syria and Palestine to the Byzantine Empire and the West. In such a situation it would seem quite possible that Isaac should issue coinage of his own, as much to emphasize his independence as to aid the economy of his island empire by providing a replacement for the regular supply of Constantinopolitan coinage, upon which the island had hitherto presumably been dependent, and of which it was now certainly deprived. There is evidence that the ancient copper mines of the island were still being worked, and the raw material therefore lay conveniently to hand.[2]

The temptation to assign coins to this usurper is, in fact, of comparatively long standing. Sabatier attributed a billon scyphate type to Isaac Comnenus,

[1] The circumstances of the usurpation of Isaac Comnenus are mentioned by Nicetas Choniates, who also gives an extremely hostile account of his reign; Bonn ed. pp. 376 ff., 443, 483 ff., 547. See also G. Hill, *A History of Cyprus* (Cambridge, 1940), 1, pp. 312 ff.

[2] The large-scale export of copper ore is mentioned by Idrisi, geographer to Roger II of Sicily (1130–54): ed. P. A. Jaubert, 2 (Paris, 1840), p. 130.

while Lambros assigned to him a whole series on the grounds that these types were found in Cyprus.[3] Wroth, however, considered that this series should be given to the Constantinopolitan Emperor Isaac II, Angelus, mainly on the grounds that its provenance was not proven as exclusively Cypriot.[4]

The only coin (that described and illustrated by Sabatier) accepted as belonging to Isaac Comnenus by all three authorities is clearly misattributed. Judging by the illustration (a line drawing), the type is as follows:

$$Obv. \quad \begin{matrix} O & \Theta\mathsf{E} \\ \Lambda & \Delta\mathsf{W} \\ \Gamma\mathsf{I} & \mathsf{P} \\ \mathsf{OC} & \mathsf{O} \\ & \mathsf{C} \end{matrix}$$

Full-length figure of Saint Theodore in short military tunic, breast-plate, and sagion; holds in left hand shield, resting on ground.

$$Rev. \quad \begin{matrix} \mathsf{IC} & \mathsf{O} \\ \Lambda\Lambda\mathsf{K} & \Delta\mathsf{OV} \\ \mathsf{IOC} & \mathsf{K}\Lambda \\ \Delta\mathsf{EC} & \mathsf{C} \\ \Pi\mathsf{O} & \end{matrix}$$

Full-length figure of an emperor in stemma, divitision, collar-piece, and jewelled loros of simplified type; holds in right hand labarum on long shaft, and in left, globus cruciger. The loros, as it drapes from the emperor's left arm is represented as a diamond-shaped length of cloth.

There are three specimens of what can only be this issue in the collection at Dumbarton Oaks (Pl. 35.9–11). The obverse type is the same as that illustrated by Sabatier, apart from small differences in the arrangement of the inscription. The reverse type is again the same as Sabatier's apart from the fact that the globus is surmounted by a patriarchal cross: the characteristic diamond form of the loros is present on one of the pieces. The reverse inscription of one specimen reads: $\begin{smallmatrix} \Delta\mathsf{E} & \Lambda\Lambda \\ \mathsf{H} & \mathsf{C} \\ \mathsf{C} & \mathsf{K} \\ & \mathsf{C} \end{smallmatrix}$, another: $\begin{smallmatrix} \mathsf{W} & \mathsf{O} \\ \mathsf{OC} & \mathsf{K} \end{smallmatrix}$, the remaining: $\begin{smallmatrix} \Theta & \Pi\mathsf{O} \\ \mathsf{E} & \mathsf{H} \\ \mathsf{W} & \mathsf{C} \\ \mathsf{POC} & \\ \mathsf{C} & \end{smallmatrix}$. The only possible conclusion is that the type is an issue of Theodore II, Ducas-Lascaris, emperor of Nicaea (1254–58), and that the full inscription reads: ΘΕΟΔWΡΟC ΔΕCΠΟΤΗC Δ&ΚΛC O ΛΛCΚΛΡIC. It must therefore be supposed that Sabatier had before him a coin which, since it was badly double struck (as in the illustration), possessed an incomplete legend, and that in attempting a reconstruction, he read the POC of ΘΕΟΔWΡΟC as the IOC of ICΛΛΚIOC. The details common to the piece given by Sabatier and the Dumbarton Oaks specimens permit of no doubt that the same issue is involved.

---

[3] Sabatier, *Description générale*, 2, p. 227, no. 1; S. P. Lambros, Ἀνέκδοτα νομίσματα τοῦ μεσαιωνικοῦ βασιλείου τῆς Κύπρου, K. Sathas, *Mesaionike Bibliotheke*, 2 (Venice, 1873), pp. 547–96 (particularly pp. 561–63).

[4] Wroth, *BMC*, 2, pp. 597–98.

It should be noted, in addition, that there is no certain indication that Isaac of Cyprus used the surname "Ducas." The relevant portion of the genealogical table of the imperial families betrays the extent of our ignorance concerning the descent of Isaac Comnenus.[5]

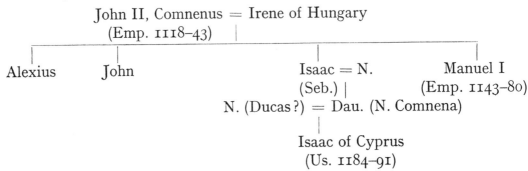

There are indications that close relatives of Isaac used the surname "Ducas" and it has been thought that it was a member of that family who married the unknown daughter of the Sebastocrator. What is more immediately important is that Nicetas Choniates, the main source of information on the usurper, refers to him as "Isaac Comnenus," and it is indeed highly probable that he would have preferred to use that illustrious name connecting him with the imperial family reigning continuously since 1081.

By far the commonest of the billon trachea generally attributed to Isaac II, Angelus is that on the reverse of which he is represented wearing stemma, divitision, collar-piece, and loros, holding a scepter cruciger and anexikakia (Pls. 20.9–13; 21.1–7). This type would certainly seem correctly assigned to the Constantinopolitan mint, for it continues the series of officina distinctions—such as the asterisk and the dot-within-circle—that had been utilized for the fourth coinage of Manuel I, and only temporarily abandoned under Andronicus I. This type appears in enormous numbers in hoards from the European provinces of the Empire.[6] Isaac Angelus has, however, had a large number of billon and copper types attributed to him, and among these there is to be found a small group of billon trachea and copper tetartera which, while themselves obviously related in fabric, style, and detail, are distinct from the Constantinopolitan types of Isaac, from those of his predecessors, and from those of his successor Alexius III. Furthermore, this group has strong connections with the island of Cyprus.

The first issues to be considered are two types of billon trachy (Pl. 19.6, 7; 8–10), and two types of copper tetartera (Pl. 19.12, 13, 14). All are among those stated by Lambros to be found in Cyprus. Wroth's objection to their

[5] C. Du Cange, *Historia Byzantina Duplici Commentario Illustrata: Familiae Byzantinae* (Paris, 1680), pp. 183–84; Hill, *op. cit.*, I, p. 312.

[6] Chap. 10.

not having been proven of exclusive Cypriot provenance is already greatly weakened, for it can now be stated without qualification that these types do not appear in hoards from the European territories of the Empire in the proportions which might be expected were they to have been issued either in the capital or in the western provinces.

The two types of billon trachy are certainly not metropolitan, for they lack the characteristic officina distinctions, and are of a broad, rounded, gently scyphate fabric which is totally different from the smaller, more irregular, deeper products of the capital. To these differences are added points of style and detail. In all four types in question, the stemma is represented in a characteristic fashion—a curved row of globules, frequently enclosed within a strong linear border; the pendilia are frequently of the form ↓.↓; the beard is short and rounded, represented by a characteristic, deeply cut border from ear to ear. In the case of metropolitan issues, the stemma is rendered merely by a line of dots; the pendilia at this period are of the form ↑↑ —even in the case of gold and electrum; the beard is longer and pointed, represented by a series of short strokes, never deeply etched. The most characteristic feature of the standing, full-length figure type in billon is that it occupies almost the entire field—repeated in an electrum type soon to be described: the imperial figure of the Constantinopolitan issues, on the other hand, is far less dominant.

The only imperial mints in the European provinces were Thessalonica, and the unidentified Greek mint which copied its current types. Both, however, were marked by their production of copper tetartera and half-tetartera— rarely billon trachea: moreover, the two tetarteron types under discussion bear no relation to the substantive Thessalonican issue of Isaac Angelus (Pl. 21.*10*, *11*). Nor do appreciable numbers of either scyphates or tetartera occur at Athens and Corinth: at Athens, three specimens of the billon scyphate (Pl. 19.*6*, *7*), and two of the copper tetarteron (Pl. 19.*12*);[7] at Corinth, one specimen of the billon scyphate (Pl. 19.*8–10*).[8]

There exists a further group of two types, a billon trachy and a tetarteron, that necessarily enter the discussion.

D. Cox, in her report on the coins found in the excavations at Curium in Cyprus, published a copper tetarteron of an Emperor Isaac.[9] The type had, in fact, already been published by F. Warren in 1892,[10] as an issue of Isaac of Cyprus, from a coin which was again of presumable Cypriot origin. The reverse type portrays a full-length figure of an Emperor Isaac, standing on a dais,

---

[7] Thompson, *The Athenian Agora*, p. 75.

[8] Edwards, *Corinth*, p. 147.

[9] D. H. Cox, *Coins from the Excavations at Curium, 1932–1953*, A.N.S. Numismatic Notes and Monographs, no. 145 (New York, 1959), p. 124, no. 731 (pl. x.).

[10] F. Warren, "Notes on Some Mediaeval Coins of Cyprus," *NC*³, 12 (1892), p. 209, no. 1 (pl. XVII, 1).

wearing stemma, divitision, and chlamys, holding in his right hand a cross on a long shaft, and in his left, a globus cruciger (Pl. 19.*15*).

There is, in the collection of the American Numismatic Society at New York, what appears to be a small hoard of billon scyphates, judging from the common patina and state of preservation. It consists of nine specimens of the scyphate type illustrated on Plate 19.*6, 7*; four specimens of Plate 19.*8–10*, and two specimens of an otherwise unpublished type featuring as the reverse type a full-length figure of an Emperor Isaac standing on a dais, wearing stemma, divitision, and chlamys, holding in his right hand a cross on a long shaft, and in his left, a globus cruciger (Pl. 19.*11*).

The figure of an emperor standing on a dais is, outside the tetarteron type published by Cox and Warren and the scyphate of the hoard, almost unknown in twelfth-century Byzantine numismatic iconography; so is the cross on long shaft. There is no doubt, on examination of the two types, that they are the issue of the same mint.

The hoard itself originally formed part of the collection of G. C. Gunther, the major part of which is known to have been collected in Cyprus. It should be noted, in addition, that one piece of this series from the British Museum Collection also came from Cyprus.[11] It might be pointed out that specimens of the undoubted Constantinopolitan type also occur in the island; but, whereas they appear elsewhere in large numbers, the types under discussion evidently do not. A provisional attribution to Isaac Comnenus is therefore called for.

The larger of the two groups assigned to Isaac Comnenus—that comprising the two billon scyphates and the two copper tetartera—is increased by the existence of a related type, theoretically, at least, in electrum. This was published in 1945 by Goodacre,[12] who evidently considered his specimen unique, although the type was among those previously mentioned by Lambros. All the characteristics of the remainder of the group are present: the form of the stemma, the pendilia, and the beard (Pl. 19.5).

The apparent division of this series into two groups, so obviously related among themselves, encourages the suspicion that there were two mints at work. This need not be excessive; although of several types the issues of each group are rare, some extremely so, and it may well be that this reflects the small nature of the original output.

As to the identity of the two mints, it would seem likely that the larger group should be assigned to the chief city, Levkosia (Nicosia).[13] The second and smaller group, in this case, might well have been issued from Limassol or Famagusta—but this suggestion rests on nothing more than general likelihood.

[11] Wroth, *BMC*, 2, p. 594, no. 34.

[12] H. Goodacre, "Notes on Some Byzantine Coins," *NC*[6], 5 (1945), p. 39, no. 10 (pl. VIII, 10); Lambros, Ἀνέκδοτα, p. 561.

[13] Hill, *op. cit.*, 1, pp. 263 ff.

CHAPTER NINE

THE ANGELI AND DUCAE

(i)

THE COINAGE OF ISAAC II, ANGELUS
1185–1195

A/ HYPERPYRON

MINT OF CONSTANTINOPLE

Obv. M̅P̅ Θ̅V̅ in upper field.

Virgin nimbate, wearing tunic and maphorion, seated upon throne with back; holds beardless, nimbate head of Christ on breast.

Rev. ICΛΛKIOCΔEC $\begin{smallmatrix}X\\\Lambda P\end{smallmatrix}$ $\begin{smallmatrix}X\\MI\end{smallmatrix}$ or $\begin{smallmatrix}\odot\\X\\M\end{smallmatrix}$ or var.

Full-length figure of emperor on left, and of Archangel Michael, beardless and nimbate, holding between them partially sheathed sword, point downward. Emperor wears stemma, divitision, collar-piece, and jewelled loros of simplified type; holds in right hand scepter cruciger. Archangel wears short military tunic, breastplate, and sagion. *Manus Dei* in upper center field.

Two main varieties:

Var. A
Rev.
Collar-piece has three jewels ⬬.

Pl. 20.*1, 2*

Var. B
Rev.
Collar-piece has six to eight jewels.

Pl. 20.*3, 4*

EL. ASPRON TRACHY

MINT OF CONSTANTINOPLE

Obv. M̅P̅ Θ̅V̅ in upper field.

Virgin nimbate, wearing tunic and maphorion, seated upon throne with back; holds beardless, nimbate head of Christ on breast.

Rev. ICΛΛKIOCΔЄC   ⊙   or   X
                  X   ΛP   X   – or var.
                  M   MI

Full-length figure of emperor on left, crowned by Archangel Michael, beardless and nimbate. Emperor wears stemma, divitision, and chlamys; holds in right hand scepter cruciger, and in left, anexikakia. Archangel wears short military tunic, breastplate, and sagion; holds jewelled scepter in left hand.

Two main varieties:

Var. A
Rev.
Portion of chlamys-border forming collar has three jewels.

Pl. 20.5, *6*

Var. B
Rev.
Portion of chlamys-border forming collar has six to eight jewels.

Pl. 20.7, *8*

BILL. ASPRON TRACHY

MINT OF CONSTANTINOPLE

Obv. M̅P̅ Θ̅V̅ in upper field.

Virgin nimbate, wearing tunic and maphorion, seated upon throne with back; holds beardless, nimbate head of Christ on breast.

Rev. ICΛΛKIOC ΔЄCΠΟΤΗC in two columnar groups.

Full-length figure of emperor wearing stemma, divitision, collar-piece, jewelled loros of simplified type, and sagion; holds in right hand scepter cruciger, and in left, anexikakia. *Manus Dei* in upper right field.

Four main varieties:

Var. A
Rev.
Collar-piece has three jewels ⌣; loros waist ⊠ or ⊡ .

Pl. 20.9–*11*

Var. B
Rev.
Collar-piece has six to eight jewels; loros waist ⊠ or ⊡ .

Pl. 20.*12, 13*

Var. C
   Rev.

Collar-piece has six to eight jewels; asterisk on sagion hanging from emperor's right arm, or on Virgin's throne, one to each side; loros waist ⊡.

Pl. *21.1–4*

Var. D
   Rev.

Collar-piece has six to eight jewels; loros waist ⊚.

Pl. *21.5–7*

Æ Tetarteron

MINT OF CONSTANTINOPLE

Obv. M͞P Θ͞V in upper field.

Full-length figure of Virgin nimbate, orans, sometimes standing on dais, wearing tunic and maphorion; beardless, nimbate head of Christ on breast.

Rev. ICΛΛΚΙΟC ΔЄCΠΟΤΗC in two columnar groups.

Full-length figure of emperor wearing stemma, divitision, and chlamys; holds in right hand scepter cruciger, and in left, anexikakia. *Manus Dei* in upper right field.

Pl. *21.8, 9*

MINT OF THESSALONICA

Obv.
     O
  X̄   X̄   – or var., in field.
  ΛΡ ΜΙ

Bust of Archangel Michael, beardless and nimbate, wearing divitision, collar-piece, and jewelled loros of simplified type; holds in right hand jewelled scepter, or spear, and in left, globus cruciger.

Rev. ICΛΛΚΙΟC ΔЄCΠΟΤΗC in two columnar groups.

Bust of emperor wearing stemma, divitision, collar-piece, and jewelled loros of simplified type; holds in right hand scepter cruciger, and in left, anexikakia.

Pl. *21.10, 11*

THE COINAGE OF ISAAC II: COMMENTARY

N Hyperpyron

Specimens occasionally have the loros-waist form ⊠ rather than the much commoner ⊡. These are probably of an early stage in the production of the

10

issue, since it is the first form that is standard during the reign of Andronicus I.[1] Rare specimens have a vertical, columnar inscription, the emperor holding a labarum-headed scepter rather than a scepter cruciger.

Æ TETARTERON

The type assigned to the metropolitan mint does not occur in appreciable numbers from the excavations at either Athens or Corinth; that assigned to Thessalonica, on the other hand, is relatively common at both sites:[2]

	Athens	Corinth
Metropolitan type	2	0
Thessalonican type	144	25

The sack of the city in 1185 by the Normans apparently, therefore, had no appreciable, long-term effect upon its production of coin.

It is uncertain, on the basis of the evidence at present available, whether the mint of uncertain Greek location—producing half-tetartera and following the current Thessalonican type—continued in production into this reign. Since the only half-tetartera of the succeeding emperor, Alexius III, are of types differing from his Thessalonican tetarteron (a trait noticed under John II and Manuel I for this mint), it would appear that the Greek mint was dismantled during either the reign of Isaac or that of Alexius.

[1] One specimen from the British Museum Collection which has the loros-waist form ⊠ depicts Isaac with a forked beard (Wroth, *BMC*, 2, p. 589, no. 3 [pl. LXXI, 17]). This, as is well known, is a characteristic of the preceding Emperor Andronicus, and what must be an engraver's error therefore tends to confirm an early date for these coins; it is hardly likely that such an error would have occurred once the new coinage was well under way.

[2] Thompson, *The Athenian Agora*, p. 75; Edwards, *Corinth*, p. 147.

(ii)

COINAGE OF UNCERTAIN ATTRIBUTION BETWEEN ISAAC ANGELUS OF CONSTANTINOPLE AND ISAAC COMNENUS OF CYPRUS

BILL. ASPRON TRACHY

Obv.
```
ĪC  X̄C
 E   N
 M   ४
 M   H
 Λ   Λ
```

Christ Emmanuel, beardless and nimbate, wearing tunic and colobion, seated upon throne with back; right hand raised in benediction, in left, holds scroll.

Rev. ICΛΛΚΙΟC ΔΕCΠΟΤ

Full-length figure of emperor wearing stemma, divitision, collar-piece, jewelled loros of simplified type, and sagion; holds in right hand scepter cruciger, and in left, anexikakia.

Pl. 21.*12*

Æ TETARTERON

Type A

Obv. EMMΛ N४HΛ – or var. ĪC X̄C in upper field.

Christ Emmanuel, beardless and nimbate, wearing tunic and colobion, seated upon throne with back; right hand raised in benediction, in left, holds scroll.

Rev. ICΛΛΚΙΟC ΔΕCΠΟΤΙC – or var. M̄P̄ in upper field.

Full-length figure of emperor on left, crowned by Virgin nimbate. Emperor wears stemma, divitision, collar-piece, and jewelled loros of simplified type; holds in right hand scepter cruciger, and in left, anexikakia. Virgin wears tunic and maphorion.

Pl. 21.*13*

Type B

Obv. EMMΛ N४HΛ – or var. ĪC X̄C in upper field.

Christ Emmanuel, beardless and nimbate, wearing tunic and colobion, seated upon throne with back; right hand raised in benediction, in left, holds scroll.

Rev. Uncertain inscription.
Full-length figure of emperor on right, crowned by nimbate figure of uncertain identity. Emperor wears stemma, divitision, collar-piece, and jewelled loros of simplified type; holds in right hand anexikakia, and in left, scepter cruciger.

Pl. 21.*14*

THE COINAGE OF UNCERTAIN ISAAC ATTRIBUTION: COMMENTARY

The billon trachy and the tetarteron types A[1] and B are obviously related by the detail and style of their obverse type. The only known exact provenance for any of these issues is for the tetarteron type B—one of which came from the excavations at Curium[2] (Cyprus), as did one of the types attributed above to Isaac Comnenus (secondary mint, tetarteron type). This is quite possibly a significant provenance, for none of these three types occurred in the excavations at Athens or Corinth and they are therefore not obvious candidates for a Thessalonican/Greek attribution. They do not, in fact, bear any clear relation to either the metropolitan or the Thessalonican series of Isaac Angelus. Were they eventually to be attributed to Isaac Comnenus, his reign would take on a numismatic character of its own: two or possibly three mints in a relatively limited area, each putting out a varied coinage of small volume, the products of each mint being marked by their own characteristic features of iconography or technique. However, any final attribution will depend on further examples and provenances.

[1] For the fullest reverse inscription known for this type, see P. D. Whitting, "A Bronze of Isaac II," *Numismatic Circular*, 60 (1952), p. 512.

[2] Cox, *Coins from the Excavations at Curium*, p. 124, no. 732 (pl. x). It should also be noted that the billon trachy and tetarteron type A are among those said by Lambros to be found in Cyprus (p. 139, note 3). The specimen illustrated here (Pl. 21.*13*) also has a Cypriot provenance.

THE COINAGE OF THEODORE MANGAPHAS, USURPER IN PHILADELPHIA

1189–1190; c. 1204–c. 1208

Stated by Nicetas Choniates to have struck "silver" coins in his own name.[1] No coins are at present attributable to this short-lived usurper, however, for the billon trachy published by H. W. Bell[2] is quite clearly a piece of Theodore II, Ducas-Lascaris, emperor of Nicaea (1254–58). The right-hand columnar inscription reads:
$$\begin{matrix} & O & \\ & \Delta \forall & \\ & K\Lambda & \\ & C\Lambda\Lambda & \\ & CK & \end{matrix}$$
. There is no evidence whatsoever that Theodore Mangaphas either possessed, or assumed the surname "Ducas." The B to either side of the standing Christ on the obverse is, in addition, typical of the later Nicaean and the Palaeologan coinage. The issue is illustrated here (Pl. 35.6).

The short duration of Theodore's first usurpation may be gauged from the fact that the *Historia de Expeditione Friderici* reports that the absence of Isaac Angelus from Constantinople on campaign against the rebel was announced to the crusading German Emperor Frederick Barbarossa by an emissary of the king of Hungary between July 11 and July 27, 1189.[3] However, the same source mentions that when the crusaders reached Philadelphia—the scene of rebellion—on April 18, 1190, they were met by a *dux* under imperial Byzantine orders, a sure sign that the rebellion was over by then.[4] Since the Hungarian report clearly concerned a relatively new state of affairs, and since Choniates reports that Isaac set out against Mangaphas without delay,[5] it appears that the entire affair cannot have much exceeded a year.

Assuming that the second usurpation began soon after the Latin conquest of April 1204, it must have ended shortly after the coronation of Theodore Lascaris in 1208, for Acropolites gives the impression that suppressing his rivals was Theodore's main subsequent task, which he promptly achieved.[6]

---

[1] Choniates; Bonn ed., p. 522: ... καὶ ἀργύρεον κέκοφε νόμισμα τὴν οἰκείαν ἐγχαράξας ἐν αὐτῷ στήλην. Presumably his coinage conformed to the Byzantine pattern; so electrum or billon trachea should be involved.

[2] H. W. Bell, *Sardis*, 11, pt. 1, *Coins* (Leiden, 1916), p. 104, no. 964 (pl. 2).

[3] *Historia de Expeditione Friderici*, ed. Chroust, pp. 28–30.

[4] *Ibid.*, p. 73.

[5] Choniates; Bonn ed., p. 522.

[6] George Acropolites; Bonn ed., pp. 13–14.

(iv)

THE COINAGE OF ALEXIUS III, ANGELUS-COMNENUS
1195–1203

N̸ HYPERPYRON

MINT OF CONSTANTINOPLE

Obv.

Full-length figure of Christ, bearded and nimbate, standing on dais, wearing tunic and colobion; holds Gospels in left hand.

Rev.

Full-length figure of emperor on left, and of St. Constantine nimbate, holding between them patriarchal cross on long shaft. Emperor wears stemma, divitision, and chlamys; holds anexikakia in right hand. Saint wears stemma, divitision, collar-piece, and jewelled loros of simplified type.

Two main varieties:

Var. I

   Obv. ĪC̄ X̄C̄ in field.

   Rev. ΛΛΕΞΙΟCΔΕCΠ Ο ΚѠΝΤΑΝΤΙ – or var.

Pl. 22.*1, 2*

Var. II

   Obv. +K̄ERO ΟΘΗΙ ĪC̄ X̄C̄ – or var. in field.

   Rev. ΛΛΕΞΙѠΔΕCΠ K̄ΕΙΟ TѠKOMΝͰNѠ – or var.

Pl. 22.*3*

EL. ASPRON TRACHY

MINT OF CONSTANTINOPLE

Obv. +K̄ERO HΘEI. ĪC̄ X̄C̄ in field.

Christ, bearded and nimbate, wearing tunic and colobion, seated upon throne without back; right hand raised in benediction, holds Gospels in left.

Rev.

Full-length figure of emperor on left and of St. Constantine nimbate, holding between them labarum—normally surmounting triangular decoration—on long shaft. Emperor and Saint wear stemma, divitision, collar-piece, and jewelled loros of simplified type; both hold scepter cruciger.

Two main varieties:

Var. I

Rev. ΛΛΕΞΙѠΔΕϹΠ Ο ΚѠΝΤΛΝΤΙ – or var.

Pl. 22.4

Var. II

Rev. ΛΛΕΞΙѠΔΕϹΠ ΚΕΙΟ ΤѠΚΟΜΝΗΝѠ – or var.

Pl. 22.5–7

BILL. ASPRON TRACHY

MINT OF CONSTANTINOPLE

Obv.

Beardless, nimbate bust of Christ, wearing tunic and colobion; holds scroll in left hand.

Rev.

Full-length figure of emperor on left, and of St. Constantine, nimbate, holding between them globus cruciger (rarely, globus surmounted by patriarchal cross). Emperor and Saint wear stemma, divitision, collar-piece, and jewelled loros of simplified type; both hold labarum-headed scepter.

Two main varieties:

Var. I

Obv. Ī͞C X͞C in field.
Rev. ΛΛΕΞΙΟϹΔΕϹΠ Ο ΚѠΝΤΛΝΤΙ – or var.

Pl. 22.8–12;
Var. II   Pl. 23.1–7
Obv. +K͞ΕRO HΘΕΙ. Ī͞C X͞C in field.

Rev. ΛΛΕΞΙѠΔΕϹΠ ΚΕΙΟ ΤѠΚΟΜΝΗΝѠ – or more rarely,

ΛΛΕΞΙѠΔΕϹΠ Ο ΚѠΝΤΛΝΤΙ

Æ Tetarteron

MINT OF CONSTANTINOPLE

Obv. M͞P Θ͞V in field.

Bust of Virgin nimbate, orans, wearing tunic and maphorion, turned to right. *Manus Dei* in upper right field.

Rev. ΛΛΕΖΙ ΔΕΣΠ

Bust of emperor wearing stemma, divitision, collar-piece, and panelled loros of simplified type; holds in right hand labarum-headed scepter, and in left, globus cruciger.

Pl. 23.8

MINT OF THESSALONICA

Obv. Θ ΓΙ
Γ͞Ε ΟC   – or var. in field.
Ϯ

Bust of St. George, beardless and nimbate, wearing tunic, breastplate, and sagion; holds spear in right hand, normally resting on left shoulder but in rare cases on the right, and in left hand (scroll?).

Rev. ΛΛΕΖΙΟC ΔΕCΠΟΤΗC – or var.

Full-length figure of emperor wearing stemma, divitision, and chlamys; holds in right hand labarum on long shaft, and in left, globus cruciger.

Pl. 23.9, 10

Æ Half-tetarteron

MINT OF THESSALONICA

Type I

Obv. Θ ΓΙ
Γ͞Ε ΟC   – or var., in field.
Ϯ

Bust of St. George, beardless and nimbate, wearing tunic, breastplate, and sagion; holds in right hand spear, over left shoulder, and in left hand (scroll?).

Rev. ΛΛΕΖΙ (or ΛΛΕΖΙШ) ΔΕΣΠ – or var.

Full-length figure of emperor wearing stemma, divitision, and chlamys; holds in right hand labarum on long shaft, and in left, globus cruciger. *Manus Dei* in upper right field.

Pl. 23.11, 12

Type II

Obv. Θ ΓΙ
Γ͞Ε ΟC   – or var., in field.
Ϯ

Bust of St. George, nimbate, wearing tunic, breastplate, and sagion; holds in right hand spear, and in left, shield.

Rev. ΛΛΕΞΙ (or ΛΛΕΞΙѠ) ΔΕCΠ, or ΛΛΕΞΙѠ ΤѠΚΟΜΝΗΝѠ – or var.
Full-length figure of emperor wearing stemma, divitision, and chlamys;
holds in right hand labarum on long shaft, and in left, globus surmounted
by patriarchal cross.

Pl. 23.13, 14

THE COINAGE OF ALEXIUS III: COMMENTARY

Ν´ HYPERPYRON

There are apparently two fairly distinct varieties within this issue. Var. I
has no inscription on the obverse other than Ī͞C X͞C, the reverse inscription
generally reading ΛΛΕΞΙΟCΔΕCΠ Θ ΚѠΝΤΑΝΤΙ. Var. II has the more elaborate
obverse inscription +K͞ERO HΘΕΙ, the reverse inscription therefore reading
ΛΛΕΞΙѠ; the name of the Saint is replaced, in this case, by the Emperor's
surname—ΤѠΚΟΜΝΗΝѠ. Var. I seems more often to have the more elaborate,
jewelled form of dais on the obverse, while var. II seems generally to have a
plain linear form. These distinctions are, however, not absolutely water-
tight: the form ΛΛΕΞΙѠ can evidently occur on var. I, while the more elaborate
form of dais is known for var. II.

Nicetas Choniates mentions the assumption of the surname "Comnenus"
by Alexius III[1]—to which he was not, in fact, entitled. It would appear
inherently more likely, in this case, that the fuller form of inscriptional
variety—the one with the surname—should form the later of the two; that
is, that the surname—which was evidently of some importance to him—
should appear on the later coins and remain, rather than on the early coins
and be dropped subsequently.

EL. ASPRON TRACHY

The two phases of inscription are less distinct for this denomination since
the obverse invocation +K͞ERO HΘΕΙ always occurs and the form ΛΛΕΞΙѠ is
therefore constant for the reverse. However, specimens do occur in which the
name Θ ΚѠΝΤΑΝΤΙ appears on the right rather than the surname ΤѠΚΟΜΝΗΝѠ,
and those former specimens are therefore probably the earlier.

There are no obvious officina distinctions for this denomination, but various
forms of the loros-waist occur: ⊠, ⊡, ◎. In addition, small devices such
as ∴ ∴, ⫶ ⫶, ✳ ✳, are occasionally to be found on the obverse directly
above the cushion of the throne. Their meaning, if any, is uncertain. A similar
series occurs on the debased hyperpyra of John III of Nicaea.[2]

---

[1] Nicetas Choniates; Bonn ed., p. 605. Confirmed by other documentary sources.
[2] Chap. 12, pp. 248–56.

Bill. Aspron Trachy

The billon trachy is, during this reign, the most difficult to understand of all the denominations. It was certainly the product of several officinae—probably four—but the official marks of distinction between them are by no means easy to discover, partly because the type is often ill struck. This degeneration of the standard of workmanship is probably to be connected with the rapidly decreasing value of the denomination during the last decade of the twelfth century—a trend apparent in documentary sources. There are evidently two phases, rather similar in character to those for the gold and electrum coinage. The first phase has no obverse inscription beyond ĪC XC and the reverse inscription ΛΛEΞIOCΔECΠ Θ KΨNϤΛNTI. The second is marked by the addition of the invocation +K͞ERO HΘEI to the obverse, and the reverse form ΛΛEΞIΨ, together with the dropping of the fuller form of the Saint's name in favor of TΨKOMΝͰNΨ.

Full discussion of the problems presented by this issue is reserved for the next Chapter.

Æ Tetarteron and Half-tetarteron

The metropolitan tetarteron type is presumably that with a bust of the Virgin as the obverse type, the Thessalonican that marked by a bust of St. George—a motif already used by that mint under Manuel and Andronicus. None of the metropolitan issue were found during the course of excavations at either Athens or Corinth: thirteen specimens of the Thessalonican series were found at Athens—although apparently none at Corinth.[3]

The practice of the Thessalonican mint in producing tetartera and half-tetartera of distinct types has already been noted, certainly for the reign of John II, and very probably for that of Manuel I. It has also been suggested that the tetarteron and half-tetarteron types were produced successively rather than simultaneously. Both observations seem confirmed by the coinage of Alexius III.

The Thessalonican series begins with an issue of tetartera: the obverse type is a nimbate bust of St. George holding in his right hand a spear which generally crosses over the body, resting on the left shoulder; in his left hand he holds what may be a scroll, a cross, or the hilt of a sword. The average weight of the twenty-one specimens in the collection at Dumbarton Oaks is 3.1 gm.—certainly a decrease in weight from the standard of the heavy tetartera of Manuel, but comparing not too unfavorably with those before and after that Emperor. The reverse inscription is normally ΛΛEΞIOC ΔECΠOTHC—although ΛΛEΞI and ΛΛEΞIΨ occur occasionally. The second issue was of half-tetarteron

---

[3] Thompson, *The Athenian Agora*, p. 75.

standard: the obverse type is the same as that for the tetarteron but the Manus Dei is added to the upper right field of the reverse in order to distinguish the denomination from the preceding issue. The average weight for the six specimens at Dumbarton Oaks is 1.5 gm. The reverse inscription is apparently ΛΛЄЗΙ (or ΛΛЄЗΙѠ) ΔЄСΠ. The third type was also a half-tetarteron; in this case, the obverse differs from both the first and the second in that St. George holds in his right hand a spear which rests on his right shoulder, and in his left hand, a shield. The Manus Dei on the reverse evidently disappears, but as a further distinction, the Emperor holds a globus surmounted by a patriarchal cross—rather than a plain cross—in his left hand. The average weight of the seven specimens at Dumbarton Oaks is 1.9 gm.—but whether this represents an official increase over the second issue is uncertain, the number of pieces involved and the difference between the two groups being too small. The reverse inscription reads ΛΛЄЗΙ (or ΛΛЄЗΙѠ) ΔЄСΠ, or ΛΛЄЗΙѠ ТѠ ΚΟΜΝΗΝѠ—or some minor variety.

It would seem possible, in consideration of the fact that two issues out of three had elapsed before the imperial surname was introduced, that the Thessalonican mint received the order for its inclusion at a distinctly later date than did the metropolitan.

(v)

ISAAC II, ANGELUS (RESTORED) WITH ALEXIUS IV, ANGELUS

1203–1204

No coins of this joint reign are known.

(vi)

ALEXIUS V, DUCAS

February–April 1204

No coins of this very short reign are known: that attributed to Alexius V by Sabatier (*Description générale*, 2, p. 231, no. 1 [pl. LVIII, 14]) is by detail and style a piece of the empire of Nicaea (see Pl. 34.*10*).

The election of Constantine Comnenus-Lascaris (brother of the future emperor Theodore) in the Great Church, after the entry of the Latins into the city and the flight of Alexius V, was never confirmed by formal coronation and cannot have produced a coinage. See: G. Ostrogorsky, *History of the Byzantine State*, trans. J. M. Hussey, 2nd ed. (Oxford, 1968), p. 428, note 2.

CHAPTER TEN

The Internal Organization of the Metropolitan Mint

In the catalogue of types given in the preceding chapters, a number of varieties have been attributed to many of the main issues. The inclusion of these varieties and the exclusion of others rest upon criteria the nature and importance of which remain as yet undiscussed.

One of the main problems remaining to be considered is whether any particular variation is of more or of less significance than another, or indeed of any significance at all: whether a collar-piece decorated with five jewels or with four, the presence or absence of a dot below the tablion, is of greater import than the form of the pendilia or of the globus cruciger. If, as a result of investigation, it is found that a particular form or variety is indeed of greater significance than another, it still remains to establish its precise nature and extent—an obvious question being whether any meaning was intended or whether it was the result of some factor in the production of the coin, or both.

Clearly, a solution is likely to be obtained only by the detailed examination of a large body of material, of the magnitude, in fact, that is provided only by hoard evidence. Fortunately this is entirely feasible for a limited number of issues—those in question being the ones identified below as the third and fourth coinages of billon trachea of the Emperor Manuel I, and the substantive types of the same denomination of Andronicus I and Isaac II.

The hoards presented here are mainly of Bulgarian provenance, the amount of material offered by that country being immense and continually increasing. The area within the present frontiers in which billon scyphate hoards mainly occur is dominated by three topographical features: the valley of the river Struma, the Thracian plain, and the plain of the river Danube. Evidence from the Struma region is of particular importance since it might be expected to reflect any influences otherwise confined to Greece—providing, as it did, one of the main routes between Greece and the inner Balkans. Similarly, the Thracian plain was the main land route between Constantinople and the West. It is obviously important that these areas be represented in the body of evidence, and, on the other hand, that the Bulgarian evidence in general should be measured against any that might be available from other regions that originally formed part of the Empire. Provided that these conditions are observed any disproportion resulting from unequal amounts of regional evidence can be, if not avoided, then reasonably evaluated.

The composition of the Bulgarian hoards containing large numbers of the coins under discussion (to the death of Manuel) is given in Table I below.

TABLE I

Hoard, and Date of Discovery		JOHN II		MANUEL I			
		1st Coinage	2nd Coinage	1st Coinage	2nd Coinage	3rd Coinage	4th Coinage
Batkoun	1937	—	—	—	—	637	1051
Belitsa	1938	1	9	12	—	28	47
Draganovo	1957	—	—	—	—	245	444
Enina	1951/2	—	—	—	—	62	91
General Nikolaevo	1960	—	—	—	1	245	368
Gradevo (I)	1936	—	2	—	—	16	71
Kaloyanovets	1960	—	1	—	1	202	367
Kroushare	1962	—	—	—	3	112	148
Loukovo	(?)	—	144	77	8	74	204
Novo Selo	1958	—	—	—	—	252	367
Ovchartsi	1958	—	—	3	2	201	379
Souvatité	1934	—	7	—	24	52	290
Tiurkmen (II)	1959	—	—	—	—	37	60
Tsruncha (A & B)	1963	—	—	—	—	38	66
Turnovo (I)	(?)	—	—	—	—	18	28
Yagoda	1962	—	1	—	1	109	160
Zlataritsa	1910	—	—	—	—	125	311

The provenances of these hoards are fully representative of all the major areas of the country in which hoards are normally found: Belitsa and Gradevo are in the Struma region; Loukovo is at the extreme western end of the Thracian plain; Batkoun, General Nikolaevo, Novo Selo, Tiurkmen, and Tsruncha are in the central southern Thracian plain, and Enina, Kaloyanovets, Kroushare, Ovchartsi, and Yagoda in the central northern part or in the Sredna Gora; Draganovo, Turnovo, and Zlataritsa are in the Danube plain; Souvatité is near the western coast of the Black Sea.[1]

A necessary preliminary to the discussion is the establishment of the correct sequence of the four coinages of Manuel I.

One striking feature of the Table is the constant appearance in large numbers of two types of Manuel, in contrast to the virtual exclusion of two others, and of the entire coinage of John II. Admittedly, hoards buried subsequent to the death of Manuel—as all these were, for they contain coins of Andronicus I— might be expected to contain a concentration of the types struck toward the end of his reign, together with fewer of his earlier types and even smaller numbers of the coins of his predecessors. Even if the two issues which are best

[1] It is unfortunately not possible to give a page reference for each of the many hoards used in this Chapter. The contents of each are listed alphabetically, according to the place of finding, in Chapter 15.

represented are considered as the last two coinages, however, this will not in itself explain the sudden and, to all intents and purposes, consistent exclusion of the preceding issues.

An obvious suggestion is that this feature is caused by geographical factors—that the coinages which do not occur in Bulgaria were struck specifically for use in other regions of the Empire. The evidence, however, is uniformly contrary. Both types of John II are rare—although the second coinage is less so than the first. Now, one of the rare issues of Manuel portrays the Emperor as beardless. Since this is not an isolated example, for the same portrait is found on the electrum trachy and on the tetarteron and half-tetarteron coinages of both the mint of Constantinople and of Thessalonica, the issue must be regarded as the first issue of the reign rather than as struck for a specific area: the reason for this characteristic pattern in the analysis of the hoards is apparently therefore chronological, not geographical.

Confirmation of this very pattern comes from three further hoards of similar type, but different provenance. The Obuda (Hungary) hoard contained 24 and 388 specimens of the types identified below as the third and fourth coinages respectively of Manuel, to the exclusion of the two remaining types of that Emperor and of both metropolitan types of John. The Zlata (Yugoslavia) hoard appears to have been of similar composition—although containing small numbers of the type identified below as the second coinage of Manuel. The Istanbul (A) hoard of 1946 included only 6 specimens of the type identified below as the second coinage of John, and 3 of the first coinage of Manuel—as opposed to 68 and 95 specimens of the two types which are common in Bulgarian hoards. The only hoards which fundamentally contradict this pattern are that from Loukovo and the Nicosia parcel: the latter containing 13 specimens of John's first coinage and 169 of his second, 80 specimens of Manuel's first coinage, 18 of his second, 11 of his third and 15 of his fourth.

On the other hand, there are strong reasons for suspecting that the early coinages of billon trachy were at some stage not so rare as might appear at first sight: hoards containing them do occur, but, significantly, not in conjunction with the later types. The hoard from Bounardzhik (Plovdiv) and the Suedinenie hoard of 1955 (both from Bulgaria), the Lazania hoard of 1938/39 from Cyprus and the Macedonian hoard of 1959 mentioned by Metcalf, are all of this early pattern; none contain issues later than the first coinage of Manuel.

The gold coinage apparently remained unaffected by whatever factors caused this phenomenon: the hoards of Gornoslav and Zgurli (1903) contained large numbers of early coins as well as late; the Corinth hoard contained all the varieties of Manuel's hyperpyron type—and thus presumably included both early and late coins of this issue.

It would therefore seem reasonable to assume that some factor other than the mere passage of time (or the production of coins for particular regions of the Empire) was responsible for a premature and almost total disappearance from the circulating medium of the billon trachea of the emperors prior to Manuel and even of certain issues of that Emperor himself.

It has already been pointed out that in 1136, toward the end of the reign of John II, the billon aspron trachy was worth $1/_{48}$ hyperpyron. In 1190, during the reign of Isaac II, on the other hand, it was worth $1/_{120}$ hyperpyron.[2] The large difference between the two values can be adequately explained only by a form of revaluation or debasement incurred by the denomination at some period between the two dates. The actual form taken by the reference of 1190 confirms this hypothesis: ... *nulla differentia existente inter nova et vetera stamina*. The occurrence of the descriptions "old" and "new" in reference to the precious metal denominations probably results from the practice of giving freshly minted coins a slight premium over older, worn coins. This usage could hardly apply to a denomination of relatively low value, the silver content of which would seem to have been 6 per cent or less. In 1190, therefore, *nova stamina* can only have been billon trachea of a new and lower value, the *vetera stamina* those of an old and higher one.

Now, Nicetas Choniates makes the interesting comment that the Emperor Manuel put adulterated silver into the nomismata which were given to the crusaders of 1147.[3] It is by no means clear what Choniates is attempting to say, but if the statement is at all accurate, he cannot have been referring to the hyperpyron, which contained only a small amount of silver in any case. There remain the electrum and the billon trachea. There is, in fact, no evidence in the table of specific gravity determinations that either the gold or electrum suffered any debasement during the reign. The billon coinage was, however, certainly silver (aspron) in color, and, to a certain extent in content. Choniates can only therefore have been referring to the billon—precisely the denomination for which there is evidence of a debasement or revaluation during the period 1136–1190. That Manuel put adulterated silver into the nomisma (the billon trachy nomisma) must therefore be a chronologically blundered reference to the lowering of the silver content of the billon alloy.

The application of this fact to the phenomenon noticed in the table of Bulgarian hoards and confirmed by evidence from Constantinople and elsewhere, is immediately obvious. The two issues of Manuel, ill represented in these hoards, together with the billon coinage of this Emperor's predecessors,

---

[2] Chap. 3, pp. 20, 21.

[3] *Ibid.*, p. 22. The case for the identification of Manuel's adulterated nomisma with the billon trachy, as argued below, is strengthened by the fact that it was the exchange-rate of precisely this denomination that, according to Odo of Deuil, caused such discontent in 1147 (Chap. 3, p. 21).

are to be identified as the *vetera stamina* of implied higher value, while the two issues of Manuel which are common in these same hoards, together with the billon coinage of his successors, are to be considered the *nova stamina* of reduced value. A discussion of whether the change occurred as a result of an illegal debasement which was followed some time later, perhaps by force of circumstances, by an official reduction in the value of the trachy, or whether the decision to alter the silver content was a publicly implemented decision, probably accompanied by a governmental attempt to call in the old coins, must be reserved for the moment. In either case the result would be superficially similar; in the first, as a result of the operation of Gresham's law, the older coins—of higher value—would tend to disappear from circulation in favor of the newer coins of lower intrinsic, but equal official value; in the second, the same coins would disappear as the result of official governmental action.

The identity of the first two coinages of Manuel would now seem clearly established. The first coinage is undoubtedly that on which he is represented as beardless and the second must be that issue which similarly appears to a minimal extent in hoards containing slightly later coins. The relative order of the other two issues—forming the third and fourth coinages—is uncertain, but on the basis of the uniform pattern of the coin hoards of the type used above, there is an obvious prima facie case for considering the issue which

TABLE II

Hoard	Region	Manuel I, Third Coinage, Total	Total identifiable as to Variety	✚	✚
Belitsa	Struma	28	19	14 (74%)	5 (26%)
Gradevo (I)	valley	16	10	7 (70%)	3 (30%)
Batkoun		223/637 sample	92	58 (63%)	34 (37%)
General Nikolaevo	Southern central	245	135	122 (90%)	13 (10%)
Novo Selo	Thracian plain	252	133	116 (87%)	17 (13%)
Tiurkmen (II)		37	36	26 (72%)	10 (28%)
Tsruncha (A & B)		38	31	21 (68%)	10 (32%)
Enina		62	56	47 (84%)	9 (16%)
Kaloyanovets	Northern central	202	178	140 (79%)	38 (21%)
Kroushare	Thracian plain	112	107	79 (74%)	28 (26%)
Ovchartsi	and Sredna Gora	201	130	76 (58%)	54 (42%)
Yagoda		109	105	77 (73%)	28 (27%)
Draganovo		245	182	128 (70%)	54 (30%)
Turnovo (I)	Danube plain	18	16	9 (56%)	7 (44%)
Zlataritsa		125	95	76 (80%)	19 (20%)
Loukovo	Western Thracian plain	74	54	47 (87%)	7 (13%)
Souvatité	Black Sea coast	52	47	36 (77%)	11 (23%)

11

consistently appears in the greater number as the fourth coinage, and that which appears in large numbers, but which does not normally exceed the other, as the third.

The issue provisionally identified as the third coinage of Manuel quite clearly divides into two main varieties. On the one, the Emperor of the reverse type holds a globus surmounted by a patriarchal cross in his left hand; on the other he holds a globus surmounted by a single-barred cross. Both occur in all major Bulgarian hoards containing the billon issues of the Emperor Manuel; see Table II on page 161.

There is no significant regional variation. The Istanbul (A) hoard reportedly contained only two specimens of the single-barred cross variety out of sixty-eight of the general type. This could, however, quite easily result from the variety not being an expected one, no detailed search therefore having been made for specimens of this description.

The most noticeable variation in the detail of the patriarchal cross variety is in the shaft of the labarum in the Emperor's right hand; this is sometimes plain, sometimes having a single dot, very rarely having two dots (Table III, *infra*):

TABLE III

Hoard	Total identifiable as to Sub-variety	Plain Shaft (A)	1 Dot on Shaft (B)	2 Dots on Shaft (C)
Batkoun	49	18	31	—
Belitsa	11	6	5	—
Draganovo	118	47	71	—
Enina	not counted	—	—	—
General Nikolaevo	not counted	—	—	—
Gradevo (I)	5	2	3	—
Kaloyanovets	127	52	73	2
Kroushare	80	32	48	—
Loukovo	36	12	24	—
Novo Selo	(c. 90)	("slightly under $^1/_2$")	48	1
Ovchartsi	65	24	41	—
Souvatité	29	16	13	—
Tiurkmen (II)	not counted	—	—	—
Tsruncha (A & B)	not counted	—	—	—
Turnovo (I)	8	2	6	—
Yagoda	66	28	38	—
Zlataritsa	56	23	30	3

The sub-variety with the plain labarum shaft is apparently almost throughout exceeded to an appreciable, although not overwhelming, extent by the sub-variety with the single dot on the labarum. This pattern may well, however, have been influenced by the fact that it is easier to establish the presence of the dot than the absence—for the lower portion of the shaft is often incompletely struck. The actual proportions may therefore have been more nearly equal than might appear. The sub-variety with the two dots on the shaft is consistently scarce.

Also variable, and common to both varieties of the labarum shaft, is the form of the chlamys-border which acts as a collar. There are three sub-varieties:

(a) ⌣—with six to eight jewels; (b) ⌣—with three jewels; (c) ⌐—a completely different form. By far the commonest in all these hoards is (a); (b) however occurs in all, with no significant regional variation; (c) is extremely rare. It is possible that (b) is more often accompanied by the presence of a diagonal fold on the chlamys than is (a), but this, in view of the small number examined in detail, is uncertain.

However, in the case of the Draganovo and Kroushare hoards, a close examination of a further variation was made—the form of the tablion, which is either of the simple form (a) ▯ or of the more complicated (b) ▣. The results would seem to suggest a distinction in the frequency with which these forms were used in the two labarum shaft varieties:

Hoards	Plain shaft		Single dot on shaft	
	(a)	(b)	(a)	(b)
Draganovo	32	2	29	18
Kroushare	24	2	25	18

The simple form of tablion (a) occurs in both shaft varieties, but the use of (b) is overwhelmingly commoner in the variety having a single dot on the shaft. This fact should be kept in mind.

The scarcer variety of the third coinage, that in which the globus is surmounted by a single-barred cross, differs in one striking aspect in its sub-varieties from that in which the globus is surmounted by a patriarchal cross. There are no less than four sub-varieties in the form of the labarum shaft, which is either plain, or has a single dot, or two dots, or three dots; see Table IV on page 164.

Apart from the introduction of the sub-variety in which the labarum shaft has three dots, the proportions in which the other three sub-varieties occur are completely different from those established for the other globus variety. The sub-variety with a single dot on the shaft occurs much less frequently, appearing in nine out of thirteen hoards only: that with a plain shaft is even scarcer. On the other hand, the sub-varieties with two and three dots to the shaft are as dominant as the other two were in the variety in which the globus is surmounted by a patriarchal cross.

11*

TABLE IV

Hoard	Total identifiable as to Sub-variety	Plain Shaft (A)	1 Dot on Shaft (B)	2 Dots on Shaft (C)	3 Dots on Shaft (D)
Batkoun	15	2	2	5	6
Belitsa	3	—	—	—	3
Draganovo	36	2	4	16	14
Enina	not counted	—	—	—	—
General Nikolaevo	not counted	—	—	—	—
Gradevo (I)	2	—	—	1	1
Kaloyanovets	25	—	2	13	10
Kroushare	27	—	3	15	9
Loukovo	7	—	1	2	4
Novo Selo	13	—	3	5	5
Ovchartsi	38	6	7	13	12
Souvatité	7	—	—	—	7
Tiurkmen (II)	not counted	—	—	—	—
Tsruncha (A & B)	not counted	—	—	—	—
Turnovo (I)	6	—	1	1	4
Yagoda	21	3	3	6	9
Zlataritsa	11	—	—	4	7

The issue provisionally identified above as the fourth coinage appears in hoards from all the main regions of Bulgaria—in numbers always exceeding those of the third coinage. Examination of the same seventeen hoards as utilized above reveals a series of remarkably consistent varieties and sub-varieties:

The proportional occurrence of these sub-varieties in Bulgarian hoards is as given in Table V on page 166.

Although there are no straightforward and obvious trends in distribution, there may be some factor beyond coincidence in the tendency of var. C to be paired with var. D in any relatively violent perturbation of the normal pattern. In the Belitsa and Souvatité hoards, and possibly the Loukovo and Novo Selo hoards, C and D are both represented in proportions well below the norm, A and B predominating markedly. This might superficially appear something of a geographical pattern, for, with the notable exception of Souvatité, a southern and western distribution might be suggested. That the matter is not quite so simple is indicated by the fact that C, if not D, is also the predominant variety at Batkoun and General Nikolaevo as well as at Kroushare and Ovchartsi, and Draganovo and Zlataritsa. A, in addition, is common in all areas, even in the north, actually predominating at Enina and Yagoda.

The Istanbul (A) hoard reveals no marked characteristics in the proportional appearances of the varieties: of the ninety-four specimens of the fourth coinage, eighteen were of the form C (a) and fifteen of D (a)—the remaining sub-varieties of D not being mentioned. It is therefore unlikely that any variety predominated overwhelmingly.

The close internal relationship of the sub-varieties of A–D is conclusively illustrated by the results of a detailed examination of the coins in the Draganovo and Kroushare hoards, checked by the considerable body of independent material available in the collection at Dumbarton Oaks.

The exceptions to the varieties and sub-varieties enumerated above are minimal in their proportions, and are apparently confined to coins having two jewels, rather than one or three, above the waist of the loros (⊞). One specimen from the Draganovo hoard had the pendilia form ‖ which probably places it within the sub-variety A (c). There are four examples in the collection at Dumbarton Oaks: the first has the globus form ✛ and the loros form ▯—which again suffices to place it in the same sub-variety as above. The second has the form ▯ and is probably therefore to be included with B (a). The two others also have the obverse asterisks and are therefore certainly to be included with C (a).

It should be pointed out that it is not claimed that the figures given below for the three bodies of material in question are unarguably fixed: subjective estimation of whether the pendilia or globus take a particular form—often carried out in unfavorable conditions including bad light, relative haste, and the uncleaned state of the coins—precludes such minute accuracy. What is claimed, however, is that the pattern of the proportions is substantially correct; see Tables VI, VII, VIII at end of Chapter.

Even more minute variations do exist—for instance, many specimens of sub-varieties A (c), B (a), and C (a), have square jewels rather than round ones, particularly on the collar-piece, on the loros-waist, and above it. That these are without particular significance is demonstrated by the further

TABLE V

Hoard	Total present	Total identifiable	A (a)	A (b)	A (c)	A (total)	B (a)	B (b)	B (total)	C (a)	C (b)	C (c)	C (total)	D (a)	D (b)	D (c)	D (d)	D (total)
Batkoun	355/1051	144	3	5	15	(23)	36	—	(36)	61	—	—	(61)	20	4	—	—	(24)
Belitsa	47	36	5	4	12	(21)	9	—	(9)	4	—	—	(4)	2	—	—	—	(2)
Draganovo	444	373	22	26	49	(97)	92	—	(92)	121	—	—	(121)	43	11	6	3	(63)
Enina	91	89	5	2	26	(33)	18	—	(18)	22	—	—	(22)	10	5	—	1	(16)
General Nikolaevo	368	193	10	8	28	(46)	46	—	(46)	58	—	—	(58)	31	9	—	3	(43)
Gradevo (I)	71	55	6	6	14	(26)	16	2	(18)	9	—	—	(9)	2	—	—	—	(2)
Kaloyanovets	367	338	11	20	63	(94)	73	—	(73)	98	—	—	(98)	46	24	6	3	(73)
Kroushare	148	144	6	7	20	(33)	29	—	(29)	54	—	—	(54)	15	7	2	—	(28)
Loukovo	204	159	18	10	32	(60)	50	—	(50)	26	1	—	(27)	19	1	—	—	(22)
Novo Selo	367	207	6	16	41	(63)	71	1	(72)	30	10	3	(43)	15	9	—	5	(29)
Ovchartsi	379	267	3	8	36	(47)	59	—	(59)	111	—	—	(111)	33	17	—	—	(50)
Souvatité	290	206	26	30	42	(98)	66	2	(68)	22	—	—	(22)	11	7	—	—	(18)
Tiurkmen (II)	60	c. 60	1	1	c. 12	(c. 14)	c. 12	—	(c. 12)	15	5	—	(20)	11	2	1	—	(14)
Tsruncha (A & B)	66	54	1	2	9	(12)	13	—	(13)	20	—	—	(20)	6	3	—	—	(9)
Turnovo (I)	28	21	—	4	1	(5)	3	—	(3)	7	—	—	(7)	2	4	—	—	(6)
Yagoda	160	159	6	15	29	(50)	26	—	(26)	44	—	—	(44)	22	17	—	—	(39)
Zlataritsa	311	242	13	13	36	(62)	53	3	(56)	73	—	—	(73)	36	3	6	6	(51)

examination of the coins of variety C in the collection at Dumbarton Oaks. Of the thirty-eight specimens of C (a) and the four of C (b), the round-jewelled form occurs in seven cases, that having some square jewels in thirteen. A characteristic feature is, however, common to both: on all the pieces that are identifiable the legs of the throne take a double, linear form (⌐⌐ ⌐⌐).

Varieties A, B, and D, on the other hand, use the single dotted form (⌐ ⌐).[4] The homogeneity of the general variety C is therefore clearly established.

Varieties A (a), A (b), and A (c) are characterized by the use of three jewels above the loros-waist; five jewels below; five jewels on the loros as it drapes from the Emperor's left arm; the globus form ⚇; the pendilia form ⁙.

Varieties B (a) and B (b) are marked by the use of a collar-piece of three jewels; one jewel above the loros-waist; five, or less commonly three, below; the dominant use of three jewels on the loros hanging from the left arm.

Varieties C (a), C (b), and C (d) are marked by the use of the asterisk in its various forms (e.g., ＊, ＊, ＊, ＊, etc.); the consistent use of three jewels below the loros-waist; the dominant occurrence of two jewels on the loros draping from the left arm.

Varieties D (a), D (b), D (c), and D (d) are characterized by the employment of the motif of a jewel within a circle.

The almost universal limitation of this general type to the four varieties and their sub-divisions can be explained only by some factor in their production, since it was obviously at this stage that their characteristics were physically fixed. Furthermore, this factor must include the die-cutters who produced them. The main possibilities are limited: that each of the four varieties was the product of the die-cutter, or cutters, of a separate mint, or that it was the product of a die-cutter, or cutters, within a single mint.

The first possibility must be discarded: it has already been noted that there is no geographical variation of significance revealed in the Bulgarian and Istanbul (A) hoards. One of the four mints postulated would have to be that of the capital—the products of which might be expected to predominate in the eastern and northern hoards. Another would have to be Thessalonica, the products of which should show some signs of limitation to the Struma Valley and western hoards. There is no pattern of distribution capable of supporting either of these hypothetical attributions and the features in question must therefore be accommodated within the context of a single mint—which can hardly be other than the metropolitan.

The four major groups A–D are defined by the use of the particular motif of three jewels above the loros-waist (A); a single jewel above the loros-waist

---

[4] The author owes this obversation to Dr. D. M. Metcalf.

(B); an asterisk (C); a jewel within a circle (D). Within the groups marked by one or the other of these occur certain characteristics which, if not confined to one group, are nevertheless frequently peculiarly common in it. A vital example confirms the independence of B which is in many respects very similar to C and D, despite its lack of asterisk or jewel-within-circle. B is, however, the only group of the three in which the use of five jewels below the loros-waist is consistently dominant. This feature, certainly, is shared with A, but in almost every other minor characteristic the two are entirely different.

The main and invariable motif must have served some purpose, for its constant appearance and the peculiar dependence of the combination of minor characteristics upon it cannot be the result of mere coincidence. The clear function of the motif is, in fact, one of distinction, and there is no reason to suppose that its original purpose was otherwise. On this assumption the only reasonable explanation for these phenomena is that they were intended to distinguish the personnel of the mint involved either in the cutting of the dies, or the general manufacturing of the coins produced from them, or both. There are no apparent reasons, or certain precedents, for the production of dies the cutters of which were capable of formal identification by the use of obligatory and fixed peculiarities in their workmanship. On the more general plane, however, there are definite—if comparatively remote—precedents for the principle of the distinction of the separate administrative divisions or "officinae" of a single mint. On the occasion of several officinae producing the same denomination the establishment of fixed distinctions would enable a check to be kept upon the design, purity, and constant average weight of the products of each.

The conclusion therefore seems unavoidable that four officinae were involved in the production of the fourth coinage of billon trachea of Manuel I, and that each officina possessed a die-cutter or cutters who were more or less permanently attached to it and responsible for the manufacture of the dies of that officina and no other. Certain deliberate distinctions in the design of the dies ensured that any given coin could be traced to its origin. On the other hand, the relative isolation of the die-cutter(s) of a particular officina was also responsible for the evolution of a whole series of small techniques in representing the different elements of the total design which remained confined to—or at least predominant in—the products of that officina. The primary distinction was deliberate and of particular import: the secondary characteristics were the result of the pattern of organization which made the primary distinction necessary.

The significance of the variations in the form of the labarum shaft in the third coinage becomes immediately evident: if four officinae were responsible for the production of the fourth coinage, it would appear a reasonable expectation that the same should be true of the third. Precisely four sub-varieties do indeed occur within the variety of this coinage marked by having a globus surmounted by a single-barred cross. The labarum shaft is plain, has a single dot, or two dots, or three. The first two sub-varieties are commoner, the latter two distinctly scarcer.

The situation as revealed within the variety marked by a globus surmounted by a patriarchal cross is somewhat different. There exist three sub-varieties, in which the labarum shaft is plain, or has a single dot, or two dots. Coins of the last named sub-variety are, however, extremely rare; pieces on which the shaft has three dots apparently do not exist.

On the analogy of the fourth coinage this difference between the varieties should be expressed in terms of an increase in the number of officinae from three to four. In this case, the earlier of the two varieties should be that in which only two main sub-varieties, together with a less important third, are represented—in fact that with the globus surmounted by a patriarchal cross.

Examination of Manuel's second and first coinages of billon trachea tends to support this hypothesis, since both form two distinct varieties and therefore probably form the products of two officinae. As regards the second coinage, the distinction between the products of each officina apparently lies in the jewelling of the collar-piece. Of the thirty-seven specimens forming the total of the Dumbarton Oaks Collection and the readily identifiable pieces from Bulgarian hoards, in twelve cases the collar-piece was decorated with four jewels (var. A) and in twenty-five it was decorated with five jewels (var. B).

Moreover, while var. A utilizes two forms of the globus cruciger (,), var. B apparently utilizes only one ( ). For the first coinage—the one portraying the beardless imperial bust—the available figures are a little more impressive. Of the twenty-nine specimens from Dumbarton Oaks and Bulgarian hoards, fifteen have a plain shaft to the labarum held in the Emperor's right hand (var. A), while fourteen have two prominent dots on the shaft (var. B). Of the sixty-four identifiable specimens from the parcel of coins originating in a hoard found at Nicosia, forty-three have the plain shaft, twenty-one have the two dots. Again, in a fashion similar to the second coinage, the two officinae apparently tend to utilize different characteristics of detail, this time to be seen in the forms of the chlamys-border making up the collar, var. A favoring a decoration of three jewels, var. B of four jewels.

The commoner of the two metropolitan types of billon trachy of John II once more divides into two main varieties: var. A with a plain shaft to the Emperor's scepter cruciger, var. B with a transverse bar or flourish to the shaft. Of the twenty-one specimens in the collection at Dumbarton Oaks, ten have the plain shaft, eleven have the bar or flourish. Of the one hundred sixty-four identifiable specimens in the parcel from Nicosia which has been mentioned above, seventy have the plain shaft, ninety-four have the bar or flourish. As in the cases of the first and second coinages of Manuel, each officina has its own characteristic techniques: the collar-piece of the officina producing var. A tends to be decorated with six jewels, that of var. A with five jewels.

At this point, the sequence, having lasted over five coinages, peters out. This is possibly due to the fact that there are insufficient numbers of the remaining metropolitan type of John II and those of Alexius I to determine the distinctions, but more probably to the fact that the main coinage of John represents the first occasion on which two officinae were used for production. It is for this reason that it is identified here as the later of the two.

The major question proceeding from this identification is therefore to account for the increase in the number of officinae during the course of Manuel's third coinage from two to four. It would seem reasonable to suppose that the change must represent some degree of increase in the volume of production, for it is unlikely that new officinae were established, at least on a large scale, without cause.

The exclusion of the first and second coinages of Manuel's billon trachea in favor of his third and fourth, from the majority of hoards laid down only a few years after the end of the reign, has already been noted and connected with the major change in the value of the denomination (from $\frac{1}{48}$ to $\frac{1}{120}$ hyperpyron), for which there is documentary evidence as occurring between 1136 and 1190. There are two main possibilities regarding the nature of this change. It may have been the relatively long-term result of a fraudulent governmental decrease in the silver content of the denomination, followed by the loss of public confidence and a decline in the value at which it circulated once issued: by 1190, at least, this trend must have been officially confirmed and an attempt made to regulate it. Alternatively, it may have been the result of a less clandestine decision taken by the authorities to decrease the silver content of the denomination and, as a corollary, to revalue the future official rate at which it circulated. Rather than allow the coins of two standards to circulate together, an obvious step would have been to recall the older pieces of higher intrinsic value and offer the new in exchange—possibly at a rate favorable to the government. In these circumstances, it would also have been in the government's interest to announce its intention of enforcing the circulation of such old pieces as remained in private hands after a mandatory period of time at the same rate as the new coins. This would have ensured that real efforts were made to turn in the old pieces. The treaty between the

Emperor Isaac and Frederick Barbarossa may preserve traces of such a measure in the stipulation that there should be no difference between the new and the old stamina.

In the first case, that of debasement, the exclusion of the earlier coins might be explained as the inevitable consequence of the operation of Gresham's law, according to which the earlier coins would have tended to disappear from circulation in favor of the newer—of the same official, but lower intrinsic, value. In the second case, that of revaluation, the same would have occurred as a result of governmental action—altogether a much more efficient method and less time consuming. For this reason, hoard evidence must be considered as favoring the second possibility: the almost total exclusion of the older coins[5] is far more plausibly accounted for by an official recall than by the gradual and piecemeal operation of Gresham's law. It should be noted in this context that between 1190 and 1199 the further decrease in the value of the denomination—from $1/_{120}$ to $1/_{184}$ hyperpyron—which is visible as a prolonged process in the degeneration of the fabric and weight of the coins themselves, had a much less drastic impact upon the pattern of hoard evidence.

The first phase of the third coinage—the first of the revalued issues—is to be identified with the variety in which the Emperor holds a globus surmounted by a patriarchal cross. Now this exists in two common sub-varieties each the product of a single officina. The third sub-variety, which should indicate the presence of a third officina, is so consistently rare that it seems certain that this workshop was either operating at well below capacity or that it was established only after the issue was under way.[6] To all intents and purposes, therefore, at the commencement of the third coinage the metropolitan mint was producing billon trachea at a volume which cannot have greatly exceeded that of the first and second coinages, although their value was approximately only a third of what it had been. In addition, the governmental recall of the older pieces was presumably under way. The consequence was inevitable: the products of two officinae were inadequate to meet the demands of a public the number of which had not only remained stable but even increased when the denomination, now of lower value than formerly, came into constant use by a larger proportion of society. The establishment of a third officina can have made little impression, to judge by the consistently small number of its products represented in hoards. A major reorganization of the system of production must have ensued, for a fourth officina was subsequently estab-

---

[5] It may be suggested that the two late hoards which contradict the main pattern of occurrence (Loukovo and the Nicosia parcel), containing large numbers of the earlier, higher value pieces, in fact represent bodies of coinage put by for their bullion—as opposed to circulating—value.

[6] For an intriguing parallel under Gallienus, cf. R. H. M. Dolley, M. A. O'Donovan, *NC*[7], 2 (1962), p. 166; H. D. Gallwey, *ibid.*, pp. 351–54; L. H. Cope, *NC*[7], 7 (1967), pp. 119, 124 (table I).

lished, the system of officina distinctions revised, and the whole signalized by the adoption of the type of the Emperor holding a globus surmounted by a single-barred cross. This formed the second phase of the third coinage. The two main officinae are, during this phase, marked by the presence of two or three dots on the labarum shaft—not the absence or presence of a single dot as in the first phase. The third officina—presumably that established at the end of the first phase—is marked by the presence of a single dot, and the fourth—that opened last of all, its products being even rarer than those of the third—is marked by a plain labarum shaft.

The explanation given above would seem to be the only one consistent with the evidence of documentary sources, of the hoards, and of the coins them-selves. A crucial sequence of mint history is thereby preserved. The pragmatic nature of Byzantine monetary policy is quite apparent: the implications and consequences of the revaluation of the billon trachy were not fully realized, and the measures taken to combat them merely a response to factors which must already have made themselves felt.

A comparison between the volume of the billon trachy coinage of Androni-cus I and that of Manuel serves no purpose: different numbers of officinae were involved at different times; the relative output of each may have changed; even the length of the short issue of Andronicus is unknown—possibly two or possibly one year, depending on whether the commencement was made with his joint reign with Alexius II or with his sole reign.

Quite clearly, however, the reign of Andronicus saw a further reorganization in the system of production of the billon trachy, and one which was consistent with the general trends evident in other aspects of this Emperor's policies. The number of officinae striking the denomination was once more reduced to two and the distinction between their products—the presence of two or of three jewels on the loros above the waist: ▯ (var. A) and: ▯ (var. B)—was far more subtle than many of those of the later years of Manuel. Furthermore, the secondary characteristics which were such a noticeable feature of the same period were, according to a detailed analysis of the coins in the Draganovo and Kroushare hoards, suppressed entirely. The tightening of control over the minutiae of the design of the coinage is confirmed in a more general fashion by the fact that all denominations issued by the metropolitan mint were made to express a single iconographic theme: the Virgin as the obverse type, the Emperor crowned by Christ as the reverse. On the other hand, the tetartera of the mint of Thessalonica, together with the half-tetartera of the unidentified Greek mint, show no signs of such conformity.

The figures for the distribution of the billon coinage of Andronicus in the various Bulgarian hoards are given in Table IX following:

TABLE IX

Hoard	Total present	Total identifiable	A	B
Batkoun	89/296	17	7	10
Draganovo	52	27	13	14
Enina	24	not counted	—	—
General Nikolaevo	101	not counted	—	—
Kaloyanovets	75	52	18	34
Kroushare	58	58	22	36
Loukovo	52	41	16	25
Novo Selo	109	not counted	—	—
Ovchartsi	78	30	14	16
Tiurkmen (II)	17	not counted	—	—
Yagoda	37	23	11	12
Zlataritsa	30	15	6	9

Once again, there is no regional variation. The consistent appearance of the two varieties, however, confirms their identification as officina distinctions. The only exceptions to these varieties were in the Kiustendil hoard of 1960, in which one specimen occurred with a single jewel on the loros above the waist—probably therefore to be grouped with the more usual variety with two jewels—and in the Kroushare hoard, where a single specimen occurred with four jewels above the loros-waist—probably to be considered with the three-jewel variety. Of the thirty-one specimens in the collection at Dumbarton Oaks, fourteen are of the two-jewel variety, thirteen of the three-jewel.

The billon trachy coinage of Isaac II occurs in the following main varieties and sub-varieties:

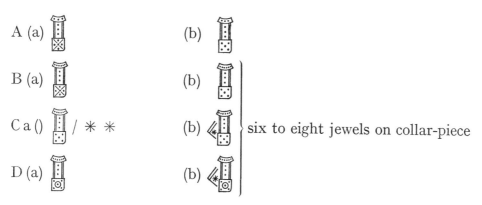

A discussion of certain other small variations is to be found below. Specimens of varieties A–D are occasionally found in which the number of jewels above the loros-waist is more or less than three, but certainly three is the norm for all varieties. The figures for the Bulgarian hoards are given in Table X on page 174.

TABLE X

Hoard and Date of discovery		Total	Total identifiable	A			B			C			D			Others
				(a)	(b)	(total)	(a)	(b)	(total)	(a)	(b)	(total)	(a)	(b)	(total)	
Batkoun	1937	44/129	29	1	9	(10)	—	6	(6)	—	8	(8)	4	1	(5)	—
Brestovo	1953	290	190	3	33	(36)	1	77	(78)	11	32	(43)	26	5	(31)	2
General Nikolaevo	1960	32	12	4	4	(8)	—	2	(2)	—	1	(1)	1	—	(1)	—
Gradevo (II)	1958	56	27	—	6	(6)	—	13	(13)	3	2	(5)	3	—	(3)	—
Iskra	1938	70	58	2	7	(9)	—	30	(30)	4	5	(9)	6	2	(8)	2
Kaloyanovets	1960	238	199	18	75	(93)	—	1	(1)	—	52	(52)	3	48	(51)	2
Kazanluk	1958	93	56	1	15	(16)	1	22	(23)	3	5	(8)	6	1	(7)	2
Kiustendil	1960	154	104	1	22	(23)	—	34	(34)	13	14	(27)	10	4	(14)	6
Loukovo	(?)	237	180	7	45	(52)	3	48	(51)	12	41	(53)	17	5	(22)	2
Momin Brod	1914	95	69	2	16	(18)	—	21	(21)	1	24	(25)	1	4	(5)	—
Muglizh (I)	1941	167	92	2	11	(13)	—	43	(43)	7	21	(28)	7	—	(7)	1
Ovchartsi	1958	2481	1767	53	302	(355)	3	808	(811)	165	308	(473)	50	25	(75)	53
Strazhitsa	1956	407	not counted				—	—	—	—	—	—	—	—	—	—
Tsruncha (A)	1963	332	274	9	34	(43)	2	105	(107)	18	52	(70)	41	7	(48)	6
Tsruncha (B)	1963	245	182	3	35	(38)	—	79	(79)	14	35	(49)	10	3	(13)	3
Turnovo (II)	1963	285	150	—	20	(20)	—	68	(68)	12	32	(44)	10	5	(15)	3
{ Uncertain Bulgarian provenance	(?)	215	112	4	6	(10)	—	42	(42)	13	27	(40)	13	4	(17)	3

It can only be assumed that this reign saw a return to the system of production as evident in the fourth and last coinage of Manuel—complete with an almost identical set of officina distinctions. The number of officinae has once more been raised to four: the primary distinctions are a collar-piece of three jewels (var. A); a collar-piece of six to twelve jewels (var. B); the asterisk motif (var. C); the jewel-within-circle (var. D). Presumably the varieties characterized by distinctions also used under Manuel (C and D) are products of the same officinae, now re-established. Var. A, by its often elegant style and the relative frequency with which the loros-waist form ⊠ is employed, should be identified as emanating from the officina that struck the var. A under Manuel: var. B therefore, by logic, must be similarly identified.

The whole organizational concept is, in fact, in direct continuation of that behind Manuel's last coinage; the reign of Andronicus, numismatically, formed nothing more than a brief interlude.

As far as the chronological sequence is concerned, the form of loros-waist as used in A (a) and B (a) is presumably in general earlier than the form ⊡ as used in A (b) and B (b), for it was the first that had been standard under Andronicus. Similarly, C (a) is probably earlier than C (b), for the practice of placing two asterisks on the obverse directly continued that customary under Manuel: the single asterisk on the Emperor's sagion (i.e., on the reverse) was something of an innovation. The varied forms of asterisk (✳, ✶, ✱, etc.) are much the same as those formerly employed.

One feature of the coinage of Isaac which does not exist (or is less apparent) under Manuel is the proportion of sub-varieties bearing characteristics other than those which are regularly recognizable. No doubt their significance, or the lack of it, was apparent to the authorities of the time, for presumably some record of them would have been kept. The most obvious examples are to be found in the decoration of the back of the Virgin's throne—∴ ∴, ∴ ∴, ∴ ∴, ✚ ✚ etc. Their precise nature remains uncertain: possibly they are variations of the asterisk motif and used by the die-cutter(s) of officina C, or possibly meaningless decorations used by those of officina B (the collar-piece is always of six to eight jewels, and these decorations rarely, if ever, appear on coins of officina D).

Others, however, although extremely rare, are more puzzling. They combine distinctions normally confined to one officina. The form ▯, that is, with a collar-piece of three jewels (A) and a jewel within circle (D)—occurs in one specimen from the Brestovo hoard. The form ▯ occurs in single specimens from the Iskra, Ovchartsi, and Tsruncha (A) hoards and that of uncertain Bulgarian provenance. It occurs twice in the Kaloyanovets hoard. Again, it must be assumed that the dominant distinction was known to the mint authorities. It should be pointed out that none of these "anomalies" is of proportions sufficient to endanger the identification of the system of officinae.

Of a different order entirely is the existence of sub-variety D (b)—▯ which frequently occurs in hoards, and in quite large numbers. To arrive at a satisfactory conclusion of the problems raised by this sub-variety it is necessary to return to the fourth and last billon coinage of Manuel. It has already been remarked that in several hoards, of which perhaps Souvatité is the best example, varieties C and D are curiously liable to be associated in any violent perturbation of the normal pattern of occurrence. Furthermore, whereas var. A is definitely distinct from B, C, and D, even in its secondary characteristics of technique, and B is distinct from A in this respect, and from C and D by its predominant use of five jewels below the loros-waist and of three jewels on the loros draping from the left arm, nevertheless, as far as the reverse design is concerned, C and D are very much alike. In two cases among the coins at Dumbarton Oaks the loros takes the form ▯ on coins otherwise of perfectly normal C (b) sub-variety. A further example, of the general variety C, occurred in the Draganovo hoard. In these three cases the motif of the jewel-within-circle is employed as a form of decoration on the products of an officina other than that to which its use is normally confined (D). With the reappearance of these two distinctions on the coinage of Isaac II, a combination of the asterisk and jewel-within-circle is formed in a way which had not previously appeared: both features are in the positions which they normally occupy as distinguishing the products of their particular officinae.

The Kaloyanovets hoard furnishes further material, being of extremely concentrated composition: ninety-three specimens of the general var. A, one specimen only of B, none of C (a), but fifty-two of C (b), three specimens only of D (a) but forty-eight of D (b). The only reasonable explanation of this extraordinary pattern is that the hoard represents a body, or bodies, of coinage taken from the mint at specific times and subsequently given little or no chance before deposition to mingle with other bodies of coinage. Once more both C and D are involved in a violent perturbation of the normal pattern of occurrence.

The evidence would seem to suggest that the officinae producing C and D were in some way related in their administration or organization, or both. A very simple explanation would be that they operated in close proximity— perhaps sharing a building—and that their products might therefore tend to be proportionally associated in any body of coinage taken directly from the mint. To take one hypothetical possibility: there would seem reason to suspect that gold, electrum, and billon nomismata were each put into purses according to some standard weight or number before leaving the mint. These purses would then have been sealed.[7] Distribution would have been effected in this form, and so they would have circulated until some smaller amount of coin was needed, when they would have been broken open and their contents eventually dispersed. In some cases, where they were in the possession of people accustomed to dealing in large sums of money, this might have happened only after a considerable lapse of time and at some distance from the point of issue. If this practice were indeed a factor of production and circulation at the time, it would seem reasonable to suppose that the filling and sealing of the purses would have taken place in the various officinae, and that they would therefore normally have contained only the products of one particular officina. According to this arrangement, the purses which came from the officina which produced var. A would have contained coins of var. A only: similarly B. If the officinae producing C and D were under the same general administration or even sharing the same premises, however, it might well happen that coins of these varieties would have been put into purses together. For this reason, hoards consisting of bodies of coinage the composition of which had been relatively undisturbed by circulation, would occasionally reflect the organizational arrangements of the mint. In particular, the com-

---

[7] Chap. 13, pp. 303–10.

position of the Kaloyanovets hoard would be explicable as, in the main, the contents of two such purses of coin: one of which had come from the officina producing var. A, the other from the premises producing both C and D. To narrow the case down even further, the last two officinae would, at the time, have been engaged in producing sub-varieties C (b) and D (b). Hoards of such concentrated composition by officina as those from Suedinenie and Souvatité would be explicable in the same fashion.

The situation as regards the arrangement of the billon trachy coinage of Alexius III is, by contrast, extremely confused. Besides the apparent existence of two chronological phases in the issue, depending upon the absence or the presence of the surname Comnenus, certain trends already evident in the coinage of Isaac are accentuated in that of his successor, reducing the identification of officina distinctions to a matter of the greatest difficulty.

It is a noticeable feature of all the hoards containing large numbers of the metropolitan coinage of Isaac and Alexius that there is not only an appreciable degeneration in the style and technique in which the majority are executed, but also a decline in standard of weight. For Isaac, these trends are subdued, and, as far as the identification of officina distinctions is concerned, of little moment. For Alexius, however, the problem is further complicated by the almost complete disappearance of such distinctions as the asterisk and the jewel-within-circle: the combination of faulty technique and uncertain officina distinctions renders it impossible to classify the issue in the detail employed for those of the period from John II to Isaac II.

The one certain variety—the product of one officina—is that in which the Emperor's collar-piece, and in most cases St. Constantine's, are decorated with three jewels only. Since it is the coins of this variety that are occasionally marked by the use of a pair of asterisks, it must be assumed that the officina producing them is to be identified with that using the asterisks as a distinction under Manuel and Isaac. For this reason, despite the uncertainty surrounding the remainder of the coins, the variety is labelled "C."

A further officina variety is probably to be found in the series of coins generally of larger module, higher weight, and finer style than the average, apparently also distinguished by the loros-waist form ⊠ for the Emperor. The collar-piece is normally decorated with five to eight jewels, and the globus frequently of the form ⬤. Since var. A of Isaac II is the least affected by the degeneration in module, weight, and style, the variety described above is probably to be identified as emanating from the same officina: it is therefore labelled "A."

The remainder should, logically, be divided somehow between those two officinae which had produced vars. B and D during the last coinage of Manuel and the coinage of Isaac. This is, however, extremely difficult. Whereas the products of the officina formerly having the asterisk as its distinction are identifiable in the coinage of Alexius—whether or not a specimen in fact bears an asterisk—because the collar-piece is always decorated with three jewels, a parallel situation does not hold good for the products of the officina formerly having a jewel-within-circle as its distinction. All the known specimens of this description have the globus and loros forms 🬀, that is, including a separate loros-end for both the Emperor and St. Constantine. Now, Metcalf draws a general distinction between coins having the forms (i) 🬀 including a single loros-end for both, and (ii) 🬀 including a separate loros-end for each.[8] Apart from the fact that the hoards from Bulgaria provide a suspiciously high number of exceptions to this arrangement, it will be seen that the sub-variety marked by the motif of the jewel-within-circle follows (i) in the form of the globus but (ii) in that of the loros-end. All that can be said is that, if anything, the rather squat style which seems to characterize the coins with the jewel-within-circle is perhaps also to be seen in (i). Both are therefore provisionally attributed to the same officina under the general variety D. A further sub-variety— 🬀 — is presumably to be grouped with (ii) under the general variety B.

It must be emphasized that the arrangement drawn up below is almost entirely provisional and that an appreciable number of exceptions have been found. Nor is it devoid of ambiguity: in particular, it is difficult to place coins of medium module for the issue with the loros-waist form ⊠ or ⊡ and the globus form ✚ —with A or with B.

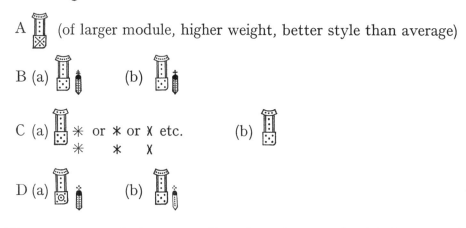

A ▯ (of larger module, higher weight, better style than average)

B (a) ▯▯   (b) ▯▯

C (a) ▯ ＊ or ＊ or ✗ etc.   (b) ▯
       ＊   ＊   ✗

D (a) ▯▯   (b) ▯▯

All, except var. C, have a collar-piece decorated with between five and eight jewels.

[8] Metcalf, *Coinage in the Balkans*, p. 121.

In view of the provisional nature of this classification and the lamentably small number of specimens identifiable even in hoards that have been satisfactorily cleaned, a table of proportional occurrences would serve little purpose. The figures for hoards containing large numbers of this issue are, however, available separately in the list of hoards.

Although the observation that the products of all officinae except A declined in module, weight, and style is not based on the actual measurement of hoard material, there is nevertheless no doubt of the fact, visual examination being quite sufficient.

The consequent isolation of the products of officina A is perhaps the strongest argument in favor of the attribution of vars. A–D to different mints—after all it is, on the face of it, odd that one officina should be producing coins of a different standard of weight from the rest. Whether the fact would be better explained by assuming a difference between the weight standards of the capital and of the provinces is a debatable point. Hoard evidence is, however, as already pointed out, consistently contrary to such an interpretation. Moreover, the same class of officina distinction as seen on the billon coinage also occurs on the gold and electrum, for which there is similarly constant evidence against an attribution to provincial mints—with rare exceptions in which this kind of distinction does not tend to occur.

The degeneration of the billon coinage should be seen against the background of a further practice revealed by hoard evidence: the widespread occurrence of drastically but neatly and regularly clipped metropolitan coins. Bulgarian hoards containing large numbers of the metropolitan billon coinage of Alexius III are as follows; hoards in which clipped coins appear are marked with an asterisk:

*Assenovgrad	(1960)	Plovdiv region	(?)
*Brestovo	(1953)	Pokrovnik	(1962)
Gradevo (I)	(1958)	*Strazhitsa	(1956)
*Kazanluk	(1958)	*Tsruncha (A & B)	(1964)
*Kiustendil	(1960)	*Turnovo (II)	(1963)
Korten	(1960)	*Tvurditsa	(?)
Kounino (II)	(1954)	Uncertain Bulg. prov. (?)	
*Loukovo	(?)	Zheleznitsa	(1964)
*Muglizh (I)	(1941)		

Metcalf suggests that the clipping of these coins was carried out by the crusaders after the conquest of 1204, in order to render them more like the deniers to which they were accustomed.[9] The hoards from Kazanluk, Muglizh, Strazhitsa,

---

[9] *Ibid.*, pp. 123, 267–68.

12*

Tsruncha, Turnovo, and Tvurditsa, however, are of a pattern containing no coins issued subsequent to 1204. The Istanbul (A) hoard similarly contained no pieces of post-conquest date. The suggestion should, therefore, be discarded. The clipped coins in question do not, however, occur in hoards deposited earlier than the reign of Alexius III, although the actual types are themselves of varying date: the practice of clipping should therefore be dated to that reign (1195–1203). The uniformly neat, regular character of the clipping which preserves the reverse design (Pl. 44. *1–15*) is of the sort that could result only from some kind of official, centralized action. Whereas provincial hoards contain only relatively small proportions of these pieces, at least one large metropolitan hoard (Istanbul A) consisted entirely of them. The process was therefore almost certainly carried out in Constantinople.

The proportions in which the products of each officina were represented in the Istanbul (A) hoard, were, as far as the fourth coinage of Manuel is concerned, entirely normal. The same apparently holds good for the coinage of Isaac II. The clipped coins of Alexius III, however, seem largely confined to the products of the officina striking var. A—those of larger module, heavier weight, and finer style than the average of vars. B, C, and D. At least eight of the thirteen specimens illustrated in Bellinger's publication of the hoard are definitely of var. A. This tendency is confirmed by the evidence of other hoards, and, moreover, seventeen of the eighteen clipped specimens of Alexius III in the collection at Dumbarton Oaks are of the same variety.

Now, the period for which there is documentary evidence for a further rapid decline in the value of the billon trachy (between 1190 and 1199 it dropped from $^1/_{120}$ hyperpyron to $^1/_{184}$ hyperpyron), apparently coincides chronologically both with the degeneration in module, weight, and style of the majority of coins, and with the appearance of an official clipping of the earlier coins and of the coins of Alexius III which had escaped this degeneration.

The only explanation consistent with the evidence is therefore that, at some point in the reign of Isaac, the authorities decided that the officinae producing vars. B–D should commence striking coins of a lighter standard of weight than that producing var. A, which continued on the traditional standard. Presumably it was hoped that by retaining a proportion of the denomination at the old standard, the value of the whole might still be maintained. The attempt failed and the value dropped by approximately a third in a matter of nine years. A situation might well have arisen where the coins of the predecessors of Alexius and his own coins of var. A would have become intrinsically worth as much as, or possibly even more than, the general market value of the denomination. The only step to take in such a position, given the official unwillingness to boost the intrinsic value of the generality of the denomination, would have been either to call in the pieces of higher value or to reduce their value to that of the rest of the denomination in some way. The governmental clipping of such coins as came into its hands was clearly a method of achieving the latter aim.

The whole episode is, in fact, a worthy accompaniment to that involving the revaluation of the billon trachy under Manuel I and is an excellent further commentary upon the limitations of contemporary monetary policy.

The organization and operation of the metropolitan mint along the lines of an officina system was not confined to the billon coinage, either in general practice, or in the consistent placing of officina distinctions upon the reverse designs of the coins. The evidence for the first appearance of those distinctions during the period under examination, that is, upon the early hyperpyra of Alexius I, has already been presented.[10] It therefore remains to collect the evidence for the gold and electrum coinage over the whole period. The assembly of such a body of evidence should be considerably aided by the fact that, drawing upon experience, it should now be easier to recognize the kind of invariable feature which was intended as an official distinction and, further, to separate it from characteristics which were merely the result of the organizational pattern of the mint, and which are sometimes confined to the products of a single officina, sometimes dominant on its products only, sometimes shared indifferently with the products of the others.

The second officina for the gold coinage disappears temporarily after the completion of the systematic recoinage evidently carried out during the first few years after the monetary reforms of 1092, but reappears in what must be the third and last coinage of John II. There were, in the Gornoslav hoard, sixty clearly preserved metropolitan specimens of this coinage. Of these, twenty-five had a collar-piece decorated with four jewels (var. A), thirty-five a collar-piece decorated with five jewels (var. B). The four-jewel series was characterized by the ligatures ΘV MP in the upper reverse field: these occurred in twenty-three cases, a reversed form VΘ MP or VΘ ᚠM occurring in the remaining two cases. On the other hand, the five-jewel series was marked by the use of the reversed form of the ligatures, which occurred in thirty-two cases, the form ΘV MP occurring in only three cases. In addition, while the use of one form of the globus cruciger (⦿) was common to both series, the simpler form ⦿ occurred on nine specimens of the four-jewel series, but was completely absent from the other. Examination of the ten specimens in the collection at Dumbarton Oaks confirms these distinctions, there being five specimens of the four-jewel series, and five of the five-jewel. All the four-jewel pieces have the ligature form ΘV MP, while two, or perhaps three pieces have the simpler globus form ⦿. All of the specimens of the five-jewel series have the reversed ligature form. It appears certain, therefore, that the main distinction is an official one, designed to separate the products of two officinae.

[10] Chap. 8, p. 92.

The existence of officina distinctions on the first two varieties of the gold coinage of Manuel I may be regarded as certain, but their classification is extremely difficult. The small, variable devices found on the imperial chlamys, below the tablion, may well form into two separate groups (• ▪ ✗ / ↑ ∫ ∫), but only close analysis will reveal the precise division. Var III, however, certainly seems to have been the product of two officinae, the distinction between their products lying in the absence (var. A) or presence (var. B) of a square dot on the divitision, directly below the point of the chlamys. Of the eighteen specimens of this variety present in the Gornoslav hoard, nine specimens showed the dot, eight lacked it. If officina distinctions are present upon the two remaining varieties (IV and V), they are not obvious, and in view of the apparently contemporary situation in the electrum coinage, to be discussed below, it may well be that only a single officina was involved in their production.

There are no distinctions to be found upon the gold coinage of Andronicus I, and almost certainly only one officina was involved in its production: this is only to be expected and is a reflection of the reforming policies pursued by this Emperor—policies which are particularly well exemplified in the coinage.

The second officina does, however, reappear once more for the gold coinage of Isaac II, the distinction between their products lying in the jewelling of the collar-piece—in very much the same fashion as on his electrum coinage. Of the nineteen specimens at Dumbarton Oaks, eleven have the collar-piece decorated with three jewels (var. A), eight with six to eight jewels (var. B). It is possible that the re-establishment of a second officina reflects the large expenses incurred by Isaac, a feature which is unfavorably commented upon by Nicetas Choniates.[11]

There is no evidence for the existence of officina distinctions on the gold coinage during the reign of Alexius III, but whether this represents a general trend toward relaxation, which is found in the billon coinage, or whether it reflects a return to a single officina remains uncertain.

The first occasion on which there is evidence for the operation of more than a single officina in the production of the metropolitan electrum coinage is to be dated to the very beginning of the reign of John II. The distinction between the products of the two officinae then in operation lies in the absence (var. A) or presence (var. B) of a dot on the chlamys, below the tablion. There were seventy-eight specimens of this general hagiogeorgaton issue in the Nicosia hoard of the early 1920's; the chlamys dot was absent in forty-seven cases, present in thirty-one. Of the eighteen specimens at Dumbarton Oaks, ten lack the dot, eight possess it.

The first electrum coinage of Manuel I must be that on which he is portrayed as beardless, and, as might be expected, emanates from two officinae, the distinc-

---

[11] For Andronicus, Choniates, Bonn ed., pp. 421–23, 429; for Isaac, *ibid.*, p. 584.

tion being the absence (var. A) or presence (var. B) of a dot on the shaft of the labarum-headed scepter in the Emperor's right hand, between the hand and the point where the shaft crosses the shoulder. There are only five specimens at Dumbarton Oaks, the dot being absent in two cases, present in three: this is precisely the type of feature that is to be expected in the circumstances, however, and its validity as a criterion need consequently not be doubted.

The coinage which has been identified as the second of the reign is very closely related in style and fabric to the first; the distinction between the products of the two officinae striking it lies in the decoration of the collar-piece. Of eight specimens in the Nicosia hoard, three examples had the collar-piece decorated with four jewels (var. A), five with five jewels (var. B).

The order of types, C, D, and E, forming the third to fifth electrum coinages of the reign, is not entirely certain, but there is one valuable fact the establishment of which gives some hope of eventually arriving at the correct succession. At some point in the production of these three coinages a third officina was brought into use.

Now, there are five varieties of the metropolitan gold coinage and five types of metropolitan electrum. It does not necessarily follow that each variety and type were absolutely contemporaneous, but even if they were not, unless there were a remarkable concentration of varieties or types at one particular part of the reign, the succession should not be too far out of step. In support of this contention it should be noted that it is the fourth variety of the gold coinage that not infrequently has a single dot in each of the limbs of the nimbus-cross on the obverse (Pl. 12. 9), not the more usual group of five dots. This feature will, then, presumably have been borrowed from the (contemporary) fourth type of the electrum coinage (Pl. 13. 10–12).

It has already been noticed, when dealing with the gold coinage, that direct evidence for the existence of two officinae disappears after var. III. The establishment of a further officina for electrum at some point between the third and fifth coinages arouses the suspicion that the officina ceasing to produce gold had merely been switched to the production of electrum. But at precisely what point did this switch occur?

The Lindos hoard of 1902, which largely consisted of electrum coins of Manuel provides some interesting figures. It contained seventy-nine specimens of type C, twenty of type D, and 105 of type E. The officina distinctions of each were carefully noted by Balling in his excellent publication of the hoard,[12] although he did not attempt to explain the reason for their existence. Type E falls into three officina varieties, according to the jewelling of the border of the chlamys which forms the collar. In thirty-seven cases the border was decorated with

[12] J. Balling, "A Byzantine Double Hoard from Lindos," *Nordisk Numismatisk Årsskrift* (1963), pp. 13–41.

three jewels (var. A); in twenty-eight cases with three jewels the central of which was within a circle (var. B); in forty cases with four to six jewels but with five and six jewels overwhelmingly dominant (var. C). Type D falls into three officina varieties, according to the number of dots on the shaft of the Emperor's labarum-headed scepter, directly below the head of the labarum. In seven cases there was a single dot (var. A); in eleven cases two dots (var. B); in two cases three dots (var. C). Type C, on the other hand, falls into two main officina varieties, with a third which is extremely rare. The distinction lies in the number of dots on the shaft of the patriarchal cross held between the Emperor and St. Theodore. In thirty cases, the shaft was plain (var. A); in forty-seven it had a single dot, frequently waisted ($\ddagger$[var. B]); in two cases only it had two dots (var. C). The coins at Dumbarton Oaks fall into much the same pattern: six with a plain shaft, four with a single dot on the shaft, one with two dots on the shaft.

The analysis above clearly suggests that type C forms the third coinage, and that the third officina—formerly producing gold—was introduced only toward its close, therefore striking very few coins. Types D and E must therefore form the fourth and fifth coinages. There is very little indication as to which is which, but the jewel-within-circle of type E is also found on the last billon coinage, and it may therefore form the fifth and last coinage of the reign. It is also the coinage in which the output of each of the three officinae seems to be of roughly uniform quantity.

Several additional points arise. The position of type C as the third metropolitan coinage tends to be confirmed by a consideration of the small Thessalonican series. There exist Thessalonican pieces of both the first and the second coinages, together with a further type portraying the Emperor and St. Demetrius. This last has an obvious claim to be considered the Thessalonican equivalent to metropolitan type C, which portrays the Emperor and St. Theodore. There are, however, no Thessalonican pieces of types D and E and no possible equivalents for them. This suggests that Thessalonica struck only three electrum coinages and then ceased production of the denomination, perhaps proceeding to strike its hyperpyron type. There is a rather striking sub-variety of type C, in which the obverse asterisks—otherwise both consistently present—are completely lacking. This sub-variety is apparently confined to coins of the officina distinguished by a plain shaft to the patriarchal cross. There were twelve such specimens in the Lindos hoard, and there are a further three at Dumbarton Oaks. There is a similarly clear sub-variety of type E, in which the shaft of the labarum held by the Emperor has a single dot. This sub-variety is apparently confined to the coins of the officina distinguished by a chlamys-collar of three jewels. There were eighteen such specimens in the Lindos hoard, and there are a further two at Dumbarton Oaks. Both these sub-varieties form the kind of characteristic that is to be expected from the organizational pattern of the mint and the consequent development, by the die-cutter or cutters of each officinae, of techniques which were peculiar to themselves.

The electrum coinage of Andronicus I betrays a return to production by two officinae, the official distinction lying in the absence (var. A) or presence (var. B) of a dot on the shaft of the labarum held by the Emperor. Of the eight specimens at Dumbarton Oaks, three lack the dot, five possess it.

The coinage of Isaac II continues this pattern. The Banya hoard, of 1927, contained thirty-five specimens of this type and there are, in addition, a further thirty pieces at Dumbarton Oaks. Of the total, in twenty-six cases the chlamys-collar is decorated with three jewels (var. A), in thirty-nine cases by six to eight jewels (var. B). Closer examination reveals that on eight of the fifteen specimens of the six–eight jewel variety at Dumbarton Oaks, there is, on each side of the Virgin's throne on the obverse, the small triangular device ∴; it occurs on none of the three-jewel variety.

For the reign of Alexius III there is no evidence for the operation of more than one officina, but, as in the case of the gold coinage, there is no possibility of discovering whether this represents the true state of affairs or results from the relaxation of control within the mint.

Production of the copper tetarteron coinage does not appear to have conformed to the officina system of the precious-metal coinage. On the other hand, since the tetarteron contained no metal of any appreciable bullion value there would have been less reason for providing a means of checking the products of each officina, and it may merely be that while the system of production conformed to that of the other denominations consistent official distinctions were not considered necessary.

Finally, it must be emphasized that it need not be supposed that what has been here termed the "officina system" should represent the uninterrupted survival into the twelfth century of a late Roman and early Byzantine organizational pattern, which use of the term might at first sight seem to suggest. Indeed, in one major aspect the twelfth-century pattern differed considerably from the earlier: for, whereas during the earlier period—say the fifth to the seventh century—the number of officinae for each metal was more or less fixed, during the twelfth century it varied considerably. All that is suggested is that the mint was organized on a departmental basis according to metal, and that each department was in some fashion divided into a number of sections, workshops, or even production lines, the number of divisions being increased or decreased as economic necessity or administrative policy (or a mixture of the two) dictated. Such a system is, after all, one obvious way of organizing a mint, and there is no reason to think that its main elements were limited in use either geographically or chronologically. The term "officina" remains a convenient shorthand.

A list of the official marks of distinction within the gold, electrum, and billon coinages of the period is appended:

A̸ HYPERPYRON

Alexius I
First coinage (commemorative)   1 *officina?*
Second coinage, var. I   2 officinae (A: ⌐ or ⌐   B: ⌐)
Second coinage, var. II   1 officina

John II
First coinage   1 officina
Second coinage   1 officina
Third coinage   2 officinae (A: ⌣ B: ⌣)

Manuel I
Var. I   2 officinae?
Var. II   2 officinae?
Var. III   2 officinae (A: ⱱ   B: ⱱ)
Var. IV   1 officina?
Var. V   1 officina?

Andronicus I
   1 officina

Isaac II
   2 officinae (A: ⌣   B: ⌣)

Alexius III
   1 officina ?

EL. TRACHY

Alexius I
   1 officina

John II
Var. I   2 officinae (A: ⱶ   B: ⱶ)
Var. II   2 officinae (A: ǁ   B: ǁ)

Manuel I
First coinage   2 officinae (A: ✦ B: ✦)
Second coinage   2 officinae (A: ⌣ B: ⌣)
Third coinage (?)   3 officinae (A: ⸢ B: ⸢ C: ⸢)
Fourth coinage (?)   3 officinae (A: ✦ B: ✦ C: ✦)
Fifth coinage (?)   3 officinae (A: ⌣ B: ⌣ C: ⌣)

Andronicus I

                2 officinae (A: ⌑   B: ⌑

Isaac II

                2 officinae (A: ⌣   B: ⌣

Alexius III

                1 officina?

BILL. TRACHY

Alexius I
   First coinage (commemorative) 1 officina
   Second coinage   1 officina
   Third coinage   1 officina
   Fourth coinage   1 officina

John II
   First coinage   1 officina
   Second coinage   2 officinae (A: ╲   B: ╲

Manuel I
   First coinage   2 officinae (A: ◇╲   B: ◇╲
   Second coinage   2 officinae (A: ⌣   B: ⌣
   Third coinage (revalued)
      first phase   3 officinae (A: ⌑   B: ⌑   C: ⌑
      second phase   4 officinae (A: ‖   B: ‖   C: ‖   D: ⌑
   Fourth coinage   4 officinae (A: ⊞   B: ⊞   C: ✳ etc. D: ⊙
                      etc.

Andronicus I

                2 officinae (A: ⊞   B: ⊞

Isaac II

                4 officinae (A: ⌣   B: ⌣   C: ✳ etc. D: ⊡
                    etc.

Alexius III

                4 officinae (A: ⊠   B: ⌑, ⌑ etc. C: ⌣, ✳ etc.
                    D: ⊡, ⌑ etc.

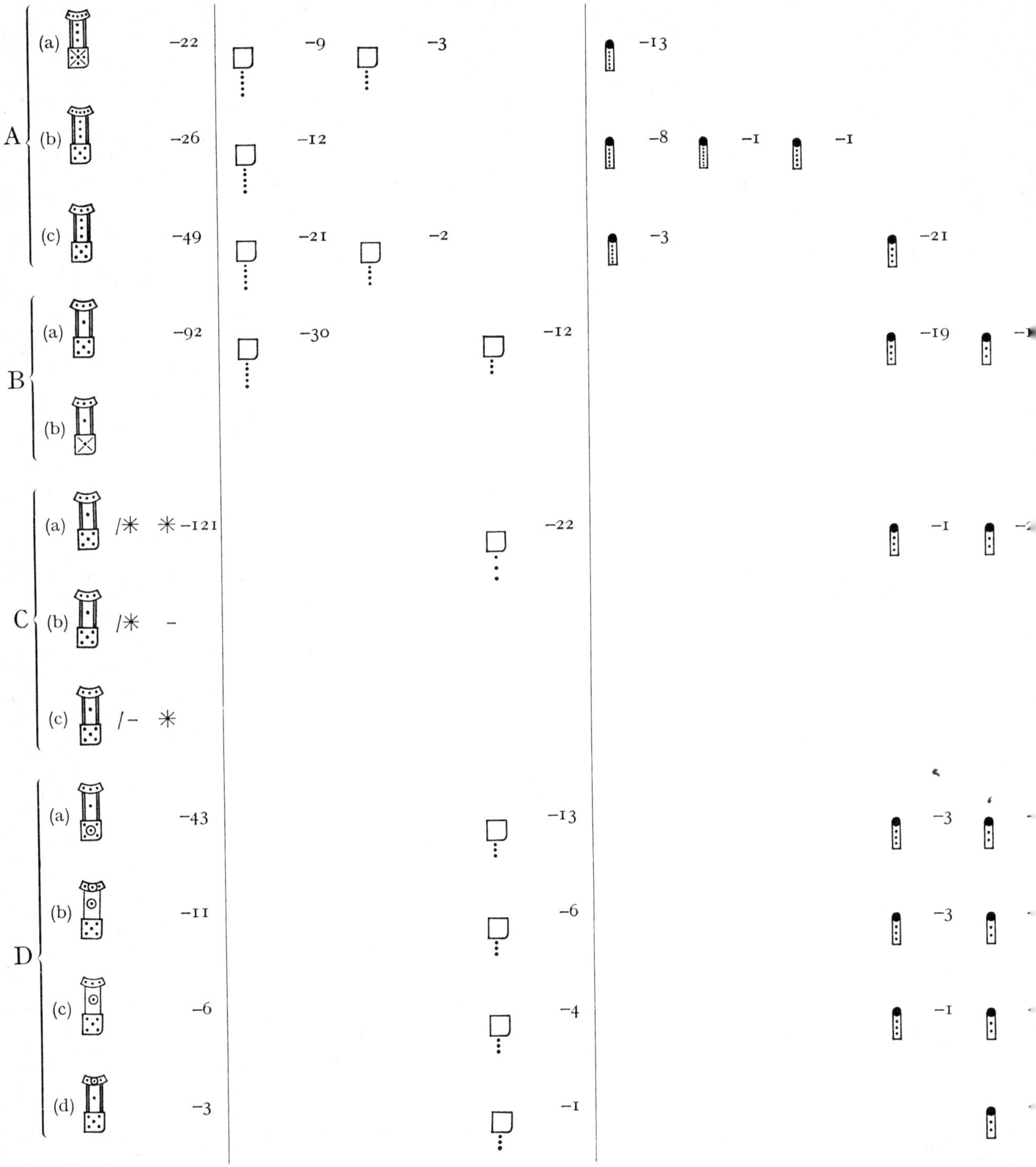
A
(a) −22 −9 −3 −13
(b) −26 −12 −8 −1 −1
(c) −49 −21 −2 −3 −21
B
(a) −92 −30 −12 −19
(b)
C
(a) /✳ ✳−121 −22 −1
(b) /✳ −
(c) /− ✳
D
(a) −43 −13 −3
(b) −11 −6 −3
(c) −6 −4 −1
(d) −3 −1

TABLE VI

TABLE VII

−3   −3   −3

−7   −2

−2   −13   −7

−13   −13   −5   −1

−30   −31   −1

−9   −8   −1

−2   −4   −1

−1   −3

KROUSH

A

(a) −6   −4   −3

(b) −7   −3   −5

(c) −20   −11   −2   −10

B

(a) −29   −7   −3   −8   −2

(b)

C

(a) /✳   ✳−54   −17   −6   −10   −1

(b) /✳   –

(c) /–   ✳

D

(a) −15   −5   −6

(b) −7   −2   −4

(c) −6   −1   −3

(d)

☩ −3	⦿ −1				‖ −3			
☩ −3		⸪⸱⸪ −1	‖ −4					
☩ −4	⦿ −9	⸪⸱⸪ −7	‖ −8					
	⦿ −18	⸪⸱⸪ −1	‖ −10	‖ −4				
	⦿ −17		‖ −24					
	⦿ −3		‖ −3					
	⦿ −9		‖ −8	‖ −3				
	⦿ −7		‖ −4	‖ −1				
	⦿ −3							

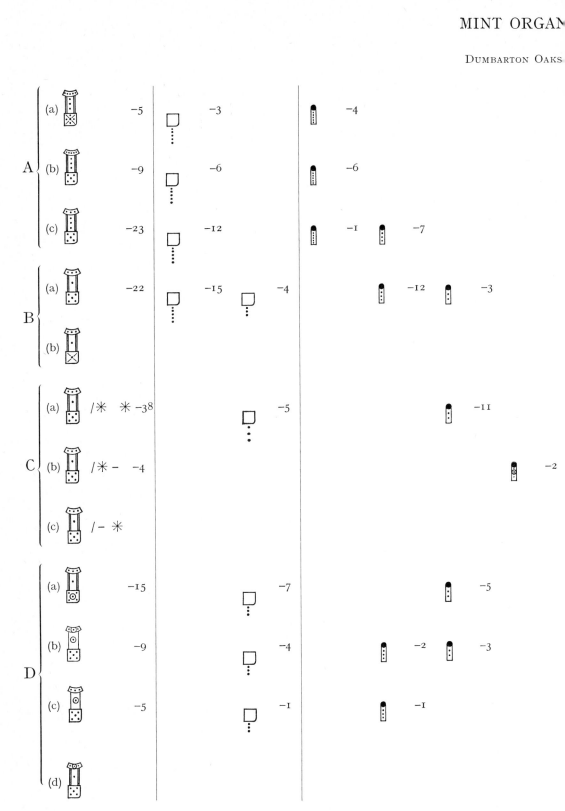

Section III

THE COINS 1204–1261

CHAPTER ELEVEN

(i)

THE IMITATIVE COINAGE OF
THE PERIOD OF THE LATIN EMPERORS

1204–1261

AND KINGS OF THESSALONICA

1204–1224

BILL. TRACHY (LARGER MODULE)

MINT OF CONSTANTINOPLE

Type A (1204–?)

Obv. M̅P̅ Θ̅V̅ in upper field.

Virgin nimbate, wearing tunic and maphorion, seated upon throne with back; holds beardless, nimbate head of Christ on breast.

Rev. MΛNOVHΛ ΔЄCΠOTHC
MΛNOVHΛ ΠOPΦVPOΓЄN } —or var. Frequently blundered and/or retrograde.

Full-length figure of emperor wearing stemma, divitision, and chlamys; holds in right hand labarum on long shaft, and in left, anexikakia.

Pl. 25. *6–10*

Type B

Obv. I̅C̅ X̅C̅ in upper field.

Christ, bearded and nimbate, wearing tunic and colobion, seated upon throne with back; holds Gospels in left hand.

Rev. MΛNOVHΛ ΔЄCΠOTHC
MΛNOVHΛ ΠOPΦVPOΓЄN } —or var. Frequently blundered and / or retrograde.

Full-length figure of emperor wearing stemma, divitision, and chlamys; holds in right hand sword, point resting on ground, and in left, globus cruciger.

Pl. 25, *11, 12*

191

Type C

Obv. M̄P̄ Θ̄V̄ in upper field.

Virgin nimbate, wearing tunic and maphorion, seated upon throne with back; holds beardless, nimbate head of Christ on breast.

Rev. ΛΛΕΞΙΟC ΔΕCΠΟΤ—or var.

Emperor seated upon throne without back, wearing stemma, divitision, collar-piece, and panelled loros of simplified type; holds in right hand labarum-headed scepter, and in left, anexikakia. *Manus Dei* in upper right field.

Pl. 25. *13*

Type D

Obv. Ī̄C̄ X̄C̄ in field.

Bust of Christ, beardless and nimbate, wearing tunic and colobion; holds scroll in left hand.

Rev. MΛNOVHΛ ΔΕCΠΟΤΗC—or var.

Full-length figure of emperor wearing stemma, divitision, collar-piece, jewelled loros of simplified type, and sagion; holds in right hand scepter cruciger, and in left, globus cruciger.

Pl. 25, *14, 15*

Type E

Obv. Ī̄C̄ X̄C̄ in field.

Bust of Christ, beardless and nimbate, wearing tunic and colobion; holds scroll in left hand.

Rev. MΛNOVHΛ ΔΕCΠΟΤΗC—or var.

Full-length figure of emperor wearing stemma, divitision, collar-piece, jewelled loros of simplified type, and sagion; holds in right hand labarum-headed scepter, and in left, globus surmounted by patriarchal cross.

Pl. 26. *1*

Type F

Obv. Ī̄C̄ X̄C̄ in field.

Christ, bearded and nimbate, wearing tunic and colobion, seated upon throne without back; right hand raised in benediction, holds Gospels in left.

Rev. MΛNOVHΛ ΔΕCΠ—or var.

Full-length figure of emperor on left, crowned by Virgin. Emperor wears stemma, divitision, and chlamys; holds in right hand labarum on long shaft, and in left anexikakia. Virgin wears tunic and maphorion.

Pl. 26. *2*

Type G

Obv. M̅P̅ Ө̅V̅ in upper field.

   Virgin nimbate, wearing tunic and maphorion, seated upon throne with back; holds beardless, nimbate head of Christ on breast.

Rev. ΛΗ🝔ИΛΜ?

   Full-length figure of emperor on left, and of beardless, nimbate military saint, holding between them labarum on long shaft. Emperor wears stemma, divitision, and chlamys; holds scepter cruciger in right hand. Saint wears short military tunic, breastplate(?), and sagion.

Pl. 26. 3

Type H

Obv. M̅P̅ Ө̅V̅ in upper field.

   Virgin nimbate, wearing tunic and maphorion, seated upon throne with back; holds beardless, nimbate head of Christ on breast.

Rev. ΛΝΔPONIKOC ΔECΠOTHC—or var. I̅C̅ X̅C̅ in upper right field.

   Full-length figure of emperor on left, crowned by Christ, bearded and nimbate. Emperor wears stemma, divitision, collar-piece, panelled loros of simplified type, and sagion; holds in right hand labarum-headed scepter, and in left, globus cruciger. Christ wears tunic and colobion; holds Gospels in left hand.

Pl. 26. 4, 5

Type I

Obv. M̅P̅ Ө̅V̅ in field.

   Full-length figure of Virgin nimbate, orans, wearing tunic and maphorion, turned to right, standing on dais. *Manus Dei* in upper right field.

Rev. ΛΝΔ TOKO. X̅C̅ in right field.

   Full-length figure of emperor on left, crowned by Christ, bearded and nimbate. Emperor wears stemma, divitision, and chlamys; holds in right hand cross on long shaft, and in left, anexikakia. Christ wears tunic and colobion; holds Gospels in left hand.

Pl. 26. 6

Type J

Obv.

   Full-length figure of Archangel (Michael?) nimbate, wearing short military tunic, breastplate(?), and sagion; holds in right hand jewelled scepter, and in left, globus cruciger.

Rev. ИШ🝔 ΔECΠ—or var.

   Full-length figure of emperor wearing stemma, divitision, and chlamys; holds in right hand sword resting on shoulder, and in left, globus cruciger.

Pl. 26. 7–9

13

Type K

Obv. ĪC X̄C in field.

Bust of Christ, bearded and nimbate, wearing tunic and colobion; holds Gospels in left hand.

Rev. ИШХ   ?

Full-length figure of emperor wearing stemma, divitision, collar-piece, jewelled loros of simplified type and sagion; holds in right hand labarum-headed scepter, and in left, globus surmounted by patriarchal cross.

Pl. 26. *10*

Type L

Obv. ĪC X̄C in field.

Christ, bearded and nimbate, wearing tunic and colobion, seated upon throne without back; right hand raised in benediction, holds Gospels in left.

Rev.   ?   KNOC

Full-length figure of emperor wearing stemma, divitision, collar-piece, panelled loros of simplified type and sagion; holds in right hand labarum-headed scepter, and in left, sword, the point of which rests on ground.

Pl. 26. *11*

Type M

Obv. X X
       P H

Full-length figure of Archangel Michael nimbate, wearing collar-piece, short military tunic (and loros?); holds in right hand sword, resting on shoulder, and in left, globus cruciger.

Rev. XVI ΔЄCΠOT

Full-length figure of emperor wearing stemma, divitision, collar-piece, panelled loros of simplified type, and sagion; holds in right hand labarum-headed scepter, and in left, globus cruciger.

Pl. 26. *12, 13*

Type N

Obv. M̄P ΘV̄ in field.

Three-quarter-length figure of Virgin nimbate, orans, wearing tunic and maphorion.

Rev.
         ĪŪ
         Δ   O
         ЄC Γ   —or var.
         ΠO Є
         T
         HC

Full-length figure of emperor on left, and of Saint George, beardless and nimbate, holding between them patriarchal cross on long shaft and three steps. Emperor wears stemma, divitision, and chlamys. Saint wears short military tunic, breastplate, and sagion; holds sword, point downward, in left hand.

Pl. 26. *14. 15*

Type O

Obv. ĪC X̄C in field.

Full-length figure of Christ, standing on dais, bearded and nimbate, wearing tunic and colobion; right hand raised in benediction, holds Gospels in left.

Rev. ΔЄC ΠΟ —or var.
(with ӀШ Ը above, Π below ΔЄC, РΦ below ΠΟ, V below)

Full-length figure of emperor, wearing stemma, short military tunic, breastplate, and sagion; holds in right hand labarum on long shaft, and in left, globus cruciger.

Pl. 27. *1, 2*

Type P

Obv. ĪC X̄C in field.

Bust of Christ, beardless and nimbate, wearing tunic and colobion; holds scroll in left hand.

Rev. X X
Λ M

Full-length figure of Archangel Michael nimbate, wearing short military tunic, breastplate, and sagion; holds in right hand jewelled scepter, and in left, globus cruciger.

Pl. 27. *3, 4*

Type Q

Obv. M̄P̄ Θ̄V̄ in upper field.

Virgin nimbate, wearing tunic and maphorion, seated upon throne with back; holds beardless, nimbate head of Christ on breast.

Rev. X
M

Full-length figure of Archangel Michael nimbate, wearing divitision and sagion; holds in right hand labarum(?) on long shaft, and in left, globus cruciger(?).

Pl. 27. *5*

13*

Type R

Obv. ĪC X̄C in field.

> Christ, bearded and nimbate, wearing tunic and colobion, seated upon throne without back; right hand raised in benediction, holds Gospels in left.

Rev. M̄P Θ̄V in field.

> Full-length figure of Virgin nimbate, orans, wearing tunic and maphorion.

Pl. 27. 6, 7

Type S

Obv. O ΛΓΙΟC ΠETPOC in two columnar groups.

> Full-length figure of Saint Peter nimbate, wearing tunic and colobion; holds in right hand scepter cruciger, and in left, two keys.

Rev. M̄P Θ̄V H ΛΓΙOCOPITICΛ in two columnar groups.

> Full-length figure of Virgin Hagiosoritissa nimbate, orans, turned to right, wearing tunic and maphorion. *Manus Dei* in upper right field.

Pl. 27. 8, 9

Type T

Obv. M̄P Θ̄V H ΛΓΙOCOPITICΛ in two columnar groups.

> Full-length figure of Virgin Hagiosoritissa nimbate, orans, turned to right wearing tunic and maphorion. *Manus Dei* in upper right field.

Rev. O ΛΓΙOC ΠETPOC O ΛΓΙOC ΠΛVΛOC in two columnar groups.

> Full-length figures of Saints Peter (on left) and Paul (on right), nimbate, wearing tunic and colobion, embracing one another. Saint Peter has short beard, Saint Paul a long one.

Pl. 27. 10, 11

MINT OF THESSALONICA

Type A (1204–?)

Obv. ĪC X̄C in field.

> Christ, bearded and nimbate, wearing tunic and colobion, seated upon throne without back; holds Gospels in left hand. Asterisk above cushion of throne, on either side.

Rev.

> Half-length figure of emperor wearing stemma, divitision, collar-piece, and panelled loros of simplified type; holds in right hand scepter cruciger and in left, globus cruciger.

Pl. 28. 1–4

Type B Obv. ĪC̄ X̄C̄
O NЯ
ЄM HΛ   —or var.
MΛ

Bust of Christ Emmanuel, bearded (*sic*) and nimbate, wearing tunic and colobion; holds scroll in left hand.

Rev.   TШKOMN

Full-length figure of emperor wearing stemma, divitision, and chlamys; holds in right hand labarum-headed scepter, and in left, globus cruciger.

Pl. 28. *5–8*

Type C

Obv. ĪC̄ X̄C̄ in field.

Christ, bearded and nimbate, wearing tunic and colobion, seated upon throne without back; right hand raised in benediction, holds Gospels in left. Cross above cushion of throne, on right.

Rev. HΛΓIΛЄΛЄNЄ OKOTΛNT—or var.

Full-length figures of Saints Helena (on left) and Constantine (on right), holding between them patriarchal cross on long shaft and step. Both wear stemma, divitision, collar-piece, and jewelled loros of simplified type; Saint Helena holds jewelled scepter, Constantine, scepter cruciger.

Pl. 28, *9, 10*

Æ TETARTERON

MINT OF CONSTANTINOPLE

Obv. M̄P̄ Θ̄V̄ in field.

Three-quarter-length figure of Virgin nimbate, orans, wearing tunic and maphorion; beardless, nimbate head of Christ on breast.

Rev. ICΛΛKIOC ΔЄCΠOT

Full-length figure of emperor wearing stemma, divitision, collar-piece, jewelled loros of simplified type and sagion; holds in right hand scepter cruciger, and in left, globus cruciger.

Pl. 27. *12, 13*

Æ HALF-TETARTERON

MINT OF THESSALONICA

Type A

Obv. M̄P̄ Θ̄V̄ in field.

Bust of Virgin nimbate, wearing tunic and maphorion.

Rev.

Leaved patriarchal cross.

Pl. 28. *11*

Type B
Obv. H ΛΓΙΛ ЄΛЄΝЄ—or var., in columnar grouping, on left.
  Full-length figure of Saint Helena nimbate, turned slightly to right, wearing stemma, divitision, collar-piece, and jewelled loros of simplified type; holds patriarchal cross, with flourish on shaft, in left hand.
Rev. ΟΛΓΙΟC ΚΟΝΓΛΝΤ—or var.
  Full-length figure of Saint Constantine, turned slightly to left, wearing stemma, divitision, collar-piece, and jewelled loros of simplified type; holds in right hand patriarchal cross, and in left, anexikakia.

Pl. 28. *12–14*

BILL. or Æ TRACHY (SMALLER MODULE)

Type A
Obv.
Rev. } As Constantinople Type A, but small module.

Pl. 29. *1–3*

Type B
Obv.
Rev. } As Constantinople Type B, but small module.

Pl. 29. *4–6*

Type C
Obv.
Rev. } As Constantinople Type C, but small module.

Pl. 29. *7–9*

Type D
Obv.
Rev. } As Thessalonica Type A, but small module.

Pl. 29. *10–12*

Type E
Obv.
Rev. } As Thessalonica Type B, but small module.

Pl. 29. *13–15*

Type F
  Obv. ⎫
          ⎬ As Thessalonica Type C, but small module.
  Rev. ⎭

Pl. 29. *16–18*

Type G
  Obv. ⎫
          ⎬ As Theodore I, Lascaris, Nicaea, First coinage, but small module.
  Rev. ⎭

Pl. 29. *19, 20*

THE COINAGE OF THE LATINS: COMMENTARY

There is no doubt that the types listed above should be differentiated from the products of the metropolitan mint during the period 1092–1204, to which they bear little or no direct relationship in metallic composition, organizational distinctions, module, fabric, weight, or style. Their precise status, however, remains to be defined.

While the view prevailed that the coinage of all rulers subsequent to the reign of Constantine VIII (1025–28) emanated from the metropolitan mint only, it was customary to ignore the problems raised by the existence of such minute pieces as those illustrated on Plate 29 or, at best, to identify in them fractions of the larger metropolitan types. The fallacy in this latter reasoning becomes obvious when it is considered that all the types represented in the smallest module also exist in a considerably larger one which is not only too large to be a fraction, but specimens of which are themselves quite distinct from the series of metropolitan billon trachea. It is therefore hardly logical to assign either large or small specimens of these types to the same series as the normal Constantinopolitan coins.

The most obvious solution is to regard the types in question as the products of provincial mints. Bellinger was, in 1958, probably the first to arrive at a tentative conclusion of this sort[1], and since then Metcalf, in a series of publications, has postulated the existence of an elaborate system of provincial mints, each producing coins of a common type, but according to its own local standard of weight.[2]

---

[1] A. R. Bellinger, "Three Hoards of Byzantine Bronze Coins," *Greek and Byzantine Studies*, I, no. 2 (Oct. 1958), p. 167; cf. Thompson, *The Athenian Agora*, p. 7.

[2] For instance, D. M. Metcalf, "Byzantine Scyphate Bronze Coinage in Greece," *Annual of the British School of Archaeology at Athens*, 56 (1961), pp. 42–63.

Before proceeding, it will be convenient to enumerate the differences between the metropolitan series and that under discussion.

The metropolitan billon trachea of the period 1092–1185, and to a lesser extent up to 1204, are either of recognizable billon alloy, or frequently bear what appears to be a silver wash; rarely fall below 25 mm. in diameter; are of a standard of weight approaching 4.0 gm.; of regular fabric, and struck from competently engraved dies of good style, with most of the design appearing. In contrast, the other series is composed of coins which are rarely, if ever, obviously of billon, or even bear a silver wash; rarely exceed a diameter of 25 mm., in many cases being as small as 15 mm., the weight varying accordingly. They are of irregular fabric and struck from badly engraved dies with blundered inscriptions, only portions of the design appearing. The metropolitan series bears a recognizable system of officially devised distinctive marks, the other series does not.

The issue listed above as Constantinopolitan type A in the large module and as type A in the small has been variously attributed to Alexius I and to Manuel I—for instance, in the *Ratto Catalogue* and by Goodacre.[3] In fact, all legible specimens read MΛNOVHΛ, or some variant spelling of that name.

Constantinopolitan/small-module type B is usually assigned to Manuel I (for instance, quite recently by Bellinger)[4] on the basis of the name MΛNOVHΛ which can occasionally be made out upon it. Gerassimov would prefer an attribution to Manuel Comnenus–Ducas of Thessalonica (1230–37) since the type is represented in several Bulgarian hoards containing coins of that empire.[5]

Constantinopolitan/small-module type C is an almost unknown type, but specimens occur bearing the name ΛΛЄ⊐IOC, and it has therefore been assigned to Alexius III by Edwards.[6]

Thessalonican type A/small-module D has been assigned to John II by Bellinger and Metcalf owing to the similarity of its reverse design to that of the second metropolitan coinage of this Emperor.[7]

Thessalonican type B/small-module E was shared between Alexius I and Manuel I in the *Ratto Catalogue*,[8] and has more recently been provisionally assigned to Isaac II by Bellinger and Metcalf on the basis of the freshly struck

[3] R. Ratto, *Monnaies byzantines et d'autres pays contemporaines à l'époque byzantine* (Sale Catalogue, Lugano, 9.xii.30) (reprint Amsterdam, 1959), no. 2077; H. Goodacre, *A Handbook of the Coinage of the Byzantine Empire* (reprint London, 1957), p. 269, nos. 36, 37; p. 279, no. 23.

[4] A. R. Bellinger, "Three More Hoards of Byzantine Copper Coins," ANS *Museum Notes*, 11 (1964), pp. 215–16, nos. 8–65; pp. 222–23, nos. 1–23.

[5] T. Gerassimov, "Contribution à l'étude de la numismatique de l'Empire byzantin de Salonique," *Studia in Honorem M. S. Drinov* (Sofia, 1960), pp. 381–98.

[6] Edwards, *Corinth*, p. 147, no. 158.

[7] A. R. Bellinger and D. M. Metcalf, "A Hoard of Byzantine Scyphate Bronze Coins from Arcadia," *NC*⁶, 19 (1959), p. 161.

[8] Ratto, *op. cit.*, nos. 2075–76, 2143.

appearance of two specimens in the Arcadia hoard of 1958—the latest metropolitan coins in the hoard being datable to 1195–1203.[9] A specimen in the possession of the author, however, reads TⱲKOMN, which suffices to rule out Isaac II as a possibility.

Thessalonican type C/small-module F has been assigned a twelfth-century date by Bertelè.[10]

Since it is these six types which are the best represented of the series in hoards, discussion will, for the moment, be confined to them.

It is in the chronological arrangement of hoards that the peculiarities of the series are most evident. The question is unfortunately somewhat hampered by the difficulties encountered in dating hoards within reasonable limits on either side of the year 1204. It is clear that any hoard containing the rather scarce billon trachea of Theodore I, Lascaris of Nicaea must have been deposited at a date subsequent to 1208, when he was formally crowned emperor: it is, in addition, doubtful whether he was in a position to issue coinage before that date. Hoards lacking coins of this emperor but containing the common billon trachea of Alexius III cannot at the moment be dated with the same degree of accuracy: they obviously cannot antedate the accession of that Emperor in 1195, but many of this pattern may have been deposited subsequent to his fall in 1203, the conquest of the city in 1204, and for at least a decade afterward. On the other hand, since the coinage of Alexius III is, as already remarked, extremely common, any hoard containing large numbers of pieces of Isaac II (1185–95) and of his predecessors, but lacking coins of Alexius III entirely, can fortunately, with some degree of confidence but by no means with certainty, be assigned to a date not later than 1195. It is clear that in particular many such hoards of Bulgarian provenance will have been deposited as a consequence of the major disturbances suffered by the area during the reign of Isaac: the revolt of the Asenid dynasty; the resulting imperial campaigns and, in addition, the passage of the Third Crusade (see Table XI on p. 202).

The pattern is quite consistent: apart from the single specimen of the general type A present in the hoard from General Nikolaevo, the six types are confined to the hoards datable by their contents as being later than 1208. Nor does the General Nikolaevo piece stand as an inexplicable anomaly, for although most hoards of this type were very probably buried before 1195, as pointed out above, there can be no certainty on the point. Four of the six hoards in which all or most of these types occur—Byaga, Dorkovo, Logodash, Lom (A), Muglizh (II), and Tri Voditsi—show definite indications of a date of deposition at least well into the second decade of the thirteenth century. They contain the later

[9] Bellinger and Metcalf, op. cit., p. 160.

[10] T. Bertelè, "Costantino il Grande e S. Elena su alcune monete bizantine," Numismatica, 14, nos. 4–6 (July–Dec. 1948), p. 95.

TABLE XI

Hoard	Total of identifiable Coins	Con. A/ Small A	Con. B/ Small B	Con. C/ Small C	Thess. A/ Small D	Thess. B/ Small E	Thess. C/ Small F
Batkoun	2113	—	—	—	—	—	—
Belitsa	100	—	—	—	—	—	—
Draganovo	752	—	—	—	—	—	—
Enina	197	—	—	—	—	—	—
General Nikolaevo	748	1	—	—	—	—	—
Iskra	84	—	—	—	—	—	—
Kaloyanovets	884	—	—	—	—	—	—
Kroushare	321	—	—	—	—	—	—
Novo Selo	744	—	—	—	—	—	—
Suedinenie	21	—	—	—	—	—	—
Tiurkmen (I & II)	128	—	—	—	—	—	—
Turnovo (I)	53	—	—	—	—	—	—
Yagoda	308	—	—	—	—	—	—
Assenovgrad	180	14	—	—	—	—	—
Brestovo	1614	99	—	—	—	—	—
Byaga (1959)	451	246	16	8	26	18	10
Dorkovo (1940)	132	64	—	2	12	2	3
Gradevo (II)	339	54	—	—	2	—	—
Kiustendil	566	44	—	—	—	—	—
Kiustendil reg. (?)	371	41	—	—	14	—	—
Logodash (1959)	302	185	8	4	16	10	6
Lom (A) (1962)	2103	882	5	—	19	27	1
Lom (B) (1962)	355	51	—	—	4	9(?)	—
Mogilitsa (1934)	18	10	—	—	—	1	—
Muglizh (II) (1960)	6559	2633	131	—	134	198	7
Oustovo (1936)	24	—	5	—	—	—	1
Pisaratsi (1927?)	69	6(?)	—	—	—	—	—
Pokrovnik	488	53	—	—	1	1	—
Preslav (1953)	25(?)	11	1	—	—	—	1
Roussé (1965)	195	175	3	—	3	1	—
Stara Zagora (1941)	348	103	1	—	1	5	—
Toulovo (?)	677	270	8	—	9	9	—
Tri Voditsi (1940)	613	321	12	16	36	24	21
Tsepina (1965)	16	1	—	—	—	—	—
Uncertain Bulg. Prov.	470	9	—	—	1	2	—
Zheleznitsa	378	55	—	—	—	—	—

(→ 1195 braces the group from Batkoun to Yagoda; 1208 → braces the group from Assenovgrad to Zheleznitsa)

Nicaean billon trachy coinage of Theodore Lascaris (Muglizh II), or the similar denomination struck by the emperors of Thessalonica (Dorkovo, Logodash, and Tri Voditsi), or both.

To all intents and purposes therefore the types under discussion did not enter the circulating medium in Bulgaria until after 1195. It is obviously important to determine whether they began to circulate at an earlier date in any other area of the Empire.

In fact, this pattern of occurrence is typical. The Zlata hoard from Yugoslavia, the Obuda hoard from Hungary, the Macedonian hoard of 1959, the Lazania hoard from Cyprus, and the Nicosia parcel are all of the type containing no coins later than 1195. None of them includes the six types in question. On the other hand, the following relatively well documented and accurately recorded hoards, dated by their inclusion of pieces of Theodore I, contain some or all of these types, often in appreciable proportions (see Table XII *infra*).

Dumbarton Oaks hoard (I)
Dumbarton Oaks hoard (II)   } Yugoslavia
Dumbarton Oaks hoard (III)
Osanica

Istanbul (B) (1946)   } Turkey in Europe
Postallar

Corinth (III) (1960)
Levkokhori (1955)   } Greece
Naousa (Paros) (1924)

Bergama   } Turkey in Asia Minor
Troad (1930's)

TABLE XII

Hoard	Total identifiable Coins	Con. A/ Small A	Con. B/ Small B	Con. C/ Small C	Thess. A/ Small D	Thess. B/ Small E	Thess. C/ Small F
D.O. (I)	101	85	—	1	4	1	1
D.O. (II)	170	84	1	3	21	17	7
D.O. (III)	360	205	10	7	24	7	4
Osanica	c. 2000	"present"	?	?	"present"	"present"	?
Istanbul (B)	448	124	58	—	2	4	—
Postallar	323	192	25(?)	4(?)	14(?)	37(?)	?
Corinth (III)	23	14	—	—	2	2	2
Levkokhori	977	745	—	—	—	—	—
Naousa (Paros)	50	1	—	—	1	—	—
Bergama	1058	36	?	?	?	?	?
Troad	140	1	23	—	—	2	—

The large proportion of the general type B in both the Istanbul (B) and Troad hoards led Bellinger to postulate the existence of a provincial mint in Asia Minor under Manuel, the products of which had remained confined to the area in which they had originally been struck and where they were still forming an important element of the circulating medium after the formation of the empire of Nicaea. In the light of further evidence, however, it can be seen that these two hoards are remarkable only to the degree in which they provide striking confirmation of a uniform pattern of occurrence, and are not in themselves the anomalies which he considered them.

The extraordinarily concentrated composition of the Yenimahalle hoard, from a village on the European side of the Bosphorus toward the Black Sea, while not of provably thirteenth-century date, provides a further indication of the general coherence of the group. The figures are as follows:

Con'ple type A	25 specimens
Con'ple type B	21 specimens
Thess. type A	53 specimens
Thess. type B	8 specimens
Thess. type C	43 specimens
Alexius III	1 specimen
Isaac II (?)	1 specimen
	152 specimens

It must be concluded therefore that these six types began to enter the circulating medium in all regions of the Empire—or of its successor states—at a date not appreciably earlier than 1195 and possibly considerably later, and that they apparently did not reach their highest proportions in the coinage until at least well into the third decade of the thirteenth century. A necessary corollary is that their actual production must also be dated to the same period, for although superficially it would be tempting to suppose that their late appearance might be due to some such phenomenon as "coin drift"—a delay in the appearance of coins in regions other than that in which they were struck owing to time taken in travelling from the point of origin—an explanation of this kind is ruled out not only by the extent of the delay (a quarter of a century and more) and the relatively small area involved (the Balkans and western Asia Minor), but finally and conclusively by their uniformly late appearance in all regions.

The unexpectedly late date given to this group of trachea is apparently confirmed by further considerations. Firstly, if the type identified here as Thessalonican A/small-module D (Pls. 28. *1–4*; 29. *10–12*) were indeed to be dated to the reign of John II, it is difficult to see how it could have anticipated the advent of the obverse type of var. C of the fourth metropolitan coinage of Manuel I (Pl. 16. *10–13*); complete with officina distinctions in the form of asterisks above the cushion of Christ's throne. In other words, it is possible but unlikely that a provincial issue should provide the direct inspiration for both the obverse type and one officina distinction of a subsequent metropolitan issue.

Secondly, although the details of the imperial chlamys on Constantinopolitan/ small-module type B (Pls. 25. *11, 12*; 29. *4–6*) are rather similar to those on the electrum trachea of Andronicus I (Pl. 18. *11, 12*), they can be exactly paralleled only on the billon coins of this same series (Constantinopolitan type F [Pl. 26. *2*]) and on the electrum scyphates (Pl. 47. *6*) of Hugh I of Lusignan, king of Cyprus 1205–1218, which is very much the same period as that to which it is suggested type B must be moved. Thirdly, there is the evidence of overstrikes. A specimen of Constantinopolitan type B from the Muglizh (II) hoard is overstruck on what can only be a coin of Isaac II, which necessarily dates the former type to not earlier than 1185. A further and more certain instance of overstriking involves a coin in the author's possession in which a specimen of Thessalonican type B is overstruck upon a coin of the first Nicaean issue of Theodore I, Lascaris. The coin which is overstruck is of the following description:

Obv. ┼╥P

Traces of nimbate head of Virgin.

Rev.

Full-length figure of emperor on left, and of a nimbate military saint, holding between them object on long shaft. Emperor wears (stemma), divitision, collar-piece, and panelled loros of simplified type; holds labarum-headed scepter in right hand. Saint wears short military tunic (and breastplate?); holds spear, resting over shoulder, in left hand.

Pl. 46. *7*

In addition to the general description, the characteristic features of the imperial loros: ▯—particularly the four jewels above the waist in the form of a cross, and the panelling of the actual waist—render it certain that the undertypes are those of the issue of Theodore already mentioned, only among specimens of which can these features be precisely paralleled (Pl. 30. *7–10*). It follows, therefore, that type B must be later than 1208.

It remains only to identify the authorities behind the issue of this series. The possibilities are, in fact, limited: at most the Constantinopolitan Emperor Alexius III; the emperors of Nicaea; the rulers of Epirus—later the emperors of Thessalonica; the tsars of Bulgaria, and the rulers of the various Latin states.

Alexius III may be immediately discounted: certainly Constantinopolitan/ small-module type C bears the name Alexius, but this is only one of the series— the same observation applies to whatever possibility there might otherwise be of an attribution to Alexius IV or V. There is, moreover, one instance of its being overstruck on Constantinopolitan type B of this series (Pl. 46. *6*). The emperors of Nicaea already have a recognized and considerable coinage in gold, electrum or silver, and billon or copper assigned to them, and although John III, Ducas-Vatatzes (1222–54) seems to have made a practice of basing his types on those of John II, Comnenus, a tentative reading of the name John accounts for only one type in the group under discussion (Thessalonican type A/small-module D). Furthermore, coins of the Nicaean emperors are uniformly rare, if widespread, in Bulgarian hoards of this period, whereas this series is exceedingly common. The short-lived empire of Thessalonica (1224–46) had only three emperors who are known to have issued coinage. The second and third of these, Manuel (1230–37) and John (1237–42, despot 1242–44), already have a considerable number of types attributed to them in view of the brevity of their reigns and, as Bertelè has remarked,[11] the style of the Thessalonican coinage is characteristically neat—quite incapable of accommodating the variations of the series under discussion. In addition, John is always represented as beardless, being still a youth at the time of his accession. Although there is reason to believe that the Asenid tsars of Bulgaria struck coins imitating Byzantine types at a period subsequent to c. 1195, it is most unlikely that they could be responsible for a series comprising so many types.

The Latin emperors of Constantinople were formerly credited with striking the coins (folleis) since identified as the latest types of the anonymous bronze, but that suggestion has long since been discarded and they therefore remain without a coinage. Yet there are two pieces of documentary evidence indicating that the Latins did strike coins. The first is a reference in the De Signis Constantinopolitanis of Nicetas Choniates, who mentions that many of the ancient statues in the hippodrome were used by the Latins, subsequent to the conquest of 1204, for the striking of coins (ἀλλὰ καὶ ταῦτα κεκόφασιν εἰς νόμισμα).[12] The second consists of a clause in the treaty of 1219 between Theodore I, Lascaris of Nicaea and Giacomo Tiepolo, the podestà of the Venetians in Romania (the lands of the former Empire): Conventum est inter hoc, quod nec Imperium meum, neque tuus dispotatus habeat licentiam formare yperperos, vel manuelatos, aut stamena equalis forme alterius partis.[13] As it was an important official document, it would appear reasonable to assume that it means precisely what it says and that the prohibition contained in it was made with regard to what had already happened or was very likely to happen. Nor was the clause a matter of mere formal custom, for it had not appeared in previous treaties between the Byzantine emperors and Venice, and it was not to appear again.

While the narrow interpretation of the clause presents no difficulties, the inferences that can be drawn from it, the various possible situations, one of which

[11] T. Bertelè, L'imperatore alato nella numismatica bizantina (Rome, 1951), p. 28.
[12] Nicetas Choniates, Bonn ed., pp. 858–59.
[13] Tafel and Thomas, Urkunden, 2 (Vienna, 1856), p. 207.

must have led up to its formulation, are unfortunately much more varied. The coinage of Theodore is well known and consists possibly—to use western terms—of gold yperperi; certainly of electrum or silver manuelati and of billon stamena. The Venetian consists of silver grossi and of billon petty deniers on the western pattern. But the terms employed in the clause are specific: Theodore will not copy Venetian yperperi, manuelati, or stamena; the Venetians will not copy Theodore's. What cannot be inferred is that Theodore had been copying the normal Venetian grossi or deniers. The imitation of the grosso became quite common in the Balkan states of a later period, but neither the specific nor a euphemistic interpretation of the clause will allow of such an inference. It is possible that Theodore had been copying Venetian yperperi, manuelati, and stamena, but this, of course, pre-supposes the Venetian issue of coinage on the Byzantine pattern. And why should Theodore copy Veneto-Byzantine coins when he was issuing his own coinage of Byzantine pattern in his own name? The Venetians could have been copying Theodore's coinage, but this again necessitates the attribution of a coinage of Byzantine pattern to them. Less directly, it might be supposed that the Venetians were considering the issue of a coinage of Byzantine pattern and, more particularly, of imitating Theodore's coinage; that Theodore, having got to know of this situation, then decided formally to bind the Venetians from doing so by inserting a clause in the treaty; that the intention of copying was therefore dropped before being put into practice. But this is the counsel of desperation and runs against the sense of the rest of the document which is markedly concrete and practical. A further possibility is that some power other than Venice had issued copies of Theodore's coinage, and that he was sufficiently perturbed to bind the Venetians from following suit. This is less unlikely than the preceding.

The possibilities which seem to be most likely, or rather least unlikely, are then, either that Venice was issuing imitations of Theodore's coinage or that a third power was doing so.

At this stage it is useful to examine the alternative courses open to a Latin power occupying former Byzantine territory, assuming that the decision to mint coins had been taken. And it should be pointed out that it is *prima facie* most improbable that at some point during the Latin occupation the necessity of striking coins should not have arisen. The territory and prosperity of the Latin empire and kingdom of Thessalonica might be much diminished, but the supply of pre-conquest coinage was necessarily decreasing with each year; the sources of Venetian and Western coinage, on the other hand, were far removed and there is no evidence for the systematic supply of any Western coinage to the Latin states. Two crucial decisions would therefore have been necessitated: the first, the form that the coins were to take, whether the Western or the Eastern. With the majority of the population of both the major cities and of the provinces remaining Greek, it would clearly have been advantageous, if not necessary, to adopt the Eastern form. Coinage, after all, is quite useless if the public refuses to accept it. It would then have been necessary to decide on the name in which the coinage was to be issued, whether that of the doge or that of the Latin emperor or the king of Thessalonica or whoever the local ruler might be. Again, the Greek population might well have found either alternative objectionable.

The evidence of documentary sources and the appearance in European hoards of large numbers of coins of these six types in question, datable to the period shortly after the conquest of 1204 and yet not attributable to the only major issuing authority of the period, Theodore Lascaris, are both explicable if it is assumed that the Latin authorities—whether Venetian or imperial—avoided the embarrassing choices before them merely by continuing to issue coins of the traditional Byzantine pattern in the names of the emperors of the preceding century. In theory, at least, they had no quarrel with any of them, except Alexius III and Alexius V. In these circumstances Theodore might well have become concerned about the possibility of his coinage being used as a model for imitation: indeed, as will be shown below, he may have had actual grounds for complaint.

Nor would this custom have been without remarkably similar precedents. The coinage of the barbarian kingdoms settled upon territory formerly occupied by the western Roman Empire had, after all, been closely imitative of the former Roman types and denominations for well over two centuries. The Arabs had, in their turn, done much the same within the provinces won from the Byzantine Empire itself. The Western invaders, besides, came from parts of Europe where immobilized types were in normal use. Most of the minting authorities in northern Italy struck coins bearing the names of emperors long since in their graves, without any attempt to keep them up to date. The same was true of much of the feudal coinage of France, where the names or monograms of Carolingian sovereigns were still in common use throughout the twelfth century. The deniers of Flanders and Brabant did not at that time bear the names of the actual rulers. Even in England an immobilized coinage had recently been introduced, with Richard I and John striking pennies unchanged in type and inscription from those of Henry II. In Syria and Palestine the gold coins issued by the Crusaders were no more than badly engraved imitations of Fatimid dinars.

It would obviously have been unwise to copy the types of the earlier emperors such as Alexius, John, and Manuel exactly, since they were of considerably higher value than the coins of the later emperors and of the Latins themselves. Consequently the Latin/Byzantine types were recognizable from the originals by some small differences in the details of design, or were of a more or less "fictional" character, having little basis in an earlier type except for the general principles of dress, the stance of the emperor depicted, and the style in which the design was rendered.

Once this identification is made, the six issues of the group under discussion can be divided into three smaller groups, two according to type, the other according to module. The first consists of two types in the name of Manuel and one in that of an Alexius. It is this that is given to Constantinople since it would seem to be the group which extends into a whole series of issues, as might be expected of an occupation lasting over half a century. Type A (Pl. 25. *6–10*) seems to have found its origin in the third billon coinage of Manuel, with the important distinction that on the obverse of the later issue the Virgin is seated upon a throne with back, rather than without, and that on the reverse the emperor holds an anexikakia, rather than a globus cruciger. A definite confirmation of this suggested connection is to be found in the fact that the shaft of the labarum, in the case of the later issue, is occasionally decorated with between one and four dots, in a pale imitation of the strict officina distinctions which characterize the earlier. The two main varieties of inscription MΛNOVHΛ ΔΕCΠΟΤΗC or ΠΟΡΦVΡΟΓΕΝΝΗΤΟC—both often incomplete, blundered, or retrograde—connect the issue with type B (Pl. 25. *11, 12*) which has the same varying feature. It is the reverse of type B which seems to have been the original of that found on the electrum scyphates of the Lusignan kings of Cyprus. Type C must be later than type B on the evidence of an overstruck specimen in the collection at Dumbarton Oaks (Pl. 25. *13*): more conveniently illustrated as regards the overstrike on Plate 46.

The second group—a very compact one—consists of three types attributable to Thessalonica during the Latin occupation (1204–24). Type A (Pl. 28. *1–4*) is undoubtedly earlier than type B (Pl. 28. *5–8*), which is in many cases overstruck upon it (e.g., Pl. 46. *5*)—to such an extent indeed that the identification of both types as emanating from the same source, though a different one from the Constantinopolitan group, is almost certain. A and B are related by a further, negative point. Of the several hundred specimens seen by the author, mainly in Bulgarian hoards, in no case has an identifiable imperial personal name occurred, although the dynastic name Comnenus occasionally appears on type B, and in spite of the fact that the neatness of many specimens seems to herald that characteristic feature of many of the issues of the Ducas subsequent to 1224. There can be little doubt that this lack—in contrast to the blundered but dominant lettering seen in the Constantinopolitan series—is deliberate, and it would seem probable that this was the solution to the embarrassing problem of whose name to put upon the coinage. In the same vein, the choice of SS. Helena and Constantine as the reverse of type C (Pl. 28. *9, 10*) was politically unexceptionable.

The attribution to Thessalonica is made on the basis of the recurrence of the extraordinary pendilia form ↓.↓ which dominates type A, and is only slightly

less common on type B, although extremely uncommon on the Constantinopolitan series, being used by the die-cutters of that mint no more than might be
accounted for by unsystematic borrowing. Precisely this unusual feature had,
however, been employed on a series of hyperpyra belonging to Alexius I which
has also been attributed to Thessalonica (Pl. 5. *7, 8*) and in which it seems to
be related to the long stem of the cross which surmounts the globus—itself a
characteristic feature of the products of that mint. The resurrection of this
technique seems too striking to have been mere coincidence and may have resulted from an intentional search through mint documents in order to discover some
way by which the products of the mint might be made distinguishable.

In attributing issues of the period to Thessalonica, it should be remembered
that the city had certainly acted as a mint of great importance during the
period preceding the conquest of 1204 (albeit mainly for tetartera, not trachea),
and that it very quickly again became so (this time mainly for trachea) directly
upon its re-occupation by the Ducas in 1224. It would seem reasonable to
suppose therefore—once the fact of a Latin coinage has been accepted—that
Thessalonica should have been a mint in the relatively short intervening period.

The source of inspiration for the obverse of type A should probably be found
in the similar design used in the second billon coinage of John II. That for the
reverse, as already mentioned, can only have been var. C of the fourth billon
coinage of Manuel I, the officina distinction in the form of asterisks above the
cushion of Christ's throne having been retained. The original of the obverse of
type B may perhaps have been the hyperpyron type of Manuel I, although
there the bust of Christ Emmanuel is represented as beardless: the bearded
representation is virtually unprecedented. The reverse seems to have been
taken from the hyperpyron type of Alexius I, even to the exaggerated form of
the chlamys-jewelling as it drapes from the Emperor's left arm, and the dot on
the shaft of the labarum-headed scepter.

The third group is composed of coins of the six types described above, but
which are distinguished by their small module and light weight (Pl. 29. *1–18*).
To these there should, however, be added a further type in the name of Theodore Lascaris of Nicaea (Pl. 29. *19, 20*). Yet a further series, in the name of
John Ducas of Thessalonica will be treated with the coinage of that empire.

The main problem presented by these coins of small module is whether or
not they should be separated from the coins of larger module, but with the
same obverse and reverse types. If they are to be considered as emanating
from the same mints as the coins of larger module, and presumably at much
the same time, then there is a clear case for simply treating them as fractions of
the larger. Unfortunately, however, the situation is not quite so straightforward.

In the first place, although it is necessary to suppose that three mints and
two major political divisions were involved in the production of this series, the

characteristics of fabric, module, and, if it may be so termed, style, are identical in all cases. Although the Latins might well be credited with a practice breaking the tradition of the preceding century, in which fractional trachea with the same obverse and reverse types as the unit had no place, the same is not true of Theodore Lascaris, whose coinage is otherwise of a strictly traditional pattern. Yet, since there manifestly does exist a small-module series of coins in his name, it would be necessary to conclude that he either initiated the practice himself or that he followed the Latins in their departure from precedent. It is also normal for fractional pieces to be issued in smaller quantities than their units—whereas in all except a very few instances the small-module coins vastly outnumber the larger ones in hoards.

Secondly, the evidence of hoards, when added to these general considerations, introduces distinct chronological complications which can only be considered as invalidating the assumption that the small coins were issued more or less contemporaneously with the large coins of identical types.

The Istanbul (B) hoard contained 124 specimens of the Constantinopolitan/ small-module type A; that is, the total included some examples at least of the small-module series. Also included were fifty-eight specimens of the Constantinopolitan type B—with, apparently, not a single coin of the small-module series. The Troad hoard contained a further twenty-three specimens of type B with, again, no coins of small module. The Yenimahalle hoard contained 150 specimens of Constantinopolitan types A and B and Thessalonican types A, B, and C—but again no coins of the small-module series. It would therefore appear that hoards within a small radius of Constantinople do not, in general, at this early date, tend to contain the small-module series in large proportions.

Further evidence comes from the region of the northern end of the valley of the river Struma, and consists of a group of six, perhaps seven, large hoards. The seventh hoard is from an uncertain Bulgarian provenance, but so closely resembles the remainder of the group in its contents that it may be provisionally attributed to the same general area. The large and small-module series of each type are arranged side by side in Table XIII below.

TABLE XIII

Hoard	Total identifiable Coins	Con. A (large)	A (small)	Thess. A (large)	D (small)	Thess. B (large)	E (small)	Theo. I (large)	G (small)
Brestovo	1614	21	78	—	—	—	—	1	—
Gradevo (II)	339	18	36	2	—	—	—	4	—
Kiustendil	566	10	34	—	—	—	—	1	—
Kiustendil reg.	371	37	4	14	—	—	—	2	—
Pokrovnik	488	18	35	1	—	1	—	3	—
Zheleznitsa	378	22	33	—	—	—	—	4	—
Uncertain prov.	470	8	1	1	—	2	—	2	—

14*

The pattern of occurrence is remarkably consistent. The commonest type is undoubtedly Constantinopolitan/small-module A. What is perhaps more important is the proportions in which the large and small series occur: although the large-module outnumbers the small in only two hoards (Kiustendil reg. and that of uncertain provenance), nevertheless the former is always represented in appreciable numbers. The total of the general type A never forms a very large proportion of the total of identifiable coins present in the hoard. The three other general types are less well represented—and, more important, present only in the large module.

There is every reason to suppose from the similarity of their content that these hoards were laid down at approximately the same time, and it follows that they should give a comparatively accurate impression of the composition of the local circulating medium. The date of deposition is presumably not too far distant from 1208, which is the first date at which the Nicaean trachea of Theodore Lascaris might have begun to appear, for only the first Constantinopolitan coinage and the first and second Thessalonican are present. At this early period, therefore, the small-module coins neither made up an overwhelming proportion of the total hoard, nor, alternatively, swamped the coins of the same types but of larger module.

An altogether different impression is given by another group of hoards, from approximately the same area, perhaps with a concentration slightly to the east—but of later date. The date is assured by their containing the later trachea of Theodore Lascaris or of his successor John Ducas-Vatatzes, or the same denomination of the emperors of Thessalonica (see Table XIV *infra*).

TABLE XIV

Hoard	Total of identifiable Coins	Con. A (large)	A (small)	Con. B (large)	B (small)	Con. C (large)	C (small)	Thess. A (large)	D (small)	Thess. B (large)	E (small)	Thess. C (large)	F (small)	Theodore I (large)	G (small)
Byaga	451	32	214	2	14	1	7	4	22	4	14	—	10	2	18
Dorkovo	132	—	64	—	—	2	—	4	8	—	2	3	—	2	—
Logodash	302	24	161	1	7	—	4	3	13	6	4	—	6	2	13
Tri Voditsi	613	321 ("very few large")		2	10	16 ("very few large")		—	36	—	24	6	15	—	23

The pattern has changed completely: the small-module coins of type A not only form a greater proportion of the total hoard, they overwhelmingly outnumber their larger counterparts. Although the remaining types of the series do not occur in the same numbers, it is nevertheless clear that the coins of larger module are generally outnumbered by the smaller.

The *prima facie* evidence of the hoards therefore suggests that the early types of the mints of Constantinople and Thessalonica, together with the first Nicaean coinage of Theodore I, were produced comparatively soon after the conquest of 1204, but that, at some appreciably later date, there was a gigantic burst of production, at all three mints, of small-module pieces bearing the same types as their earlier and larger counterparts. This is, of course, possible, but considering the political divisions involved, unlikely. It is particularly unlikely that the official mint of Thessalonica would have been allowed to continue the small-module series of Latin design subsequent to the recovery of the city by the Ducas in 1224—a date much too early to account for the changes in the circulating medium that took place between the deposition of the two groups of hoards analyzed above.

Yet the comparatively late date at which these coins of small module were apparently produced is confirmed by the existence—and presence in late hoards —of a similar series with the types and in the name of John Comnenus-Ducas, emperor of Thessalonica 1237–42 (Pls. 40. *12*—41. *18*). The large number of types involved in this latter series strongly suggests that its production was not necessarily limited to the few years of John's short reign, but the approximate date at which both series seem to have flourished is very much the same.

It would therefore seem necessary to dissociate this small-module series from the larger module one with the same obverse and reverse types, however unwelcome this might be on general principles.

But if this is the case, then what were these small coins, and from where did they come? Unfortunately neither question can be answered with any assurance on the basis of the present state of the evidence: at best, tentative suggestions can be put forward.

The small module and often wretched manufacture of this series, together with the constant and drastic clipping down of larger, regular coins, as seen in such late hoards as those from Logodash, Dorkovo, Mogilitsa, Oustovo, Preslav, and Tri Voditsi, suggests that it perhaps ought to be viewed as something in the way of an "unofficial" imitative coinage—produced in order to supplement the meager supplies of the official mints, and at least tolerated by the authorities themselves. A parallel might be found in the "barbarous" radiate and diademed coins of small module and clipped fabric which the western provinces of the Roman Empire produced in vast quantities at various times during the late third to fifth centuries.

Hoard evidence suggests that Greece and Bulgaria were the areas in which the small-module coinage tended to dominate the circulating mediums of the third to the fifth or sixth decades of the thirteenth century. Whether the production of a similar series in the name of John Ducas of Thessalonica conveys any hint as to the major source, or sources, of both series remains to be seen. The small-module series of John Ducas contains an astonishing number of types for a short reign of seven years at most; it is generally reckoned that his authority to strike coins ended with his demotion to the rank of despot after a mere five years. Yet there are no less than fifteen types at a conservative count, and others will very probably come to light in future: the large number of types should not disguise the fact that each survives in a remarkably small number of specimens, frequently less than half a dozen, some being apparently unique. In the circumstances, therefore, it will be surprising if additional types do not turn up occasionally as they have done so far. With the appearance of each new type it becomes increasingly difficult to believe that the series is an official one the production of which was confined to the short period of his rule. It should be pointed out that, whereas the regular coinage of John Ducas (Pl. 40. *1–5, 6–10*) is of a relatively conservative character in its choice of iconographical themes, the small-module coinage (Pls. 40. *12–15*; 41. *1–18*) provides several astonishing departures from tradition: the emperor holding a large banner; the winged emperor; the winged emperor atop the towered walls of a city. As Bertelè has convincingly shown, there are strong reasons for supposing that such themes betray Western influences. Might this not give some clue as to who actually produced the coins, or for whose benefit they were produced?

Although the two major series of small-module coins, that with Latin and Lascarid obverse and reverse types, and that with the Thessalonican, are almost certainly connected—whether by a common source or merely by a common standard—it has been thought less confusing and more in conformity with the present state of evidence to classify them as separate from their counterparts of large module, but not to remove them from their vicinity. Consequently, the pieces with Latin and Lascarid types have been listed as an appendage to the Latin coinage, and those with Thessalonican types together with the regular coinage of John Ducas.

Whatever the solution of the problem outlined above, if the main suggestions of this Chapter are accepted, the general scheme of the thirteenth-century coinage is now radically altered and an understanding of the climate which produced the extraordinary clause in the treaty of 1219 is at least facilitated. Coinage was being copied on a large scale. Theodore was concerned lest his own might suffer—indeed, if the small-module coins with his types were not, in fact, produced by his moneyers, he had legitimate cause for concern. Moreover the copiers were the Latin authorities, placed in the position of an alien minority ruling a still overwhelmingly Greek population. Unwilling or incapable of producing a viable coinage of their own, they resorted to continuing the types and themes of the preceding century.

A precise allocation of responsibility for the production of the Latin imitative series—as between the Venetians and the local imperial or royal authorities—is, unfortunately, not possible on the basis of present evidence. Although it is perhaps tempting to see the Venetians as solely responsible and the treaty clause as the inevitable result, the actual phrasing employed in it does not justify such a direct inference. Theodore may merely have been hoping to put pressure on the local authorities *via* the Venetians, or he may simply have decided to anticipate any Venetian moves toward following an example already set by the local authorities. What is certain is that the treaty clause was not a piece of verbiage produced without adequate reason—to fill up paper. Something of appreciable moment must have occurred to justify the inclusion of a clause which, although less specific than one might now wish, nevertheless remains unparalleled in the text of any other treaty between Byzantium and the West.

The first three issues only of the Latin mint of Constantinople having been discussed, it remains to deal with the remainder. Unfortunately the relative order is completely lost, and probably unrecoverable.

Type D has already been the occasion of some disagreement. It was attributed by Wroth to Manuel Comnenus-Ducas of Thessalonica,[14] but Bertelè has since correctly pointed out that the blundered—frequently retrograde—inscription, and the heavy, crude style disqualify it from any consideration as the product of that mint, and prefers an attribution to Manuel I, Comnenus.[15] The evidence of hoards, however, clearly confirms the type in a thirteenth-century context: Assenovgrad (1 specimen), Dorkovo (5), Oustovo (1), Pisaratsi (1), and Tri Voditsi (22). All except the first are datable at least to the third decade of the thirteenth century, and it would therefore seem reasonable to attribute the type to the Latin series.

Type E is clearly related to the previous by fabric, module, and style. Examples occurred in the Troad hoard (1 specimen) and that from Preslav (1?).

Type F, again of the same stylistic group, occurred in the hoards from Mogilitsa (2 specimens ?) and Tri Voditsi (7).

Type G is known apparently only from a specimen in the collection at Dumbarton Oaks.

Type H occurred in the hoards from Preslav (1 specimen) and Tri Voditsi (6).

Type I is again apparently known only from a single specimen, in the Bibliothèque Nationale, but is of the same style as the preceding types and is related by its unusual obverse to types S and T.

Types J and K have been attributed by Bertelè to Constantine Ducas, Sebastocrator of Thessaly (*c.* 1289–1303), who is not otherwise known to have issued coinage.[16] There were two specimens of type J in the Preslav hoard, and

[14] W. Wroth, *Catalogue of the Coins of the Vandals, Ostrogoths and Lombards and of the Empires of Thessalonica, Nicaea and Trebizond in the British Museum* (London, 1911), pp. 198–99, nos. 3, 4 (type 2).

[15] T. Bertelè, "Monete di Giovanni Comneno Duca imperatore di Salonicco (1237–1244)," *Numismatica*, 16 (1950), p. 79, note 65.

[16] *Idem*, "Monete bizantine inedite o rare," *Zeitschrift für Numismatik*, 36 (1926), pp. 35–36, nos. 112, 113.

seven in the Tri Voditsi hoard, and, although both are of a late pattern, it is most unlikely to be that late: a date somewhere in the fourth to sixth decades of the thirteenth century is far more acceptable in view of their contents. The type should therefore be attributed to the Latin occupation. Despite the lack of the nimbus, the person depicted under the name Constantine can only be the saint of that name. The choice of this unusual type was possibly motivated by the same kind of consideration as demonstrated by Thessalonican type C.

Type L is also apparently known only from a Dumbarton Oaks specimen.

Type M is apparently known from two specimens: one in the collection of the American Numismatic Society, the other at Dumbarton Oaks. The obverse type is similar to that used for type J.

Type N has been attributed by Bertelè to John II, Comnenus,[17] but, although the design is almost certainly based upon the reverse type of the electrum issue of that Emperor, such an attribution is impossible in view of the crude style of the rendering. An alternative attribution to John III, Ducas-Vatatzes of Nicaea is possible, but the emperor is portrayed here with a rounded beard, not with a forked one as is normal for John III. The type would, however, be at home in the context of the preceding series.

Type O was attributed to John II in the *Ratto Catalogue*, an attribution also recently followed by Bertelè.[18] It is, however, of thirteenth-century date: there was one in the Istanbul (B), three in the Oustovo, and ten in the Tri Voditsi hoard. It is, in addition, known to be overstruck on Thessalonican type C of this series (Pl. 46. *8*). An attribution to John III, Ducas-Vatatzes of Nicaea is a possibility, but an unlikely one for the same reasons of portraiture as in the preceding type, N. The triangular shaped object to be seen in the field, to the left of the standing figure of Christ, is a puzzling feature and can be explained only by considering it as an attempt to represent, in perspective, the corner of the dais upon which Christ often stands—an attempt which has, however, become disassociated from the actual figure. The reverse type has apparently been taken from the first metropolitan billon coinage of John II.

Type P has already come under discussion: Wroth placed it (correctly) with type D which it very much resembles in fabric, module, and style; his further attribution to Thessalonica during the period 1243–46[19] must be rejected on the same grounds as his attribution of type D to Manuel Comnenus-Ducas; the style is too crude. The type is quite definitely a thirteenth-century one, however, for specimens have occurred in the hoards from Dorkovo (4 specimens), Mogilitsa (1), Oustovo (1), Preslav (2), and Tri Voditsi (16). It also appeared in the equally late Postallar hoard (8 specimens). A single specimen said to have

[17] *Ibid.*, pp. 12–13, nos. 36–38.
[18] Ratto, *Monnaies byzantines*, nos. 2101–02; Bellinger, "Three More Hoards," p. 222.
[19] Wroth, *BMCV*, pp. 202–203.

come from the Souvatité hoard—which is otherwise dated by coins of Alexius III—is probably intrusive, for its bright orange patina distinguishes it from the rest of the coins.

Type Q is apparently known only from a single specimen in the collection at Dumbarton Oaks, but clearly fits into this series with regard to type, module, fabric, and style.

Type R occurred in the hoards from Dorkovo (4 specimens), Preslav (1), and Tri Voditsi (8). It also apparently occurred in the Postallar hoard (3 specimens).

Type S has apparently not yet been found in hoards, but type T, to which it is obviously related by the unusual type of the Virgin Hagiosoritissa, occurred in the hoards from Dorkovo (3 specimens), Mogilitsa (1), and Tri Voditsi (12).

There can be no doubt that the late pattern of hoards—Dorkovo, Mogilitsa, Oustovo, Pisaratsi, Preslav, and Tri Voditsi—represents the circulating medium of the third to sixth decades of the thirteenth century, and the appearance in them of coins in the names of emperors such as Andronicus, Constantine, and Manuel, together with the associated anonymous types, can have resulted only from the continuation of the Latin imitative series: for there were no emperors at all of that period named Andronicus or Constantine, and the only Manuel (of Thessalonica) could not have struck both the fine, neat coins that are provably products of his reign and the crude, blundered coins of this series. The term "imitative" is no more than partly applicable in the case of many of the later types, for, whereas H and I certainly have some foundation in the coinage of Andronicus I, and N and O are similarly based upon types struck by John II, many, such as J, K, and L, are purely fictional in that they are neither struck in the name of the reigning emperor nor based on any previous issue.

The tetarteron type given to the Latin mint of Constantinople (Pl. 27. *12*, *13*) is so assigned because of the similarity in points of detail between the representation of the Virgin, on the obverse, and that on types N and R of the trachea. The jewelled border along the front of the maphorion common to all these types apparently does not appear on twelfth-century issues. The inscription on this tetarteron type is mostly blundered, but probably reads: ICΛΛKIOC.

The half-tetarteron types (Pl. 28. *11–14*) are assigned to Thessalonica on the grounds that there had been a long tradition for the striking of this denomination at the mint: type C of the trachea, moreover, also portrays SS. Helena and Constantine. The figures on the half-tetarteron type B are both turned slightly to one side, Helena to the right, Constantine to the left: the same rather unusual posture is adopted by Theodore Comnenus-Ducas on his half-tetarteron types (Pl. 38. *12–15*). That these types are halves, and not the unit, is clear from the weight of the specimens in the collection at Dumbarton Oaks. The two specimens of type A weigh 1.85 and 1.39gm., the six specimens of type B weigh 1.74, 1.69, 1.67, 1.54, 1.46, and 1.35gm..

THE IMITATIVE COINAGE OF THE PERIOD OF THE ASENID TSARS OF BULGARIA

c. 1195–?

BILL. TRACHY

Type A (As Manuel I, 4th coinage, var. C)

Obv. ĪC XC in field.

Christ, bearded and nimbate, wearing tunic and colobion, seated upon throne without back; holds Gospels in left hand. Asterisk above cushion of throne on either side.

Rev. MΛNȢHΛ ΔECΠOT—or var. M̄P ΘV̄ in upper right field.

Full-length figure of emperor on left, crowned by Virgin nimbate. Emperor wears stemma, divitision, collar-piece, and jewelled loros of simplified type; holds in right hand labarum-headed scepter (occasionally scepter cruciger), and in left, globus cruciger. Virgin wears tunic and maphorion.

Pl. 24.*1–9*

Type B (As Isaac II, var. A)

Obv. M̄P ΘV̄ in upper field.

Virgin nimbate, wearing tunic and maphorion, seated upon throne with back; holds beardless, nimbate head of Christ on breast.

Rev. ICΛΛKIOC ΔECΠOTHC in two columnar groups.

Full-length figure of emperor wearing stemma, divitision, collar-piece, jewelled loros of simplified type, and sagion; holds in right hand scepter cruciger, and in left, anexikakia. *Manus Dei* in upper right field.

Pl. 24.*10–14*

Type C (As Alexius III, var. II)

Obv.+KERO HΘEI. ĪC XC in field.

Beardless, nimbate bust of Christ wearing tunic and colobion; holds scroll in left hand.

Rev. ΛΛEΞIШΔECΠ $\overset{\text{Θ}}{\underset{\text{K}}{\text{Ū}}}$ TШKOMΗNШ — or var.

Full-length figure of emperor on left, and of Saint Constantine nimbate, holding between them globus cruciger. Emperor and saint each wear stemma, divitision, collar-piece, and jewelled loros of simplified type, and hold labarum-headed scepter (occasionally scepter cruciger, or jewelled).

Pl. 24.*15*, Pl. 25.*1–5*

THE COINAGE OF THE BULGARIANS: COMMENTARY

The information gained from the identification of the Latin imitative series itself reveals chronological anomalies in the behavior of another small group of trachea.

This group consists of three main types and is closely based on the metropolitan series: the fourth coinage of Manuel, and the substantive types of Isaac II and Alexius III. Unlike the Latin series, they are more or less direct copies. Fortunately for the sake of distinction, however, the strict system of jewelling on the imperial loros and collar-piece which marks the metropolitan series is not adhered to in the case of the imitative coins. In addition, whereas the metropolitan coins of Alexius III always have the loros waists ⊠ ▦ or ⦂ ▦ or ⊡ ▦, the imitative series adds the easily recognizable varieties (a) ⦂ ⦂, (b) ▦ ▦, and (c) ▩ ▩. In general, the imitative coins are distinguishable from the metropolitan by differences of fabric, module, and style. The fabric of the former is irregular, frequently marred by striking cracks, the module is often smaller, and the style has been described by Metcalf as "linear"—in addition, the inscription is mostly crudely effected and blundered. It is sometimes difficult to distinguish the originals from the copies in the case of Alexius III/type C coins, for the degeneration in style and technique which affected the coins of the metropolitan mint under that Emperor diminishes the differences between the two. However, examination of a series will often have the effect of emphasizing the peculiarities of each.

With the recognition of the Latin series commencing in 1204 or soon after, hoards deposited during the decades to either side of 1200 can now be recognized with a good deal more certainty than hitherto possible. The group of hoards containing issues of the emperors up to, and frequently including, those of Isaac II, has already been noted and dated to some point in the reign of that Emperor. Now, hoards including coins of both Alexius III and the Latin series can be given a definite post-1204 date (whether or not they include coins of Theodore of Nicaea), while those including the coins of Alexius III but not the Latin series can—with a good deal of probability, but not certainty—be dated to the reign of Alexius, or very shortly after, before the Latin coins amounted to an appreciable part of the circulating medium.

A list of the larger Bulgarian hoards of pre-conquest date, giving the relative numbers of metropolitan and imitative coins of the series in question is given in Table XV on page 220.

The figures are as conclusive as those for the Latin series: to all intents and purposes, the imitative series in question—even the "Manuel" type—did not begin to arrive in the circulating medium in Bulgaria until either late in the reign of Isaac II or during the reign of Alexius III. A pre-1195 date cannot be

TABLE XV

	Hoard	Manuel I, 4th Coinage (metropolitan)	Imitative Series	Andronicus I (metropolitan)	Isaac II (metropolitan)	Imitative Series	Alexius III (metropolitan)	Imitative Series
→1195	Batkoun	1051	—	296	129	—	—	—
	Belitsa	47	—	3	—	—	—	—
	Draganovo	444	—	52	11	—	—	—
	Enina	91	1	24	19	—	—	—
	Iskra	8	—	5	70	—	—	—
	Kaloyanovets	367	—	75	238	—	—	—
	Kroushare	148	—	58	—	—	—	—
	Novo Selo	367	—	109	16	—	—	—
	Tiurkmen (II)	60	—	17	3	—	—	—
	Turnovo (I)	28	—	7	—	—	—	—
	Yagoda	160	—	37	—	—	—	—
→1204	Kartal (1914)	17	1	3	6	—	5	—
	Kazanluk	18	188	2	93	310	191	239
	Muglizh (I)	27	204	9	167	202	234	308
	Pirdop	2	2	—	20	6	32	—
	Plovdiv reg.	—	—	—	23	—	67	—
	Strazhitsa	34	—	6	407	2(?)	531	4(?)
	Tsruncha (A)	41	105	11	332	150	533	52
	Tsruncha (B)	25	95	9	245	115	379	39
	Turnovo (II)	—	4	—	285	22	336	—
	Tvurditsa	11	34	—	24	59	73	15

entirely excluded, for the Batkoun-Yagoda pattern of hoards were mostly, if not all, buried during the early years of the reign of Isaac (1185–95), but it is at least certain that these hoards do not generally include the imitative series.

Metcalf has suggested that this series emanated from a number of provincial mints in Greece and assumed that they are to be dated to the reigns of the emperors in whose name the coins purport to have been issued. Both points are considerably undermined by the late appearance of this series—for why should imperial (even provincial) mints strike numbers of coins in the names of deceased emperors? The postulated Greek origin is rendered invalid by the fact that the Struma valley hoards show no signs of overwhelming numbers of these coins penetrating up from Greece either prior to 1195 or subsequently (see Table XVI on p. 221).

Judging by the figures, the metropolitan coinage of Manuel disappeared very quickly from circulation, probably owing to its relatively high silver content, and it is for this reason that the proportions for the metropolitan type of Manuel and its imitation are so disparate. However, despite the comparatively late date of these hoards (probably well into the second decade of the thirteenth century), the figures for Isaac and Alexius show appreciably less difference be-

TABLE XVI

Hoard	Manuel I, 4th Coinage (met.)	Imitative Series	Isaac II (met.)	Imitative Series	Alexius III (met.)	Imitative Series
Brestovo	19	386	290	157	370	267
Gradevo (II)	—	105	56	10	83	23
Kiustendil	20	75	154	25	183	50
Kiustendil reg.	1	183	9	80	27	14
Pokrovnik	9	118	66	51	98	85
Zheleznitsa	1	103	22	54	49	90
Uncertain prov.	25	47	215	12	117	18

tween the two series: in fact there is a definite tendency for the metropolitan coins to outnumber the imitations.

The figures for the pre-conquest hoards from Bulgaria show considerable variation, although hoards such as that from the region of Plovdiv may be considered as bodies of coinage taken from the metropolitan region and not allowed to mix with the local currency. Yet neither of the two large hoards from north of the Balkan range—Strazhitsa or Turnovo—contain large numbers of the imitative series. The two large hoards from Tsruncha, in the southwestern Thracian plain, similarly do not contain overwhelming proportions of that series, though certainly greater than the Strazhitsa/Turnovo hoards. On the other hand, both hoards from the region of the Sredna Gora—Kazanluk and Muglizh (I)—contain large proportions of the imitative series, outnumbering the metropolitan even in the cases of Isaac and Alexius. This pattern is possibly confirmed by the (later) hoard from nearby Korten in which there were no specimens of Manuel's metropolitan fourth coinage, but thirty-nine imitations, six specimens of Isaac's metropolitan type with eight imitations, and twelve specimens of the metropolitan type of Alexius, together with no less than seventy-two imitations. Twelve pieces of a Latin issue date the hoard to the post-conquest period.

The late appearance of this series, as already pointed out, suggests that, although pre-conquest in date, it was not imperial. It appeared between c. 1195 and 1204 and seems strongest in the region of the northern Thracian plain and the Sredna Gora. It was precisely at this period that the latter areas fell under the rule of the Asenid tsars. Moreover, copies of imperial types of the late tenth or the eleventh century have been found in considerable numbers in Bulgaria. The total of evidence at present available would therefore seem to suggest that this series in fact forms a Bulgarian imitative coinage—whether officially inspired or merely tolerated cannot be ascertained. The official Bulgarian coinage, in the name of the ruling tsar, apparently does not commence until the reign of Ivan II, Asen (1218–41), although Kaloyan, as early as 1203–1204 had demanded, and obtained, the right of coining in his own name from Innocent III.[20] The series in question would clearly fill the hiatus admirably.

It is easy to see why the fourth metropolitan coinage of Manuel was chosen, in that it must have formed the major element of the circulating medium until well into Isaac's reign. Var. C was no doubt selected as the most distinctive. Whether these three main types were produced in chronological succession or all at one time is impossible to say. As to the identity of the mint concerned— although there might have been more than one—the obvious candidate is Verroë (Stara Zagora), the largest city of the area in question, which must have fallen into Bulgarian hands at some time subsequent to 1191.[21] That it, rather than Turnovo, should be the site of a mint is not surprising at this early period in the organization of the second Bulgarian empire, for the latter city must have taken some time to develop.

The fact that type A, at least, was being struck at a date subsequent to the death of Manuel, in whose name it was allegedly struck, would seem confirmed by the evidence of a coin in the collection at Dumbarton Oaks, The reverse inscription of this piece clearly reads: — ѠѦƎΓΝѦѠΤ (Pl. 24.9). Now, the first emperor bearing the family name Angelus was Isaac II (1185–95), and if, as seems likely from appearances, the coin is genuine (although clipped and flattened), it must have been produced after 1185. But the obverse and reverse types are those of Manuel's fourth metropolitan coinage, var. C.

---

[20] *Bullarium Diplomatum et Privilegiorum Sanctorum Romanorum Pontificum*, 3, ed. A. Tomassetti (Turin, 1858), no. XXXVIII, p. 188: *Ad petitionem… publicam in regno tuo cudendi monetam tuo charactere insignitam, liberam tibi concedimus facultatem.*

[21] When Isaac fled back to the city after being ambushed in the passes of the Balkan range (Nicetas Choniates, Bonn ed., p. 562).

(iii)

SUMMARY

The "horizontal" complexity of the coinage of the twelfth century—the need to accommodate within a single reign trachea of wildly differing fabric, module, style, and weight—has now been replaced with a "vertical" one; the distinction of several chronological waves of imitative coins overlying the original imperial issues. It is for this reason that hoards deposited subsequent to the appearance of the last of them present an incredibly confused picture, containing as they do, both the original issues and all the various imitations based on them.

The main defense of the arrangement postulated in the preceding sections of this Chapter is therefore not only that it can be seen to work in the chronological listing of hoards, but that in itself such a radical reinterpretation makes a good deal more sense than the situation previously accepted.

Once this distinction is made, it is quite plain that the monetary system of the Comneni and Angeli together with the organization of its production was essentially very simple. The main mint throughout, as far as the coinage of gold, electrum and billon trachea was concerned, was Constantinople itself. The coinage of copper tetartera and half-tetartera was, however, divided between two main mints, Constantinople and Thessalonica, with a probable temporary third somewhere in the central Greek provinces.

It is only with the reigns of Isaac II and his successor Alexius III that complications begin to appear. At some point during that period the first wave of the imitative coinages appeared: based on the almost direct copying of the Byzantine series, it apparently originated in the areas of the Empire recently lost to the Asenid tsars of Bulgaria.

With the Latin conquest of 1204, the pattern speedily becomes confused, despite the fact that the coinages of the empires of Nicaea and later Thessalonica are easily recognizable. Three further imitative series must now be distinguished, with one of them having chronological complications in addition. The series issued by the Latins in Constantinople is marked by its reversion to the types of previous emperors, but with slight and presumably deliberate distinctions in the iconography of the obverse or reverse types, or both: the name of the emperor by whom the original was issued is normally prominent, although frequently badly blundered. The Thessalonican series is necessarily of shorter duration but produced on much the same lines as that of the capital. A different technique is, however, used with regard to the imperial name, for in all but a few cases it is deliberately omitted. The third series is that consisting of coins of small module, struck in direct imitation of the early Constantinopolitan and Thessalonican Latin coins, together with the main Nicaean type of Theodore Lascaris.

223

CHAPTER TWELVE

THE COINAGE OF THE EMPIRES OF NICAEA AND THESSALONICA

The three major successor states to the Empire of the Comneni and Angeli—Nicaea, Thessalonica, and Trebizond—all issued coinage in some quantity. While those of Nicaea and Thessalonica were modelled largely upon the pattern of the Alexian reformed coinage, that of Trebizond, which was geographically and politically an isolated unit, was overwhelmingly of a pattern more akin to those of the Seljuk sultans of Rum and the Armenian kings of Cilicia. For this reason it will not be dealt with in this publication.

The obvious similarities between the coinage of the twelfth-century Empire and that of its thirteenth-century successors tend to conceal one difference of fundamental importance. While the circulating medium of the earlier period was composed of a relatively small number of issues, each of considerable volume, that of the later was, on the contrary, made up of a very great number of issues, most of them apparently struck in minimal quantities and now known only from very few surviving examples. Although this observation does not perhaps apply to the first Nicaean emperor Theodore I, Comnenus-Lascaris (1208–22), it certainly does to his successors John III, Ducas-Vatatzes (1222–54), Theodore II, Ducas-Lascaris (1254–58), and Michael VIII, Palaeologus (1258/59–61). The emperors of Thessalonica, Theodore Comnenus-Ducas (1224–30), Manuel (1230–37), and John (1237–44) are all represented, despite the brevity of their reigns, by a disproportionately large number of types, with completely new ones still occasionally appearing. It has therefore been impossible to treat the coinages of the successor states with anything like the degree of completeness which, it is hoped, has been achieved for the earlier emperors.

It should also be pointed out that the lists of types contained in this section include only those which have been (in the author's opinion) adequately published and photographed, or of which he has personal knowledge. Although this further limits the degree of completeness, it was thought that the alternative—long lists of types, many of which owe their existence to over-enthusiastic reconstruction, the over-indulged desire to discover varieties differing from those already known, or simple misattribution—has been a serious drawback to the study of this series for some considerable time. It is hoped, on the other hand, that the body of proven material described and illustrated here will provide a concentrated point of reference which will be of some use for the substantial amount of work which remains to be done in this field.

The detailed study of the monetary history of the period is faced with problems which are no less formidable. While the general form of the monetary system remains unaltered from the twelfth century, there were undoubtedly considerable changes in the values of particular denominations. Unfortunately there is much less documentary evidence for the thirteenth century than for the twelfth, and for this reason the precise denominational structure remains obscure. The same lack of sources renders the recovery of the contemporary terminology at best a patchy affair, although fortunately it seems, insofar as it is recoverable, to be a direct continuation of that of the preceding period.

References to νομίσματα,[1] νομίσματα χρυσᾶ,[2] νομίσματα (χρυσᾶ) ἐξάγια[3] and νομίσματα ὑπέρπυρα (ἐξάγια),[4] together with such Latin transliterations as yperperi,[5] all involve the standard gold coin of the day, the hyperpyron nomisma. During the early years of the century the only hyperpyra in circulation would have been those of the Comneni and Angeli of the pre-conquest period, but with the third and fourth decades the hyperpyra of the Nicaean emperor John III would rapidly have come to form the bulk of the circulating medium of precious metal, particularly since they represented an alloy slightly—but appreciably—lower than that of the earlier rulers.

A Latin document of 1219 and a Greek one of 1208 mention respectively the stamenum[6] and a sum in nomismata to be paid διὰ τραχέων.[7] Both involve the billon scyphate.

The manuelatus continues to put in an appearance in Latin documents: thus *manuelatos bonos* in 1207[8] and *manuelatos* in 1219.[9] On the basis of the Pisan document of 1199, which has been discussed in a previous chapter, the obvious step would be a straightforward identification of the manuelatus with the electrum trachy. There is, however, another possibility: the term may here refer to the hyperpyron. The reference of 1219 is to ... *yperperos vel manuelatos aut stamena.* ... Unfortunately the passage is capable of two interpretations. In the first place, three denominations would be involved—yperperus, manuelatus and stamenum. On the other hand, *manuelatus* could quite well qualify *yperperus* in which case two denominations only would be involved: the yperperus manuelatus and the stamenum. In view of the unequivocal

---

[1] E.g., Miklosich and Müller, *Acta et Diplomata*, 6, pp. 152, 157, 159, 168, 170, 171, 172, 173.

[2] *Ibid.*, 4, pp. 47, 50, 61.

[3] *Ibid.*, p. 78.

[4] *Ibid.*, pp. 52, 74, and *passim*.

[5] E.g., Tafel and Thomas, *Urkunden*, 2, pp. 43, 53, 60, 90.

[6] *Ibid.*, p. 207.

[7] Miklosich and Müller, *op. cit.*, 4, p. 183.

[8] Tafel and Thomas, *op. cit.*, 2, p. 58.

[9] *Ibid.*, p. 207.

evidence of the Pisan document mentioned above, however, it is probably wiser to accept the former interpretation, and three denominations.

The term νόμισμα τρικέφαλον (often abbreviated to Γκλ′)[10] occurs in dated documents of 1213 and 1216 from the Monastery of Patmos,[11] and of 1208, 1232, and 1237 from that of Lembo.[12] Although the later references are quite possibly to the hyperpyra of John III, which portray the three figures of Christ, the emperor, and the Virgin, those of 1208, 1213, and 1216—to be assigned to the reign of Theodore I—are much less decisive. It is possible that they refer to either hyperpyra or electrum trachea of the pre-conquest emperors, but it should be remembered that the electrum or silver trachea of Theodore I himself are also capable of this description.

[10] For the explanation of the abbreviation Γκλ′, see F. Dölger, "Chronologisches und Prosopographisches zur byzantinischen Geschichte des 13. Jahrhunderts," *BZ*, 27 (1927), pp. 296–97, note 4.

[11] Miklosich and Müller, *op. cit.*, 6, pp. 164, 175.

[12] *Ibid.*, 4, pp. 183, 79, 90.

(i)

THE EMPIRE OF NICAEA

The situation confronting Theodore Lascaris on his flight from the City in 1204 was perhaps even more disastrous than that which Alexius I had faced in 1081: the latter had, at least, control of the capital upon which to base his reconstitution of the state.

Asia Minor, which was to be the basis of Theodore's reconstruction was, on the other hand, in utter chaos. A number of members of the great families of the Empire had established themselves as independent sovereigns: Alexius and David Comnenus—even before the fall of the City—in Trebizond; Sabbas Asidenus in Sampson near Miletus; Manuel Mavrozomes in the Maeander valley; Theodore Mangaphas in Philadelphia once more; Leo Gavalas in Rhodes; and a Byzantine educated Italian named Aldobrandini in Attalia.[13]

All but the last few years of the reign of Theodore I were spent in suppressing these dynasts and campaigning against the Latins on the one side, the Seljuks on the other. At his death in 1222, the frontiers of the Nicaean empire in Asia Minor were already largely established. His successor, John III, was therefore little concerned with this area, beyond extending his rule over the northwest and the islands off the coast. Interest was henceforth centered on Europe where by 1246 he was in possession of Thrace up to the Maritsa—reconquered from the Bulgarians—and of Thessalonica, which had been the site of the only other serious attempt to reconstitute the Byzantine Empire in its old form with its former frontiers. In turn, at his death in 1254, the empire extended from the Adriatic to Amastris on the Pontic coast and to the Cnidan peninsula on the Aegean. Only the recovery of Constantinople remained, and with this, in 1261, the goal of the successor states for over half a century was finally attained.

THE COINAGE OF THEODORE I, COMNENUS-LASCARIS

1208–1222

N HYPERPYRON

MINT OF NICAEA OR MAGNESIA

Obv. KERO HΘEI . ΪĊ X̄C̄ in field.

Christ, bearded and nimbate, wearing tunic and colobion, seated upon throne without back; right hand raised in benediction, holds Gospels in left.

---

[13] The main Byzantine authors for this highly obscure period are Nicetas Choniates (Bonn ed., p. 842) and George Acropolites (Bonn ed., pp. 12–14).

Rev. (ΘΕΟΔШΡΟC ΚΟΜΝΗΝΟC ?) in two columnar groups.
Full-length figure of emperor wearing stemma, divitision, and chlamys; holds in right hand labarum-headed scepter, and in left, globus cruciger. *Manus Dei* in upper right field.

Pl. 30.*1*

Æ TRACHY

MINT OF MAGNESIA

Type A
Obv. ĪC X̄C in upper field.
Christ, bearded and nimbate, wearing tunic and colobion, seated upon throne without back; holds Gospels in left hand.
Rev. ΘΕΟΔШΡΟCΔΕCΠΟΤ Ο,ΘΕΟΔШΡΟC—or var.
Full-length figure of emperor on left, and of St. Theodore, bearded and nimbate, holding between them long shaft, at the head of which a star. Emperor wears stemma, divitision, jewelled loros of simplified type, and sagion; holds sheathed sword, point downward, in right hand. Saint wears short military tunic, breastplate, and sagion; holds sheathed sword point downward, in left hand.

Pl. 30.*2, 3*

Type B
Obv. ĪC X̄C Ο ΕΜΜΑΝΰΗΛ in two columnar groups.
Bust of Christ Emmanuel, beardless and nimbate, wearing tunic and colobion; holds scroll in left hand.
Rev. ΘΕΟΔШΡΟCΔΕC Ο,ΘΕΟΔШΡΟC—or var.
Full-length figure of emperor on left, and of St. Theodore, bearded and nimbate, holding between them patriarchal cross on long shaft, at the base of which three steps. Emperor wears stemma, divitision, and chlamys; holds sheathed sword, point downward, in right hand. Saint wears short military tunic, breastplate, and sagion; holds sheathed sword, point downward, in left hand.

Pl. 30.*4–6*

BILL. TRACHY

MINT OF NICAEA

First coinage
Obv. M̄P Θ̄V in field.
Virgin nimbate, wearing tunic and maphorion, seated upon throne without back; holds beardless, nimbate head of Christ on breast.

Rev. ΘΕΟΔWΡΟC ΟΘΕΟΔWΡΟC—or var.

Full-length figure of emperor on left, and of St. Theodore, bearded and nimbate, holding between them patriarchal cross on long shaft. Emperor wears stemma, divitision, collar-piece, and panelled loros of simplified type; holds labarum-headed scepter in right hand. Saint wears short military tunic and breastplate; holds spear in left hand, resting over shoulder.

Pl. 30.*7–10*

Second coinage

Obv. ĪC X̄C in field.

Christ, bearded and nimbate, wearing tunic and colobion, seated upon throne without back; holds Gospels in left hand. Asterisk above cushion of throne, on either side.

Rev. ΘΕΟΔWΡΟC ΔΕCΠΟΤΗC ΚΟΜΝΗΝΟC Ο ΛΛCΚΛΡΗC in two columnar groups.

Full-length figure of emperor wearing stemma, divitision, and chlamys; holds in right hand scepter cruciger, and in left, anexikakia. Asterisk frequently on left, or right, or both, of inside of chlamys as it hangs from emperor's arms.

Pl. 31.*1–5*

MINT OF MAGNESIA

Type A

Obv. ĪC X̄C in field.
      + +

Full-length figure of Christ, bearded and nimbate, wearing tunic and colobion; holds Gospels in left hand.

Rev. (ΘΕΟΔWΡΟC ΟΘΕΟΔWΡΟC ?)

Full-length figure of emperor on left, and of St. Theodore, bearded and nimbate, holding between them labarum on long shaft. Emperor wears stemma, divitision, collar-piece, and jewelled loros of simplified type; holds in right hand anexikakia, sword hangs point downward to left of waist. Saint wears short military tunic and breastplate; holds spear in left hand, resting over shoulder, sword hangs point downward to right of waist.

Pl. 31.6, 7

Type B (As Æ type B)

Obv. ĪC X̄C Ο ΕΜΜΛΝΥΗΛ in two columnar groups.

Bust of Christ Emmanuel, beardless and nimbate, wearing tunic and colobion; holds scroll in left hand.

Rev. (ΘΕΟΔѠΡΟC   ΟΘΕΟΔѠΡΟC ?)

Full-length figure of emperor on left, and of St. Theodore, bearded and nimbate, holding between them patriarchal cross on long shaft, at the base of which three steps. Emperor wears stemma, divitision, and chlamys; holds sheathed sword, point downward, in right hand. Saint wears short military tunic, breastplate, and sagion; holds sheathed sword, point downward, in left hand.

Pl. 31.*8, 9*

Type C

Obv. ĪC X̄C Ο ЄΜΜΑΝΫΗΛ in two columnar groups.

Bust of Christ Emmanuel, beardless and nimbate, wearing tunic and colobion; holds scroll in left hand.

Rev. (ΘΕΟΔѠΡΟC   ΟΘΕΟΔѠΡΟC ?)

Full-length figure of emperor on left, and of St. Theodore, bearded and nimbate, standing on dais, holding between them labarum(?) on long shaft. Emperor wears stemma, divitision, and chlamys; holds in right hand labarum-headed scepter. Saint wears short military tunic and breastplate; holds spear in left hand, resting over shoulder.

Pl. 31.*10*

THE COINAGE OF THEODORE I: COMMENTARY

GENERAL

The date at which Theodore began to issue coinage is uncertain, but his position during the first few years after 1204 was so precarious as to render it most unlikely that he would have done so from the beginning. His ecclesiastical coronation in 1208,[14] involving the formal rejection of the fiction of his administering the empire in the name of his absent father-in-law, the ex-Emperor Alexius III, probably marks the *terminus ante quem*. Several years more may have elapsed, however, before he could make full use of the imperial prerogative which he claimed by striking coinage.

The adoption of the surname "Comnenus" was presumably made on the basis of his marriage to Anna, a daughter of Alexius III:[15] confirmation of the style is available from documentary sources—his signature to the treaty of 1219 with the Venetian podestà reads: *Theodorus, in Cristo Deo fidelis Imperator et moderator Grecorum Comnanus Lascarus.*[16]

---

[14] A. Heisenberg, *Neue Quellen zur Geschichte des lateinischen Kaisertums und der Kirchenunion*, 2 (Munich, 1923), pp. 8–11. Proclaimed in 1205, he had previously held the title of Despot.

[15] Acropolites; Bonn ed., p. 12.

[16] Tafel and Thomas, *op. cit.*, 2, p. 207.

The forked beard with which Theodore is depicted on his coins is mentioned by George Acropolites, the historian of the empire:[17] both of Theodore's successors, John III and Theodore II, seem to have continued the fashion.

It has long been customary to accept the conjecture that the main or only mint of the empire was at Nicaea itself as the official capital. Acquiescence is largely based, however, on the fact that no evidence has as yet been brought out either for or against the hypothesis: yet several considerations, both general and particular, not only undermine it but, moreover, indicate the area in which the main mint was actually sited.

A glance at the map of the frontiers of the empire, although necessarily only approximate, quickly shows that the city of Nicaea lay between the areas under the control of the Latins on the one side, the Seljuks on the other. The area under Latin control began slightly to the south of Adramyttium and included Achyra, Cyzicus, and Nicomedia.[18] The researches of Charanis have shown that the Seljuk frontier began only a little west of Nicaea itself: Claudiopolis, Dorylaeum, and Cotyaeum all certainly seem to have been in Seljuk hands.[19] Consequently the cities of Amastris, Heraclea, Nicaea, and even Brusa must have been part of a corridor only a few miles wide between two always potential, sometimes actual, hostile frontiers. Nicaea would surely have been an inconvenient and unsafe site for the mint—with all the convoys of bullion to and from the city that this would have entailed.

There is, in addition, conclusive evidence demonstrating that it was not the area around Nicaea that formed the basis of the considerable prosperity of the empire, but that lying between the rivers Hermus and Maeander, forming the themes of Neocastra and Thracesion. Included were the cities of Smyrna and Ephesus on the coast, and Magnesia, Nymphaeum, and Sardis in the hinterland.[20]

Smyrna, the chief center of the empire's military and mercantile marine, also lay in a fertile region largely composed of the estates of senior court functionaries and members of the imperial family itself. Documents from the Monastery of Lembo[21] nearby provide an illuminating commentary upon the social and economic conditions prevailing in the region.

[17] Acropolites; Bonn ed., p. 34.

[18] Information on the approximate frontier line can be gleaned from Acropolites (Bonn ed.; pp. 30–31, 41).

[19] P. Charanis, "On the Asiatic Frontiers of the Empire of Nicaea," *Orientalia Christiana Periodica*, 13 (1947), pp. 58–62. *Pace* Charanis, neither Laodicea nor Chonae seems to have been a permanent possession of the empire of Nicaea (cf. Choniates, Bonn ed., p. 842; Acropolites, Bonn ed., pp. 153–54).

[20] What follows is based largely on the valuable study of the region by H. Ahrweiler-Glykatzi, "L'histoire et la géographie de la région de Smyrne entre les deux occupations turques (1081–1317) particulièrement au XIIIe siècle," *Travaux et mémoires*, 1 (1965), pp. 1–204.

[21] Published in Miklosich and Müller, *op. cit.*, 4, pp. 1–289.

Ephesus, the capital of the Thracesion theme, evidently remained a port of considerable influence, although subordinated to Smyrna.

Mme Ahrweiler argues convincingly that Magnesia was the capital of the theme of Neocastra and documentary sources mention it as a considerable center of international trade.

It is apparent from the sources that John III, Theodore II, and Michael VIII (before the recovery of the City) preferred the city of Nymphaeum above all others as the imperial residence, particularly during the autumn and winter months.[22] Both John and Theodore, and their closer relations, were buried in the various monasteries of their foundation in the areas under discussion.[23]

Sardis, to judge by the evidence of coin finds from the excavations there—about which more below—seems to have shared fully in the prosperity of these two themes.

Nevertheless, it must be admitted that ancient and mediaeval mints were not invariably sited with regard to economy or convenience, and the general evidence above, although suggestive, does not, taken on its own, warrant the re-siting of what must have been an important permanent section of the bureaucracy away from the official capital. However, both documentary and numismatic evidence particularly favor such an alteration and place the mint within the prosperous region between the Hermus and Maeander; in fact, within the city of Magnesia.

It is the main historian of the reign of Michael VIII, George Pachymeres, who gives the interesting information that it was at Magnesia that John III had his main treasury, and that, although Theodore II had an additional one at Astytzium on the Scamander (to facilitate the payment of the military in the European provinces?), Magnesia must also have acted as his main treasury, for a detachment of Varangian mercenaries was already stationed there as its guard when Michael Palaeologus began manoeuvering for power in 1258, immediately after the death of Theodore.[24] Theodore himself had referred to the city as "golden Magnesia."[25]

The billon trachea of Theodore I quite clearly fall into two groups on the basis of module, style, and details of iconography. The one consists of the (Nicaean) "first" and "second" coinages (Pls. 30.7–10; 31.1–5), the other of (Magnesian) types A–C (Pl. 31.6–10). The module of the first group seems to average at about 25 mm., the second at about 30 mm. It is, however, in the details of the military dress worn by St. Theodore that the differences between

[22] E.g., Acropolites; Bonn ed., pp. 91, 109, 187.

[23] Ibid., p. 164.

[24] George Pachymeres; Bonn ed., 1, pp. 68, 71. An interesting parallel to the cohors ad monetam of early first-century Lugdunum (CIL xiii. 1499).

[25] Ed. N. Festa, Theodori Ducae Lascaris Epistulae CCXVII (Florence, 1898), p. 265.

the two groups are the most obvious. On the coins of the first group the Saint's breastplate is made up of small dots, suggesting the effect of chain mail; moreover, the tunic drapes out uninterruptedly from under the bottom of the breastplate. On pieces of the second the breastplate is composed of linear segments suggesting scale armor; between the bottom of the breastplate and the tunic there are three strips of what would be leather in the classical military dress.

Turning from the billon to the silver trachea, it is at once evident that it is the technique used in the second billon group that is used also in the silver: the stylistic connection between the coins of different metals is so close that they might well have been engraved by the same hand. It is therefore not mere coincidence that type B of the billon is of exactly the same design as type B of the silver.

The best known of all the billon types is the (Nicaean) "first" coinage. Among other points this type appears constantly—albeit in small quantities—in almost all of the Bulgarian hoards that are demonstrably of thirteenth-century date. The (Nicaean) "second" coinage, which has only recently been correctly attributed to Theodore I by Bellinger,[26] is definitely scarcer in this area, but does appear in an appreciable number of the hoards presented in this publication. Of these, several[27] are certainly of late date, containing most or all of the commoner Latin types, or those of the empire of Thessalonica, or both. There is, therefore, a good *prima facie* case for considering the one as later than the other on this evidence alone. In fact, a specimen from the Istanbul (B) hoard clearly shows an overstriking (Pl. 46.9) which confirms the suggestion. The three (Magnesian) types A–C, however, appear in only one of these Bulgarian hoards, and then in the most minute quantity (Tri Voditsi: one specimen type B, one type C, from a total of 136 identifiable coins).

On the other hand, the excavations at Sardis brought to light fourteen coins of Theodore I,[28] which in view of the paucity of twelfth-century pieces might legitimately be taken as confirmation of the flourishing state of the area under the Lascarids. An analysis of the types represented is of extreme interest in view of the fact that no hoard seems to have been involved:

Æ, Type A	1 specimen
Bill., (N) First coinage	1 specimen
(M) Type A	1 specimen
(M) Type B	7 specimens
(M) Type C	4 specimens
	14 specimens

[26] Bellinger, "Three More Hoards," pp. 221–22.
[27] For instance, those from: Lom (B), Muglizh (II), Toulovo, Tri Voditsi, and Tsepina.
[28] Bell, *Sardis*, pp. 105–107. Subsequent excavation has brought to light many more.

Of the two billon groups, the second, that connected with the silver (of which there was also a single specimen) predominates overwhelmingly.

The provenance of the only published hoard of the silver of Theodore I confirms the evidence: over two hundred pieces of both types were found at Torbalı, a small town between Smyrna and Aydin (Tralles).[29] The site is within a few miles of Smyrna, Magnesia, Nymphaeum, and Sardis.

The conclusion therefore seems inescapable that of the two billon groups, the one connected with the silver, together with the silver itself, is related to the area between the Hermus and the Maeander: the area containing the treasury at Magnesia. They should therefore be attributed to the mint of that city.

The obvious corollary is to attribute the remaining two billon types to Nicaea, and in support of this suggestion is the fact of their repeated appearance in Bulgarian hoards.

The problem still remaining is to discover whether the issue of the two billon groups was contemporaneous or successive, and, if the former, whether there is any evidence for the continued existence of both mints during the following reigns.

Unfortunately no direct evidence is available. However, there is no obvious division within the coinage of John III that would suggest the operation of two mints. Given the increasing prosperity of the Hermus-Maeander region and the fact that the treasury was situated at Magnesia until the recovery of Constantinople, it would appear unlikely that the mint of the former city should cease or even decrease production—rather the opposite. In view of the fact that the (Nicaean) first coinage must be considered a very early issue indeed owing to the pattern of its appearance in Bulgarian hoards and its overstriking by the second, and that the mint of Magnesia cannot have come into operation until after the suppression of Asidenus and Mangaphas (between 1208 and 1211),[30] it would on general grounds appear more likely that Magnesia succeeded and replaced, rather than accompanied, Nicaea.

The known provenances of the gold of John III are at this point worthy of some consideration, although qualified by their uncertain reliability.

A hoard of about a thousand pieces, including hyperpyra of John III, Theodore II, and Michael VIII, was found near Smyrna in 1839. Part was purchased by H. P. Borrell, a British merchant residing in that city.[31]

---

[29] Chap. 15, pp. 389–90.

[30] Acropolites treats these campaigns as subsequent to the coronation of 1208 (Bonn ed., pp. 13–14), and Lascaris was certainly well in possession of the areas formerly occupied by these dynasts at the time of the Latin campaigns of 1211–14. For Mangaphas, see also Chap. 9, p. 149.

[31] H. P. Borrell, "Unedited Coins of the Lower Empire," *NC*, 4 (1841), pp. 15–22. Although Borrell is also known to have purchased over a wide area, it is interesting to note the large proportion of coins of the empire in the British Museum Collection that is derived from him (Wroth, *BMCV*, particularly for John III).

At about the same time part of a hoard of precisely the same composition came into the hands of the Paris dealer Rollin: it reportedly came from Brusa (Prusa).[32]

As Metcalf has already commented,[33] the highly characteristic composition of these two hoards, together with the fact that no further hoard of similar type has come out of Asia Minor during the intervening hundred and twenty years, immediately arouses the strong suspicion that both had the same origin. It is, of course, impossible to be certain, but it is more likely that Smyrna, rather than Brusa, was the point of origin, for it must be noted that Borrell bought his part on the spot, Rollin at some remove. The discovery of such a large hoard near Smyrna might tend to confirm the view that this was the area in which the mint was situated and, in any case, until further evidence comes to light Magnesia should be considered the site of the sole mint of the empire of Nicaea subsequent to a move postulated during the reign of Theodore I.

Such a move conforms well with what is known of the political situation. The treaty of 1214 between Theodore and the Latins, although formalizing the frontiers also confirmed the near isolation of the Amastris-Brusa corridor. It would not then be surprising if the move had taken place as a consequence of this treaty. It would have been marked by the commencement of the second billon group and the silver which is so closely connected with it.

The later appearance of St. Tryphon, patron saint of Nicaea, upon the coinage does not necessarily contradict the argument for re-siting the mint. It is not denied that Nicaea remained the official capital of the empire, and its patron (the object of the intense personal devotion of Theodore II) might be represented on the coinage whether or not actually struck in that city.

N̸ HYPERPYRON

The attribution of this coin to Theodore I is, on the evidence, likely but by no means certain. No. 2056 in the *Ratto Catalogue*; the reverse inscription was recorded as reading: ΛΛΕΞΙW ΔΕCΠΟΤΗ ΤW ΚΟΜΝΗΝW, and the piece was therefore attributed to Alexius I. The inscription is, however, to judge from the photograph, extremely fragmentary: only Ε and W can be made out on the left, ΚΟ on the right. Besides being of much cruder style than normal for the coinage of Alexius I, it does not seem to have been noticed that the emperor depicted has a forked beard. This fashion, as far as numismatic representation is concerned, is unknown before the reign of Andronicus I. The coin bears not the slightest resemblance to the issues of that Emperor. The next ruler to affect the fashion

[32] Rollin, "Monnoies d'or des empereurs de Nicée pendant l'occupation de Constantinople par les princes croisés," *RN* (1841), pp. 171–76.

[33] D. M. Metcalf, "John Vatatzes and John Comnenus: Questions of Style and Detail in Byzantine Numismatics," *Greek, Roman and Byzantine Studies*, 3 (1960), p. 204.

is Theodore I and when the style of this coin is compared with that of coins of the (Nicaean) billon second coinage there is a noticeable similarity. The two letters Є and Ѡ on the left and ΚΟ on the right are the ones frequently surviving in the normally fragmentary inscriptions of the billon coins (e.g., Pl. 31.*3, 5*). A provisional attribution to Theodore has therefore been made. The Ratto coin seems to be unique, but its present whereabouts is unknown.

It is of some interest that this issue is clearly taken from that of Alexius I: the same kind of practice is found for Theodore's silver coinage and for the gold of the following reign. Presumably this is the result of the formation of a mint lacking precedent or tradition: recourse therefore being had to the repertoire of the preceding century.

Æ TRACHY

The relative order of the two silver issues is unknown—so, unfortunately, is the value that the denomination held vis-à-vis the hyperpyron upon which it presumably depended.

Type B seems to be a copy of the electrum hagiogeorgaton of John II. The dot below the tablion—the presence or absence of which distinguishes the work of different officinae in John's coinage—is included in that of Theodore.

A further type, which has come to light since this book went to press, is to be found in the Supplementary Note, at the end of the volume (pp. 405–408).

BILL. TRACHY

It has already been mentioned that the (Nicaean) first coinage has been found overstruck by the second, thus establishing the order of issue. Dr. Metcalf of the Ashmolean Museum, Oxford, has informed the author that he has recently purchased a specimen with the same sequence of overstriking.

The obverse of the second coinage apparently follows var. C of the fourth billon coinage of Manuel in including asterisks above the cushions of Christ's throne—as also does the Thessalonican Latin issue type A.

As mentioned in the preceding chapter, the (Nicaean) first coinage is also found in a small module, associated with the Latin imitative coinage. The original Nicaean pieces—of larger module—always have the loros-waist form ⊞, and ◩, ⬓ or rarely ⬓ between the collar-piece and the waist. The Latin copies—of smaller module—occasionally have the panelled waist form, but more commonly ⬚ and rarely ▦. The pattern above the waist is either ⬓ or ⬓.

The sequence of the Magnesian issues remains completely uncertain.

THE COINAGE OF JOHN III, DUCAS-VATATZES

1222–1254

N HYPERPYRON

MINT OF MAGNESIA

First coinage

Obv. KЄRO HӨЄI. IͨC XͨC in field.

Christ, bearded and nimbate, wearing tunic and colobion, seated upon throne without back; right hand raised in benediction, holds Gospels in left.

Rev. +IͦWΔЄCΠ. ӨV MͦP in upper right field.

Half-length figure of emperor on left, and of Virgin nimbate, holding between them patriarchal cross on long shaft. Emperor wears stemma, divitision, collar-piece, and panelled loros of simplified type; holds anexikakia in right hand. Virgin wears tunic and maphorion. *Manus Dei* in upper left field.

Pl. 31.*11, 12*

Second coinage

Obv. IͨC XͨC in field.

Christ, bearded and nimbate, wearing tunic and colobion, seated upon throne without back; right hand raised in benediction, holds Gospels in left.

Rev. IͦW ΔЄCΠOTH TW(ͫ) ΠOPΦVPOΓЄNNHTW (usually abbreviated) in two columnar groups. MͦP ӨV in upper right field.

Full-length figure of emperor on left, crowned by Virgin nimbate. Emperor wears stemma, divitision, collar-piece, and panelled loros of simplified type; holds in right hand labarum on long shaft, and in left, anexikakia. Virgin wears tunic and maphorion.

Pl. 31.*13–15*; 32.*1–5*

Æ TRACHY

MINT OF MAGNESIA

Type A

Obv. IͨC XͨC in field.

Christ, bearded and nimbate, wearing tunic and colobion, seated upon throne with back; holds Gospels in left hand.

Rev. IѠΔЄСПОТ Ο,ΚѠѰΛΝΤΙΝ

Full-length figure of emperor on left, and of St. Constantine, bearded and nimbate, holding between them long shaft at head of which a star and transverse bar. Emperor wears stemma, divitision, collar-piece, and jewelled loros of simplified type; holds scepter cruciger in right hand. Saint, similarly dressed, but with sagion in addition, holds anexikakia in left hand.

Pl. 32.6

Type B

Obv. M͞P Θ͞V in upper field.

Virgin nimbate, wearing tunic and maphorion, seated upon throne with back; holds beardless, nimbate head of Christ on breast.

Rev. IѠΔЄСПОΤΙC   I͞C X͞C   ΟΧΛΛΚΙΤΙC — or var.

Full-length figure of emperor, on left, crowned by Christ Chalcitis. Emperor wears stemma, divitision, collar-piece, panelled loros of simplified type, and sagion; holds in right hand labarum-headed scepter, and in left globus cruciger. Christ wears tunic and colobion, holds Gospels in left hand.

Pl. 32.7

Type C

Obv. I͞C X͞C in field.

Christ, bearded and nimbate, wearing tunic and colobion, seated upon throne without back; right hand raised in benediction, holds Gospels in left.

Rev. IѠΔЄСПОΤΗ   Ο,ΘЄΟΔѠP

Full-length figure of emperor on left, and of St. Theodore, bearded and nimbate, holding between them long shaft, at the head of which a star. Emperor wears stemma, divitision, jewelled loros of simplified type, and sagion; holds sheathed sword, point downward, in right hand. Saint wears short military tunic, breastplate, and sagion; holds sheathed sword, point downward, in left hand.

Pl. 32.8

Type D

Obv. I͞C X͞C Ο ЄΜΜΛΝȢΗΛ in two columnar groups.

Bust of Christ Emmanuel, beardless and nimbate, wearing tunic and colobion; holds scroll in left hand.

Rev. IⱲ OΛΓIOC

Full-length figure of emperor on left, and of St. Theodore(?), bearded and nimbate, holding between them patriarchal cross on long shaft and three(?) steps. Emperor wears stemma, divitision, and panelled chlamys; holds sheathed sword, point downward, in right hand. Saint wears short military tunic, breastplate and sagion; holds sheathed sword, point downward, in left hand.

Pl. 32.9

Type E

Obv. H̅P̅ Θ̅V̅ in upper field.

Virgin nimbate, wearing tunic and maphorion, seated upon throne with back; holds beardless, nimbate head of Christ on breast.

Rev.
I̅Ⱳ ☒
Δ Δ
EC Ɐ
ΠO K

Full-length figure of emperor on left, and of St. Constantine(?) bearded, holding between them long shaft at the head of which a cross within circle, and at the base of which a globe. Emperor wears stemma, divitision, jewelled loros of simplified type, and sagion; holds scepter cruciger in right hand. Saint, similarly dressed, but with triangular ornaments to stemma, holds scepter cruciger in left hand.

Pl. 32.*10, 11*

Type F

Obv. I̅C̅ X̅C̅ O EMMANɃHΛ in two columnar groups.

Bust of Christ Emmanuel, beardless and nimbate, wearing tunic and colobion; holds scroll in left hand.

Rev.
I̅Ⱳ O
ΔEC Δ
ΠO Ɐ
KΛ
C

Full-length figure of emperor, standing on dais, wearing stemma, divitision, jewelled loros of simplified type, and sagion; holds in right hand labarum-headed scepter, and in left, globus cruciger. *Manus Dei* in upper right field.

Pl. 32.*12*

Type G

Obv. I̅C̅ X̅C̅ O EMMANɃHΛ in two columnar groups.

Bust of Christ Emmanuel, beardless and nimbate, wearing tunic and colobion; holds Gospels (sic) in left hand.

Rev.
```
IW   O
ΔE   Δ
CΠ   Я
OT   K
     Λ
```

Full-length figure of emperor, wearing stemma, divitision, jewelled loros of simplified type, and sagion; holds in right hand labarum-headed scepter, and in left, anexikakia. *Manus Dei* in upper right field.

Pl. 32.*13*

Type H

Obv.

Full-length figure of Archangel Michael(?), wearing divitision, panelled loros of simplified type, and sagion; holds in right hand scepter(?) and in left, globus cruciger.

Rev.
```
O
Δ
K
Λ
```

Full-length figure of emperor, wearing stemma, divitision, jewelled loros of simplified type, and sagion; holds in right hand labarum-headed scepter, and in left, patriarchal cross on three steps.

Pl. 32.*14*

Type I

Obv. H ΘV in upper field.

Virgin nimbate, wearing tunic and maphorion, seated upon throne with back; holds beardless, nimbate head of Christ on breast.

Rev.

Full-length figure of emperor on left, crowned by Christ, beardless and nimbate. Emperor wears stemma, divitision, collar-piece, and jewelled loros of simplified type; holds in right hand anexikakia, and in left, globus cruciger. Christ wears tunic and colobion; holds scroll(?) in left hand. Two asterisks between figures.

BILL. TRACHY

MINT OF MAGNESIA

Type A

Obv. Λ X in upper field.

Three-quarter length figure of Archangel Michael, wearing short military tunic, breastplate, and sagion; holds in right hand sword, resting over shoulder, and in left, globus.

Rev. I͞Ѡ̄ . I͞C X͞C in upper field.
Δ
Є
C
Π
O

Full-length figure of emperor on left, crowned by Christ, bearded and nimbate. Emperor wears stemma, divitision, and chlamys; holds in right hand anexikakia, and in left, globus cruciger. Christ wears tunic and colobion, holds Gospels in left hand.

Pl. 33.*1*

Type B

Obv. O
Λ   ГЄ
ПI   ѠP
OC

Figure of St. George, beardless and nimbate, wearing short military tunic, breastplate, and sagion; holds in right hand spear, and in left, shield.

Rev. IѠΔЄ

Full-length figure of emperor on left, crowned by Christ, bearded and nimbate. Emperor wears stemma, divitision, and chlamys; holds in right hand labarum-headed scepter, and in left, globus cruciger. Christ wears tunic and colobion; holds Gospels in left hand.

Pl. 33.*2*

Type C

Obv. H͞T͞P   Ѳ͞V in field.
+   +

Full-length figure of Virgin nimbate, wearing tunic and maphorion; holds beardless, nimbate head of Christ on breast.

Rev. O . I͞C X͞C in upper field.
Δ

Full-length figure of emperor on left, crowned by Christ, bearded and nimbate. Emperor wears stemma, divitision, and panelled chlamys; holds in right hand labarum-headed scepter, and in left, anexikakia. Christ wears tunic and colobion; holds Gospels in left hand.

Pl. 33.*3*

Type D

Obv. I͞C   X͞C in field.
+   +

Full-length figure of Christ, bearded and nimbate, wearing tunic and colobion; right hand raised in benediction, holds Gospels in left.

Rev. ΙѠΔΠ

Figure of emperor on left, and of Virgin nimbate, holding between them patriarchal cross on long shaft. Emperor wears stemma, divitision, jewelled loros of simplified type, and sagion; holds in right hand labarum-headed scepter. Virgin wears tunic and maphorion.

Pl. 33.*4*

Type E

Obv. ĪC X̄C O ЄMMΛΝȢHΛ in two columnar groups.

Bust of Christ Emmanuel, beardless and nimbate, wearing tunic and colobion; holds scroll in left hand.

Rev. ĪѠ O
ΔЄ K
Ѡ

Full-length figure of emperor on left, and of St. Constantine bearded, holding between them patriarchal cross on long shaft, at the base of which, three steps. Emperor wears stemma, divitision, jewelled loros of simplified type, and sagion; holds labarum-headed scepter in right hand. Saint similarly dressed; holds scepter cruciger in left hand.

Pl. 33.*5*

Type F

Obv. ĪC X̄C in field.

Christ, bearded and nimbate, wearing tunic and colobion, seated upon throne without back; right hand raised in benediction, holds Gospels in left.

Rev. ĪѠ O
ΔЄC Δ
ΠOT Ȣ
HC KΛ
C

Full-length figure of emperor, wearing stemma, divitision, and chlamys; holds in right hand labarum on long shaft, and in left, globus surmounted by patriarchal cross.

Pl. 33.*6*

Type G

Obv. M̄P̄ Θ̄V̄ in upper field.

Virgin nimbate, wearing tunic and maphorion, seated upon throne with back; holds beardless, nimbate head of Christ on breast.

Rev. ĪѠ Δ
Ȣ
K

Full-length figure of emperor, wearing stemma, divitision, collar-piece, jewelled loros of simplified type, and sagion; holds in right hand labarum-headed scepter, and in left, globus cruciger.

Pl. 33.*7, 8*

Type H

Obv. I̅C̅ X̅C̅
      X   KI
      ΛΛ TH

Full-length figure of Christ Chalcitis, standing on dais, wearing tunic and colobion; right hand raised in benediction, holds Gospels in left.

Rev. I̅W̅ O
            Δ
            Ȣ
          KΛ
           C

Full-length figure of emperor standing on dais, wearing stemma, divitision, jewelled loros of simplified type, and sagion; holds in right hand labarum-headed scepter, and in left, sheathed sword, point downward.

Pl. 33.*9*

Type I

Obv. M̅R̅ Θ̅V̅ in upper field.

Virgin nimbate, wearing tunic and maphorion, seated upon throne with back; holds nimbate, beardless head of Christ on breast.

Rev. IWΔECΠ ·ΔȢK

Full-length figure of emperor, wearing stemma, divitision, collar-piece, jewelled loros of simplified type, and sagion; holds in right hand anexikakia, and in left, globus surmounted by labarum which he holds by the shaft.

Pl. 33.*10*

Type J

Obv. I̅C̅ X̅C̅ in field.

Bust of Christ, beardless and nimbate, wearing tunic and colobion; holds scroll in left hand.

Rev.

Half-length figure of emperor, wearing stemma, divitision, panelled loros of simplified type, and sagion; holds in right hand labarum-headed scepter, and in left, globus surmounted by patriarchal cross.

Pl. 33.*11*

Type K

Obv. ⊘ P̅I
      ΔI O
      HH C

Full-length figure of St. Demetrius, nimbate, wearing short military tunic, breastplate, and sagion; holds in right hand spear, and in left, shield.

Rev. IШΔECΠ   OΔ&KΛ

Full-length figure of emperor, seated upon throne with back, wearing stemma, divitision, collar-piece, and panelled loros of simplified type; holds in right hand scepter cruciger, and in left, globus cruciger.

Pl. 33.*12*

Type L

Obv. M̅P̅ Θ̅V̅ in field.

Half-length figure of Virgin nimbate, orans, wearing tunic and maphorion.

Rev. I̅Ш̅

Half-length figure of emperor on left, and of Virgin nimbate (holding between them labarum on long shaft?) Emperor wears stemma, divitision, collar-piece, and jewelled loros of simplified type; holds scepter cruciger in right hand. Virgin wears tunic and maphorion.

Pl. 33.*13*

Æ TETARTERON

Type A

Obv.

Square formed of four interlaced bands ornamented with pellets.

Rev.
```
I̅Ш̅   O
ΔEC  Δ   —or var.
ΠO   &
 T   K
 H   Λ
 C   C
```

Full-length figure of emperor wearing stemma, short military tunic, breastplate, and sagion; holds in left hand sword, resting over shoulder, and in right, sheath, point downward.

Pl. 34.*1, 2*

Type B

Obv.

Head of cherub with four wings; triangle of three pellets in field to either side.

Rev.
```
I̅Ш̅   O
 Δ   Δ
 E   &   —or var.
 C   K
 Π
```

Full-length figure of emperor wearing stemma, divitision, and chlamys; holds in right hand labarum-headed scepter, and in left, globus cruciger.

Pl. 34.*3*

Type C

Obv. ⊗ 𝕁 in field.

Bust of St. George, beardless and nimbate, wearing tunic, breastplate and sagion; holds in right hand spear resting over shoulder, and in left, shield.

Rev.

IŪ O
ΔEC ΔƲ
ΠO K   —or var.
Λ
C

Full-length figure of emperor wearing stemma, divitision, collar-piece, jewelled loros of simplified type, and sagion; holds in right hand labarum on long shaft, and in left, anexikakia.

Pl. 34.*4, 5*

Type D

Obv.

Cross within crescent-shaped ornament decorated with pellets.

Rev. IŴΔECΠ —or var.

Half-length figure of emperor wearing stemma, divitision, collar-piece, and panelled loros of simplified type; holds in right hand labarum-headed scepter, and in left, globus surmounted by patriarchal cross.

Pl. 34.*6*

Type E

Obv. ĪC X̄C in field.

Bust of Christ, beardless and nimbate, wearing tunic and colobion; holds scroll in left hand.

Rev.

O
Δ
Ʋ

Full-length figure of emperor, wearing stemma, divitision, collar-piece, and jewelled loros of simplified type; holds in right hand labarum on long shaft, and in left, globus surmounted by patriarchal cross.

Pl. 34.*7*

Type F

Obv. ✳ ✳ in field.

Figure of Virgin nimbate, orans, wearing tunic and maphorion, turned slightly to right.

Rev. IŴΔEC OΔƲ

Full-length figure of emperor wearing stemma, divitision, and jewelled loros of simplified type; holds in right hand labarum-headed scepter, and in left, globus surmounted by patriarchal cross, which he holds by the shaft.

Pl. 34.*8*

THE COINAGE OF JOHN III: COMMENTARY

A͞/ HYPERPYRON

The outstanding question with regard to the hyperpyra of John III is that of arriving at a satisfactory method for distinguishing them from the Thessalonican series of John II.

The three types of hyperpyron struck by John II in large module, thin, spread fabric, and elegant style, are undoubtedly to be assigned to the metropolitan mint (Pl. 9.*1–9*). These coins, however, have their counterparts in a small series of coins, of the same types, but distinguishable by their smaller module, thicker fabric, and less neat style. This series has been assigned to the mint of Thessalonica. Unfortunately there are a number of coins, of two types, with rather similar characteristics, one of which, if only on hoard evidence, should be attributed to John III of Nicaea. The third coinage of John II, in both the large and the small series, need not come under discussion, for its attribution has not been seriously called into question and, in fact, there is no reason to suspect that it should be. However, the precise frontiers between the first and second coinages of John II, in the Thessalonican series, and the first and second of John III, have been a matter of discussion for some considerable time.

The question was opened by Rollin in 1841 as a result of the purchase of some coins which were supposed to have been part of a hoard from near Brusa. It has already been noted that there is reason to suspect that in fact it may have been part of a hoard which was almost certainly found near Smyrna in 1839. Whatever their precise origin, the hoard of which they were a part contained coins of Theodore (II) of Nicaea, of small module and thick fabric, showing as the reverse type the emperor standing, crowned by the Virgin, together with coins of two varieties of Michael VIII. The bulk of the hoard, however, consisted of coins with the same obverse and reverse types as those of Theodore, and of similar module and fabric, but with an abbreviated form of the reverse inscription I͞W ΔЄCΠΟΤΗ ΤѠ(Ɪ) ΠΟΡΦVΡΟΓЄΝΝΗΤѠ. Despite their superficial resemblance to the coins of John II, Rollin recognized that there was a fundamental difference between that large, spread series and these smaller, thicker coins. He therefore attributed them to John III.[1]

Wroth, when writing the *British Museum Catalogue* of Byzantine coins (published in 1908), assigned both series to John II,[2] but by 1911, when the catalogue including the coinage of the empire of Nicaea was published, he had come to agree with Rollin.[3] He further questioned whether certain other coins of similar module and fabric, but of different type, should not also be similarly reattributed, but finally decided to leave them as they were.

[1] Rollin, "Monnoies d'or," pp. 173–74.
[2] Wroth, *BMC*, 2, pp. 558–60, nos. 20–40.
[3] Wroth, *BMCV*, pp. 210–13, nos. 1–24.

In 1960, the debate was reopened by Metcalf's article, in which he came to the conclusion that this further series of small, thick coins, depicting the half-length figures of the emperor and Virgin, holding between them a patriarchal cross, should also be given to John III.[4] This was later modified in the light of subsequent hoard evidence and one sub-variety only given to John III, the rest to John II.[5]

Discussion continues,[6] and clearly a thorough examination of the question in the light of contemporary documentary sources will not be out of place. It should in the first place be noted that, although the question of debasement may complicate these attributions, it cannot be considered a decisive criterion.

As is well known, Pachymeres gives a detailed account of the decline in the precious-metal content of the hyperpyron during the thirteenth and early fourteenth centuries.[7] According to him, at first, during the reign of John III, the hyperpyron was of 16 carats (two-thirds) fine, remaining at that level under his successor (Theodore II). During the reign of Michael VIII, after the recapture of Constantinople, the standard was reduced by a further carat, to 15, because of heavy expenses incurred, particularly toward the "Italians." This reduction was apparently contemporaneous with the adoption of the "Virgin-within-walls" obverse type. During the reign of Michael's successor (Andronicus II) the standard, although at first of 14 carats, later reached the state then (c. 1308) obtaining, where the quantity of gold and alloy were equal (i.e., 12 carats gold, 12 alloy).

Although very closely confirmed by the coin list of Pegolotti, which will be dealt with below, the evidence for the reign of John III at least has been treated with a reverence which is unjustified.

It has been shown by specific gravity determinations that the hyperpyra of the Comneni and Angeli were struck on a standard somewhere between 19 and 21 carats, and it has been argued that the official 20 $\frac{1}{2}$ carat standard of the Hohenstaufen augustalis probably also represents the standard of the twelfth-century hyperpyron. It may be presumed on the evidence of Pachymeres that any hyperpyra struck by Theodore I would have continued at

[4] Metcalf, "John Vatatzes and John Comnenus," p. 209.

[5] Metcalf, *Coinage in the Balkans*, p. 94.

[6] E.g., T. Bertelè, "Il titolo degli iperperi della zecca di Nicea," *Thirteenth International Congress of Byzantine Studies* (Oxford, 1966), *Supplementary Papers, Summaries*, pp. 95–97—a remarkably overconfident "exposure" of Metcalf's "elementi esteriori... fragili e fallaci."

[7] George Pachymeres; Bonn ed., 2, pp. 493–94: Ἀλλὰ καὶ τὸ νόμισμα διὰ τὴν χρείαν ἐκιβδηλεύετο. Πρότερον μὲν γὰρ ἐπὶ Ἰωάννου τοῦ Δούκα τὸ δίμοιρον τοῦ ταλάντου τῶν νομισμάτων χρυσὸς ἦν ἄπεφθος, ὃ δὴ καὶ ὁ ἐξ ἐκείνου διετήρει· ὕστερον δὲ ἐπὶ Μιχαήλ, τῆς Πόλεως ἁλούσης, διὰ τὰς τότε κατ'ἀνάγκην δόσεις, καὶ μᾶλλον πρὸς Ἰταλούς, μετεγγράφατο μὲν τὰ τῶν παλαιῶν σημείων, τῆς Πόλεως χαραττομένης ὄπισθεν, καθυφίετο δὲ καὶ παρὰ κεράτιον τὸ ἐκ χρυσοῦ νομιζόμενον, ὡς πεντεκαίδεκα πρὸς τὰ εἰκοσιτέσσαρα γίνεσθαι. Μεταλλάξαντος δ'ἐκείνου, πρότερον μὲν εἰς δεκατέσσαρα περιέστη πρὸς δέκα, νῦν δὲ ἀλλὰ καὶ ἐφ'ἡμισείας τὸ ἄπεφθον καταμίγνυται....

that level. However, the only information that one is entitled to draw from Pachymeres' evidence concerning John III is that at some point in his reign he adopted a lower standard of 16 carats. Pachymeres does not say that this occurred at the very beginning of the reign, or, alternatively, when John began to strike hyperpyra—two points in time which might not be coincidental. It is therefore quite possible that John commenced with a standard of $20^1/_2$ carats and then, at some uncertain stage of the reign, but probably at a relatively early one, dropped to 16 carats. It might, in fact, be plausibly argued that if Frederick of Hohenstaufen copied the Byzantine standard of $20^1/_2$ carats in 1231, it is more likely than not that it was still in use.

As far as differentiating between the coins of John II and John III is concerned, therefore, all that can be said is that coins betraying a gold content of about 16 carats must be attributed to John III, but that, while the majority of coins containing about $20^1/_2$ carats gold will necessarily be attributed to John II, it is quite possible that some will belong to John III.

John II, first coinage/John III, first coinage is comparatively easily dealt with. As Metcalf noticed,[8] there are, within this general group, two sub-varieties (Pl. 9.*10*; 31.*11, 12*), one having the obverse inscription KЄRO HΘЄI as well as IC XC, which is common to both. The coins with the inscription occasionally have the various devices above the cushions of Christ's throne that are found also on the undoubted coinage of John III, but not on that of John II: for instance, two coins in the British Museum have ∴ ∴ and ✳ ✳.[9] This sub-variety should therefore be assigned to John III. Coins without the obverse inscription (Pl. 9.*10*) should remain with John II, as being the counterparts of the first metropolitan coinage. Four specimens of the small, thick coins without the obverse inscription were included in the Gornoslav hoard which was apparently deposited early in the reign of Isaac II (1185–95) and therefore appears to confirm the division suggested above. Two of these four coins had the pendilia form ‖ which, since he considered it later than the reign of John II, was one of the reasons behind Metcalf's assignment of the whole group to John III. This form cannot be considered a reliable criterion of chronology in the light of the evidence above.

As Metcalf himself noticed, however, the attribution of this sub-variety to John III has not as yet been borne out by hoard evidence: that is, it has never been found in conjunction with undoubted coins of John III (or of John II for that matter). This might well be explained if the debasement of the coinage were a factor to be taken into account. In this case, some coins at least of the first coinage of John III could easily be of a standard higher than that of most, or all, of the second.

[8] Metcalf, "John Vatatzes and John Comnenus," p. 208.
[9] Wroth, *BMC*, 2, p. 556, nos. 8, 9. See also *infra*, pp. 253, 254.

The situation as regards the second Thessalonican coinage of John II and the second of John III is less clear-cut. Since, however, the mint of Thessalonica is represented in both the first and the third coinage of John II, it would seem logical to assume that some coins at least of the small, thick series should be attributed to the earlier Emperor.

Now, under Theodore I some of the elongation of the figures on the reverse side of the coinage—which is a typical feature of the twelfth century—still remains. But under John III, continuing into the reigns of his successors, the figures become much more heavily rendered and squat. This trend is apparent with even a superficial glance at Plates 30 to 36.

The hyperpyra of Theodore II—beyond doubt correctly attributed owing to the presence of the surnames Ducas, or Lascaris, or both—are immediately recognizable as the product of this stylistic trend (Pl. 34.9–14). The figures of both emperor and Virgin, on the reverse, are squat and heavy; the collar-piece is decorated with between seven and nine jewels; the loros-waist is broad and contains four panels horizontally, three vertically (▦); the inscription is clumsy and much abbreviated. On the obverse small devices or letters frequently occur above the cushions of the throne. The coins themselves are of small module and thick fabric, with bevelled edges.

Precisely these features are anticipated in many of the coins which are generally attributed to John III (Pl. 32.3–5), and which are recognizably illustrated by both Rollin and Borrell in their accounts of the Brusa and Smyrna "hoards." There is therefore every reason why they should be confirmed in their attribution.

A further group of coins (Pls. 31.13–15; 32.1, 2) betrays slightly different characteristics. The style in which the emperor and Virgin are rendered is less squat; the collar-piece is frequently decorated with three jewels only; the loros-waist is not so wide as in the previous group and the panels of which it is comprised are less standardized in number; the inscription is slightly neater and less abbreviated. The average module of this group is perhaps slightly larger than of the previous, the flans consequently slightly thinner, and the bevelled edges less noticeable.

This group must nevertheless also be attributed to John III since many have devices such as a cross above the cushions of the throne on the obverse.

It would be quite in conformity with the stylistic trends of the reign of John III if these coins were assigned to a date early in the reign before the evolution of the squat, standardized representations which continued into the reign of Theodore II. In point of fact such an attribution is only logical when it is considered that type and inscription are both copied from John II, and it might be expected that earlier copies should show a greater similarity to the originals than the later.

This attribution of the two groups of coins above of course leaves few specimens to be attributed to the Thessalonican mint of John II, but this should not be unexpected, for the other types attributed to Thessalonica are all extremely scarce, while the quantity of coins struck by John III may have been overstressed by the dispersal of one or several large hoards.

It would seem widely admitted that in the general striking of gold hyperpyra John III was attempting to emphasize his position as emperor, and in his copying the types of John II was deliberately attempting to recall the prosperous state of the Empire at that period.

Yet there do exist specimens that are, in all probability, the products of Thessalonica during the reign of John II. One such piece is illustrated (Pl. 9.*11*). The figures on the reverse are tall and elegant (cf. Pl. 9.*12–14*, which are certainly of John II); the arrangement of the neat inscription is precisely the same

as that seen in the coinage of the metropolitan mint (Pl. 9.*4, 5*; $\overline{\text{IW}}$ ΦV / ΔEC PO / ΠOT ΓE / TW NH / Π T); the

throne on the obverse is exactly as that found on the metropolitan coins. The flan is regular.

The stage should now have been reached where the detailed information contained in the *Pratica della mercatura* of the Florentine merchant Francesco Balducci Pegolotti can be studied with some profit. In a list of gold coins in circulation during the late thirteenth and the early fourteenth century, there occur a number of references to Byzantine hyperpyra. A translation of the relevant portion follows, while the original text is given as an *Appendix* at the end of this reign (pp. 255–56):[10]

> Perperi of yellowish gold [are] of 18 carats.
> Palaeologid gold perperi [are] of 15$\frac{1}{2}$ carats; and they can be recognized by the fact that one of the two figures on one side has a face on its breast and the circle of the large figure which is on the other side is not round but elongated.
> Latin gold perperi [are] of 16$\frac{1}{2}$ carats; and they can be recognized by the fact that of the two figures which are on one side, one holds a pestle in his hand hanging down between the two figures, and the single figure which is on the other side has on the left side above the throne on which it sits 4 dots made thus ⦂, and such as ∴, and such as ⦂, and this one is of a rather worse class than the others.
> Common gold perperi are of 16$\frac{3}{4}$ carats; and they can be recognized by the fact that the pestle which one of the two figures holds in its hand has below

---

[10] The author is indebted for this translation to Philip Grierson and to Mrs. Fanny Bonajuto, Associate in Research at Dumbarton Oaks.

it a dot: ⚥, and the single figure on the other side has a dot above the left side of the throne on which it sits, and it is an issue which is newer than the others, and it is worse by a florin in the ounce.

Good perperi, and they can be recognized from this, that the majesty on either side has above the throne on which it sits on the right arm a half-moon with three dots made thus ⸫☾•, and these are better than tari gold by 20 soldi by the florin in the ounce, according to the Apulian ounce in Florence, since all perperi are sold in Florence by the Apulian ounce.

Perperi of another class which have on the arm a half-moon and a dot like this •☽, and it is worse by 6 pennies in the florin to the ounce than those of the fifth class described above, but when mixed with these the other two classes mentioned above make good tari gold, that is $16^2/_3$ carats fine gold to the ounce.

Perperi of another class have under the right arm a little cross, and above it nothing, and it is worse than the others already mentioned by 6 pennies in the florin to the ounce.

Kneeler perperi are of 14 carats.

Old perperi with 3 saints [are] of $13^1/_2$ carats.

New perperi with a rose and star [are] of $11^3/_4$ carats.

Perperi of Philadelphia [are] of 12 carats.

The latest perperi [are] of 11 carats.

The extent of the debasement covered by Pegolotti thus commences at 18 carats and ends with 11 carats, although concentrating between $16^3/_4$ and 11. This, of course, is very much on the same scale as that listed by Pachymeres, who also identifies the chronological range as lying between John III and Andronicus II. The issues involved should therefore be capable of identification with relative ease.

To start, for the moment, with the "Palaeologid perperi" of $15^1/_2$ carats. On the information of Pachymeres, they should be an issue of Michael VIII, and clearly this correlation is correct. The obverse of the main issue of this Emperor depicts the Virgin, orans, within the walls of Constantinople (Pl. 45.*13*). The plan of the walls in this issue is frequently far more pear-shaped than on later ones with the same subject: this is presumably what is meant by "elongated." As for the figure with a face on its breast, the Archangel Michael, on the left of the reverse, stands behind the kneeling Emperor, whose head obscures the former's chest.

"Kneeler perperi" of 14 carats should similarly be an issue of Andronicus II, and are clearly to be identified with the first issue of the reign—before the association of Michael IX as co-Emperor in 1295—on the reverse of which the Emperor kneels before Christ, who is standing (Pl. 45.*14*).

"Old perperi with three saints," of $13^1/_2$ carats fine, can only be the earlier coins—of visibly better metal—of the co-emperorship of Andronicus II and

Michael IX (1295–1320), on the reverse of which Christ, standing, crowns the kneeling Emperors (Pl. 45.*15*).

"New perperi, with a rose and star," of $11^3/_4$ carats are presumably the later coins of this same issue, on the obverse of which the Virgin has to either side of her devices very like a rose or star: ✳ ✳ (Pl. 45.*16*).

"The latest perperi," of 11 carats, might well be those of the co-emperorship of Andronicus II and III (Pl. 46.*3*), or less likely, those of Andronicus III, Anna of Savoy, and John V (Pl. 46.*4*), or John V or VI.

"Perperi of Philadelphia," of 12 carats, are something of a puzzle, but in the context should involve some issue of the co-emperorship of Andronicus II and Michael IX—the period of the "three saints" coinage.

It is to be observed that many of the later coins of this issue have the letters K N or $\frac{C}{K}$ $\frac{\Pi}{N}$ (Pl. 46.*1*) in the obverse field. The obvious conclusion is that they identify the city of which the walls are shown: K(Ш)N(CTANTINOV)Π(OΛΙ)C, reading counter-clockwise from K. Now Π Φ is a further combination of letters (Pl. 46.*2*): it is tempting to suggest that, whether rightly or wrongly, they were popularly understood as the signature of Philadelphia: Π(OΛIC) Φ(IΛAΔEΛΦEIA), one of the only Byzantine towns in Asia Minor still, at that time, resisting the incursions of the Ottoman Turks.

There remain to be discussed the "yellowish perperi" of 18 carats; "Latin perperi" of $16^1/_2$ carats; "common gold perperi" of $16^3/_4$ carats; "good perperi" of $16^2/_3$ carats, and two other classes which are apparently of much the same issue.

"Latin" and "common" gold perperi both have two figures on one side, and a single figure seated upon a throne on the other: "good" perperi, together with the two following classes, have a single figure seated upon a throne on one side, the other side not being described. The only issues answering the requirements of chronology, gold-content, and iconography are the hyperpyra of John III, Theodore II, and Michael VIII having as the obverse type Christ seated upon a throne without back, and as the reverse the emperor crowned by the Virgin (Pls. 31, 32, 34, 36).

The entries for the "Latin" and the "common" perperi both mention a "pestle"—held by one of the figures on the reverse—which hangs down between the two figures. A glance at the illustrations immediately reveals the origin of this somewhat curious description: the long, cylindrical shape of the anexikakia held by the emperor in his left hand.

The various dots, half-moons and crosses above the throne, or on its arm, by the seated figure of Christ on the obverse, are clearly to be identified with the various devices and letters found in that position.

With the clarification of these points, it should be possible to extract further information from the details of the list given by Pegolotti.

"Latin" perperi are said to be recognizable by the fact that they have the dotted devices ∴, ∴, ∶∙ above the left-hand side of the throne. This is presumably the variety illustrated (Pl. 32,2). It will be noticed that the device appears on the observer's right-hand side, but, as will appear from the figures below, Pegolotti evidently considers iconographical positions from the heraldic point of view, that is, as they would be seen by the person actually seated on the throne.

"Common" gold perperi have a dot below the pestle, and a further one above the (heraldic) left-hand side of the throne. The illustration (Pl. 32.4) must be the variety involved: the loros-end hanging from the emperor's left arm does indeed have a dot below it (▦ ⎛⎞) and there is a dot above the throne.

As it happens, the validity of the general stylistic trends noticed above can be tested from the information given here, for Pegolotti mentions that these common gold perperi are newer than the others of the same general issue, and that they are also of lower gold content. This should be expected on the basis of the fact that over the whole period the newer the coin the more debased it is. There are fourteen specimens of the varieties with dots above the throne at Dumbarton Oaks: -/∙, nine specimens; ∙/-, three; ∙/∙, two. Of this total all except one specimen are of the squat style; have the collar-piece of between seven and nine jewels; the standardized form of broad loros-waist ▦; the clumsy and much abbreviated inscription—all of which have been suggested as stylistic criteria by which the later coins might be recognized.

"Good" perperi, and those of a slightly inferior class, have the devices ⟨C⟩∙ and ∙𝔇 respectively, above the (heraldic) right-hand side of the throne. Although these cannot as yet be precisely paralleled, coins with a plain half-moon (𝔇) above the throne are known (Pl. 32.3).

The last variety of hyperpyra of this type is recognizable by the little cross which is to be found under the (heraldic) right arm of the figure of Christ on the obverse. There are five specimens at Dumbarton Oaks with these small crosses: +/-, three specimens; +/+, two (Pl. 31.13–15). According to Pegolotti, they are inferior by six pennies in the florin to the ounce to "the others already mentioned." Whether "already mentioned" refers to the "good" perperi or to the perperi following them is impossible to ascertain, but their general chronological position is clear, for four of the five specimens have early stylistic features: the more elongated style, the collar-piece of three jewels. It is interesting to note that of these four coins none has the dot below the "pestle"; instead they all have a simpler form of loros-end: ⎛⎞.

The degree of accuracy achieved by Pegolotti's list is completely uncertain and likely to remain so. The basis for his estimations is unknown and might be anything from official information through general market value to private assay. Assay of a few pieces only would obviously achieve little, for the alloy would hardly be identical even in coins of the same melting: it is the average of each melting which is the crucial figure.

Furthermore, the precise nature of the variant devices above the throne must similarly remain uncertain, for this reign at least, pending further evidence. It is unlikely that they were formally designed to impart any particular information as to mint, metal content, or chronology, for the existence of such a large proportion without them tends to make any such suggestion suspect. It is possible, on the other hand, that they resulted from some aspect of their production and were seized upon by the acute merchant class as informal guides to metal content and chronology.

The reference to "Latin perperi" is suggestive in view of what is known of the imitative proclivities of the Latin authorities. It is possible that the description has some very general meaning such as *tempore Latinorum imperatorum*, but then all gold coins struck between the reigns of Theodore I and Theodore II conformed to that limitation. As implied above, one plausible interpretation is that coins of this variety were actually struck by the Latins in imitation of a "well-liked trade-coin," as Metcalf remarked, on different grounds, of the same series,[11] and in spite of the Veneto-Byzantine treaty of 1219.

The "perperi of yellowish gold" of 18 carats are very probably to be identified with some early issue of John III or of Theodore I: it can hardly be an accurate description of the hyperpyra of the twelfth century which normally achieved a higher standard.

It is interesting to note that John is represented on his gold as having a rounded beard, but on his silver and copper as having a forked one. This is obviously the result of the fact that the Emperor from whose coins these hyperpyra were copied (John II) had a rounded beard. The distinction continued into the following reigns.

Æ TRACHY

There is, at the present state of knowledge, little that can be said of these issues: both the sequence and their relative value remain unknown. Types A, B, and C are, by their large, spread fabric and neat, bejewelled style, to be attributed to an early stage of the reign since they closely resemble the coinage of Theodore I in these features. The later issues, to judge from the grey color of the metal, suffer from some degree of debasement.

Type I was illustrated in the Hess-Leu *Sale Catalogue 24* (16.iv.64) as no. 473. It is clearly linked to type G of the billon trachy by the characteristic decorations on the back of the throne, on the obverse.

---

[11] Metcalf, *Coinage in the Balkans*, p. 127. The first coinage might also be involved.

A further type, which has come to light since this book went to press, is to be found in the Supplementary Note at the end of the volume (p. 406).

BILL. TRACHY

Information on the billon trachy is similarly lacking. While most of the types having a bust of the emperor as the reverse design seem to belong to the mint of Thessalonica, type J must be counted an exception. The characteristic technique by which Christ's hair is rendered on the obverse can best be paralleled on the products of the mint of Magnesia (cf. Pl. *32.9, 12*). Type K is attributed to the same mint, despite the presence of St. Demetrius on the obverse, in consideration of the fact that the square panelling of the emperor's throne is also to be paralleled on the products of the mint (cf. Pl. *33.7, 8*). Presumably St. Demetrius lost his strictly Thessalonican status in 1246, with the Nicaean conquest of that city.

A further type, which has come to light since this book went to press, is to be found in the Supplementary Note at the end of the volume (p. 406–07).

Æ TETARTERON

An article by H. Goodacre ("The Flat Bronze Coinage of Nicaea," *NC*[5], 18 [1938], pp. 159–64) represents a summary of what was then known of the types forming this general series. It does, however, perpetuate one serious error: no. 3 (p. 160) attributed to John III—largely on the authority of Sabatier—is, in fact, to be given to Theodore II (type A). It is improbable that this type was struck at all by John Vatatzes.

Appendix

Perperi d'oro ingiallati a carati 18.

Perperi d'oro paglialoccati a carati 15½; e conoscesi chè l'una delle due figure dall'un lato à uno viso nel petto, e lo cerchio della grande figura ch'è dall'altro lato non è tondo anzi è lungo.

Perperi latini d'oro a carati 16½; e conosconsi chè le due figure che sono dall'uno lato l'una tiene uno pestello in mano pendente a basso tr'ambedue le figure, e l'una figura ch'è dall'altro lato si à dal lato manco sopra alla carriera dove siede 4 punti così fatti: ∴, e tale: ∴, e tale: ⋮, ed è questi alquanti piggiore ragione che gli altri.

Perperi comunali d'oro sono a carati 16¾; e conosconsi chè 'l pestello che tiene in mano l'una delle due figure è di sotto uno punto: ⚲, e la figura sola dall'altro lato à uno punto sopra la carriera dove siede dal lato manco, ed è uno conio ch'è più nuovo che gli altri, ed è piggiore da fiorino 1 d'oro l'oncia.

Perperi buoni, e conosconsi a questo, che la maestra d'ogni lato à sopra la ciarriera ove siede in sul braccio ritto una lunetta con tre punti così fatti: ⊂, e questi cotali sono migliori che oro di terì da soldi 20 a fiorino l'oncia all'oncia di Puglia in Firenze, però che tutti perperi si vendono in Firenze all'oncia di Puglia.

Perperi d'un'altra ragione che ànno in sul braccio una lunetta e uno punto così fatta: •⟩, ed è peggio denari 6 a fiorino l'oncia di quelli della quinta ragione detti di sopra, ma mescolate con queste l'altre due ragione sopradette rispondono come buono oro di terì, cioè a carati 16⅔ d'oro fine per oncia.

Perperi d'un'altra ragione ch'ànno sotto il braccio ritto una crocellina, e in sul braccio non ànno segnale niuno, ed è peggio che gli altri detti a dietro denari 6 a fiorino l'oncia.

Perperi inginocchiati sono a carati 14.

Perperi vecchi 3 santi a carati 13 e ½.

Perperi nuovi di rosa et di stella a carati 11 e ¾.

Perperi di Filadelfe a carati 12.

Perperi nuovi nuovi a carati 11.

> Francesco Balducci Pegolotti, *La pratica della mercatura*, Florence, fourth decade of the thirteenth century (ed. Evans, pp. 288–89).

....perperi, i quali sono di lega di carati 11 d'oro fine per oncia, e lo rimanente della lega infino in 24 carati sì ne sono li 6 carati d'argento fine e li 7 di rame per ogni oncia.

> Pegolotti, *ed. cit.*, p. 40.

THE COINAGE OF THEODORE II, DUCAS-LASCARIS

1254–1258

Ν̸ HYPERPYRON

MINT OF MAGNESIA

Obv. I̅C̅ X̅C̅ in field.

Christ, bearded and nimbate, wearing tunic and colobion, seated upon throne without back; right hand raised in benediction, holds Gospels in left.

Rev. Inscription in two columnar groups. M̅P̅ Θ̅V̅ in upper field.

Full-length figure of emperor on left, crowned by Virgin nimbate. Emperor wears stemma, divitision, collar-piece, and panelled loros of simplified type; holds in right hand labarum on long shaft, and in left, anexikakia. Virgin wears tunic and maphorion.

Three main reverse inscriptional varieties, all much abbreviated:

Var. A.

    Rev. ΘΕΟΔΩΡΟC ΔΕCΠΟΤΗ(Ⱨ) ΤⲰ(Ⳁ) ΠΟΡΦVΡΟΓΕΝΝΗΤⲰ in two columnar groups.

                                    Pl. 34.9

Var. B.

Rev. ΘΕΟΔѠΡΟC ΔΕCΠΟΤΗ(Ħ)C Ο ΛΛCΚΛΡΙC in two columnar groups.

Pl. 34.*10, 11*

Var. C.

Rev. ΘΕΟΔѠΡΟC ΔΕCΠΟΤΗ(Ħ)C ΔႡΚΛC Ο ΛΛCΚΛΡΙC in two columnar groups.

Pl. 34.*12–14*

Æ TRACHY

MINT OF MAGNESIA

Type A

Obv. ĪC X̄C in field.

Christ, bearded and nimbate, wearing tunic and colobion, seated upon throne without back; right hand raised in benediction, holds Gospels in left.

Rev. ΘΕΟΔѠΡΟC ΔΕCΠΟĦC ⊘ ꝥVΦ ΔႡΚΛC Ο ΛΛCΚΛΡΙC in two columnar groups.

Full-length figure of emperor on left, and of St. Tryphon, beardless and nimbate, holding between them labarum on long shaft, at the base of which, lys. Emperor wears stemma, divitision, jewelled loros of simplified type, and sagion; holds in right hand scepter cruciger. Saint wears tunic and colobion.

Pl. 35.*1, 2*

Type B

Obv. ĪC X̄C in field.

Full-length figure of Christ, bearded and nimbate, wearing tunic and colobion; holds Gospels in left hand.

Rev.   ΘΕ   ʘ
       ΟΔѠ   ΛΛ
       POC   C

Full-length figure of emperor on left, and of beardless, nimbate military saint, holding between them patriarchal cross on long shaft. Emperor wears stemma, divitision, jewelled loros of simplified type, and sagion; holds in right hand scepter cruciger. Saint wears short military tunic, breastplate, and sagion.

Pl. 35.*3*

17

Type C

Obv. $\frac{\varnothing}{P}V$ ↑N Lys in lower field to either side.

Full-length figure of St. Tryphon, beardless and nimbate, wearing tunic and colobion; holds cross in right hand.

Rev. ΘΕΟΔШΡΟϹ ΔΕϹΠΟΤΗϹ ΔΥΚΛϹ Ο ΛΛϹΚΛΡΙϹ in two columnar groups. Full-length figure of emperor wearing stemma, divitision, and panelled chlamys; holds in right hand labarum-headed scepter, and in left, globus surmounted by patriarchal cross.

Pl. 35.4, 5

BILL. TRACHY

MINT OF MAGNESIA

Type A

Obv. $\overline{IC}$ $\overline{XC}$ in field.
　　　 B　 B

Full-length figure of Christ, bearded and nimbate, wearing tunic and colobion, standing on dais; right hand raised in benediction, holds Gospels in left.

Rev. ΘΕΟΔШΡΟϹ ΔΕϹΠΟΤΗϹ ΔΥΚΛϹ Ο ΛΛϹΚΛΡΙϹ in two columnar groups. Full-length figure of emperor on left, crowned by Virgin nimbate. Emperor wears stemma, divitision, jewelled loros of simplified type, and sagion; holds in right hand scepter cruciger, and in left, globus cruciger. Virgin wears tunic and maphorion.

Pl. 35.6

Type B

Obv. $\frac{\varnothing}{P}V$ ↑ Lys in lower field to either side.

Full-length figure of St. Tryphon, beardless and nimbate, wearing tunic and colobion; holds cross in right hand.

Rev. ΘΕΟΔШΡΟϹ ΔΕϹΠΟΤΗϹ ΔΥΚΛϹ Ο ΛΛϹΚΛΡΙϹ in two columnar groups. Full-length figure of emperor wearing stemma, divitision, and panelled chlamys; holds in right hand labarum-headed scepter, and in left, globus cruciger. *Manus Dei* in upper right field.

Pl. 35.7, 8

Type C

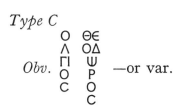

Obv. —or var.

Full-length figure of St. Theodore, bearded and nimbate, wearing short military tunic, breastplate and sagion; holds in right hand spear, and in left, shield.

Rev. ΘΕΟΔѠΡΟC ΔΕCΠΟΤΗC ΔȢΚΛC Ο ΛΛCΚΛΡΙC in two columnar groups. Full-length figure of emperor wearing stemma, divitision, jewelled loros of simplified type, and sagion; holds in right hand labarum on long shaft, and in left, globus surmounted by patriarchal cross.

Pl. 35.9–11

Type D

Obv. Ⓐ 𝔉
          B   B

Full-length figure of St. George, beardless and nimbate, wearing short military tunic, breastplate, and sagion; holds in right hand spear resting over shoulder, and in left, shield, resting on ground.

Rev.   (ΛΛCΚ?)

Full-length figure of emperor seated upon throne with back, wearing stemma, divitision, jewelled loros of simplified type, and sagion; in act of drawing sword with right hand from a sheath, held in his left, across knees.

Pl. 35.12, 13

Æ TETARTERON

MINT OF MAGNESIA

Type A
  Obv.
      Lys. Pellet in upper and lower field to either side.

              ΘΕ   ΔΕC
              ΔѠ   Π
  Rev. ΡΟ   Ο
          C   Ħ
              C

Full-length figure of emperor wearing stemma, divitision, and chlamys; holds in right hand labarum on long shaft, and in left, anexikakia.

Pl. 35.14

17*

Type B
Obv.

✱ within crescent-shaped ornament decorated with pellets.

Rev. Θ ϵ O Δ Ⲱ

Full-length figure of emperor, wearing stemma, divitision, collar-piece, and jewelled loros of simplified type; holds in right hand labarum-headed scepter, and in left, globus surmounted by patriarchal cross, which he holds by the shaft.

Pl. 35.*15*

THE COINAGE OF THEODORE II: COMMENTARY

AV HYPERPYRON

The re-attribution of var. A from Theodore I to Theodore II as suggested by Metcalf,[1] is confirmed by the style of the apparently unique example in the Bibliothèque Nationale. It is perhaps the earliest of the three varieties, unless the letters A, B, Γ, A, found above the cushion of the throne on the obverse represent annual sequence marks during this reign, in which case it would, of course, come later. Although Wroth expressed doubts as to the existence of var. C,[2] there are in fact at least four specimens known: in the collections of the Bibliothèque Nationale, Dumbarton Oaks, and Mr. P. D. Whitting; the other came from the Corinth excavations of 1925.[3]

BILL. TRACHY

Type A, attributed by Bell to Theodore "Ducas-Mangaphas," is clearly an issue of Theodore Ducas-Lascaris (Chap. 9, p. 149).

Type C, attributed by Sabatier to Isaac "Ducas-Comnenus" of Cyprus, is of similar origin (Chap. 8, p. 139).

The attribution of type D to this emperor is not certain, but seems to be strongly indicated by stylistic evidence. The B B in the field of the obverse places it in the late Nicaean or the Palaeologan periods. The hemispherical rendering of the imperial face on the reverse, together with the stemma jutting out over the temples, are definite Nicaean traits. The only convincing possibilities are Theodore II and Michael VIII: a provisional attribution to the former—who reigned the longer at Nicaea—is preferred, but the latter should be kept in mind.

[1] Metcalf, "John Vatatzes and John Comnenus," pp. 209–10.

[2] Wroth, *BMCV*, p. 205.

[3] A. R. Bellinger, *Catalogue of the Coins Found at Corinth, 1925* (New Haven, Conn., 1930), p. 74.

The significance of the lily (particularly as seen on the silver trachy type C and the billon type B) and its connection with St. Tryphon have been explained by Laurent.[4]

A further type, which has come to light since this book went to press, is to be found in the Supplementary Note at the end of the volume (p. 407).

JOHN IV, LASCARIS

1258/59

No coins of this short reign are known; probably none were issued. The two types attributed to John IV by P. D. Whitting and P. J. Donald ("Two Coins of John IV of Nicaea," Spink's *Numismatic Circular*, 75, no. 2 [Feb. 1967], p. 32) are, respectively, a coin of Michael Shishman with Ivan-Stephen, and a billon trachy of John III, Ducas-Vatatzes, under whom it has been classified as type E in this publication.

THE COINAGE OF MICHAEL VIII, PALAEOLOGUS

1258/59–1261

N HYPERPYRON

MINT OF MAGNESIA

Obv. IC XC in field.

Christ, bearded and nimbate, wearing tunic and colobion, seated upon throne without back; right hand raised in benediction, holds Gospels in left.

Rev.

```
X   O
H   ΠΛ
ΔЄ  ΛЄ  .  MP ΘV in upper field.
Π   OΛ
T   Γ
```

Full-length figure of emperor on left, crowned by Virgin nimbate. Emperor wears stemma, divitision, collar-piece, and panelled loros of simplified type; holds in right hand labarum on long shaft, and in left, anexikakia. Virgin wears tunic and maphorion.

Pl. 36.*1*

[4] V. Laurent, "L'Emblème du lis dans la numismatique byzantine: son origine," *Centennial Publication of the American Numismatic Society*, ed. H. Ingholt (New York, 1958), pp. 417–27.

Æ TRACHY

MINT OF MAGNESIA

Obv. IC XC in field.

Full-length figure of Christ, standing on dais, bearded and nimbate, wearing tunic and colobion; right hand raised in benediction, holds Gospels in left.

Rev.
    X   O
    M   Π
  ΔЄC   Λ
  ΠO   Γ
    T   ╯

Full-length figure of emperor wearing stemma, divitision, and panelled chlamys; holds in right hand labarum on long shaft, and in left, globus cruciger. *Manus Dei* in upper right field.

Pl. 36.2

BILL. TRACHY

MINT OF MAGNESIA

Type A

Obv. ⊘̄Ρ̄V   Φ̄Ṳ̄ Lys in lower field to either side.

Full-length figure of St. Tryphon, beardless and nimbate, wearing tunic and colobion; holds cross in right hand.

Rev.
    X
    M   Π
    Δ   Λ   . M̄Ρ̄ Θ̄V̄ in upper field.
    Π   Γ
    H

Full-length figure of emperor on left, crowned by Virgin nimbate. Emperor wears stemma, divitision, collar-piece, and jewelled loros of simplified type; holds in right hand scepter cruciger, and in left, anexikakia. Virgin wears tunic and maphorion.

Pl. 36.3

Type B

Obv. IC XC in field.

Christ, bearded and nimbate, wearing tunic and colobion, seated upon throne without back; right hand raised in benediction, holds Gospels in left.

Rev.
```
    X
    M
    ΔЄ
    C
    ПO
    H
    C
```

Full-length figure of emperor wearing stemma, divitision, and panelled chlamys; holds in right hand labarum-headed scepter, and in left, globus surmounted by patriarchal cross.

Pl. 36.*4*

Æ TETARTERON

MINT OF MAGNESIA

Obv. ĪC X̄C̄ in field.

Full-length figure of Christ, standing on dais, bearded and nimbate, wearing tunic and colobion; right hand raised in benediction, holds Gospels in left.

Rev.
```
  X   O
  H   П
      Λ
      ΛЄ
  OΛ
  Г
```

Full-length figure of emperor wearing stemma, divitision, collar-piece, jewelled loros of simplified type, and sagion; holds in right hand labarum-headed scepter, and in left, anexikakia. *Manus Dei* in upper right field.

Pl. 36.*5, 6*

THE COINAGE OF MICHAEL VIII: COMMENTARY

Ν̄ HYPERPYRON

The recent publication by Iliescu of an apparently unique coin of this issue[1] renders it very unlikely that the issue having as the obverse type the Virgin seated upon a throne with back, and as the reverse type Christ, the Archangel Michael, and the Emperor (Pl. 45.*12*), should be given to the short period of Michael's rule before the recovery of Constantinople. Rather, as suggested by Iliescu, and confirmed by Pachymeres, it would seem more likely that the latter type represents the first Constantinopolitan issue and that its abandonment signified the lowering of the gold content by a further carat.

[1] O. Iliescu, "Le dernier hyperpère de l'empire byzantin de Nicée," *Byzantinoslavica*, 26, 1 (1965), pp. 94–99.

Æ Trachy

The reasons for the attribution of this type to the period before the recovery of the City are its obvious stylistic similarities to the silver trachy type C of Theodore II on the one hand, and the strongly Nicaean flavor of the copper tetarteron of Michael, with which it shares a common obverse type.

Bill. Trachy

Type B is again similar to the silver trachy type C of Theodore II in points of style and detail: the exaggerated jewelling; the panelled chlamys; the broad stemma extending over the temples. It also has the ligature Ⱨ, which is peculiarly common during the reign of Theodore II, as part of the reverse inscription.

Æ Tetarteron

The obvious similarity of this issue to the tetartera of John III and Theodore II, together with the apparent absence of the denomination from the undoubted Constantinopolitan coinage of Michael VIII, seems to require an attribution to the empire of Nicaea. The obverse type—that of Christ standing on a square dais (souppedion)—which appears on type A of the billon trachy coinage of Theodore II, as well as on the silver trachy and copper tetarteron of Michael VIII, is particularly prominent upon the imperial seals of the Palaeologi.[2] A seal of John III published by V. Laurent[3] is remarkable for the similarity of its reverse type to that of the silver trachy and billon trachy type B of Michael VIII assigned to the empire of Nicaea. A further seal, of Michael VIII himself, published by J. Ebersolt,[4] is even closer in its resemblance and must surely be dated very early in the reign.

COINS OF THE EMPIRE OF NICAEA, OF UNCERTAIN ATTRIBUTION

Æ Tetarteron

Type A
Obv.

Letter Ꞵ decorated with pellets; triangle of three pellets in field to either side.

---

[2] E.g., G. Schlumberger, "Bulles d'or byzantines conservées aux archives vaticanes," *RN*[3], 12 (1894), pp. 194–99 (pl. IV).

[3] V. Laurent, *Les sceaux byzantins du Médailler Vatican* (Vatican City, 1962), p. 10, no. 14 (pl. XLIV).

[4] J. Ebersolt, "Sceaux byzantins du Musée de Constantinople," *RN*[4], 18 (1914), p. 214, no. 160 (pl. VII. 6).

Rev.

Full-length figure of emperor seated upon throne with back; wears
stemma, divitision, collar-piece, and jewelled loros of simplified type;
holds in right hand scepter cruciger, and in left, anexikakia.

Pl. 36.7

Type B

Obv. ĪC X̄C in field.

Cross composed of shaft and two barred sections, one of two, one of
three bars.

Rev.　　　　ΔЄ

Half-length figure of emperor wearing stemma, divitision, jewelled loros
of simplified type, and sagion; holds in right hand labarum-headed
scepter, and in left, globus cruciger.

Pl. 36.8

Type C

Obv. ĪC X̄C O XΛΛKHTHC in two columnar groups.

Full-length figure of Christ Chalcitis, bearded and nimbate, wearing
tunic and colobion; holds Gospels in left hand.

Rev.　ĪC　X̄C
　　　　N　K

Patriarchal cross on base

Pl. 36.9

Type D

Obv. M̄P Θ̄V in field.

Half-length figure of Virgin nimbate, orans, wearing tunic and maphorion.

Rev.

Cross, radiate, with lunate ornaments at ends, decorated with pellets.

Pl. 36.*10*

Type E

Obv.　I　C̄
　　　　X　C̄

Cross, decorated with pellets.

Rev.

Two letter B's, back to back, decorated with pellets; pellet in each loop
of letter.

Pl. 36.*11*

NICAEA, UNCERTAIN ATTRIBUTION: COMMENTARY

Type A, listed by Sabatier as "incertaine,"[1] unfortunately remains so. The reverse forked beard and stemma extending over the temples make a Nicaean attribution inevitable, as do general considerations of fabric, module, and style.

Type B was attributed by Sabatier to Alexius V, Ducas, and as pointed out earlier (Chap. 9, p. 156) should be reattributed to the empire of Nicaea for the same reasons as the preceding type.

Since this book went to press the author has seen, in the collection of Mr. P. D. Whitting, a recently acquired specimen of what is apparently this issue, but with a simple patriarchal cross, on three steps, as the obverse type. It is at least plausible to assume that this is what the very unusual design of the piece illustrated (Pl. 36.8) was originally intended to represent. Whether, in this case, the extension of the shaft of the cross down through the steps and out beyond was the result of accident or design remains unclear.

The new specimen does not provide a definite answer to the question of attribution, but it is possible that the inscription in the top left field reads: $\overline{\text{U}}$ — in which case the issuer will have been John III.

Types C–E are all of Nicaean fabric and module, and can best be paralleled on the coinages of those emperors, particularly John III and Theodore II. The decoration with pellets is also characteristic. Christ Chalcitis, present on the obverse of Type C, is found in the coinage of John III. Types D and E were also published as "incertaines" by Sabatier.[2]

THE FAMILY NAMES OF THE EMPERORS OF NICAEA

The names used by Theodore I have already been noted (p. 230).

Although John III is now almost invariably accredited with the names "Ducas-Vatatzes," contemporary documentary sources and the coinage never term him more than "Ducas." His formal signature runs: Ἰωάννης ἐν Χριστῷ τῷ Θεῷ πιστὸς βασιλεὺς καὶ αὐτοκράτορ Ῥωμαίων, ὁ Δούκας.[3]

Theodore II is termed "Lascaris" or "Ducas-Lascaris" on the coinage, both forms appearing in contemporary sources.[4]

For Michael VIII, see *infra.*, p. 295.

---

[1] Sabatier, *Description générale*, 2, p. 339, no. 11 (pl. LXX. 17).

[2] *Ibid.*, p. 338, no. 6 (pl. LXX. 12); p. 339, no. 12 (pl. LXX. 18).

[3] E.g., Miklosich and Müller, *op. cit.*, 4, pp. 4, 22, 26.

[4] For the longer form, see *ibid.*, p. 221.

THE EMPIRE OF THESSALONICA

The short and turbulent history of the empire of Thessalonica began during the last days of 1224, when the city was recaptured from the Latins by the hitherto ruler of Epirus, Theodore Comnenus-Ducas.[1]

Theodore's brilliant reign as emperor was ended in 1230 by his defeat, capture, and later blinding at the hands of the Bulgarian tsar Ivan II, Asen, at Klokotnitsa in the Rhodope. He was shortly afterward deprived of the throne by his brother Manuel, who nevertheless held onto his pretensions if not his authority.

Manuel, after an undistinguished reign, was in turn deposed upon the reappearance of Theodore in 1237. The latter, however, refused to resume his former position, instead installing as emperor his young son, John (1237–44).

The battle of Klokotnitsa had deprived the empire of Thessalonica of its chance of hegemony over the successor states to the old, undivided Empire, and its commanding position was resumed by the empire of Nicaea. In 1242, the Emperor John was forced to renounce his title in favor of the Nicaean emperor, John Ducas-Vatatzes, and was in return allowed the inferior status of despot.

The short reign of John's brother and successor, the despot Demetrius (1244–46) was concluded by the definitive occupation of the city by the Nicaean emperor.

The coinage of the empire of Thessalonica closely follows the traditional denominational pattern, but there were apparently no issues of gold. The coinage in silver, billon, and copper was therefore probably based on the old twelfth-century hyperpyron, although to what extent that continued in circulation is completely obscure.

Despite its traditional denominational lines, the coinage of Thessalonica—mostly of elegant style and competent manufacture—introduces several new iconographical themes, notably the representation of the ΠΟΛΙΣ ΘΕССΑΛΟΝΙΚΗ as a walled town with three towers, held between the emperor and his various patrons—perhaps derived from Byzantine prototypes; and the wing or winged emperor, which may well be ultimately derived from western sources.[2]

[1] The most complete history of the empire of Thessalonica is undoubtedly to be found in D. M. Nicol, *The Despotate of Epiros* (Oxford, 1957)—which has, however, been modified by L. Stiernon with regard to the date of the coronation of Theodore: "Les origines du despotat d'Epire (suite). La date du couronnement de Théodore Doukas," *Actes du XIIe Congrès International d'Études Byzantines*, 2 (Belgrade, 1964), pp. 197–202. See also p. 296.

[2] Bertelè, *L'imperatore alato*, pp. 39 ff., 52 ff.

It is tempting to suppose that the fine, large-module, billon issues of Theodore, Manuel, and John Comnenus-Ducas—and of John Ducas-Vatatzes after 1246—were produced on the basis of one type to a year. But such an arrangement would be exceedingly difficult to prove at all conclusively.

THE COINAGE OF THEODORE, COMNENUS-DUCAS

1224–1230

Æ TRACHY

Type A

Obv. IC XC in field.

Christ, bearded and nimbate, wearing tunic and colobion, seated upon throne without back; right hand raised in benediction, holds Gospels in left.

Rev. ΘΕΟΔѠΡΟCΔ𝖸ΚΛ ΟΛΓΙΟCΔΙΜΙΤΡΙΟC—or var.

Full-length figure of emperor on left, and of St. Demetrius, beardless and nimbate, holding between them cross within circle, surmounting triangular decoration on long shaft. Emperor wears stemma, divitision, and jewelled loros of traditional type. Saint (standing on dais) wears short military tunic, breastplate, and sagion; holds sword, resting over shoulder, in left hand.

Pl. 37.*1, 2*

Type B

Obv. M͞P Θ͞V H ΛΓΗΟCѠΡΗΤΗCΛ in two columnar groups.

Full-length figure of Virgin Hagiosoritissa, nimbate, orans, facing, wearing tunic and maphorion.

Rev. ΘΕΟΔѠΡΟCΔΕCΠΟ ΟΛΓΙΟCΔΙΜΙΤΡΙΟC—or var.

Full-length figure of emperor on left, and of St. Demetrius beardless and nimbate, giving a castle with three towers into the hands of the emperor. Emperor wears stemma, divitision, collar-piece, and jewelled loros of simplified type. Saint (standing on dais) wears short military tunic, breastplate, and sagion. *Manus Dei* in upper center field.

Pl. 37.*3, 4*

Type C

Obv. M͞P Θ͞V in upper field.

Virgin nimbate, wearing tunic and maphorion, seated upon throne with back: holds beardless, nimbate head of Christ on breast.

Rev. ΘЄΟΔΨΡΟC ΔȣΚΛC—or var. Ī̄C X̄C In upper field.

Full-length figure of emperor on left, crowned by Christ, bearded and nimbate. Emperor wears stemma, divitision, jewelled loros of simplified type, and sagion; holds in right hand sheathed sword, point downward, and in left, anexikakia. Christ wears tunic and colobion; holds Gospels in left hand.

Pl. 37.5, *6*

BILL. TRACHY

Type A

Obv. Ī̄C X̄C Ο ЄΜΜΛΝȣΗΛ in two columnar groups.

Bust of Christ Emmanuel, beardless and nimbate, wearing tunic and colobion; holds scroll in left hand.

Rev. ΘЄΟΔΟΡΟCΔȣΚ ΟΛΓΙΟCΔΙΜΙΤΡ—or var.

Full-length figure of emperor on left, and of St. Demetrius, beardless and nimbate, holding between them cross within circle, surmounting triangular decoration on long shaft. Emperor wears stemma, divitision, and chlamys. Saint wears short military tunic, breastplate, and sagion; holds sword, resting over shoulder, in left hand.

Pl. 37.*7–9*

Type B

Obv. Ī̄C X̄C in field.

Christ, beardless and nimbate, wearing tunic and colobion, seated upon throne without back; right hand raised in benediction, left hand raised holding scroll.

Rev. ΘЄΟΔΟΡΟCΔЄCΠΟΤ ΟΛΓΙΟCΔΙΜΙΤΡΙ—or var.

Full-length figure of emperor on left, crowned by St. Demetrius, beardless and nimbate. Emperor wears stemma, divitision, collar-piece, and panelled loros of simplified type; holds in right hand scepter cruciger, and in left, anexikakia. Saint (standing on dais) wears short military tunic, breastplate, and sagion; holds sheathed sword, point downard, in left hand.

Pl. 37.*10–12*

Type C

Obv. M̄P̄ Θ̄V̄ in upper field.

Virgin nimbate, wearing tunic and maphorion, seated upon throne with back; holds beardless, nimbate head of Christ on breast.

Rev. ΘΕΟΔШΡΟCΔΕCΠΤ ΟΛΓΙΟCΘΕΟΔШΡ—or var.

Full-length figure of emperor on left, and of St. Theodore, bearded and nimbate, holding between them cross within circle, surmounting triangular decoration on long shaft. Emperor wears stemma, divitision, collarpiece, and jewelled loros of simplified type; holds sheathed sword, point downward, in right hand. Saint wears short military tunic, breastplate, and sagion; holds shield, resting on ground, in left hand.

Pl. 38.*1*, *2*

Type D

Obv. Ī͞C X͞C in field.

Christ, bearded and nimbate, wearing tunic and colobion, seated upon throne without back; right hand raised in benediction, holds Gospels in left.

Rev. ΘΕΟΔШΡΟCΔ૪Κ $\overset{X}{M}$ —or var.

Full-length figure of emperor on left, and of Archangel Michael nimbate, giving a castle with three towers into the hands of the emperor. Emperor wears stemma, divitision, collar-piece, and jewelled loros of simplified type; holds labarum-headed scepter in right hand. Archangel wears divitision, collar-piece, and panelled loros of simplified type; holds jewelled scepter in left hand. *Manus Dei* in upper center field.

Pl. 38.*3*, *4*

Type E

Obv. $\overset{\overline{MP}}{*} \overset{\overline{\Theta V}}{*}$ in field.

Full-length figure of Virgin nimbate, wearing tunic and maphorion.

Rev. (ΘΕΟΔШΡΟC?)Δ૪. Ī͞C X͞C in upper right field, asterisk in lower field.

Full-length figure of emperor on left, crowned by Christ, bearded and nimbate. Emperor wears stemma, divitision, collar-piece, panelled loros of simplified type, and sagion; holds in right hand scepter cruciger, and in left, anexikakia. Christ wears tunic and colobion; holds Gospels in left hand.

Pl. 38.*5*

Type F

Obv. $\begin{matrix} O & \Delta I \\ \Lambda\Gamma & MH \\ IO & TP \\ C & IO \\ & C \end{matrix}$ —or var.

St. Demetrius, beardless and nimbate, in act of drawing sword, seated upon throne without back: wears tunic, breastplate, and sagion; holds hilt of sword in right hand and sheath in left, horizontally across knees.

Rev. ΘΕΟΔѠΡΟСΔЄС—or var. M̄P̄ Θ̄V̄ in upper field.

Half-length figure of emperor on left, and of Virgin nimbate, holding between them patriarchal cross on long shaft, at base of which a small globe. Emperor wears stemma, divitision, collar-piece, and panelled loros of simplified type; holds scepter cruciger in right hand. Virgin wears tunic and maphorion. *Manus Dei* in upper left field.

Pl. 38.*6, 7*

Type G

Obv. Ī꜀ X̄C̄ *or* Ī꜀ X̄C̄ Ο ЄΜΜΛΝȣΗΛ in two columnar groups.

Bust of Christ Emmanuel, beardless and nimbate, wearing tunic and colobion; holds scroll in left hand.

Rev. ΘΕΟΔѠΡΟС ΔЄСΠΟΤΗС ΚΟΜΝΗΝΟС Ο ΔȣΚΛС in two columnar groups.

Full-length figure of emperor wearing stemma, divitision, collar-piece, panelled loros of simplified type, and sagion; holds in right hand labarum-headed scepter, and in left, globus surmounted by single *or* double-barred cross. *Manus Dei* in upper right field.

Pl. 38.*8, 9*

Æ TETARTERON

Obv.
+ΘЄ
ΟΔѠΡΟС
ΔЄСΠΟΤ
ΗСΟΔΟV
ΚΛС

Rev. ΘΕΟΔѠΡΟСΔȣΚΛС ΟΛΓΙΟСΔΙΜΙΤ—or var.

Half-length figure of emperor on left, and of St. Demetrius, beardless and nimbate. Between them a patriarchal cross-crosslet, on long shaft decorated with crescent and pellet, the base of the shaft ending in three steps. Emperor wears stemma, divitision, collar-piece, and jewelled loros of simplified type; holds anexikakia in left hand. Saint wears tunic, breastplate, and sagion; holds in right hand sword, resting over shoulder, and in left, shield.

Pl. 38.*10, 11*

Æ HALF-TETARTERON

Type A
Obv. M̄P̄ Θ̄V̄ in field.

Bust of Virgin nimbate, orans, wearing tunic and maphorion.

Rev. ΔЄCΠOTI ΘЄOΔΨPOC

Full-length figure of emperor turned slightly to left, wearing stemma, divitision, collar-piece, and jewelled loros of simplified type; holds in right hand globus cruciger, and in left, labarum on long shaft.

Pl. 38.*12*

Type B

Obv.
```
    O    Δ
   ΛΓ   HM
   HO   TP
    C
```

Half-length figure of St. Demetrius, beardless and nimbate, wearing tunic, breastplate, and sagion; holds in right hand spear, resting over shoulder, and in left, shield.

Rev. ΘЄOΔΨPOC KOMNHИOC

Full-length figure of emperor turned slightly to right, wearing stemma, divitision, collar-piece, and jewelled loros of simplified type; holds in right hand scepter, and in left, globus cruciger.

Pl. 38.*13*

Type C

Obv. O ΛΓHOC ΔHMHTP—or var. in two columnar groups.

Half-length figure of St. Demetrius, beardless and nimbate, wearing tunic, breastplate, and sagion; holds in right hand spear, resting over shoulder, and in left, shield; *or*, shield in right hand and spear in left.

Rev. ΘЄOΔΨPOC O ΔYKΛC—or var. in two columnar groups.

Full-length figure of emperor turned slightly to left, wearing stemma, divitision, collar-piece, and jewelled loros of simplified type; holds in right hand globus cruciger, and in left, labarum-headed scepter.

Pl. 38.*14, 15*

THE COINAGE OF THEODORE DUCAS: COMMENTARY

GENERAL

The date of Theodore's ecclesiastical coronation as Emperor of the Romans is uncertain: early 1225, or between late 1227 and early 1228, have both been suggested.[3] If the latter were eventually confirmed, then it is almost certain that the issue of coinage began before the coronation, since it is most unlikely— even by Thessalonican standards—that the varied and splendid series of coins bearing Theodore's name could be fitted into the short period 1227/28–30.

[3] *Supra*, p. 267, note 1.

It is known from documentary sources that Theodore assumed the full imperial titulature, signing for instance in June 1228 as: Θεόδωρος ἐν Χριστῷ τῷ Θεῷ πιστὸς βασιλεὺς καὶ αὐτοκράτωρ ʽΡωμαίων Κομνηνὸς ὁ Δούκας.[4] Despite the fact that he was entitled to the use of the surname "Angelus," that somewhat dubious distinction was apparently kept in the background: he is referred to on his coinage —when any surname is used—as Theodore Comnenus, or Ducas, or Comnenus-Ducas. This generally suffices to distinguish him from Theodore I, Comnenus-Lascaris or Theodore II, Ducas-Lascaris, of Nicaea. Even if this were not so, the fine, elegant style of the mint of Thessalonica is quite unmistakable.

Unfortunately neither the relative value nor the sequence of issues is certain for any of the denominations in the following lists.

Æ TRACHY

The facing Virgin Hagiosoritissa on the obverse of type B differs from the profile figure normally found.[5] A single specimen of this type has, according to Mme Oikonomides, been found in copper (billon). Silver, however, certainly seems the norm.

Type C was attributed by Wroth to Theodore II, Ducas-Lascaris of Nicaea,[6] but the fine, elegant style, the rather deep scyphate fabric, and the relatively small module, require a Thessalonican attribution. The titulature ΘΕΟΔWΡΟC ΔYΚΛC is more often used by Theodore of Thessalonica than by Theodore II of Nicaea, who generally couples the surname with ΛΛCΚΛΡΙC. The lys on the obverse of Wroth no. 3 and the letters on that of no. 4 can also be paralleled by similar devices and letters on types A and B, and on the billon coinage.

One of the most interesting characteristics of this elegant group of issues is the recurrence on type A of the loros of traditional type: that directly descended from the Roman consular trabea. It had last appeared on a billon issue of John II (Pl. 11.3, 4) which also seems to be separate from the metropolitan coinage on the basis of hoard occurrence. Prior to that it had appeared on both the pre-reform folleis and the post-reform tetartera of Alexius I which are assigned to the mint of Thessalonica (Pls. 3.2; 8.10–15). The recurrence, at lengthy intervals, of this form of dress on the products of this mint, when taken together with other similar evidence, can only be an indication of the systematic preservation of mint documents or master dies.[7]

The same garment is found on type G of the billon trachea of Manuel of Thessalonica (Pl. 39.10, 11) and on types A and B of the same denomination of John III, Ducas-Vatatzes, minted at Thessalonica (Pl. 42.1–4).

[4] Miklosich and Müller, *Acta et Diplomata*, 5 (Vienna, 1887), p. 15.
[5] E.g., Pl. 27.8–11. Cf. T. Bertelè, "La Vergine Aghiosoritissa nella numismatica bizantina," *Revue des études byzantines*, 16 (1958) (= Mélanges S. Salaville), pp. 233–34.
[6] Wroth, *BMCV*, p. 222, nos. 3, 4.
[7] Chap. 13, p. 302.

18

BILL. TRACHY

Type C was attributed to Theodore II of Nicaea by Sabatier,[8] but for the same reason as silver type C—the fine style—must be attributed instead to Theodore of Thessalonica. The bearded military saint is in fact St. Theodore, and not St. Demetrius, as given by Sabatier.

Type E is certainly Thessalonican and—since John Ducas is always represented beardless—must belong to either Theodore or Manuel. The former has been preferred because of the surname "Ducas" which is the only legible part of the reverse inscription. Whereas Theodore frequently used the name, Manuel is apparently known to numismatics only by the inscription MΛNЧHΛ ΔЄCΠOTHC. The alternative attribution should, however, be kept in mind.

Æ TETARTERON

The four flat copper pieces at Dumbarton Oaks which remain unmutilated weigh 4.12, 3.98, 3.72 and 2.63 gm. and therefore plainly qualify for this denomination. The reverse type is very much a throw-back and finds its nearest parallel in a miliaresion type of Nicephorus III, Botaneiates.

Æ HALF-TETARTERON

The nine pieces of these three types at Dumbarton Oaks weigh between 2.07 gm. and 1.35 gm., averaging at 1.83 gm. They are therefore to be identified as halves of the above. They are certainly to be assigned to Thessalonica—not to the empire of Nicaea—because only the former uses the combination of surnames "Comnenus" and "Ducas." This is a valuable attribution to be able to establish, for the only other coins of this denomination which are distinguishable from the unit by iconographical types as well as by weight, have also been assigned to this mint. The obverse bust type of St. Demetrius is closely paralleled by those of SS. Demetrius and George on the half-tetartera of John II and tetartera and half-tetartera of Alexius III. The reverse type depicting Theodore turned slightly to the left, or to the right, is very similar to those of SS. Constantine and Helena on the series of anonymous Latin types (Pl. 28. *12–14*).

THE COINAGE OF MANUEL, COMNENUS-DUCAS

1230–1237

Æ TRACHY

Type A

    Obv. I̅C̅ X̅C̅ in field.

       Bust of Christ, bearded and nimbate, wearing tunic and colobion; right hand raised in benediction, holds Gospels in left.

[8] Sabatier, *Description générale*, 2, p. 299, no. 14 (pl. LXVI, 2).

Rev. MΛNЧHΛΔ. M̄P̄ ⊖V̄ in upper field.

Full-length figure of emperor on left, crowned by Virgin nimbate. Emperor wears stemma, divitision, jewelled loros of simplified type, and sagion; holds in right hand labarum-headed scepter, and in left, anexika-kia. Virgin wears tunic and maphorion.

Pl. 39.*1*

Type B

Obv. ĪC X̄C Ш (*sic*) ЄMMΛNЧHΛ in two columnar groups.

Bust of Christ Emmanuel, beardless and nimbate, wearing tunic and colobion; holds scroll in left hand.

Rev. MΛNЧHΛΔЄCПOT OΛ(ΓIOCΔIMITPIOC?)

Full-length figure of emperor on left, and of St. Demetrius, beardless and nimbate, holding between them labarum, surmounting triangular decoration on long shaft. Emperor wears stemma, divitision, and chlamys; holds sheathed sword, point resting on ground, in right hand. Saint, similarly dressed, holds sheathed sword, point resting on ground, in left hand.

Pl. 39.*2*

BILL. TRACHY

Type A

Obv.
```
   O     Δ
  ΛΓ    HM
  IO    IT
   C    OC
```

Bust of St. Demetrius, beardless and nimbate, wearing tunic, breastplate, and sagion; holds in right hand spear, resting over shoulder, and in left, hilt of sword (or cross?).

Rev. MΛNЧHΛ. ĪC X̄C in upper field.

Full-length figure of emperor on left, crowned by Christ, bearded and nimbate. Emperor wears stemma, divitision, and panelled chlamys; holds in right hand scepter cruciger, and in left, anexikakia. Christ wears tunic and colobion; holds Gospels in left hand.

Pl. 39.*3*

Type B

Obv. M̄P̄ ⊖V̄ in upper field.

Virgin nimbate, wearing tunic and maphorion, seated upon throne with back; holds beardless, nimbate head of Christ on breast.

Rev. MΛNЪHΛΔЄCПOT $\begin{matrix} \mathsf{X} \\ \mathsf{M} \\ \mathsf{X} \\ \mathsf{P} \end{matrix}$ —or var.

Full-length figure of emperor on left, and of Archangel Michael nimbate, holding between them labarum on long shaft. Emperor wears stemma, divitision, collar-piece, and panelled loros of simplified type. Archangel wears short tunic and (sagion?) held wrapped around him.

Pl. 39.*4, 5*

Type C

Obv. $\overline{\mathsf{MP}}$ $\overline{\Theta V}$ in field.
 ✳ ✳

Bust of Virgin nimbate, orans, wearing tunic and maphorion.

Rev. MΛNЪHΛΔЄCП $\begin{matrix} \mathsf{OΛ} \\ \mathsf{ΓI} \\ \mathsf{OC} \end{matrix}$ (ΔIMITPIOC ?)—or var.

Full-length figure of emperor on left, and of St. Demetrius(?), beardless and nimbate, giving globus surmounted by patriarchal cross into the hands of the emperor. Emperor wears stemma, divitision, collar-piece, and jewelled loros of simplified type; holds scepter cruciger in right hand. Saint wears divitision and chlamys; holds spear in left hand.

Pl. 39.*6*

Type D

Obv. $\begin{matrix} \mathsf{X} \\ \mathsf{P} \end{matrix}$ $\begin{matrix} \mathsf{X} \\ \mathsf{M} \end{matrix}$

Half-length figure of Archangel Michael nimbate, wearing divitision, collar-piece, and panelled loros of simplified type; holds in right hand sword, resting over shoulder, and in left, sheath.

Rev. MΛNЪHΛΔЄ OKШNCTΛNTINOC—or var.

Full-length figure of emperor on left, and of St. Constantine (with forked beard), holding between them patriarchal cross on long shaft at the base of which, three steps. Emperor wears stemma, divitision, collar-piece, and jewelled loros of simplified type; holds palm-frond in right hand. Saint, similarly dressed, holds palm-frond in left hand.

Pl. 39.*7*

Type E

Obv. Ī̄C X̄C in field.

Facing bust of Christ, beardless and nimbate, wearing tunic and colobion; holds scroll in left hand.

Rev. (MΛΝႸΗΛ?)Δ Ᵽ (ˣM?)

Full-length figure of emperor on left, crowned by nimbate Archangel (Michael?), holding between them sheathed sword, point downward. Emperor wears stemma, divitision, collar-piece, and jewelled loros of simplified type; holds scepter cruciger in right hand. Archangel wears tunic and (colobion?).

Pl. 39.*8*

Type F

Obv.

Bust of St. Theodore, bearded and nimbate, wearing tunic, breastplate, and sagion; holds in right hand spear, resting over shoulder, and in left, shield.

Rev. MΛΝႸΗΛ   ΟΛ

Half-length figure of emperor on left, and of beardless, nimbate military Saint (Demetrius?), holding between them sheathed sword, point downward. Emperor wears stemma, divitision, collar-piece, and jewelled loros of simplified type. Saint wears tunic, breastplate, and sagion. In upper center field a cloud, with a star in the center, out of which extends *Manus Dei*, crowning the emperor.

Pl. 39.9

Type G

Obv. ˣᎪ ˣM

Full-length figure of Archangel Michael nimbate, wearing short military tunic, breastplate, and sagion; holds in right hand sword which he is in the act of unsheathing—the sheath held horizontally in the left hand.

Rev. MΑΝႸΗΛΔΕϹΠΟΤΙ ΠΟΛΙϹ ΘΕϹϹΛ ΛΟΝ ΙΚΗ ΟΛΓΙΟϹΔΗΜΗΤΡΙΟϹ—or var.

Emperor on left, and St. Demetrius, beardless and nimbate, seated upon throne without back, holding between them the city of Thessalonica represented as a walled town with three towers. Emperor wears stemma, divitision, and jewelled loros of traditional type; holds labarum-headed scepter in right hand. Saint wears tunic, breastplate, and sagion; holds sword, resting over shoulder, in left hand.

Pl. 39.*10, 11*

THE COINAGE OF MANUEL DUCAS: COMMENTARY

Æ Trachy

Type B is apparently known only from the specimen in the Ashmolean Museum, Oxford.

Bill. Trachy

Type D has already been the cause of some confusion. It was apparently first published by Edwards, in 1936,[1] and assigned to a previously unknown co-emperorship of Manuel I and Andronicus Comnenus which, it is suggested, took place some time between 1143 and 1153.

Such a co-emperorship is both historically and numismatically in the highest degree unlikely. The period is relatively well documented both by official administrative documents and by Byzantine historians—some of whom, such as Nicetas Choniates, wrote a good deal later, but with access to official sources: there would therefore have been no reason to omit such an important constitutional event. The first electrum, billon, and copper coinages of the reign all portray Manuel as beardless: yet this coin which would necessarily antedate the disgrace of Andronicus in 1153—i.e., still early in the reign—has a bearded Manuel.

There is little doubt that the type is, in fact, an issue of the empire of Thessalonica. The neat, elegant style—superior even to the metropolitan coinage of Manuel I—and the bust of the Archangel Michael on the obverse, which can be very closely paralleled on type B of the coinage of John III, Ducas-Vatatzes struck at Thessalonica between 1246 and 1254, both require such an attribution.

This suggestion is confirmed by a coin published by Longuet in 1943.[2] The obverse and reverse types are the same as those on the piece published by Edwards; the figure on the right-hand side of the reverse even has the forked beard which lends a superficial plausibility to its identification as Andronicus Comnenus. The inscription reads not ΛΝΔΡΟΝΙΚΟC but ΟΚШΝCΤΛΝΤΙΝΟC— which is as might be expected when it is considered that it is only St. Constantine of the whole repertoire of saints represented upon the Byzantine coinage who is portrayed as wearing the combination of stemma, divitision, and loros. The Saint's lack of nimbus can also be paralleled upon the silver trachy type E of John Ducas-Vatatzes, and upon the billon trachy type E of the same Emperor.

[1] K. M. Edwards, "A Remarkable Coin of Manuel I Comnenus," *Classical Studies in Honor of E. Capps* (Princeton, 1936), pp. 103–05.

[2] H. Longuet, "Deux monnaies de Manuel l'Ange Comnène Ducas, empereur de Thessalonique (1230–1262 [sic])," *RN*[5], 7 (1943), pp. 137–44.

Two further pieces, reading ΜΛΝΟVΗΛΔC ΟΛΓΙΟCΚΟCΤ, have recently been published by Bertelè, whose attribution is also to Manuel Ducas rather than to Manuel I, Comnenus.[3]

It can therefore only be assumed that Edward's attribution was based on the misreading of an inscription that was either blundered, or faulty, or both.

The attribution of type E to Manuel rather than to Theodore is based on an attempted reconstruction of the faint traces of inscription remaining on the piece illustrated.

Type F is similarly attributed on the basis of a retrograde inscription found on a clipped specimen of the issue, from the Mogilitsa hoard.

A further type, which has come to light since this book went to press, is to be found in the Supplementary Note at the end of the volume (p. 407).

THE COINAGE OF JOHN, COMNENUS-DUCAS
EMPEROR 1237–42, DESPOT 1242–44

Bill. Trachy (Series I)

Type A

Obv. Γ
OΛ
ΔΗ

St. Demetrius nimbate, seated upon throne without back.

Rev. ΙШΛΝΝΙCΔЄC

Full-length figure of emperor on left, and of Virgin nimbate, holding between them cross within circle, surmounting triangular decoration on long shaft. Emperor wears stemma, divitision, collar-piece, and panelled loros of simplified type; holds anexikakia in right hand. Virgin wears tunic and maphorion.

Pl. 40.*1*

Type B

Obv. Γ Δ Lys in field to either side.
⊗ ΘЄO

Full-length figure of St. Theodore, bearded and nimbate, wearing short military tunic, breastplate, and sagion; holds in right hand spear, and in left, shield.

---

[3] T. Bertelè, "L'imperatore con una palma su una bulla e monete bizantine del sec. XIII," *Polychronion: Festschrift Franz Dölger zum 75. Geburstag*, ed. P. Wirth (Heidelberg, 1966), pp. 82–89. Bertelè also makes a persuasive case for accepting as an authentic type of Manuel what appears to have been a billon scyphate, first published by Tanini in 1791, and described as depicting on the obverse a bust of Christ Emmanuel, and on the reverse a full-length figure of the Emperor holding a palm-frond and scepter. While regarding the existence of such a type as probable, the author would prefer to note the fact and defer a formal listing until an actual specimen should turn up.

Rev. IѠ

Full-length figure of emperor on left, crowned by beardless, nimbate military saint (Demetrius?). Emperor wears stemma, divitision, collar-piece, and panelled loros of simplified type; holds in right hand labarum-headed scepter, and in left, anexikakia. Saint wears short military tunic, breastplate, and sagion; holds sword, point resting on ground, in left hand.

Pl. 40.*2*

Type C

Obv. M̅P̅ Ө̅V̅ in field.

Virgin nimbate, wearing tunic and maphorion, seated upon throne without back; holds beardless, nimbate head of Christ on breast.

Rev. IѠΛΝΝΙC

Full-length figure of emperor wearing short military tunic (breastplate?), and sagion; holds in right hand labarum on long shaft, and in left, globus cruciger.

Pl. 40.*3*

Type D

Obv. I̅C̅ X̅C̅ in field.

Bust of Christ, beardless and nimbate, wearing tunic and colobion; holds scroll in left hand.

Rev. •IѠΛΝΙCΔЄCΠO OΛΓIOCΔIMIT

Half-length figure of emperor on left, and of St. Demetrius, beardless and nimbate, holding between them patriarchal cross. Emperor wears stemma, divitision, collar-piece, and jewelled loros of simplified type. Saint wears tunic, breastplate, and sagion.

Pl. 40.*4*

Type E

Obv. ⊘ Ѡ
     ӨЄ P
     ѠΔ ⌐

Half-length figure of St. Theodore, bearded and nimbate, wearing tunic, breastplate, and sagion; holds in right hand sword, resting over shoulder, and in left, sheath(?).

Rev. IѠΔЄCΠO ⊘ΔΗMΗT

Half-length figure of emperor on left and of St. Demetrius, beardless and nimbate, holding between them large cross within circle, surmounting triangular decoration on long shaft. Emperor wears stemma, divitision, collar-piece, and jewelled loros of simplified type. Saint wears tunic, (breastplate?), and sagion. Emperor holds shaft with left hand, the Saint with both hands.

Pl. 40.*5*

BILL. TRACHY (Series II)

Type F

Obv. ⊘ $^{\Delta}_{HM}$

Half-length figure of St. Demetrius, beardless and nimbate, wearing tunic, breastplate, and sagion; holds in right hand sword, resting over shoulder, and in left, sheath.

Rev. IШ• Δ $\overline{\text{MP}}\atop\overline{\Theta V}$

Full-length figure of emperor on left, crowned by Virgin nimbate. Emperor wears stemma, divitision, collar-piece, and panelled loros of simplified type; holds in right hand labarum on long shaft, and in left, anexikakia. Virgin wears tunic and maphorion.

Pl. 40.6

Type G

Obv.

Eagle with wings outstretched, head turned to left.

Rev. IШΔ ⊘ΔIM

Half-length figure of emperor on left, and of St. Demetrius, beardless and nimbate, holding between them patriarchal cross-crosslet on long shaft, at base of which, three steps. Emperor wears stemma, divitision, collar-piece, and jewelled loros of simplified type. Saint wears tunic, breastplate, and sagion; holds spear in left hand.

Pl. 40.7

Type H

Obv. $\overline{\oslash}$ ΔΙ

St. Demetrius, beardless and nimbate, seated upon throne without back; wears tunic (breastplate?), and sagion; holds in right hand sword, and in left, sheath, held horizontally across knees. Lys above cushions of throne, to either side.

Rev. IШΔ ЄСΠ

Half-length figure of emperor wearing stemma, divitision, panelled loros of simplified type, and sagion; holds in right hand scepter cruciger, and in left, globus cruciger.

Pl. 40.8

Type I

Obv. $^{X}_{M}$

Half-length figure of Archangel Michael nimbate, wearing divitision, loros, and sagion; holds in right hand sword, resting over shoulder, and in left, globus cruciger.

Rev. IШΛΝΝΙC ΔΕCΠΟΤΗC

Emperor seated upon throne without back. Wears stemma, divitision, collar-piece, and panelled loros of simplified type; holds in right hand scepter cruciger, and in left, anexikakia.

Pl. 40.*9, 10*

Æ HALF-TETARTERON

Obv.
+ïШΔ
KOMNH
NOCOΔO
VKΛC

Rev. ĪC X̄C in field.

Cross potent on three steps.

Pl. 40.*11*

BILL. OR Æ TRACHY (Series III [small module])

Type A
Obv.
Rev.
} As billon trachy type A (Series I), but small module.

Pl. 40.*12, 13* (*rev.* only)

Type B
Obv.
Rev.
} As billon trachy type B (Series I), but small module.

Pl. 40.*14* (*rev.* only)

Type C
Obv. | *Var. A* As billon trachy type E (Series I), but small module.
Rev. | *Var. B* As above, but full-length figures on reverse.

(A) Pl. 40.*15*
(B) Pl. 41.*1* (*rev.* only)

Type D
Obv.
Rev.
} As billon trachy type F (Series II), but small module.

Pl. 41.*2*

Type E

Obv.

Rev.

As billon trachy type G (Series II), but small module.

Pl. 41.*3, 4* (*revs.* only)

Type F

Obv.

Head of cherub, nimbate, with four wings.

Rev. IⱲ OΛΓ

Full-length figure of emperor on left, and of beardless, nimbate saint (Demetrius?) in military dress, holding between them cross, surmounted by globule, on long shaft. Emperor wears stemma, divitision, collar-piece, and jewelled loros of simplified type. Saint wears short military tunic, breastplate, and sagion; holds sword, resting over shoulder, in left hand.

Pl. 41.*5, 6*

Type G

Obv. IC XC
NI KΛ

Patriarchal cross, radiate, on step.

Rev.

Full-length figure of beardless emperor on left, and of beardless, nimbate saint (Demetrius?) in military dress, holding between them castle with two towers. Emperor wears stemma, divitision, jewelled loros of simplified type, and sagion. Saint wears short military tunic, breastplate, and sagion.

Pl. 41.*7, 8* (*rev.* only)

Type H

Obv. M̅P̅ Θ̅V̅ in field.

Virgin seated upon throne without back.

Rev. ΔЄСΠΟΤ IⱲANNIC

Full-length figure of emperor wearing stemma, divitision, collar-piece, and jewelled loros of simplified type; holds in right hand scepter, and in left, anexikakia. *Manus Dei* in upper right field.

Pl. 40.*9* (*rev.* only)

Type I

Obv.

As *rev.*, incuse.

Rev.

Full-length figure of beardless emperor wearing stemma, divitision, and chlamys; holds in right hand labarum-headed scepter, and in left, globus cruciger.

Pl. 41.*10*

Type J
Obv.

Cross, radiate, decorated with pellets.

Rev.   ΔЄ

Full-length figure of beardless emperor wearing stemma, short military tunic (breastplate?), and sagion; holds in right hand sword, resting over shoulder, and in left, castle with three towers.

Pl. 41.*11*

Type K
Obv.

Outstretched wing.

Rev. I̅Ѡ̅Δ in left field.

Half-length figure of emperor wearing stemma, divitision, and jewelled loros of traditional type; holds in right hand large standard decorated with two crosses-within-circle, and in left, cross on long shaft.

Pl. 41.*12, 13*

Type L
Obv.

Large letter B.

Rev. I̅Ѡ̅Δ in left field.

As preceding type.

Type M
Obv.

Large letter B on left, and standard decorated with two crosses-within-circle on right.

Rev. M̅P̅ Θ̅V̅ in field.

Virgin nimbate, wearing tunic and maphorion, seated upon throne without back; holds beardless, nimbate head of Christ on breast.

Pl. 41.*14*

Type N
Obv.

As *rev.*, incuse.

Rev. (IѠ?)

Half-length figure of beardless emperor wearing stemma, divitision, collar-piece, and jewelled loros of simplified type; holds in right hand labarum-headed scepter, and in left, anexikakia.

Pl. 41.*15, 16* (*revs.* only)

Type O

Obv. M̅P̅ Θ̅V̅ in field.
       * *

    Bust of Virgin nimbate, orans, wearing tunic and maphorion.

Rev. IѠ in upper right field.

    Full-length figure of winged emperor, wearing stemma, divitision, collar-piece, and panelled loros of simplified type; holds in right hand labarum-headed scepter, and in left, anexikakia.

Pl. 41.17

Type P
Obv.

    Obscure.

Rev.

    Winged, beardless, imperial bust surmounting the towered walls of a city.

Pl. 41.18 (rev. only)

Type Q

Obv. ✸

Rev. M̅P̅ Θ̅V̅ in field.
       * *

    Full-length figure of Virgin nimbate, orans, wearing tunic and maphorion.

THE COINAGE OF JOHN DUCAS: COMMENTARY

GENERAL

John Ducas, still a youth at the time of his accession, is always portrayed as beardless.

In a similar fashion to his father, Theodore, and indeed to most of his nearer relations, John apparently used only the surnames "Comnenus" and "Ducas" —not "Angelus," to which he was also entitled.[1]

BILL. TRACHY

As shown by the plates, the scyphate coinages of both Theodore and Manuel Ducas are characterized by their large module, regular fabric, and fine style. Coins of the same denomination struck by John Ducas-Vatatzes during the period 1246–54 form a direct continuation of the series, the first two of his types (Pl. 42.<i>1–4</i>) being of particularly fine workmanship.

---

[1] As on John's half-tetarteron type. See also: V. Laurent, "Bulle et monnaies inédites de Jean Ducas Comnène, empereur de Thessalonique (1240–1244)," *Cronica Numismatică și Arheologică*, 125/126 (1943), pp. 3–14; D. I. Polemis, *The Doukai* (London, 1968), nos. 42–46, 48, 52–54.

Although there are isolated specimens of the coinage of Theodore and Manuel that fall below the average in respect of module, fabric, and style, there is nothing to give warning of the flood of small, irregular, and generally inferior types that apparently accompany the normal scyphate coinage of the reign of John Comnenus-Ducas.

The normal coinage—that is, of the module, fabric, and style common to both John's predecessors and his successor—is composed of five types (Series I, A–E, Pl. 40.*1–5*).

A further four types (Series II, F–I, Pl. 40.*6–10*) are clearly interrelated by a slightly different combination of characteristics: they are of quite small module (*c.* 20–24 mm.), but of rather thicker fabric than the previous group, and of good style with small, deeply engraved dies. The iconography of this series is perhaps rather more adventurous than that of the preceding—the obverse design of type G (an eagle) being striking and unprecedented (taken from the augustalis?): the reverse is taken from the tetarteron type of Theodore. Since it is impossible to assign this second series to another mint (the "empire" by now consisting of little more than the city of Thessalonica), or, on the present evidence, to assume that it either preceded or succeeded the first (thus breaking the sequence of the normal coinage), it might plausibly be suggested that it represents a fractional coinage: presumably the half. Although the few surviving specimens of these two series betray no obvious differences of weight-standard (despite their different module), it must be remembered that the scyphate denomination was, technically at least, of billon—and that there might therefore be some small difference of metallic composition.

The third group of coins (Series III, Pls. 40.*12–15*; 41.*1–18*) is altogether another proposition. The large number of types of which it is composed is all the more extraordinary when it is considered that John's reign lasted only seven years and, moreover, that it is generally agreed that his right to issue an autonomous coinage ceased with his demotion to the rank of despot, after a mere five years of reign.[2] This results in an apparent average of over three types per year, with the strong probability that further types will come to light in the future. There is also a further anomaly in that of these fifteen types, five are more or less identical with those also represented in the two series of larger module—three from the first, two from the second.

Comparison of the small-module coins in Series III with the similar pieces in the Latin imitative series (Pl. 29.*1–20*) immediately arouses the suspicion that the two are related in some way—whether by common origin, or standard, or both.[3] Such a connection is strongly confirmed by the evidence of hoards.

[2] See, for instance, Bertelè, "Monete di Giovanni di Salonicco," p. 74.
[3] Chap. 11, pp. 213–14.

The Dorkovo hoard contained fourteen trachea definitely identifiable as Thessalonican. Of these, five coins were of Theodore and Manuel: originally all of normal large module, three had been so drastically clipped that only fractions of the designs remained.[4] The remaining nine pieces, which were all of John, were of the small-module series.

The Logodash hoard contained a single piece of Theodore: it had been similarly clipped.

The Mogilitsa hoard contained a further specimen—of Manuel: it also had been clipped.

The Oustovo contained twelve certain Thessalonican trachea: the eight specimens that were of Theodore and Manuel had all been clipped. Of the four coins of John, the only piece of Series I, the regular coinage, had suffered a similar fate: the remainder were of small module.

The Preslav hoard contained three coins of John, all of the small module.

The Tri Voditsi hoard contained nineteen definite Thessalonican trachea. Of the fifteen pieces of Theodore and Manuel, five had been clipped, as had all three large-module pieces of John. There was one piece of John's small-module series.

It is therefore evident that in this class of hoard the large Thessalonican pieces have a definite tendency to be reduced by clipping to the module of the small series—whether that of Thessalonica or of the similar Latin pieces which make up the bulk of these hoards.

Now, *pace* Bertelè, the identification of the Thessalonican small-module series with a genuine fractional coinage, carries little conviction in the light of these figures. Firstly, as previously noted for the Latin series, fractions are normally struck in smaller quantities than their units. Secondly, although occasional examples of such units are sometimes deliberately cut into fractions (as Bertelè suggests of the piece illustrated, Pl. 40.*1*), the situation as seen in these hoards is that the majority of the large pieces have been reduced in module. This has much more the appearance of a clash of separate standards.

Such a situation would be quite understandable if, as suggested when dealing with the similar Latin series, the small-module coins form a coinage of emergency, manufactured in order to alleviate the shortage of regular trachea—

[4] A selection of clipped billon trachea from these hoards is illustrated (Pl. 45. *1–10*): it will be noticed that this rough clipping bears no resemblance to that practiced by the imperial authorities under Alexius III upon the coinage of his predecessors (Pl. 44. *1–15*). The Thessalonican types are as follows:

Pl. 45.   *1* (Theodore Ducas, type B, from the Oustovo hoard)
   2 (Theodore Ducas, type D, from the Oustovo hoard)
   3–5 (Theodore Ducas, type F, from the Tri Voditsi hoard)
   6 (Manuel Ducas, type C, from the Oustovo hoard)
   7, 8 (Manuel Ducas, type D, from the Oustovo hoard)
   9, 10 (John Ducas, type D, from the Oustovo and Tri Voditsi hoards)

the plentiful circulation of which during the third to fifth decades of the thirteenth century seems to have been largely confined to Asia Minor and Constantinople and Thessalonica and their immediate environs.

As to the source of the small "Thessalonican" coins, it is presumably bound up with that of the Latin series. At least the attribution of the former to an unofficial source explains the existence of so many types, for it is not now necessary to suppose that their production was coterminous with the reign of John Comnenus-Ducas.

The attribution of type Q to this emperor is less certain than that of the other types, but seems justified by considerations of module, style, and technique. Of its late date there is little doubt: single specimens occurred in both the Oustovo and Tri Voditsi hoards.[5]

As Bertelè has already remarked, the type attributed by Sabatier to John V as no. 3 of that Emperor, depicting the standing figures of Saint Demetrius on the obverse and of an Emperor John on the reverse, is probably to be identified with no. 644 in the *Photiadès Catalogue*; there more plausibly attributed to John Ducas.[6] The Sabatier piece is described as flat, the Photiadès one as scyphate, both as small. There need be no real contradiction, for scyphate coins of the Thessalonican series are frequently found flattened. The existence of the type may therefore be accepted as very probable, but in default of actual known specimens it has not been formally listed here.

Æ HALF-TETARTERON

The two published examples of this type weigh 1.68 and 1.98 gm.,[7] which, in view of the known weights for tetartera and their halves, ensures the identification of these pieces as examples of the latter.

THE COINAGE OF DEMETRIUS, COMNENUS-DUCAS

DESPOT 1244–1246

No named coins of the despot Demetrius, John's successor, are known, and it is probable that none were struck. It is possible, however, that the billon trachea of neat, elegant style, of the following description, are to be attributed to the mint of Thessalonica during the period 1242–46.

---

[5] The type has already been published: H. Longuet, "Die unedierten byzantinischen Münzen des Wiener Kabinettes," *NZ*, 77 (1957), pp. 56–57, no. 328 (pl. VI).

[6] W. Frœhner, *Monnaies byzantines de la collection Photiadès Pacha* (Sale Catalogue, Paris, 23–24. v. 1890), p. 46.

[7] Bertelè, "Monete di Giovanni di Salonicco," p. 65.

Obv. I͞C X͞C in field; sometimes with O EMMΛNȢHΛ in two columnar groups. Bust of Christ, beardless and nimbate, wearing tunic and colobion; holds scroll in left hand.

Rev. X̄/Ꝓ   X̄/M in lower field.

Full-length figure of Archangel Michael nimbate, wearing divitision, collar-piece, and panelled loros of simplified type; holds in right hand labarum on long shaft, and in left, globus cruciger.

Pl. 41.*20, 21*

Certainly they are not of the period of Isaac II, to whom they were attributed by Wroth,[1] nor can they be confused with the somewhat similar Constantinopolitan Latin type P (Pl. *27.3, 4*). Their style demands a thirteenth-century Thessalonican attribution of some kind, and a late date is confirmed by the presence of a specimen, along with other Thessalonican pieces, among the finds from the recent excavations at Lake Prespa.

SCYPHATE, SMALL-MODULE ISSUE OF UNCERTAIN THESSALONICAN ATTRIBUTION

An apparently unique example of this issue was published by Bertelè (*Imperatore alato*, p. 33, no. 52). The description is as follows:

Obv.

Wing, from which extends an arm holding a sword; above and below, an asterisk.

Rev.

Full-length figure of emperor, bearded, on right, and of beardless, nimbate saint (Demetrius?) in military dress, holding between them partially sheathed sword, point downward. Emperor wears stemma, divitision, collar-piece, and jewelled loros of simplified type; holds scepter in left hand. Saint wears short military tunic, breastplate, and sagion; holds (spear?) in right hand.

Pl. 41.*19*

That the emperor is bearded precludes an attribution to John Comnenus-Ducas—to whose coinage this issue is otherwise related by its obverse type.

---

[1] Wroth, *BMC*, 2, p. 595, no. 37.

THESSALONICA UNDER THE EMPERORS OF NICAEA

1246–1261

THE COINAGE OF JOHN III, DUCAS-VATATZES

1246–1254

BILL. TRACHY

Type A

Obv. M̄P̄ Θ̄V̄ in field.
    +   +

Bust of Virgin nimbate, wearing tunic and maphorion.

Rev. I̅W̅ ΔЄ / CΠ / OT / HC —or var.

Full-length figure of emperor, wearing stemma, divitision, and jewelled loros of traditional type; holds in right hand labarum on long shaft, and in left, anexikakia. In left field, an outstretched wing; in upper right field, *Manus Dei*.

Pl. 42.*1, 2*

Type B

Obv. Ρ ᵡM in field.

Bust of Archangel Michael nimbate, wearing divitision, collar-piece, and panelled loros of simplified type; holds in right hand sword, resting over shoulder, and in left, globus cruciger.

Rev. I̅W̅ ΔЄC / ΠO / TH / C —or var.

Emperor seated upon throne without back, wearing stemma, divitision, and jewelled loros of traditional type; holds in right hand scepter cruciger, and in left, anexikakia. In left field, an outstretched wing; in upper right field, *Manus Dei*.

Pl. 42.*3, 4*

Type C

Obv. Γ / OΛ / ΔH / MH P̄I / OC / ✳ —or var.

290

St. Demetrius, beardless and nimbate, seated upon throne without back;
wears tunic, breastplate, and sagion; holds in right hand hilt of sword,
and in left, sheath, horizontally across knees.

Rev. I͞Ѡ O Δ ᴚ —or var.

Full-length figure of emperor wearing short military tunic, breastplate,
and sagion; holds in right hand labarum on long shaft, and in left,
anexikakia. Large asterisk in upper right field.

Pl. 42.5, *6*

Type D

Obv. Γ O͡Λ I ᴘ͡ι O C —or var.

Bust of St. Demetrius, beardless and nimbate, wearing tunic, breastplate,
and sagion; holds sword, resting over shoulder, in right hand.

Rev. I͞Ѡ O Δ ᴚ K —or var.

Full-length figure of emperor, wearing stemma, divitision, and chlamys;
holds labarum on long shaft in left hand.

Pl. 42.7, *8*

Type E

Obv. M͞P Θ͞V in field.

Virgin nimbate, wearing tunic and maphorion, seated upon throne without back; holds beardless, nimbate head of Christ on breast. Lys above
cushion of throne, to either side.

Rev. I͞Ѡ Δ Π Τ O Δ M Τ —or var.

Full-length figure of emperor on left, and of St. Demetrius, beardless
and nimbate, holding between them patriarchal cross. Emperor wears
stemma, divitision, collar-piece, and jewelled loros of simplified type.
Saint wears short military tunic, breastplate, and sagion.

Pl. 42.9, *10*

Type F

Obv. I͞C X͞C in field.

Bust of Christ, bearded and nimbate, wearing tunic and colobion; holds
Gospels in left hand.

19*

Rev.
$$\overline{I\omega} \quad \Gamma$$
$$\Delta \quad \begin{matrix} O\Lambda \\ \Delta \\ M \\ T \end{matrix}$$
$$\Pi$$
—or var.

Full-length figure of emperor on left, and of St. Demetrius, beardless and nimbate, holding between them castle with three towers. Emperor wears stemma, divitision, collar-piece, and jewelled loros of simplified type; holds labarum-headed scepter in right hand. Saint wears short military tunic, breastplate, and sagion; holds sword, point resting on ground, in left hand.

Pl. 42.*11, 12*

Type G

Rev.
$$\overline{MP} \quad \overline{\Theta V}$$
$$* \quad *$$
in field.

Full-length figure of Virgin nimbate, orans, wearing tunic and maphorion

Rev.
$$\overline{IW} \quad \oslash$$
$$\begin{matrix} \Delta\Pi \\ O\Delta \\ K \end{matrix} \quad \begin{matrix} \Delta I \\ M \\ T \end{matrix}$$
—or var.

Full-length figure of emperor on left, and of St. Demetrius, beardless and nimbate, holding between them labarum surmounting triangular decoration on long shaft. Emperor wears stemma, divitision, and chlamys; holds sword, point resting on ground, in right hand. Saint wears divitision and chlamys; holds sword, point resting on ground, in left hand.

Pl. 43.*1, 2*

Type H

Obv.
$$\Gamma \quad P$$
$$\begin{matrix} \oslash \\ \Gamma\epsilon \\ \omega \end{matrix} \quad \begin{matrix} \Pi I \\ O \\ C \end{matrix}$$
—or var.

Bust of St. George, beardless and nimbate, wearing tunic, breastplate, and sagion; holds in right hand spear, resting over left shoulder, and in left, shield.

Rev.
$$\overline{IW} \quad \Delta$$
$$\Delta \quad \begin{matrix} M \\ \overline{P} \end{matrix}$$
$$\begin{matrix} \Pi \\ T \end{matrix}$$
—or var.

Half-length figure of emperor on left, and of St. Demetrius, beardless and nimbate, holding between them cross-within-circle surmounting triangular decoration on long shaft. Emperor wears stemma, divitision, collar-piece, and jewelled loros of simplified type. Saint wears tunic, breastplate, and sagion.

Pl. 43.*3, 4*

Type I

Obv. O Ꝑ|
△ ŌC —or var.
M

Full-length figure of St. Demetrius, bearded and nimbate, wearing short military tunic, breastplate, and sagion; holds in right hand spear, and in left, shield.

Rev. ĪŪ O —or var.
△

Half-length figure of emperor wearing stemma, divitision, collar-piece, and panelled loros of simplified type; holds in right hand labarum on long shaft, and in left, globus cruciger.

Pl. 43.5, 6

Type J

Obv. O Π

Full-length figure of St. Peter, bearded and nimbate, turned to left; holds two keys in right hand.

Rev.

Half-length figure of emperor, wearing stemma, divitision, collar-piece, and panelled loros of simplified type; holds in right hand labarum-headed scepter, and in left, globus surmounted by patriarchal cross.

Pl. 43.7

Type K

Obv. ĪC X̄C in field.

Bust of Christ, beardless and nimbate, wearing tunic and colobion; holds scroll in left hand.

Rev.

Half-length figure of emperor wearing stemma, divitision, collar-piece, and panelled loros of simplified type; holds in right hand labarum-headed scepter, and in left, globus cruciger.

Pl. 43,8, 9

THE COINAGE OF JOHN III: COMMENTARY

BILL. TRACHY

John III is distinguishable from John Comnenus-Ducas by his forked beard.

As remarked when dealing with the coinage of Theodore Comnenus-Ducas, types A and B are examples of the tendency of the Thessalonican mint to use the traditional rather than the simplified pattern of loros.

Because of the splendid style in which both these types are rendered it is clear that they belong at the very beginning of the short period during which John III ruled Thessalonica, and it is therefore probable that they were intended as something of a commemorative coinage—to mark the advent of the new regime in the city.

Their attribution to John Ducas, Sebastocrator of Neopatras (c. 1268–89) —as made, for example, by Lambros and followed by Wroth[1]—is most unlikely. There was an unrecognized example of type B in the (earlier) Arta hoard.

There is, in the collection at the British Museum, an apparently unique specimen of type F in silver.

Lathoud and Bertelè have suggested that the presence of St. Peter upon the obverse of type J formed a contemporary allusion to the negotiations carried on between John III and the papacy during the closing years of his reign on the subject of the reconciliation of the churches.[2] It should be remarked, however, that a similar figure of the Saint appears on the Latin coinage of Constantinople, although the authorities there had everything to fear from a favorable conclusion to these negotiations. It is, of course, impossible to decide which of the two first used the type of St. Peter, and to build a whole edifice of theological and political speculation upon his appearance is to go much further than the small amount of evidence warrants.

Although the large number of types (eleven) attributed to this relatively short reign might perhaps appear excessive, it should be noted that several— such as types D, J, and K—seem to continue the fabric, module, and technique of Series II of John Comnenus-Ducas (Pl. 40.6–10). That is, they are of rather smaller module and thicker fabric than the rest, and also struck from slightly smaller dies. This is particularly noticeable of type K (Pl. 43.8, 9). They may, therefore, have been struck as a parallel series to the other types rather than as a part of one succession.

The attribution of type K, at least, to Thessalonica seems to be supported by the small amount of hoard evidence available. No less than five specimens occurred in the Dorkovo hoard, and there was a further specimen in the Tri-Voditsi hoard.

[1] S. P. Lambros, "Monnaies et bulles inédites de Néopatras et de Carytaena," RN², 14 (1869/70), pp. 187–88. Wroth, BMCV, pp. 227–28. Metcalf (Coinage in the Balkans, p. 234) finds, in the appearance of single coins of these two types at excavations at Trikkala, proof of their attribution to Neopatras: but they might just as well have come from Thessalonica.

The fact that both types (and that of Theodore II) were copied by Constantine Asen, tsar of Bulgaria (1257–77), perhaps also slightly favors John III at Thessalonica. Cf. N. A. Moushmov, Monetite i Pechatite na Bulgarskite Tsare (Sofia, 1924), pp. 78–83, nos. 16–29.

[2] D. Lathoud and T. Bertelè, "Les clefs de Saint Pierre sur une monnaie de Jean III Doucas Vatatzès, empereur de Nicée (1222–1254)," Unitas, yr. 1, no. 3 (1948), pp. 189–96.

THE COINAGE OF THEODORE II, DUCAS-LASCARIS

1254–1258

BILL. TRACHY

Obv.

Large cross with floriate ends to limbs; in center, small linear cross.

Rev.  —or var.

Full-length figure of emperor on left, and of St. Demetrius, beardless and nimbate, holding between them castle with three towers, surmounted by large asterisk. Emperor wears stemma, divitision, collar-piece, and jewelled loros of simplified type; holds labarum-headed scepter in right hand. Saint wears short military tunic, breastplate, and sagion; holds spear, resting over shoulder, in left hand.

Pl. 43.*10*

THE COINAGE OF MICHAEL VIII, PALAEOLOGUS

1258/59–1261

Although there are a number of types of this Emperor attributable to the mint of Thessalonica, there is no adequate method of distinguishing those struck before the recapture of Constantinople from those struck subsequently: the series will therefore not be treated in this publication. It should be remarked, however, that most of the types attributed to the various rulers of Epirus of this name are, in fact, to be identified as Thessalonican issues of Michael VIII. Since this Emperor's formal signature invariably includes the family name "Ducas," it is quite possible that even the coin struck in the name of a "Michael Ducas," and attributed by Bertelè to Epirus, should be involved in this reappraisal.[1]

---

[1] For Bertelè's article, see p. 296. Michael's signature runs: Μιχαὴλ ἐν Χριστῷ τῷ Θεῷ πιστὸς βασιλεὺς καὶ αὐτοκράτωρ Ῥωμαίων, Δούκας Ἄγγελος Κομνηνὸς ὁ Παλαιολόγος. E.g., Miklosich and Müller, *op. cit.*, 5, pp. 13, 260.

(iv)

OTHER RULERS

THE COINAGE OF THE "DESPOTS" OF EPIRUS

The only coin at all plausibly attributed to the "despots" of Epirus is that published by T. Bertelè ("Una moneta dei despoti di Epiro," *Numismatica,* 17–18 [1951–52], pp. 17–18). In view of the observations of L. Stiernon ("Les origines du despotat d'Épire. A propos d'un livre récent," *Revue des études byzantines,* 17 [1959], pp. 90–126), it is almost certain that the coin in question should be assigned to Michael II (*c.* 1231–68) rather than to Michael I (*c.* 1205–15). The coin from the Arta hoard attributed to Michael II and his son Nicephorus is double-struck, giving "Nicephorus" the appearance of being in a junior position. The figure on the right is very probably that of St. Constantine, but the issuer (although probably a Thessalonican emperor) is unidentifiable.

Although a model treatment in its time, Mattingly's article on the Arta hoard ("A Find of Thirteenth-century Coins at Arta in Epirus," *NC*[5], 3 [1923], pp. 31–46) badly needs reconsideration.

THE COINAGE OF LEO AND JOHN GAVALAS, RULERS OF RHODES

c. 1204–*c.* 1250

The coinage of these brothers consists of thin, flat, copper pieces. They are treated by G. Schlumberger in his *Numismatique de l'Orient latin* (Paris, 1878; reprint, Graz, 1954), pp. 215–16.

THE COINAGE OF IVAN II, ASEN, TSAR OF BULGARIA

1218–1241

The scyphate coin illustrated (Pl. 46.*10, 11*) has, on occasion, been treated as belonging to the Byzantine series. It has, however, already been correctly attributed to Ivan II, Asen (Moushmov, *Monetite i Pechatite na Bulgarskite Tsare,* pp. 69–71 [nos. 4–6]).

Comparison of these pieces with coins of the empire of Thessalonica (e.g., Pl. 37.7–9) shows the main source of inspiration, but the star on the long shaft can be paralleled only on the coins of the empire of Nicaea (e.g., Pl. 30.*2*, *3*). It is tempting to consider this issue as having been struck after the battle of Klokotnitsa (1230), largely for use in the territories conquered from the empire of Thessalonica. Two specimens occurred in the Arta hoard (Class XIII): a small find of four specimens has been reliably reported to the author as coming from Prilep: a single specimen occurred in a hoard from Levski (Plovdiv reg.). Examples may also have been included in a hoard of twenty-nine billon trachea of Ivan Asen which was found at Ochrida (Gerassimov, *IAI*, 29 [1966], p. 213). Finally, according to Mme Oikonomides, eight specimens have recently come from a hoard found during excavations at Lake Prespa.

A rather similar type was struck in gold (Gerassimov, "Purvata zlatna moneta na Tsar Ivan Asen II," *IBAI*, 8 [1934], pp. 361–68).

THE COINAGE OF "STEFAN DUCAS REX"

The billon scyphate illustrated (Pl. 47.*1*) has sometimes been attributed to Stephen Gabrielopoulus the sebastocrator of Thessaly (died 1333), which is absurd. The full reverse inscription reads: CTЄΦΑΝΟCΡΙƷΟΔ ΘΚШΝCΤΑΝΤΙΝΟC, but is generally abbreviated to some extent. The imperial portion of the inscription can be expanded only to Στέφανος ρίξ ὁ Δούκας, and, as such, must refer to the Serbian tsar Stephen Radoslav (*c.* 1228–33), who is referred to in precisely these terms by both Serbian and Byzantine sources.[1] He had married a daughter of Theodore Ducas of Thessalonica, and it was presumably as a result of this (backed, perhaps, by his descent from Euphrosyne Ducaina, wife of Alexius III) that he took the family name of Ducas.

The source of inspiration for the reverse type of the issue is undoubtedly Thessalonican, not, as occasionally supposed, Nicaean or pre-conquest Byzantine. It is to be found in the billon scyphate type D of Manuel Ducas, Stephen's relation by marriage and his contemporary on the throne (Pl. 39.7). The type is reproduced with only minor alterations on the Serbian issue, and better preserved specimens than that illustrated even include the forked beard for St. Constantine that caused difficulties in the correct attribution of the original (*supra*, pp. 278–79).

---

[1] The correct attribution was first made by K. Stockert: "Zwei unedierte Bronzemünzen von Serbien," *NZ*, 47 (1915), pp. 195–96. For the documentary evidence for Radoslav's entitulature, see: F. Miklosich, *Monumenta Serbica Spectantia Historiam Serbiae Bosnae Ragusii* (Vienna, 1858), p. 20; Miklosich and Müller, *op. cit.*, 3 (Vienna, 1865), pp. 66–67. There is a brief but useful survey of the problem of attribution (as between Radoslav and Gabrielopoulus) by M. Lascaris in "Bulletin yougoslave," *Byzantion*, 14 (1939), pp. 423–24. See also: Polemis, *The Doukai*, p. 93, note 9. For the mythical despot Melissenus, P. Lemerle, *L'Emirat d'Aydin, Byzance et l'Occident* (Paris, 1957), p. 119.

A further type of this Serbian ruler, in silver, seems to reproduce the main features of the reverse design of the silver scyphate type C of Theodore Ducas (Pl. 37. *5,6*). In this case, the left-hand columnar inscription actually reads: CTЄФANOC PIƷ O ΔꙊKAC.[2]

The attribution of this small series in billon and silver to the reign of Stephen Radoslav requires that its date should be approximately the same as that suggested for the rather similar series in billon and gold which is given to Ivan II, Asen of Bulgaria. It is, in the circumstances, tempting to infer an element of rivalry, although the point is obviously incapable of anything like proof.

[2] The Serbian type is most conveniently described and illustrated by R. Marić in: *Studije iz Srpske Numizmatike* (Belgrade, 1956), pp. 64–67; "Iz Numizmatičke Zbirke," *Zbornik Radova Narodnog Muzeja*, 3 (1962), p. 24.

Section IV

GENERAL CONSIDERATIONS

CHAPTER THIRTEEN

APODESMOI AND *APOKOMBIA*

The radical changes in the Byzantine monetary system, which were initiated by the Alexian reform of 1092 and the withdrawal of old currency which apparently accompanied it, must have necessitated drastic alterations in the organization of function and personnel within the mint.

Probably as a result of the new and unprecedented character of the reformed coinage, the reverse designs of the first regular scyphate types in gold, electrum, and billon from the metropolitan mint all represented the same iconographical device of the Emperor, standing, with a columnar inscription to either side. The latter was an innovation at the mint of the capital, the only precedent being that on the "St. Demetrius" scyphates of the Thessalonican pre-reform coinage. The iconographical distinction between the denominations which was to mark the series in the future was maintained in this case by the differing regalia and robing on each denomination. For the twelfth century, therefore, the coronation series of 1092 represents the only occasion on which genuine coins of different scyphate denominations reproduced the same iconographical types. This in itself marks both the ceremonial nature of these coins and the more practical realism which subsequently insisted on rendering it impossible to forge a gold coin by the plating of a genuine electrum or billon one.

Similarly, owing to the new pattern of the coinage, the degree of variation permitted to the die-cutters was, in general, extremely small. True, the development of the left-hand inscriptional ending from T to T, to TH was allowed, or even ordered, as was the increasing amount of exaggeration in the chlamys-jewelling; but on the other hand, the general arrangement of the inscription and the individual elements of design are remarkably uniform. This strict attention to the details of the design was adhered to throughout the twelfth century, and in the vast majority of cases where major variations in detail did occur they were intended, whether as distinctions between officinae of the same mint, or between different organizational phases of a coinage, or between separate mints. The attention paid to the inscription was less long-lasting: control was loosened for the billon coinage even during the reign of Alexius, but that exercised over the gold and electrum remained throughout the reign of John. It is only with the reign of Manuel that there are definite signs of a relaxation, probably resulting from the tremendous amount of inscription which had to be inserted into such a small space: this is particularly true for the gold coinage

301

and for type D of the electrum coinage. It is clear, in these two cases, that the imperial image was engraved first and then such space as was left was unsystematically crammed with the vertical inscription.

To the contrary, a good deal less attention throughout seems to have been paid to the obverse, the side bearing a religious design. Balling and Bellinger have both noticed[1]—for the coinages of Manuel I and Theodore I respectively— that this die, or parts of it, were frequently recut when worn or damaged, without much trouble being taken to imitate the detail or style of the original.

It might be expected by analogy with near contemporary Western examples that the authorities at the mint should keep such documents relating to the issue, design, purity, and quantity of coinage as came into their hands. There is strong circumstantial evidence in the history of the Thessalonican mint to support such a supposition. The characteristic pendilia form ⅃⅃ which is noticeable on hyperpyra of Alexius I attributed to that mint, makes a concerted reappearance on the Latin series struck there after the conquest of 1204. The use of the traditional form of loros—discontinued at the metropolitan mint during the reign of Constantine IX—continues on the copper tetartera of Thessalonica during the reign of Alexius, again on the billon of John II, and then reappears only after a long interval on the silver trachea of Theodore Comnenus-Ducas and the billon of Manuel Comnenus-Ducas and of John Ducas-Vatatzes. Such resurrections of old but characteristic techniques can hardly have occurred except by deliberate reference to documentary records or master dies which had been retained. It is obvious, on a more general plane, that the establishment and continuance of the elaborate system of officina distinctions employed at the metropolitan mint must have been based on something more substantial than the memory of individuals.

The instructions sent out by the central authorities to the provincial mints were sufficiently detailed, in the case of the hyperpyra of Alexius I, not only to decide on elaborate differences to distinguish provincial products from each other and from those of the metropolis, but also to enforce such common details as the presence of two folds of the chlamys on the Emperor's left shoulder.

The degree of control exercised over the mint of Thessalonica by the central authorities seems understandably to have varied as between the precious and the base-metal coinages. As mentioned above, the precious-metal coinage struck at the provincial mint seems generally to have been modelled very closely upon that of the capital, but with the addition of small, deliberate distinctions; its quantity was apparently small and production was probably sporadic. On the other hand, the tetartera and half-tetartera which formed the basic product of Thessalonica were entirely distinct in type from those of the capital. At

---

[1] Balling, "Lindos," pp. 14–15; A. R. Bellinger, "A Hoard of Silver Coins of the Empire of Nicaea," *Centennial Publication of the American Numismatic Society*, ed. H. Ingholt (New York, 1958), p. 76.

no time is this more evident than during the reign of Andronicus I, when the metropolitan coinage of all denominations conforms to a single iconographical theme; the Virgin on the obverse, the Emperor crowned by Christ on the reverse. In complete contrast, the two Thessalonican types portray the Virgin and St. George as their obverse, and the unaccompanied imperial, full-length figure and bust as their reverse.

The only other aspect of the internal organization of the metropolitan mint which is recoverable with any degree of certainty is what has been termed above as the officina system. The presence of this pattern of organization, together with the further evidence about to be discussed, has considerable bearing on the question of the circulation of coinage in bulk.

That sums of copper and silver coin circulated in sealed, or at least tightly bound, bags or purses during the fourth and fifth centuries, is attested by both documentary sources and pictorial representations. Jones has remarked upon the purses marked ✱$\overline{XII}\triangle$ (12, 500 denarii) depicted in the Piazza Armerina mosaics, and quotes passages from Epiphanius stating that "the follis makes up 125 silver coins; and it is called among the Romans a sack," and that "the follis weight is also called a *balantion* (βαλάντιον), and it makes up 250 denarii." The existence of at least two such standard sums is confirmed by Epiphanius himself, who distinguishes in another passage between the φόλλις κατὰ τὸν ἀργυρισμόν and κατὰ τὸν δηναρισμόν.[2]

The evidence for gold is equally strong. A purse marked ∞CCC (1,300 pieces) is depicted in the mosaics of the Constantinian basilica of Aquileia,[3] and in the light of further examples in the *Chronographer* of 354 may be considered as containing gold. Three purses are illustrated in the *Chronographer*: the Caesar Constantius Gallus has at his feet one marked $\overset{S}{\infty}$ (1,000 solidi); the personification of Constantinople has one marked ∞ (1,000 pieces); Roma has ∞CCCC (1,400 pieces).[4] The insignia of the *comites sacrarum largitionum* and *rerum privatarum* as illustrated in the *Notitia Dignitatum*[5] include several purses, of which some appear to bear numerals. Finally, the consular diptych of Boethius (487) at Brescia depicts several purses marked 8 8 (2,000 pieces).[6]

It is true, however, that most of the examples above occur in a very general context, as in the case of the personifications, or a ceremonial one, as in that

[2] A. H. M. Jones, "The Origin and Early History of the *Follis*," *Journal of Roman Studies*, 49, 1–2 (1959), pp. 34–38; see also L. Ruggini, "A proposito del *follis* nel IV secolo," *Atti della Accademia nazionale dei Lincei, Rendiconti*[8], 16 (1961), pp. 306–19. For references to *pecunia clusa* or *obsignata* and the *sacculum vel argentum signatum*, see D. 16,iii(xxv); 16,iii(xxix); 19,ii(xxxi).

[3] G. C. Menis, *I mosaici christiani di Aquileia* (Udine, 1965), pl. 69.

[4] H. Stern, *Le calendrier de 354; étude sur son texte et ses illustrations* (Paris, 1953), pls. 15, 3, 2.

[5] *Notitia Dignitatum*, ed. O. Seeck (Berlin, 1876), pp. 35, 37, 148, 154.

[6] R. Delbrueck, *Die Consulardiptychen und verwandte Denkmäler* (Berlin, 1929), 1 (Text), pp. 103–06, 2 (Plates), p. 7.

of the consular largess of Gallus and Boethius. The widespread use of such a system, including sums smaller than a thousand solidi, remains unproven.

Fortunately, precisely this latter information can be gleaned from a series of documentary sources which also extend the period of reference into the mid-seventh century.

In April 363, the Emperor Julian issued the following edict:[7]

Emperor Julian Augustus, to Mamertinus, Praetorian Prefect:

The buying and selling of solidi is impeded if anyone clips, diminishes, or—to use the word suitable for such avarice—nibbles them away, for some persons refuse them as being light and inadequate. It therefore pleases us to appoint a zygostates [weigher], as the Greek word terms him, in each city, who, on account of his faithfulness and industry, will neither deceive nor be deceived, so that if a dispute shall have arisen between a seller and a buyer of solidi, it may be settled according to his judgment and reliability.

The sense of the edict is sufficiently clear as to need no explanation.

In January 559, the Emperor Justinian issued an edict headed as follows:[8]

So that in future, the zygostatai and chrysones of Egypt shall have no license to collect the [charge called] obryza, but that coined gold in these regions shall correspond to that of this great city [i.e., Constantinople], they shall place their seals according to the undiminished weight in the coined [metal].

The Emperor goes on to say in the preface that he intends to abolish a charge called obryza which had grown up recently in Egypt and now amounted in Alexandria to the sum of nine solidi in the pound, thereby harmfully affecting both public and private affairs.

In the paragraph—the second—which is of particular relevance to this examination, Justinian names the zygostatai and chrysones as the chief perpetrators of this fraudulent charge, ruling that they are to be put under bond by their superiors and that they are to encourage dealings in the ἀπόλυτον Αἰγύπτιον χάραγμα (surely loose, unsealed gold coin), even if defective, but when required, they are to indicate, in writing, the true weight of the gold in the containers which they seal, not, as hitherto customary, indicating an amount more than that actually therein. The Emperor proceeds to fix the punishment for infringement, and once more to warn that payments made to officials of the treasury in Alexandria must not be subject to the charge.

Oxyrhynchus Papyrus 1886[9] (late fifth or early sixth century) records the bringing of an accusation of what is apparently the same fraudulent practice as that described by Justinian. It mentions that one Aurelius Joseph had taken a

---

7 *Codex Theodosianus*, 12, vii (ii).
8 Justinian: Edict 11.
9 *The Oxyrhynchus Papyri*, 16, eds. Grenfell, Hunt, and Bell (London, 1924), pp. 90–91, no. 1886.

certain sum of money in gold to the public *zygostates* Anastasius, on a condition unfortunately lost in the manuscript. However, having handed over his money, Joseph received the weigher's seal, but when, for whatever reason, the seal was broken, the sum was found to be short by fifty-two keratia.

Quite clearly, on the basis of these extracts, what had been happening was that the *zygostatai* (and *chrysones*) had received, or had arrogated to themselves, the right of authenticating sums circulating in purses by the imposition of their seals, but had been, in Egypt at least, illegally demanding or exacting a fee for doing so. The amount of money in the sealed purse was therefore equivalent to the sum handed over to the *zygostates* minus the fee exacted, for since the fee was illegal in any case its exaction could not be admitted. Although the phrasing of the edict is complex and the sense not as clear as it might be, there can be little doubt that this illegal fee was that termed *obryza*.

The complete identity of the seal (σφραγίς) with the actual purse of gold coin the value of which it authenticated is established beyond question by the events described in one of the tales of the Egyptian solitaries[10]—a class of work circulating widely during the second half of the fourth or the fifth century.

The particular episode almost inevitably involves a *zygostates*—their public image must have been quite appalling.

A man came to the public weigher one day with a "seal of five hundred nomismata" (. . . σφραγίδα πεντακοσίων νομισμάτων), requesting him to take the seal (Λαβὲ τὴν σφραγίδα) and to give it to him little by little as he needed it. There was thought to have been no witness to the request, but in fact a noble of the town had both heard and seen it. Some time later the former possessor of the seal came to the *zygostates* and requested part of it (Δός μοι ἐκ τῆς σφραγίδος, i.e., "from out of the seal") since he was in need. The *zygostates*, not knowing of the witness, denied all knowledge of the transaction. The cheated man, however, met the noble who had witnessed the original request and recounted his story. The noble told the man that he had only to bring his suit before St. Andrew (there was an oratory nearby) and he would receive satisfaction. When the time for the confrontation came, the noble went to the oratory, undressed, and began to act as if possessed. As the *zygostates* and his accuser arrived, the noble began to shout out the truth of the affair: Ἰδοὺ ὁ φαῦλος οὗτος ἔλαβε τὰ πεντακόσια νομίσ-ματα τοῦ ἀνθρώπου—"Look! this dreadful fellow has taken the man's five hundred nomismata." The noble threw himself at the *zygostates* and took him by the throat: Δὸς τὰ πεντακόσια νομίσματα τοῦ ανθρώπου—"Hand over the man's five hundred nomismata!" The *zygostates*, terrified: Ἐγὼ φέρω αὐτά—"I will bring them." The noble: Ἄρτι φέρε αὐτά—"Fetch them immediately." The *zygostates* brought them (αὐτά). The noble told the owner of the solidi (. . .τῷ

[10] F. Nau, "Histoire des solitaires égyptiens (MS Coislin 126, fol. 167 sqq.)," *Revue de l'Orient chrétien*[2], 2 (1907), no. 48, pp. 176–77.

κυρίῳ τῶν νομισμάτων·) to put six pieces on the altar—presumably as a thanksgiving. Thus, the story ends with a splendid moral punch.

It has to be admitted that the extensive quotation of this edifying tale has been undertaken with a view to something other than its original intent. For it is the references to the "seal" that are of considerable monetary interest.

That a seal should really be worth five hundred solidi is rather unlikely, if not impossible. Although Nau, who published and translated the manuscript, did not comment on the fact, the publishers and translators of Oxyrhynchus Papyrus 1886 did, and came to the conclusion—since the problem coincided with their own—that σφραγίς should be translated as "bond" (in the legal, documentary sense of the term). To do this they also had to exercise considerable ingenuity in translating the verb λύω as "discharge," rather than simply as "unfasten" or "loosen" (with reference to the "seal"), as the events recorded in the document otherwise clearly suggest. But the relationship between the "seal" and the five hundred solidi of the tale above is much more direct than "bond" would allow: the "seal" actually is five hundred solidi, as the nobleman conveniently and continually affirms in the text. "Seal" and "five hundred solidi" are interchangeable.

This relationship is explicable only on the assumption that the "seal" was, in fact, a sealed purse of solidi. The sense of the tale then becomes immediately apparent. The owner of the purse had taken it to the *zygostates* as he would have taken it to a banker, merely wishing to make periodic withdrawals in cash, from cash.

Finally, for this early period, mention must be made of two references in the *Life* of St. John the Almsgiver, the archbishop of Alexandria, written by Leontius, bishop of Cypriot Neapolis, at some time subsequent to 641.

At one point in the *Life*, the Archbishop is made to tell a tale in which he was given an *apokombion* of a hundred nomismata (....δίδωσίν μοι ἀποκόμβιν ἑκατὸν νομισμάτων).[11] At another, he was given a gift of seven and one-half pounds of gold, and a little further on the sum is identified as being contained in an *apokombion* (....τὸ ἀποκόμβιν τοῦ ποσοῦ).[12]

The word κομβίον is normally translated as "buckle"—i.e., something that fastens. This suggests that these *apokombia* were merely further examples of sealed purses.

The number of references to these sealed purses in Egyptian sources, or sources involving Egypt, should not be taken as indicating that their use was confined to that province, for Justinian, in the edict quoted above, expressly states that Egyptian practice must be brought into line with that of the capital,

[11] *Sammlung ausgewählter kirchen- und dogmengeschichtlicher Quellenschriften*, 5 (1893), ed. H. Gelzer, p. 16.
[12] *Ibid.*, p. 54.

that is, that such purses must be inscribed and sealed according to the weight of coin actually inside. It would therefore seem certain that during the late Roman and early Byzantine period, the circulation of convenient sums in sealed purses of pounds, half pounds, or hundreds of solidi, was both frequent and widespread. Consequently, when the same custom appears during the middle and later Byzantine periods, it should not be considered an innovation, merely a continuation.

The legal code known as the *Basilika*, completed during the reign of Leo VI (886–912), draws a distinction, in the section on usufruct involving slaves, between nomismata spent one by one (ἑκάτερος) and those spent together, at the same time, in an *apokompion* (Εἰ δὲ τὰ εἴκοσι νομίσματα ἅμα ἐν ἀποκομπίῳ δέδω-κεν ....).[13] The assumption that coins in an *apokompion* will be spent together tends to confirm the suggestion made above that a sealed or tightly bound purse is involved. It is interesting to find that even a sum as small as twenty nomismata could be considered worth sealing.

The *Life* of St. Nicholas of Myra as compiled by Symeon the Logothete (fl. *c.* 960), mentions an *apodesmos* of gold (e.g., ...τὸν ἀπόδεσμον τοῦ χρυσίου)[14] on several occasions in the well-known story where the Saint endows three destitute virgins. An *apodesmos*, similarly to an *apokombion*, can only be a purse that has been bound up or sealed (ἀποδεσμεύω = bind fast).

At Constantinople in the year 950, during the week before Palm Sunday, Bishop Liutprand of Cremona, on behalf of his master Berengar, witnessed the annual payment of the chief officials of the Empire, the Emperor himself participating in the ceremony. Liutprand describes the event in some detail:[15] A table was brought in on which were coins which had been tied up in purses— each having the amount it contained written on the outside (*mensa, quae numismata loculis colligata, prout cuique debebatur, numeris extrinsecus in loculis scriptis retinebat*). The payments actually mentioned were of twenty-four pounds of gold, of twelve pounds, and of seven down to a single pound.

The Emperor Constantine Porphyrogenitus (913–959) mentions in the *De Caerimoniis* that when the sovereigns made their procession to the Great Church, they donated purses of gold (χρυσᾶ βαλάντια) to the higher ecclesiastical officials, and *apokombia* to the patriarch. A gloss on this passage, as reconstructed by Vogt,[16] records that the *apokombion* was of ten pounds, and if there was only one emperor, he gave the full amount; if, however, there were more than one, the sum was divided. The division was made so that the senior

[13] *Basilika*, 16, i (xxv).
[14] G. Anrich, *Hagios Nikolaos, der heilige Nikolaos in der griechischen Kirche*, I, *Texte* (Berlin, 1913), pp. 240–41.
[15] Ed. J. Becker, *Die Werke Liudprands von Cremona* (Hanover, 1915), pp. 157–58.
[16] *De Caerimoniis*, I, 1; ed. Vogt (Paris, 1935), vol. I (text), p. 14, vol. I (commentary), pp. 64–66.

20*

emperor gave the most, the junior emperors giving lesser but equal amounts. Thus, if there were two emperors other than the senior, the former would have given two sums of three pounds, the senior, four pounds: if there were three emperors besides the senior, the three would each have given two pounds, the senior, four pounds. Presumably each emperor presented one *apokombion*.

An appendix to the *De Caerimoniis*, dealing with imperial requirements in the field, mentions the provision of κεντινάρια, μιλιαρήσια, σακκία for expenses, largess, and rewards.[17] The kentenarion is normally one hundred pounds in gold; the miliaresion at this period, a silver coin. The juxtaposition found here, however, suggests that purses (*sakkia*) of one hundred and one thousand nomismata respectively were involved. A further instance, involving σακκία χάραγμα κεντινάρια καὶ μιλιαρήσια σακκία[18] reinforces the suggestion, for why should the purses of gold be of a particular amount (the kentenarion of one hundred pounds) and those of silver miliaresia of indeterminate quantity? The phrase should probably be translated "purses of coined money, [that is] purses of a hundred and a thousand pieces."

Although the last three occasions involve ceremonial payments, the earlier two are quite clearly matters of normal circulation: the situation therefore differs in no respect from that prevalent in the period stretching from the late fourth to the mid-seventh century.

Turning to representational art, two mosaics in Hagia Sophia take the circulation of sealed purses into the eleventh and twelfth centuries. The so-called panel of Constantine IX and Zoë (Pls. 48, 49) represents the Emperor and Empress, dressed in stemma, collar-piece, divitision, and panelled loros of simplified type, to either side of a seated Christ. The Empress holds a document on which the imperial signature can be seen. The Emperor actually holds a sealed purse, in two tones of ivory-white tesserae: the cord is dark red, the seal a greyish blue. The purse itself may therefore have been either of a cloth, such as linen, or of leather; the seal was presumably of lead.

Whittemore, who published the mosaic, brought forward reasons proving beyond doubt that the Emperor originally represented had not been Constantine IX, but one of Zoë's earlier husbands, Romanus III or Michael IV. He finally came to the conclusion that it had been Romanus, on the grounds that his name fitted into the space available in the inscription better than Michael's.[19]

The Emperor Romanus had a short and undistinguished reign, but one of his few accomplishments was his establishment—upon learning that the revenues

[17] *De Caerimoniis; Appendix;* Bonn ed., p. 471.
[18] *Ibid.,* p. 473.
[19] T. Whittemore, *The Mosaics of Hagia Sophia at Istanbul: The Imperial Portraits of the South Gallery* (Oxford, 1942), pp. 17–18.

of the Great Church were insufficient—of an annual imperial grant to it amounting to eighty pounds of gold.[20] The fact that the Emperor and Empress hold not only a purse, but also a signed document, strongly suggests that the event commemorated in the mosaic was not the donation of a purse to the Patriarch on the occasion of the Emperor's visit to the Church—which was purely customary—but, in particular, the establishment of the annual imperial grant—for which a signed document would certainly have been necessary.

The John II and Irene panel (Pl. 50) repeats the theme in its main aspects. The purse is of ivory-white and ochre tesserae—the cord of dark red. It is apparently not sealed, merely loosely tied. The document, on the other hand, is both tied and sealed, but not signed. John is not recorded as having made any extraordinary gifts to the Church, but such negative evidence can in no way be considered decisive.

The chronicler Nicetas Choniates mentions the use of sealed purses (*phaskolia*) incidentally, during his account of the reign of Manuel I.[21]

Finally, the Emperor John VI, Cantacuzene, writing of the coronation of 1325, gives an interesting description of the distribution of largess on that occasion. He states that what were called *epikombia* were thrown to the crowd, and that these purses (*apodesmoi*) were pieces of linen, each having bound inside it three gold pieces, three silver, and three copper.[22]

Such *epikombia* were obviously made up particularly for the coronation ceremonies, but there is no reason to suppose—after an existence stretching back a thousand years—that the general circulation of sealed purses had declined.

It was suggested by Seeck that these purses were formally sealed in the various officinae of the mint. This is clearly not the whole story, for, during the early period at least, the sealing was also within the competence of the local *zygostatai*. However, in view of the number of imperial payments which were provably made in sealed purses—presumably on these occasions involving newly minted coins—Seeck's suggestion is eminently plausible as far as it goes. For if coin was sealed when it left the mint, the obvious place for this process to have taken place was, indeed, in the officinae.

---

[20] Cedrenus; Bonn ed., 2, p. 486: .... ὀγδοήκοντα χρυσίου λίτρας ἀνὰ πᾶν ἔτος χορηγεῖσθαι τούτοις τετύπωκεν ἀπὸ τοῦ βασιλικοῦ ταμιείου εἰς προσθήκην. It replaced a grant of forty pounds.

[21] Choniates; Bonn ed., p. 267: ...ὁ δὲ ὡς κερδοσυλλέκτης προεδρεύει καὶ τὰ φασκώλια σφραγῖδι διασημαίνεται ἃ ἤμελλον εἰσφέρεσθαι βασιλεῖ.

An interesting series of documents from Egypt, datable to the close of the eleventh century, shows the circulation of sealed purses of coin to have been a commonplace there: S. D. Goitein, "Bankers' Accounts from the Eleventh Century A.D.," *Journal of the Economic and Social History of the Orient*, 9, 1–2 (Nov. 1966), pp. 28–66. Cf. the later Italian *fiorino di suggello*.

[22] Cantacuzene, I, 41; Bonn ed., 1, p. 203: ....εἰς τὸν δῆμον ῥίπτονται ἃ λέγουσιν ἐπικόμβια. Δύναται δὲ τοῦτο ἀπόδεσμος τινὰς εἶναι ἐν ὀθονίων τμήμασι δεδεμένους, ἔνδον ἔχοντας νομίσματα χρυσᾶ τῶν βασιλικῶν τρία καὶ ἐξ ἀργύρου τοσαῦτα ἢ καὶ πλείω, καὶ ὀβολοὺς ἀπὸ χαλκοῦ τοσούτους.

Although there are too few hoards of gold or electrum nomismata for there to be any hope of deriving any indication as to the accuracy of this suggestion, the composition of several hoards of billon trachea does seem to point to the existence of some such system for this denomination. Two in particular show a very strong concentration of the products of individual officinae. Both the fourth billon coinage of Manuel I and the only substantive type of Isaac II have been divided into the products of four officinae—including two which were apparently closely connected in their administration or by physical proximity. The contents of the Souvatité and Kaloyanovets hoards both reflect this pattern of organization, and it may be conjectured that they consist mainly of the contents of purses the seals of which had remained unbroken until the time of deposition.[23]

The examination carried out above is not only of some interest in itself for the study of the monetary history of the Empire, but also bears relevance to recent attempts at estimating the actual amount of coin issued by individual emperors.[24] The statistics involved in such estimations are based on the supposition that it is possible to obtain a random sample of the issue under investigation. From the number of die-identities present in such a random sample of, say, hyperpyra of Alexius I or Manuel I, it should be possible via the average number of pieces struck by a single die, to calculate the total number of pieces originally issued.

While the actual statistical steps involved in reaching a conclusion of this kind have been accepted as correct in theory, it has been pointed out that, in practice, the small number of pieces involved in the samples so far used heavily overemphasized the eventual numerical importance of each die-identity, and that the calculation of the average number of coins struck by a single die is, except within the wide limits of practical possibility, little more than guess-work.[25]

If, in addition, large amounts of coin circulated in sealed purses, the collection of a random sample must be considered as gravely compromised, for it is obvious that the use of such a system would not only have appreciably prolonged the life of coin but also, at best, have significantly retarded the rate at which bodies of it became so sufficiently dispersed as to form a representative circulating medium. At worst, hoards will tend to contain clusters of coin in varying stages of dispersal: a factor which will have been emphasized by the high value of both the gold and electrum coinage and their consequent comparatively slow rate of circulation.

[23] Chap. 10, pp. 176–77.

[24] See, particularly, Metcalf, *Coinage in the Balkans*, pp. 7–10, 82–83, 99–100.

[25] P. Grierson, "Byzantine Coinage as Source Material," *Thirteenth International Congress of Byzantine Studies* (Oxford, 1966), *Main Papers*, 10, pp. 5–7.

Even if difficulties of this kind were overcome the result would not necessarily be of economic significance, for the precious-metal coinage of an emperor of this period is not represented by either his gold or his electrum alone, but by the sum of both. Moreover, there is no proof—indeed, there are indications to the contrary—that the proportion of electrum to gold remained stable over several reigns, or even throughout any one reign. Judging by the number of officinae, the proportion of electrum tended to increase during the reigns of the Comnenian emperors; although, since its bullion and official values were more or less identical, no broad economic conclusions can be drawn from that.

Only if large numbers of the coins surviving were provably isolated finds might a sufficiently large sample, with a good claim to being random, finally be assembled: but when it is considered that the dispersal of a relatively small number of hoards might significantly affect the pattern of survival—and in some cases demonstrably already has affected it[26]—the possibility of the random sample becomes purely chimerical.

Of the normal methods for the distribution of coinage to the provinces during this period, nothing definite is known, but some system there must have been, for the existence of two main areas of circulation for the lower denominations is beyond doubt. The capital apparently used both billon trachea and copper tetartera; Asia Minor and the Balkans north of the Rhodope employed billon trachea almost exclusively (although tetartera were admittedly issued by Isaac Comnenus in Cyprus), while Thessalonica and Greece did likewise with the copper tetarteron and its half. Had distribution merely been left to the chances of trade, the division could hardly have been so systematic. On the other hand, the metropolitan gold and electrum seem to have been in use everywhere, although no doubt supplemented to some extent in Thessalonica and its environs by the small, occasional issues of that city.

Nor is the relative length of life of the particular denominations once put into circulation any more apparent. It might be expected that the denominations of high intrinsic value and slow circulation, which were also liable to be hoarded as bullion—that is, gold and electrum—might tend to have a longer life than those in frequent, day-to-day use—the billon and copper. The composition of hoards such as Gornoslav, Zgurli, and Novo Selo seems to confirm a long life for the gold; moreover, of that from Novo Selo a longer life for gold than for billon. But it should be remembered that the reign of Alexius I represents a complete recoinage, and this may well account, at least in part, for the large numbers of his hyperpyra in hoards deposited over half a century after

---

[26] For instance, the recent flood of hyperpyra of Andronicus II and Michael IX results from the discovery of a single large hoard somewhere near Istanbul. One may suspect, although not prove, that the commonness of the hyperpyra of John III of Nicaea also stems from the discovery and dispersal of very few—perhaps a single—large hoards.

his death. A further explanation may be that the proportion of hyperpyra tended to decline in favor of that of electrum during the twelfth century, and particularly during the reign of Manuel I. It should also be pointed out that any comparison between gold and billon is rendered invalid by the revaluation of the latter denomination during the reign of Manuel and the subsequent withdrawal of the earlier pieces. The further rapid and unsystematic decline in the value of the denomination during the reigns of Isaac II and Alexius III meant that even the revalued pieces of Manuel and Andronicus I tended to disappear relatively speedily—probably as a result of the higher proportion of silver which they contained. If they were not melted down by the public, they were clipped by the government. The billon coinage of Isaac and Alexius itself probably tended to disappear when the Bulgarian and Latin imitative coinages flooded the circulating medium, and they and the larger Latin pieces almost certainly did when the small module series did likewise. The large billon pieces of Theodore Comnenus-Ducas and his successors suffered a far more brutal clipping in the thirteenth century than had those of Manuel, Andronicus, Isaac, and Alexius in the twelfth. What the life of the denomination would have been had it remained stable is therefore a matter of conjecture.

The continuity between the Byzantine state and its late Roman predecessor is perhaps never more evident than in its attitude toward precious metal and the coinage struck from it.[27] The manoeuverings in the stages leading up to the establishment of the *Nea Logarike*, during the reign of Alexius I, make it quite clear that the imperial government was as interested as ever to control as much of it as possible as frequently as possible. The *Book of the Prefect*, datable to the first half of the tenth century, forbids jewelers—who were particularly likely to have large amounts—to possess more than a pound of gold at a time, or even to work at home. It was forbidden on the one hand to hoard gold and, on the other, to refuse genuine imperial pieces or to pare or clip them down. The bankers and their assistants suffered a particularly strict control. The export of gold had, of course, been forbidden in both the *Code* of Justinian (4, lxiii [ii]) and the *Basilika* (56, i [xx]). There is no reason to suspect that any of these provisions had been relaxed by the twelfth century. In this century a chronicler could—still with justification—echo the sentiments of Cosmas Indicopleustes in the sixth, in stating "It is not permissible to impress any other mark on gold coin but that of the Emperor of the Romans."[28]

As to the Empire's sources of gold, it must have relied almost entirely upon supplies from abroad. When it became increasingly less capable of attracting

[27] Cf. J. P. C. Kent, "Gold Coinage in the Later Roman Empire," in *Essays in Roman Coinage Presented to Harold Mattingly* (Oxford, 1956), pp. 190–204.

[28] Zonaras; Bonn ed., 3, p. 230: Οὐδὲ γὰρ ἐξῆν ἐν χρυσῷ νομίσματι χαρακτῆρα ἕτερον ἐντυποῦσθαι ἢ τὸν τοῦ βασιλέως Ῥωμαίων.

such supplies during the second half of the thirteenth century, the gold coinage suffered accordingly. Normally, some probably came from the Urals through to Cherson, but one would have expected this route to have been interrupted during the second half of the eleventh century by the movements of the nomadic Patzinaks and Cumans. A certain amount probably came from the Caucasus through Trebizond, but this too must have been adversely affected by the arrival of the Seljuk Turks. It is therefore very probable that the undoubted increase in the trade with the West during the twelfth century also played a large part in maintaining the supply of gold, for there are indications that Senegalese gold which had travelled over the Sahara to North Africa was being exported to the Italian merchant cities and thence probably into the Byzantine Empire. The treaty of IIII between the Pisans and the Empire[29] exempted the former from paying the tax called *kommerkion* on gold and silver which they were exporting into the Empire. Such an exemption would hardly have been worthwhile to both sides if the amount involved had not been significant. It is known that the Genoese were obtaining gold from North Africa, and it may be assumed that the Pisans and Venetians were also.

It would indeed be interesting to know to what degree, if any, fluctuations in the free market ratio of gold and silver were allowed to affect the currency. That new gold and electrum coins were apparently given a small premium over old ones does not at all imply that the value of the large denominations was allowed to fluctuate freely. The one unofficial mention, in a set of Pisan documents, of the value of electrum coins (of the standard of Manuel) puts it at eight keratia—which was also the official rate of long standing.

With regard to the general level of development in Byzantine monetary policies, there seems to have existed an odd mixture of pragmatic organizational efficiency and naïveté of theory.

It has already been noted that the authorities seem to have been unprepared for the results of the revaluation of the billon trachy during the reign of Manuel and the withdrawal of old currency which apparently accompanied it, although once the inevitable increase in demand occurred the steps taken to accommodate it—the eventual establishment of extra officinae—seem to have been accomplished neatly and without organizational confusion. Similarly, the governmental response to the swift decline in the value of the billon coinage during the reign of Isaac II and Alexius III was to commence the clipping of the older coins, which by now were individually worth intrinsically more than the general market value. But this in itself was a response to a decline which

---

[29] Müller, *Documenti*, p. 44: Κομμέρκιον εἰς τὸ εἰσαγόμενον παρ' ὑμῶν χρυσάφιον καὶ ἀσήμιον οὐ μὴ παρέχητε τὸ σύνολον. The Latin version, *ibid.*, p. 53, reads: *Commertium de auro et argento quod afferetur a vobis non dabitis ullo modo.* The best account of the Saharan gold trade is in: E. W. Bovill, *The Golden Trade of the Moors* (Oxford, 1958), esp. pp. 66–92, 191–202.

seems to have been triggered by the issue of coin on two standards of weight—and possibly even silver content.

Contemporary comments on events of monetary interest exhibit a similar inability to comprehend the wider aspects while reporting the basic events with some fidelity. It is true that the instance of Zonaras reporting on the Alexian monetary reform may not be altogether typical, for the historian was no friend to the Comneni. All the main points of the reform are mentioned: the striking of nomismata in gold, "half-gold" (electrum) and "copper" (billon); the abolition of the follis. And yet the chronicle manages to convey the impression of the perpetration of a further example of imperial fraud. The same is true of his treatment of the introduction of the tetarteron by Nicephorus II.

Nor is Nicetas Choniates any different when dealing with what must be the revaluation of the billon by Manuel: again he rationalizes it as fraud, practiced this time upon the crusaders of 1147.

This kind of approach seems to be based in the consideration that any monetary change must necessarily be for the worse—as of course it had been previously, and was later to be again. It should, however, be recognized and taken into account by numismatists and monetary historians when using Byzantine documentary sources.

CHAPTER FOURTEEN

THE COINAGE AND THE ECONOMY

The virtual impossibility of obtaining a reasonably accurate estimate of the number of precious-metal coins in circulation at any one time, or less ambitiously, of the number issued by any one ruler, has been pointed out in the previous chapter. Nor is it any more feasible to attempt an estimate of the relative proportions of the gold, electrum, and billon in circulation, or issued by a ruler, for although the number of officinae involved in the production of each denomination might at first sight appear a tempting basis for such a process, the prospect is vitiated by the fact that there is no guarantee that an officina producing gold or electrum did so at the same rate as one striking billon. Moreover, the proportion of the lowest denominations, the copper tetarteron and its half, must necessarily remain entirely unknown, for, apart from their having been issued in large numbers at more than one mint, they do not seem to have been subject to officina distinctions.

Less absolutely, but with a high degree of confidence, it may be assumed that the precious-metal coinage of the reformed system was not formally or otherwise limited in its circulation—either internally to the military or the bureaucracy, or both, or externally to the foreign mercantile classes or international subsidies, or both. Surviving Byzantine and Latin documentary sources, confirmed by the evidence of hoard material, show that not only did these coins circulate freely within the Empire, but they were in widespread use. Indeed, whatever the actual number of precious-metal coins struck by Alexius and his successors, it seems very probable that it was on the increase until well into the second half of the twelfth century. The single officina used for the issue of gold (once the general recoinage of the first few years of the reform had been accomplished) was raised to two during the last coinage of John II, both remaining in use until well into the reign of Manuel. Although once more reduced to a single officina at the end of the third of Manuel's five precious-metal coinages, the second officina was revived by Isaac. The single officina for the electrum was increased to two at the beginning of John's reign, both remaining, with a third being added at the end of Manuel's third coinage— probably that which was ceasing to issue gold at about the same time. Although the third officina was abandoned during the reign of Andronicus, when the organization of the metropolitan mint underwent a thoroughgoing reform, the other two continued production into the reign of Isaac. While there is no guarantee that an increase or a decrease in the number of officinae necessarily reflected trends in the amount of coin issued, yet the example of the billon coinage under Manuel (where the revaluation of the denomination and the withdrawal of the older coins resulted in the creation of two new officinae to cater for the subsequent increasing demand) should not be forgotten.

Lopez, enquiring into the question of whether the adherence by the Byzantines to a standard coin of high weight and purity was the economic benefit that it is customarily assumed to have been, came to the conclusion that although it promoted stability, it tended to preclude expansion.[1]

Conversely, it now seems legitimate to enquire whether a radical monetary reform resulting in the emission of a plentiful and stable precious-metal coinage for approximately a century could have taken place in a state which is usually assumed to have been in full economic decline—or, in view of the apparent contradiction, whether a reassessment of the economic situation might not be called for. In other words, whether the customary view of an economic decline might not be as unsoundly based as the factor which has been quoted as best illustrating it: the wholesale debasement of the coinage.

One of the fundamental factors which must be dealt with before there is any hope of a satisfactory answer to this question is, of course, the debasement of the gold coinage during the fourth to ninth decades of the eleventh century, for it is on the basis of this that the customary approach to the coinage, and to a certain extent the economy, of the twelfth century is made.

Cipolla, analyzing the causes of debasement in the mediaeval period, has concluded that it was viewed as the most expedient way of dealing with a number of problems, the most important of them being: the long-term increase in the demand for money—resulting from the long-term growth of population, or of income, or of the degree in which money was used (or a mixture of these); the growth of governmental expenditure (without, presumbly, a corresponding increase in revenue); the pressure of social groups in the direction of profit-inflation; disequilibrium in the balance of payments.[2]

The debasement of the gold coinage apparently began under the Emperor Michael IV (1034–41), who had been a money-changer earlier in life, and even then had been suspected of false coining. It was not, at this stage, a dramatic debasement—a matter of 4 carats or so of alloy. The principle of debasement seems to have been definitively adopted and systematized by Constantine IX (1042–55), but even at the end of his reign the standard of fineness still stood at approximately 18 carats. It is only with the reigns of Michael VII (1071–78) and Nicephorus III (1078–81) that the dramatic crash came, plummeting from

[1] R. S. Lopez, "The Dollar of the Middle Ages," *Journal of Economic History*, 11 (1951), pp. 209–34.
[2] C. M. Cipolla, "Currency Depreciation in Medieval Europe," *Ec. Hist. Rev.*², 15 (1962/63), pp. 413–22.

17 or 18 carats to 8 within a decade. Nor was this the nadir, for during the
first decade of the reign of Alexius I (i.e., between 1081 and the reform of
1092), the nomisma histamenon and nomisma tetarteron both seem to have
lost whatever gold they had still contained at his accession.

The progress of debasement was therefore by no means a steady one: after
the first steps under Michael IV and Constantine IX, the gold content of the
coinage remained stable throughout the sixth and seventh decades of the century—then in a further two decades gold almost disappeared from the coinage.

In assessing the causes of this debasement two facts seem to be of crucial
importance: firstly, that the Emperor Basil II left 200,000 pounds of gold in the
treasury on his death in 1025; secondly, that the main debasement began with
Michael VII, who came to the throne in 1071. It may be objected that the
figure (as estimated by Psellus) is worthy of no more consideration than that
normally given to mediaeval estimates of large amounts. On the other hand,
Psellus, as an imperial official, was in a position to know the true facts of the
situation. At any rate, the amount was enormous in contemporary eyes, and
possibly came to several years' revenue.

That the debasement began so soon after Basil's death and certainly before
the exhaustion of his accumulated reserves can only mean that the first stage
was caused by nothing more than the irresponsibility of Michael IV or his
advisors. Psellus lays the blame for the exhaustion of Basil's treasure upon the
reckless extravagance of Constantine IX and his wife Zoë. Certainly their faults
cannot have improved the situation, and both they and their successors can be
blamed for not restoring the traditional standard, but at least the coinage was
not further debased to any large extent. The second—and far more serious—
stage of debasement began with Michael VII, who came to power in 1071, in
the aftermath of the serious defeat of Manzikert. As a result of his and his
successor's sheer incompetence, Asia Minor was, largely unnecessarily, lost to the
Seljuk Turks and imperial authority in the remaining provinces, to all intents
and purposes, vanished. Provincial governors did as they pleased, the peace
was broken by continual revolt, the powerful landed nobility succeeded in
evading their tax obligations. The revenue inevitably suffered, while imperial
expenses (both necessary and unnecessary) either remained stable or, more
probably, increased. The second stage of the debasement therefore speedily
followed.

It is superfluous to attempt to account for either stage of the debasement of
the eleventh century by postulating deep-seated, long-term trends acting adversely on the Byzantine economy: general trends such as a disequilibrium in
the balance of payments, or more particular ones such as the capture of Byzantine markets and carrying-trade by the Italian merchant cities. The trouble in
which the Empire found itself at this period was, insofar as it affected the

coinage, fundamentally of a political and short-term nature, not of an economic and long-term one: the radical cause was the irresponsibility, incompetence, and apathy of the central government. Because the trouble was of this kind, the situation was, in the main, retrievable by short-term methods.

And the situation clearly was retrieved, there being little doubt as to where the turning-point lay. The first years of the reign of Alexius I looked as if they might see the dismemberment of the Empire, and to all appearances merely continued the chaos prevalent under his two predecessors. But by 1091/92, events had begun to take a more encouraging turn. Asia Minor, with the exception of a few coastal cities, had been almost entirely lost for the moment, but the Normans had been repulsed from Epirus and Thessaly (1085), the Patzinaks from Bulgaria and Thrace (1091), the Seljuk pirate Tzachas from the Bosphorus itself and the islands of the Aegean (1091). The central authorities were once more in control, however precarious that control might be.

It was at precisely this point that the Emperor was able to perform two significant public actions: to crown his son John (b. 1087) emperor, which implies that he felt himself sufficiently strong to be able to alienate the Ducas faction (which had helped him to power) by infringing the rights of Constantine Ducas his young co-Emperor; and further, to reform the coinage according to an unprecedented pattern. The coronation issue of 1092 forms the first recognizable occasion on which the new coinage was struck.

In perspective, the sequence of events strongly confirms the analysis made above: the political collapse after Manzikert was closely followed by the monetary one—the second, and catastrophic, stage of debasement; the political recovery was closely followed by the monetary one—the reform. Although the picture is undoubtedly a simplified one—if only for the very good reason that a collapse on the scale of that undergone by the Empire could not have occurred without leaving the administration and the economy shaken—nevertheless the pattern of events suggests that it is essentially correct.

The remainder of the reign of Alexius was spent in what was in some aspects a restoration, but in many others a radical reform of the civil and military administration of the Empire: a subject which as Mme Ahrweiler has remarked is "encore insuffisamment traité"—although its main lines have now been admirably delineated by her research. The author takes the liberty of quotation:

> ... Alexis Ier, outre les mesures exceptionnelles qu'il prit tout de suite (confiscation de biens privés, alliances étrangères, etc.), procéda à une modification complète des rouages administratifs de l'Empire qui aboutit à une réforme radicale de toutes les institutions byzantines. Elle touche le gouvernement central et l'appareil provincial, conditionnant ainsi le fonctionnement et la constitution de l'armée de terre et de mer de l'Empire; autrement dit, elle constitue l'ensemble des mesures militaires, juridiques,

économiques et financières, dont l'application, inaugurée par Alexis Ier et généralisée par ses successeurs, donna à l'Etat byzantin l'aspect qu'il gardera jusqu'à la fin de l'Empire.[3]

To mention even the main lines of these reforms—except to point out how neatly the establishment of the *Nea Logarike*, in its correctly understood form, fits into the general scheme of the reign—is beyond the scope of this study.

The stability of the reformed coinage was something of an achievement in view of the rather complicated form of its gold, electrum, and billon denominations. The first alteration—then only a minor one, the revaluation of the billon—must have occurred at some point in the middle of Manuel's reign (*c.* 1160?). The reigns of the Angelus brothers saw two departures from the "honest" monetary system of the Comneni—one of them of some importance. This involved the debasement of the electrum denomination by Isaac, attested both by specific gravity determination and the chronicler Nicetas Choniates. Although the debasement does not seem to have been of any great extent under Isaac, a fair proportion of the coins of Alexius seem to be appreciably sub-standard, being not only deficient in gold but also having appreciable amounts of copper in the alloy. The standard of the hyperpyron remained unaffected and that denomination was issued, by Isaac at least, in some quantity.[4] There may have been a decrease in the issue of both gold and electrum under Alexius, reflected in the apparent disappearance of the second officina for both denominations. Unfortunately there is, in the first place, no reliable criterion for discovering whether the debasement of the electrum was carried out in the face of adverse economic factors, or whether it resulted from another example of imperial irresponsibility as exercised by Michael IV in the eleventh century. Similarly, the apparent disappearance of the second officinae may only be a further example of the relaxation in the system of officina distinctions that is to be seen in the billon coinage. An accurate assessment is also precluded by the shortness of the period involved—probably little more than the last decade of the twelfth century. The continuity of the monetary history of the Empire comes to a sudden end in 1204, and the coinages of Latin Constantinople and Thessalonica and of the empires of Nicaea and Thessalonica cannot be expected to provide any detailed information concerning the volume of coinage issued in the immediately preceding period, except insofar as they eloquently demonstrate the catastrophic nature of the events of that year.

Whatever the adverse pressures at work on the monetary system during the reigns of the Angeli, for the coinage, as for much else, there is no disguising the utterly decisive nature of the sack of the city and the partition of its ter-

---

[3] H. Ahrweiler-Glykatzi, *Byzance et la mer* (Paris, 1966), p. 198.

[4] On the distinction between the rôle and history of the standard and petty coinage, see: C. M. Cipolla, *Money, Prices, and Civilization in the Mediterranean World* (Princeton, 1956), pp. 13–37.

ritories, although the issue of coinage by the successor states along outwardly traditional lines tends to lend a superficial mask to the fact.

The successor states were plainly incapable of providing their inhabitants with a plentiful and stable coinage. The merits of stability in itself have been debated, but it was nevertheless certainly the aim of the monetary policy of the Byzantine Empire and therefore of its successors.

The coinage of the Latin empire and kingdom of Thessalonica was confined entirely to the base metal denominations and, judging by hoard evidence, can never have been an important element of circulation outside Constantinople and Thessalonica. The scyphate billon coinages of the Bulgarian and Serbian tsars rarely appear in hoards, even those from the areas in which they were originally issued. The coinage of the Thessalonican empire of the Ducas—despite its neat style and regular fabric—can scarcely have been of any importance outside that city itself, for even hoards from the nearby Rhodope contain only relatively small amounts. Despite the fact that the empire issued silver, much of it appears to have been base, and no gold coinage at all can be attributed to the Ducae with any degree of confidence, although it is tolerably certain that they would have issued a standard coinage had they been at all able, if only for reasons of prestige. The circulating medium of the European provinces outside the two main cities largely consisted, during the third to sixth decades of the century, of the crude small-module pieces that have been identified above as forming an unofficial coinage of emergency.

Monetarily, as well as eventually politically, it was the empire of Nicaea that acted as the real successor to the old Empire. It was the only successor state to strike a gold coinage in any quantity, and in addition struck an appreciable electrum or silver coinage, at least in its early years: its billon is as common as that of Thessalonica, even in hoards from the Rhodope. That it was Nicaea and not Thessalonica that issued a precious-metal coinage is of some interest in itself, for as a large and active emporium the empire of Nicaea had nothing to rival Thessalonica, long the second city of the old Empire. On the other hand, Nicaea did possess the prosperous agricultural area contained in the themes of Neocastra and Thracesion, as well as the relatively minor, but prosperous, cities of Smyrna, Nymphaeum, and Magnesia: it may well have been this sound agricultural basis, which Thessalonica with its limited hinterland lacked, that gave the extra economic strength seen in the Lascarid precious-metal coinage.

Even so, despite the economic resources that were wisely exploited by the emperors of Nicaea,[5] it was during this very period that the hyperpyron began its long and irretrievable decline. Under John III, the gold content fell to approximately 16 carats and although stabilized for several decades began to decline again under the Palaeologid emperors, after the recovery of Con-

[5] E.g., Nicephorus Gregoras, 2, vi; Bonn ed. 1, pp. 42–43.

stantinople. During the reign of Michael VIII the standard fell by a further carat of fineness, and during the long reign of his son Andronicus II, it reached a bare 11 carats of gold, 6 of silver and 7 of copper.[6] As the gold content fell, the amount of coin issued also dwindled, and so, losing 10 carats of fineness within a century, the hyperpyron as a gold coin barely survived into the reigns of Andronicus III and John V. In this there is a complete contrast with what seems to have happened during, and as a result of, the debasement of the eleventh century. The decline in quantity also extended to the base-metal, petty coinage—which again it had not done on the previous occasion. Meanwhile, as a result of processes no doubt connected with those that caused the fall of the hyperpyron, the Italian mercantile cities began to issue their own coinage, of pure gold, in increasing quantities; Genoa and Florence in 1252, Venice in 1285.[7]

The great crisis of the bezant was essentially a phenomenon of the post-conquest period, separated from the temporary, earlier crisis by a full century of monetary stability and abundance.[8]

[6] See Chap. 12, p. 256.

[7] For the latest study of this connection, see: A. M. Watson, "Back to Gold—and Silver," *Ec. Hist. Rev.*[2], 20 (1967), pp. 1–34.

[8] Crises of the bezant which have been postulated at various times for the sixth and tenth centuries are based on misunderstandings of monetary practices and policies which were largely independent of economic necessity: see C. Diehl, "Une crise monétaire au VIe siècle," *Revue des études grecques*, 32 (1919), pp. 158–66; R. S. Lopez, "La crise du besant au Xe siècle et la date du Livre du Préfet," *Annuaire de l'Institut de Philologie et d'Histoire Orientales et Slaves*, 10 (1950) (= Mélanges Henri Grégoire, 2), pp. 403–18.

SECTION V
MATERIALS

CHAPTER FIFTEEN

LIST OF HOARDS

The following list is entirely subjective in its composition. It contains hoards from Bulgaria that have actually been examined by the author; a certain number of hoards from other areas that have also been personally examined; a few which are of particular interest and which have been published with a degree of attention to detail sufficient to provide accurate and reliable information. While it is to be regretted that more are not capable of the latter description, it is hoped that this publication will go some way toward providing a point of reference which will be of some aid in the future.

ARCADIA HOARD

Bellinger and Metcalf, *NC*[6], 19 (1959), pp. 155–64.
Said to have been found in 1958, and to have consisted of 204 "bronze" scyphates.
Location: dispersed.
Recte 204 billon trachea of the following description:

Manuel I

Third coinage   3 specimens (worn; all first phase).
Fourth coinage   2 specimens? (worn; var. A[c] – 1; var. D[a] – 1).

Andronicus I

1 specimen (worn; var. B).

Isaac II

70 specimens (incl., var. C[a] – 1; ∴ ∴ on back of throne – 1).

Alexius III

42 specimens

"Bulgarian" Imitative

Type A   37 specimens?
Type B   ?
Type C   7 specimens

Latin Imitative (larger module)

MINT OF CONSTANTINOPLE

Type A   4 specimens

MINT OF THESSALONICA

Type B   2 specimens

Latin Imitative (smaller module)

Type A   35 specimens
Type D   1 specimen

ASSENOVGRAD HOARD

Gerassimov, *IAI*, 26 (1963), p. 257.

Said to have been found in 1960, and to have consisted of 170 "copper" scyphates of Manuel I, Isaac II, Alexius III, and Theodore I.

Location: Assenovgrad, Archaeological Museum.

Recte 175 billon trachea and 5 copper tetartera of the following description:

BILL. TRACHEA

Manuel I

Third coinage   2 specimens (very worn; both first phase).
Fourth coinage 2 specimens (very worn, var. A[c] – 1; var. B[a] – 1).

Andronicus I

3 specimens (two very worn).

Isaac II

40 specimens. Identifiable: var. A(b) – 4; var. B(b) – 2; var.
                  C(a) – 3, C(b) – 2; var. D(a) – 5;
                  rest uncertain. 1 specimen reg-
                  ularly clipped.

Alexius III

*c.*52 specimens. Identifiable: var. A – 14; var. B(a) – 2, B(b) –
                  "present"; var. C(b) – 2; var.
                  D(a) – 2, D(b) – "present"; rest
                  uncertain. 3 specimens regularly
                  clipped.

"Bulgarian" Imitative

Type A	21 specimens
Type B	17 specimens
Type C	c.21 (incl. 1 specimen overstruck on Seljuk copper coin: *obv.* inscr., *rev.* horse with asterisk beneath. 1 specimen apparently a mule: *obv.* type A, *rev.* type C).

Latin Imitative (larger module)

MINT OF CONSTANTINOPLE

Type A	1 specimen
Type D	1 specimen

Latin Imitative (smaller module)

Type A	13 specimens

Theodore I, Comnenus-Lascaris

MINT OF NICAEA

Type A	2 specimens

Æ TETARTERA

Manuel I

MINT OF THESSALONICA

Type A	5 specimens (all very worn).

BANYA HOARD

Moushmov, *IBAI*, 5 (1928/29), p. 383.

Said to have been found in 1927 and to have consisted of 36 "gold" coins of Isaac II and 70 to 80 "copper" coins of the same period. The copper coins were not retained by the authorities.

Location: Plovdiv, Archaeological Museum.

Recte 36 electrum trachea of the following description:

Manuel I

MINT OF THESSALONICA

Type C	1 specimen (no inscr., gilded, probable contemporary forgery).

Isaac II

MINT OF CONSTANTINOPLE

> 35 specimens, incl. var. A – 24; var. B – 11.

BATKOUN HOARD

Gerassimov, *IBAI*, 12 (1938), p. 451.

Said to have been found in 1937 and to have consisted of 10 kilos of "copper" scyphates of Manuel I, Andronicus I, and Isaac II.

Location: Pazardzhik, Archaeological Museum.

Recte 2120 Constantinopolitan billon trachea of which a sample 711 were subjected to a more detailed analysis:

Manuel I

Third coinage 637 specimens
(sample)   223 specimens. Identifiable: first phase – 58, incl. var. A – 18; var. B – 31; rest uncertain.
second phase – 34, incl. var. A – 2; var. B – 2; var. C – 5; var. D – 6; rest uncertain.

Fourth coinage 1051 specimens
(sample)   355 specimens. Identifiable: var. A(a) – 3, A(b) – 5, A(c) – 15; var. B(a) – 36; var. C(a) – 61; var D(a) – 20, D(b) – 4; rest uncertain.

Andronicus I

296 specimens
(sample)   89 specimens. Identifiable: var. A – 7; var. B – 10; rest uncertain.

Isaac II

129 specimens
(sample)   44 specimens. Identifiable: var. A(a) – 1, A(b) – 9; var. B(b) – 6; var. C(b) – 8; var. D(a) – 4, D(b) – 1; rest uncertain.

Unidentifiable

7 specimens

BELITSA HOARD

Gerassimov, *IBAI*, 12 (1938), p. 455.
Said to have been found in 1938 and to have consisted of "copper" scyphates
of Manuel I and Isaac II.
Location: Sofia, Archaeological Museum.
Recte 101 Constantinopolitan billon trachea of the following description:

John I

First coinage	1 specimen
Second coinage	9 specimens

Manuel I

First coinage	12 specimens, incl. both vars. A and B.
Third coinage	28 specimens. Identifiable: first phase – 14, incl. var. A – 6; var. B – 5; rest uncertain. second phase – 5, incl. var. D – 3; rest uncertain.
Fourth Coinage	47 specimens. Identifiable: var. A(a) – 5, A(b) – 4, A(c) – 12; var. B(a) – 9; var. C(a) – 4; var. D(a) – 2; rest uncertain.

Andronicus I

3 specimens. Identifiable: var B – 2; other uncertain.

Unidentifiable

1 specimen

BERGAMA HOARD

Mosser, ANS Numismatic Notes and Monographs, No. 67 (New York, 1935),
p. 64.
Described as 1059 "copper" coins.
Location: Istanbul?
Recte 1059 billon trachea of the following description:

Manuel I

First coinage?	1 specimen?
Third coinage	1 specimen
Fourth coinage	162 specimens

Isaac II

221 specimens

Alexius III

481 specimens

Latin Imitative (larger module?)

MINT OF CONSTANTINOPLE

Type A   36 specimens

Theodore I, Comnenus-Lascaris

MINT OF NICAEA

First coinage   156 specimens

Uncertain

1 specimen

BRAURON HOARD

Metcalf, *NC*[7], 4 (1964), pp. 257–58.

Said to have been found in 1956, and to have consisted of 205 "bronze folles" of John II, Manuel I, Andronicus I, and Isaac II, together with 1 scyphate coin.

Location: Athens.

Recte 205 copper tetartera and half-tetartera and 1 billon trachy, the identifiable coins being of the following description:

BILL. TRACHY

Latin Imitative (smaller module)

Type A   1 specimen (broken half-piece).

Æ TETARTERA

John II

MINT OF THESSALONICA

1 specimen (broken half-piece).

Manuel I

MINT OF CONSTANTINOPLE

First coinage   1 specimen

MINT OF THESSALONICA

Type A   5 specimens
Type B   1 specimen (broken half-piece).

Andronicus I

MINT OF THESSALONICA

Type A   3 specimens?

Isaac Comnenus (Cyprus)

MAIN MINT

Type A   1 specimen

Isaac II

MINT OF THESSALONICA

                         2 specimens

Æ HALF-TETARTERA

Manuel I

MINT OF THESSALONICA

Type A   1 specimen (broken half-piece).

UNCERTAIN GREEK MINT

Type A   *c.*86 specimens
Type C   1 specimen

Uncertain attribution

2 specimens

BRESTOVO HOARD

Gerassimov, *IAI*, 20 (1955), p. 606.
Said to have been found in 1953 and to have consisted of "copper" coins of
    Manuel I and Andronicus I, of which 620 were retained by the authorities.
Location: Blagoevgrad, Archaeological Museum.
Recte 1620 billon trachea of the following description:

Manuel I

Third coinage   17 specimens. Identifiable: first phase – 12, incl. var. A – 4; var. B – 7; var. C – 1. second phase – 5, incl. var. C – 2; var. D – 2; other uncertain.

Fourth coinage   19 specimens. Identifiable: var. A(b) – 3, A(c) – 2; var. B(a) – 4; var. C(a) – 6; var. D(a) – 2; rest uncertain. Several specimens regularly clipped.

Andronicus I

8 specimens. Identifiable: var. A – 2; var. B – 5; other uncertain.

Isaac II

290 specimens. Identifiable: var. A(a) – 3, A(b) – 33; var. B(a) – 1, B(b) – 77; var. C(a) – 11, C(b) – 32; var. D(a) – 26, D(b) – 5; ⁖ ⁖ on back of throne – 1; – 1; rest uncertain. Several specimens regularly clipped.

Alexius III

370 specimens. Identifiable: var. A – 40 (incl. 4 of chronological var. I); var. B(a) – 5, B(b) – 21; var. C(a) – 1, C(b) – 40; var. D(a) – 12, D(b) – 32; – 6; rest uncertain.

"Bulgarian" Imitative

Type A   386 specimens
Type B   157 specimens
Type C   267 specimens

Latin Imitative (larger module)

MINT OF CONSTANTINOPLE
Type A   21 specimens

Latin Imitative (smaller module)

Type A   78 specimens

Theodore I, Comnenus-Lascaris

MINT OF NICAEA

First coinage   1 specimen

Unidentifiable
6 specimens

BYAGA HOARD

Gerassimov, *IAI*, 25 (1962), p. 229.
Said to have been found in 1959 and to have consisted of "copper" scyphates
    of Manuel I and Alexius III, of which 430 were retained by the author-
    ities.
Location: Plovdiv, Archaeological Museum.
Recte c. 463 billon trachea of the following description:

Manuel I
Fourth coinage   1 specimen (var. B[a]; very worn).

Isaac II
1 specimen (var. B[b]).

Alexius III
24 specimens

"Bulgarian" Imitative
Type A   6 specimens
Type B   8 specimens
Type C   67 specimens

Latin Imitative (larger module)

MINT OF CONSTANTINOPLE

Type A   32 specimens
Type B   2 specimens
Type C   1 specimen

MINT OF THESSALONICA

Type A   4 specimens
Type B   4 specimens (incl. 1 overstruck on preceding type).

Latin Imitative (smaller module)

Type A	214 specimens
Type B	14 specimens
Type C	7 specimens
Type D	22 specimens
Type E	14 specimens
Type F	10 specimens
Type G	18 specimens

Theodore I, Comnenus-Lascaris

MINT OF NICAEA

First coinage   2 specimens

Unidentifiable
c.12 fragments and clipped pieces of coin.

CORINTH (I) HOARD

Metcalf, *NC⁷*, 4 (1964), p. 252.
Found in February 1937, and said to have consisted of 518 "bronze folles"
    of John II and Manuel I.
Location: Corinth.
Recte 518 copper tetartera and half-tetartera of the following description:

Æ TETARTERA

John II

MINT OF THESSALONICA

39 specimens

Æ HALF-TETARTERA

John II

MINT OF THESSALONICA

Type A   1 specimen

Manuel I

MINT OF THESSALONICA

Type A   33 specimens

UNCERTAIN GREEK MINT

Type A   445 specimens

CORINTH (II) HOARD

Harris, *AJA*, 43 (1939), pp. 268–77.
Location: Corinth.
Found in 1938, consisting of 30 Constantinopolitan hyperpyra of Manuel I of
the following description:

Var. I	2 specimens
Var. II	9 specimens
Var. III	1 specimen
Var. IV	3 specimens
Var. V	15 specimens

CORINTH (III) HOARD

Robinson, *Hesperia*, 31 (1962), p. 131.
Location: Corinth.
Found in 1960, consisting of 1 anonymous copper follis and 22 billon trachea:

Æ FOLLIS

Anonymous Type J 1 specimen

BILL. TRACHEA

"Bulgarian" Imitative

Type B	1 specimen

Latin Imitative (smaller module)

Type A	14 specimens
Type D	2 specimens
Type E	2 specimens
Type F	2 specimens
Type G	1 specimen

DOLNI VURBISHTA HOARD

Unpublished.
The date of finding seems to be unknown.
Location: Turnovo, Archaeological Museum.
99 billon trachea of the following description:

Manuel I

Third coinage   6 specimens, incl. 1 regularly clipped.
Fourth coinage   1 specimen (regularly clipped).

Andronicus I

1 specimen (regularly clipped).

Isaac II

28 specimens

Alexius III

33 specimens

"Bulgarian" Imitative

Type A   4 specimens
Type B   15 specimens
Type C   8 specimens

Latin Imitative (larger module)

MINT OF THESSALONICA
Type B   1 specimen

Latin Imitative (smaller module)

Type A   1 specimen
Type E   1 specimen

DORKOVO HOARD

Gerassimov, *IBAI*, 14 (1940–42), pp. 282–83.
Said to have been found in 1940, and to have consisted of 3 kilos of "copper" coins of Andronicus I, Alexius III, and Manuel of Thessalonica.
Location: Pazardzhik, Archaeological Museum.
Recte 3 kilos of billon trachea (but including 1 half-tetarteron), of which the 132 identifiable pieces were of the following description:

BILL. TRACHEA

Manuel I

Fourth coinage   2 specimens (both very worn).

Isaac II

2 specimens

Alexius III

1 specimen

"Bulgarian" Imitative

Type A   1 specimen
Type B   1 specimen
Type C   1 specimen

Latin Imitative (larger module)

MINT OF CONSTANTINOPLE

Type C   2 specimens (both clipped).
Type D   5 specimens (all clipped).
Type H   3 specimens (all clipped).
Type P   4 specimens
Type R   4 specimens
Type T   3 specimens

MINT OF THESSALONICA

Type A   4 specimens
Type C   3 specimens (all clipped).

Latin Imitative (smaller module)

Type A   64 specimens
Type D   8 specimens
Type E   2 specimens

Theodore I, Comnenus-Lascaris

MINT OF NICAEA
First coinage   2 specimens

Theodore Comnenus-Ducas

Type G   1 specimen (clipped).

Manuel Comnenus-Ducas

Type F   2 specimens (1 clipped).
Type G   2 specimens (1 clipped).

John Comnenus-Ducas
(Series III)

Type E	1 specimen
Type H	1 specimen
Type J	2 specimens
Type K	2 specimens
Type O	2 specimens
Type P	1 specimen

John III, Ducas-Vatatzes

MINT OF THESSALONICA

Type K	5 specimens

Æ HALF-TETARTERON

John Comnenus-Ducas
1 specimen (fragment).

DRAGANOVO HOARD

Gerassimov, *IAI*, 22 (1959), p. 361.

Said to have been found in 1957, and to have consisted of 3½ kilos of "copper" scyphates of Manuel I, Isaac II, and Alexius III.

Location: Turnovo, Archaeological Museum.

Recte 752 Constantinopolitan billon trachea of the following description:

Manuel I

Third coinage   245 specimens. Identifiable: first phase – 128, incl. var. A – 47; var. B – 71; rest uncertain.
second phase – 54, incl. var. A – 2; var. B – 4; var. C – 16; var. D – 14; rest uncertain.

Fourth coinage   444 specimens. Identifiable: var. A(a) – 22, A(b) – 26, A(c) – 49; var. B(a) – 92; var. C(a) – 121; var. D(a) – 43, D(b) – 11, D(c) – 6, D(d) – 3; rest uncertain.

Andronicus I

52 specimens. Identifiable: var. A – 13; var. B – 14; rest uncertain.

Isaac II
11 specimens. Identifiable: var. A(a) – 5; var. B(a) – 2; var.
C(b) – 1; rest uncertain.

DUMBARTON OAKS (I) HOARD

Unpublished.
Said to have been found in central Yugoslavia.
Location: Dumbarton Oaks.
101 billon trachea of the following description:

"Bulgarian" Imitative
Type C   2 specimens

Latin Imitative (larger module)
MINT OF CONSTANTINOPLE
Type A   3 specimens

Latin Imitative (smaller module)
Type A   82 specimens
Type C   1 specimen
Type D   4 specimens
Type E   1 specimen
Type F   1 specimen
Type G   7 specimens

DUMBARTON OAKS (II) HOARD

Unpublished.
Said to have been found in central Yugoslavia.
Location: Dumbarton Oaks.
170 billon trachea of the following description:

Alexius III
1 specimen

"Bulgarian" Imitative
Type A   1 specimen
Type B   2 specimens
Type C   26 specimens

22*

Latin Imitative (larger module)

MINT OF CONSTANTINOPLE

Type A   20 specimens
Type C   1 specimen (clipped).

MINT OF THESSALONICA

Type A   6 specimens (incl. 1 clipped).
Type B   17 specimens
Type C   5 specimens (incl. 3 clipped).

Latin Imitative (smaller module)

Type A   64 specimens
Type B   1 specimen
Type C   2 specimens
Type D   15 specimens
Type F   2 specimens
Type G   4 specimens

Theodore I, Comnenus-Lascaris

MINT OF NICAEA

First coinage   3 specimens

DUMBARTON OAKS (III) HOARD

Unpublished.
Said to have been found in central Yugoslavia.
Location: Dumbarton Oaks.
369 billon trachea of the following description:

Manuel I

Fourth coinage   3 specimens (A[a], B[a], D[a]—all worn).

Isaac II

1 specimen (A[a] – worn).

Alexius III

3 specimens (incl. var. [Ca] – 1).

"Bulgarian" Imitative

Type A   6 specimens
Type B   2 specimens
Type C   53 specimens

Latin Imitative (larger module)

MINT OF CONSTANTINOPLE

Type A	7 specimens
Type B	1 specimen (clipped).
Type C	3 specimens (clipped).
Type D	1 specimen (clipped).
Type P	1 specimen (clipped).

MINT OF THESSALONICA

Type A	4 specimens
Type B	1 specimen
Type C	2 specimens (clipped).

Latin Imitative (smaller module)

Type A	198 specimens
Type B	9 specimens
Type C	4 specimens
Type D	20 specimens
Type E	6 specimens
Type F	2 specimens
Type G	26 specimens

Theodore I, Comnenus-Lascaris

MINT OF NICAEA

First coinage	7 specimens

Unidentifiable

9 specimens

ENINA HOARD

Gerassimov, *IAI*, 20 (1955), p. 603.

Said to have been found in 1951/52, and to have consisted of 200 "copper" coins of Manuel I, Andronicus I, and Isaac II.

Location: Sofia, Archaeological Museum.

Recte 169 Constantinopolitan billon trachea, to which must be added a further 28 pieces which remained in the Archaeological Museum at Kazanluk when the others were forwarded to Sofia. The description of the two parcels combined is as follows:

Manuel I

Third coinage   62 specimens. Identifiable: first phase – 47 ⎱ rest
                   second phase – 9 ⎰ uncertain.

Fourth coinage   91 specimens. Identifiable: var. A(a) – 5, A(b) – 2, A(c) – 26;
                   var. B(a) – 18; var. C(a) – 22;
                   var. D(a) – 10, D(b) – 5, D(d) – 1;
                   rest uncertain.

Andronicus I

24 specimens

Isaac II

19 specimens

"Bulgarian" Imitative

Type A   1 specimen

GENERAL NIKOLAEVO HOARD

Gerassimov, *IAI*, 26 (1963), pp. 257–58.
Said to have been found in 1960, and to have consisted of 770 "copper" coins
    of Manuel I and Andronicus I.
Location: Plovdiv, Archaeological Museum.
Recte 748 Constantinopolitan billon trachea, of the following description:

Manuel I

Second coinage   1 specimen
Third coinage   245 specimens. Identifiable: first phase – 122 ⎱ rest
                   second phase – 13 ⎰ uncertain.
Fourth coinage   368 specimens. Identifiable: var. A(a) – 10, A(b) – 8, A(c) –
                   28; var. B(a) – 46; var. C(a) – 58;
                   var. D(a) – 31, D(b) – 9, D(d) – 3;
                   rest uncertain.

Andronicus I

101 specimens

Isaac II

32 specimens. Identifiable: var. A(a) – 4, A(b) – 4; var.
B(b) – 2; var. C(b) – 1; var.
D(a) – 1; rest uncertain.

Latin Imitative (larger module)

MINT OF CONSTANTINOPLE

Type A   1 specimen

GORNOSLAV HOARD

Gerassimov, *IAI*, 26 (1963), p. 262. Dzhambov, *Arkheologiya*, yr. III, bk. 4
     (1961), pp. 1–5.
Said to have been found in 1961, and to have consisted of 786 gold coins of
     Alexius I, John II, Manuel I, and Andronicus I.
Location: Plovdiv, Archaeological Museum.
Recte 786 gold hyperpyra of the following description:

Alexius I (239 specimens)

MINT OF CONSTANTINOPLE

Var. I(A)   47 specimens, incl. small jewelling – 16 (inscr. var. [i] – 9,
                                             [ii] – 5, [iii] – 2).
                          med. jewelling – 3 (all inscr. var. [iii]).
                          large jewelling – 28 (all inscr. var. [iii]).
Var. I(B)   48 specimens, incl. small jewelling – 34 (inscr. var. [i] – 15,
                                             [ii] – 9, [iii] – 10).
                          med. jewelling – 13 (all inscr. var. [iii]).
                          large jewelling – 1 (inscr. var. [iii]).
Var. II   85 specimens, incl. 5 with ligature ⋈ for ⋈.

MINT OF THESSALONICA

Var. I   21 specimens, incl. 2 with erased attempt to decorate chlamys-
                                  border on two sides on left (inscr. var.
                                  [i] – 18, [ii] – 3).
Var. II   1 specimen (inscr. var. [i]).
Var. III   9 specimens (inscr. var. [i] – 1, [ii] – 8).
Var. IV (A)   6 specimens (inscr. var. [i] – 1, [iii] – 5).
Var. IV (B)   4 specimens, incl. 1 with dot on labarum-shaft and below
                                  tablion (inscr. var. [i] – 3, [iii] – 1).
Var. V   6 specimens
When this hoard was examined the author was still unaware of the existence
     of Thessalonican var. VI and it is therefore possible that some examples
     were included with Constantinopolitan var. II. The 3 specimens of var.
     IV(B) with the inscr. var. (i) are all from the same reverse die.

MINT OF PHILIPPOPOLIS

Var. I   9 specimens (inscr. var. [i] – 6, [ii] – 3).
Var. II   1 specimen

UNKNOWN MINT   2 specimens

John II (274 specimens)

MINT OF CONSTANTINOPLE

First coinage   133 specimens
Second coinage   73 specimens
Third coinage   61 specimens. Identifiable: var. A – 25, incl. ΘV ΜΡ – 23, VΘ ΡΜ etc. – 2; var. B – 35, incl. ΘV ΜΡ – 3, VΘ ΡΜ etc. – 32; globus form ⸪ – 9.

MINT OF THESSALONICA

First coinage   4 specimens (pendilia form: ‖ – 2, ⅄⅄ – 2).

Third coinage   3 specimens (pendilia form: ‖ – 1, ⅃⅃ – 2).

Manuel I (264 specimens)

MINT OF CONSTANTINOPLE

Var. I   62 specimens (• ▪ ✕ ꜀ ʃ �, below tablion).
Var. II   80 specimens (• ▪ ✕ ꜀ ʃ �, below tablion).
Var. III   18 specimens. Identifiable: var. A – 8; var. B – 9; other uncertain.

Var. IV   65 specimens
Var. V   35 specimens, incl. dot on chlamys ≪, and below tablion – 25; dot on chlamys, none below tablion – 5; no dot on chlamys, none below tablion – 2; cross on chlamys ≪, dot below tablion – 3. Large number of die-identities in this var.

Uncertain var.   2 specimens

MINT OF THESSALONICA

     2 specimens (*obv.* & *rev.* dies identical).

Andronicus I

8 specimens

Isaac II

1 specimen (loros-waist ⊠).

GRABOVAC HOARD

Metcalf, *Coinage in the Balkans*, pp. 115–16 (a provisional publication only).
See under "ZLATA HOARD."

GRADEVO (I) HOARD

Gerassimov, *IBAI*, 11 (1937), p. 322.
Said to have been found in 1936, and to have consisted of *c.* 200 "copper"
    scyphates of Manuel I and Alexius III.
Location: Sofia, Archaeological Museum.
Recte 104 billon trachea (only part of the original hoard) of the following de-
    scription:

John II

Second coinage   2 specimens (var. A).

Manuel I

Third coinage   16 specimens. Identifiable: first phase – 7, incl. var. A – 2;
                            var. B – 3
                       second phase – 3, incl. var. C – 1;
                       var. D – 1; other uncertain.
Fourth coinage   71 specimens. Identifiable: var. A(a) – 6, A(b) – 6, A(c) – 14;
                        var. B(a) – 16, B(b) – 2; var.
                        C(a) – 9; var. D(a) – 2; rest un-
                        certain.

Andronicus I

4 specimens (var. A – 2; var. B – 2).

Alexius III

9 specimens

"Bulgarian" Imitative

Type A   1 specimen

Latin Imitative (larger module)

MINT OF CONSTANTINOPLE
Type A   1 specimen

GRADEVO (II) HOARD

Gerassimov, *IAI*, 25 (1962), p. 226.

Said to have been found in 1958, and to have consisted of 349 "copper" coins of Manuel I and Andronicus I.

Location: Blagoevgrad, Archaeological Museum.

Recte 351 billon trachea of the following description:

Manuel I

Third coinage   1 specimen (first phase, var. B).

Andronicus I

1 specimen (var. B).

Isaac II

56 specimens. Identifiable: var. A(b) – 6; var. B(b) – 13; var. C(a) – 3; C(b) – 2; var. D(a) – 3; rest uncertain.

Alexius III

83 specimens. Identifiable: var. A – 4; var. B(a) – 2, B(b) – 2; var. C(a?) – 2; var. D(a) – 2, D(b) – 9; rest uncertain.

"Bulgarian" Imitative

Type A	105 specimens
Type B	10 specimens
Type C	23 specimens

Latin Imitative (larger module)

MINT OF CONSTANTINOPLE

Type A   18 specimens (incl. 2 with 4 dots on shaft of labarum).

MINT OF THESSALONICA

Type A   2 specimens

Latin Imitative (smaller module)

Type A   36 specimens

Theodore I, Comnenus-Lascaris

MINT OF NICAEA
First coinage   4 specimens (incl. 2).

Unidentifiable
12 specimens

ISKRA HOARD

Tsonchev, *Godishnik na Narodniya Arkheologicheski Mouzei, Plovdiv*, 4 (1960),
   pp. 206–14.
Said to have been found in 1938, and to have consisted of 84 "copper" coins
   of the period of Manuel I–Isaac II.
Location: Plovdiv, Archaeological Museum.
Recte 84 Constantinopolitan billon trachea of the following description:

Manuel I
Third coinage   1 specimen
Fourth coinage   8 specimens. Identifiable: var. B(a) – 1; var. C(a) – 2; var.
                                   D(a)–1, D(b)–3; other uncertain.

Andronicus I
5 specimens

Isaac II
70 specimens. Identifiable: var. A(a) – 2, A(b) – 7; var.
                          B(b) – 30; var. C(a) – 4, C(b) – 5;
                          var. D(a) – 6, D(b) – 2; ∴ ∴ on
                          back of throne – 1; – 1;
                          rest uncertain.

ISTANBUL (A) HOARD

Bellinger, ANS *Museum Notes*, 11 (1964), pp. 207–13.
Found before 1946, and described as consisting of 1088 "copper" scyphates
   of the Emperors John II–Alexius III, struck with small dies that had been
   specifically prepared for the small flans seen in this hoard.
Location: University of Nebraska.

Recte 1088 regularly clipped Constantinopolitan billon trachea of the emperors mentioned above. Bellinger's assertion that these coins were struck on small flans from small dies is quite untenable. As Metcalf has rightly pointed out, they were struck from dies of normal size and on large flans, but were subsequently clipped (*Coinage in the Balkans*, p. 268). On the other hand, Metcalf's further assertion (*op. cit.*, p. 123) that the clipping was carried out by the Latin authorities after 1204, in order to render them more like the Western denier, is equally untenable, and makes no sense in the light of the monetary policies attributed to the Latin emperors in this publication. The clipping was carried out during the reign of Alexius III in response to monetary factors which have been treated above, Chap. 10, pp. 179–81.

John II
Second coinage   7 specimens

Manuel I
First coinage   3 specimens
Third coinage   68 specimens (incl. at least 2 specimens of the second phase).
Fourth coinage   95 specimens (incl. var. C[a] – 19; var. D[a] – 15).

Andronicus I
8 specimens

Isaac II
713 specimens

Alexius III
194 specimens

ISTANBUL (B) HOARD

Bellinger, ANS *Museum Notes*, 11 (1964), pp. 213–22.
Found before 1946, and described as consisting of 469 "copper" scyphates of the Emperors Alexius I–Theodore I.
Location: University of Nebraska.
Recte 469 billon trachea of the following description:

Alexius I
Third coinage   1 specimen (worn [No. 1]).

John II
Second coinage   2 specimens (worn [Nos. 2,3]).

Manuel I
First coinage   2 specimens (worn [Nos. 4,5]).
Fourth coinage   2 specimens (worn [Nos. 6,7]).

Isaac II
6 specimens (incl. regularly clipped pieces [Nos. 218–19, 221–24]).

Alexius III
24 specimens (incl. regularly clipped pieces [Nos. 228–51]).

"Bulgarian" Imitative
Type A   26 specimens (Nos. 66–91).

Latin Imitative (larger module)
MINT OF CONSTANTINOPLE
Type A   124 specimens (but incl. some pieces of smaller module, type A [Nos. 92–215]).
Type B   58 specimens (Nos. 8–65).
Type O   1 specimen (No. 448).

MINT OF THESSALONICA
Type A   2 specimens (Nos. 216–17).
Type B   4 specimens (Nos. 220, 225–27).

Latin Imitative (smaller module)
Type A   (Present but included with Con'ple larger module, type A).

Theodore I, Comnenus-Lascaris
MINT OF NICAEA
First coinage   1 specimen ([No. 252]).
Second coinage   194 specimens (Nos. 254–447).

MINT OF MAGNESIA
1 specimen (uncertain type but *rev.* very similar to that of coins of this group [No. 253]).

Unidentifiable
21 specimens (Nos. 449–69).

KALENTZI HOARD

Metcalf, *NC*[7], 4 (1964), p. 255.
Said to have been found in 1927, and to have consisted of 86 "bronze folles" of Manuel I.
Location: Athens.
Recte 86 copper half-tetartera of Manuel I of the following description:

Manuel I

MINT OF THESSALONICA
Type B   1 specimen

UNCERTAIN GREEK MINT
Type A   11 specimens
Type B   54 specimens

Unidentifiable
20 specimens

KALOYANOVETS HOARD

Gerassimov, *IAI*, 26 (1963), p. 259.
Said to have been found in 1960, and to have consisted of 889 "copper" scyphates of Manuel I, Andronicus I, and Isaac II.
Location: Stara Zagora, Archaeological Museum.
Recte 884 Constantinopolitan billon trachea of the following description:

John II
Second coinage   1 specimen (var. A).

Manuel I
Second coinage   1 specimen
Third coinage   202 specimens. Identifiable: first phase – 140, incl. var. A – 52; var. B – 73; var. C – 2; rest uncertain.
second phase – 38, incl. var. B – 2; var. C – 13; var. D – 10; rest uncertain.
Fourth coinage   367 specimens. Identifiable: var. A(a) – 11, A(b) – 20, A(c) – 63; var B(a) – 73; var. C(a) – 98; var. D(a) – 46, D(b) – 24, D(d) – 3; rest uncertain.

Andronicus I

75 specimens. Identifiable: var. A – 18; var. B – 34; rest uncertain.

Isaac II

238 specimens. Identifiable: var. A(a) – 18, A(b) – 75; var. B(b) – 1; var. C(b) – 52; var. D(a) – 3, D(b) – 48; – 2; rest uncertain.

KARTAL HOARD

Moushmov, *IBAD*, 4 (1914), pp. 274–75.

Said to have been found in 1914, and to have consisted of *c.* 100 "copper" scyphates of the period of the Comneni.

Location: Sofia, Archaeological Museum.

Recte 39 billon trachea (only part of the original hoard) of the following description:

Manuel I

Third coinage 7 specimens (first phase – 6, second phase – 1).

Fourth coinage 17 specimens. Identifiable: var. A(b) – 2, A(c) – 3; var. B(a) – 4; var. C(a) – 5; var. D(b) – 1; rest uncertain.

Andronicus I

3 specimens. Identifiable: var. A – 1; var. B – 1; other uncertain.

Isaac II

6 specimens. Identifiable: var. A(a) – 1, A(b) – 2; var. C(b) – 1; var. D(a) – 1; other uncertain.

Alexius III

5 specimens

"Bulgarian" Imitative

Type A 1 specimen

KASTRI HOARD

Metcalf, *NC*[7], 4 (1964), pp. 255–56.
Said to have been found in 1952, and to have consisted of 910 "bronze coins."
Location: Athens.
Recte The identifiable copper tetartera and half-tetartera which were counted
   were as follows:

Æ TETARTERA

John II

MINT OF THESSALONICA
                9 specimens (incl. 2 broken halves).

Isaac II

MINT OF THESSALONICA
                22 specimens

Æ HALF-TETARTERA

Manuel I

UNCERTAIN GREEK MINT
Type A   51 specimens
Type B   622 specimens
Type C   61 specimens

Andronicus I

UNCERTAIN GREEK MINT
                48 specimens

KAZANLUK HOARD

Gerassimov, *IAI*, 25 (1962), p. 226.
Said to have been found in 1958, and to have consisted of 1060 "copper"
   scyphates of Manuel I, Isaac II, and Alexius III.
Location: Kazanluk, Archaeological Museum.
Recte 1060 billon trachea of the following description:

John II

MINT OF THESSALONICA
> 1 specimen (very worn).

Manuel I

Third coinage   8 specimens. Identifiable: first phase   – 6 ⎫ other uncer-
                                        ⎪ tain. 3 speci-
                                        ⎧ mens regular-
                     second phase – 1 ⎭ ly clipped.

Fourth coinage   18 specimens. Identifiable: var. A(c) – 2; var. B(a) – 3; var. C(a) – 4; rest uncertain. 7 specimens regularly clipped.

Andronicus I
> 2 specimens (both regularly clipped).

Isaac II
> 93 specimens. Identifiable: var. A(a) – 1, A(b) – 15; var. B(a) – 1, B(b) – 22; var. C(a) – 3, C(b) – 5; var. D(a) – 6, D(b) – 1; ∴ ∴ on back of throne – 2; rest uncertain.

Alexius III
> 191 specimens. Identifiable: var. A – 20; var. B(a) – 8, B(b) – 7; var. C(a) – 10, C(b) – 34; var. D(a) – 4, D(b) – 25; ▮ – 3; rest uncertain.

"Bulgarian" Imitative

Type A   188 specimens
Type B   310 specimens
Type C   239 specimens

Unidentifiable
> 10 specimens, incl. 2 fragments.

23

KHISSAR HOARD

Moushmov, *IBAI*, 1 (1921/22), p. 242. Metcalf, *HBN*, 16 (1962), p. 273.
Said to have consisted of 1 scyphate of Michael VII, 58 of Nicephorus III, 1 electrum scyphate of Alexius I, and 5 gold scyphates of the same Emperor. The electrum coins were presumably debased trachea, the gold coins certainly included metropolitan reformed hyperpyra (var. I[A]).
Location: dispersed?

KIUSTENDIL HOARD

Gerassimov, *IAI*, 26 (1963), p. 259.
Said to have been found in 1960, and to have consisted of 577 "copper" scyphates of Manuel I, Andronicus I, Isaac II, and Alexius III.
Location: Kiustendil, Archaeological Museum.
Recte 566 billon trachea, to which must be added a further 34 specimens which remained uncleaned. The description is as follows:

Manuel I

Third coinage 12 specimens. Identifiable: first phase – 7, incl. var. A – 2; var. B – 4; other uncertain. second phase – 5, incl. var. C – 3; rest uncertain. 5 specimens of the coinage regularly clipped.

Fourth coinage 20 specimens. Identifiable: var. A(a) – 1, A(b) – 1, A(c) – 2; var. B(a) – 6; var. C(a) – 4; var. D(a) – 2, D(b) – 1; rest uncertain. 9 specimens regularly clipped.

Andronicus I
2 specimens (var. B – 1; 𝕀𝕀 – 1).

Isaac II
154 specimens. Identifiable: var. A(a) – 1, A(b) – 22; var. B(b) – 34; var. C(a) – 13, C(b) – 14; var. D(a) – 10, D(b) – 4; ∴ ∴ on back of throne – 6. 8 specimens regularly clipped.

Alexius III

183 specimens. Identifiable: var. A – 22; var. B(a) – 5, B(b) – 7; var. C(b) – 20; var. D(a) – 4, D(b) – 22; ⬥–3; ⬥–1; rest uncertain. 9 specimens regularly clipped.

"Bulgarian" Imitative

Type A	75 specimens
Type B	25 specimens
Type C	50 specimens

Latin Imitative (larger module)

MINT OF CONSTANTINOPLE

Type A   10 specimens

Latin Imitative (smaller module)

Type A   34 specimens

Theodore I, Comnenus-Lascaris

MINT OF NICAEA

First coinage   1 specimen

Uncleaned and unidentifiable

34 specimens

KIUSTENDIL REGION HOARD

Unpublished.
Location: Sofia, Archaeological Museum.
371 billon trachea of the following description:

Manuel I

Fourth coinage   1 specimen

Isaac II

9 specimens (incl. 2 specimens regularly clipped).

23*

Alexius III

27 specimens. Identifiable: var. A – 2; var. B(b) – 2; var. C(b) – 6; var. D(b) – 1; rest uncertain.

"Bulgarian" Imitative

Type A	183 specimens
Type B	80 specimens
Type C	14 specimens

Latin Imitative (larger module)

MINT OF CONSTANTINOPLE

Type A	37 specimens

MINT OF THESSALONICA

Type A	14 specimens

Latin Imitative (smaller module)

Type A	4 specimens

Theodore I, Comnenus-Lascaris

MINT OF NICAEA

First coinage 2 specimens (both ⊠).

KORTEN HOARD

Gerassimov, *IAI*, 26 (1963), p. 259.
Said to have been found in 1960, and to have consisted of 2 kilos of "copper" scyphates of Isaac II and Alexius III.
Location: Nova Zagora, Archaeological Museum.
Recte 149 billon trachea of the following description:

Isaac II

6 specimens   (var. A[b] – 1; var. B[b] – 2; var. C[a] – 1, C[b] – 1; var. D[a] – 1).

Alexius III

12 specimens. Identifiable: var. B(a) – 1, B(b) – 1; var. D(a) – 1, D(b) – 4; rest uncertain.

"Bulgarian" Imitative

Type A   39 specimens
Type B   8 specimens
Type C   72 specimens

Latin Imitative (larger module)

MINT OF CONSTANTINOPLE
Type A   1 specimen

Latin Imitative (smaller module)

Type A   11 specimens

KOUNINO (I) HOARD

Gerassimov, *IAI*, 20 (1955), p. 610.
Said to have been found in 1954, and to have consisted of 389 "copper" scyphates of Manuel I, Andronicus I, Isaac II, and Alexius III.
Location: Sofia, Archaeological Museum.
Recte 349 billon trachea of the following description:

Isaac II

*c.*35 specimens

Alexius III

*c.*98 specimens

"Bulgarian" Imitative

Type A   10 specimens
Type B   *c.*35 specimens
Type C   *c.*78 specimens

Latin Imitative (larger module)

MINT OF CONSTANTINOPLE
Type A   *c.*5 specimens

Latin Imitative (smaller module)

Type A   *c.*88 specimens

KOUNINO (II) HOARD

Unpublished?

Location (1964/65): in the possession of Professor Milchev of the Kliment Okhridski University at Sofia.

106 billon trachea of the following description:

Manuel I

Fourth coinage   2 specimens (1 regularly clipped).

Isaac II

5 specimens (1 regularly clipped).

Alexius III

3 specimens

"Bulgarian" Imitative

Type A	10 specimens
Type B	6 specimens
Type C	47 specimens

Latin Imitative (smaller module)

Type A   27 specimens

Unidentifiable

6 specimens

KROUSHARE HOARD

Gerassimov, *IAI*, 27 (1964), p. 238.

Said to have been found in 1962, and to have consisted of 320 "copper" scyphates of Manuel I and Andronicus I.

Location: Sliven, Archaeological Museum.

Recte 321 Constantinopolitan billon trachea of the following description:

Manuel I

Second coinage   3 specimens. Identifiable: var. A – 2, incl. $\overset{\cdot\cdot}{\bullet}$ – 1; other uncertain.

Third coinage   112 specimens. Identifiable: first phase – 79, incl. var. A – 32;
                                         var. B – 48; rest uncertain.
                                         second phase – 28, incl. var.
                                         B – 3; var. C – 15; var. D – 9;
                                         other uncertain.
Fourth coinage   148 specimens. Identifiable: var. A(a) – 6, A(b) – 7, A(c) – 20;
                                         var. B(a) – 29; var. C(a) – 54;
                                         var. D(a) – 15, D(b) – 7, D(c) – 6;
                                         rest uncertain.

Andronicus I
58 specimens (var. A – 22; var. B – 35; ▯ – 1).

LAKITÉ HOARD

Unpublished.
Location: Assenovgrad, Archaeological Museum.
A curious collection of 12 pieces of widely divergent date and denomination.

Aʹ HYPERPYRON

John II

MINT OF THESSALONICA
Third coinage   1 specimen

EL. TRACHY

Isaac II
1 specimen (var. B).

BILL. TRACHEA

John II

MINT OF CONSTANTINOPLE
Second coinage   2 specimens (both var. B).

Isaac II
6 specimens

"Bulgarian" Imitative
Type B   1 specimen

Æ FOLLIS

Constantine X, Ducas

MINT OF THESSALONICA(?)

B.M.C. Type 3   1 specimen

LAZANIA HOARD

Mattingly, *Report of the Dept. of Antiquities, Cyprus, 1937–39*, pp. 22–23.
784 Constantinopolitan billon trachea of the following description:

John II

First coinage	403 specimens
Second coinage	229 specimens

Manuel I

First coinage	152 specimens

LEVKOKHORI HOARD

Metcalf, *Annual of the British School of Archaeology at Athens*, 56 (1961) pp. 60–62.
Location: Athens.
Said to have been found in 1955, and to have consisted of 990 "bronze"
    scyphates (billon trachea) of the following description:

Isaac II
38 specimens (incl. specimens of the "Bulgarian" imitative
    series?).

Alexius III
91 specimens (incl. specimens of the "Bulgarian" imitative
    series?).

"Bulgarian" Imitative

Type A	90 specimens
Type B	?
Type C	?

Latin Imitative (smaller module)

Type A	745 specimens
Type G	1 specimen?

Theodore I, Comnenus-Lascaris

MINT OF NICAEA

First coinage   12 specimens (but incl. some of the small-module type G?).

Uncertain and Unidentifiable

13 specimens

LINDOS HOARD

Balling, *Nordisk Numismatisk Årsskrift* (1963), pp. 13–41.
Found in 1902, the hoard was originally said to have consisted of 309 Byzantine "silver" coins, 14 gold coins, and 3 "bronze." When the hoard was transferred to the Royal Collection of Coins and Medals in Copenhagen in 1947, only the following were left and described by Balling in an exemplary fashion: 14 solidi of the Emperors Justin II to Constantine IV, 1 dinar of the Almohad dynasty, 204 electrum scyphates of Manuel I, 2 pennies of Henry II of England, and 3 silver fragments. But cf. Mosser, *op. cit.*, pp. 50–51, under "Lindos." The 204 Constantinopolitan electrum trachea are of the following description:

Manuel I

Type C	79 specimens (var. A – 30 [incl. 12 without *obv.* asterisks]; var. B – 47; var. C – 2).
Type D	20 specimens (var. A – 7; var. B – 11; var. C – 2).
Type E	105 specimens (var. A – 37 [incl. 18 with single dot on *rev.* labarum-shaft]; var. B – 28; var. C – 40).

LOGODASH HOARD

Gerassimov, *IAI*, 25 (1962), p. 231.
Said to have been found in 1959, and to have consisted of 479 "copper" coins of Manuel I, Alexius III, and Theodore and Manuel "Angelus-Ducas."
Location: Blagoevgrad, Archaeological Museum.
Recte 301 billon trachea of the following description, in addition to 1 small antique (fourth-century) copper coin:

Isaac Comnenus (Cyprus)

MAIN MINT

Type A   1 specimen (very worn).

Isaac II

3 specimens

Alexius III

3 specimens (var. C[b?]).

"Bulgarian" Imitative

Type A	18 specimens
Type B	5 specimens
Type C	26 specimens

Latin Imitative (larger module)

MINT OF CONSTANTINOPLE

Type A   24 specimens (incl. 1 with two dots on labarum-shaft, 1 with single dot).

Type B   1 specimen

MINT OF THESSALONICA

Type A   3 specimens

Type B   6 specimens (incl. 1 overstruck on preceding type?).

Latin Imitative (smaller module)

Type A	161 specimens
Type B	7 specimens
Type C	4 specimens (incl. 2 originally of large module but clipped?).
Type D	13 specimens
Type E	4 specimens
Type F	6 specimens
Type G	13 specimens

Theodore I, Comnenus-Lascaris

MINT OF NICAEA

First coinage   2 specimens (both ▦).

Theodore Comnenus-Ducas

Type D   1 specimen (drastically clipped so that only fragment of design appears).

LOM (A) HOARD

Gerassimov, *IAI*, 27 (1964), p. 239.
Found in 1962, consisting of 3633 "copper" coins, buried in an urn and
    described as of Manuel I, Isaac II, Alexius III, and Theodore I.
Location (1964/65): in the possession of Professor Milchev of the Kliment
    Okhridski University at Sofia.
Recte 3633 billon trachea, of which 2111 were subjected to a more detailed
    analysis:

Manuel I

Fourth coinage   1 specimen (var. D[a], regularly clipped).

Isaac II

13 specimens (incl. 2 specimens regularly clipped).

Alexius III

52 specimens

"Bulgarian" Imitative

Type A	245 specimens
Type B	146 specimens
Type C	687 specimens

Latin Imitative (larger module)

MINT OF CONSTANTINOPLE

Type A	16 specimens
Type B	5 specimens

MINT OF THESSALONICA

Type A	16 specimens
Type B	12 specimens
Type C	1 specimen

Latin Imitative (smaller module)

Type A	866 specimens
Type D	3 specimens
Type E	15 specimens
Type G	15 specimens (all apparently have ⠔ loros-waist).

Theodore I, Comnenus-Lascaris

MINT OF NICAEA

First coinage　　10 specimens (all have ▦ loros-waist).

Unidentifiable

8 specimens

LOM (B) HOARD

Found at much the same time as the preceding and in close proximity. Described as consisting of 1376 "copper" coins of the same emperors.
Location: as preceding.
Recte 1376 billon trachea, of which 355 were subjected to a more detailed analysis:

Manuel I

Fourth coinage　　3 specimens (all regularly clipped).

Andronicus I

1 specimen

Isaac II

35 specimens (incl. 1 specimen regularly clipped).

Alexius III

109 specimens

"Bulgarian" Imitative

Type A　　70 specimens
Type B　　24 specimens
Type C　　46 specimens

Latin Imitative (larger module)

MINT OF CONSTANTINOPLE

Type A　　11 specimens

MINT OF THESSALONICA

Type A　　3 specimens
Type B　　9(?) specimens

Latin Imitative (smaller module)

Type A	40 specimens
Type D	1 specimen

Theodore I, Comnenus-Lascaris

MINT OF NICAEA

First coinage	2 specimens (both ⊞ loros-waist).
Second coinage	1 specimen

LOUKOVO HOARD

Unpublished?

Location: Sofia, Archaeological Museum.

974 billon trachea of the following description:

John II

Second coinage   144 specimens (both vars., A and B, present).

Manuel I

First coinage   77 specimens (both vars., A and B, present).

Second coinage   8 specimens (incl. var. A – 2 [globus ⦂●]; var. B – 5 [globus ✝●]).

Third coinage   74 specimens. Identifiable: first phase – 47, incl. var. A – 12; var. B – 24; rest uncertain. second phase – 7, incl. var. B – 1; var. C – 2; var. D – 4.

Fourth coinage   204 specimens. Identifiable: var. A(a) – 18, A(b) – 10, A(c) – 32; var. B(a) – 50; var. C(a) – 26, C(b) – 1; var. D(a) – 19, D(b) – 1, D(c) – 2; rest uncertain.

Andronicus I

52 specimens. Identifiable: var. A – 16; var. B – 25; rest uncertain.

Isaac Comnenus (Cyprus)

MAIN MINT

Type A	1 specimen

Isaac II

237 specimens. Identifiable: var. A(a) – 7, A(b) - 45; var. B(a) – 3, B(b) – 48; var. C(a) – 12, C(b) – 41; var. D(a) – 17, D(b) – 5; ⁘ ⁘ on back of throne – 2; rest uncertain.

Alexius III

141 specimens. Identifiable: var. A – 43 (incl. several regularly clipped); var. B(a) – 4, B(b) – 11; var. C(a) – 4, C(b) – 12; var. D(a) – 5, D(b) – 5, ⚬ – 4; rest uncertain.

"Bulgarian" Imitative

Type A	20 specimens
Type B	8 specimens
Type C	7 specimens

Latin Imitative (smaller module)

Type A	1 specimen

"MACEDONIA" HOARD

Metcalf, *Coinage in the Balkans*, pp. 102–03.
Found in 1959(?).
Location: Messrs. Bitale, Athens.
Consisted of 28 Constantinopolitan billon trachea of the following description:

Manuel I

First coinage	28 specimens (both vars., A and B, present).

MOGILITSA HOARD

Gerassimov, *IBAI*, 11 (1937), p. 316.
Said to have been found in 1934, and to have consisted of over 21 thirteenth-century coins.
Location: Sofia, Archaeological Museum.
Recte 23 billon trachea of the following description:

"Bulgarian" Imitative

Type C	1 specimen

Latin Imitative (larger module)

MINT OF CONSTANTINOPLE

Type F	2 specimens? (both clipped).
Type P	1 specimen (clipped).
Type T	1 specimen

Latin Imitative (smaller module)

Type A	10 specimens
Type E	1 specimen
Type G	1 specimen

Manuel Comnenus-Ducas

Type F	1 specimen (clipped? reads ЯИΛM).

Unidentifiable

5 specimens

MOMIN BROD HOARD

Moushmov, *IBAD*, 4 (1914), p. 275.
Said to have been found in 1914, and to have consisted of 106 "copper" scyphates of Isaac II.
Location: Sofia, Archaeological Museum.
Recte 106 billon trachea of the following description:

John II

Second coinage	1 specimen (var. A; very worn).

Manuel I

First coinage	3 specimens (all very worn).
Second coinage	2 specimens (both very worn).
Fourth coinage	1 specimen (a torn half-piece; very worn).

Isaac II

95 specimens. Identifiable: var. A(a) – 2, A(b) – 16; var. B(b) – 21; var. C(a) – 1, C(b) – 24; var. D(a) – 1, D(b) – 4; rest uncertain.

Alexius III

1 specimen

"Bulgarian" Imitative

Type B   1 specimen

Latin Imitative (larger module)

MINT OF CONSTANTINOPLE

Type A   1 specimen

MINT OF THESSALONICA

Type B   1 specimen

MUGLIZH (I) HOARD

Gerassimov, *IBAI*, 15 (1946), pp. 236–37.
Said to have been found in 1941 and to have consisted of "copper" scyphates,
  of which 640 were of John II, Manuel I, and Alexius III.
Location: Kazanluk, Archaeological Museum.
Recte 1203 billon trachea of the following description:

Manuel I

Second coinage   1 specimen (var. B; globus ✚̇ ; very worn).
Third coinage   18 specimens (many very worn, 8 specimens regularly clip-
                      ped).
Fourth coinage   27 specimens (many very worn; 17 specimens regularly clip-
                      ped).

Andronicus I

9 specimens (3 specimens regularly clipped).

Isaac II

167 specimens. Identifiable: var. A(a) – 2, A(b) – 11; var.
                B(b) – 43; var. C(a) – 7, C(b)
                – 21; var. D(a) – 7; ∴ ∵ on
                back of throne – 1. 9 specimens
                regularly clipped.

Alexius III

234 specimens (3 specimens regularly clipped).

"Bulgarian" Imitative

Type A   204 specimens
Type B   202 specimens
Type C   308 specimens

Unidentifiable

33 specimens

MUGLIZH (II) HOARD

Gerassimov, *IAI*, 26 (1963), p. 260.
Said to have been found in 1960, and to have consisted of over 16 kilos
   (*c.* 8000 pieces) of "copper" coins of Manuel I, Andronicus I, Isaac II, and
   Alexius III.
Location: Stara Zagora, Archaeological Museum.
Recte 6923 billon trachea of the following description:

Manuel I

Third coinage   1 specimen (second phase; very worn, regularly clipped).
Fourth coinage   1 specimen (var. A[c]).

Isaac II

24 specimens

Alexius III

49 specimens

"Bulgarian" Imitative

Type A   847 specimens
Type B   431 specimens
Type C   1887 specimens

Latin Imitative (larger module)

MINT OF CONSTANTINOPLE
Type A   171 specimens
Type B   7 specimens (incl. 1 overstruck on Isaac II).

MINT OF THESSALONICA

Type A	28 specimens
Type B	30 specimens (several specimens read TⱲKOMNH to right; 11 specimens are overstruck, 7 apparently on preceding type).
Type C	4 specimens

Latin Imitative (smaller module)

Type A	2462 specimens
Type B	124 specimens
Type D	106 specimens
Type E	168 specimens
Type F	3 specimens
Type G	151 specimens (most have loros-waist ⊡, but ▨ occurs at least once).

Theodore I, Comnenus-Lascaris

MINT OF NICAEA

First coinage   32 specimens (all but 1 have loros-waist ▦, and ▨ or ▤).

Second coinage   33 specimens (1 specimen, with exceptionally well-preserved

$$\begin{array}{cc} \Theta\epsilon & \text{KO} \\ \Delta\text{Ⱳ} & \text{MNH} \\ \text{C} & \text{NOC} \\ & \Lambda\Lambda \\ & \text{C} \end{array}$$

inscr. reads: the reverse of another is overstruck on the obverse of a coin of Alexius III—two diademed heads, emperor's labarum, ⊙ between figures, still remaining in view).

Unidentifiable

364 specimens

NAOUSA (PAROS) HOARD

Metcalf, *Annual of the British School of Archaeology at Athens*, 56 (1961), pp. 56–57.
Location: Athens.
Said to have been found in 1924, and to have consisted of 50 "bronze" scyphates (billon trachea) of the following description:

Isaac II

10 specimens (incl. specimens of the "Bulgarian" imitative series?).

Alexius III

14 specimens (incl. specimens of the "Bulgarian" imitative series?).

"Bulgarian" Imitative

Type A	23 specimens
Type B	?
Type C	?

Latin Imitative (larger module)

MINT OF CONSTANTINOPLE

Type A	1 specimen

MINT OF THESSALONICA

Type A	1 specimen

Theodore I, Comnenus-Lascaris

MINT OF NICAEA

First coinage	1 specimen

NICOSIA (I) HOARD

Unpublished.
Said to have been found in the early 1920's, and to have consisted then of 117 electrum trachea, of which several have since been sold.
Location (1965): in the hands of Messrs. Spink and Son Ltd., London.
110 electrum trachea of the following description:

John II

Var. I
Var. II } 78 specimens (var. A – 47; var. B – 31).

24*

Manuel I

MINT OF CONSTANTINOPLE
First coinage   2 specimens
Second coinage   8 specimens (var. A – 3; var. B – 5).
Type D   1 specimen

MINT OF THESSALONICA
Type C   21 specimens

NICOSIA (II) HOARD

Unpublished.
Reliably reported to the author as having been found near the cathedral at
    Nicosia, and to have consisted of several thousand billon trachea up to
    and including the Emperor Manuel I. Parcels of this hoard have come
    onto the market on several occasions: the one listed here, consisting of
    306 Constantinopolitan billon trachea, is now in the hands of Mr. P. D.
    Whitting, London, and seems to be a representative sample:

John II

First coinage   13 specimens
Second coinage   169 specimens. Identifiable: var. A – 70; var. B – 94; rest
                                  uncertain.

Manuel I

First coinage   80 specimens. Identifiable: var. A – 43; var. B – 21; rest un-
                                  certain.
Second coinage   18 specimens
Third coinage   11 specimens
Fourth coinage   15 specimens

NOVO SELO HOARD

Gerassimov, *IAI*, 25 (1962), p. 227.
Said to have been found in 1958, and to have consisted of 17 gold coins and
    750 "copper" coins of Alexius I, John II, and Isaac II.
Location: Plovdiv, Archaeological Museum.
Recte 17 Constantinopolitan gold hyperpyra, 744 Constantinopolitan billon
    trachea, and perhaps a half dozen unidentifiable and corroded billon pieces.

A̸ Hyperpyra

Alexius I

Var. II   3 specimens

John II

First coinage   3 specimens
Second coinage   4 specimens
Third coinage   3 specimens

Manuel I

Var. II   2 specimens (1 has ✗ below tablion).

Andronicus I
1 specimen

Isaac II
1 specimen (loros-waist ▨).

Bill. Trachea

Manuel I

Third coinage   252 specimens. Identifiable: first phase – 116, incl. var. A –
"slightly under half" (of *c.* 90);
var. B – 48; var. C – 1.
second phase – 17, incl. var.
B – 3; var. C – 5; var. D – 5;
rest uncertain.

Fourth coinage 367 specimens. Identifiable: var. A(a)–6, A(b) – 16, A(c) –41;
var. B(a) – 71, B(b) – 1; var.
C(a) – 30, C(b) – 10, C(c) – 3;
var. D(a) –15, D(b) – 9, D(d) –5;
rest uncertain.

Andronicus I
109 specimens

Isaac II
16 specimens

Unidentifiable
*c.*6 specimens

OBUDA HOARD

Kerényi, *Budapest Régiségei. A Budapesti Történeti Muzeum Évkönyve*, 16 (1950), pp. 541–47. Metcalf, *Coinage in the Balkans*, p. 112.
Location: Budapest?
475 Constantinopolitan billon trachea of the following description:

Manuel I

Third coinage　　24 specimens
Fourth coinage　388 specimens

Andronicus I

57 specimens

Isaac II

6 specimens

OSANICA HOARD

Metcalf, *Coinage in the Balkans*, p. 116 (a provisional publication only). See under "ZLATA HOARD."

OUSTOVO HOARD

Gerassimov, *IBAI*, 11 (1937), p. 324.
Said to have been found in 1936, and to have consisted of "copper" scyphate coins, including those of the empire of Thessalonica.
Location: Sofia, Archaeological Museum.
Recte 26 billon trachea of the following description:

Latin Imitative (larger module)

MINT OF CONSTANTINOPLE

Type B	2 specimens
Type D	1 specimen
Type O	3 specimens (all clipped).
Type P	1 specimen

Latin Imitative (smaller module).

Type B	3 specimens
Type F	1 specimen

Theodore Comnenus-Ducas

Type B	1 specimen (clipped).
Type D	1 specimen (clipped).

Manuel Comnenus-Ducas

Type C	2 specimens (clipped).
Type D	2 specimens (both clipped).
Type F	1 specimen (clipped?).
Type G	1 specimen (clipped).

John Comnenus-Ducas

(Series I)

Type D	1 specimen (clipped).

(Series III)

Type B	1 specimen
Type G	1 specimen
Type M	1 specimen
Type Q	1 specimen

Unidentifiable

2 specimens

OVCHARTSI HOARD

Gerassimov, *IAI*, 25 (1962), p. 227.
Said to have been found in 1958, and to have consisted of 3900 "copper" coins
   of Manuel I and Isaac II.
Location: Nova Zagora, Archaeological Museum.
Recte 3151 billon trachea of the following description:

Manuel I

First coinage	3 specimens (2 very worn).
Second coinage	2 specimens (var. A–1, globus ⦂●; var. B – 1, globus ✝●).
Third coinage	201 specimens. Identifiable: first phase – 76, incl. var. A – 24; var. B – 41; rest uncertain. second phase – 54, incl. var. A – 6; var. B – 7; var. C – 13; var. D – 12; rest uncertain.

Fourth coinage   379 specimens. Identifiable: var. A(a) – 3, A(b) – 8, A(c) – 36; var. B(a) – 59; var. C(a) – 111; var. D(a) – 33, D(b) – 17; rest uncertain.

Andronicus I

78 specimens. Identifiable: var. A – 14; var. B – 16; rest uncertain.

Isaac II

2481 specimens. Identifiable: var. A(a) – 53, A(b) – 302; var. B(a) – 3, B(b) – 808; var. C(a) – 165, C(b) – 308; var. D(a) – 50, D(b) – 25; ∴ ∴ or ∴ ∴ on back of throne – 49; ∴ ∴ on back of throne – 2; ✤ ✤ on back of throne – 1; – 1; rest uncertain.

"Bulgarian" Imitative

Type B   2 specimens
Type C   2 specimens

Latin Imitative (smaller module)

Type A   2 specimens

PAZARDZHIK HOARD

Gerassimov, *IBAI*, 11 (1937), pp. 322–23.
Said to have been found in 1936, and to have consisted of 700 "copper" scyphates of Manuel I, of which the authorities retained only 260.
Location: Pazardzhik, Archaeological Museum.
Recte 214 billon trachea of the following description:

Manuel I

Third coinage   1 specimen

Isaac II

13 specimens

Alexius III

20 specimens

"Bulgarian" Imitative

Type A   55 specimens
Type B   34 specimens
Type C   50 specimens

Latin Imitative (larger module)

MINT OF CONSTANTINOPLE
Type A   4 specimens
Type D   1 specimen

Latin Imitative (smaller module)

Type A   17 specimens

Unidentifiable

19 specimens

PIRDOP HOARD

Unpublished?
Location: Sofia, Archaeological Museum.
62 billon trachea of the following description:

Manuel I

Fourth coinage   2 specimens (both var. C[a]).

Isaac II

20 specimens. Identifiable: var. A(b) – 1; var. B(b) – 9; var.
C(b) – 2; var. D(a) – 1; ∴ ∴ on
back of throne – 1; rest uncertain. 1 specimen regularly clipped.

Alexius III

32 specimens

"Bulgarian" Imitative

Type A   2 specimens
Type B   6 specimens

PISARATSI HOARD

(Moushmov, *IBAI*, 5 [1928/29], p. 383?)

Probably part of a hoard said to have been found in 1927 at Makhala Pisaratsi, and to have consisted of 10 "gold" coins and 300 to 400 "copper" coins of John II. If such is the case, the gold coins were probably hyperpyra of John III of Nicaea, for the part of the hoard which is preserved is conspicuously of a late date.

Location: Sofia, Archaeological Museum.

Recte 70 billon trachea (only part of the original hoard) of the following description:

Manuel I

First coinage   2 specimens (both very worn).

Isaac II

2 specimens (1 regularly clipped).

Alexius III

8 specimens

"Bulgarian" Imitative

Type A   15 specimens
Type B   8 specimens
Type C   25 specimens

Latin Imitative (larger module)

MINT OF CONSTANTINOPLE
Type A   2(?) specimens
Type D   1 specimen (clipped).

Latin Imitative (smaller module)

Type A   4(?) specimens

Manuel Comnenus-Ducas

Type A(?)   1 specimen

John III, Ducas-Vatatzes

MINT OF THESSALONICA

Type K(?)   1 specimen

Unidentifiable

1 specimen

PLOVDIV (BOUNARDZHIK) HOARD

Tsonchev, *Godishnik na Narodniya Arkheologicheski Mouzei, Plovdiv*, 4 (1960),
   pp. 206–14.
Said to have been found in 1955, and to have consisted of 21 "copper" coins
   of Alexius I.
Location: Plovdiv, Archaeological Museum.
Recte 21 billon trachea of the following description:

Alexius I

MINT OF PHILIPPOPOLIS

21 specimens

PLOVDIV REGION HOARD

Unpublished?
Location: Plovdiv, Archaeological Museum.
94 Constantinopolitan billon trachea of the following description:

Alexius I

Third coinage   1 specimen (worn).

Manuel I

Third coinage   3 specimens

Isaac II

23 specimens (var. A[b] – 2; var. B[b] – 11; var. C[a] – 2,
          C[b] – 3; var. D[a] – 3; ∴ ∴ on back of
          throne – 1; ✠ ✠ on back of throne – 1).

Alexius III

67 specimens. Identifiable: var. A – 15; var. B(b) – 5; var.
          C(a) – 2, C(b) – 8; var. D(a) – 3,
          D(b) – 6; rest uncertain.

POKROVNIK HOARD

Gerassimov, *IAI*, 27 (1964), pp. 239–40.

Said to have been found in 1962, and to have consisted of 488 "copper" scyphates of Manuel I, Isaac II, Alexius III, and Theodore I. Commendably and unusually, the essential distinction between the "regular" imperial types and the "barbarous" imitations based on them was recognized in the report.

Location: Blagoevgrad, Archaeological Museum.

Recte 488 billon trachea of the following description:

Manuel I

Third coinage   2 specimens (both first phase, var. B).

Fourth coinage   9 specimens (var. A[c] – 2; var. C[a] – 9. 1 specimen regularly clipped).

Andronicus I

1 specimen (var. B).

Isaac II

66 specimens. Identifiable: var. A(b) – 15; var. B(b) – 18; var. C(a) – 7, C(b) – 8; var. D(a) – 3; rest uncertain.

Alexius III

98 specimens. Identifiable: var. A – 14; var. B(a) – 1, B(b) – 7; var. C(a) – 4, C(b) – 9; var. D(a) – 2, D(b) – 11; ⚭ – 2; loros-waists ⠌ ⊞ – 1; rest uncertain.

"Bulgarian" Imitative

Type A   118 specimens
Type B   51 specimens
Type C   85 specimens

Latin Imitative (larger module)

MINT OF CONSTANTINOPLE

Type A   18 specimens (incl. 3 specimens with two dots on labarum-shaft, 1 specimen with a single dot).

MINT OF THESSALONICA
Type A   1 specimen
Type B   1 specimen

Latin Imitative (smaller module)
Type A   35 specimens

Theodore I, Comnenus-Lascaris

MINT OF NICAEA
First coinage   3 specimens (– 1).

POSTALLAR HOARD

Mosser, ANS Numismatic Notes and Monographs, No. 67 (New York, 1935),
    pp. 68–69.
Location: Istanbul.
Said to have consisted of 2 illegible gold coins and 374 "copper" scyphates
    (billon trachea) of the following description—insofar as it can be recon-
    structed from the inadequate report:

Alexius III
31 specimens (no doubt including pieces of the "Bulgarian"
imitative series).

Latin Imitative (larger and smaller module)
MINT OF CONSTANTINOPLE
Type A/A   192 specimens
Type B/B   25 specimens?
Type C/C   4 specimens?

MINT OF THESSALONICA
Type A/D   14 specimens?
Type B/E   37 specimens?

MINT OF CONSTANTINOPLE (large module only)
Type P   8 specimens
Type R   3 specimens

Theodore I, Comnenus-Lascaris

MINT OF NICAEA

First coinage   9 specimens

Uncertain

53 specimens (incl. John III and Michael VIII?).

PRESLAV HOARD

Gerassimov, *IAI*, 20 (1955), p. 607.

Said to have been found in 1953, and to have consisted of 2 gold coins of John Ducas-Vatatzes and 12 "copper" coins—11 of Manuel "Angelus" of Thessalonica, and 1 of Alexius III.

Location: Sofia, Archaeological Museum.

Recte 2 gold hyperpyra of John Ducas-Vatatzes and about 40 billon trachea. The identifiable coins were as follows:

Ν HYPERPYRA

John III, Ducas-Vatatzes

Second coinage   2 specimens (both "late" style; 1 has dot above *obv.* throne, on right).

BILL. TRACHEA

Latin Imitative (larger module)

MINT OF CONSTANTINOPLE

Type E   1 specimen (?)
Type H   1 specimen
Type J   2 specimens
Type P   2 specimens (both clipped).
Type R   1 specimen

Latin Imitative (smaller module)

Type A   11 specimens
Type B   1 specimen
Type F   1 specimen

John Comnenus-Ducas

(Series III)

Type E   1 specimen
Type N   2 specimens

ROUSSÉ HOARD

Unpublished?

Said to have been found in 1965 and to have contained about 400 coins.

Seen by the author in Sofia, at the Archaeological Museum, but may since
have been returned to locality of finding.

195 billon trachea of the following description:

"Bulgarian" Imitative

Type A   1 specimen
Type C   6 specimens

Latin Imitative (smaller module)

Type A   175 specimens
Type B   3 specimens
Type D   3 specimens
Type E   1 specimen
Type G   6 specimens (loros-waist ⊞ – 1; ⊡ – 5).

SOFIA HOARD

Schlumberger, *Comptes-rendus de l'Académie des Inscriptions et Belles-Lettres*[4],
25 (1897), pp. 303–04. Metcalf, *HBN*, 16 (1962), p. 273.

The sum of evidence at present available seems to suggest that the hoard
consisted of at least 206 coins of the Emperors Romanus III–Alexius I.
Those of Alexius apparently included numbers of both metropolitan issues
of debased trachea, and one reformed hyperpyron—similarly of the metropolitan mint (var. I[B]).

SOUVATITÉ HOARD

Gerassimov, *IBAI*, 11 (1937), p. 317.

Said to have been found in 1934, and to have consisted of 805 "copper"
scyphates of Manuel I.

Location: Sofia, Archaeological Museum.

Recte 407 billon trachea (presumably only part of the original hoard) of the
following description:

John II

MINT OF CONSTANTINOPLE

Second coinage   7 specimens (var. A – 3; var. B – 4).

MINT OF THESSALONICA

1 specimen (worn).

Manuel I

Second coinage   24 specimens. Identifiable: var. A – 4 (✚ – 2; ⁚ – 2); var.
B – 11 (all ✚).

Third coinage   52 specimens. Identifiable: first phase – 36, incl. var. A – 16;
var. B – 13; rest uncertain.
second phase – 11, incl. var.
D – 7; rest uncertain.

Fourth coinage   290 specimens. Identifiable: var. A(a) – 26, A(b) – 30, A(c)
– 42; var. B(a) – 66, B(b) – 2;
var. C(a) – 22; var. D(a) – 11,
D(b) – 7; rest uncertain.

Andronicus I

5 specimens (var. A – 3; var. B – 2).

Isaac II

9 specimens. Identifiable: var. A(b) – 1; var. B(b) – 6; rest
uncertain.

Alexius III

8 specimens

"Bulgarian" Imitative

Type A   9 specimens

Latin Imitative (larger module)

MINT OF CONSTANTINOPLE

Type P   1 specimen (clipped, bright orange patina—intrusive?).

Unidentifiable

1 specimen

STARA ZAGORA HOARD

Gerassimov, *IBAI*, 15 (1946), p. 237.

Said to have been found in 1941, and to have consisted of 8 kilos of "copper" scyphates of John II, Manuel I, and Alexius III.

Location: Stara Zagora, Archaeological Museum.

Recte 8 kilos of billon trachea, encrusted with dirt, corroded, and in many cases fused together. A brief examination gave the following results:

Manuel I

Fourth coinage	6 specimens

Andronicus I

2 specimens (1 specimen regularly clipped).

Isaac II

8 specimens

Alexius III

13 specimens

"Bulgarian" Imitative

Type A	41 specimens
Type B	25 specimens
Type C	133 specimens

Latin Imitative (larger module)

MINT OF CONSTANTINOPLE

Type A	14 specimens
Type B	1 specimen

MINT OF THESSALONICA

Type A	1 specimen
Type B	2 specimens

Latin Imitative (smaller module)

Type A	89 specimens
Type E	3 specimens
Type G	4 specimens

Theodore I, Comnenus-Lascaris

MINT OF NICAEA

First coinage	6 specimens

STRAZHITSA HOARD

Gerassimov, *IAI*, 22 (1959), p. 359.

Said to have been found in 1956, and to have consisted of 35 kilos (*c.* 12 000 coins) of "copper" scyphates of Manuel I, Isaac II, and Alexius III.

Location: Turnovo, Archaeological Museum.

Recte No doubt 35 kilos of billon trachea. A sample thousand pieces were subjected to a brief examination, and the following results were obtained:

John II

Second coinage   1 specimen (extremely worn).

Manuel I

Third coinage   8 specimens (worn; 4 specimens regularly clipped).
Fourth coinage   34 specimens (worn; 17 specimens regularly clipped).

Andronicus I

6 specimens (3 specimens regularly clipped).

Isaac II

407 specimens

Alexius III

531 specimens

"Bulgarian" Imitative

Type B   2 specimens?
Type C   4 specimens?

Unidentifiable

7 specimens

SUEDINENIE HOARD

Gerassimov, *IAI*, 21 (1957), p. 325.

Said to have been found in 1955, and to have consisted of 12 gold coins of Alexius I and John II, and "copper" scyphates of John II.

Location: Stara Zagora, Archaeological Museum.

Some of the gold coins being away on exhibition in Sofia, the author was able to examine 5 gold hyperpyra and 21 billon trachea, of the following description:

N HYPERPYRA

Alexius I

MINT OF CONSTANTINOPLE
Var. II   3 specimens

MINT OF THESSALONICA
Var. V   1 specimen (long stem to globus cruciger, and pendilia ⌡ ⌡).

John II

Second coinage   1 specimen

BILL. TRACHEA

Alexius I

Third coinage   1 specimen

John II

Second coinage   20 specimens (all var. A; 19 certainly have six jewels to the collar-piece; 1 may have seven jewels. A very compact group as regards patina and state of preservation: possibly fresh from the mint).

"THESSALY" HOARD

Metcalf, *Annual of the British School of Archaeology at Athens*, 56 (1961), pp. 57–60.
Location: Athens.
Said to have been found in 1957, and to have consisted of over 600 "bronze" scyphates (billon trachea), of which 143 were described by Metcalf:

Manuel I

Third coinage   1 specimen
Fourth coinage   5 specimens

Andronicus I

1 specimen

Isaac II

32 specimens

388 COINAGE AND MONEY 1081-1261

COINAGE AND MONEY 1081-1261

Alexius III

37 specimens

"Bulgarian" Imitative

Type A	17 specimens
Type B	1 specimen
Type C	1 specimen

Latin Imitative (larger module)

MINT OF CONSTANTINOPLE

Type A	5 specimens

Latin Imitative (smaller module)

Type A	35 specimens
Type D	3 specimens
Type E	1 specimen
Type G	1 specimen

Theodore I, Comnenus-Lascaris

MINT OF NICAEA

First coinage	1 specimen

Uncertain (barbarous)

2 specimens

TIURKMEN (I) HOARD

Tsonchev, *Godishnik na Narodniya Arkheologicheski Mouzei, Plovdiv*, 4 (1960), pp. 206–14.

Said to have been found in 1953, and to have consisted of 11 "copper" coins of Manuel I.

Location: Plovdiv, Archaeological Museum.

Recte 11 Constantinopolitan billon trachea of the following description:

Manuel I

Third coinage	4 specimens (all first phase).
Fourth coinage	3 specimens (var. A[c] – 1; var. B[a] – 2).

Andronicus I
1 specimen

Isaac II
3 specimens (var. B[b] – 1; var. C[b] – 1; other uncertain).

TIURKMEN (II) HOARD

Gerassimov, *IAI*, 25 (1962), p. 233.
Said to have been found in 1959, and to have consisted of 116 "copper" scyphates of Manuel I, Andronicus I, and Isaac II. The close similarity between the contents of this hoard and the preceding render it very probable that they both represent parts of the same hoard, despite the apparent difference in the dates of finding.
Recte 117 Constantinopolitan billon trachea of the following description:

Manuel I
Third coinage — 37 specimens. Identifiable: first phase–26; second phase–10.
Fourth coinage — 60 specimens. Identifiable: var. A(a) – 1, A(b) – 1, A(c) – c. 12; var. B(a) – c. 12; var. C(a) – 15, C(b) – 5; var. D(a) – 11, D(b) – 2, D(c) – 1.

Andronicus I
17 specimens

Isaac II
3 specimens (var. A[a] – 1, A[b] – 1; var. B[b] – 1).

TORBALI HOARD

Bellinger, *Centennial Publication of the American Numismatic Society*, pp. 73–81.
Said to have been found about 1946, and to have consisted of 247 silver scyphates of Theodore I.
Location: Dumbarton Oaks.
Recte 247 silver trachea of the following description:

Theodore I, Comnenus-Lascaris

Type A   100 specimens
Type B   145 specimens

John III, Ducas-Vatatzes

Type D   1 specimen

Theodore II, Ducas-Lascaris

Type B   1 specimen

TOULOVO HOARD

Unpublished?
Location: Kazanluk, Archaeological Museum.
834 billon trachea of the following description:

Manuel I

Third coinage   3 specimens (all very worn; 2 specimens regularly clipped).
Fourth coinage 7 specimens (all very worn; 6 specimens regularly clipped).

Andronicus I

1 specimen

Isaac II

23 specimens (3 specimens regularly clipped).

Alexius III

42 specimens (2 specimens regularly clipped).

"Bulgarian" Imitative

Type A   65 specimens
Type B   64 specimens
Type C   161 specimens

Latin Imitative (larger module)

MINT OF CONSTANTINOPLE

Type A   11 specimens
Type B   1 specimen

MINT OF THESSALONICA

Type A	7 specimens
Type B	9 specimens (2 specimens overstruck on preceding type).

Latin Imitative (smaller module)

Type A	259 specimens
Type B	7 specimens
Type D	2 specimens
Type G	3 specimens

Theodore I, Comnenus-Lascaris

MINT OF NICAEA

First coinage	8 specimens
Second coinage	4 specimens (1 specimen apparently overstruck on Latin imitative, Thessalonica type A).

Unidentifiable

157 specimens (incl. 2 antique copper).

TRI VODITSI HOARD

Gerassimov, *IBAI*, 14 (1940–42), p. 285.

Said to have been found in 1940, and to have consisted of two kilos of "copper" scyphates of Manuel I, Andronicus I, and Isaac II.

Location: Pazardzhik, Archaeological Museum.

Recte 2 kilos of billon trachea, and 1 copper tetarteron. The identifiable coins were as follows:

BILL. TRACHEA

Manuel I

Third coinage	1 specimen
Fourth coinage	1 specimen

Isaac II

1 specimen

"Bulgarian" Imitative

Type B	2 specimens
Type C	37 specimens

Latin Imitative (larger module)

MINT OF CONSTANTINOPLE

Type A	(see small-module A).
Type B	2 specimens (both clipped).
Type C	(see small-module C).
Type D	22 specimens (all clipped).
Type F	7 specimens (all clipped).
Type H	6 specimens (all clipped).
Type J	7 specimens (several clipped).
Type O	10 specimens (all clipped).
Type P	16 specimens (several clipped).
Type R	8 specimens (several clipped).
Type T	12 specimens (several clipped).

MINT OF THESSALONICA

Type C	6 specimens

Latin Imitative (smaller module)

Type A	321 specimens (but incl. a "very few" of Con'ple large-module A).
Type B	10 specimens
Type C	16 specimens (but incl. a "very few" of Con'ple large-module C).
Type D	36 specimens
Type E	24 specimens
Type F	15 specimens
Type G	23 specimens

Theodore I, Comnenus-Lascaris

MINT OF NICAEA

Second coinage	4 specimens (all clipped).

MINT OF MAGNESIA

Type B	1 specimen (clipped).
Type C	1 specimen (clipped).

John III, Ducas-Vatatzes

MINT OF MAGNESIA

Type G	2 specimens

MINT OF THESSALONICA

Type K	1 specimen

Theodore Comnenus-Ducas

Type A   1 specimen (clipped).
Type C   1 specimen
Type F   4 specimens (all clipped; 2 read ΘЄΟΔѰΡΟC).
Type G   5 specimens

Manuel Comnenus-Ducas

Type D   2 specimens
Type G   2 specimens

John Comnenus-Ducas

(Series I)

Type D   3 specimens (all clipped).

(Series III)

Type E   1 specimen
Type Q   1 specimen

Æ TETARTERON

Manuel I

MINT OF THESSALONICA
Type A   1 specimen

TROAD HOARD

Bellinger, ANS *Museum Notes*, 11 (1964), pp. 222–24.
Found in the thirties(?) and described as consisting of 140 "copper" scyphates
    of the Emperors Manuel I–Theodore I.
Location: Yale University Library.
Recte 140 billon trachea of the following description:

Latin Imitative (larger module)

MINT OF CONSTANTINOPLE
Type A   1 specimen (No. 25).
Type B   23 specimens (Nos. 1–23).
Type E   1 specimen (No. 24).

MINT OF THESSALONICA
Type B   2 specimens (Nos. 26–27).

Theodore I, Comnenus-Lascaris

MINT OF NICAEA

First coinage   4 specimens (Nos. 28–31).
Second coinage   109 specimens (Nos. 32–140).

TSEPINA HOARD

Gerassimov, *IAI*, 29 (1966), p. 212 (under "Dorkovo").
Location: seen by the author in Sofia, at the Archaeological Museum, but may
    since have been returned to locality of finding.
Found in 1965, consisting of 16 billon trachea of the following description:

Manuel I

Fourth coinage   2 specimens

Isaac II

2 specimens

Alexius III

4 specimens

"Bulgarian" Imitative

Type A   4 specimens
Type B   1 specimen

Latin Imitative (smaller module)

Type A   1 specimen

Theodore I, Comnenus-Lascaris

MINT OF NICAEA

Second coinage   2 specimens (1 a torn half-piece).

TSRUNCHA (A) HOARD

Gerassimov, *IAI*, 27 (1964), p. 244.
Found in 1963 and said to have consisted of 4 kilos (1252 pieces) of "copper"
    scyphates of Manuel I, Andronicus I, Isaac II, and Alexius III.

Location: Pazardzhik, Archaeological Museum.
Recte 1248 billon trachea of the following description:

Manuel I

Third coinage   23 specimens. Identifiable: first phase – 12 ⎫ rest   uncertain.
                                                              ⎬ 2 specimens reg-
                   second phase – 6 ⎭ ularly clipped.

Fourth coinage 41 specimens. Identifiable: var. A(a) – 1, A(c) – 9; var.
                   B(a) – 7; var. C(a) – 12; var.
                   D(a) – 3, D(b) – 2; rest uncertain.
                   8 specimens regularly clipped.

Andronicus I
11 specimens (4 specimens regularly clipped).

Isaac II
332 specimens. Identifiable: var. A(a) – 9, A(b) – 34; var.
                   B(a) – 2, B(b) – 105; var. C(a)
                   – 18, C(b) – 52; var. D(a) – 41,
                   D(b) – 7; ∴ ∴ on back of throne
                   – 5; – 1; rest uncertain.
                   4 specimens regularly clipped.

Alexius III
533 specimens. Identifiable: var. A – 87; var. B(a) – 7, B(b)
                   – 12; var. C(a) – 15, C(b) – 96;
                   var. D(a) – 17, D(b) – 27; – 4;
                   rest uncertain. 10 specimens reg-
                   ularly clipped.

"Bulgarian" Imitative
Type A   105 specimens
Type B   150 specimens
Type C   52 specimens

Unidentifiable
1 specimen

TSRUNCHA (B) HOARD

Gerassimov, *IAI*, 27 (1964), p. 244.

Found in 1963, at much the same time and in the same place as the preceding hoard; said to have contained 3 kilos (922 pieces) of "copper" scyphates of Manuel I, Andronicus I, Isaac II, and Alexius III.

Location: Pazardzhik, Archaeological Museum.

Recte 923 billon trachea of the following description:

Manuel I

Third coinage   15 specimens. Identifiable: first phase – 9⎱rest   uncertain.
⎰3 specimens reg-
second phase–4⎰ularly clipped.

Fourth coinage   25 specimens. Identifiable: var. A(b) – 2; var. B(a) – 6; var. C(a) – 8; var. D(a) – 3, D(b) – 1; rest uncertain. 2 specimens regularly clipped.

Andronicus I

9 specimens (1 specimen regularly clipped).

Isaac II

245 specimens. Identifiable: var. A(a) – 3, A(b) – 35; var. B(b) – 79; var. C(a) – 14, C(b) – 35; var. D(a) – 10, D(b) – 3; ⠃ ⠃ on back of throne – 3; rest uncertain. Several specimens regularly clipped.

Alexius III

379 specimens. Identifiable: var. A – 48; var. B(a) – 4, B(b) – 6; var. C(a) – 12, C(b) – 63; var. D(a) – 10, D(b) – 27; ⚏ – 6; ⚏ – 1; rest uncertain. 1 specimen possibly regularly clipped.

"Bulgarian" Imitative

Type A   95 specimens
Type B   115 specimens
Type C   39 specimens

Unidentifiable

1 specimen

TURNOVO (I) HOARD

Unpublished?
Location: Sofia, Archaeological Museum.
53 Constantinopolitan billon trachea of the following description:

Manuel I

Third coinage 18 specimens. Identifiable: first phase – 9, incl. var. A – 2; var. B – 6; other uncertain. second phase – 7, incl. var. B – 1; var. C – 1; var. D – 4; other uncertain.

Fourth coinage 28 specimens. Identifiable: var. A(b) – 4, A(c) – 1; var. B(a) – 3; var. C(a) – 7; var. D(a) – 2, D(b) – 4; rest uncertain.

Andronicus I

7 specimens

TURNOVO (II) HOARD

Gerassimov, *IAI*, 27 (1964), p. 244.
Said to have been found in 1963, and to have consisted of 50 "copper" scyphates of Isaac II and Alexius III—presumably only part of the hoard.
Location: Turnovo, Archaeological Museum.
Recte 648 billon trachea of the following description:

Isaac Comnenus (Cyprus)

MAIN MINT
Type A 1 specimen (worn).

Isaac II

285 specimens. Identifiable: var. A(b) – 20; var. B(b) – 68; var. C(a) – 12, C(b) – 32; var. D(a) – 10, D(b) – 5; ⁚ ⁚ on back of throne – 3; rest uncertain. 3 specimens regularly clipped.

Alexius III

336 specimens. Identifiable: var. A – 11; var. B(a) – 2, B(b) – 8; var. C(a) – 6, C(b) – 29; var. D(a) – 4, D(b) – 17; ⚬ – 3; rest uncertain.

"Bulgarian" Imitative

Type A   4 specimens
Type B   22 specimens

TVURDITSA HOARD

Unpublished?
Location: Nova Zagora, Archaeological Museum.
217 billon trachea of the following description:

Manuel I

Third coinage   1 specimen (first phase, var. B).
Fourth coinage   11 specimens. Identifiable: var. B(a) – 1; var. C(a) – 4; var. D(d) – 1; rest uncertain. 6 specimens regularly clipped.

Isaac II

24 specimens. Identifiable: var. A(a) – 1, A(b) – 1; var. B(b) – 9; var. C(a) – 2, C(b) – 3; var. D(a) – 2, D(b) – 3; ∴ ∴ on back of throne – 1; rest uncertain. 2 specimens regularly clipped.

Alexius III

73 specimens. Identifiable: var. A – 6; var. B(b) – 6; var. C(a) – 7, C(b) – 13; var. D(a) – 2, D(b) - 23.

"Bulgarian" Imitative

Type A   34 specimens
Type B   59 specimens
Type C   15 specimens

HOARD OF UNCERTAIN BULGARIAN PROVENANCE
(Struma valley?)

Unpublished?
Location: Sofia, Archaeological Museum.
471 billon trachea of the following description:

Manuel I

Third coinage 13 specimens. Identifiable: first phase − 4⎫ rest uncertain.
second phase − 5⎭

Fourth coinage 25 specimens. Identifiable: var. A(a) − 1, A(b) − 3, A(c) − 2; var. B(a) − 8; var. C(a) − 7; var. D(a) − 1, D(b) − 1; rest uncertain. Several specimens regularly clipped.

Andronicus I

9 specimens

Isaac II

215 specimens. Identifiable: var. A(a) − 4, A(b) − 6; var. B(b) − 42; var. C(a) − 13, C(b) − 27; var. D(a) − 13, D(b) − 4; ⁘ ⁘ on back of throne − 1; ∴ ∴ on back of throne − 1; 🖼 − 1; rest uncertain.

Alexius III

117 specimens. Identifiable: var. A − 7; var. B(a) − 1, B(b) − 3; var. C(a) − 1, C(b) − 1; var. D(b) − 4; ▮ − 1; rest uncertain.

"Bulgarian" Imitative

Type A 47 specimens
Type B 12 specimens
Type C 18 specimens

Latin Imitative (larger module)

MINT OF CONSTANTINOPLE

Type A 8 specimens

MINT OF THESSALONICA
Type A   1 specimen
Type B   2 specimens

Latin Imitative (smaller module)

Type A   1 specimen

Theodore I, Comnenus-Lascaris

MINT OF NICAEA

First coinage   2 specimens (and).

Unidentifiable

1 specimen

YAGODA HOARD

Gerassimov, *IAI*, 27 (1964), p. 241.

Said to have been found in 1962, and to have consisted of 308 "copper" scyphates of Manuel I and Andronicus I.

Location: Kazanluk, Archaeological Museum.

Recte 308 Constantinopolitan billon trachea of the following description:

John II

Second coinage   1 specimen (var. B, collar of five jewels).

Manuel I

Second coinage   1 specimen (var. B, globus).

Third coinage   109 specimens. Identifiable: first phase – 77, incl. var. A – 28; var. B – 38; rest uncertain.
second phase – 28, incl. var. A – 3; var. B – 3; var. C – 6; var. D – 9; rest uncertain.

Fourth coinage   160 specimens. Identifiable: var. A(a) – 6, A(b) – 15, A(c) – 29; var. B(a) – 26; var. C(a) – 44; var. D(a) – 22, D(b) – 17; other uncertain.

Andronicus I

37 specimens. Identifiable: var. A – 11; var. B – 12; rest uncertain.

YENIMAHALLE HOARD

Unpublished.

Location (1967): in the possession of Mr. P. D. Whitting, London.

152 billon trachea of the following description:

Isaac II?

1 specimen?

Alexius III

1 specimen

Latin Imitative (larger module)

MINT OF CONSTANTINOPLE

Type A	25 specimens
Type B	21 specimens

MINT OF THESSALONICA

Type A	53 specimens
Type B	8 specimens
Type C	43 specimens

ZGURLI HOARD

Tacchella, *RN*⁴, 7 (1903), pp. 380–82.

Location: presumably dispersed.

A very large number of gold scyphates—hyperpyra—of the Emperors Alexius I–Isaac II. Tacchella reports having examined 240 pieces, giving the following analysis:

Alexius I	– 55 specimens
John II	– 65 specimens
Manuel I	– 62 specimens
Andronicus I	– 11 specimens
Isaac II	– 47 specimens

ZHELEZNITSA HOARD

Gerassimov, *IAI*, 27 (1964), p. 238.
Said to have been found in 1962, and to have consisted of 378 "copper" scyphates of Manuel I, Isaac II, Alexius III, and Theodore I.
Location: Blagoevgrad, Archaeological Museum.
Recte 378 billon trachea of the following description:

Manuel I

Fourth coinage   1 specimen (var. C[a] – ✳ ✱).

Isaac II

22 specimens. Identifiable: var. A(a) – 1, A(b) – 2; var. B(b) – 7; var. C(a) – 3; var. D(b) – 1; ∴ ∴ on back of throne – 1; ∷ ∷ on back of throne – 1; rest uncertain.

Alexius III

49 specimens. Identifiable: var. A – 1; var. B(b) – 1; var. C(b) – 7; var. D(b) – 9; rest uncertain.

"Bulgarian" Imitative

Type A   103 specimens
Type B   54 specimens
Type C   90 specimens

Latin Imitative (larger module)

MINT OF CONSTANTINOPLE
Type A   22 specimens (incl. 5 specimens with two dots on labarum-shaft).

Latin Imitative (smaller module)

Type A   33 specimens (incl. 1 specimen with a single dot on labarum-shaft).

Theodore I, Comnenus-Lascaris

MINT OF NICAEA
First coinage   4 specimens (– 1; – 1).

ZLATA HOARD

Metcalf, *Coinage in the Balkans*, p. 115 (a provisional publication only).
Location: Belgrade?
This hoard, together with those from Grabovac and Osanica in much the same
area of Yugoslavia, provides valuable confirmation of the chronological
developments in the pattern of the circulating medium that have already
been noticed in Bulgarian hoards. The Zlata hoard contains large numbers
of billon trachea of Manuel's last two metropolitan coinages, but only a
few of his first two and of his predecessor John. Andronicus is well represented, but there are very few of Isaac II. The Grabovac hoard contains
large numbers of billon trachea of Isaac II and Alexius III, in addition.
Whereas all the coins of the Zlata hoard are of large module, regular
fabric, and fine style, those from Grabovac betray the degeneration in all
three aspects that affected the products of the metropolitan mint *c.* 1190–
1203. The Osanica hoard consists mainly of what can only be the "Bulgarian" imitative series of coins, together with coins of the Latin imitative
series: Constantinople type A/small-module A; Thess. types A and B/small-
module D and E. It is dated by coins of the first Nicaean issue of Theodore I. Metcalf noticed the differences in the quality of the contents of
each of these hoards, but assumed a largely geographical—horizontal—
explanation, rather than a chronological—vertical—one.

ZLATARITSA HOARD

Filov, *IBAD*, 2 (1911), pp. 278–80.
Said to have been found in 1910, and to have consisted of 470 "copper"
scyphates of Manuel I and Andronicus I.
Location: Sofia, Archaeological Museum.
Recte 467 Constantinopolitan billon trachea of the following description:

Manuel I

Third coinage	125 specimens. Identifiable: first phase – 76, incl. var. A – 23; var. B. – 30; var. C – 3; rest uncertain.
	second phase – 19, incl. var. C – 4; var. D – 7; rest uncertain.
Fourth coinage	311 specimens. Identifiable: var. A(a) – 13, A(b) – 13, A(c) – 36; var. B(a) – 53, B(b) – 3; var. C(a) – 73; var. D(a) – 36, D(b) – 3, D(c) – 6, D(d) – 6; rest uncertain.

26*

Andronicus I

30 specimens. Identifiable: var. A – 6; var. B – 9; rest uncertain.

Alexius III

1 specimen

SUPPLEMENTARY NOTE

The following specimens and coin-types have come to the attention of the author since this book went to press.

ALEXIUS I

EL. DEBASED TRACHY

MINT OF CONSTANTINOPLE

Obv. IC XC in field.

Christ, bearded and nimbate, wearing tunic and colobion, seated upon throne with back; holds Gospels in left hand.

Rev. ΠΟΤΤШΚΟΜΝΗΝШ

Full-length figure of emperor wearing stemma, divitision, collar-piece, and jewelled loros of simplified type; holds in right hand labarum on long shaft, on which X, and in left, globus cruciger.

Pl. 51.*1*

Known only from an apparently unique specimen in the Münzkabinett, Berlin, the type has every appearance of being a transitional issue from the first few days or weeks of the reign. The reverse design has very obvious connections with two electrum trachy types of Nicephorus III (Pls. 47.*5*; 51.*2*). It possesses the X on the labarum-shaft which characterizes the former, but, like the latter, lacks the "tear-drop" ornament below the globus cruciger. The obverse is very close to that of the second trachy of Nicephorus, but the jewelling on the edges of the back of the throne can be precisely paralleled only on the first coinage of Alexius himself (e.g., Pl. 51.*3*).

It is possible, but to judge from the photograph very unlikely, that the piece is a contemporary forgery.

THEODORE I

Æ TRACHY

MINT OF NICAEA

Obv. IC XC in field.

Full-length figure of Christ, standing on dais, bearded and nimbate, wearing tunic and colobion; holds Gospels in left hand. ✳ ✳ in field.

405

Rev.   ΔO

Full-length figure of emperor on left, and of St. Theodore, bearded and nimbate, holding between them patriarchal cross on long shaft at base of which a large globe. Emperor wears stemma, divitision, collar-piece, and jewelled loros of simplified type; holds sheathed sword in right hand. Saint wears short military tunic and breastplate; holds sheathed sword in left hand.

Pl. 51.5

Quite clearly a copy of the electrum type C of Manuel I, the thirteenth-century character of the issue is betrayed only by stylistic considerations and by the late form of loros-waist (▨). The details of the Saint's dress place the issue with the "Nicaean" group rather than with the "Magnesian." See *supra*, p. 233.

JOHN III

Æ TRACHY

MINT OF MAGNESIA

Obv. I͞C X͞C
    +   + in field.

Bust of Christ, beardless and nimbate, wearing tunic and colobion; holds scroll in left hand.

Rev. W̄ O
    C Δ
       ᴚ
       K
       Λ
       C

Full-length figure of emperor wearing stemma, divitision, jewelled loros of simplified type, and sagion; holds in right hand labarum on long shaft, and in left, globus surmounted by patriarchal cross.

(Ashmolean Museum, Oxford)

The reverse design, and in particular the shape of the sagion as it drapes from the emperor's left arm, closely resembles that of the billon type C of Theodore II (Pl. 35.9–*11*). This probably indicates a date late in John's reign for the issue.

BILL. TRACHY

MINT OF MAGNESIA

Obv. ⊘ ⅁

Three-quarter-length figure of St. George, nimbate, wearing tunic, breast-plate, and sagion; holds in right hand spear, resting over shoulder, and in left, shield.

Rev. IⱲ   O   CⱭK

Half-length figure of emperor wearing stemma, divitision, collar-piece, and panelled loros of simplified type; holds in right hand labarum-headed scepter, and in left, globus cruciger.

Pl. 51.*6*

THEODORE II

BILL. TRACHY

MINT OF MAGNESIA

Obv. ӀC̄ X̄C
OЄ NɎ
M   H

Bust of Christ Emmanuel, beardless and nimbate, wearing tunic and colobion; holds scroll in left hand.

Rev. Ᵽ
Δ
OC   KⱯ
CC   C

Full-length figure of emperor on left, and of beardless, nimbate saint (Tryphon?), holding between them long shaft, at the head of which lys, and at the base, small globe. Emperor wears stemma, divitision, jewelled loros of simplified type, and sagion; holds labarum(?) on long shaft in right hand. Saint wears tunic and colobion; holds jewelled scepter, with triple head, in left hand.

(Ashmolean Museum, Oxford)

MANUEL COMNENUS-DUCAS

BILL. TRACHY

MINT OF THESSALONICA

Obv. KЄRO HΘЄӀ . ӀC̄ X̄C̄ in field.

Bust of Christ, beardless and nimbate, wearing tunic and colobion; holds scroll in left hand.

Rev. MⱭNɎHⱭΔЄC ПOT OKⱲ

Full-length figure of emperor on left, crowned by St. Constantine. Emperor wears stemma, divitision, jewelled loros of simplified type, and sagion; holds anexikakia in left hand. Saint, similarly dressed, holds scepter (cruciger?) in left hand.

Pl. 51.*7,8*

JOHN COMNENUS-DUCAS (Series I and III)

BILL. TRACHY

MINT OF THESSALONICA

Obv.

Cross-within-circle, surmounting triangular decoration on long shaft, between outstretched wings. On either wing, below forepart, a human head.

Rev.

Full-length figure of emperor on left, crowned by bearded, nimbate bishop-saint (Nicholas?). Emperor wears stemma, divitision, collar-piece, and jewelled loros of simplified type; holds in right hand scepter cruciger, and in left, anexikakia. Saint wears customary episcopal vestments, of which omophorion is plainly visible; holds Gospels in left hand.

An extraordinary issue, recently published (in the large-module) by Mme Oikonomides ("Contribution à l'étude de la numismatique byzantine du XIIIᵉ siècle," *RN*⁶, 9 [1967], p. 261, no. 77). If, as seems probable from the illustration, the emperor is beardless, he will be John Comnenus-Ducas. A small-module piece, apparently of identical obverse and reverse type, is to be found in: Bertelè, *L'imperatore alato*, p. 34, no. 53. It seems improbable that the obverse type should have any political significance.

KEY TO PLATES
and
INDEXES

Key to Plates

ANS — American Numismatic Society
BM — British Museum [followed by
  Wroth Catalogue Number]
BN — Bibliothèque Nationale
DO — Dumbarton Oaks

DO(W) — Dumbarton Oaks (Whittemore
  Loan)
JHU — Johns Hopkins University, Baltimore
  (Garrett Collection)
O — Oxford, Ashmolean Museum

PLATE 1

Alexius I. Pre-reform (1081–92). Debased Trachy

1	Constantinople	First coinage	El.	4.30 gm.	DO
2	Constantinople	First coinage	El.	4.42 gm.	DO
3	Constantinople	First coinage	El.		O (Goodacre Loan)
4	Constantinople	First coinage	El.	4.41 gm.	DO
5	Constantinople	Second coinage	El.	4.39 gm.	DO
6	Constantinople	Second coinage	Æ	4.52 gm.	DO
7	Constantinople	Second coinage	Æ	4.38 gm.	DO(W)
8	Constantinople	Second coinage	Bill.	4.34 gm.	DO(W)
9	Thessalonica	First coinage	El.	3.43 gm.	DO
10	Thessalonica	Second coinage	Æ	3.64 gm.	DO
11	Thessalonica	Second coinage	Æ	4.05 gm.	DO(W)
12	Thessalonica	Second coinage	Bill.	4.19 gm.	DO(W)

PLATE 2

Alexius I. Pre-reform (1081–92). Debased Tetarteron

1	Constantinople	First coinage	El.	3.82 gm.	DO
2	Constantinople	First coinage	Æ	3.92 gm.	DO
3	Constantinople	Second coinage	Æ	4.05 gm.	DO
4	Constantinople	Second coinage	Æ	3.81 gm.	DO(W)
5	Constantinople	Second coinage	Æ	3.78 gm.	DO
6	Thessalonica	First coinage	Æ	3.61 gm.	DO
7	Thessalonica	First coinage	Æ	3.77 gm.	DO
8	Thessalonica	First coinage	Æ	3.04 gm.	DO(W)
9	Thessalonica	First coinage	Æ	3.16 gm.	DO(W)
10	Thessalonica	Second coinage	Æ	3.65 gm.	DO
11	Thessalonica	Second coinage	Æ	3.79 gm.	DO
12	Thessalonica	Second coinage	Bill.	3.14 gm.	DO

Light-weight Scyphate

13	Constantinople		Æ	1.89 gm.	DO

Miliaresion or Fraction

14	Constantinople	Type A	Æ	2.07 gm.	BM 31
15	Constantinople	Type B	Æ	0.97 gm.	DO

411

16	Constantinople	Type B	Æ	0.74 gm.	DO
17	Thessalonica		Æ	1.06 gm.	BM 37 (Alexius III)

Follis

18	Constantinople	First coinage	Æ	6.99 gm.	DO
19	Constantinople	First coinage	Æ	5.56 gm.	DO
20	Constantinople	Second coinage	Æ	5.20 gm.	DO
21	Constantinople	Second coinage	Æ	5.94 gm.	DO
22	Constantinople	Third coinage	Æ		Private Collection

PLATE 3

Alexius I. Pre-reform (1081–92). Follis

1	Thessalonica	Type A	Æ	7.35 gm.	DO
2	Thessalonica	Type B	Æ	2.96 gm.	BM 55
3	Eastern(?)		Æ	6.42 gm.	DO

Alexius I. Post-reform (1092–1118). Hyperpyron

4	Constantinople	Second coinage (IA [i])	Aʋ	4.23 gm.	DO
5	Constantinople	Second coinage (IA [ii])	Aʋ	4.41 gm.	DO(W)
6	Constantinople	Second coinage (IA [iii])	Aʋ	4.30 gm.	DO(W)
7	Constantinople	Second coinage (IA [iii])	Aʋ	4.04 gm.	DO
8	Constantinople	Second coinage (IA [iii])	Aʋ	4.41 gm.	DO
9	Constantinople	Second coinage (IB [i])	Aʋ		Sale Catalogue (Unidentified)
10	Constantinople	Second coinage (IB [ii])	Aʋ	4.42 gm.	DO(W)

PLATE 4

Alexius I. Post-reform (1092–1118). Hyperpyron

1	Constantinople	Second coinage (IB [iii])	Aʋ	4.22 gm.	DO
2	Constantinople	Second coinage (IB [iii])	Aʋ	4.46 gm.	DO(W)
3	Constantinople	Second coinage (II)	Aʋ	4.37 gm.	DO(W)
4	Constantinople	Second coinage (II)	Aʋ	4.40 gm.	DO
5	Constantinople	Second coinage (II)	Aʋ	4.37 gm.	DO(W)
6	Thessalonica	Var. I	Aʋ	4.25 gm.	DO
7	Thessalonica	Var. I	Aʋ	4.35 gm.	DO(W)
8	Thessalonica	Var. I	Aʋ		Gornoslav Hoard
9	Thessalonica	Var. I	Aʋ		Gornoslav Hoard
10	Thessalonica	Var. I	Aʋ	4.36 gm.	DO(W)

PLATE 5

Alexius I. Post-reform (1092–1118). Hyperpyron

1	Thessalonica	Var. II	Aʋ	4.19 gm.	DO
2	Thessalonica	Var. II	Aʋ		Gornoslav Hoard
3	Thessalonica	Var. IV(A)	Aʋ		Gornoslav Hoard
4	Thessalonica	Var. IV(A)	Aʋ		Gornoslav Hoard
5	Thessalonica	Var. IV(B)	Aʋ		Gornoslav Hoard
6	Thessalonica	Var. IV(B)	Aʋ		Gornoslav Hoard

7	Thessalonica	Var. V	Aʹ	4.33 gm.	DO
8	Thessalonica	Var. V	Aʹ		Gornoslav Hoard
9	Thessalonica	Var. VI	Aʹ	4.38 gm.	DO
10	Thessalonica	Var. VI	Aʹ	4.34 gm.	DO(W)
11	Philippopolis(?)	Var. I	Aʹ		Gornoslav Hoard
12	Philippopolis(?)	Var. I	Aʹ		Gornoslav Hoard
13	Philippopolis(?)	Var. II	Aʹ		Gornoslav Hoard
14	Unknown mint		Aʹ		Gornoslav Hoard

PLATE 6

Alexius I. Post-reform (1092–1118). Aspron Trachy

1	Constantinople	First coinage	El.	4.38 gm.	BN
2	Constantinople	Second coinage	El.		BN
3	Constantinople	Second coinage	El.	4.50 gm.	DO
4	Constantinople	Second coinage	El.	4.36 gm.	DO(W)
5	Constantinople	Second coinage	El.		O
6	Thessalonica		El.	4.25 gm.	DO(W)
7	Thessalonica		El.		BN
8	Thessalonica		El.	4.34 gm.	DO
9	Thessalonica		El.	4.35 gm.	BM 23

Aspron Trachy

10	Constantinople	First coinage	Bill.		O (Goodacre Loan)
11	Constantinople	First coinage	Bill.	3.11 gm.	DO

PLATE 7

Alexius I. Post-reform (1092–1118). Aspron Trachy

1	Constantinople	Second coinage	Bill.		O (Goodacre Loan)
2	Constantinople	Third coinage	Bill.		O (Goodacre Loan)
3	Constantinople	Third coinage	Bill.	3.94 gm.	DO(W)
4	Constantinople	Third coinage	Bill.	3.50 gm.	DO
5	Constantinople	Fourth coinage	Bill.	3.99 gm.	DO
6	Constantinople	Fourth coinage	Bill.	3.83 gm.	DO
7	Thessalonica		Bill.		Whitting Collection
8	Philippopolis		Bill.		Whitting Collection
9	Philippopolis		Bill.	4.11 gm.	DO

Tetarteron

10	Constantinople	Type A	Æ	4.69 gm.	DO
11	Constantinople	Type A	Æ	4.38 gm.	DO

PLATE 8

Alexius I. Post-reform (1092–1118). Tetarteron

1	Constantinople	Type B	Æ	3.01 gm.	DO
2	Constantinople	Type B	Æ	3.49 gm.	DO(W)
3	Constantinople	Type C	Æ	3.91 gm.	DO(W)
4	Constantinople	Type C	Æ	3.72 gm.	DO

5	Constantinople	Type D	Æ	3.99 gm.	DO
6	Constantinople	Type D	Æ	3.83 gm.	DO(W)
7	Thessalonica	First coinage	Æ	4.03 gm.	DO
8	Thessalonica	First coinage	Æ	3.87 gm.	DO
9	Thessalonica	Second coinage	Æ	4.02 gm.	DO
10	Thessalonica	Third coinage	Æ	3.98 gm.	DO
11	Thessalonica	Third coinage	Æ	3.36 gm.	DO
12	Thessalonica	Third coinage	Æ	1.10 gm.	DO
13	Thessalonica	Type D	Æ	2.87 gm.	DO
14	Thessalonica	Type D	Æ	2.37 gm.	DO
15	Thessalonica	Type D	Æ	0.90 gm.	DO
16	Thessalonica	Type E	Æ	2.44 gm.	BM 46

Half-tetarteron

17	Thessalonica		Æ	2.15 gm.	DO

PLATE 9

John II (1118–43). Hyperpyron

1	Constantinople	First coinage	AV	4.02 gm.	DO
2	Constantinople	First coinage	AV	4.05 gm.	DO
3	Constantinople	First coinage	AV	4.35 gm.	DO
4	Constantinople	Second coinage	AV	4.22 gm.	DO
5	Constantinople	Second coinage	AV	4.40 gm.	DO(W)
6	Constantinople	Third coinage (A)	AV	4.26 gm.	DO(W)
7	Constantinople	Third coinage (A)	AV	4.34 gm.	DO
8	Constantinople	Third coinage (B)	AV	4.43 gm.	DO
9	Constantinople	Third coinage (B)	AV	4.11 gm.	DO
10	Thessalonica	First coinage	AV	4.49 gm.	DO(W)
11	Thessalonica	Second coinage	AV	4.55 gm.	DO
12	Thessalonica	Transitional coinage	AV		BN
13	Thessalonica	Third coinage	AV	4.30 gm.	DO(W)
14	Thessalonica	Third coinage	AV	4.35 gm.	DO(W)

PLATE 10

John II (1118–43). Aspron Trachy

1	Constantinople	Var. I(A)	El.	4.36 gm.	DO
2	Constantinople	Var. I(B)	El.	4.45 gm.	DO
3	Constantinople	Var. II(A)	El.	4.40 gm.	DO
4	Constantinople	Var. II(B)	El.	4.39 gm.	DO
5	Thessalonica		El.	4.13 gm.	DO
6	Thessalonica		El.		BN

Aspron Trachy

7	Constantinople	First coinage	Bill.	3.59 gm.	DO
8	Constantinople	First coinage	Bill.	3.92 gm.	DO
9	Constantinople	Second coinage (A)	Bill.	3.67 gm.	DO
10	Constantinople	Second coinage (A)	Bill.	3.27 gm.	DO
11	Constantinople	Second coinage (B)	Bill.	5.00 gm.	DO

PLATE 11

John II (1118–43). Aspron Trachy

1	Constantinople	Second coinage (B)	Bill.	3.81 gm.	DO
2	Constantinople	Second coinage (B)	Bill.	4.56 gm.	DO
3	Thessalonica		Bill.	4.46 gm.	DO
4	Thessalonica		Bill.		BN

Tetarteron

5	Constantinople	Type A	Æ	4.15 gm.	DO
6	Constantinople	Type A	Æ	3.33 gm.	DO
7	Constantinople	Type A	Æ/Bill.	4.14 gm.	DO
8	Constantinople	Type B	Æ	4.57 gm.	DO
9	Constantinople	Type B	Æ	3.52 gm.	DO
10	Constantinople	Type B	Æ	3.30 gm.	DO
11	Thessalonica		Æ	2.62 gm.	DO
12	Thessalonica		Æ	2.63 gm.	DO

Half-tetarteron

13	Thessalonica	Type A	Æ	1.74 gm.	DO
14	Thessalonica	Type A	Æ	2.30 gm.	DO
15	Thessalonica	Type B	Æ	2.92 gm.	DO
16	Thessalonica	Type B	Æ	1.58 gm.	DO
17	Thessalonica	Type B	Æ	1.51 gm.	DO

PLATE 12

Manuel I (1143–80). Hyperpyron

1	Constantinople	Var. I	N	3.91 gm.	DO
2	Constantinople	Var. I	N	4.20 gm.	DO
3	Constantinople	Var. I	N	4.15 gm.	DO
4	Constantinople	Var. I	N	4.47 gm.	DO
5	Constantinople	Var. II	N	4.34 gm.	DO(W)
6	Constantinople	Var. II	N	4.21 gm.	DO(W)
7	Constantinople	Var. III (A)	N	4.28 gm.	DO(W)
8	Constantinople	Var. III (B)	N	4.43 gm.	DO(W)
9	Constantinople	Var. IV	N	4.34 gm.	DO(W)
10	Constantinople	Var. V	N	4.48 gm.	DO(W)
11	Constantinople	Var. V	N	4.42 gm.	DO
12	Thessalonica		N		Hess-Leu Sale 5.iv.55, no. 245

PLATE 13

Manuel I (1143–80). Aspron Trachy

1	Constantinople	First coinage	(A)	El.	4.33 gm.	DO
2	Constantinople	First coinage	(B)	El.	4.56 gm.	DO(W)
3	Constantinople	Second coinage	(A)	El.	4.19 gm.	DO
4	Constantinople	Second coinage	(B)	El.	4.32 gm.	DO
5	Constantinople	Type C	(A)	El.	4.47 gm.	DO(W)
6	Constantinople	Type C	(A)	El.	4.56 gm.	DO(W)

7	Constantinople	Type C	(B)	El.	4.17 gm.	DO(W)
8	Constantinople	Type C	(B)	El.	4.17 gm.	DO
9	Constantinople	Type C	(C)	El.	4.11 gm.	DO
10	Constantinople	Type D	(A)	El.	4.10 gm.	DO(W)
11	Constantinople	Type D	(B)	El.	4.47 gm.	DO(W)
12	Constantinople	Type D	(C)	El.	3.96 gm.	DO(W)

PLATE 14

Manuel I (1143–80). Aspron Trachy

1	Constantinople	Type E (A)	El.	4.24 gm.	DO(W)
2	Constantinople	Type E (A)	El.	4.21 gm.	DO(W)
3	Constantinople	Type E (B)	El.	4.56 gm.	DO(W)
4	Constantinople	Type E (C)	El.	4.54 gm.	DO(W)
5	Thessalonica	First coinage	El.	2.64 gm.	DO
6	Thessalonica	Second coinage	El.	3.59 gm.	DO
7	Thessalonica	Type C	El.	3.98 gm.	DO
8	Thessalonica	Type C	El.	4.42 gm.	DO
9	Thessalonica	Type C	El.	4.23 gm.	DO

Aspron Trachy

10	Constantinople	First coinage (A)	Bill.	2.87 gm.	DO
11	Constantinople	First coinage (A)	Bill.	4.05 gm.	DO
12	Constantinople	First coinage (B)	Bill.	3.51 gm.	DO
13	Constantinople	First coinage (B)	Bill.	3.38 gm.	DO

PLATE 15

Manuel I (1143–80). Aspron Trachy

1	Constantinople	Second coinage (A)	Bill.	5.67 gm.	DO
2	Constantinople	Second coinage (A)	Bill.	5.44 gm.	DO
3	Constantinople	Second coinage (B)	Bill.	3.84 gm.	DO
4	Constantinople	Second coinage (B)	Bill.	3.19 gm.	DO
5	Constantinople	Third coinage (Ph. 1: [A])	Bill.	2.88 gm.	DO
6	Constantinople	Third coinage (Ph. 1: [A])	Bill.	4.78 gm.	DO(W)
7	Constantinople	Third coinage (Ph. 1: [B])	Bill.	3.44 gm.	DO
8	Constantinople	Third coinage (Ph. 1: [B])	Bill.	3.25 gm.	DO
9	Constantinople	Third coinage (Ph. 1: [B])	Bill.	4.91 gm.	DO(W)
10	Constantinople	Third coinage (Ph. 1: [C])	Bill.	4.07 gm.	DO
11	Constantinople	Third coinage (Ph. 2: [B])	Bill.	4.89 gm.	DO
12	Constantinople	Third coinage (Ph. 2: [C])	Bill.	4.15 gm.	DO
13	Constantinople	Third coinage (Ph. 2: [D])	Bill.	4.47 gm.	DO(W)

PLATE 16

Manuel I (1143–80). Aspron Trachy

1	Constantinople	Fourth coinage (A [a])	Bill.	4.58 gm.	DO
2	Constantinople	Fourth coinage (A [a])	Bill.	3.84 gm.	DO
3	Constantinople	Fourth coinage (A [b])	Bill.	3.88 gm.	DO

4	Constantinople	Fourth coinage (A [b])	Bill.	3.79 gm.	DO
5	Constantinople	Fourth coinage (A [c])	Bill.	3.24 gm.	DO
6	Constantinople	Fourth coinage (A [c])	Bill.	4.92 gm.	DO
7	Constantinople	Fourth coinage (B [a])	Bill.	4.41 gm.	DO
8	Constantinople	Fourth coinage (B [a])	Bill.	3.96 gm.	DO
9	Constantinople	Fourth coinage (B [a])	Bill.	2.72 gm.	DO
10	Constantinople	Fourth coinage (C [a])	Bill.	3.66 gm.	DO
11	Constantinople	Fourth coinage (C [a])	Bill.	3.08 gm.	DO
12	Constantinople	Fourth coinage (C [b])	Bill.	5.85 gm.	DO
13	Constantinople	Fourth coinage (C [b])	Bill.	4.32 gm.	DO
14	Constantinople	Fourth coinage (D [a])	Bill.	3.68 gm.	DO(W)
15	Constantinople	Fourth coinage (D [a])	Bill.	3.66 gm.	DO

PLATE 17

Manuel I (1143–80). Aspron Trachy

1	Constantinople	Fourth coinage (D [b])	Bill.	3.98 gm.	DO
2	Constantinople	Fourth coinage (D [b])	Bill.	3.85 gm.	DO
3	Constantinople	Fourth coinage (D [c])	Bill.	4.39 gm.	DO
4	Constantinople	Fourth coinage (D [c])	Bill.	4.28 gm.	DO

Tetarteron

5	Constantinople	First coinage	Æ	2.88 gm.	DO
6	Constantinople	First coinage	Æ/Bill.	4.04 gm.	DO
7	Constantinople	Type B	Æ	3.83 gm.	DO
8	Constantinople	Type B	Æ	3.42 gm.	DO
9	Constantinople	Type C	Æ	3.68 gm.	DO
10	Constantinople	Type C	Æ	4.01 gm.	DO(W)
11	Constantinople	Type D	Æ	3.16 gm.	DO
12	Constantinople	Type D	Æ	4.87 gm.	DO(W)
13	Thessalonica	Type A	Æ	5.40 gm.	DO
14	Thessalonica	Type A	Æ	4.03 gm.	DO
15	Thessalonica	Type B	Æ	5.00 gm.	DO
16	Thessalonica	Type B	Æ	2.94 gm.	DO

Half-tetarteron

17	Thessalonica	Type A	Æ	2.69 gm.	DO
18	Thessalonica	Type A	Æ	2.94 gm.	DO
19	Thessalonica	Type B	Æ	2.86 gm.	DO
20	Thessalonica	Type B	Æ	3.45 gm.	DO

PLATE 18

Manuel I (1143–80). Half-tetarteron

1	Uncertain Gk. mint	Type A	Æ	1.49 gm.	DO
2	Uncertain Gk. mint	Type A	Æ	1.81 gm.	DO
3	Uncertain Gk. mint	Type B	Æ	1.53 gm.	DO
4	Uncertain Gk. mint	Type B	Æ	2.26 gm.	DO
5	Uncertain Gk. mint	Type C	Æ	1.99 gm.	DO
6	Uncertain Gk. mint	Type C	Æ	1.69 gm.	DO

7	Uncertain Gk. mint	Type D	Æ	1.85 gm.	DO
8	Uncertain Gk. mint	Type D	Æ	1.75 gm.	DO

Andronicus I (1183–85). Hyperpyron

9	Constantinople		*N*	4.16 gm.	DO(W)
10	Constantinople		*N*	4.39 gm.	DO

Aspron Trachy

11	Constantinople	(Var. A)	El.	4.20 gm.	DO(W)
12	Constantinople	(Var. B)	El.	3.81 gm.	DO

Aspron Trachy

13	Constantinople	(Var. A)	Bill.	3.67 gm.	DO
14	Constantinople	(Var. A)	Bill.	3.83 gm.	DO
15	Constantinople	(Var. B)	Bill.	3.46 gm.	DO
16	Constantinople	(Var. B)	Bill.	5.58 gm.	DO(W)

PLATE 19

Andronicus I (1183–85). Tetarteron

1	Constantinople		Æ	4.29 gm.	DO(W)
2	Thessalonica	Type A	Æ	4.49 gm.	DO
3	Thessalonica	Type B	Æ	2.55 gm.	BM 19

Half-tetarteron

4	Uncertain Gk. mint		Æ	1.38 gm.	DO

Isaac of Cyprus (1184–91). Aspron Trachy

5	Main mint (Nicosia?)		El.		O (Goodacre Loan)

Aspron Trachy

6	Main mint (Nicosia?)	Type A	Bill.	3.69 gm.	DO
7	Main mint (Nicosia?)	Type A	Bill.	3.50 gm.	DO
8	Main mint (Nicosia?)	Type B	Bill.		ANS
9	Main mint (Nicosia?)	Type B	Bill.		ANS
10	Main mint (Nicosia?)	Type B	Bill.	4.42 gm.	DO
11	Secondary mint		Bill.		ANS

Tetarteron

12	Main mint (Nicosia?)	Type A	Æ	2.48 gm.	DO
13	Main mint (Nicosia?)	Type B	Æ		O (Goodacre Loan)
14	Main mint (Nicosia?)	Type B	Æ		BM (Not in Wroth)
15	Secondary mint		Æ		Cox, *Curium*, no. 731

PLATE 20

Isaac II (1185–95). Hyperpyron

1	Constantinople	(Var. A)	*N*	4.36 gm.	DO
2	Constantinople	(Var. A)	*N*	4.60 gm.	DO
3	Constantinople	(Var. B)	*N*		BN
4	Constantinople	(Var. B)	*N*	4.26 gm.	DO

Aspron Trachy

5	Constantinople	(Var. A)	El.	3.17 gm.	DO(W)
6	Constantinople	(Var. A)	El.	4.60 gm.	DO(W)

7	Constantinople	(Var. B)	El.	4.40 gm.	DO(W)
8	Constantinople	(Var. B)	El.	4.04 gm.	DO(W)

Aspron Trachy

9	Constantinople	(Var. A [a])	Bill.	4.51 gm.	DO
10	Constantinople	(Var. A [b])	Bill.	5.11 gm.	DO
11	Constantinople	(Var. A [b])	Bill.	3.96 gm.	DO
12	Constantinople	(Var. B [a])	Bill.	3.54 gm.	DO(W)
13	Constantinople	(Var. B [b])	Bill.	3.09 gm.	DO

PLATE 21

Isaac II (1185–95). Aspron Trachy

1	Constantinople	(Var. C [a])	Bill.	2.81 gm.	DO
2	Constantinople	(Var. C [a])	Bill.	2.49 gm.	DO(W)
3	Constantinople	(Var. C [b])	Bill.	3.97 gm.	DO
4	Constantinople	(Var. C [b])	Bill.	3.74 gm.	DO
5	Constantinople	(Var. D [a])	Bill.	2.55 gm.	DO
6	Constantinople	(Var. D [a])	Bill.	2.53 gm.	DO
7	Constantinople	(Var. D [b])	Bill.	2.72 gm.	DO

Tetarteron

8	Constantinople		Æ	3.28 gm.	DO
9	Constantinople		Æ	3.62 gm.	DO(W)
10	Thessalonica		Æ	3.61 gm.	DO
11	Thessalonica		Æ	3.73 gm.	DO(W)

Uncertain Attribution — Isaac II, Isaac Comnenus. Aspron Trachy

12	Uncertain		Bill.		Whitting Collection

Tetarteron

13	Uncertain	Type A	Æ	2.81 gm.	DO
14	Uncertain	Type B	Æ	2.84 gm.	DO

PLATE 22

Alexius III (1195–1203). Hyperpyron

1	Constantinople	(Var. I)	Aʹ	4.43 gm.	DO
2	Constantinople	(Var. I)	Aʹ	4.11 gm.	DO
3	Constantinople	(Var. II)	Aʹ	4.35 gm.	DO

Aspron Trachy

4	Constantinople	(Var. I)	El.	4.53 gm.	DO
5	Constantinople	(Var. II)	El.	3.39 gm.	DO
6	Constantinople	(Var. II)	El.	4.23 gm.	DO
7	Constantinople	(Var. II)	El.	4.18 gm.	DO

Aspron Trachy

8	Constantinople	(Var. I/A)	Bill.	3.53 gm.	DO
9	Constantinople	(Var. II/A)	Bill.	3.48 gm.	DO
10	Constantinople	(Var. II/A ?)	Bill.	2.58 gm.	DO
11	Constantinople	(Var. II/B [a])	Bill.	3.19 gm.	DO
12	Constantinople	(Var. II/B [b])	Bill.	3.47 gm.	DO

PLATE 23

Alexius III (1195–1203). Aspron Trachy

1	Constantinople	(Var. II/B [b])	Bill.	3.25 gm.	DO
2	Constantinople	(Var. II/B [b]/D [b])	Bill.	3.02 gm.	DO
3	Constantinople	(Var. II/C [a])	Bill.	3.12 gm.	DO
4	Constantinople	(Var. II/C [b])	Bill.	2.79 gm.	DO
5	Constantinople	(Var. II/D [a])	Bill.	3.01 gm.	DO
6	Constantinople	(Var. II/D [a])	Bill.	2.66 gm.	DO
7	Constantinople	(Var. II/D [b])	Bill.	4.77 gm.	DO

Tetarteron

8	Constantinople	Æ		BN
9	Thessalonica	Æ	3.57 gm.	DO
10	Thessalonica	Æ	4.56 gm.	DO

Half-tetarteron

11	Thessalonica	Type I	Æ	1.20 gm.	DO
12	Thessalonica	Type I	Æ	1.47 gm.	DO
13	Thessalonica	Type II	Æ	1.18 gm.	DO
14	Thessalonica	Type II	Æ	2.38 gm.	DO

PLATE 24

"Bulgarian" imitative. Trachy

1	Uncertain	Type A	Bill.	3.06 gm.	DO(W)
2	Uncertain	Type A	Bill.	2.74 gm.	DO
3	Uncertain	Type A	Bill.	3.25 gm.	DO
4	Uncertain	Type A	Bill.	2.25 gm.	DO
5	Uncertain	Type A	Bill.	3.47 gm.	DO
6	Uncertain	Type A	Bill.	2.71 gm.	DO
7	Uncertain	Type A	Bill.	2.30 gm.	DO
8	Uncertain	Type A	Bill.	2.68 gm.	DO
9	Uncertain	Type A	Bill.	2.98 gm.	DO
10	Uncertain	Type B	Bill.	2.64 gm.	DO
11	Uncertain	Type B	Bill.	2.17 gm.	DO
12	Uncertain	Type B	Bill.	2.51 gm.	DO
13	Uncertain	Type B	Bill.	2.77 gm.	DO
14	Uncertain	Type B	Bill.	2.23 gm.	DO
15	Uncertain	Type C	Bill.	2.20 gm.	DO

PLATE 25

"Bulgarian" imitative. Trachy

1	Uncertain	Type C	Bill.	2.73 gm.	DO
2	Uncertain	Type C	Bill.	2.43 gm.	DO
3	Uncertain	Type C	Bill.	2.32 gm.	DO
4	Uncertain	Type C	Bill.	3.50 gm.	DO
5	Uncertain	Type C	Bill.	2.46 gm.	DO

Latin imitative (larger module). Trachy

6	Constantinople	Type A	Bill.	3.28 gm.	DO
7	Constantinople	Type A	Bill.	2.29 gm.	DO
8	Constantinople	Type A	Bill.	3.79 gm.	DO
9	Constantinople	Type A	Bill.	3.55 gm.	DO
10	Constantinople	Type A	Bill.	4.72 gm.	DO
11	Constantinople	Type B	Bill.	3.52 gm.	DO
12	Constantinople	Type B	Bill.	4.16 gm.	DO
13	Constantinople	Type C	Bill.	2.38 gm.	DO
14	Constantinople	Type D	Bill.	3.93 gm.	DO
15	Constantinople	Type D	Bill.	4.30 gm.	DO

PLATE 26

Latin imitative (larger module). Trachy

1	Constantinople	Type E	Bill.	3.43 gm.	DO
2	Constantinople	Type F	Bill.	2.72 gm.	DO
3	Constantinople	Type G	Bill.	3.21 gm.	DO
4	Constantinople	Type H	Bill.	2.94 gm.	DO
5	Constantinople	Type H	Bill.	3.61 gm.	DO
6	Constantinople	Type I	Bill.		BN
7	Constantinople	Type J	Bill.	3.67 gm.	DO
8	Constantinople	Type J	Bill.	3.62 gm.	DO
9	Constantinople	Type J	Bill.	3.33 gm.	DO
10	Constantinople	Type K	Bill.	3.32 gm.	DO
11	Constantinople	Type L	Bill.	1.99 gm.	DO
12	Constantinople	Type M	Bill.	2.92 gm.	DO
13	Constantinople	Type M	Bill.		ANS
14	Constantinople	Type N	Bill.	3.36 gm.	DO
15	Constantinople	Type N	Bill.	4.03 gm.	DO

PLATE 27

Latin imitative (larger module). Trachy

1	Constantinople	Type O	Bill.	3.63 gm.	DO
2	Constantinople	Type O	Bill.	3.60 gm.	DO
3	Constantinople	Type P	Bill.	3.79 gm.	DO
4	Constantinople	Type P	Bill.	3.28 gm.	DO
5	Constantinople	Type Q	Bill.	5.22 gm.	DO
6	Constantinople	Type R	Bill.	3.42 gm.	DO
7	Constantinople	Type R	Bill.	3.60 gm.	DO
8	Constantinople	Type S	Bill.	3.46 gm.	DO
9	Constantinople	Type S	Bill.	3.88 gm.	DO(W)
10	Constantinople	Type T	Bill.	3.76 gm.	DO
11	Constantinople	Type T	Bill.	3.39 gm.	DO

Tetarteron

12	Constantinople		Æ	3.76 gm.	DO
13	Constantinople		Æ	2.70 gm.	DO

PLATE 28

Latin imitative (larger module). Trachy

1	Thessalonica	Type A	Bill.	2.83 gm.	DO
2	Thessalonica	Type A	Bill.	2.76 gm.	DO
3	Thessalonica	Type A	Bill.	2.36 gm.	DO
4	Thessalonica	Type A	Bill.	2.76 gm.	DO
5	Thessalonica	Type B	Bill.	1.92 gm.	DO
6	Thessalonica	Type B	Bill.	2.46 gm.	DO
7	Thessalonica	Type B	Bill.	2.22 gm.	DO
8	Thessalonica	Type B	Bill.	2.30 gm.	DO
9	Thessalonica	Type C	Bill.	3.85 gm.	DO
10	Thessalonica	Type C	Bill.	3.04 gm.	DO

Half-tetarteron

11	Thessalonica	Type A	Æ	1.85 gm.	DO
12	Thessalonica	Type B	Æ	1.54 gm.	DO
13	Thessalonica	Type B	Æ	1.74 gm.	DO
14	Thessalonica	Type B	Æ	1.67 gm.	DO

PLATE 29

Latin imitative (smaller module). Trachy

1	Uncertain	Type A	Bill.	2.26 gm.	DO
2	Uncertain	Type A	Bill.	1.64 gm.	DO
3	Uncertain	Type A	Bill.	1.24 gm.	DO
4	Uncertain	Type B	Bill.	0.97 gm.	DO
5	Uncertain	Type B	Bill.	1.12 gm.	DO
6	Uncertain	Type B	Bill.	1.42 gm.	DO
7	Uncertain	Type C	Bill.	2.57 gm.	DO
8	Uncertain	Type C	Bill.	1.63 gm.	DO
9	Uncertain	Type C	Bill.	1.19 gm.	DO
10	Uncertain	Type D	Bill.	1.20 gm.	DO
11	Uncertain	Type D	Bill.	1.05 gm.	DO
12	Uncertain	Type D	Bill.	1.60 gm.	DO
13	Uncertain	Type E	Bill.	1.59 gm.	DO
14	Uncertain	Type E	Bill.	1.22 gm.	DO
15	Uncertain	Type E	Bill.	1.94 gm.	DO
16	Uncertain	Type F	Bill.	1.20 gm.	DO
17	Uncertain	Type F	Bill.	1.30 gm.	DO
18	Uncertain	Type F	Bill.	1.67 gm.	DO
19	Uncertain	Type G	Bill.	1.91 gm.	DO
20	Uncertain	Type G	Bill.	1.68 gm.	DO

PLATE 30

Theodore I (1208–22). Hyperpyron

1	Nicaea/Magnesia		N	Ratto, no. 2056

Trachy

2	Magnesia	Type A	Æ	4.07 gm.	DO(W)
3	Magnesia	Type A	Æ	4.35 gm.	DO(W)
4	Magnesia	Type B	Æ	4.23 gm.	DO(W)
5	Magnesia	Type B	Æ	4.21 gm.	DO(W)
6	Magnesia	Type B	Æ	4.34 gm.	DO(W)

Trachy

7	Nicaea	First coinage	Bill.	3.64 gm.	DO
8	Nicaea	First coinage	Bill.	3.58 gm.	DO
9	Nicaea	First coinage	Bill.	3.29 gm.	DO
10	Nicaea	First coinage	Bill.	2.41 gm.	DO

PLATE 31

Theodore I (1208–22). Trachy

1	Nicaea	Second coinage	Bill.		Bellinger "Three More Hoards" (Pl. XXXVII. 6)
2	Nicaea	Second coinage	Bill.		*Ibid.* (Pl. XXXVII. 7)
3	Nicaea	Second coinage	Bill.	2.86 gm.	DO
4	Nicaea	Second coinage	Bill.	4.81 gm.	DO
5	Nicaea	Second coinage	Bill.		O
6	Magnesia	Type A	Bill.	4.18 gm.	Bell, *Sardis*, no. 974
7	Magnesia	Type A	Bill.	3.30 gm.	*Ibid.*, no. 976
8	Magnesia	Type B	Bill.	3.97 gm.	DO(W)
9	Magnesia	Type B	Bill.	4.58 gm.	Bell, *Sardis*, no. 982
10	Magnesia	Type C	Bill.	2.54 gm.	*Ibid.*, no. 984

John III (1222–54). Hyperpyron

11	Magnesia	First coinage	N	4.28 gm.	DO(W)
12	Magnesia	First coinage	N	4.61 gm.	DO
13	Magnesia	Second coinage	N	4.15 gm.	DO(W)
14	Magnesia	Second coinage	N	4.17 gm.	DO(W)
15	Magnesia	Second coinage	N	4.02 gm.	DO(W)

PLATE 32

John III (1222–54). Hyperpyron

1	Magnesia	Second coinage	N	4.31 gm.	DO
2	Magnesia	Second coinage	N	4.30 gm.	DO(W)
3	Magnesia	Second coinage	N	3.90 gm.	DO
4	Magnesia	Second coinage	N	4.50 gm.	DO
5	Magnesia	Second coinage	N	4.26 gm.	DO

Trachy

6	Magnesia	Type A	Æ	2.69 gm.	BM 25
7	Magnesia	Type B	Æ	3.28 gm.	BM 26
8	Magnesia	Type C	Æ		JHU
9	Magnesia	Type D	Æ	2.57 gm.	DO(W)
10	Magnesia	Type E	Æ	2.70 gm.	DO
11	Magnesia	Type E	Æ	2.67 gm.	DO(W)

12 Magnesia	Type F	Æ		JHU
13 Magnesia	Type G	Æ	2.71 gm.	DO
14 Magnesia	Type H	Æ	2.68 gm.	DO

PLATE 33
John III (1222–54). Trachy

1 Magnesia	Type A	Bill.	4.06 gm.	DO
2 Magnesia	Type B	Bill.	1.72 gm.	Bell, *Sardis,* no. 969
3 Magnesia	Type C	Bill.	3.36 gm.	DO
4 Magnesia	Type D	Bill.	1.73 gm.	DO
5 Magnesia	Type E	Bill.	4.46 gm.	DO(W)
6 Magnesia	Type F	Bill.	3.69 gm.	DO
7 Magnesia	Type G	Bill.		Tri Voditsi Hoard
8 Magnesia	Type G	Bill.	1.80 gm.	DO
9 Magnesia	Type H	Bill.	3.01 gm.	BM 30
10 Magnesia	Type I	Bill.	3.07 gm.	DO
11 Magnesia	Type J	Bill.	3.26 gm.	DO
12 Magnesia	Type K	Bill.	3.96 gm.	DO
13 Magnesia	Type L	Bill.		Yale University Collection

PLATE 34
John III (1222–54). Tetarteron

1 Magnesia	Type A	Æ	2.15 gm.	DO
2 Magnesia	Type A	Æ	2.15 gm.	DO
3 Magnesia	Type B	Æ	3.41 gm.	DO
4 Magnesia	Type C	Æ	2.68 gm.	DO
5 Magnesia	Type C	Æ	2.96 gm.	DO
6 Magnesia	Type D	Æ	2.34 gm.	DO
7 Magnesia	Type E	Æ		ANS
8 Magnesia	Type F	Æ		BN

Theodore II (1254–58). Hyperpyron

9 Magnesia	Var. A	N		BN
10 Magnesia	Var. B	N		BN
11 Magnesia	Var. B	N	4.30 gm.	BM 1
12 Magnesia	Var. C	N		Whitting Collection
13 Magnesia	Var. C	N	4.19 gm.	DO
14 Magnesia	Var. C	N		BN

PLATE 35
Theodore II (1254–58). Trachy

1 Magnesia	Type A	Æ	2.86 gm.	DO
2 Magnesia	Type A	Æ	2.76 gm.	DO
3 Magnesia	Type B	Æ	2.54 gm.	DO(W)
4 Magnesia	Type C	Æ	2.73 gm.	DO
5 Magnesia	Type C	Æ	1.68 gm.	DO

Trachy

6	Magnesia	Type A	Bill.		BN
7	Magnesia	Type B	Bill.	3.81 gm.	DO
8	Magnesia	Type B	Bill.	1.28 gm.	DO
9	Magnesia	Type C	Bill.	4.34 gm.	DO
10	Magnesia	Type C	Bill.	2.94 gm.	DO
11	Magnesia	Type C	Bill.	2.14 gm.	DO
12	Magnesia	Type D	Bill.	2.79 gm.	DO
13	Magnesia	Type D	Bill.	4.12 gm.	DO

Tetarteron

14	Magnesia	Type A	Æ		BN
15	Magnesia	Type B	Æ		BN

PLATE 36

Michael VIII (1258/59–61). Hyperpyron

1	Magnesia		$\mathcal{N}$	4.12 gm.	Iliescu, "Le dernier hyperpère," p.95, no.2

Trachy

2	Magnesia		$\mathcal{R}$	1.67 gm.	DO

Trachy

3	Magnesia	Type A	Bill.	2.24 gm.	DO
4	Magnesia	Type B	Bill.	4.25 gm.	DO

Tetarteron

5	Magnesia		Æ	1.52 gm.	DO
6	Magnesia		Æ	1.74 gm.	DO

Uncertain Nicaean Attribution. Tetarteron

7	Magnesia	Type A	Æ	2.53 gm.	DO
8	Magnesia	Type B	Æ	1.93 gm.	DO
9	Magnesia	Type C	Æ	2.30 gm.	DO
10	Magnesia	Type D	Æ	2.31 gm.	DO
11	Magnesia	Type E	Æ	1.91 gm.	DO

PLATE 37

Theodore Comnenus-Ducas (1224–30). Trachy

1	Thessalonica	Type A	$\mathcal{R}$	2.62 gm.	DO
2	Thessalonica	Type A	$\mathcal{R}$	1.87 gm.	DO
3	Thessalonica	Type B	$\mathcal{R}$	2.48 gm.	DO
4	Thessalonica	Type B	$\mathcal{R}$	2.23 gm.	DO
5	Thessalonica	Type C	$\mathcal{R}$		Whitting Collection
6	Thessalonica	Type C	$\mathcal{R}$	3.19 gm.	BM 4 (Theodore II)

Trachy

7	Thessalonica	Type A	Bill.	3.74 gm.	DO
8	Thessalonica	Type A	Bill.	3.54 gm.	DO
9	Thessalonica	Type A	Bill.	3.38 gm.	DO
10	Thessalonica	Type B	Bill.	3.30 gm.	DO
11	Thessalonica	Type B	Bill.	4.70 gm.	DO
12	Thessalonica	Type B	Bill.	3.33 gm.	DO

PLATE 38

Theodore Comnenus-Ducas (1224–30). Trachy

1	Thessalonica	Type C	Bill.	3.27 gm.	DO
2	Thessalonica	Type C	Bill.	3.07 gm.	DO
3	Thessalonica	Type D	Bill.	6.24 gm.	DO
4	Thessalonica	Type D	Bill.	4.62 gm.	DO
5	Thessalonica	Type E	Bill.	2.39 gm.	DO
6	Thessalonica	Type F	Bill.	2.88 gm.	DO
7	Thessalonica	Type F	Bill.	2.69 gm.	DO
8	Thessalonica	Type G	Bill.	3.53 gm.	DO
9	Thessalonica	Type G	Bill.	3.62 gm.	DO

Tetarteron

10	Thessalonica		Æ	3.98 gm.	DO
11	Thessalonica		Æ	3.72 gm.	DO

Half-tetarteron

12	Thessalonica	Type A	Æ	1.35 gm.	DO
13	Thessalonica	Type B	Æ	1.47 gm.	DO
14	Thessalonica	Type C	Æ	2.04 gm.	DO
15	Thessalonica	Type C	Æ	2.07 gm.	DO

PLATE 39

Manuel Comnenus-Ducas (1230–37). Trachy

1	Thessalonica	Type A	Ꜫ	1.87 gm.	DO
2	Thessalonica	Type B	Ꜫ		O

Trachy

3	Thessalonica	Type A	Bill.	2.19 gm.	DO
4	Thessalonica	Type B	Bill.	2.77 gm.	DO
5	Thessalonica	Type B	Bill.	2.55 gm.	DO
6	Thessalonica	Type C	Bill.	2.26 gm.	DO
7	Thessalonica	Type D	Bill.		Edwards, "A Remarkable Coin of Manuel I"
8	Thessalonica	Type E	Bill.	1.83 gm.	DO
9	Thessalonica	Type F	Bill.	3.35 gm.	DO
10	Thessalonica	Type G	Bill.	1.77 gm.	DO
11	Thessalonica	Type G	Bill.	3.81 gm.	DO

PLATE 40

John Comnenus-Ducas (1237–44). Trachy

1	Thessalonica	Type A	(Ser. I)	Bill.	1.49 gm.	DO
2	Thessalonica	Type B	(Ser. I)	Bill.	2.59 gm.	DO
3	Thessalonica	Type C	(Ser. I)	Bill.	2.47 gm.	DO
4	Thessalonica	Type D	(Ser. I)	Bill.	1.81 gm.	DO
5	Thessalonica	Type E	(Ser. I)	Bill.	1.86 gm.	DO
6	Thessalonica	Type F	(Ser. II)	Bill.	2.26 gm.	DO

7 Thessalonica	Type G	(Ser. II)	Bill.	1.69 gm.	DO
8 Thessalonica	Type H	(Ser. II)	Bill.	2.01 gm.	DO
9 Thessalonica	Type I	(Ser. II)	Bill.	2.63 gm.	DO
10 Thessalonica	Type I	(Ser. II)	Bill.	2.05 gm.	DO

Half-tetarteron

11 Thessalonica	Æ	1.68 gm.	DO

Trachy

12 Thessalonica	Type A	(Ser. III)	Bill.	1.24 gm.	DO
13 Thessalonica	Type A	(Ser. III)	Bill.		Oustovo Hoard
14 Thessalonica	Type B	(Ser. III)	Bill.		Oustovo Hoard
15 Thessalonica	Type C (A)	(Ser. III)	Bill.	1.24 gm.	DO

PLATE 41

John Comnenus-Ducas (1237–44). Trachy

1 Thessalonica	Type C (B)	(Ser. III)	Bill.		Tri Voditsi Hoard
2 Thessalonica	Type D	(Ser. III)	Bill.	1.07 gm.	DO
3 Thessalonica	Type E	(Ser. III)	Bill.		Dorkovo Hoard
4 Thessalonica	Type E	(Ser. III)	Bill.		Tri Voditsi Hoard
5 Thessalonica	Type F	(Ser. III)	Bill.	1.02 gm.	DO
6 Thessalonica	Type F	(Ser. III)	Bill.	0.47 gm.	DO
7 Thessalonica	Type G	(Ser. III)	Bill.	1.46 gm.	DO
8 Thessalonica	Type G	(Ser. III)	Bill.		Oustovo Hoard
9 Thessalonica	Type H	(Ser. III)	Bill.		Dorkovo Hoard
10 Thessalonica	Type I	(Ser. III)	Bill.	0.53 gm.	DO
11 Thessalonica	Type J	(Ser. III)	Bill.	1.12 gm.	DO
12 Thessalonica	Type K	(Ser. III)	Bill.	1.49 gm.	DO
13 Thessalonica	Type K	(Ser. III)	Bill.	0.94 gm.	DO
14 Thessalonica	Type M	(Ser. III)	Bill.		Oustovo Hoard
15 Thessalonica	Type N	(Ser. III)	Bill.		Preslav Hoard
16 Thessalonica	Type N	(Ser. III)	Bill.		Preslav Hoard
17 Thessalonica	Type O	(Ser. III)	Bill.	1.04 gm.	Bertelè, *L'imperatore alato*, p. 19, no. 1
18 Thessalonica	Type P	(Ser. III)	Bill.		Dorkovo Hoard

Uncertain Thessalonican Attribution. Trachy

19 Thessalonica	Bill.	1.31 gm.	DO

Demetrius Comnenus-Ducas? (1244–46). Trachy

20 Thessalonica	Bill.	2.50 gm.	DO
21 Thessalonica	Bill.	3.03 gm.	DO

PLATE 42

John III (1246–54). Trachy

1 Thessalonica	Type A	Bill.	2.46 gm.	DO
2 Thessalonica	Type A	Bill.	2.45 gm.	DO
3 Thessalonica	Type B	Bill.	4.19 gm.	DO
4 Thessalonica	Type B	Bill.	2.74 gm.	DO

5	Thessalonica	Type C	Bill.	1.79 gm.	DO
6	Thessalonica	Type C	Bill.	2.02 gm.	DO
7	Thessalonica	Type D	Bill.	2.26 gm.	DO
8	Thessalonica	Type D	Bill.	1.57 gm.	DO
9	Thessalonica	Type E	Bill.	2.98 gm.	DO
10	Thessalonica	Type E	Bill.	2.48 gm.	DO
11	Thessalonica	Type F	Bill.	2.61 gm.	DO
12	Thessalonica	Type F	Bill.	2.46 gm.	DO

PLATE 43

John III (1246–54). Trachy

1	Thessalonica	Type G	Bill.	2.38 gm.	DO
2	Thessalonica	Type G	Bill.	3.01 gm.	DO
3	Thessalonica	Type H	Bill.	2.07 gm.	DO
4	Thessalonica	Type H	Bill.	2.58 gm.	DO
5	Thessalonica	Type I	Bill.	2.38 gm.	DO
6	Thessalonica	Type I	Bill.	3.74 gm.	DO
7	Thessalonica	Type J	Bill.	2.48 gm.	DO
8	Thessalonica	Type K	Bill.	1.79 gm.	DO
9	Thessalonica	Type K	Bill.	2.14 gm.	DO

Theodore II (1254–58). Trachy

10	Thessalonica	Bill.	2.86 gm.	DO

PLATE 44

Clipped Coins (Manuel I–Alexius III)
Manuel I

1	Constantinople	First coinage (B)	Bill.	2.04 gm.	DO
2	Constantinople	Third coinage (Ph. 1: [A])	Bill.	1.79 gm.	DO
3	Constantinople	Third coinage (Ph. 2: [D])	Bill.	2.04 gm.	DO
4	Constantinople	Fourth coinage (A [c])	Bill.	1.03 gm.	DO
5	Constantinople	Fourth coinage (B [a])	Bill.	2.05 gm.	DO
6	Constantinople	Fourth coinage (C [a])	Bill.	1.58 gm.	DO

Andronicus I

7	Constantinople	(Var. A)	Bill.	1.70 gm.	DO
8	Constantinople	(Var. B)	Bill.	1.24 gm.	DO

Isaac II

9	Constantinople	(Var. A [b])	Bill.	2.27 gm.	DO
10	Constantinople	(Var. B [b])	Bill.	2.07 gm.	DO
11	Constantinople	(Var. C [b])	Bill.	2.54 gm.	DO

Alexius III

12	Constantinople	(Var. I/A)	Bill.	1.54 gm.	DO
13	Constantinople	(Var. I/A)	Bill.	1.86 gm.	DO

| *14* Constantinople | (Var. II/A) | Bill. | 1.15 gm. | DO |
| *15* Constantinople | (Var. II/A) | Bill. | 2.06 gm. | DO |

PLATE 45

Clipped Coins (Empire of Thessalonica)
Theodore Comnenus-Ducas

1 Thessalonica	Type B	Bill.	Oustovo Hoard
2 Thessalonica	Type D	Bill.	Oustovo Hoard
3 Thessalonica	Type F	Bill.	Tri Voditsi Hoard
4 Thessalonica	Type F	Bill.	Tri Voditsi Hoard
5 Thessalonica	Type F	Bill.	Tri Voditsi Hoard

Manuel Comnenus-Ducas

6 Thessalonica	Type C	Bill.	Oustovo Hoard
7 Thessalonica	Type D	Bill.	Oustovo Hoard
8 Thessalonica	Type D	Bill.	Oustovo Hoard

John Comnenus-Ducas

| *9* Thessalonica | Type D | Bill. | Oustovo Hoard |
| *10* Thessalonica | Type D | Bill. | Tri Voditsi Hoard |

Roger II of Sicily, Ducat

11   Æ/Bill. DO

Debased Hyperpyra, Thirteenth-fourteenth Centuries

12 Michael VIII	ANS
13 Michael VIII	DO
14 Andronicus II	DO
15 Andronicus II, Michael IX	DO
16 Andronicus II, Michael IX	DO

PLATE 46

Debased Hyperpyra, Thirteenth-fourteenth Centuries

1 Andronicus II, Michael IX	DO
2 Andronicus II, Michael IX	DO
3 Andronicus II, Andronicus III	DO
4 Andronicus III, John V, Anna of Savoy	DO

Overstrikes

5 Latin imitative (Large module) Thess. B over Thess. A	DO
6 Latin imitative (Large module) Con'ple C over Con'ple B	DO
7 Latin imitative (Large module) Thess. B over Theodore I, Nicaea	Author's Collection
8 Latin imitative (Large module) Con'ple O over Thess. C	Whitting Collection
9 Theodore I, Nicaea, second coinage, over Nicaea, first	Bellinger, "Three More Hoards" (Pl. XXXVII. 10)

Ivan II, Asen

| *10* Bill. trachy | Grierson Collection |
| *11* Bill. trachy | DO |

PLATE 47

Stefan "Rex"

1 Bill. trachy				Grierson Collection

Miscellaneous Eleventh Century

2 Romanus IV	Æ	Follis	Thessalonica	DO
3 Nicephorus III	Æ	Follis	Thessalonica	DO
4 Nicephorus Basilacius	Æ	Follis	Thessalonica	DO
5 Nicephorus III	El.	Debased trachy	Con'ple	DO

Hugh I Lusignan, of Cyprus

6 El. Besant		ANS

PLATE 48

Hagia Sophia. "Constantine IX" and Zoë

PLATE 49

Hagia Sophia. "Constantine IX" and Zoë, detail of *Apokombion*

PLATE 50

Hagia Sophia. John II and Irene

PLATE 51

Supplementary Material

Alexius I. Pre-reform (1081–92). Debased Trachy
1 Constantinople	El.	Berlin Münzkabinett

Nicephorus III (1078–81). Debased Trachy
2 Constantinople	El.	DO

Alexius I. Pre-reform. Debased Trachy
3 Constantinople	El.	Berlin Münzkabinett

Alexius I. Post-reform (1092–1118). Aspron Trachy
4 Thessalonica	El.	Berlin Münzkabinett

Theodore I (1208–22). Trachy
5 Nicaea	Ær	Whitting Collection

John III (1222–54). Trachy
6 Magnesia	Bill.	Whitting Collection

Manuel Comnenus-Ducas (1230–37). Trachy
7 Thessalonica	Bill.	Fitzwilliam Museum, Cambridge
8 Thessalonica	Bill.	Whitting Collection

Indexes

INDEX I

RULERS, MINTS, AND DENOMINATIONS

Main Descriptions and Commentaries only. *See also* Index V

Alexius I, Pre-reform, 1081–92
    Cpl. El.("N"), 71, 76, 405 (trachy),
      72, 76 (tetarteron); Æ, 73, 77
      (scyphate), 73–74, 77 (flat); Æ,
      74–75, 77, 80
    Thess. El.("N"), 71–72, 76 (trachy),
      73, 76–77 (tetarteron); Æ, 74, 77
      (flat); Æ, 75–76, 78–80
    Eastern(?)/Thess.(?) Æ, 76, 80
Alexius I, Post-reform, 1092–1118
    Cpl. N, 81–82, 89–94; El., 84–85, 96;
      Bill., 85–86, 97; Æ, 87–88, 98–101
    Thess. N, 82–83, 90–95; El., 85, 96–
      97; Bill., 86, 98; Æ, 88–89, 98–101
    Philippopolis(?) N, 83–84, 91, 95;
      Bill., 87, 95–96, 98
    Uncertain Gk(?) Æ, 99–100
    Unknown N, 84, 96
John II (1118–43)
    Cpl. N, 102–03, 107; El., 104, 108;
      Bill., 104–05, 108–09; Æ, 106, 109
    Thess. N, 103, 107–08; El., 104,
      108; Bill., 105, 108–09; Æ, 106–07,
      109–10
Manuel I (1143–80)
    Cpl. N, 111–12, 122–24; El., 112–
      15, 124–25; Bill., 116–19, 126; Æ,
      119–20, 126–27
    Thess. N, 112, 124; El., 115–16, 125–
      26; Æ, 120–21, 127–30
    Uncertain Gk. Æ, 121–22, 127–30
Alexius II (1180–84)
    No coinage, 131

Andronicus I (1183–85)
    Cpl. N, 132, 134–35; El., 132; Bill.,
      133; Æ, 133, 135
    Thess. Æ, 133–34, 135
    Uncertain Gk. Æ, 134, 135
Isaac of Cyprus (1184–91)
    Main El., 136, 142; Bill., 136–37,
      140–41; Æ, 137, 140–41
    Secondary Bill., 137, 142; Æ, 138,
      141–42
Isaac II (1185–95)
    Cpl. N, 143, 145–46; El., 143–44;
      Bill., 144–45; Æ, 145, 146
    Thess. Æ, 145, 146
    Uncertain Gk(?) Æ, 146
Uncertain Isaac
    Bill., 147, 148; Æ, 147–48
Theodore Mangaphas (1189–90, *c.* 1204–
    c. 1208)
    No coinage identified, 149
Alexius III (1195–1203)
    Cpl. N, 150, 153; El., 150–51, 153;
      Bill., 151, 154; Æ, 152, 154
    Thess. Æ, 152–53, 154–55
Isaac II (rest.), Alexius IV (1203–04)
    No coinage, 156
Alexius V (1204)
    No coinage, 156
Latin Imitative (Cpl., 1204–61; Thess.,
    1204–24)
    Large module
    Cpl. N (?), 254; Bill., 191–96, 199–
      209, 215–17, 223; Æ, 197, 217

Thess. Bill., 196–97, 199–210, 223; Æ, 197–98, 217

Small module

Bill./Æ, 198–99, 199–209, 210–14, 223

"Bulgarian" Imitative (*c.* 1195–?)

Bill., 218–22, 223

Theodore I (1208–22)

Nicaea/Magnesia N(?), 227–28, 235–36

Nicaea R, 405–06; Bill., 228–29, 232–34, 236

Magnesia R, 228, 233–34, 236; Bill., 229–30, 232–34, 236

John III (1222–54)

Magnesia N, 237, 246–54, 255–56; R, 237–40, 254–55, 406; Bill., 240–44, 255, 406–07; Æ, 244–45, 255, 266

Thess. R, 294; Bill., 290–94

Theodore II (1254–58)

Magnesia N, 256–57, 260; R, 257–58, 261; Bill., 258–59, 260–61, 407; Æ, 259–60

Thess. Bill., 295

John IV (1258/59)

No coinage, 261

Michael VIII (1258/59–61)

Magnesia N, 261, 263; R, 262, 264; Bill., 262–63, 264; Æ, 263, 264

Thess. Coinage not treated, 295

Uncertain Attribution

Æ, 264–66

Theodore Comnenus-Ducas (1224–30)

Thess. R, 268–69, 273; Bill., 269–71, 274; Æ, 271–72, 274

Manuel Comnenus-Ducas (1230–37)

Thess. R, 274–75, 278; Bill., 275–77, 278–79, 407

John Comnenus-Ducas (Emp. 1237–42, Desp. 1242–44)

Thess. Bill. (large), 279–82, 285–88, 408; Æ, 282, 288; Bill./Æ (small), 282–85, 286–88, 408

Demetrius Comnenus-Ducas (Desp. 1244–46)

No named coinage identified, 288–89

Uncertain Attribution

Bill./Æ (small), 289

Michael II Comnenus-Ducas (*c.* 1231–68)

Arta(?) Bill. (?), 296

Leo, John Gavalas (*c.* 1204–*c.* 1250)

Æ, 296

Ivan II Asen (1218–41)

N, 297; Bill., 296–97

"Stefan Ducas Rex" ([Radoslav], *c.* 1228–33)

R, 298; Bill., 297–98

INDEX II

Hoards

Place, Country, and Date of Finding; Denominations present; Latest Ruler represented

Main Entries only. *See also* Map at end of Volume, and Index V

Where hoards contain Latin material, which is not closely datable, an attempt has been made at an approximate indication of their predominant chronological character: the assemblage has therefore been termed "early," "middle," or "late." The first indicates that the Latin pieces of large module form a relatively high proportion of the Latin issues present, or that the total of Latin issues forms a relatively low proportion of the total hoard, or both; the second that the Latin pieces of small module form a relatively high proportion of the total of Latin issues present and of the hoard itself; the third that there are present, in addition, an appreciable number of the rarer and evidently later Constantinopolitan Latin issues (types D–T). Such a classification is clearly not an absolute one and is to a considerable degree based on subjective criteria.

Key: Bulg. — Bulgaria   Tr. (A) — Turkey in Asia Minor
       Cyp.   — Cyprus   Tr. (E) — Turkey in Europe
       Gr.   — Greece   Yug.   — Yugoslavia

Arcadia (Gr.), 1958; Bill.; Alexius III/ Latin (early); 325–26

Assenovgrad (Bulg.), 1960; Bill., Æ; Theodore I/Latin (early); 326–27

Banya (Bulg.), 1927; El.; Isaac II; 327–28

Batkoun (Bulg.), 1937; Bill.; Isaac II; 328

Belitsa (Bulg.), 1938; Bill.; Andronicus I; 329

Bergama (Tr.[A]); Bill.; Theodore I/ Latin (early); 329–30

Brauron (Gr.), 1956; Æ, Bill.; Isaac II/ Latin (early); 330–31

Brestovo (Bulg.), 1953; Bill.; Theodore I/ Latin (early); 331–33

Byaga (Bulg.), 1959; Bill.; Theodore I/ Latin (middle); 333–34

Corinth (Gr.) I, 1937; Æ; Manuel I; 334

Corinth (Gr.) II, 1938; *N*; Manuel I; 335

Corinth (Gr.) III, 1960; Bill., Æ; Latin (middle); 335

Dolni Vurbishta (Bulg.); Bill.; Alexius III/ Latin (early); 335–36

Dorkovo (Bulg.), 1940; Bill., Æ; John III/Latin (late); 336–38

Draganovo (Bulg.), 1957; Bill.; Isaac II; 338–39

"Dumbarton Oaks" I (fr. cent. Yug.); Bill.; Latin (middle); 339

"Dumbarton Oaks" II (fr. cent. Yug.); Bill.; Theodore I/Latin (middle); 339–40

"Dumbarton Oaks" III (fr. cent. Yug.); Bill.; Theodore I/Latin (middle); 340–41

Enina (Bulg.), 1951/52; Bill.; Isaac II/ "Bulgarian"; 341–42

General Nikolaevo (Bulg.), 1960; Bill.; Isaac II/Latin (early); 342–43

Gornoslav (Bulg.), 1961; *N*; Isaac II; 343–44

Grabovac (Yug.); Bill.; Alexius III; 345, 403

Gradevo (Bulg.) I, 1936; Bill.; Alexius III/Latin (early); 345

Gradevo (Bulg.) II, 1958; Bill.; Theodore I/Latin (early); 346–47

Iskra (Bulg.), 1938; Bill.; Isaac II; 347

Istanbul (Tr.[E]) A; Bill.; Alexius III; 347–48

Istanbul (Tr.[E]) B; Bill.; Theodore I/ Latin (early); 348–49

Kalentzi (Gr.), 1927; Æ; Manuel I; 350

Kaloyanovets (Bulg.), 1960; Bill.; Isaac II; 350–51

Kartal (Bulg.), 1914; Bill.; Alexius III/ "Bulgarian"; 351

Kastri (Gr.), 1952; Æ; Isaac II; 352

Kazanluk (Bulg.), 1958; Bill.; Alexius III/ "Bulgarian"; 352–53

Khissar (Bulg.), 1922; El. ("*N*"), *N*; Alexius (post-reform); 354

Kiustendil (Bulg.), 1960; Bill.; Theodore I/Latin (early); 354–55

Kiustendil Reg. (Bulg.); Bill.; Theodore I/Latin (early); 355–56

Korten (Bulg.), 1960; Bill.; Alexius III/ Latin (early); 356–57

Kounino (Bulg.) I, 1954; Bill.; Alexius III/Latin (early); 357

Kounino (Bulg.) II; Bill.; Alexius III/Latin (early); 358

Kroushare (Bulg.), 1962; Bill.; Andronicus I; 358–59

Lakité (Bulg.); A', El., Bill., Æ; Isaac II/"Bulgarian"; 359–60

Lazania (Cyp.); Bill.; Manuel I; 360

Levkokhori (Gr.), 1955; Bill.; Theodore I/Latin (early); 360–61

Lindos (Gr.), 1902; El.; Manuel I; 361

Logodash (Bulg.), 1959; Bill., Æ; Theodore Comnenus-Ducas/Latin (middle); 361–62

Lom (Bulg.) A, 1962; Bill.; Theodore I/Latin (middle); 363–64

Lom (Bulg.) B, 1962; Bill.; Theodore I/Latin (early); 364–65

Loukovo (Bulg.); Bill.; Alexius III/Latin (early); 365–66

Macedonia (Gr.); Bill.; Manuel I; 366

Mogilitsa (Bulg.), 1934; Bill.; Manuel Comnenus-Ducas/Latin (late); 366–67

Momin Brod (Bulg.), 1914; Bill.; Alexius III/Latin (early); 367–68

Muglizh (Bulg.) I, 1941; Bill.; Alexius III/"Bulgarian"; 368–69

Muglizh (Bulg.) II, 1960; Bill.; Theodore I/Latin (middle); 369–70

Naousa (Gr.), 1924; Bill.; Theodore I/Latin (early); 370–71

Nicosia (Cyp.) I, 1920's; El.; Manuel I; 371–72

Nicosia (Cyp.) II; Bill.; Manuel I; 372

Novo Selo (Bulg.), 1958; A', Bill.; Isaac II; 372–73

Obuda (Hungary); Bill.; Isaac II; 374

Osanica (Yug.); Bill.; Theodore I/Latin (early); 374–403

Oustovo (Bulg.), 1936; Bill.; John Comnenus-Ducas/Latin (late); 374–75

Ovchartsi (Bulg.), 1958; Bill.; Isaac II/Latin (early); 375–76

Pazardzhik (Bulg.), 1936; Bill.; Alexius III/Latin (early); 376–77

Pirdop (Bulg.); Bill.; Alexius III/"Bulgarian"; 377

Pisaratsi (Bulg.), 1927; A', Bill.; John III/Latin (early); 378–79

Plovdiv (Bulg.), 1955; Bill.; Alexius I; 379

Plovdiv Reg. (Bulg.); Bill.; Alexius III; 379

Pokrovnik (Bulg.), 1962; Bill.; Theodore I/Latin (early); 380–81

Postallar (Tr.[E]); A', Bill.; Michael VIII (?)/Latin (late); 381–82

Preslav (Bulg.), 1953; A', Bill.; John III/Latin (late); 382–83

Roussé (Bulg.), 1965; Bill.; Latin (middle); 383

Sofia (Bulg.), 1897; El. ("A'"), A'; Alexius I (post-reform); 383

Souvatité (Bulg.), 1934; Bill.; Alexius III/"Bulgarian" (+ Latin?); 383–84

Stara Zagora (Bulg.), 1941; Bill.; Theodore I/Latin (middle); 385

Strazhitsa (Bulg.), 1956; Bill.; Alexius III/"Bulgarian" (?); 386

Suedinenie (Bulg.), 1955; A', Bill.; John II; 386–87

Thessaly (Gr.), 1957; Bill.; Theodore I/Latin (early); 387–88

Tiurkmen (Bulg.) I, 1953; Bill.; Isaac II; 388–89

Tiurkmen (Bulg.) II, 1959; Bill.; Isaac II; 389

Torbalı (Tr.[A]), c. 1946; Æ; Theodore II; 389–90

Toulovo (Bulg.); Bill.; Theodore I/Latin (middle); 390–91

Tri Voditsi (Bulg.), 1940; Bill., Æ; John III/Latin (late); 391–93

Troad (Tr.[A]), 1930's; Bill.; Theodore I/Latin (early); 393–94

Tsepina (Bulg.), 1905; Bill.; Theodore I/Latin (early); 394

Tsruncha (Bulg.) A, 1963; Bill.; Alexius III/"Bulgarian"; 394–95

Tsruncha (Bulg.) B, 1963; Bill.; Alexius III/"Bulgarian"; 396–97

Turnovo (Bulg.) I; Bill.; Andronicus I; 397

Turnovo (Bulg.) II, 1963; Bill.; Alexius III/"Bulgarian"; 397–98

Tvurditsa (Bulg.); Bill.; Alexius III/ "Bulgarian"; 398

Uncertain Bulg. Provenance; Bill.; Theodore I/Latin (early); 399–400

Yagoda (Bulg.), 1962; Bill.; Andronicus I; 400

Yenimahalle (Tr.[E]); Bill.; Alexius III/ Latin (early); 401

Zgurli (Bulg.); N; Isaac II; 401

Zheleznitsa (Bulg.), 1962; Bill.; Theodore I/Latin (early); 402

Zlata (Yug.); Bill.; Isaac II; 403

Zlataritsa (Bulg.), 1910; Bill.; Alexius III; 403–04

Other Hoards used

Arta (Gr.); Bill.; Michael VIII
Cyprus (?); Bill.; Isaac of Cyprus
Gurdzhaani (Georgia); N; John II   } See Index V for references
Ochrida (Yug.); Bill.; Ivan II
"Brusa"   }
"Smyrna" } (Tr.[A]); N; Michael VIII

INDEX III

IMPERIAL CEREMONIAL COSTUME

Type-references to be made via the Key to Plates. *See also* Index V

A. Stemma, divitision, chlamys: Pls. 1.*1–4, 5–8*; 2.*1–2, 6–9*; 3.*4–5.14*; 7.*2–4*; 8.*3–4, 7–8, 9, 17*; 10.*1–4, 5–6*; 11.*8–10, 11–12, 13–14*; 12.*1–11, 12*; 14.*1–4, 7–9, 10–13*; 15.*5–13*; 17.*11–12*; 18.*11–12*; 19.*1, 5, 6–7, 11, 12, 15*; 20.*5–8*; 21.*8–9*; 22.*1–3*; 23.*9–10, 11–12, 13–14*; 25.*6–10, 11–12*; 26.*2, 3, 6, 7–9, 14–15*; 28.*5–8*; 29.*1–3, 4–6, 13–15*; 30.*1, 4–6*; 31.*1–5, 8–9, 10*; 32.*9*; 33.*1, 2, 3, 6*; 34.*3*; 35.*4–5, 7–8, 14*; 36.*2, 4*; 37.*7–9*; 39.*2, 3*; 41.*10*; 42.*7–8*; 43.*1–2*; 46.*10–11*; 51.*3*

B(a). Stemma, divitision, traditional loros: Pls. 3.*2*; 8.*10–12, 13–15*; 11.*3–4*; 37.*1–2*; 39.*10–11*; 41.*12–13*; 42.*1–2, 3–4*

B(b). Stemma, divitision, collar-piece, simplified loros: Pls. 1.*9, 10–12*; 2.*3–5, 10–12, 17*; 3.*1*; 6.*1, 6–9, 10–11*; 7.*5–6, 7, 8–9, 10–11*; 8.*1–2, 16*; 9.*1–3, 4–5, 6–9, 10, 11, 12, 13–14*; 10.*9–11.2*; 11.*5–7, 15–17*; 13.*1–2, 3–4, 5–9*; 14.*5, 6*; 16.*1–17.4*; 17.*5–6, 9–10, 13–14, 15–16, 17–18*; 18.*1–2, 3–4, 7–8, 13–16*; 19.*3*; 20.*1–4*; 21.*10–11, 13, 14*; 22.*4–7*; 22.*8–23.7*; 23.*8*; 24.*1–9*; 24.*15–25.5*; 25.*13*; 28.*1–4, 9–10, 12–14*; 29.*7–9, 10–12, 16–18, 19–20*; 30.*7–10*; 31.*6–7, 11–12*; 31.*13–32.5*; 32.*6*; 33.*12, 13*; 34.*6, 7, 8, 9–14*; 35.*15*; 36.*1, 3, 7*; 37.*3–4, 10–12*; 38.*1–2, 3–4, 6–7, 10–11, 12, 13, 14–15*; 39.*4–5, 6, 7, 8, 9*; 40.*1, 2, 4, 5, 6, 7, 9–10, 12–13, 14, 15*; 41.*1, 2, 3–4, 5–6, 9, 15–16, 17, 19*; 42.*9–10, 11–12*; 43.*3–4, 5–6, 7, 8–9, 10*; 47.*1*; 51.*1, 4, 5, 6*

28*

B(c). Stemma, divitision, (collar-piece), simplified loros, sagion: Pls. 8.*5–6*; 15.*1–4*; 17.*7–8*; 18.*9–10*; 20.*9*–21.*7*; 21.*12*; 24.*11–14*; 25.*14–15*; 26.*1, 4–5, 10, 11, 12–13*; 27.*12–13*; 30.*2–3*; 32.*7, 8, 10–11, 12, 13, 14*; 33.*4, 5, 7–8, 9, 10, 11*; 34.*4–5*; 35.*1–2, 3, 6, 9–11, 12–13*; 36.*5–6, 8*; 37.*5–6*; 38.*5, 8–9*; 39.*1*; 40.*8*; 41.*7–8*; 51.*7–8*

C. Stemma, scaramangion or divitision, sagion: Pls. 6.*2–5*; 7.*1*; 13.*10–12*; 19.*2, 4, 8–10, 13–14*

D. Stemma, short military tunic, (breastplate), sagion: Pls. 2.*13*; 10.*7–8*; 17.*19–20(?)*; 18.*5–6(?)*; 27.*1–2*; 34.*1–2*; 40.*3*; 41.*11*; 42.*5–6*

INDEX IV

RELIGIOUS FIGURES

In the order: Christ, Virgin, Saints (alphabetically), Cherub

CHRIST

Two basic varieties of representation: the one bearded, with long hair parted in the middle of the head and falling to either side, holding Book of the Gospels; the other beardless, with short and apparently curly hair, holding scroll. The latter is frequently labelled "Emmanuel," although the implied distinction is not without exception (e.g., Pls. 2.*3–5*; 28.*5–8*; 32.*13*). A rare variety of the former, consisting of a standing figure, is occasionally labelled "Chalcitis," that is, similar to the image over the Bronze Gate of the Great Palace (Pls. 32.*7*; 33.*9*; 36.*9*). Pls. 1.*1–4, 5–8, 9, 10–12*; 2.*1–2, 3–5, 10–12, 18–19, 20–21, 22*; 3.*4*–5.*14*; 6.*1, 6–9, 10–11*; 7.*1, 2–4, 5–6, 7, 8–9, 10–11*; 8.*1–2, 3–4, 5–6, 7–8, 16*; 9.*1–3, 4–5, 6–9, 10, 11, 12, 13–14*; 10.*1–4, 5–6*; 10.*9*–11.*2*; 11.*5–7, 11–12, 13–14*; 12.*1–11, 12*; 13.*1–2, 3–4, 5–9, 10–12*; 14.*1–4, 5, 6, 10–13*; 15.*1–4*; 16.*1*–17.*4*; 17.*5–6, 9–10, 19–20*; 18.*5–6, 9–10, 11–12, 13–16*; 19.*1, 8–10, 13–14*; 21.*12, 13, 14*; 22.*1–3, 4–7*; 22.*8*–23.*7*; 24.*1–9*; 24.*15*–25.*5*; 25.*11–12, 14–15*; 26.*1, 2, 10, 11*; 27.*1–2, 3–4, 6–7*; 28.*1–4, 5–8, 9–10*; 29.*4–6, 10–12, 13–15, 16–18*; 30.*1, 2–3, 4–6*; 31.*1–5, 6–7, 8–9, 10, 11–12*; 31.*13*–32.*5*; 32.*6, 7, 8, 9, 12, 13*; 33.*1, 2, 3, 4, 5, 6, 9, 11*; 34.*4–5, 7, 9–14*; 35.*1–2, 3, 6*; 36.*1, 2, 4, 5–6, 9*; 37.*1–2, 5–6, 7–9, 10–12*; 38.*3–4, 5, 8–9*; 39.*1, 2, 3, 8*; 40.*4*; 41.*20–21*; 42.*11–12*; 43.*8–9*; 46.*10–11*; 47.*1*; 51.*1, 3, 4, 5, 7–8*

VIRGIN

Several major varieties of representation, with the Virgin either possessing, or lacking, an icon or medallion of the head or bust of the infant Christ at breast level. Both varieties include an orans type. In a much rarer variety, the Virgin faces to the right, orans, toward the *Manus Dei*. This is the type occasionally labelled "Hagiosoritissa"—although in one case the same designation is applied to a facing orans figure, without the *Manus Dei* (cf. Pls. 27.*8–9, 10–11*; 37.*3–4*). Pls. 2.*6–9, 13, 14, 15–16, 20–21*; 3.*1*; 6.*2–5, 6–9, 7*; 8.*9, 17*; 9.*1–3, 4–5, 6–9, 10, 11, 12, 13–14*; 10.*7–8*; 11.*3–4, 8–10*; 13.*1–2, 3–4*; 14.*1–4, 5, 6, 7–9*;

15.*5–13*; 16.*1–17.4*; 17.*7–8*, *11–12*; 18.*9–10*, *11–12*, *13–16*; 19.*1*, 2, 4, 5, *6–7*, *11*, *12*, *15*; 20.*1–4*, *5–8*; 20.*9–21.7*; 21.*8–9*, *13*; 23.*8*; 24.*1–9*, *10–14*; 25.*6–10*, *13*; 26.2, 3, *4–5*, 6, *14–15*; 27.5, *6–7*, *8–9*, *10–11*, *12–13*; 28.*11*; 29.*1–3*, *7–9*, *19–20*; 30.*7–10*; 31.*11–12*; 31.*13–32.5*; 32.7, *10–11*; 33.*3*, 4, *7–8*, *10*, *13*; 34.*8*, *9–14*; 35.*6*; 36.*1*, 3, *10*; 37.*3–4*, *5–6*; 38.*1–2*, 5, *6–7*, *12*; 39.*1*, *4–5*, 6; 40.*1*, 3, 6, *12–13*; 41.*2*, *14*, *17*; 42.*1–2*, *9–10*; 43.*1–2*

SAINTS

St. Constantine

Bearded, dressed in stemma, divitision, and loros—occasionally sagion as well. Holds normal imperial insignia. Somewhat confusingly often lacks nimbus, and appears with a further imperial saint—Helena. First appearance under Alexius III. Pls. 22.*1–3*, *4–7*; 22.*8–23.7*; 24.*15–25.5*; 26.*7–9*, *10*; 28.*9–10*, *12–14*; 29.*16–18*; 32.6, *10–11*; 33.*5*; 39.*7*; 51.*7–8*

St. Demetrius

Beardless, with short curly hair, usually in military dress (short tunic, breastplate, and sagion), but on occasion in divitision and chlamys (Pls. 39.*2*, 6; 43.*1–2*). Usually holds one or two of following: sword, sword and sheath, spear, shield, cross (?). First appearance under Alexius I. Pls. 1.9, *10–12*; 2.*17*; 11.*15–17*; 14.*7–9*; 33.*12*; 37.*1–2*, *3–4*, *7–9*, *10–12*; 38.*6–7*, *10–11*, *13*, *14–15*; 39.*2*, 3, 6, 9, *10–11*; 40.*1*, 2, 4, 5, 6, 7, 8, *12*, *14*, *15*; 41.*1*, 2, *3–4*, *5–6(?)*, *7–8(?)*, *19(?)*; 42.*5–6*, *7–8*, *9–10*, *11–12*; 43.*1–2*, *3–4*, *5–6*, *10*

St. George

Beardless, with short curly hair, always in military dress (short tunic, breastplate, and sagion). Usually holds one or two of following: sword, spear, shield, scroll (?). First appearance under John II. Pls. 10.*1–4*, *5–6*; 17.*13–14*; 18.*3–4*; 19.3, *6–7*; 23.*9–10*, *11–12*, *13–14*; 26.*3(?)*, *14–15*; 33.*2*; 34.*4–5*; 35.*3(?)*, *12–13*; 43.*3–4*; 51.6

St. Helena

Dressed in stemma, divitision, and loros. Holds scepter or cross. Pl. 28.*9–10*, *12–14*

St. Michael

Winged, beardless, with short curly hair. Three main varieties of dress: military (short tunic, breastplate, and sagion); imperial (divitision and loros), and a rarer form (apparently tunic and colobion). These seem to have been the object of some confusion (e.g., Pl. 26.*12–13*). Usually holds one or two of following: scepter, globus cruciger, sword, sword and sheath, labarum. First appearance under Isaac II. Pls. 20.*1–4*, *5–8*; 21.*10–11*; 26.*7–9*, *12–13*; 27.*3–4*, 5; 32.*14*; 33.*1*; 38.*3–4*; 39.*4–5*, 7, *8*, *10–11*; 40.*9–10*; 41.*20–21*; 42.*3–4*

St. Nicholas (?)

Bearded, dressed in episcopal vestments (sticharion, felonion, and omophorion, only the last being really distinguishable). Holds Book of Gospels. *See* p. 408

St. Paul

With long beard, dressed in tunic and colobion. Appears embracing St. Peter only on late Latin type (T). Pl. 27.*10–11*

St. Peter

With short beard, dressed in tunic and colobion. Alone, he holds keys or scepter cruciger and keys. Pls. *27.8–9, 10–11*; *43.7*

St. Theodore

With forked beard and short curly hair. Always in military dress (short tunic, breast-plate, and sagion). Holds one or two of following: sword, sword and sheath, spear, shield. Almost certainly to be identified throughout as Theodore Stratelates rather than Theodore Tiro. First appearance under Manuel I. Pls. *13.5–9*; *30.2–3, 4–6, 7–10*; *31.6–7, 8–9, 10*; *32.8, 9(?)*; *35.9–11*; *38.1–2*; *39.9*; *40.2, 5, 15*; *51.5*

St. Tryphon

Beardless, with short curly hair, dressed in tunic and colobion. Holds cross, or scepter(?), and is usually accompanied by his particular attribute, the lys. Appears only under Theodore II and Michael VIII, at Magnesia. Pls. *35.1–2, 7–8*; *36.3*

CHERUB

Since the creature depicted on Plates *34.3* and *41.5–6* apparently has four wings, it seems to qualify as a cherub rather than as a seraph, which should have six. Appears only under John III at Magnesia, and John Comnenus-Ducas at Thessalonica.

INDEX V

GENERAL

ACCOUNT, documents of, 26 (Greek), 18, 22–23, 26 (western); system of, 6–7 (pre-reform), 24–25, 26 (post-reform)

Achyra, 231

Acropolites, George, on appearance of Theodore I, 231

Adramyttium, 231

Adrianople, 46, 78

Ahrweiler, H., on tetarteron, 5 n. 6; on Smyrna and area, 232; on extent and radical nature of Alexian reforms, 318–19

albus, 31

Aldobrandini, 227

alek'sati (stamenoni), 28

alloy, *see* composition (metallic)

Amastris, 227, 231, 235

American Numismatic Society, collection, 142, 216, 418, 421, 424, 429, 430

ἀνεξικακία, 67

Angelus

Alexius III (called Comnenus)
coinage and commentary, 150–55;
coins wrongly attributed to, 41;
distinctive marks on billon, 177–80, 187;
governmental clipping of coin under, 179–81

Alexius IV
no coinage, 156

Isaac II
coinage and commentary, 143–46;
debasement of electrum, 19;
distinctive marks on gold, 182, 186, on electrum, 185, 187, on billon, 173–77, 187

annual sequence, 260, 268

"anonymous bronze," introduced by John
    I, 77; studies on, 80 n. 9
Antioch, Byzantine mint (?), 80; coins
    from excavations, 80; *see also* Index I
ἀντιστροφή, *see* στροφή
ἀπόδεσμος, 307
ἀποκόμβιον, ἀποκόμπιον, 306–09
ἀπόλυτον Αἰγύπτιον χάραγμα, 304
Aquileia, mosaic, 303
Arcadia (hoard), 201, *see also* Index II
argentum signatum, 303 n. 2
Argyrus, Romanus III
    last emp. to issue unalloyed gold, 6, 47;
    mosaic (originally) of, 308–09;
    παλαιὸν λογάριον of, 29–30
Armenians (Cilician), 138, 224
Arta (hoard), 294, 296, 297, *see also*
    Index II
Artavasdus, Nicephorus (*proedros*), 53, 55
Asen
    Constantine, 294 n. 1;
    Ivan I (Kaloyan), 221–22;
    Ivan II, 296–97 (coinage); 221, 267,
    298
Ashmolean Museum Oxford, collection, 40,
    278, 406, 407, 413, 423, 426
Asidenus, Sabbas, 227, 234
ἄσπρον τραχὺ νόμισμα
    (billon)
        identification, composition, value, and
        history, to Alexius III, 20–23, 25,
        28, 29–31; in *Palaia kai Nea Logarike*,
        58, 64; revaluation under Manuel I,
        160, 170–71; degeneration under Isaac
        II and Alexius III, 177, 179–180;
        clipping under Alexius III, 180–81;
        during thirteenth century, 286–87;
        Latin and Bulgarian imitative series
        of, 199–217, 219–222, 223; under
        empire of Nicaea, 225; under empire
        of Thessalonica, 267; *see also* Index I,
        (ἱ)στάμενον, τραχύ
    (electrum)
        identification, value, and history, to

Alexius III, 18–20, 23, 25, 29–31;
    composition, 10–12, 19; in *Palaia kai
    Nea Logarike*, 53–54, 56–58, 64; as Æ
    under empire of Nicaea, 225–26; as
    Æ under empire of Thessalonica,
    267; *see also* Index I, μανοηλάτον,
    τραχύ, τρικέφαλον
Assenovgrad (hoard), 179, 202 (table XI),
    215, *see also* Index II, Map
"Astrampsychus" on trikephalon, 49 n. 30
Astytzium, 232
Athens, coins from excavations, 80, 98–
    101, 109, 110, 127–29, 135, 141, 146,
    148, 154
Attaleiates, Michael, 29
Attalia, 227
augustalis, introduction by Frederick II,
    15; metallic composition, 15
Augustus Caesar, 50
aurum coctum, 34
aurum de Palaeola, 16
Avlona, 43

ΒΑΛΑΝΤΙΟΝ, 303, 307
Balling, J., on Lindos hoard, 183, 302
Banya (hoard), 185, *see also* Index II,
    Map
Basil I, 66
Basil II
    leaves treasury full, 5–6, 317;
    menologium of, 67
Basilacius, Nicephorus
    revolt and possible coin of, 78–79
Basilika, 16, i (xxv), on *apokompion*, 307;
    56, i (xx), on export of gold, 312
Batkoun (hoard), 158 and table I, 161
    table II, 162 table III, 164 table IV,
    165, 166 table V, 173 table IX, 174
    table X, 202 table XI, 220 table XV,
    see also Index II, Map
Belitsa (hoard), 158 and table I, 161 table
    II, 162 table III, 164 and table IV,
    166 table V, 202 table XI, 220 table
    XV, *see also* Index II, Map

Bell, H. W., on supposed coin of Theodore Mangaphas, 149, 260; *see also* Sardis

Bellinger, A. R., on anonymous bronze, 80; on possible provincial mints, 199; on Latin type B (Cpl.), 200, 203–04; on first coinage (Nicaea), 233; on recutting of dies, 302; with Metcalf on Latin type B (Thess.), 200

Belyaev, D. F., on loros, 66

Bergama (hoard), 203 and table XI, *see also* Index II, Map

Berlin Münzkabinett, collection, 76, 405, 430

Bertelè, T., on Comnenian denominational system, 4; on Latin type C (Thess.), 201; on Western influences, 214, 267; on Latin types D, J, and K (Cpl.), 215; on Latin types N and O, 216; on gold content of hyperpyra of empire of Nicaea, 247 n. 6; on Manuel Ducas type D, 279; on possible type of Manuel Ducas, 279 n. 3; on small-module types of John Ducas, 287, 288; on uncertain Thessalonican type, 289; on possible coin of Michael II of Epirus, 296; on winged motif, 408, 427

Bibliothèque Nationale, collection, 40, 215, 260, 413, 414, 415, 418, 420, 421, 424, 425

bisanti di Cipri, composition, 19; details of costume on, 205

Blachernae, 67

Blake, R. P., on dimitraton, 125

Boethius, consular diptych of, 303, 304

Bohemund (son of Robert Guiscard), 44–45, 47, 97

Book of the Prefect, 312

Borrell, H. P., on "Smyrna" hoard, 234–35, 249

Botaneiates, Nicephorus III
extends debasement, 6, 316;
system of account under, 6–7;
depletion of treasury by, 44;

revolt of, 78;
details of coin design influence Alexius I, 90; Theodore Ducas, 274

Bovill, E. W., on Saharan gold trade, 313 n. 29

Brauron (hoard), 127, 129, *see also* Index II, Map

Brestovo (hoard), 174 table X, 175, 179, 202 table XI, 211 table XIII, 221 table XVI, *see also* Index II, Map

British Museum, collection, 41, 96–97, 146 n. 1, 248, 294, 411, 412, 413, 414, 418, 423, 424, 425

Brusa, 231; "hoard," 235, 246, 249, *see also* Index II

Bryennius, Nicephorus
(elder), 78–79;
(younger, Caesar) on the usurpation of the elder, 78–79

Bulgarians, imitative coinage and commentary, 218–22, 223

buoni (perperi), 251, 253, 255

Byaga (hoard), 201, 202 table XI, 212 table XIV, *see also* Index II, Map

CAESAR, crown of, 68

Camaterus, Demetrius, 53

camelaucion, 67

Cantacuzene, John VI, on *epikombia*, 252

carat (as degree of fineness), 19, 250–54, 255–56

Carnello, Gyslando, characteristic phraseology in docs., 36–37

Castoria, 44

χάραγμα (nomisma), as monetary term, 38, 51, table 1, 59; as fiscal practice under *Palaia Logarike*, 51, 52, 53, 55, 60–61 table 3, under *Nea Logarike*, 56–58, 63 table 7, 64

Charanis, P., on Asiatic frontiers of empire of Nicaea, 231

Chartres, Fulcher of, on tartaron, 24, 28

Chatillon, Renauld of, 138

χιᾶτον (trachy), 38

χλαμύς, 65, *see also* Index III

Choniates, Nicetas, on debasement of electrum by Isaac II, 19; on revaluation of billon by Manuel I, 22; on appearance of Andronicus I, 135; on Isaac Comnenus, 138 n. 1, 140; on Theodore Mangaphas, 149; on assumption of name "Comnenus" by Alexius III, 153; on Latins striking coinage, 206; on *phaskolia*, 309

χωρία, 53–56, 58

Chronographer of 354, 303

chrysones, 304, 305

χρυσοῦν (nomisma), 35–36, 38

Cipolla, C. M., on causes of debasement, 316; on monetary history, 319 n. 4

Claudiopolis, 231

clipping of coins, 179–81, 287, 312

Cnidan peninsula, 227

Codex, Iustinianus, see Justinian I; *Theodosianus, see* Theodosius II

Codinus, George, *de Officiis* formerly attributed to, 65

"coin drift," 204

Coislin MS 79; 65, 66, 67

Coislin MS 126; 305–06

collar-piece, 68; various forms of, on Aʹ of Alexius I, 81–84, 90–91, 95; on Aʹ of John II, 181; on Aʹ of Manuel I, 123; on Aʹ of Isaac II, 182; on El. of Manuel I, 183–84; on El. of Isaac II, 185; on bill. of John II, 170; on bill. of Manuel I, 169, 163, 164; on bill. of Isaac II, 173; on bill. of Alexius III, 177–78; on Æ of Manuel I, 121

comites rerum privatarum and *sacrarum largitionum*, 303

comet (of 1106), 97

commemorative issue in electrum and billon (Alexius I, Irene, John II), 40–41, 46, 81, 84, 85, 89, 97

Comnena, Anna, on first Norman war, 43–44, 47; on Treaty of Deavolis, 47–48; on stemma/crown, 67–68; on revolt of Bryennius and Basilacius, 78–79; on revolt of Theodore and Gregory Gavras, 93; on comet (of 1106), 97

Comnenus

  Alexius I

    coinage and commentary, 71–80 (pre-reform), 81–101 (post-reform), 405; state of empire and coinage at accession, 3–4, 6; monetary reform—system, 14–25; monetary reform—date of introduction, 39–46; taxation reforms (*Palaia kai Nea Logarike*), 50–64; coins imitated by Latins, 210; coins imitated by Theodore I, 235–36

  Alexius II

    no coinage, 131

  Alexius and David, 227

  Andronicus I

    coinage and commentary, 132–35; distinctive marks on electrum, 185, 187; on billon, 172–73, 187; coins imitated by Latins, 215, 217

  Isaac I

    state of gold coinage under, 6

  Isaac

    (sebastocrator, brother of Alexius I), 44

  Isaac

    (sebastocrator, son of Alexius I), 31

  Isaac

    (sebastocrator, son of John II), 138, 140

  Isaac

    (usurper in Cyprus) coinage and commentary, 136–42

  John II

    coinage and commentary, 102–10; commemorative issue (with Alexius I and Irene), 40–41; Greek mint closed for reign, 129; sequence of billon issues, 169–70;

distinctive marks on gold, 181, 186; on electrum, 182, 186; on billon, 169–70;

coins imitated by Latins, 210, 216;

coins imitated by Theodore I, 236; by John III, 246–50;

mosaic of, 309

Manuel I

coinage and commentary, 111–30;

revaluation of billon by, 22, 170–72;

distinctive marks on gold, 182, 186; and sequence of electrum, 182–85, 186, and billon, 162–69, 187;

coins imitated by Latins, 209–10, 215;

coins imitated by Theodore I, 405–06

Comnenus-Ducas

Constantine (sebastocrator), 215

Demetrius (despot)

no named coinage, 288–89

John (emperor then despot)

coinage and commentary, 279–88, 408

John (sebastocrator), 294

Manuel

coinage and commentary, 274–79, 407

Michael I ("despot" of Epirus), 296

Michael II ("despot" of Epirus)

possible coin of, 296

Nicephorus (son of Michael II), 296

Theodore

coinage and commentary, 268–74

Comnenus-Lascaris

Constantine (despot), abortive election of, 156

Theodore I

coinage and commentary, 227–36, 405–06;

coins useful in dating hoards, 201, 212;

treaty with Venetian podestà, 206–08;

coins imitative of Alexius I, 235–36, John II, 236, Manuel I, 405–06

composition (metallic), of pre-reform issues, 41, 43, 76–77; of hyperpyron, 10–13, 15–17, 247, 250–51, 255–56; of

electrum trachy, 10–13, 19; of billon trachy, 21; Nicholas Oresme on, 49 n. 30

comunali (perperi), 250–51, 253, 255

Constantine VII

ivory of, 66;

on imperial costume, 65–68;

on purses of coin, 307–08

Constantine VIII, 6, 199

Constantinople, personification of, 303; for products of mint of, *see* Index I

Constantius Gallus, 303, 304

copper mines, 138

Corfu, 43

Corinth, coins from excavations, 93, 98–101, 109, 110, 127–29, 135, 141, 146, 148, 154, 260; sacked by Normans, 129; supposed mint at, 92–93; I (hoard), 129; II (hoard), 203 and table XII; III (hoard), 13 n. 3, 122–24, 159; *see also* Index II, Map

Cosmas I (patriarch), 3

Cosmas Indicopleustes, 312

costume (imperial ceremonial), 65–68, *see also* Index III

Cotyaeum, 231

countermark (Arabic), 80

Cox, D. H., on coins from excavations at Curium, 141, 142, *see also* Curium

Cremona, Liutprand bishop of, on ceremonial payment of Byzantine officials, 307

Crete, duke of, 31

crown (stemma), description of, 67–68

Crusade, First, 39, 80; Second, 21; Third, 21, 138, 148; Fourth, 156, 206

Cumans, 46, 313

Curium, coins from excavations, 141, 148, 418

Cyprus, possible hoard from, 142

Cyzicus, 231

Dais, attempt at perspective, 216; on Palaeologan seals, 264

Dalassena, Anna, 44

Danube valley and plain, 151, 158, 161 table II

debasement, Michael IV–Nicephorus III, 5 n. 7, 6; supposed widespread under Comneni, 3–4; by Alexius I prior to reform, 41, 43, 76–77; of electrum by Isaac II and Alexius III, 19; of gold by John III and successors, 247, 250–254, 255–56; of silver by John III, 254; of silver by emperors of Thessalonica, 320; general causes of, 316–18

De Caerimoniis, on imperial costume, 65–68

de Jerphanion, G., on θωράκιον, 66

Demetrius, Saint, significance of on coins of Alexius I, 41–46; of John II, 110; of Manuel I, 125–26; *see also* Index IV

δημόσιος κανών, δημόσιον, 51–64

De Officiis, on imperial costume, 65–68

Deuil, Odo bishop of, on exchange rates, 21, 28

διβιτήσιον, 67, *see also* Index III

δικέρατον, under *Palaia Logarike*, 51–52, 59 table 2, 60–61 table 3, 61 table 4, 62 table 6; under *Nea Logarike*, 55–58, 64, 63 table 7

dimidium staminum, 28

dimitraton, 26, 125–26

Diogenes, Romanus IV, 6

διοίκησις, fiscal situation in *dioikeseis* of Thrace and Macedonia, 53–55

distinctive marks (official), for internal sequences, 90–91, 123, 260; for "officinae," 91–93, 162–187; for mints, 93–96, 124; of uncertain nature, 153, 175, 248, 250–54, 255–56, 273

distribution of coin, 311

Dölger, F., on dates in *Palaia kai Nea Logarike*, 50; on abbreviation Γκλ', 226 n. 10

Dorkovo (hoard), 201, 202 and table X, 212 table XIV, 213, 215, 216, 217, 287, 294, 427, *see also* Index II, Map

Dorylaeum, 231

δουκᾶτον (trachy), 29

Draganovo (hoard), 158 and table I, 161 table II, 162 table III, 163, 164 table IV, 165, 166 table V, 172, 173 table IX, 175, 202 table XI, 220 table XV, *see also* Index II, Map

drakhani (dimitrati), 125–26

Ducaina
Euphrosyne, 297
Irene on commemorative issue (with Alexius I and John II), 40

Du Cange, C., on derivation of term hyperpyron, 34; of term trikephalon, 31

Ducas
Alexius V
no coinage, 156
Constantine X
chrysobull of, 29; reintroduces named copper, 78; trachy of, 29–30
Constantine (son of Michael VII), 41, 318
John III (called Vatatzes)
coinage and commentary, 237–56, 290–94, 406–07; treasury at Magnesia, 232
Michael VII
extends debasement, 6, 47, 316; trachy of, 29–30
Stephen (Radoslav)
coinage of, 297–98

Ducas-Angelus-Comnenus-Palaeologus
Andronicus II, 251, 252
Michael VIII
coinage and commentary, 261–64; coinage of Thessalonica not treated, 295
Michael IX, 251, 252

Ducas-Lascaris
Theodore II
coinage and commentary, 256–61, 295, 407; treasury at Astytzium, 232

ducat (ducalis), of Roger II, 42–43, 45

Dumbarton Oaks, Collection, 41, 43, 77, 80, 92, 95, 125, 139, 165, 167, 170, 173, 175, 181, 182, 183, 184, 215, 216, 217, 222, 260, 274, 411–30 *passim*; I (hoard), 203 table XII; II (hoard), 203 table XII; III (hoard), 203 table XII; *see also* Index II

Dyrrhachium, 43, 44, 46, 78

EBERSOLT, J., on θωράκιον, 66; on seal of Michael VIII, 264

ecclesiastical property, confiscation of by Alexius I, 44

Edwards, K. M., on Latin type C (Cpl.), 200; on supposed coin of Manuel and Andronicus, 278; *see also* Corinth

Egyptian solitaries (Coislin MS 126), 305–06

Ehrenkreutz, A. S., on tetarteron, 5 n. 6

ek' ust' avi (stamenoni), 28

ἐλατικόν, under *Palaia Logarike*, 52, 61 table 5, 62 table 6; under *Nea Logarike*, 55–58, 64, 63 table 7

Emmanuel (Christ), probable pun with name Manuel, 126; with beard, 210, *see also* Index IV

Enina (hoard), 158 and table I, 161 table II, 162 table III, 164 table IV, 165, 166 table V, 173 table IX, 202 table XI, 220 table XV, *see also* Index II, Map

Ephesus, 231, 232

ἐπικόμβιον, *see* ἀποκόμβιον

Epiphanius, on *balantion*, 303

exchange rates, of hyperpyron with western coins, 14; of trachy (billon) with western coins, 21

FAMILY NAMES, of Isaac of Cyprus, 140; of Theodore Mangaphas, 149; of Alexius III, 153; of Theodore I, 230; of John III, 266; of Theodore II, 266; of Michael VIII, 295; of Stephen Radoslav, 297; of Theodore Ducas, 273; of John Ducas, etc., 285

Fatimid dinar, standard for tetarteron (?), 5; crusaders' imitations of, 208

Filadelphe (perperi di), 251, 252, 256

fiorino di suggello, 309 n. 21

Fitzwilliam Museum, Cambridge, Collection, 430

follis, *see* φόλλις (ph)

forgery (contemporary) of Manuel I, 327

Frederick I, Barbarossa, 21, 149

Frolow, A., on derivation of term hyperpyron, 34; on derivation of term trikephalon, 31; on monetary terminology of Pantocrator typicon, 35

frontiers of empire of Nicaea, 227, 231

GABRIELOPOULUS, STEPHEN (sebastocrator), 297

Gavalas, Leo and John (Rhodes), coinage of, 296

Gavras, Theodore and Gregory, 93

General Nikolaevo (hoard), 158 and table I, 161 table II, 162 table III, 164 table IV, 165, 166 table V, 173 table IX, 174 table X, 201, 202 table XI, *see also* Index II, Map

Genoa, docs. on exchange rates, 14 n. 1

Gerassimov, T. D., on Latin type B (Cpl.), 200; on Ivan II, 297

Γκλ', 226

globus cruciger, various forms of, on *N* of Alexius I, 82–83, 95; on *N* of John II, 181; on bill. of Manuel I, 169, 165, 167; on bill. of Alexius III, 177–78

Goitein, S. D., on the use of sealed purses in Egypt, 309 n. 21

gold, governmental control of, 312; possible sources of, 312–13

Golden Gate, 67

Goodacre, H., collection, 411, 413, 418; on supposed gold commemorative issue of Alexius I, 40; on electrum issue attributed to Isaac of Cyprus, 142; on Latin type A (small module), 200; on copper coinage of empire of Nicaea, 255

Gornoslav (hoard), 13 n. 3, 90–96, 107,
122–24, 159, 181, 182, 248, 311, 412,
413, *see also* Index II, Map

Gradevo I (hoard), 158 and table I, 161
table II, 162 table III, 164 table IV,
166 table V, 179; II (hoard), 174 table
X, 202 table XI, 211 table XIII, 221
table XVI; *see also* Index II, Map

Great Church, 3, 67, 309

Greek mint (of uncertain identity), isolation of products of, 128–30, *see also*
Index I

Gresham's law, operation of, 7, 8, 171

Grierson, P., collection, 429, 430; on coin
(supposed) of Nicephorus Bryennius,
79; on debasement, 5 n. 7; on tetarteron,
5 n. 6

Guiscard, Robert, 43–45

Gunther, G. C., collection, 142

Gurdzhaani (hoard), 93

HAFSIDS, gold coinage of, 16

ἁγιογεωργάτον (nomisma), electrum issue
of John II, 32, 34; *see also* stafratus

half-tetarteron, identification of, 109–
110; *see also* τεταρτηρόν, weight(s) and
Index I

Henry IV (German emperor), 44, 47

Heraclea, 231

Hermus River, 231, 232, 234

Hess-Leu, 254

ἑξάγιον (nomisma), 225

ἑξάφολλον, under *Palaia Logarike*, 51–52,
60–61 table 3, 61 table 4; under *Nea
Logarike*, 55–58, 64, 63 table 7

(ἱ)στάμενον (nomisma), origin, 5; becomes
scyphate, suffers debasement, 6; under
Comneni and Angeli, 20–23, 28; *see also*
ἄσπρον τραχὺ νόμισμα (billon)

*Historia de Expeditione Friderici Im-
peratoris*, on value of staminum, 21–
22; on Theodore Mangaphas, 149

Hohenstaufen, Frederick II of, introduces
augustalis, 15–16

Holy Apostles, church of, 67

ὁρμαθοί, 68

ὑπέρπυρον (nomisma), identification and
exchange rates of, 14; derivation of term
and use in docs., 34–37, 225; metallic
composition of, 10–13, 15–17; place in
Comnenian monetary system, 17–18;
debased by John III and successors,
247–254, 255–256; *see also* Index I

ὑπομνηστικά, of John Tzirithon, 53–57; of
George Spanopoulus, 57–58

IDRISI, on copper ore from Cyprus, 138
n. 2

Iliescu, O., on hyperpyron type of Michael
VIII, 263

ingiallati (perperi), 250, 254, 255

inginocchiati (perperi), 251, 256

imitative coinage, "Bulgarian," 219–22,
223, under Ivan II and Constantine
Asen, 296–97, 294 n. 1; Latin, 199–217,
223; Nicaean tendency toward, 236,
246–50, 294, 406; Serbian, 297–98

inscriptions, used as mint distinction on
Aʹ of Alexius I, 81–84, 90–95; possible
chronological criterion on coinage of
Alexius I, 90–91, 97, 101; Zacos and
Veglery on, 101; control loosened on Aʹ
and El. of Manuel I, 123–24, 301–02;
possible chronological criterion on coinage of Alexius III, 153–155; distinctive
usages of Latin mints of Cpl. and Thess.,
209

insignia (official), in *Notitia Dignitatum*,
303

Ioannina, 44

Irene (wife of John II), 20, Pl. 50

Isauria, 138

Iskra (hoard), 174 table X, 175, 202 table
XI, 220 table XV, *see also* Index II,
Map

Istanbul, A (hoard), 159, 162, 180; B
(hoard), 203 and table XII, 211, 216,
233, 423, 429; *see also* Index II, Map

JOHN I
introduces "anonymous bronze," 77, 80
Johns Hopkins University, Collection, 423, 424
Jones, A. H. M., on follis in fourth century, 303
Julian
introduces *zygostatai*, 304
Justinian I
Cod. Iust. 4, lxiii (ii), on export of gold, 312;
11, x (i), on value of solidi, 38
Dig. Iust. 16, iii (xxv); 16, iii (xxix); 19, ii (xxxi), on sealed purses, 303 n. 2
Edict 11, on *obryza* etc., 38, 304

ΚΑΙΝΟΥΡΓΙΟΝ trikephalon, 33, 34, 37–38; hyperpyron, 36, 37–38
Kalentzi (hoard), 127, *see also* Index II, Map
Kaloyanovets (hoard), 158 and table I, 161 table II, 162 table III, 164 table IV, 166 table V, 173 table IX, 174 table X, 175, 176, 177, 202 table XI, 220 table XV, *see also* Index II, Map
καμπάγια, 68
Kartal (hoard), 220 table XV, *see also* Index II
Kastri (hoard), 127, *see also* Index II, Map
Kazanluk (hoard), 174 table X, 179, 220 table XV, 221, *see also* Index II, Map
Kent, J. P. C., on Roman attitude to gold coin, 312 n. 26
κεράτιον, weight and unit of value, 5, 17 n. 8, 26
Khissar (hoard), 90, *see also* Index II, Map
Kiustendil (hoard), 173, 174 table X, 179, 202 table XI, 211 table XIII, 221 table XVI, *see also* Index II, Map
Kiustendil region (hoard), 202 table XI, 211 table XIII, 212, 221 table XVI, *see also* Index II

Klokotnitsa, battle of, 267, 297
κομμέρκιον, 313
Kondakov, N. P., on scaramangion/ scaranicon, 67
Korten (hoard), 179, 221, *see also* Index II, Map
Kounino II (hoard), 179, *see also* Index II, Map
Kroushare (hoard), 158 and table I, 161 table II, 162 table III, 163, 164 table IV, 165, 166 table V, 172, 173 and table IX, 202 table XI, 220 table XV, *see also* Index II, Map

LAKITÉ (HOARD), 107, *see also* Index II
Lambros, S. P., on coinage of Isaac of Cyprus, 139, 140, 142; on supposed coinage of John of Neopatras, 294
Larissa, siege of, 44
Lascaris, John IV
no coinage, 261
Lathoud, D., on St. Peter on coin of John III, 294
latini (perperi), 250, 254, 255
Latins, imitative coinage and commentary, 191–217, 223; frontiers with empire of Nicaea, 231; possible gold issue, 254
Laurent, V., on derivation of term trikephalon, 31; on "just weight of trachy hyperpyron," 30, 35; on seal of John III, 264; on significance of lys on coins of Theodore II, 261
Lazania (hoard), 21, 108–09, 159, 203, *see also* Index II, Map
Leo III, 51
Leo VI
novel 52 of, on value of solidi, 38
λεπτὰ ψηφία, in *Nea Logarike*, 56–58, 64
Levkokhori (hoard), 203 and table XI, *see also* Index II, Map
Levkosia, 142; *see* Nicosia
Levski (hoard), 297
Levunium, battle of, 46
life of coin, 311–12

ligatures, ꓵ and ꓵꓧ on _N_ of Alexius I, 91; ꓮ and ꓮ on _N_ of Manuel I, 123–24; ꓧ on Magnesian coinage of Theodore II and Michael VIII, 264; _see also_ List of Ligatured Letters

Lindos (hoard), 124, 183–84, _see also_ Index II, Map

λίτρα, trikephalon, 33, 34; hyperpyron, 36

λογάριον (παλαιὸν ῥωμανᾶτον), 29–30

Logodash (hoard), 201, 202 and table XI, 212 table XIV, 213, 287, _see also_ Index II, Map

λογοθέτης τοῦ γενικοῦ, 57

Lom, A (hoard), 201, 202 table XI; B (hoard), 202 table XI, 233 n. 27; _see also_ Index II, Map

Longuet, H., on billon issue of Manuel Ducas, 274

Lopez, R. S., on augustalis, 15–16; on "crisis" of the bezant, 4 n. 2, 321 n. 8; on stability of coinage, 316; on supposed debasement under Comneni and Angeli, 4

λῶρος, types of, 66; survival of traditional type on Thessalonican issues, 101, 109, 273, 302; _see also_ Index III

loros-waist, possible chronological criterion on issues of Isaac II, 145–46, 174

Loukovo (hoard), 158 and table I, 159, 161 table II, 162 table III, 164 table IV, 166 table V, 173 table IX, 174 table X, 179, _see also_ Index II, Map

Lübeck, Arnold of, on electrum manlat, 49 n. 30

λύσεις, of Alexius I in _Palaia kai Nea Logarike_, 55–58

Lusignan (Cyprus), composition of bisanti of, 19; details of costume on bisanti of Hugh I, 205

lys, significance of on coins of empire of Nicaea, 261

MACEDONIA, fiscal situation in _dioikesis_ of, 53–55; (hoard), 159, 203; _see also_ Index II

Maeander River and Valley, 227, 231, 232, 234

Magnesia, identification of mint at, 232–35; _see also_ Index I

μανδύας, 65

Mangaphas, Theodore probable coinage and length of usurpation of, 149, 227, 234

μανοηλᾶτον/ manuellatus, under Comneni and Angeli, 19–20, 23, 27, 49 n. 30; under empire of Nicaea, 225

Manzikert, battle of, 317

mappa, 67

Maritsa River, 227

Mattingly, H., on Arta hoard, 296; on Lazania hoard, 21

Mavrozomes, Manuel, 227

μέγας δομέστικος, 46

μέγας λογαριαστής, 34

Melissenus despot, non existence of, 297 n. 1 Nicephorus, 79

menologium of Basil II, 68

Metcalf, D. M., on _N_ of Alexius I and date of Alexian reform, 39–40, 91–94; on _N_ of Manuel I, 124; on Æ of Manuel I, 127–129; on detail of fourth billon coinage of Manuel I, 167 and n. 4; on supposed Æ of Alexius II, 131; on twelfth-thirteenth century billon issues, 199, 219, 220; on overstrike of Theodore I, 236; on "Brusa" and "Smyrna" hoards and _N_ of the empire of Nicaea, 235, 247, 248, 254, 260; with Bellinger on Latin type B (Thess.), 200

Michael IV commences debasement, adopts scyphate fabric, 6, 47, 316, 317

μιχαηλᾶτον (trachy), 29–30, 47

Miletus, 33, 227

military dress, 68; _see also_ Index III

μιλλιαρήσιον, prior to debasement, 5; during period of debasement, 7; denomination of account after monetary reform, 24, 25, 26; in *Palaia kai Nea Logarike*, 51–64; *see also* Index I

mints, *see* under individual entries and Index I

mint organization, 157–87, 301–03

Mogilitsa (hoard), 174 table X, *see also* Index II, Map

monasteries, involved in *Palaia kai Nea Logarike*, 54

monastic documents (typica, chartularies, etc.), from: Cosmosotira, 31; Iviron, 26, 125–26; Lavra, 31, 34; Lembo, 226, 231; Our Lady of Pity, 33; Our Lady of the Altars of Elijah, 29; Pantocrator, 20, 23–24, 29, 32, 35–36; Petritzos, 28, 29; Rodosto, 29; St. John (Patmos), 26–27, 31–32, 34, 226; St. Mamas, 32–33; St. Paul, 33; Virgin Full of Grace, 30

monetary policy, 172, 181, 313–14

monetary system, prior to debasement, 5; during period of debasement, 6–7; subsequent to Alexian reforms, 14–25

monetary terminology, to 1204, 26–38; after 1204, 225–26

monogram (as *rev.* type), on Æ of emperors prior to Alexius I, 78–79; on pre-reform Æ of Alexius I, 79–80; on post-reform Æ of Alexius I, 100–01; on Æ of Manuel I, 127–28

Monomachus, Constantine IX
μονομαχᾶτον (trachy), 29–30;
mosaic of, 66, Pls. 48–49;
reign crucial in system of tax payment, 52–53;
systematizes debasement and scyphate fabric, 6, 316, 317

Morrisson, C., on τραχὺ χιᾶτον, 38

mosaics, at Aquileia, 303; at Piazza Armerina, 303; "Constantine IX" (originally Romanus III) and Zoë, 66, 308–09, Pls. 48–49; John II and Irene, 309, Pl. 50

Moushmov, N. A., on Bulgarian coinage, 294 n. 1, 296

Muglizh, I (hoard), 174 table X, 179, 220 table XV, 221; II (hoard), 201, 202 table XI, 205, 233 n. 27; *see also* Index II, Map

Muwahids, gold coinage of, 16

NAOUSA (HOARD), 203 and table XII, *see also* Index II, Map

Nau, F., on *sphragis* (Coislin MS 126), 305–06

Neapolis, Leontius, bishop of Cypriot, on *apokombion*, 306

Neocastra, theme of, 231, 232

Nicaea, mint and economic position of in empire of Nicaea, 231–35

Nicomedia, 231

Nicosia, I (hoard), 108, 124–25, 182, 183; II (hoard), 109, 159, 169, 170, 203; *see also* Index II, Map

Normans, ducat of Roger II, 42–43; first Norman war, 43–45, 318; second Norman war, 47, 97; sack of Corinth, 129; sack of Thessalonica, 146

Notitia Dignitatum, on official insignia, 303

νουμίον, traditional smallest monetary division, 24, 25, 50 n. 6; referring to Æ tetarteron, 23, 25, 29; in *Palaia kai Nea Logarike* as Æ tetarteron (?), 24, 56–58

Novo Selo (hoard), 158 and table I, 161 table II, 162 table III, 164 table IV, 166 table V, 173 table IX, 202 table XI, 220 table XV, 311, *see also* Index II, Map

novi pesantes (perperi), 36–37

nuovi nuovi (perperi), 251, 252, 256

Nymphaeum, 231, 232, 234

OBRYZA, 304, 305

Obuda (hoard), 159, 203, *see also* Index II

Ochrida (hoard), 297, *see also* Index II

Oikonomides, M., 273, 297, 408

Oresme, Nicholas, on monetary alloys, 49 n. 30

Osanica (hoard), 203 and table XII, *see also* Index II, Map

Ostrogorsky, G., on Constantine Lascaris, 156

Oustovo (hoard), 202 table XI, 213, 215–17, 287 and n. 4, 288, 427, 429, *see also* Index II, Map

Ovchartsi (hoard), 158 and table I, 161 table II, 162 table III, 164 table IV, 165, 166 table V, 173 table IX, 174 table X, 175, *see also* Index II, Map

overstriking, "Bulgarian" imitative type C on Seljuk coin, 327; Latin imitative type B (Cpl.) on Isaac II, 205, 369; Latin imitative type C (Cpl.) on type B (Cpl.), 209, 429; Latin imitative type O (Cpl.) on type C (Thess.), 216, 429; Latin imitative type B (Thess.) on type A (Thess.), 209, 333, 362, 370, 391, 419; Latin imitative type B (Thess.) on Theodore I first coinage (Nic.), 205, 429; Theodore I second coinage (Nic.) on Alexius III, 370; Theodore I second coinage (Nic.) on first coinage, 233, 236, 429; Theodore I second coinage (Nic.) on Latin imitative type A (Thess.), 391

Oxyrhynchus Papyrus (1886), on *sphragis*, 304–05, 306

PACHYMERES, GEORGE, on debasement, John III–Andronicus II, 247–48, 251, 263; on site of treasury under John III, 232

Pacourianus, Gregory (*megas domestikos*), 29–30, 46

paglialoccati (perperi), 250, 251, 255

Palaeologus
  Andronicus III, 252;
  John V, 252;
  for Michael VIII, Andronicus II, and Michael IX, *see* Ducas-Angelus-Comnenus-Palaeologus

Παλαιὰ καὶ Νέα Λογαρική (Alexian taxation reform), 50–64

παλαιόν, logarion, 29–30; trachy, 56; trikephalon, 32, 33, 34; hyperpyron, 36; significance of term, 37–38

palm frond, Bertelè on, 279. n. 3

παρακολουθήματα (*dikeraton, hexafollon, synetheia, elatikon*), under *Palaia Logarike*, 51–55, 59–62 (tables 1–6); under *Nea Logarike*, 55–58, 63 table 7, 64; examples of calculation of, 58, 64

Patzinaks, 3, 46, 318

Paulicians, 46

pecunia clusa, obsignata, 303 n. 2

Pegolotti, Francesco Balducci, on gold content of augustalis, 15; on gold content of *bisanti di Cipri*, 19; list of debased perperi, 250–54, 255–56

pendilia, on *N* of Alexius I, 81, 83, 95; on *N* of Manuel I, 124; on coinage of Isaac Angelus and Isaac Comnenus, 141; revival of Alexian types on Latin issues, 95, 209–10, 302; *see also* πρεπεν-δούλια

pensa (recta) de Constantinopoli, in Pisan docs., 37

perperi, list of by Pegolotti, 250–54, 255–56

pestello/pestle, 250, 252, 253, 255

φασκώλια, 309

φίβλα, 65

Philadelphia, 149, 227; *see also Filadelphe (perperi di)*

Philaretus, 80

Philippopolis (Plovdiv), identification of temporary mint at, 95–96, 98; *see also* Index I

Phocas, Nicephorus II
  introduces tetarteron, 5

φόλλις, prior to debasement, 5; during period of debasement, 7; denomination of account after monetary reform, 24, 25, 26; superseded by keration, 26; in *Palaia kai Nea Logarike*, 51–64; as purse, 303; *see also* Index I

Photiadès Catalogue, 288

Piazza Armerina, mosaic at, 303

Pirdop (hoard), 220 table XV, *see also* Index II, Map

Pisa, docs. of account etc., 18, 22–23, 28, 37; treaty with Alexius I (1111), 313

Pisaratsi (hoard), 202 table XI, 215–17, *see also* Index II, Map

Plovdiv, (Bounardzhik) hoard, 96, 159; (region) hoard, 179, 220 table XV, 221; *see also* Index II, Map

Pokrovnik (hoard), 179, 202 table XI, 211 table XIII, 221 table XVI, *see also* Index II, Map

ΠΟΛΙC ΘΕCCΑΛΟΝΙΚΗ, derivation of representation, 267

Postallar (hoard), 203 and table XII, 216–17, *see also* Index II, Map

πρεπενδούλια, 68

Preslav (hoard), 202 table XI, 213, 215–17, 287, 427, *see also* Index II, Map

Prespa (Lake), coins from excavations at, 297, 408

Prilep, find of coins at, 297

Prodromus, Theodore, on ὑπέρπυρον μανοηλᾶτον, 27

πρόσωπα, involved in *Palaia kai Nea Logarike*, 54–56, 58

προτιμηταῖον, trikephalon, 32, 33; significance, 37–38

προτιμώμενον, trikephalon, 32, 33; hyperpyron, 35–36; significance, 37–38

"RADIATE CROSS," in nimbus of Christ on Thessalonican issues, 108, 124

Ratto Catalogue, 200, 216, 235–36, 422

recutting of dies, 91, 108, 302

restrictions, (supposed) on internal circulation of gold coin, 8, 315

revaluation, of billon trachy by Manuel I, 170–72

Rhabdas, on value of (electrum) trachy, 19 n. 15

Rhodes, 227, 296 (*see also* Lindos)

ῥωμανᾶτον, logarion, 29–30; nomisma, 47

Richard I, king of England, 138, 208

Romanus II and Eudocia, ivory of, 66

Roger (duke of Apulia), 42–43

Roger II (king of Sicily), 42–43, 138 n. 2

Rollin, G., on "Brusa" hoard and coinage of John III, 235, 246, 249

Roma, personification of, 303

rosa et di stella (*perperi di*), 251, 252, 256

Roussé (hoard), 202 table XI, *see also* Index II, Map

SABATIER, J., on el. commemorative issue of Alexius I, 40; on supposed Æ tetarteron of Alexius I, 100; on supposed bill. trachy of Isaac of Cyprus, 138–39, 260; on supposed tetarteron of Alexius V, 156; on supposed tetarteron of John III, 255; on tetartera of uncertain attribution, 266; on supposed bill. trachy of Theodore II, 274; on supposed bill. trachy of John V, 288

sacculum, 303 n. 2

σαγίον (*sagum*), 67, 68, *see also* Index III

saints, as coin types, 45 and n. 25, *see also* Index IV

σακκία, 308

σάκκος, 67

Saloman (ex king of Hungary), 46

Sampson, 227

San Germano, Richard of, on introduction of augustalis, 15

Sardis, city, 231, 232; coins from excavations, 233, 234, 423, 424

Savoy, Anna of, 252

Schindler, L., on Comnenian denominational system, 4; on staminum, 20

Schlumberger, G., on coinage of Gavalas brothers, 296; *see also* weights

scyphate fabric, introduction and possible significance, 6; denoted by term τραχύ, 29–31

sealed purses, 303–10

seals (Palaeologan), 264

sebastocrator, crown of, 68

Seeck, O., on sealed purses, 309

Selymbria, 78

Senegal (source of gold), 16, 313

Shishman, Michael, 261

Silistria, battle at, 46

σκαραμάγγιον / σκαράνικον, 67, *see also* Index III

σκηπτρᾶτον (trachy), 29–30

small-module coins, Latin, 210–14, 223; John Comnenus-Ducas, 286–88, 408

Smyrna, city, 46, 231, 232, 234; "hoard," 234–35, 249

Sofia (hoard), 41, 90, *see also* Index II, Map

souppedion (dais), 264, *see also* dais

Souvatité (hoard), 158 and table I, 161 table II, 162 table III, 164 and table IV, 165, 166 table V, 177, 217, *see also* Index II, Map

Spanopoulus, George (*logothetes tou genikou*), *hypomnestikon* of, 57–58

specific gravity, of pre-reform coins, 41; of post-reform coins (A/ and El.), 10–12; methodology and use, 12–13

σφραγίς, 305–06

Sredna Gora, hoards from, 221

stafratus, 27

staminum, *see* (i)στάμενον

standard (held by emperor), 284

star, *see* comet

Stara Zagora (hoard), 202 table XI, *see also* Index II, Map

Statuta Officiorum, on metallic composition of augustalis, 15

stauro-manuellatus, 27

στέμμα, 67–68; *see also* Index III

Stiernon, L., on the "despotate" of Epirus, 267 n. 1, 296

Strazhitsa (hoard), 174 table X, 179, 220 table XV, 221, *see also* Index II, Map

στροφή, 51, 60–61 table 3

Struma Valley, as topographical feature, 157, 158, 161 table II; hoards from, 211–13, 220, 221 table XVI

Suedinenie (hoard), 95, 177, 202 table XI, *see also* Index II, Map

Svoronos, N. G., on supposed debasement under Comneni, 4, 47; on date of composition of *Palaia kai Nea Logarike*, 50

Symeon (*logothetes*), on *apodesmos*, 307

συνήθεια, under *Palaia Logarike*, 52, 61 table 5, 62 table 6; under *Nea Logarike*, 55–58, 63 table 7

ΤΑΒΛΙΟΝ, ornament on chlamys, 65; varieties of on coinage, 81, 163

tari (Sicilian), 15, 251, 255, 256

Taronites, Gregory, 93, *see also* Gavras

Taticius, 46

taxes, δημόσιος κανών, παρακολουθήματα 51–64; κομμέρκιον, 313

Templars, 138

terminology, *see* monetary terminology

τεταρτηρόν (nomisma, noummion), prior to debasement, 6; during period of debasement, 6–7; under Comneni and Angeli, 23–25, 28–29; *see also* half-tetarteron, νουμίον, weight(s) and Index I

Theoctistus, abbot of Patmos, 32

Theodora, 6

Theodosius II

 Cod. Theod. 12, vii (i) for *aurum coctum*, 34,

   12, vii (ii) for *zygostatai*, 304

θεοτόκιον (nomisma), 26–27, 31–32

Thessalonica, mint, probably opened for copper under Constantine X, 78–79; opened for precious metal during first Norman war, 43–46; taken by John III, 227; representation of ΠΟΛΙС on coins, 267; *see also* Index I

Thompson, M., on "anonymous bronze," 80; *see also* Athens

θωράκιον, 66

Thrace, revolt of Nicephorus Bryennius, 78; Patzinak attacks, 46; fiscal situation in *dioikesis* of, 53–55; monetary situation in, 96; as topographical feature, 157, 158, 161 table II, 221; taken by John III, 227

Thracesion, theme of, 231, 232

Tiepolo, Giacomo, Venetian podestà, treaty with Theodore I (1219), 206

Tiurkmen, I and II (hoards), 202 table XI; II, 158 and table I, 161 table II, 162 table III, 164 table IV, 166 table V, 173 table IX, 220 table XV; *see also* Index II, Map

Torbalı (hoard), 234, *see also* Index II, Map

Toulovo (hoard), 202 table XI, 233 n. 27, *see also* Index II, Map

trabea, 66

τραχύ (nomisma), meaning of term and varieties of, 29–31

Trajanopolis, 78

Tralles, 234

transitional types, El. ("A'") of Alexius I, 405; A' of John II, 108

treasury, left full by Basil II, 5; left empty by Nicephorus III, 44; of empire of Nicaea, 232, 234

Trebizond, 224, 227

tre santi (perperi), 251–52, 256

τρικέφαλον (nomisma), meaning of term and instances of use, 31–34, 49 n. 30; under empire of Nicaea, 226

trimenus (perperus) = trikephalon, 31, 34

Tri Voditsi (hoard), 201, 202 and table XI, 212 table XIV, 213, 215–17, 233, 233 n. 27, 287, 287 n. 4, 288, 294, 424, 427, 429, *see also* Index II, Map

Troad (hoard), 203 and table XI, 211, *see also* Index II

Tsepina (hoard), 202 table XI, 233 n. 27, *see also* Index II

Tsruncha, A (hoard), 174 table X, 175, 220 table XV, 221; B (hoard), 174 table X, 220 table XV, 221; A and B, 158 and table I, 161 table II, 164 table IV, 166 table V, 179, 180; *see also* Index II, Map

Turks, Ottoman, 252; Seljuk, 3, 46, 91, 224, 231, 318; coin overstruck by "Bulgarian" imitative type C, 327

Turnovo, I (hoard), 158 and table I, 161 table II, 162 table III, 164 table IV, 166 table V, 202 table XI, 220 table XV; II (hoard), 174 table X, 179, 180, 220 table XV, 221; *see also* Index II, Map

Tvurditsa (hoard), 179, 180, 220 table XV, *see also* Index II, Map

Tzachas, emir of Smyrna, 46, 318

Tzirithon, John, *hypomnestikon* of, 53–57

UNCERTAIN ATTRIBUTION (COINS OF), of Isaac Comnenus or Isaac Angelus, 147–48; of the empire of Nicaea, 264–66; of the empire of Thessalonica, 289

uncertain Bulgarian provenance (hoard of), 174 table X, 175, 179, 202 table XI, 211 table XIII, 212, 221 table XVI, *see also* Index II

uncertain mint, products of, 96, *see also* Index I

VALENTINIAN I

novel of, concerning value of old solidi (*Cod. Iust.* 11, x[i]), 38

Valentinian III

novel 14(i) of, concerning value of old solidi, 37–38

Varangians, 232

Venice, docs. on exchange rates, 14 n. 1; docs. of account etc., 18, 27, 36–37, 225; treaty with Theodore I, 206–08, 214–15

Verroë (Stara Zagora), 222

veteres pesantes (perperi), 36–37

Vogt, A., on ceremonial *apokombia*, 307–08

volume of coinage, 310–11, 315–16

WARREN, F., on coinage of Isaac Comnenus 141, 142

weight(s), average, of tetartera and half-tetartera, 109–10, 127, 154–55, 217, 274, 288; *see also* Key to Plates; copper coin, Laurent on ΔΙΚΑΙΟC CTAΘMOC Tȣ ΤΡΑΧΕΟC VΠΕΡΠVΡΟV, 30, 35; Schlumberger on + ΠΑΛΑΙΟΝ ΟΛΟΤΡΑΧΟΝ ΕΛΑΦΡΟΝ, 29

Whitting, P. D., on "anonymous bronze," 80; on supposed coins of John IV and Michael VIII, 261; collection, 109, 260, 261, 266, 372, 401, 413, 419, 424, 425, 429, 430

wing/winged emperor, derivation of motif, 267

Wroth, W., on supposed striking of coins by crusaders, 80; on supposed coins of Manuel Comnenus-Ducas, 215, 216; on distinction between gold of John II and John III, 246; on supposed coin of Theodore II, 273; on supposed coin of Isaac II, 289; on supposed coin of John of Neopatras, 294

YAGODA (HOARD), 158 and table I, 161 table II, 162 table III, 164 table IV, 165, 166 table V, 173 table IX, 202 table XI, 220 table XV, *see also* Index II, Map

Yale University, Collection, 424

Yenimahalle (hoard), 204, 211, *see also* Index II, Map

ZACHARIÄ VON LINGENTHAL, on dates referred to in *Palaia kai Nea Logarike*, 50

Zacos, G. and Veglery, A., on eleventh-century coin inscriptions, 101

Zakythinos, D. A., on supposed debasement under Comneni, 47

Zgurli (hoard), 159, 311, *see also* Index II, Map

Zheleznitsa (hoard), 179, 202 table XI, 211 table XIII, 221 table XVI, *see also* Index II, Map

Zlata (hoard), 159, 203, *see also* Index II, Map

Zlataritsa (hoard), 158 and table I, 161 table II, 162 table III, 164 table IV, 165, 166 table V, 173 table IX, *see also* Index II, Map

Zonaras, John, on monetary reform of Alexius I, 48–49, 314; on coining of gold, 312

zygostatai, 304–06

PLATES

PLATE 1

ALEXIUS I, PRE-REFORM

CONSTANTINOPLE

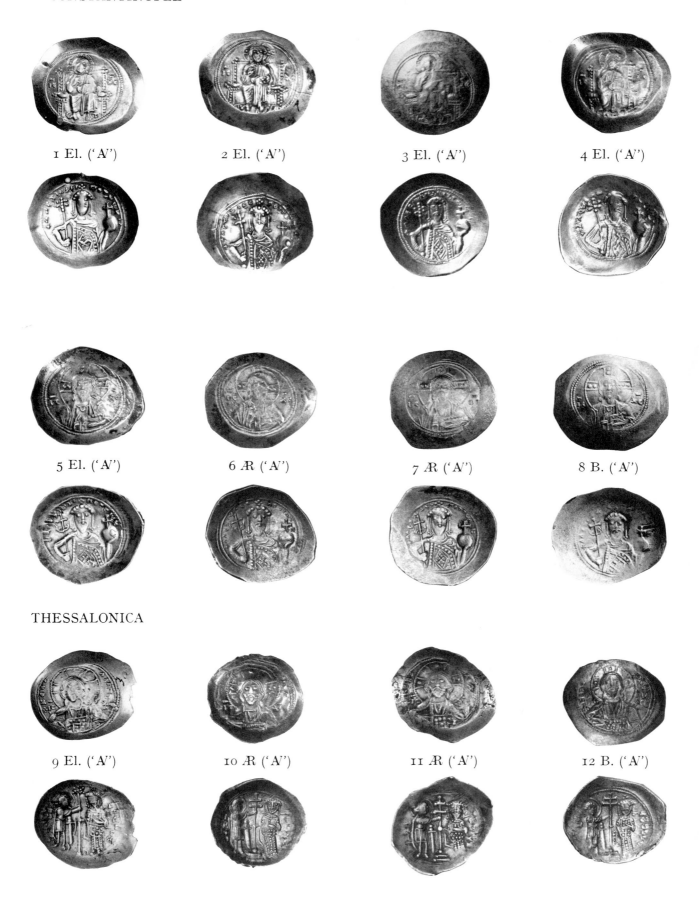

1 El. ('A'')　　2 El. ('A'')　　3 El. ('A'')　　4 El. ('A'')

5 El. ('A'')　　6 Æ ('A'')　　7 Æ ('A'')　　8 B. ('A'')

THESSALONICA

9 El. ('A'')　　10 Æ ('A'')　　11 Æ ('A'')　　12 B. ('A'')

PLATE 2

ALEXIUS I, PRE-REFORM

CONSTANTINOPLE

THESSALONICA

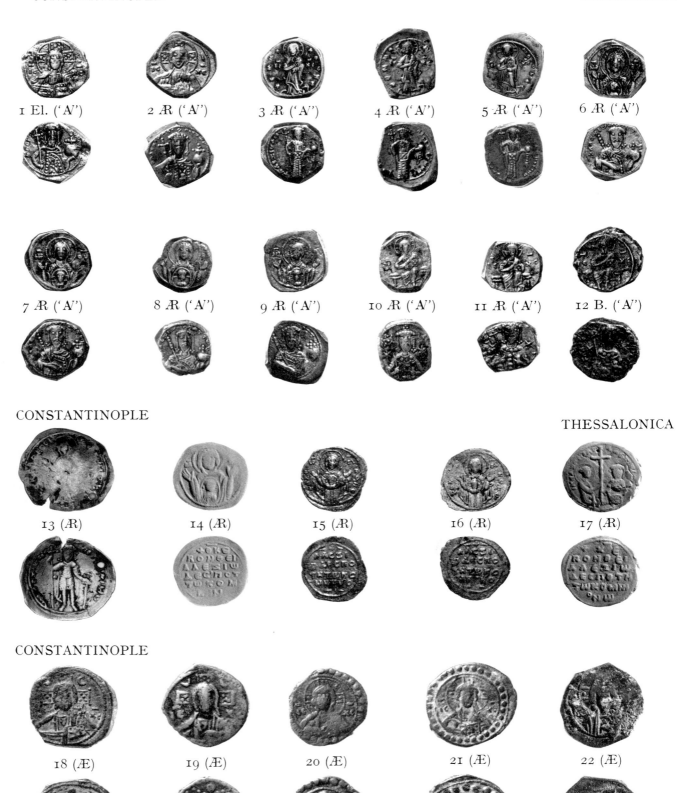

1 El. ('A'')   2 Æ ('A'')   3 Æ ('A'')   4 Æ ('A'')   5 Æ ('A'')   6 Æ ('A'')

7 Æ ('A'')   8 Æ ('A'')   9 Æ ('A'')   10 Æ ('A'')   11 Æ ('A'')   12 B. ('A'')

CONSTANTINOPLE

THESSALONICA

13 (Æ)   14 (Æ)   15 (Æ)   16 (Æ)   17 (Æ)

CONSTANTINOPLE

18 (Æ)   19 (Æ)   20 (Æ)   21 (Æ)   22 (Æ)

PLATE 3

ALEXIUS I, PRE-REFORM

THESSALONICA   EASTERN ?

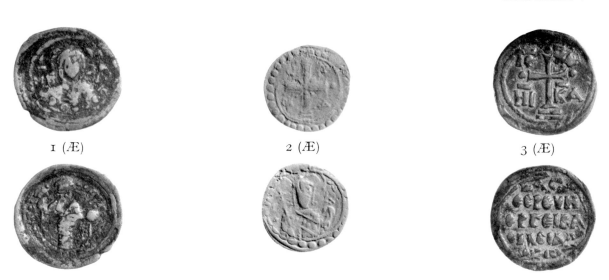

1 (Æ)   2 (Æ)   3 (Æ)

ALEXIUS I, POST-REFORM

CONSTANTINOPLE

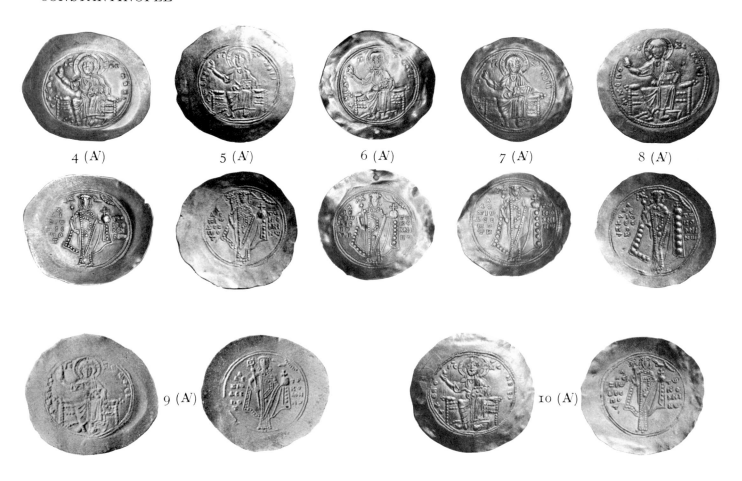

4 (A′)   5 (A′)   6 (A′)   7 (A′)   8 (A′)

9 (A′)   10 (A′)

PLATE 4

ALEXIUS I, POST-REFORM

CONSTANTINOPLE

1 (A′) 2 (A′)

3 (A′) 4 (A′) 5 (A′)

THESSALONICA

6 (A′) 7 (A′) 8 (A′) 9 (A′) 10 (A′)

PLATE 5

ALEXIUS I, POST-REFORM

THESSALONICA

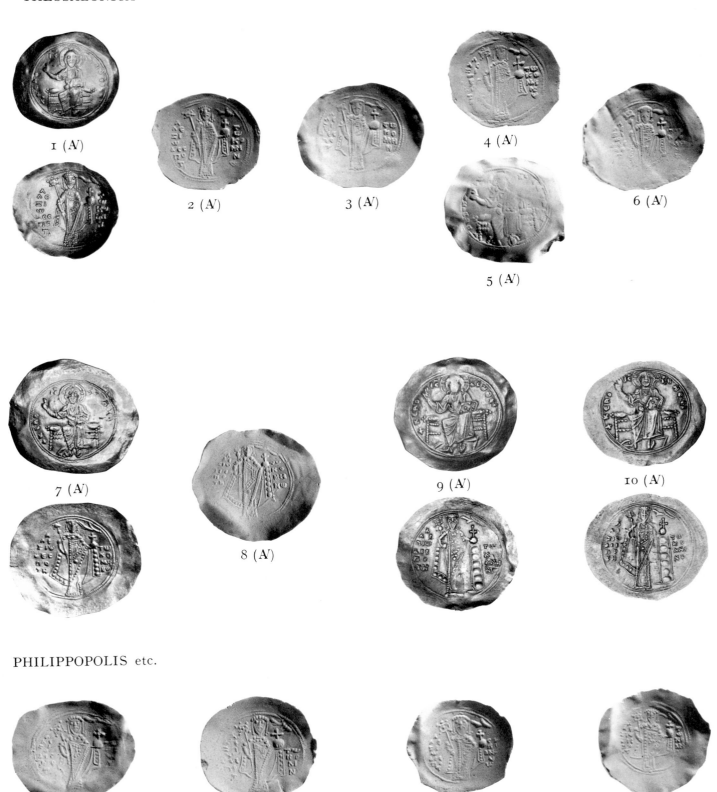

1 (A′)

2 (A′)

3 (A′)

4 (A′)

5 (A′)

6 (A′)

7 (A′)

8 (A′)

9 (A′)

10 (A′)

PHILIPPOPOLIS etc.

11 (A′)

12 (A′)

13 (A′)

14 (A′)

PLATE 6

ALEXIUS I, POST-REFORM

CONSTANTINOPLE

1 (El.) 2 (El.) 3 (El.) 4 (El.) 5 (El.)

THESSALONICA

6 (El.) 7 (El.) 8 (El.) 9 (El.)

CONSTANTINOPLE

10 (B.) 11 (B.)

PLATE 7

ALEXIUS I, POST-REFORM

CONSTANTINOPLE

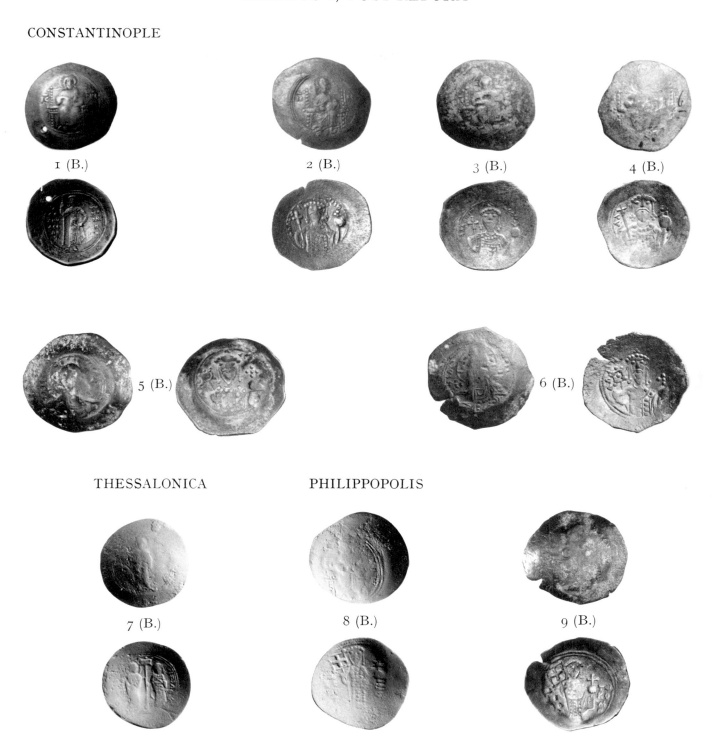

1 (B.) 2 (B.) 3 (B.) 4 (B.)

5 (B.) 6 (B.)

THESSALONICA PHILIPPOPOLIS

7 (B.) 8 (B.) 9 (B.)

CONSTANTINOPLE

10 (Æ) 11 (Æ)

PLATE 8

ALEXIUS I, POST-REFORM

CONSTANTINOPLE

1 (Æ) 2 (Æ) 3 (Æ) 4 (Æ) 5 (Æ) 6 (Æ)

THESSALONICA

7 (Æ) 8 (Æ) 9 (Æ) 10 (Æ) 11 (Æ) 12 (Æ)

13 (Æ) 14 (Æ) 15 (Æ) 16 (Æ)

17 (Æ)

PLATE 9

JOHN II

CONSTANTINOPLE

1 (A/)   2 (A/)   3 (A/)   4 (A/)   5 (A/)

6 (A/)   7 (A/)   8 (A/)   9 (A/)

THESSALONICA

10 (A/)   11 (A/)   12 (A/)   13 (A/)   14 (A/)

PLATE 10

JOHN II

CONSTANTINOPLE

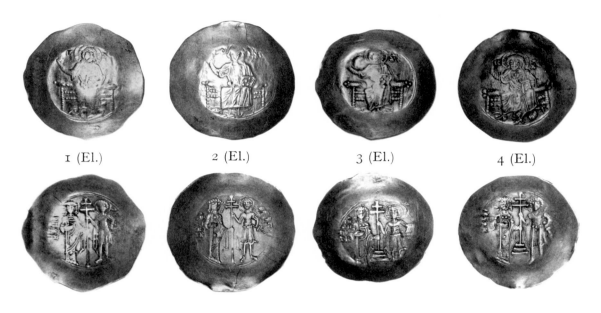

1 (El.) 2 (El.) 3 (El.) 4 (El.)

THESSALONICA

5 (El.) 6 (El.)

CONSTANTINOPLE

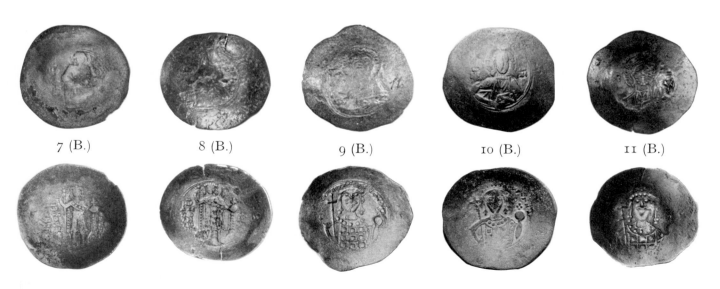

7 (B.) 8 (B.) 9 (B.) 10 (B.) 11 (B.)

PLATE II

JOHN II

CONSTANTINOPLE

THESSALONICA

1 (B.)   2 (B.)   3 (B.)   4 (B.)

CONSTANTINOPLE

5 (Æ)   6 (Æ)   7 (Æ)   8 (Æ)   9 (Æ)   10 (Æ)

THESSALONICA

11 (Æ)   12 (Æ)

13 (Æ)   14 (Æ)   15 (Æ)   16 (Æ)   17 (Æ)

PLATE 12

MANUEL I

CONSTANTINOPLE

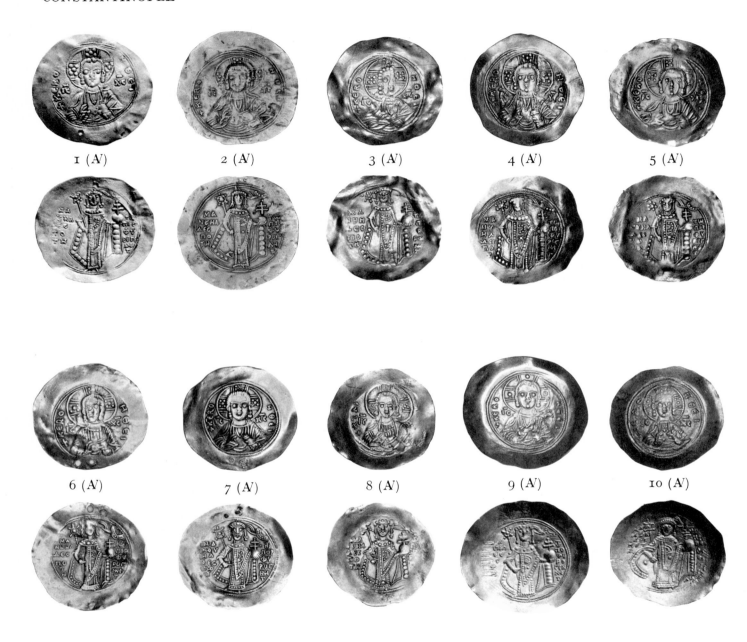

1 (A′)   2 (A′)   3 (A′)   4 (A′)   5 (A′)

6 (A′)   7 (A′)   8 (A′)   9 (A′)   10 (A′)

THESSALONICA

11 (A′)   12 (A′)

PLATE 13

MANUEL I

CONSTANTINOPLE

1 (El.)   2 (El.)   3 (El.)   4 (El.)

5 (El.)   6 (El.)   7 (El.)   8 (El.)   9 (El.)

10 (El.)   11 (El.)   12 (El.)

PLATE 14

MANUEL I

CONSTANTINOPLE

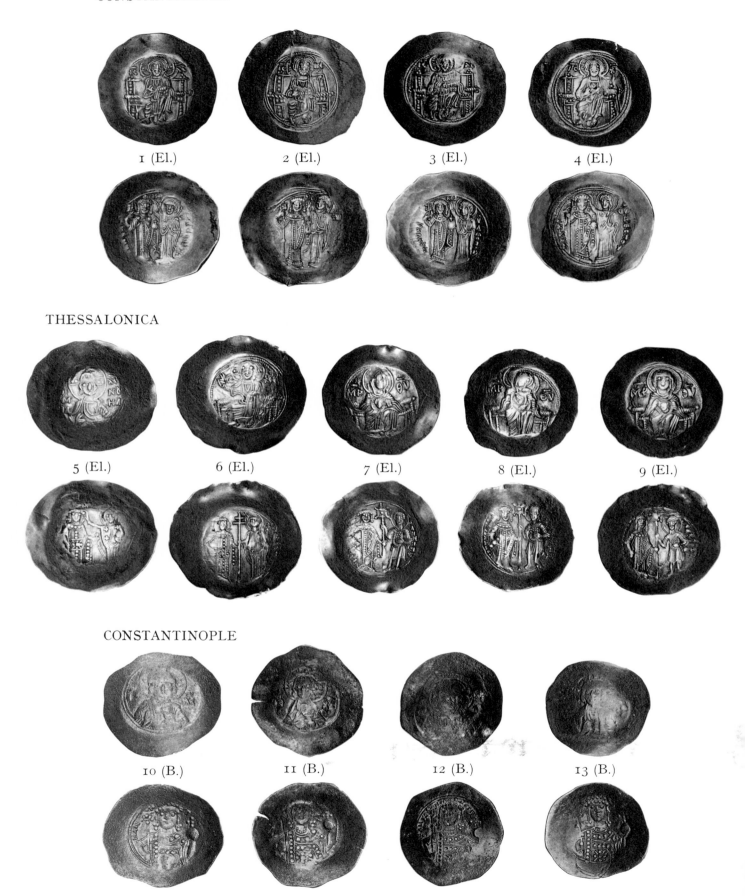

1 (El.)   2 (El.)   3 (El.)   4 (El.)

THESSALONICA

5 (El.)   6 (El.)   7 (El.)   8 (El.)   9 (El.)

CONSTANTINOPLE

10 (B.)   11 (B.)   12 (B.)   13 (B.)

PLATE 15

MANUEL I

CONSTANTINOPLE

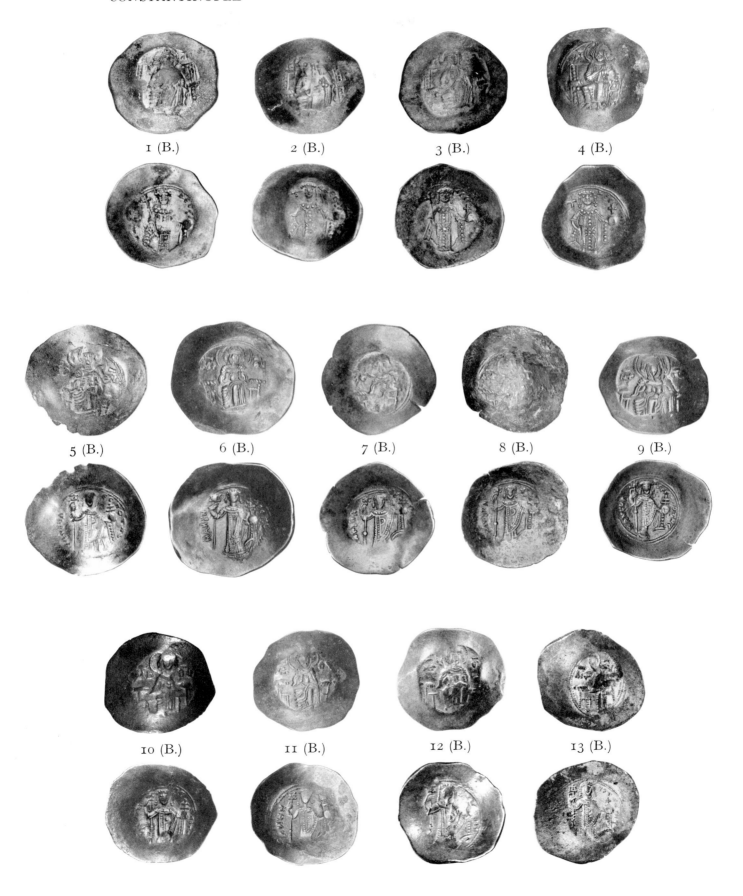

1 (B.)   2 (B.)   3 (B.)   4 (B.)

5 (B.)   6 (B.)   7 (B.)   8 (B.)   9 (B.)

10 (B.)   11 (B.)   12 (B.)   13 (B.)

PLATE 16

MANUEL I

CONSTANTINOPLE

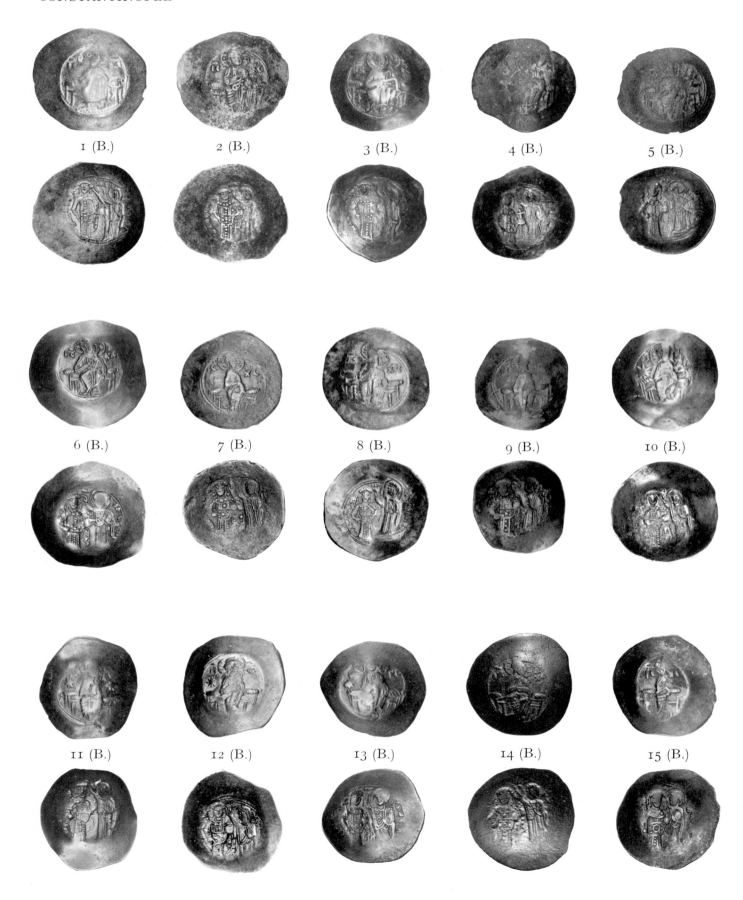

1 (B.) 2 (B.) 3 (B.) 4 (B.) 5 (B.)

6 (B.) 7 (B.) 8 (B.) 9 (B.) 10 (B.)

11 (B.) 12 (B.) 13 (B.) 14 (B.) 15 (B.)

PLATE 17

MANUEL I

CONSTANTINOPLE

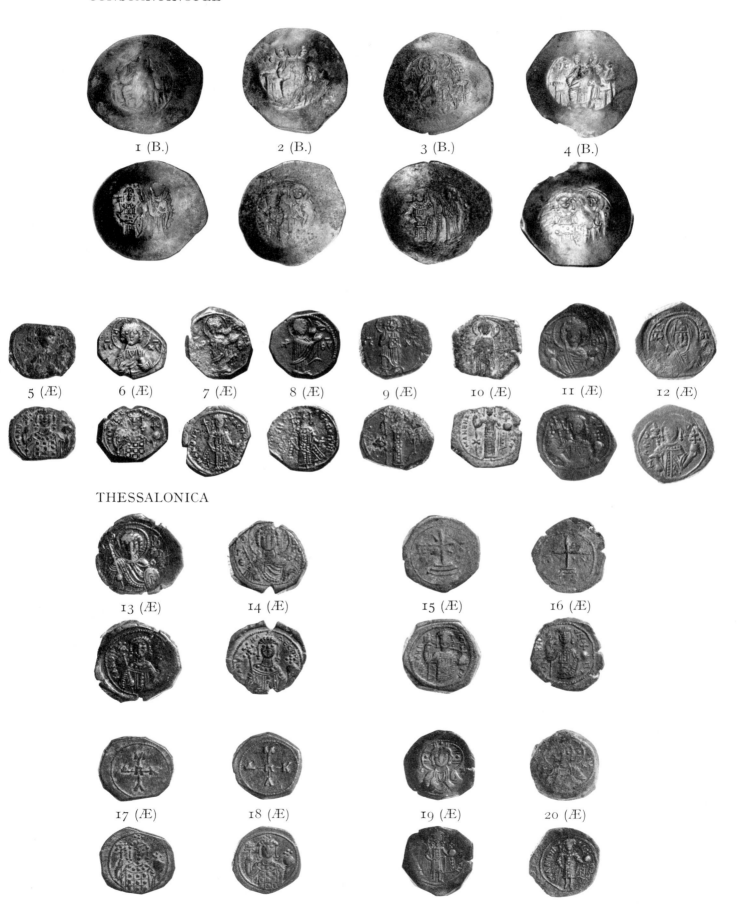

1 (B.)   2 (B.)   3 (B.)   4 (B.)

5 (Æ)   6 (Æ)   7 (Æ)   8 (Æ)   9 (Æ)   10 (Æ)   11 (Æ)   12 (Æ)

THESSALONICA

13 (Æ)   14 (Æ)   15 (Æ)   16 (Æ)

17 (Æ)   18 (Æ)   19 (Æ)   20 (Æ)

PLATE 18

MANUEL I

UNCERTAIN GREEK MINT

1 (Æ)   2 (Æ)   3 (Æ)   4 (Æ)   5 (Æ)   6 (Æ)   7 (Æ)   8 (Æ)

ANDRONICUS I

CONSTANTINOPLE

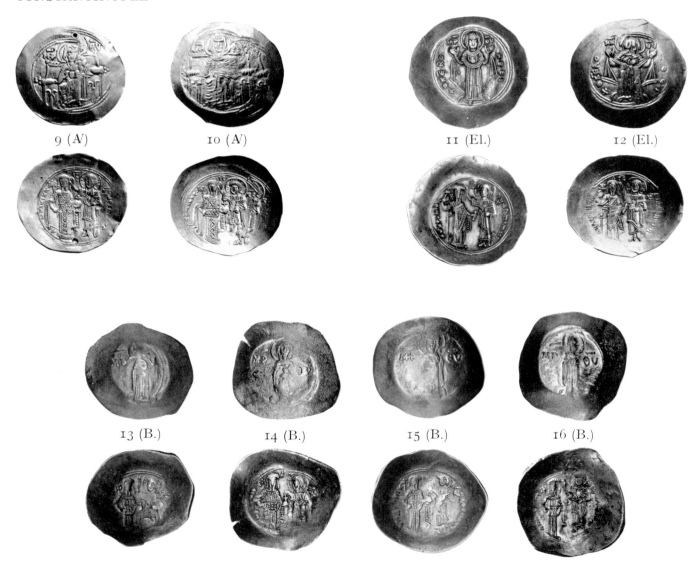

9 (A/)   10 (A/)   11 (El.)   12 (El.)

13 (B.)   14 (B.)   15 (B.)   16 (B.)

PLATE 19

ANDRONICUS I

CONSTANTINOPLE THESSALONICA etc.

 1 (Æ)   2 (Æ)  3 (Æ) 4 (Æ)

ISAAC OF CYPRUS

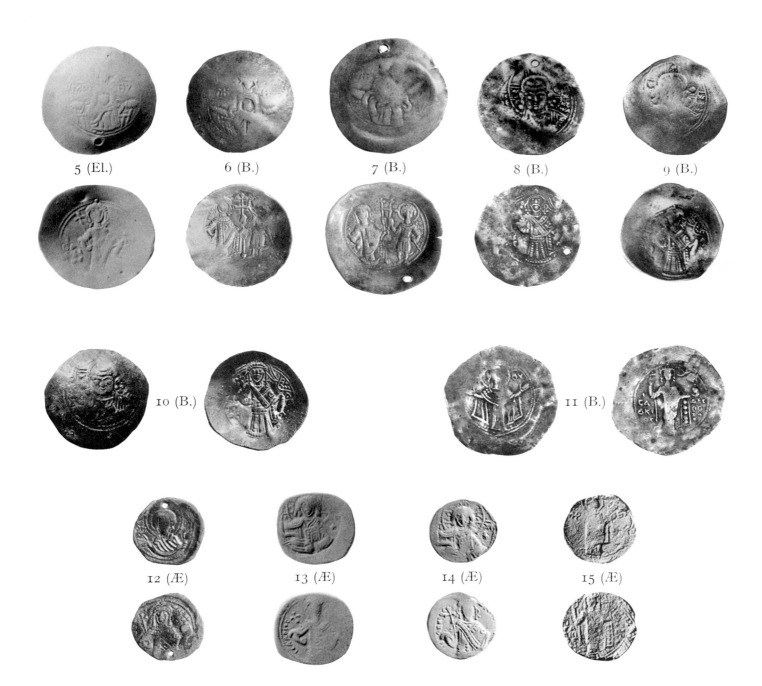

5 (El.) 6 (B.) 7 (B.) 8 (B.) 9 (B.)

10 (B.) 11 (B.)

12 (Æ) 13 (Æ) 14 (Æ) 15 (Æ)

PLATE 20

ISAAC II

CONSTANTINOPLE

1 (A/) 2 (A/) 3 (A/) 4 (A/)

5 (El.) 6 (El.) 7 (El.) 8 (El.)

9 (B.) 10 (B.) 11 (B.) 12 (B.) 13 (B.)

PLATE 21

ISAAC II

CONSTANTINOPLE

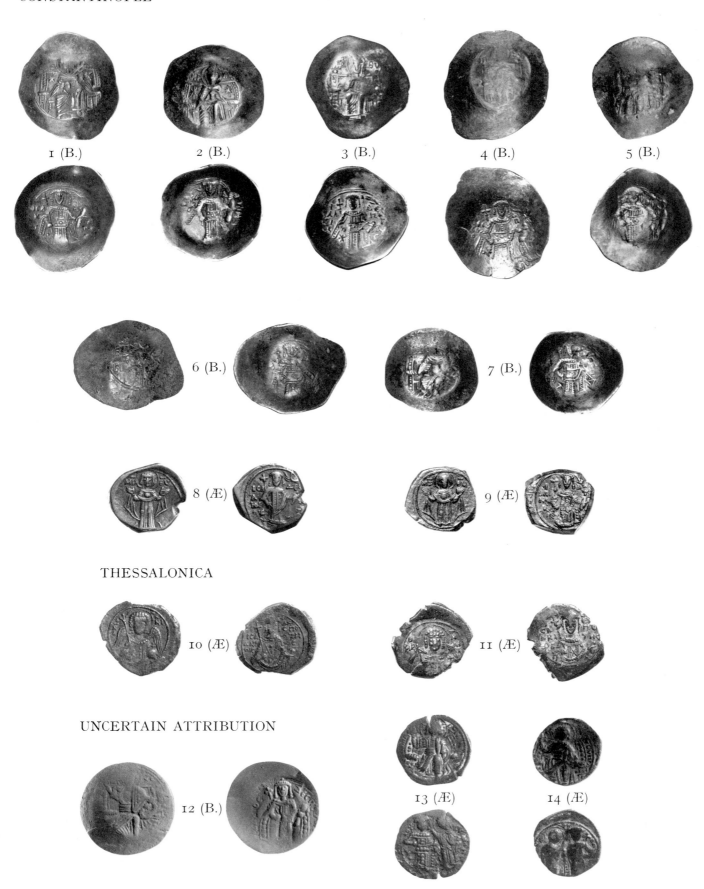

1 (B.) 2 (B.) 3 (B.) 4 (B.) 5 (B.)

6 (B.) 7 (B.)

8 (Æ) 9 (Æ)

THESSALONICA

10 (Æ) 11 (Æ)

UNCERTAIN ATTRIBUTION

12 (B.) 13 (Æ) 14 (Æ)

PLATE 22

ALEXIUS III

CONSTANTINOPLE

1 (A')   2 (A')   3 (A')

4 (El.)   5 (El.)   6 (El.)   7 (El.)

8 (B.)   9 (B.)   10 (B.)   11 (B.)   12 (B.)

PLATE 23

ALEXIUS III

CONSTANTINOPLE

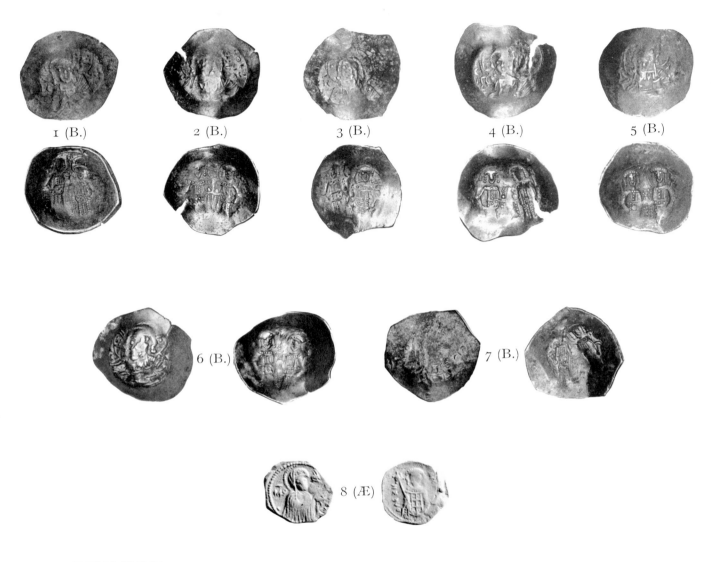

1 (B.)   2 (B.)   3 (B.)   4 (B.)   5 (B.)

6 (B.)   7 (B.)

8 (Æ)

THESSALONICA

9 (Æ)   10 (Æ)   11 (Æ)   12 (Æ)   13 (Æ)   14 (Æ)

PLATE 24

"BULGARIAN" IMITATIVE

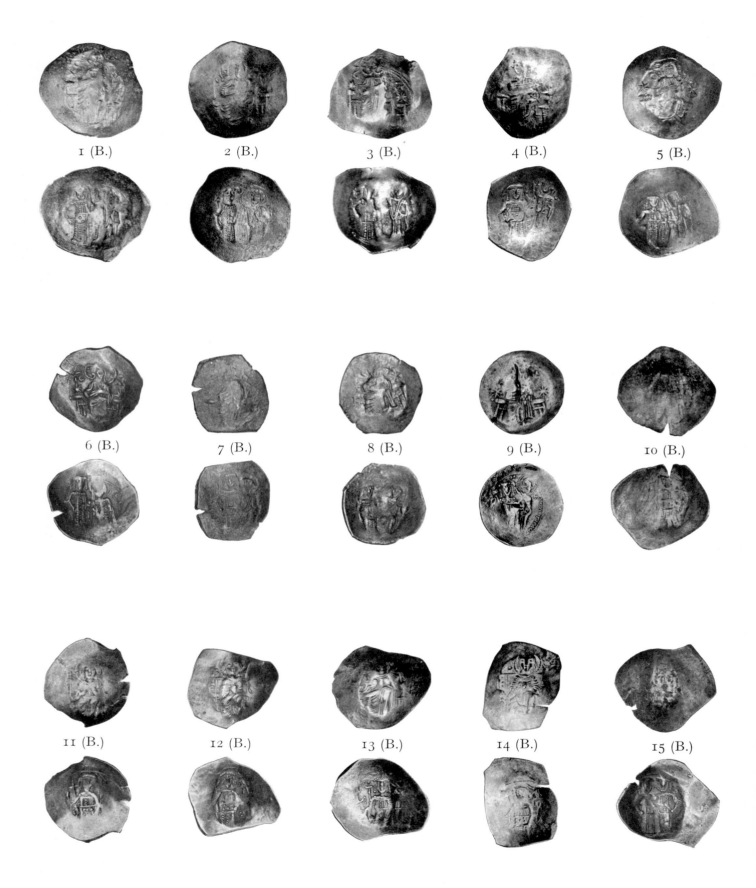

1 (B.)   2 (B.)   3 (B.)   4 (B.)   5 (B.)

6 (B.)   7 (B.)   8 (B.)   9 (B.)   10 (B.)

11 (B.)   12 (B.)   13 (B.)   14 (B.)   15 (B.)

PLATE 25

"BULGARIAN" IMITATIVE

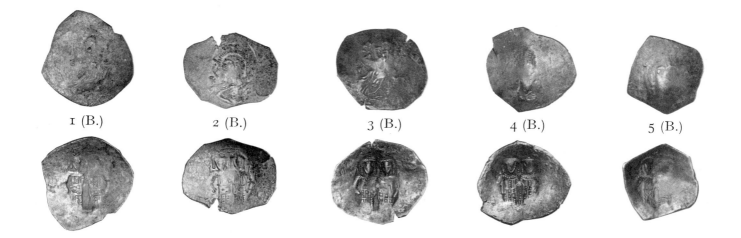

1 (B.) 2 (B.) 3 (B.) 4 (B.) 5 (B.)

LATIN IMITATIVE

CONSTANTINOPLE

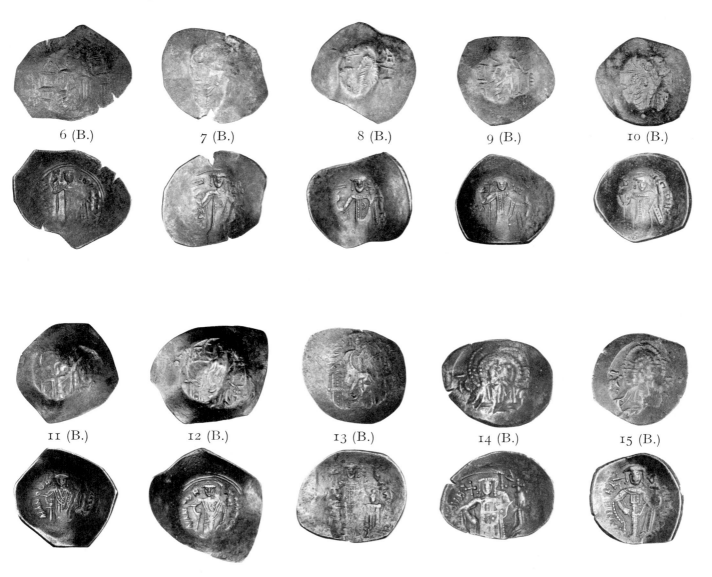

6 (B.) 7 (B.) 8 (B.) 9 (B.) 10 (B.)

11 (B.) 12 (B.) 13 (B.) 14 (B.) 15 (B.)

PLATE 26

LATIN IMITATIVE

CONSTANTINOPLE

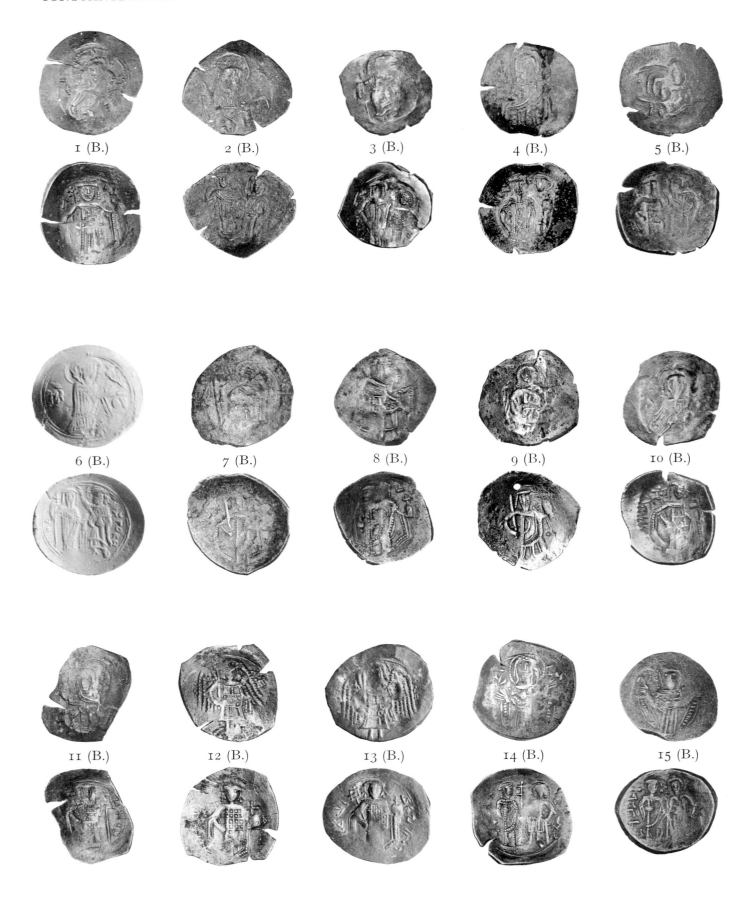

1 (B.) 2 (B.) 3 (B.) 4 (B.) 5 (B.)

6 (B.) 7 (B.) 8 (B.) 9 (B.) 10 (B.)

11 (B.) 12 (B.) 13 (B.) 14 (B.) 15 (B.)

PLATE 27

LATIN IMITATIVE

CONSTANTINOPLE

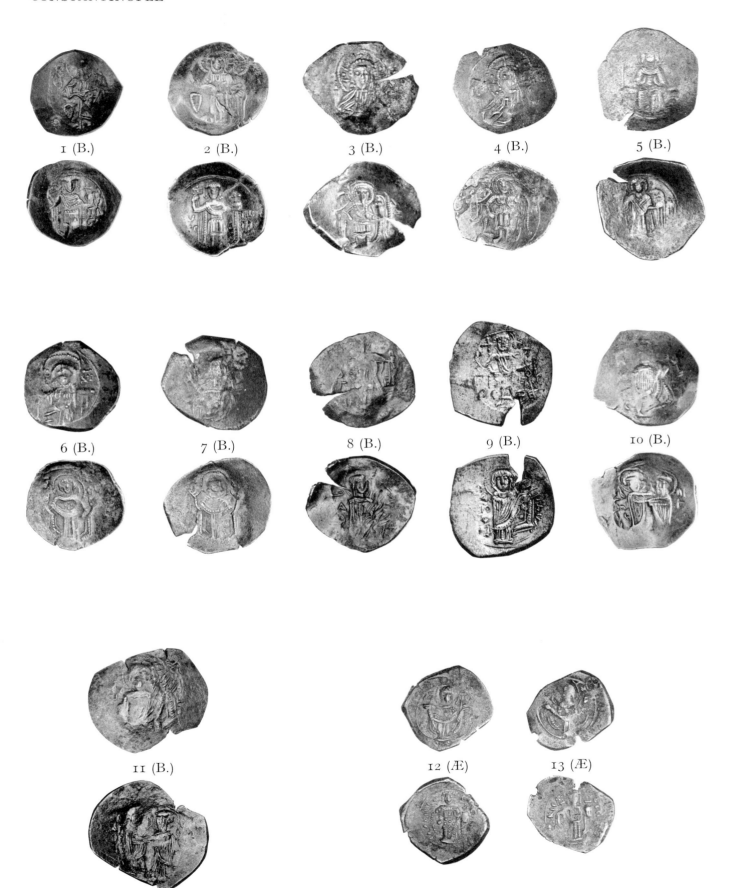

1 (B.)   2 (B.)   3 (B.)   4 (B.)   5 (B.)

6 (B.)   7 (B.)   8 (B.)   9 (B.)   10 (B.)

11 (B.)   12 (Æ)   13 (Æ)

PLATE 28

LATIN IMITATIVE

THESSALONICA

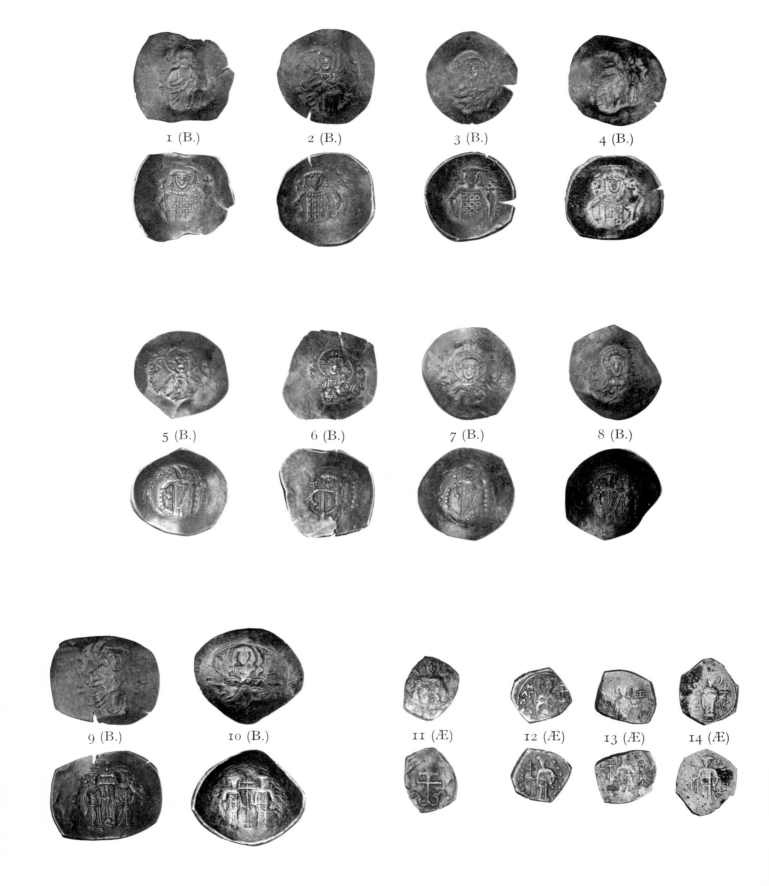

1 (B.)   2 (B.)   3 (B.)   4 (B.)

5 (B.)   6 (B.)   7 (B.)   8 (B.)

9 (B.)   10 (B.)   11 (Æ)   12 (Æ)   13 (Æ)   14 (Æ)

PLATE 29

LATIN SMALL-MODULE

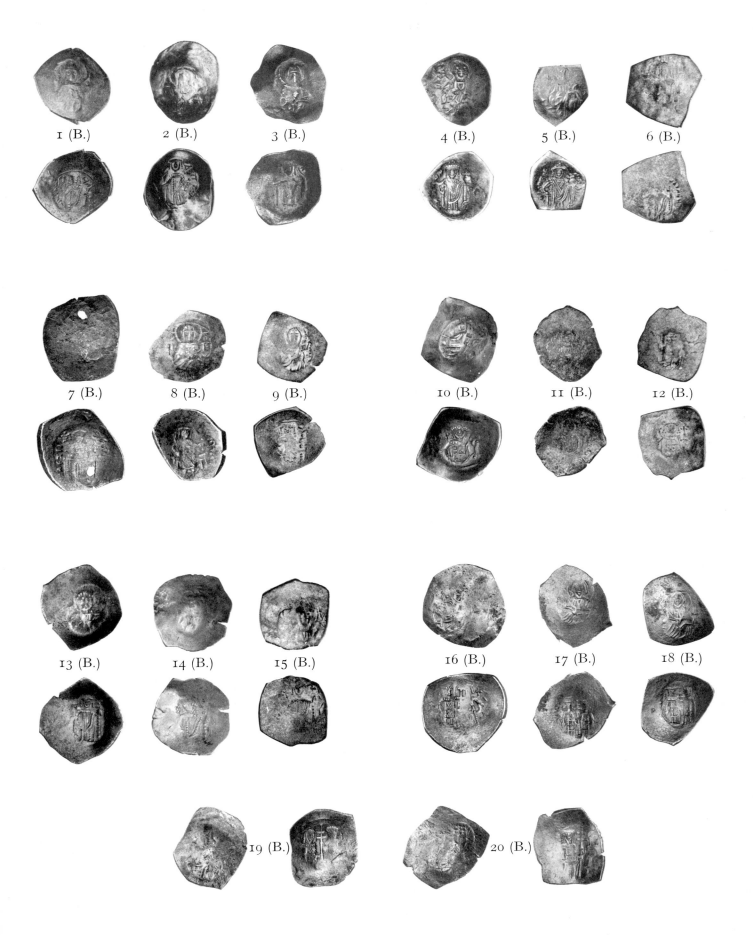

1 (B.) 2 (B.) 3 (B.)

4 (B.) 5 (B.) 6 (B.)

7 (B.) 8 (B.) 9 (B.)

10 (B.) 11 (B.) 12 (B.)

13 (B.) 14 (B.) 15 (B.)

16 (B.) 17 (B.) 18 (B.)

19 (B.) 20 (B.)

PLATE 30

THEODORE I

NICAEA or MAGNESIA

1 (A')

MAGNESIA

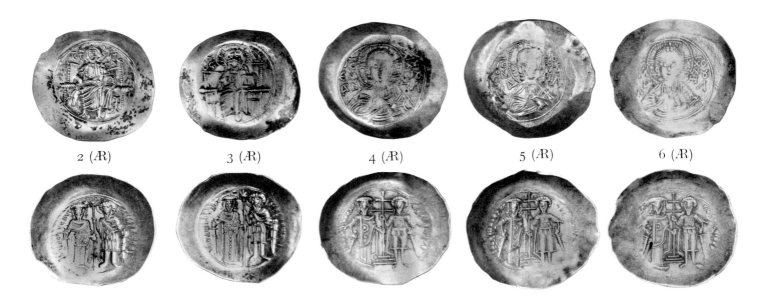

2 (Æ)   3 (Æ)   4 (Æ)   5 (Æ)   6 (Æ)

NICAEA

7 (B.)   8 (B.)   9 (B.)   10 (B.)

PLATE 31

THEODORE I

NICAEA

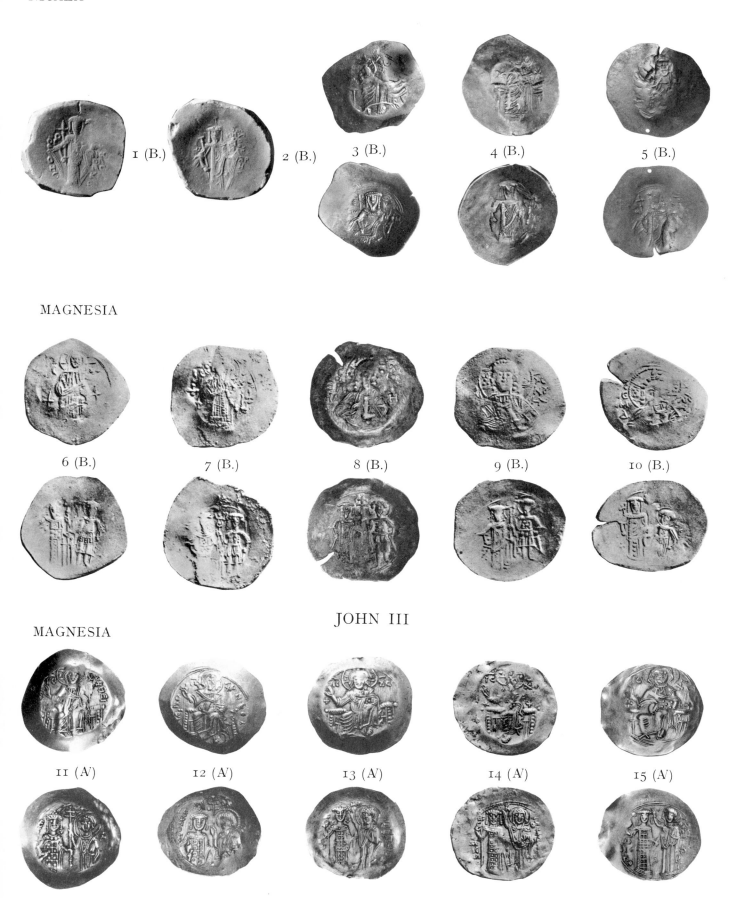

1 (B.)   2 (B.)   3 (B.)   4 (B.)   5 (B.)

MAGNESIA

6 (B.)   7 (B.)   8 (B.)   9 (B.)   10 (B.)

JOHN III

MAGNESIA

11 (A′)   12 (A′)   13 (A′)   14 (A′)   15 (A′)

PLATE 32

JOHN III

MAGNESIA

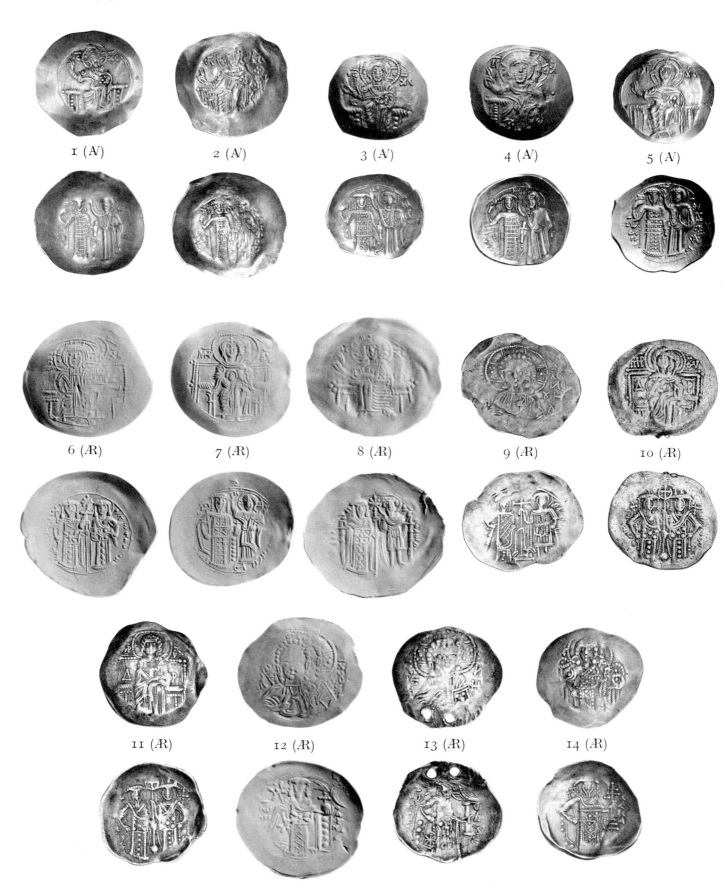

1 (A')   2 (A')   3 (A')   4 (A')   5 (A')

6 (Æ)   7 (Æ)   8 (Æ)   9 (Æ)   10 (Æ)

11 (Æ)   12 (Æ)   13 (Æ)   14 (Æ)

PLATE 33

JOHN III

MAGNESIA

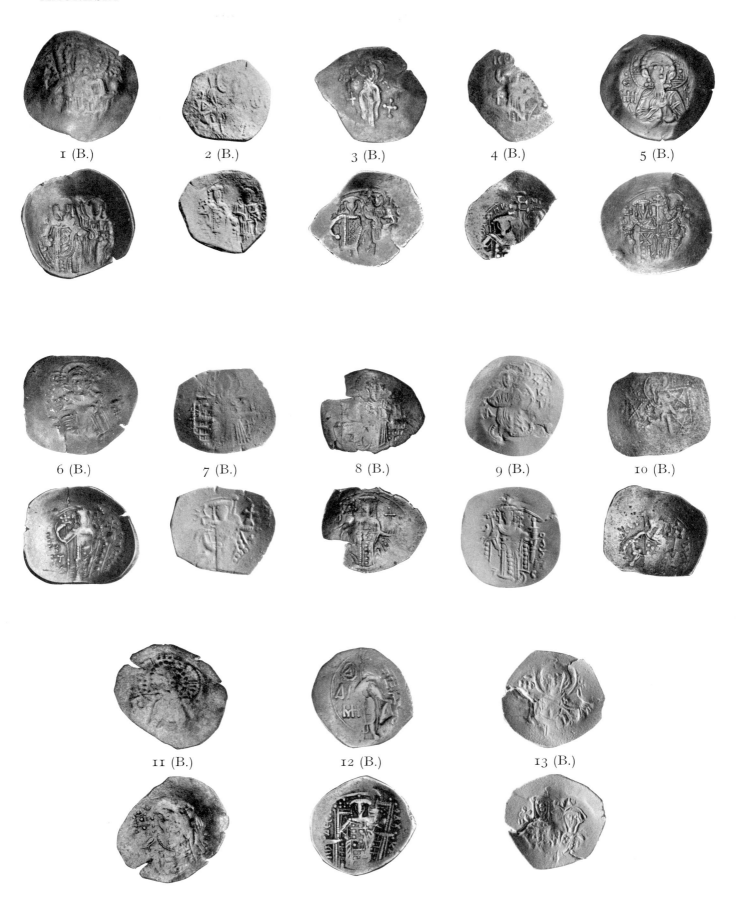

1 (B.)   2 (B.)   3 (B.)   4 (B.)   5 (B.)

6 (B.)   7 (B.)   8 (B.)   9 (B.)   10 (B.)

11 (B.)   12 (B.)   13 (B.)

PLATE 34

JOHN III

MAGNESIA

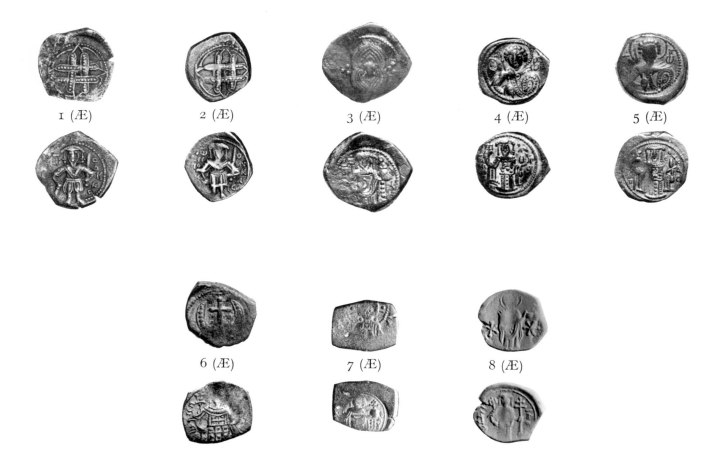

1 (Æ) 2 (Æ) 3 (Æ) 4 (Æ) 5 (Æ)

6 (Æ) 7 (Æ) 8 (Æ)

THEODORE II

MAGNESIA

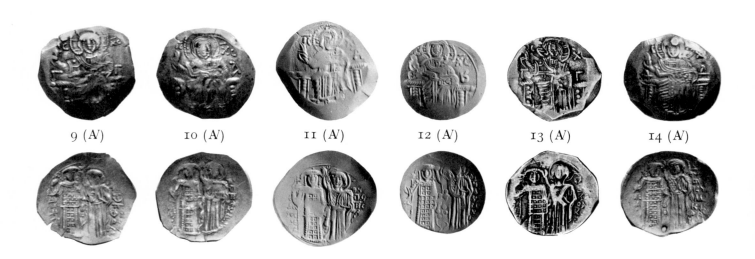

9 (A/) 10 (A/) 11 (A/) 12 (A/) 13 (A/) 14 (A/)

PLATE 35

THEODORE II

MAGNESIA

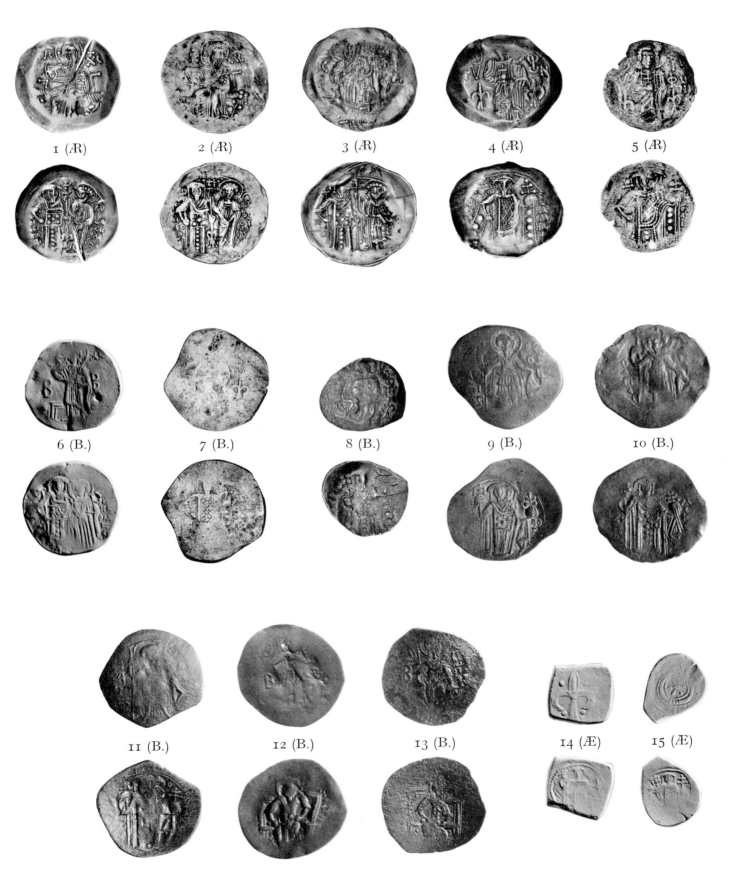

1 (Æ) 2 (Æ) 3 (Æ) 4 (Æ) 5 (Æ)

6 (B.) 7 (B.) 8 (B.) 9 (B.) 10 (B.)

11 (B.) 12 (B.) 13 (B.) 14 (Æ) 15 (Æ)

PLATE 36

MICHAEL VIII

MAGNESIA

1 (A/)   2 (Æ)   3 (B.)   4 (B.)

5 (Æ)   6 (Æ)

UNCERTAIN NICAEAN ATTRIBUTION

MAGNESIA

7 (Æ)   8 (Æ)   9 (Æ)   10 (Æ)   11 (Æ)

PLATE 37

THEODORE COMNENUS-DUCAS

THESSALONICA

1 (Æ)   2 (Æ)   3 (Æ)   4 (Æ)

5 (Æ)   6 (Æ)

7 (B.)   8 (B.)   9 (B.)   10 (B.)

11 (B.)   12 (B.)

PLATE 38

THEODORE COMNENUS-DUCAS

THESSALONICA

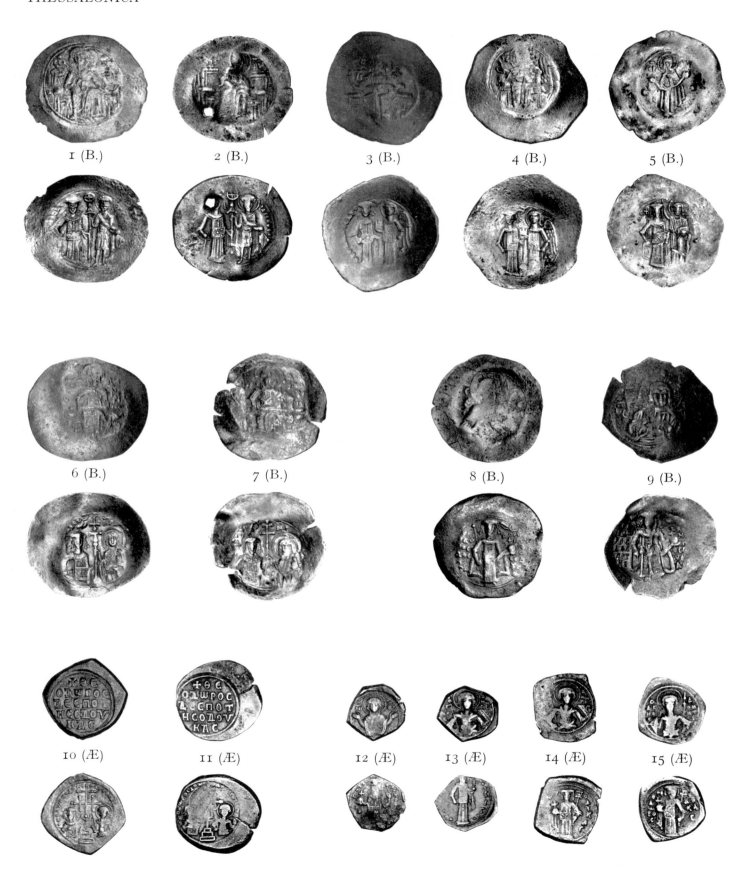

1 (B.) 2 (B.) 3 (B.) 4 (B.) 5 (B.)

6 (B.) 7 (B.) 8 (B.) 9 (B.)

10 (Æ) 11 (Æ) 12 (Æ) 13 (Æ) 14 (Æ) 15 (Æ)

PLATE 39

MANUEL COMNENUS-DUCAS

THESSALONICA

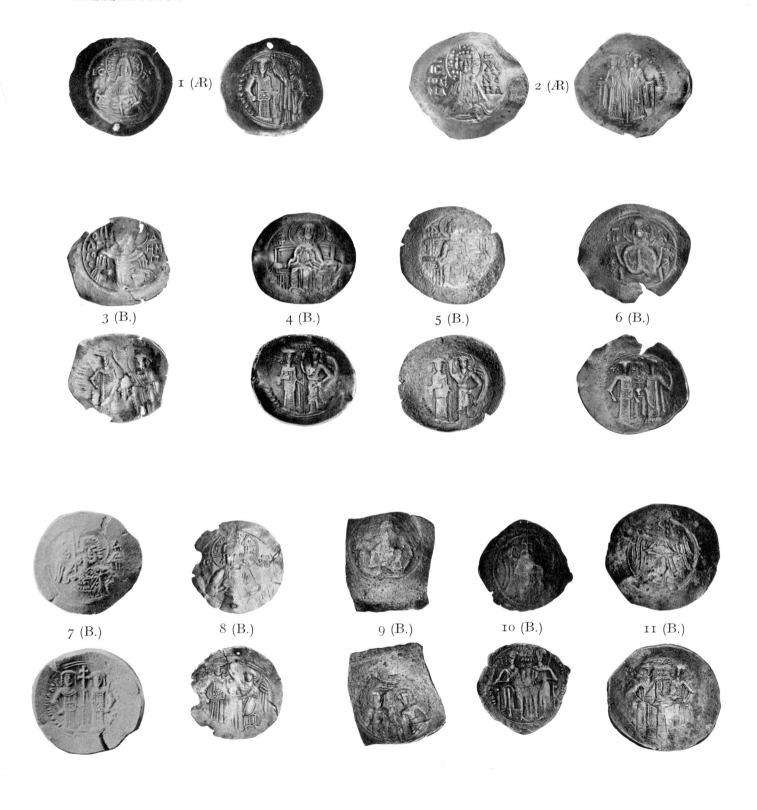

1 (Æ)   2 (Æ)

3 (B.)   4 (B.)   5 (B.)   6 (B.)

7 (B.)   8 (B.)   9 (B.)   10 (B.)   11 (B.)

PLATE 40

JOHN COMNENUS-DUCAS

THESSALONICA

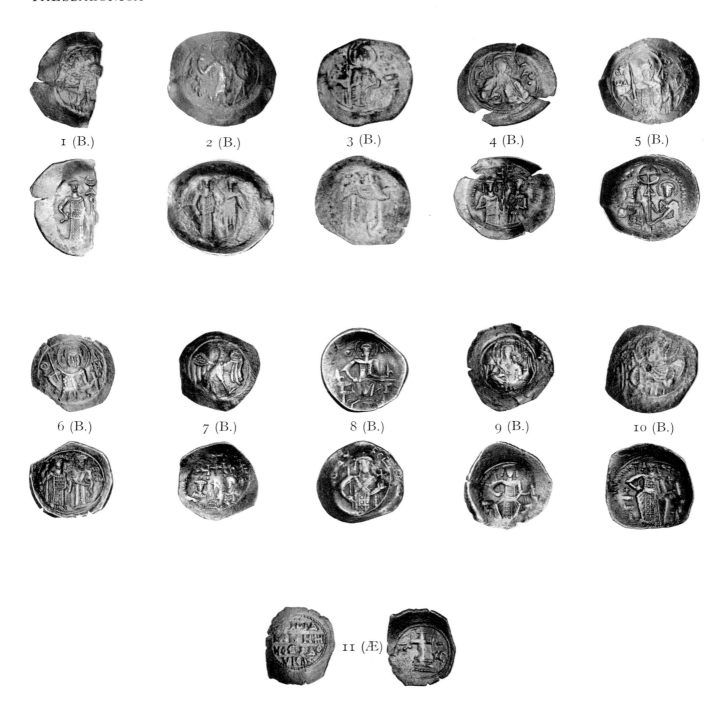

1 (B.)   2 (B.)   3 (B.)   4 (B.)   5 (B.)

6 (B.)   7 (B.)   8 (B.)   9 (B.)   10 (B.)

11 (Æ)

  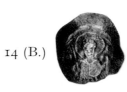 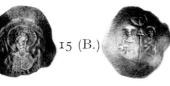

12 (B.)   13 (B.)   14 (B.)   15 (B.)

PLATE 41

JOHN COMNENUS-DUCAS ETC.

THESSALONICA

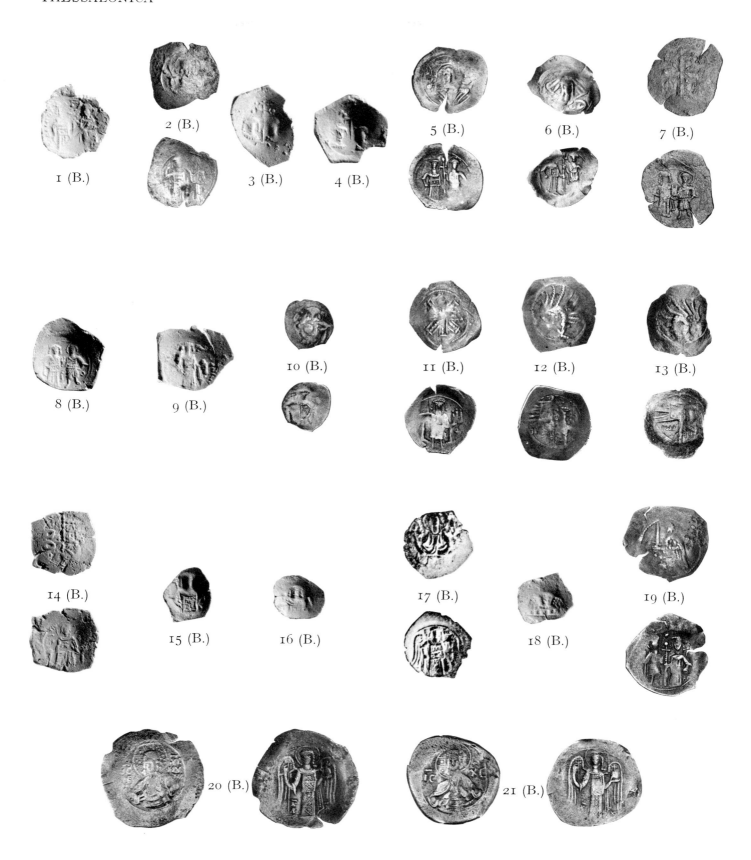

1 (B.)
2 (B.)
3 (B.)
4 (B.)
5 (B.)
6 (B.)
7 (B.)

8 (B.)
9 (B.)
10 (B.)
11 (B.)
12 (B.)
13 (B.)

14 (B.)
15 (B.)
16 (B.)
17 (B.)
18 (B.)
19 (B.)

20 (B.)
21 (B.)

PLATE 42

JOHN III

THESSALONICA

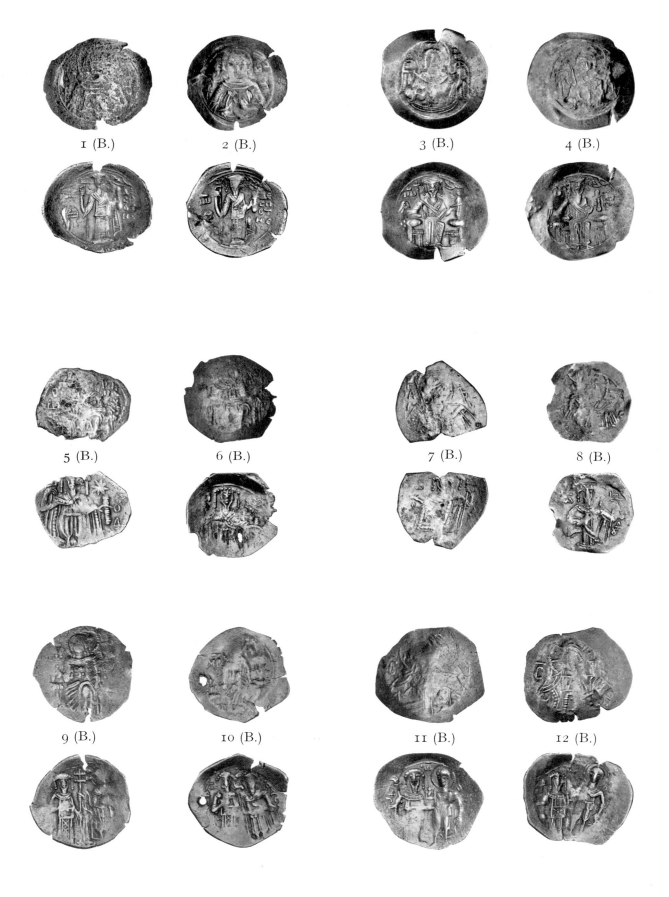

1 (B.) 2 (B.) 3 (B.) 4 (B.)

5 (B.) 6 (B.) 7 (B.) 8 (B.)

9 (B.) 10 (B.) 11 (B.) 12 (B.)

PLATE 43

JOHN III

THESSALONICA

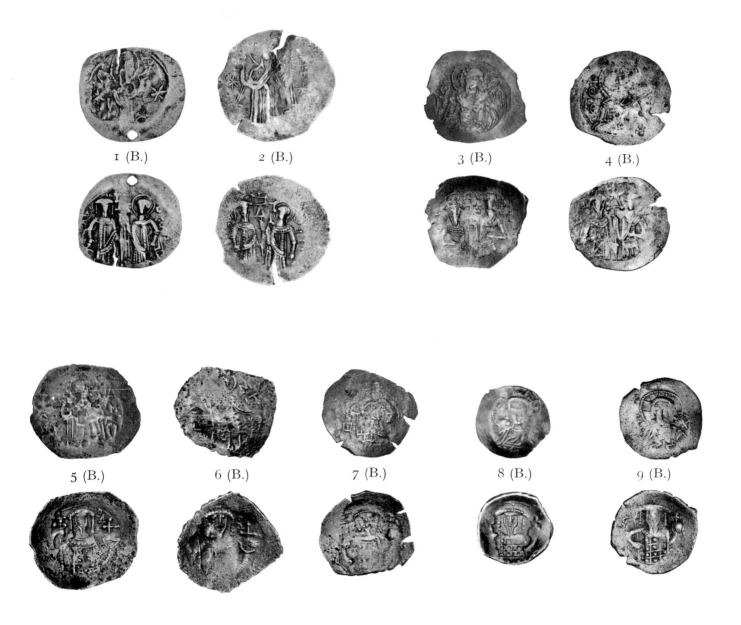

1 (B.)   2 (B.)   3 (B.)   4 (B.)

5 (B.)   6 (B.)   7 (B.)   8 (B.)   9 (B.)

THEODORE II

10 (B.)

PLATE 44

CLIPPED COINS

CONSTANTINOPLE

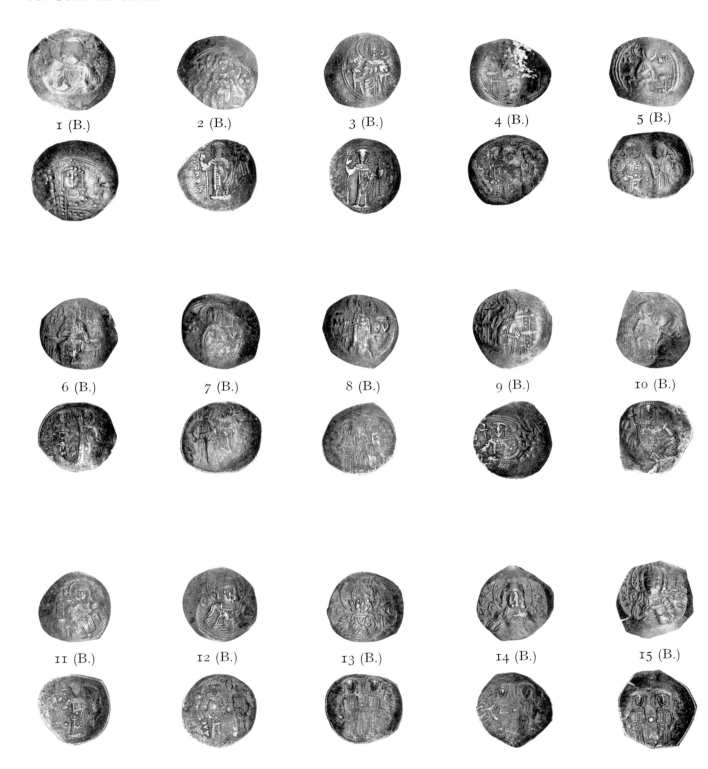

1 (B.)   2 (B.)   3 (B.)   4 (B.)   5 (B.)

6 (B.)   7 (B.)   8 (B.)   9 (B.)   10 (B.)

11 (B.)   12 (B.)   13 (B.)   14 (B.)   15 (B.)

PLATE 45

CLIPPED COINS

THESSALONICA

1 (B.)   2 (B.)   3 (B.)   4 (B.)   5 (B.)

6 (B.)   7 (B.)   8 (B.)   9 (B.)   10 (B.)

ROGER II OF SICILY, DUCAT

11 (Æ)

DEBASED HYPERPYRA

12 (A')   13 (A')   14 (A')   15 (A')   16 (A')

PLATE 46

DEBASED HYPERPYRA

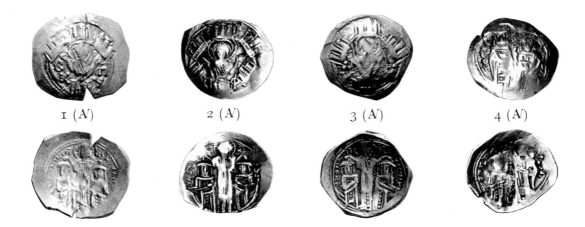

1 (A′)   2 (A′)   3 (A′)   4 (A′)

OVERSTRIKES

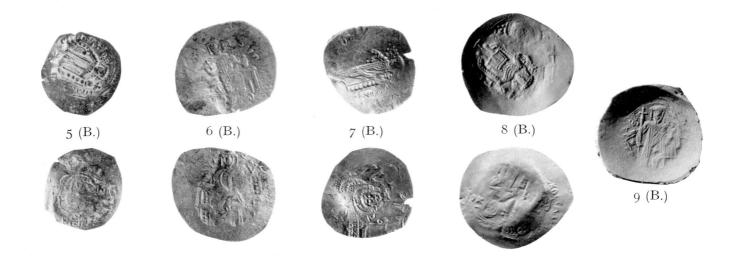

5 (B.)   6 (B.)   7 (B.)   8 (B.)   9 (B.)

IVAN II ASEN

10 (B.)   11 (B.)

PLATE 47

STEFAN "REX"

1 (B.)

MISCELLANEOUS ELEVENTH CENTURY

2 (Æ) 3 (Æ) 4 (Æ) 5 (AV)

HUGH I OF CYPRUS, BESANT

6 (El.)

PLATE 48

Hagia Sophia: "Constantine IX" and Zoë

PLATE 49

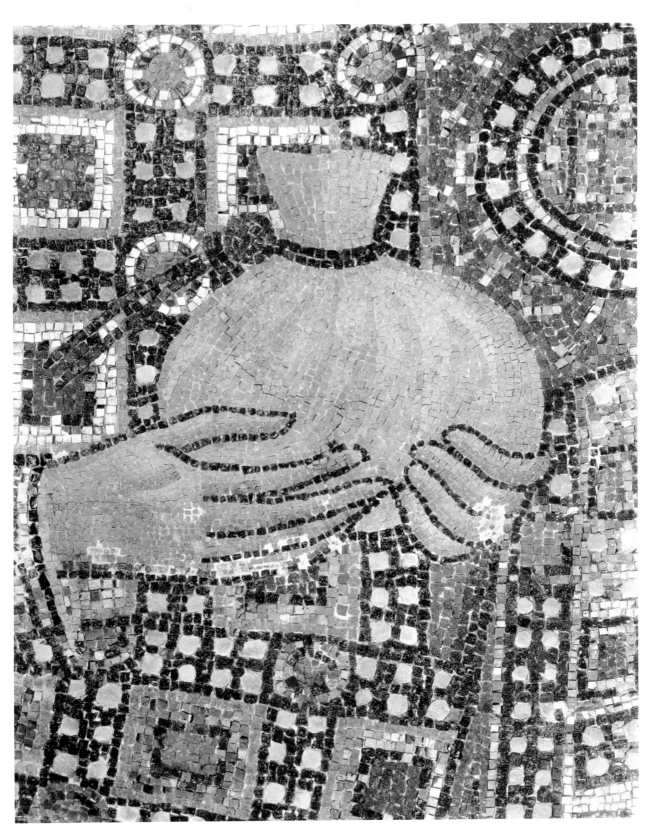

Hagia Sophia: "Constantine IX" and Zoë, detail of *Apokombion*

PLATE 50

Hagia Sophia: John II and Irene

PLATE 51

SUPPLEMENTARY MATERIAL

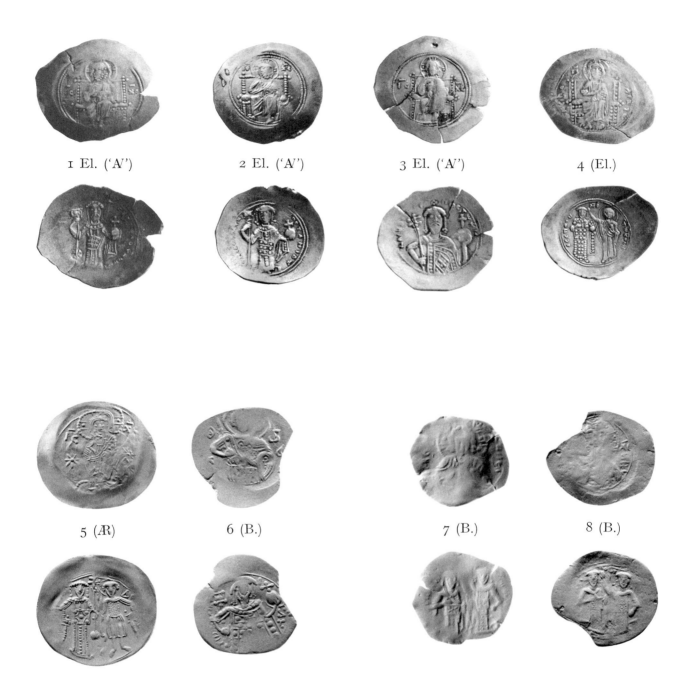

1 El. ('A/')　　　　2 El. ('A/')　　　　3 El. ('A/')　　　　4 (El.)

5 (Æ)　　　　6 (B.)　　　　7 (B.)　　　　8 (B.)